Cities in Full

Cities in Full
Recognizing and Realizing the Great Potential of Urban America

By
Steve Belmont

Planners Press
American Planning Association
Chicago, Illinois
Washington, D.C.

Text appearing on pages 393-394
Excerpts from CHANGING PLANS FOR AMERICA'S INNER CITIES by Zane L. Miller and Bruce Tucker.

Text appearing on page 316
Excerpt from FIXING BROKEN WINDOWS by George Kelling and Catherine Coles, p. 99-100.

Text appearing on pages 105, 106
From CRABGRASS FRONTIER by Kenneth Jackson, copyright © 1985 by Kenneth Jackson. Used by permission of Oxford University Press.

Text appearing on pages 6, 8, 30, 43, 44, 45, 46, 67, 407
From THE DEATH AND LIFE OF GREAT AMERICAN CITIES by Jane Jacobs, copyright © 1961 by Jane Jacobs. Used by permission of Random House.

Illustration Credits

All photos, tables, and figures credited to Steve Belmont except where noted.

Copyright 2002 by the American Planning Association
122 S. Michigan Ave., Suite 1600, Chicago, IL 60603

ISBN (paperback): 1-884829-52-X
ISBN (hardbound): 1-884829-53-8

Library of Congress Catalog Card Number 2001 135202

Printed in the United States of America

Dedications

To my parents
To the memory of HWM

Contents

Acknowledgements

Among the many public employees and officials who provided essential information, some stand apart for their uncommon generosity: George Minicucci at the New York City Planning Department, Larry Harris at the Cincinnati Planning Department, Janese Chapman at Detroit's Historical Designation Advisory Board, Donna Etienne at Ramsey County Human Services in St. Paul, John Dillery at Metro Transit in Minneapolis, and Oakland council member Nancy Nadel.

Many thanks to Sylvia Lewis and Sherrie Voss Matthews at Planners Press for their guidance, and special thanks to Michael Brooks, Ph.D., professor of urban planning at Virginia Commonwealth University in Richmond, for his encouragement and advice.

Steve Belmont
September 10, 2001

Introduction:
Diminished Expectations
and Stunted Visions

Surely cities do not have to reclaim all their lost glory—all the population, density, economic mass, and social and political hegemony of the first half of this century... PAUL GROGAN[1]

Less than a decade ago pundits were questioning the relevance of American cities, revisiting Louis Mumford's and Frank Lloyd Wright's suggestion that cities should be allowed to die their natural death. After rioting decimated much of South Central Los Angeles in 1992, George Will challenged HUD Secretary Jack Kemp's assertion that Los Angeles and other American cities deserve federal support. Political scientist Dr. Irving Baker said of our many cities that depend on federal money for viability, "Those cities...are expendable." In 1995 the urban affairs writer at the *Dallas Morning News* raised the specter of modern-day ghost towns—disposable cities abandoned after they've run their course. The "urban civilization without cities" predicted by Irving Kristol in 1972 seemed plausible and, in some places, imminent.[2] Americans had decided that suburbs were preferable for nearly all activities that sustain and enrich human life.

But it appears cities have survived their darkest days, thanks in large measure to the growing problems of suburbs. In August 1999, the *New York Times* reported that unbearable congestion on Miami's roadways causes commuters to rethink their life choices. Ralph Paulino, for one, decided to move from a distant suburb to a neighborhood close to his downtown job. "I'm a happy man," he told the *Times*, referring to his new lifestyle.[3] David Gillece, a real estate executive and former president of the Baltimore Economic Development Corporation, said in the spring of 1999, "I certainly believe that there are an awful lot of structural forces in place that suggest central cities should make a comeback." At a June 1999 "smart growth" conference in Minneapolis, environmentalists and elected officials from across the nation voiced a hopeful theme: "the stars are aligned" for a fundamental change in the way we develop our metro- politan areas, a change that favors cities and older suburbs. In April 2000, at the annual convention of the American Planning Association, journalist Ray Suarez announced, "I think an urban moment may be upon us once again."[4]

The age of electronic information bodes well for cities, contrary to popular assumption. William Mitchell, dean of architecture at the Massachusetts Institute of Technology, notes that the "locational freedom" granted by telecommunications and cybercommunications allows some workers to live farther than ever from cities, but many others "are selecting the city and its amenities—neighborhoods oriented to people on foot, concert halls, museums . . ." Peter Hall, author of *Cities of Tomorrow*, is equally optimistic: "The more you multiply electronic technology, the more you create demand for face-to-face contact."[5] These opinions are validated by the explosive growth of new-media industries in San Francisco's Multimedia Gulch and in Manhattan's Silicon Alley. In the first quarter of 2000, "dot-com" companies accounted for 25 percent of all the commercial leases executed in Manhattan's hot real estate market, eclipsing the traditional leader—the banking and finance sector.[6]

Many long-struggling cities have reversed their population declines in this era of falling crime rates and rising socio-economic indicators. The low unemployment rates that raise our hope for inner-city neighborhoods also favor downtown; in a tight labor market, businesses need every advantage to attract workers, including locations proximate to public transportation. In the closing years of the millennium, many of the nation's downtown office markets thrive as never before. "The state of the city is great," proclaimed Minneapolis Mayor Sharon Sayles Belton in her 1999 State of the City address.[7] Crime is down, downtown is booming, neighborhoods are thriving, and residential property values are up. "What can I say?" asked the mayor, "When you're hot, you're hot!"

WHEN YOU'RE NOT, YOU'RE NOT

The mayor was excessively jubilant. Crime is down, she said, but in the year that had just ended, Minneapolis' rate of violent crime was higher than in any year prior to 1986, more than 20 times as high as the rate in many of the suburbs with which Minneapolis competes for middle-class families. Downtown is booming? Historic buildings continue to fall, making way for parking garages. Downtown's last remaining cinema shut down less than two months after the mayor's gleeful proclamation. Neighborhoods are thriving? Some are healthy, but many others bear the scars of vandalism and abandonment in a city that has lost 50,000 residents (net loss) since 1970. Property values are up? Not everywhere, and not nearly enough in the city's marginal neighborhoods to compensate for three decades of decline and stagnation. The median value of houses in Minneapolis is about three-fourths that of houses in the surrounding suburbs.

In her State of the City address, the mayor also boasted that Minneapolis had recently won HUD's designation as an Empowerment Zone. But the city had to demonstrate substantial socioeconomic distress in order to achieve this dubious distinction. This is a sorry rather than salutary state of affairs.

Three decades ago, urban America was troubled by escalating crime rates and middle-class flight, but conditions were enviable then compared to now. America's cities are so grossly eviscerated that to restore them to their 1970 condition seems an unsurpassable goal, and true revitalization—the restoration of the vitality lost since World War II—seems beyond the imaginations of those who control the fate of our cities. State and federal officials relegate cities to a permanently diminished status, and urban policymakers—those who labor on behalf of cities—labor within the confines of a stunted vision. Paul Grogan, president and cofounder of CEOs for Cities and author of *Comeback Cities: A Blueprint for Urban Neighborhood Revival*, predicates his blueprint on the proposition that "cities do not have to reclaim all their lost glory." Many of America's policymakers, journalists, and academics have tacitly decided that the American city is just about as good as it will ever be.

We will reverse the social and environmental damage wrought by present-day metropolitan development practices only by exploiting the great potential of our cities, a potential that couldn't be more in doubt. The standardized and familiar prescriptions of metropolitan progressives—neo-traditional planners and "smart growth" advocates—will not reverse the automobile dependence of the American metropolis because they will not revitalize cities. The smart-growth agenda—light rail transit, mixed-use development, growth boundaries, smaller suburban lots, urban infill— will help to stabilize cities but, as currently formulated, the agenda will prevent or long delay true revitalization. The "smart growth" agenda lacks depth and focus, and it really isn't very smart.

Let's imagine that the agenda is adopted at the dawn of the new millennium and widely executed. Then, 50 years hence, historians will note that America's cities bottomed out at the turn of the millennium and thereafter slowly ascended. But the ascent has been shallow, they will say, compared to the deep decline of the latter 20th century. The historians will confidently speculate that America's cities will never regain their peak stature.

This pale urban future is the best we can realistically hope for, unless the stunted vision of today's progressive policymakers is cast aside for a better one. A brighter future is possible, but only if America's urban leaders comprehend the great potential of cities and exploit the rare opportunity presented by the alignment of factors favorable to revitalization. This book explores the great potential of the American city and outlines the essential elements for its revitalization.

Chapter 1 revisits Jane Jacobs' much acclaimed, but much ignored, prescription for urban vitality, for cities will achieve their great potential only if the lost attributes prescribed by Jacobs are restored to them. Chapter 2 builds upon the lessons of Jane Jacobs, exploring neighborhoods that adhere to her precepts and neighborhoods that do not. The essential attributes of vibrant neighborhoods are sacrificed in urban America to an irrational process of decentralization that bleeds the core of the metropolis. Chapter 3 examines the inevitable forces of decentralization and shows how and why we must turn them from forces of decay into forces of renewal.

Chapters 4, 5, and 6 delineate the recentralization agenda for commerce, housing, and transportation infrastructure. The decentralization of any one of these elements of the metropolis reinforces the decentralization of the other two. Recentralization of all three is necessary to realize the great potential of cities and thereby reverse the social and environmental damage inflicted on the entire metropolis by automobile dependence.

Any discussion about the recentralization of commerce, housing, and transportation infrastructure is moot if repellent social and economic conditions remain centralized in urban neighborhoods, but current strategies to deconcentrate poverty are ineffective if not counterproductive. Chapter 7 examines the deficiencies of current low-income housing policy, and Chapter 8 offers a strategy more in tune with the best interests of cities and their metropolitan areas.

The recentralization agenda encompasses the entire metropolis, from downtown to the outer frontier, but the urban neighborhood—the focus of the final section—is ground zero in the action plan. Chapter 9 exposes the neighborhood political forces that sometimes thwart the best interests of the city, and Chapter 10 offers a blueprint for neighborhood revitalization—the primary component of smart metropolitan growth.

Part

I

The Great Unrecognized Potential
of the American City

CHAPTER

1

Jane Jacobs Revisited

We have pitifully few outstandingly successful residential districts in our American Cities ...JANE JACOBS[1]

Maples and elms arch over the streets of Willard-Hay, a neighborhood of single-family houses, flower gardens, and well-tended lawns two miles northwest of downtown Minneapolis. Built mostly in the streetcar era on 5,000-square-foot lots, the neighborhood's houses vary in size, shape, and color, but a veil of trees softens the contrasts, and front porches lend a measure of visual unity. Critics of modern suburbia lament the disappearance of front porches and the loss of neighborliness implied; double-wide garage doors dominate the fronts of suburban houses, displacing outdoor socializing to fenced back yards. But in Willard-Hay, front porches are plentiful and still used by residents. Garages are relegated to back yards, accessible from alleys.

One-family detached houses constitute 70 percent of Willard Hay's housing stock, and in the mid-1990s, three-quarters of those detached houses were owner-occupied, compared to about two-thirds of housing units nationwide. High ownership rates bring high levels of care and maintenance, so it is unsurprising that only 11 percent of Willard-Hay's detached houses were classified "substandard" by the Minneapolis Planning Department in 1994. Willard-Hay is far from unique among Minneapolis neighborhoods; detached houses constitute a majority of housing units in most of the city's 81 neighborhoods, and the owner-occupancy rate for detached houses throughout the city is a lofty 89 percent.[2] City officials and neighborhood residents value owner-occupancy as an effective impetus to property maintenance and neighborhood stability, and, by extension, as a positive factor in quality of life.

Minneapolis was decreed to be one of the nation's five most livable cities by *Saturday Review* magazine in 1976, in an issue that noted Minneapolis' moderate housing densities and its "many neighborhoods of splendid, serene charm...softened by plenty of shade trees." In Minneapolis, "there are no down-and-out slums of the Chicago...variety," and Minneapolis has avoided the "fear of street crimes [that] has paralyzed many cities..."[3] *Money* magazine ranked the Minneapolis-St. Paul metropolis as one of the nation's 10 best in four of its five annual surveys of U.S. cities in the period 1989 through 1993.[4] *New York Times* cultural correspondent Paul Goldberger cited Minneapolis as an example of America's several low-density cities that "provide middle-class residents with close-in neighborhoods of detached houses with ample, and private, yards, allowing them to live what is essentially a suburban life within city limits." These neighborhoods, according to Goldberger, offer "a sense of relative freedom from the serious problems of crime and poverty that are so conspicuous in such cities as...New York."[5]

It is unsurprising that many Minneapolitans attribute their city's vaunted quality of life to its low-density neighborhoods of detached houses, big yards, and abundant trees; Americans traditionally associate leafy low-density living environments with high social, economic, and moral status. In the realm of violent crime, Minneapolitans long considered their city above the fray, a cousin to Denver or Seattle, perhaps, but not to high-crime big cities like New York.

But in 1995 Minneapolis' murder rate soared high above New York's—nearly 70 percent higher. Minneapolis' record-setting violence was announced to the world on the front page of the *New York Times* in June 1996, in an article noting that this city of "woodsy neighborhoods" had lost its urban innocence. The city that had nicknamed itself the Minneapple—the manageable Midwestern version of the Big Apple—had more recently acquired the nickname Murderapolis.[6] Then in July 1996 the *Minneapolis Star Tribune* noted, on a front page story, its hometown's declining position in *Money* magazine's annual ranking of U.S. cities. Minneapolis and its highly livable neighborhoods had enjoyed two decades of national media acclaim, but, the article noted, "those days may be gone for good." A month later another front-page story in the *Star Tribune* announced, "A pall hangs over the City of Lakes, as stagnant and enervating as the summer's humidity." That story reported a poll that disclosed a negative attitude and loss of faith: Fifty-eight percent of Minneapolis respondents feared that the quality of life in their city would deteriorate over the next 10 years.[7]

So it was that Minneapolis residents came to the sad realization that their leafy city of owner-occupied houses and spacious green lawns had entered the arena of urban despair; the "Minneapple" had lost its polish. In 1997 Minneapolis residents who perused *Money* magazine's annual survey of U.S. cities found their own ranked 118th, lower than Detroit.

MURDER AMONG DETACHED HOUSES

When television crews report murders in Minneapolis, one-family detached houses and tree-lined streets are the typical backdrop. And so they were in June 1996, when news crews visited Willard-Hay's Newton Avenue, which got the city's attention because two people were shot to death on that street in two separate incidents, within a week of one another. The Newton Avenue murders were noteworthy because they occurred not only within a week, but also within a block of one another, and one of the victims was a boy of just 11 years, killed in a drive-by shooting as he sat on the front porch of a Newton Avenue house.[8]

In reality, Newton Avenue North is a troubled street in a precarious neighborhood, a neighborhood where boarded-up houses and weed-infested vacant lots have emerged among the many orderly detached houses—a neighborhood invaded by drugs and crime. By the 1990s Willard-Hay was contributing disproportionately to its city's crime rate— in 1991 the neighborhood contained 2.3 percent of the city's population, and produced 3.7 percent its major crimes.[9] In 1995 Willard-Hay produced five murders, yielding a neighborhood rate of 60 murders per 100,000 population, more than double the citywide record-setting rate. (Three of Willard-Hay's five murders occurred at addresses occupied by one-family detached houses.) Willard-Hay's 1995 murder rate was not anomalous; the neighborhood produced five murders again the following year, including the two within a week and within a block of one another on Newton Avenue.[10]

In June 1996 a newspaper reporter visited the Newton Avenue block visited twice by murder that month, and described the everyday lives of residents: "[G]unshots ring through the 1900 block of Newton Avenue North every day,...violence has touched many of their lives and, worst of all,...their children can't play outside."[11] Willard-Hay's high rate of owner-occupancy failed to keep these problems at bay. The high owner-occupancy rate merely subjected a large number of working-class home-owners to an erosion of property value.

JANE JACOBS' PRESCRIPTION

In 1961 Jane Jacobs predicted Willard-Hay would degenerate into a "gray area." She told Minneapolis officials how to prevent the decline. The officials ignored her advice, and now they pour immense resources—police protection, social services, and housing improvement funds—into the neighborhood to stem the decay.

Jacobs didn't discuss Willard-Hay or Minneapolis specifically, but she discussed low-density urban housing generally in the most insightful and frequently-cited book ever written about urban America: *The Death and Life of Great American Cities*. She warned that low-density neighborhoods like Willard-Hay "will not generate city liveliness or public life—their populations are too thin—nor will they help maintain city sidewalk safety....densities of this kind ringing a city are a bad long-term bet, destined to become gray area."[12]

Social and economic conditions trump housing density and other physical conditions as determinants of neighborhood vitality. Socioeconomic privation breeds the disorder and criminal activity that undermines the public realm and repels the middle class. Where social and economic conditions are favorable they interact with high densities and three other physical conditions prescribed by Jacobs—commingled land uses, small blocks, and variously aged buildings—to create appealing urban environments. Appealing environments are necessary to attract and retain non-poor households to urban neighborhoods, and neighborhoods remain above despair as long as they retain a preponderance of non-poor households.

In spite of the poverty and social chaos associated with cities in the United States, more than a few Americans appreciate an urban environment, not only as a place to visit but as a place to live. Many Americans who can well afford suburban living choose to live in cities. In fact, much of the nation's most coveted housing is found in city neighborhoods that possess the four physical attributes prescribed by Jane Jacobs. The high price of housing in these high-density, high-vitality, high-appeal neighborhoods indicates that demand outweighs supply. Zoning restrictions and historical landmark designations, rather than market forces, prevent housing supplies from growing toward demand in the nation's premier urban neighborhoods.

Many suburbanites reject the innate physical characteristics of cities; they value big lawns, seclusion, and easy automobile access to everyday destinations. Other suburbanites reject not the innate physical characteristics of cities, but the inferior social condition of cities in the United States, and middle-class families with school-age children reject city schools. In metropolitan areas with growing populations, good housing in a decent neighborhood in an urban rather than suburban environment is available to a shrinking fraction of households. Suburban officials and developers attempt to narrow the supply-demand gap by reproducing some of the ambiance of the city in suburbia; the "new urbanism" is a primarily suburban movement that is gaining popularity. But urban vitality cannot be created in automobile-age suburbs, and the suburban interpretation of the urban environment could never compete with the real thing if it weren't for the superior social condition of suburbs and the exorbitant cost of housing in the nation's remaining high-vitality urban neighborhoods.

As suburban officials try to urbanize their suburbs, city officials suburbanize their cities in pursuit of that segment of the metropolitan housing market that is predisposed to suburban living. The pursuit of suburbanites is the renunciation of urban vitality, but policymakers and developers will continue to suburbanize cities until they recognize and respect the differences between physical development that is appropriate to land near the center of the metropolis and development appropriate to land remote from the center. Forty years ago Jane Jacobs outlined the fundamental characteristics of physical development that is appropriate to land near the center—city land. She prescribed and explained the attributes without which urban vitality is unattainable. These attributes—high densities, commingled land uses, small blocks, and variously aged buildings—should be maintained in the few city places endowed with them, and created in the many city places deprived. For cities in pursuit of vitality, these physical attributes are, as Jacobs wrote, *indispensable.*[13]

Of the four attributes prescribed by Jacobs, the density factor warrants special attention because it represents the greatest deficiency of the American city, and the most daunting political challenge.

DENSITY AND AUTOMOBILE DEPENDENCE

High densities—both commercial and residential—are essential to urban vitality because they minimize the automobile dependence of the occupants of cities: residents, workers, and visitors. Urban vitality is incompatible with automobile dependence, which is defined here as a condition evidenced by the daily use of automobiles by a majority of households for routine trips. The incompatibility of cities with automobile dependence was noted by Jane Jacobs in 1961:

> Traffic arteries, along with parking lots, gas stations, and drive-ins, are powerful and insistent instruments of city destruction. To accommodate them, city streets are broken down into loose sprawls, incoherent and vacuous for anyone afoot.[14]

City residents are as automobile dependent today as their suburban brethren, except where two amenities coexist:

1. Neighborhood commercial streets that provide frequently purchased goods and services within walking distance of residences.

2. Good transit that provides access to major employment centers and to specialized goods, services, and cultural amenities, mostly in and near downtown.

Under these conditions—proximity to a healthy commercial street, and good transit connections to a comprehensive high-vitality downtown—automobile dependence is minimized. These conditions cannot exist in the absence of high downtown and neighborhood densities. The subject of housing density recurs throughout this text, so definitions are in order:

Gross Housing Density describes the number of dwelling units per acre or square mile of land within specific boundaries, usually a neighborhood, a district, or a city. Gross density takes into account all land area—residential and nonresidential, including public right-of-way—within the area's boundaries. (The measure sometimes called "neighborhood housing density" is referred to here as gross housing density.)

Net Housing Density refers to the number of dwelling units per acre of land devoted exclusively to housing—land within the property lines of the lot or lots occupied by housing. Net densities exclude nonresidential land such as parks, schools, commercial development, and public right-of-way. (The net housing density of a neighborhood is double the gross housing density if one-half of the neighborhood's land is private land occupied by housing.) Net densities provide a more accurate clue about housing types than gross densities do. Furthermore, transit researchers have compiled important data, cited later, based on net densities.

Low density is defined most generally as a housing density incapable of sustaining good transit and basic neighborhood retailing within walking distance of most households; *high density* sustains both.

A net housing density of at least 15 dwelling units per acre—nearly double the density of most detached-house neighborhoods—is required to sustain a high level of bus service (120 buses per day on routes spaced no more than one-half mile apart). And densities much higher than that are necessary to overcome automobile dependence. In the American city, fewer than half of all vehicle trips originating in a neighborhood will be made on transit unless the neighborhood's net housing density exceeds 60 dwelling units per acre.[15]

High housing densities are required also to sustain a full range of frequently purchased, or convenience, goods and services in neighborhood commercial areas within walking distance of households. Jane Jacobs suggested that a net housing density in excess of 100 units per acre is required to sustain neighborhood commercial vitality.[16] A net housing density of 110 units per acre allows 10,000 people to live on a piece of land 2,000 feet square, assuming half the land is devoted to housing, and assuming an average of two people per housing unit. If that square piece of land were bisected by a commercial street, then all 10,000 residents would live within 1,000 feet of it. Such a compact arrangement would ensure the vitality of the commercial street because most of the 10,000 residents would patronize it routinely, walking rather than driving.

THE DEATH OF NEIGHBORHOOD COMMERCE

Willard-Hay is more suburban in character today than in its pre-World War II days because its inhabitants no longer sustain the high-quality transit and the full range of neighborhood retailing they sustained a couple generations ago; they're dependent on cars. Willard Hay is representative of thinly populated, devitalized neighborhoods common in cities across America, from Buffalo to Los Angeles.

Most American cities have population densities of less than 7,500 people per square mile; in 2000, 40 of the nation's 50 most populous cities had overall population densities below that threshold (Figure 1-1) and densities drop off further in America's less populous cities. In order to achieve a population density as low as 7,500 persons per square mile, a city must possess at least one of the following three defects: an inordinate number of one-person households, an unusually small fraction of land area occupied by housing, or a sizable inventory of one-family detached houses. The typical American city has too many detached houses.

Minneapolis, for example, has an overall population density of 6,970 people per square mile in 2000, and 44 percent of its housing stock is one-

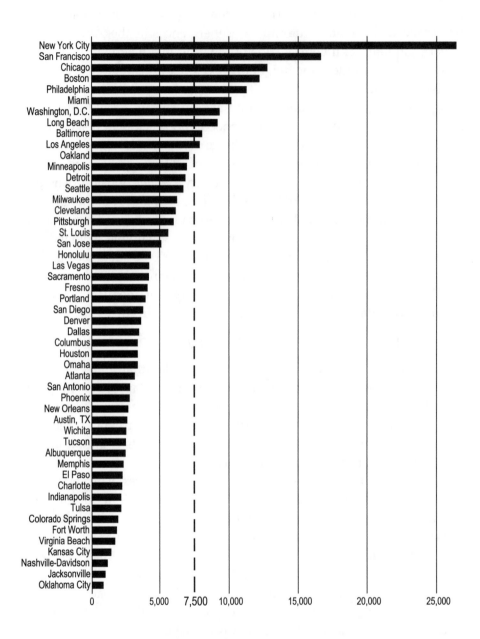

Figure 1-1. Population densities—2000: Inhabitants per square mile in America's 50 most populous cities.

Source of data: Census 2000, PL94-171 Summary File.

family detached houses. Duplexes and detached houses combined account for more than half (58 percent) of Minneapolis' housing units. The city's average net housing density is only 13 units per acre, a semi-suburban density.[17] (Net densities in most neighborhoods, including Willard-Hay, are even lower than that; the citywide average is spiked by higher densities at the edges of downtown and near the University of Minnesota.) If a city's entire housing stock consisted of townhouses on traditional townhouse lots it would have net housing densities in the range of 16 to 20 units per acre, and an overall population density exceeding 8,000 persons per square mile. Cities with population densities less than 7,500 people per square mile invariably include sizable neighborhoods of detached houses and duplexes—suburban housing that no longer sustains the essential elements of urban life—good public transportation and full-service neighborhood commercial streets.

Prior to the 1950s, before car ownership was universal, neighborhoods of Willard-Hay's density sustained a full range of convenience retail and service establishments on their commercial streets. Drugstores, hardware stores, and large grocery stores traditionally anchored neighborhood retail areas, drawings enough customers to sustain bakeries, dry cleaners, shoe repair shops, and other retail and service businesses. But the traditional anchors and their entourage of smaller businesses followed the middle class in its post-war flight. Market analysts reported in 1996 that only 28 percent of Minneapolis' 57 neighborhood commercial areas have a supermarket, 35 percent have a drug store, and only 30 percent have a hardware store. And only one of Minneapolis' 57 neighborhood commercial areas combines all three of these traditional anchors. In all of Minneapolis, according to the analysis, there remains *only one* full-service neighborhood commercial area. This diminishes quality of life, according to the analysts:

> Most of the Minneapolis neighborhood commercial areas are not providing the range of convenience and neighborhood oriented goods and services needed or desired by most residents living within their trade areas. Almost all lack some of the basic goods and services needed or desired by most residents on a regular basis. This makes it necessary for residents to go to other commercial areas on a regular basis.[18]

Larger trade-area populations are necessary today to sustain a neighborhood's traditional level of retail activity, especially in cities with high rates of automobile ownership and large numbers of residents who commute to suburban jobs. In Minneapolis and similar low-density cities, a neighborhood commercial area with the traditional array of goods and services requires a trade-area population of at least 10,000 today, double the number required in the 1950s. (A much larger population is required to sustain a neighborhood commercial street with an enhanced range of amenities including a cinema.)[19] In 1995, the average trade-area population for the 57 neighborhood commercial areas in Minneapolis was only 5,575—a number sufficient to sustain a full-service commercial area in the 1950s, but just half the number required today. At today's neighborhood densities, the 10,000 people required to sustain a traditional neighborhood commercial area are spread so thin that only a small fraction lives within a reasonable walking distance. Remote residents depend on vehicles for convenience shopping, and in today's retail environment the shoppers who get into their cars are won by modern large-scale retailers on major arterial streets (usually suburban) rather than by small-scale neighborhood merchants. The relatively few car owners who live within walking distance of a neighborhood commercial street will usually ignore it unless it offers the complete range of frequently purchased products and services in a compact arrangement. Commercial streets that offer less than that will lose car owners to big new supermarkets and discount department stores that offer convenient parking, low prices, and broad product selections. At these venues, shoppers succumb to the convenience of one-stop shopping and buy not only those products that are unavailable in their neighborhoods, but also those products that are available.

Neighborhood commercial streets began to lose businesses by the mid-1950s, and the businesses that remained became increasingly dependent on patrons arriving in cars. The number of grocery stores in Minneapolis declined in the 1950s while the number of gas stations increased. In 1962, the Minneapolis Planning Commission recommended off-street parking as a means of maintaining the viability of struggling neighborhood commercial areas.[20] But the decline continued. The torching of commercial buildings during the race riots of the 1960s was the coup de grace to neighborhood retailing in urban America. In Philadelphia, a 1964 traffic dispute precipitated rioting on a celebrated community commercial street; 31 years later the *Philadelphia Inquirer* recounted the incident and its enduring consequences:

A simple traffic dispute between a police officer and a local woman turned into a riot that would permanently destroy what was once the commercial heart of black North Philadelphia. Days of looting followed what would come to be known as the Columbia Avenue Riots. The commercial strip, nicknamed "Jump Street" because of its energy and jazz bars...would never rebound.[21]

The assassination of Dr. Martin Luther King, Jr. in 1968 triggered burning and looting in more than 100 cities. In Washington, D.C., approximately 20,000 rioters inflicted an estimated $15 million in property damage including the destruction of half the property along Fourteenth Street. Many of the city's businesses relocated to the suburbs, and nearly 5,000 central-city jobs were permanently lost. "Patterns of commerce that had developed over decades and sustained black neighborhoods were snuffed out in three days," according to Washington journalists Harry Jaffe and Tom Sherwood.[22]

The Official Renunciation of Neighborhood Commerce

In the decades since the 1960s, city governments have filled the retail void in some of their long-deprived communities, assembling land and turning it over to developers who build upon that land one-story supermarkets and discount department stores surrounded by parking lots, just like in the suburbs. These suburb-style developments are intended to provide local jobs and shopping opportunities, and to stem the flow of central-city dollars to suburban retailers. The new large-scale developments, which are found on major arterial streets for a mostly drive-in trade, could not be provided for every neighborhood, but only for broader districts. Thus the scale of basic retailing expanded from the *neighborhood* level to the *district* level. Neighborhood-level commercial streets were left to languish.

Commercial streets in low-density middle-class neighborhoods live on in altered form to comply with present-day realities. Once-continuous rows of storefronts are gapped with parking lots and gas stations. Some of the remaining commercial buildings retain their traditional uses, but many have found new uses: antiques shops, health-food stores, and coffee houses, all of which draw customers from beyond walking distance, customers for whom off-street parking is necessary. In low-density low-income neighborhoods many commercial buildings are boarded up, but others continue to serve original or new uses. Rather than antiques shops and health-food stores, however, one is likely to find check-cashing joints, storefront missions, social service agencies, and auto parts and repair shops. Laura Washington, editor and publisher of the *Chicago Reporter*, describes the paucity of neighborhood commerce in a Chicago gray area called Englewood, a neighborhood of "two-flats and aging single-family homes." Her description fits most of America's urban gray areas:

> The nearest supermarket is miles away, so you're stuck with the neighborhood grocer, a raggety storefront where things never go on sale. You must pay the "black tax," that surcharge on the cost of groceries, dry cleaning, insurance and the other basics...
>
> Want to take the family out to dinner for a special occasion? Your only options in the neighborhood are chicken shacks and burger joints....
>
> You're living from paycheck to paycheck, and you could use a checking account. But there are no banks nearby....
>
> Despite a record-breaking economic boom, new businesses are not locating in your neighborhood...[23]

In low-density neighborhoods, non-poor as well as poor, the commercial area lacks the full range of retail and service establishments that would allow neighborhood residents to do their routine shopping without a car. And in both cases, many if not most customers drive to the commercial area in cars that are accommodated in off-street parking lots.

Parking lots are more plentiful than stores on West Broadway Avenue, the main commercial thoroughfare for Willard-Hay and the five other neighborhoods in Minneapolis' Near North district. The mile-and-a-half portion of West Broadway that borders Willard-Hay has only 34 consumer retail and service establishments where twice as many existed in the mid-1950s (excluding automobile sales and repair businesses). Today's inventory includes three gas station/convenience stores and five hair salons, but the two drugstores and three hardware stores that were here in 1955 have disappeared. Willard-Hay's segment of West Broadway has also lost its general merchandise ("variety") stores, shoe stores, appliance stores, furniture stores, furriers, meat markets, sporting goods stores, bowling alleys, dry cleaners, and its flower shop.[24]

Willard-Hay's surviving businesses share once-lively West Broadway with storefront missions, auto repair shops, used-car lots, parking lots, vacant lots, and vacant buildings. Willard-Hay's former Paradise Theater is among West Broadway's vacant buildings—a video rental shop now provides entertainment to neighborhood residents. Movie theaters that once energized neighborhood commercial streets are all but extinct from low-density neighborhoods. The Paradise Theater has been vacant since the late 1970s, but nearby Delisi's Italian restaurant and Art Song's ribs and chicken wings held out until the mid-1990s, when they too locked their doors and boarded their windows.

West Broadway borders the northern edge of Willard-Hay and is beyond walking distance of those residents in the southerly portion of the neighborhood, but those residents were served by a second commercial street—Plymouth Avenue—until the late 1960s when rioting and fires ravaged the businesses there. Before the turmoil, Willard-Hay's portion of Plymouth Avenue had about 50 consumer retail and service businesses similar to those found on West Broadway. Today it has only eight, five of which are in a new suburban-style strip behind a parking lot.[25] Those segments of West Broadway and Plymouth Avenue that traverse or border the Willard-Hay neighborhood once offered approximately 120 retail and service establishments to the neighborhood's residents. Now they offer about one-third as many. Willard-Hay residents can no longer walk to a lively commercial street for routine goods and services, let alone luxuries, entertainment, recreation, and relaxation.

DENSITY EXTREMES

The power of high residential densities to sustain neighborhood commercial vitality is most evident in New York City's Upper East Side, where Census Tract 126 (CT-126) represents an extreme housing density, an extreme opposite that of the Willard-Hay neighborhood (Table 1-1). (New York City does not officially recognize its neighborhoods, some of which are loosely defined, as geographic entities; nor does the city compile data on them. Manhattan's census tracts most closely resemble Minneapolis' neighborhoods in magnitude of population.) CT-126, which has New York City's highest housing density, is located a mile and a half north of the heart of Midtown Manhattan, covering the 10 blocks bounded by First and Third avenues on the east and west, and by Seventy-fourth and Sixty-ninth streets on the north and south. With a population about 40 percent higher than Willard-Hay's, CT-126 occupies less than 7 percent as much land area (Figure 1-2). The population density of CT-126 is more than 21 times that of Willard-Hay, and CT-126's net

Table 1-1. Density Spectrum: Net Housing Densities

Density Range	Example	Housing Types	Net Density
Very High 150 and up	Census Tract 126, Manhattan	Low-rise, mid-rise, and high-rise apartments; very few flats and townhouses	330
	Upper East Side and Upper West Side	Low-rise, mid-rise, and high-rise apartments; flats, townhouses	210
High 75-149	Brooklyn Heights, Brooklyn, New York	Mostly low-rise apartments, flats, and townhouses; some mid-rise and high-rise apartments	125
	Commercial Threshold	**Commercial street within 1,000 feet of 10,000 residents (1)**	**110**
	Beacon Hill, Boston	Low-rise apartments, flats, and townhouses	95
Moderate 25-74	**Transit Threshold**	**More than half of vehicle trips are made on public transportation (2)**	**60**
	Lafayette Courts,	Public housing with high-rise and low-rise buildings	40
	Baltimore	(Demolished for redevelopment at lower density)	
	Richmond district, San Francisco	Townhouses, virtual townhouses, low-rise apartments, and flats	30
Low 10-24	New York townhouses (generically)	One-family townhouses on lots measuring 25 feet X 100 feet	17
	Transit Threshold	**Good Bus Service supported: 120 buses per day; 1/2 mile route spacing (3)**	**15**
	Willard-Hay n'borhood, Minneapolis	One-family detached houses, duplexes, and small apartment buildings	10
Very Low Below 10	R1 zoning district, Minneapolis	One-family detached houses on 6,000 square-foot lots	7
	Typical post-war Suburban subdivision	One-family detached houses on lots ranging from 6,000 to 15,000 square feet	3 – 7

Numbered Notes:

(1) Stipulations: the neighborhood is square in shape, bisected by the commercial street; 50 percent of land area is devoted to housing; two persons per housing unit, on average.

(2) Source: Regional Plan Association, "Where Transit Works," Regional Plan News, August 1976, p. 6.

(3) Source: Parsons Brinckerhoff Quade & Douglas, Inc., Transportation Research Board of the National Research Council, TCRP Report 16, Transit and Urban Form (Washington D.C.: National Academy Press, 1996), Volume 1, Part 1, Table 6, p. 15.

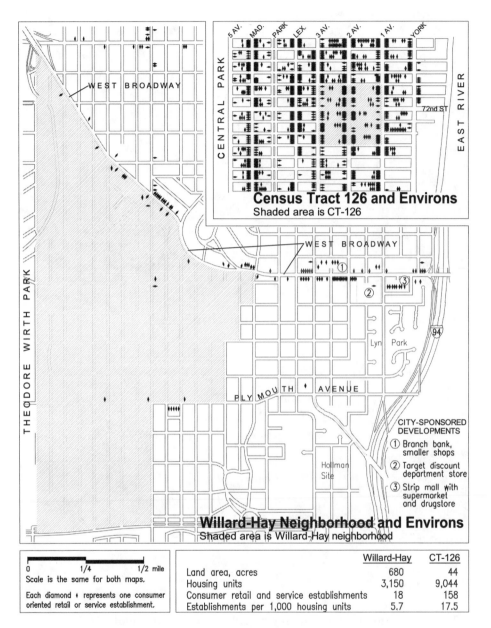

Census Tract 126 and Environs
Shaded area is CT-126

CITY-SPONSORED
DEVELOPMENTS
① Branch bank,
   smaller shops
② Target discount
   department store
③ Strip mall with
   supermarket
   and drugstore

Willard-Hay Neighborhood and Environs
Shaded area is Willard-Hay neighborhood

Scale is the same for both maps.

Each diamond ♦ represents one consumer oriented retail or service establishment.

	Willard-Hay	CT-126
Land area, acres	680	44
Housing units	3,150	9,044
Consumer retail and service establishments	18	158
Establishments per 1,000 housing units	5.7	17.5

Figure 1-2. Minneapolis—Willard-Hay neighborhood, and Manhattan—CT-126. CT-126 has nearly three times as many housing units as Willard-Hay, on less than 7 percent as much land area. High housing density in CT-126 sustains consumer businesses within easy walking distance of all residents.

Source for business locations: author's surveys, April 23–30, 2001. Automobile sales and service businesses not counted, except gas stations with convenience stores. (These are plentiful in Willard-Hay and environs.) Private schools, child-care facilities, and realty, law, and financial service offices not counted. (These are plentiful in CT-126 and environs.)

1-3a. First Avenue, Census Tract 126, Manhattan (1999)

1-3b. West Broadway, Willard-Hay neighborhood, Minneapolis (2000)

Figure 1-3. Commercial streets—CT-126 and Willard-Hay.
High residential density in CT-126 sustains a rich variety of retailers on the
ground floors of apartment buildings and tenements. Willard Hay's primary
commercial street is vacuous; the surrounding low-density housing no longer
sustains neighborhood commerce as it once did.

housing density is about 330 housing units per acre, 33 times as dense as Willard-Hay's 10 units per acre.[26]

Housing is the dominant land use in CT-126, where retail activity occurs on the ground floors of apartment buildings and tenements, mostly on the tract's three north-south avenues—First, Second, and Third (Figure 1-3a). Medical and dental offices, laundries and tailor shops occupy ground-floor space on east-west streets. CT-126 has nearly three times as many housing units as Willard-Hay (with fewer occupants per unit, on average), and nearly nine times as many consumer-oriented business establishments.

Residents of CT-126 (and other tracts in the Upper East Side) find all frequently purchased goods and services within easy walking distance of their homes. Residents of Willard-Hay must leave their neighborhood to get convenience items; many travel more than a mile to the nearest drugstore or hardware store. CT-126's superior commercial inventory is attributable in part to its greater affluence, but its high housing density is its dominant advantage. Consumer amenities that are absent from CT-126, or in short supply, such as exercise clubs and cinemas, are available nearby. Intense commercial development continues from the northern to the southern border of the Upper East Side—a two-mile stretch—and beyond.

In Willard-Hay, West Broadway's businesses are widely separated from each other by the avenue's many vacant buildings and lots, too widely separated to walk among (Figure 1-3b). Consequently it is not only difficult for most Willard-Hay residents to get to West Broadway without a car, but for those who live near West Broadway the trek from store to store is arduous. Once in their cars, it is easiest for car owners to leave the neighborhood for routine errands.

Willard-Hay's automobile-dependent residents shop mostly in adjacent suburbs or in a modern strip development—three commercial superblocks developed with City of Minneapolis assistance—centered a half-mile east of Willard-Hay's border, a full mile east of the middle of the neighborhood. This suburban-style development, on West Broadway near Interstate 94, includes a supermarket and a drugstore (on the block farthest from Willard-Hay), and also some fast-food restaurants, some auto repair businesses, and a discount department store. The discount department store—a Target store—has some 60,000 square feet of sales area and a range of merchandise traditionally represented by a dozen stores. The Target store is the merchandising and sales-area equivalent of perhaps 20 stores of the type and size once prominent on West Broadway and still alive in CT-126. A parking lot of some 500 spaces accommodates Target's customers.

Most of West Broadway's businesses vacated before the Target store was built, but when city officials were forced by circumstances into action they decided to suburbanize retailing in Willard-Hay's Near North district to consolidate it into one automobile-oriented location. They combined six small blocks into three superblocks large enough to accommodate parked cars adjacent to the new businesses. The officials chose not to re-urbanize neighborhood retailing by increasing housing densities to a level that would support traditional commercial arrays along the full length of West Broadway. That is why West Broadway is alive today with vehicles but not pedestrians.

In March 2000, the elected leaders of Minneapolis adopted a comprehensive plan that fully endorses the automobile's encroachment onto formerly pedestrian-oriented commercial streets like West Broadway: "These corridors must balance both a pedestrian and automobile orientation in their design and development." Consistent with this vision, the plan's implementation strategy includes the development of "parking facilities [for] improved customer access." Vacuous as they are, neighborhood commercial areas have too much commercial space according to the city's official plan: "Many areas of the city have an oversupply of commercial space."[27] The planning department cites West Broadway as one of several derelict commercial streets ripe for unspecified and unknown "alternative land use." The city's vision of commercial retrenchment is consistent with its intent to "maintain areas that are predominantly developed with single and two family structures," but this stunted vision is strikingly incompatible with the plan's definition of a great city: "A great city is a place where you can walk."[28]

You can walk if you live in CT-126 and its environs because the area's businesses are within easy walking distance of their trade-area populations, and each other.* No land on the Upper East Side is farther than a half mile from a comprehensive retail array. Eighty percent of Upper East

*The primary trade area served by CT-126's businesses extends westward to Central Park and eastward to the East River. This compact trade area measures perhaps a half mile from north to south by slightly less than a mile from east to west, with CT-126 near the center. And this densely populated trade area is home to roughly 50,000 people— enough to sustain the full range of convenience commercial amenities and much more. Although the limits of the trade area for CT-126's businesses cannot be precisely drawn, the trade area is evidently compact enough to dissuade most residents from using private vehicles for routine shopping.

Side land lies within 1,000 feet of at least one of the district's four avenues that are lined almost continuously with consumer retail and service establishments. (The four avenues are First, Second, Third, and Lexington. Madison Avenue is lined for much of its length with specialty stores, and York Avenue intersperses commercial land uses with institutional. Fifth and Park avenues accommodate many medical and dental practices, but few retail establishments, between Fifty-ninth and Ninety-sixth streets.)

Virtually all of Willard-Hay (and the trade area served by its businesses) is farther than a half mile from the superblocks on West Broadway—the Near North district's only full-service retail array.* Seventy percent of the larger Near North district is farther than a half mile from the superblocks. Routine shopping in Willard-Hay and its surrounding neighborhoods is an endeavor that necessarily involves automobiles.

Walkability

Four interrelated factors ensure that Upper East Side residents will walk rather than drive to the businesses in their district. First, distances among households and businesses are short. Second, automobile ownership rates are low. Third, off-street parking is scarce. And fourth, the streets and avenues of the Upper East Side are safe, lively, and appealing to people on foot.

The east-west streets of the Upper East Side are tree-shaded and tranquil, lined with high-stoop townhouses and low-rise pre-war apartment buildings of brick and stone masonry, softened by townhouse gardens and an occasional vest-pocket park. Commercial avenues are bordered by continuous rows of storefronts modulated by large display windows, pedestrian-oriented signage, and closely spaced entrances. On Second Avenue between Seventy-third and Seventy-fourth streets (in CT-126) a row of eight tenements accommodates 12 businesses, an average of one storefront every 17 feet. This fine-grained quality is found throughout the Upper East Side, where rich varieties in architectural scale and style combine with colorful outdoor displays of fruit and flowers, and with the aromas of exotic restaurants, to produce an environment in which one prefers walking to driving. It is unsurprising under these circumstances

---

*The trade area served by Willard-Hay's dispersed businesses extends beyond the neighborhood's boundaries, encompassing four times as much land as CT-126's trade area, but containing less than a third as many residents. Since there are no full-service retail concentrations in Willard-Hay, the neighborhood's residents and the larger trade-area population served by its businesses go to the suburbs or the new commercial superblocks near Interstate 94 for their routine shopping.

that CT-126's retail and service amenities include two shoe repair shops but no car repair garages or gas stations.

The avenues of the Upper East Side are rarely broken by gas stations or surface parking lots—the grim land uses that so profusely adulterate the commercial streets of low-density districts. In all of CT-126 there are no such land uses; off-street parking is limited to the basements of newer apartment buildings, a few townhouse garages, and a solitary on-grade multiple-vehicle garage. And that garage occupies only 7,500 square feet of land, less than one percent of the private land area in CT-126. The streets and avenues of the Upper East Side are almost completely devoid of the unappealing land uses that extend physical and psychological walking distances among homes and businesses in most of America's urban neighborhoods.

Research published in 1984 indicates that 500 feet is, for nearly all able-bodied people, an acceptable walking distance for routine purposes, and 40 percent consider 1,000 feet to be a reasonable walking distance. However these distances decrease in ominous settings and increase along stimulating urban streets.[29] Diversions of the sort found on the streets and avenues of the Upper East Side reduce the psychological distance of a walk, but the standard features of gray-area commercial streets—parking lots and vacant buildings, or parking lots and big blank walls in the case of suburb-style commercial developments—add psychological distance to excessive physical distance.

Darkness of night increases psychological distances on depopulated streets, but residential and commercial streets in high-density neighborhoods generate reassuring nighttime activity. Though more stolid than Manhattan' Upper West Side and its downtown neighborhoods, the Upper East Side provides a sure sense of nighttime street safety to the many residents shopping, walking their dogs, or visiting the district's restaurants. Many Upper East Side restaurants, drugstores, and grocery stores remain open late into the night, some 24 hours. The safety and comfort of Upper East Side pedestrians is abetted by hundreds of doormen tending the lobbies of their apartment buildings around the clock, eyes on the street.

THE EROSION OF TRANSIT

One might expect a low-income neighborhood's low rate of car ownership to enliven its commercial street with a captive market, but car ownership rates in low-income neighborhoods are not all that low, unless their housing densities are high. Automobile ownership in Minneapolis' Near North district extends well into the universe of households in poverty. In a majority of the district's census tracts, the number of households owning one or more vehicles is higher than the number of households above the poverty threshold, according to 1990 census data.

Poor and non-poor households in suburbs and in suburbanized cities must buy and maintain automobiles as soon as they can afford them, and many of those who can't afford them find ways to possess them. In the central-city counties of the Twin Cities metropolitan area—Hennepin and Ramsey—23 percent of welfare recipients own cars. As Minneapolis' poverty rate climbed from 13.5 percent to 18.5 percent in the decade of the 1980s, the city lost 1,176 households, but it gained about 14,000 automobiles.[30] Urban devitalization is, in large measure, suburbanization.

Rising affluence generally brings rising rates of automobile ownership, but high residential densities counteract the effect of affluence on rates of ownership and use.[31] Because of their high densities, New York City's richest residential districts have lower rates of vehicle ownership than Minneapolis' poorest. New York's Upper East Side, the most affluent of 59 Community Districts in the five boroughs, had a 1990 median household income of $53,000 (and a median family income of $94,350). Yet less than 30 percent of the district's households owned personal vehicles in 1990. By contrast, nearly two-thirds (64.3 percent) of the households in Minneapolis' low-density Near North district owned vehicles in 1990 in spite of a median household income barely more than a third as high as the Upper East Side's, and a poverty rate more than six times as high.[32]

Corollary to the Upper East Side's low rate of automobile ownership is its high rate of transit use. According to 1990 census data, 57.7 percent of Upper East Side commutes were on public transportation, with the subway accounting for a majority of transit trips. Another 21.6 percent of workers walked to their workplaces; only 8.6 percent of commutes were in single-occupancy cars. (The remaining 12.1 percent worked at home, carpooled, or used taxis, bikes, or in-line skates.) Commuters from Minneapolis' low density Near North neighborhoods, by contrast, used public transportation for only 21 percent of commutes in spite of lesser affluence. Fifty-seven percent of Near North's employed residents drove alone to work each day in 1990. Housing densities explain the differences in commuting habits.

In a 1976 report called *Where Transit Works*, transit analysts outlined the results of their groundbreaking research into the factors that produce high rates of transit use. The analysts summarized their findings (which were reexamined and validated as recently as 1996):

> Residents will be more likely to use public transportation:
> **1.** The higher the density and the larger the size of a downtown or another cluster of nonresidential activity;
> **2.** the closer their neighborhood is to that nonresidential concentration;
> **3.** the higher the residential density of their neighborhood;
> **4.** the better the transit service.[33]

The first three of these are land-use factors, which affect the fourth—a service factor. The three land-use factors, if favorable, enable a transit authority to provide high-quality service cost-efficiently. Notice that high densities account for two of the three land-use conditions that maximize transit use. High downtown density is even more important than high neighborhood density, as will be discussed in Chapter 4, but high housing densities also are essential to sustain transit service of sufficient quality to compete effectively with automobiles (Figure 1-4).

Quality of transit service is measured primarily by service frequency and route spacing. No point in CT-126 is more than 400 feet from a transit route; buses travel all three of the tract's avenues and one of its streets (Seventy-second). Willard-Hay's route spacing leaves some residents as far as 1,400 feet from the nearest bus line, a problem compounded by long service intervals (headways). After decades of service reductions, evening and weekend headways of one hour are not uncommon among the bus routes that serve Willard-Hay.[34]

A total of 178 downtown-bound buses (on four routes) serve Willard-Hay's 680 acres each weekday, compared to about 360 midtown-bound buses per day (on two routes) in CT-126's forty-four acres. Residents of CT-126 get double the bus service on 7 percent as much land area, and fewer than half of Upper East Side transit users ride the bus; most ride the Lexington Avenue subway one block west of CT-126.[35] Density of transit service corresponds with density of population, and in low-density neighborhoods like Willard-Hay, the combination of long headways and wide route spacing encourages car ownership, even among the poor.

Less than two miles from the biggest downtown between the Great Lakes and the Rocky Mountains, Willard-Hay lacks the population density to sustain two essentials of urban life: good transit and neighborhood commerce. These are the vital elements that distinguish urban neighborhoods from suburban neighborhoods. They were available in the Willard-

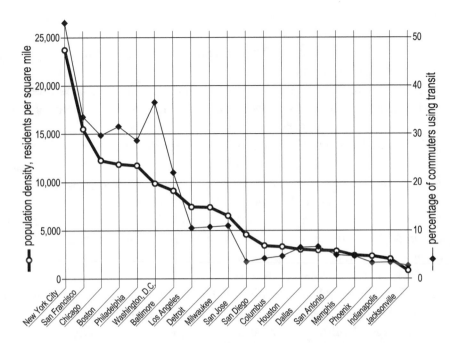

Figure 1-4. Population densities and rates of transit commuting in America's most populous 20 cities—1990. Residential population density is one of three land-use factors that determine the feasibility of transit communing for city residents.
Source of data: U.S. Census Bureau, Summary Tape File 3, DP-3, 1990.

Hay of the 1950s and earlier, but today's Willard-Hay burdens its residents with automobile dependence. In that respect, Willard-Hay is more suburban today than in its formative years as a streetcar suburb.

APPROPRIATE DENSITIES

Between the density extremes of automobile-dependent Willard-Hay and high-amenity CT-126 lies the range of densities appropriate for most American urban neighborhoods. Willard-Hay's low density cannot sustain the essentials of urban life, and CT-126's inventory of high density housing cannot attract very many middle-class families with children because such high densities preclude one-family houses, except in very small numbers. Only 39 of CT-126's 9,026 housing units are one-family houses (townhouses), and 53 units are flats in townhouses subdivided into two, three, or four units, according to 1990 census data. Eighty-six percent of the tract's housing units are in apartment buildings with 20 or more units. The average housing unit in CT-126 housed only 1.4 persons in 1990 compared to a national average of 2.4 persons per housing unit.[36] CT-126 densities are appropriate for near-downtown sectors of big cities, but most neighborhoods must provide a better balance among housing types while maintaining densities sufficient to sustain retail amenities and good transit. Such neighborhoods can be found, and they are among the most appealing in America.

New York City's Brooklyn Heights, for example, provides a rich mix of housing types including 19th-century and contemporary townhouses, low-rise, mid-rise, and a few high-rise apartment buildings, mostly on quiet, narrow, tree-shaded streets. With a net housing density of about 125 units per acre, less than half the density of CT-126, Brooklyn Heights is populated densely enough to produce transit ridership rates above 50 percent and to sustain one of the liveliest commercial streets in New York City—Montague Street—within walking distance of all the neighborhood's residents.[37] All four prerequisites to urban vitality prescribed by Jane Jacobs—high density, commingled land uses, small blocks, and variously aged buildings—are abundantly present in Brooklyn Heights.

In Philadelphia, Rittenhouse Square offers much the same variety of housing types and commercial amenities, and the same can be said of San Francisco's Nob Hill, Russian Hill, and Pacific Heights neighborhoods. In San Francisco, as in other cities, high neighborhood densities correlate with high appeal as evidenced by affluence. (A high-appeal neighborhood is loosely defined here as one in which the housing inventory includes more than a few units valued at double the metropolitan-area median.) Apartments sell routinely for more than double the metro-area median in San Francisco's highest-density residential sector, which includes the famous neighborhoods mentioned above.[38]

High-density neighborhoods in Chicago, Washington, D.C., and Boston support the generalization that the nation's highest-density neighborhoods are among its most appealing. Boston's Beacon Hill accommodates nearly 10,000 residents in its captivating red brick townhouses and low-rise apartment buildings, which constitute a net housing density of nearly 100 units per acre. Beacon Hill devotees Barbara Moore and Gail Weesner write that their beloved neighborhood is "an unusually stable and close-knit community," and they add, "We live within walking distance of most urban amenities and services." By 1999, townhouse prices in Beacon Hill had broken the $4 million threshold, attesting to the enduring appeal of the neighborhood.[39]

San Francisco and Toronto* are routinely cited as exemplary and highly livable North American cities that have retained affluent and middle class households, and both have population densities above 15,000 inhabitants per square mile—more than double the densities of most U.S. cities. Both cities offer lively neighborhood commercial streets and highly evolved transit systems. San Francisco's rate of transit use is more than double that of Minneapolis and other low-density cities. And the Bay City's high appeal is evidenced by the fact that its median house value is higher than that of its metropolitan area, whereas Minneapolis and most other U.S. cities have median house values lower than those of their metro areas.[40]

DENSITY AVERSION

In spite of the several exemplary high-density neighborhoods in North America's highest-density cities, and in spite of San Francisco's and Toronto's avoidance of the widespread urban despair that troubles many low-density cities, aversions to densities higher than suburban densities persist in the United States, even in central cities. But those aversions are less rational today than they were a century ago when they established deep roots.

America's long-standing aversion to high residential densities peaked in a 19th- and early 20th-century period of massive immigration and urban housing shortage, when high densities were associated with the dark squalor of tenement slums, especially in New York City where population pressures were greatest and densities were highest. Representative of the era's tenement critics was housing reformer Henry Morgenthau, who in 1909 characterized the tenement environment as "an evil that breeds physical disease, moral depravity, discontent, and socialism..."[41] (Physical disease, moral depravity, discontent, and political liberalism are commonly associated today with New York City and San Francisco—the nation's most densely populated cities.)

While some of New York's housing reformers campaigned for improvements in tenement design, others excoriated tenements in any form, blaming high densities for poverty and deficient character, prescribing

---

* Toronto is now one of six communities in the City of Toronto, which absorbed the five other municipalities of Metropolitan Toronto in 1998, increasing the city's land area from 38 to 243 square miles and decreasing its population density from 17,400 to 9,800 residents per square mile. Still, this is a density higher than that of any central metropolitan land area of equal size in the United States outside of New York City, which anchors a metropolitan area four times as populous as Toronto's, and Chicago, which anchors a metro area twice as populous as Toronto's.

low-density living as the cure. Environmental determinist Elgin Gould indicted the New York tenement as corrosive to health, morality, family, and civic integrity, and then he prescribed suburban homeownership, by then (1909) made feasible by streetcar lines, as a cure for the social and economic problems of the immigrant poor. Gould believed that suburban homeownership would convert slum dwellers of deficient character into "reflective, careful, prudent..." citizens. Reformer Lawrence Veiller prescribed the one-family detached house to cure irresponsible living among the working poor, and to put their minds right: "It is useless to expect a conservative point of view in the workingman, if his home is but three or four rooms in some huge building..."[42]

Veiller got the attention of politicians in 1900 with his detailed architectural model of a Lower East Side block of tenements, providing for his audience the day's equivalent of a helicopter ride over the real thing.[43] The model exposed a fundamental deficiency of the tenements: They covered so much land area—often 90 percent of their narrow lots—that daylight could scarcely reach the rooms that didn't front on the block's bordering streets. Air shafts between buildings were so narrow that residents of neighboring buildings might have opened their windows to shake hands. Small patches of back yard were, on many tenement lots, exploited for additional buildings—"back buildings"—so that only the access lanes to outdoor privies remained unbuilt. Many tenement rooms got their only daylight and outside air from these fouled and constricted back yards. Other rooms, having no windows facing the exterior, had to make do with whatever stale air they could borrow from adjacent rooms.[44]

In 1901 the eminent tenement critic Jacob Riis reported, "The death of a child in a tenement was registered at the Bureau of Vital Statistics as 'plainly due to suffocation in the foul air of an unventilated apartment...'" Not only were tenement lots overcrowded with buildings, many tenement dwellings were overcrowded with people. Jacob Riis reported, "In Essex Street two small rooms in a six-story tenement were made to hold a 'family' of father and mother, twelve children and six boarders."[45] The sanitation, hygiene, and privacy of these huddled masses were poorly accommodated. The 2,781 tenants of Lawrence Veiller's infamous block shared 264 water closets, which translates to 2.3 dwellings and 10.5 people per water closet. The block's 39 tenement buildings provided no baths for their tenants.[46] In his history of New York City's housing, architect/historian Richard Plunz describes the tenement district's sanitation deficiency:

The water closets were either privies or larger "school sinks," depending on whether the excrement was removed by hand or drained from the vault into the street sewer. Typically, hand removal was infrequent, or the sewer would be clogged up. School sinks were especially infamous sources of filth and disease.[47]

Unwholesome conditions in the tenement districts included accumulated filth, poor drainage, and the comingling of residences with stables and other noxious land uses. Riis cited the example of a family "who fed hogs in the cellar that contained eight or ten loads of manure…"[48]

Three terms—*congestion, crowding*, and *high density*—were used pejoratively and interchangeably by housing reformers to take blame for the maladies of tenement districts. In a 1909 tract entitled *The Public Health as Affected by Congestion of Population*, housing reformer Benjamin Marsh wrote, "the death rates from consumption in the *overcrowded* wards in lower Manhattan were even two or three times higher than the death rates in sections of the city that had a *normal density*…" (Emphasis added.) Marsh concluded that congestion (or overcrowding or high density) was cause rather than corollary and must be eliminated in order to eliminate disease.[49]

Social pathologies and diseases were not *caused* by high housing and population densities, but were *exacerbated* by the crowding of dwelling units onto lots, and people into dwelling units. In neighborhoods where building heights did not exceed six stories, a net residential density in excess of 300 dwelling units, and 2,000 people, per acre did indeed constitute a crowding of units on lots and of people in units. High densities exacerbated the accumulation of filth insofar as a large number of people generate more filth than a smaller number of people on a given parcel of land over a given period of time. But the filth rather than the high density caused the spread of disease, and improvements in sanitation rather than reductions in density caused improvements in public health. High housing densities also contributed to the rapid spread of fires prior to the adoption of building codes and improved construction practices.[50] High densities caused neither disease nor fire, but exacerbated the spread of both.

The perception that high densities caused diseases and social problems dissipated somewhat in the light of evidence. Jacob Riis noted that new buildings, subjected by city officials to basic standards of sanitation, were less deadly than older, smaller buildings: "as the building grew taller, the death rate fell." While some housing reformers were preoccupied with the high-density tenements of New York City, others noticed the equally squalid condition of poor people in lower-density environments in cities such as Chicago and Washington, D.C., where single houses had been converted into multiple-unit buildings, and shanties had taken over back yards. The inhabitants of these environments also suffered room overcrowding and deficient sanitation—the maladies commonly associated with New York City's high-density tenement slums.[51]

By 1910 a sufficient number of modern apartment buildings had been built and occupied by New York City's non-poor residents to demonstrate that spacious apartments served by elevators, with adequate sanitation and good exposure to daylight, lent a high degree of livability to high-density housing. It became apparent that high density and crowding are distinct phenomena, yet the two terms continued to be used interchangeably. Jane Jacobs noted the confusion and superstition surrounding high densities and crowding in *Death and Life*:

> One reason why low city densities conventionally have a good name, unjustified by the facts, and why high city densities have a bad name, equally unjustified, is that high densities of dwellings and overcrowding of dwellings are often confused. High densities mean large numbers of dwellings per acre of land. Overcrowding means too many people in a dwelling for the number of rooms it contains.[52]

The blocks between Manhattan's Fifth and Park avenues are densely developed, with net housing densities as high as 150 dwelling units per acre, but the opulent residences in those prestigious blocks are anything but crowded. It is understandable that New York's 19th-century housing reformers had failed to distinguish between high residential densities and crowding, the two conditions almost always coexisted. New York's early apartment buildings for middle-class and affluent households, built in the latter half of the 19th century, were not associated with high residential densities because they were situated in areas of lower residential density—amidst townhouses and churches, and in some cases adjacent to commercial buildings. The legendary Dakota was built in 1884 in a field of open space. New York's highest-density neighborhoods—the tenement slums—happened to be the most crowded as well.

The net housing density on Veiller's notoriously crowded Lower East Side tenement block was 329 dwelling units per acre, nearly identical to the net density of the Upper East Side's CT-126. The tenement buildings of the Lower East Side rarely if ever exceeded six stories in height, but modern apartment buildings in CT-126's ten blocks reach a maximum height of about 40 stories, and apartment buildings exceeding a dozen stories are found on every block in the tract. Spacious apartments with good sanitary facilities and ample exposure to daylight and fresh air are the norm among the housing stock of CT-126.

High housing densities did not and do not cause any of the problems for which they were blamed in the tenement era, not even political liberalism. Among New York City's 59 Community Districts, the politically conservative Upper East Side is the most densely populated.[53]

URBAPHOBIA—THE PERSISTENCE OF DENSITY AVERSION

In the early decades of the 20th century, apartments gained popularity among affluent urbanites who appreciated the convenience and freedom from property maintenance they offered, but the proliferation of apartment buildings alarmed some tenement critics, who adopted an opposition to multifamily housing in any form. Lawrence Veiller applied his anti-tenement sentiment to apartment buildings generally, and he became one of the leaders of the National Housing Association, formed in 1909 to curtail the spread of multifamily housing.[54] Veiller and other critics attributed to apartment buildings the same moral evils, such as drinking and gambling, that they had earlier attached to tenements. A Harvard professor warned that apartments would cause the physical degeneration of humankind: "the atmosphere of the...apartment house is one destined to create a race of adults that is unhealthful, puny, and socially highly artificialized." Cities in general were the real target of apartment critics such as Charles L. Hayes, who said, "Motherhood and childhood require freedom from the nerve-racking city life …"[55]

Apartment critics wielded enough influence to affect urban land use policy nationwide. America's earliest zoning laws had been formulated to separate housing from obnoxious nonresidential land uses, but in the 1910s cities began to enact zoning restrictions to separate various housing types from one another. In the 1920s the U.S. Department of Commerce promoted exclusionary zoning to protect emerging detached-house districts from apartment buildings, and by the mid-1920s many cities had enacted such zoning. Some state courts invalidated these early single-house zoning regulations, but others upheld them. California's Supreme Court decided in 1925 that detached-house districts promote family life, moral welfare, and mental fitness. North Dakota's Supreme Court upheld detached-house zoning in 1926, having concluded that apartment buildings were responsible for crime and juvenile delinquency. In 1926, the U.S. Supreme Court validated the practice of restricting certain zoning districts to detached houses.[56]

The Depression and World War II brought new rounds of crowding to many city neighborhoods, and the presupposition that high residential densities are unwholesome for humankind lingered on.[57] The irrational attitude lives on today, perpetuated even by those entrusted with the dissemination of knowledge and wisdom about urban planning. In their 1993 edition of a widely distributed planning text, planners/architects/professors Simon and Stanley Eisner and Arthur Gallion echo the tenement critics of a century earlier in their enthusiasm for suburban life, in their denunciation of high residential densities:

> The desirability of low density for a residential environment is obvious; it has been demonstrated in all places and for all people on the face of the earth. Low density does not forestall blight, but with the exception of apartment development with commodious space and enriched facilities, high density has induced blight.[58]

Extreme in their environmental determinism, the textbook authors are most unscholarly in their denunciation of high densities, citing no examples of blight-inducing high-density development. Perhaps they were thinking of tenements, which did not induce blight although many accommodated and succumbed to it. Or perhaps Eisner, Eisner, and Gallion had public housing in mind, but even that remained blight-free until the 1960s when federal policies and court rulings forced a change in the socioeconomic composition of the projects. Philadelphia's Raymond Rosen development, for one of many examples, was anything but blighted in the 1950s, before it was forced to accept disruptive households into its highrise buildings. On the eve of the 1995 demolition of five Raymond Rosen highrises, the *Philadelphia Inquirer* described the 1950s tidy tranquility of the project:

> Life in the complex was a setting of quiet nights and lawnside tea parties. There were manicured lawns and state-of-the-art elevators, safe playgrounds and clean sidewalks. "It was beautiful then, the nicest," said Betty Boyd, 60, who moved into one of the high-rises when she was 19 ...[59]

Eisner, Eisner, and Gallion, who deride apartments as "cubicles," go on to proclaim the incompatibility of high housing densities and neighborliness: "There are very few high-density 'neighborhoods'—just high-rise buildings and congestion."[60] Once again they provide no evidence. If any evidence exists to demonstrate that high-density urban neighborhoods are less conducive to neighborliness than low-density neighborhoods, they fail to cite it. Highrise apartment buildings do not somehow strip individual humans of their neighborly tendencies unless those buildings are inhabited by uncivil tenants, as is the case in some of the nation's public housing.

On the east side of Manhattan, between Midtown and Downtown, lies a high-density neighborhood called Kips Bay, whose housing stock consists of townhouses and highrise apartment buildings. An attorney named Jackson Koffman has lived in one of the highrises for 18 years and he describes his building and its environs in terms that might surprise urbaphobes: "It's like a small town...a cohesive community..." And it's not a bad place raise children; Koffman says the gregarious kids in his building foster neighborliness, and he proudly adds, "I'm godfather to a couple of kids here." Realtor Douglas Elliman characterizes Kips Bay as "a family neighborhood."

Neighborliness is almost a defining characteristic of New York's highest-density neighborhoods. Chance encounters among neighbors spark greetings and conversations on the streets of the Upper East Side and Upper West Side, America's most densely populated residential districts, where residents take to the sidewalks nightly to walk their dogs and visit neighborhood shops and restaurants. Residents develop friendships with the proprietors of establishments that are sustained by high densities. Screenwriter Nora Ephron describes the social climate of her beloved city:

> New York is a series of little villages that we all live in, sort of three square blocks where we know the dry cleaner and the butcher and...the florist....You see the same fathers and kids going to school in the morning and mothers pushing their kids...You can live...a kind of wonderful life in this city ...[61]

Neighborly bonds are strengthened by impromptu social encounters in New York's many restaurants, coffee shops, exercise clubs and neighborhood pubs. Bar-restaurant owner Earl Greer describes his Upper East Side clientele as neighborhood residents who meet neighbors, get to know the staff, and become regular customers: "The Upper East Side is one giant social club. You see the same faces and people whenever you go out. If you meet someone casually there's a good chance you'll meet them again." Upper East Side bar manager Wayne Rambharose says, "Most people who come in here live in the neighborhood and think its appealing that this is their neighborhood place." Another Upper East Side host—nightclub owner Mark Grossich—has clubs in several neighborhoods, but finds that his highest-density location produces the greatest bonds of loyalty: "Out of all our locations, Upper East Siders are probably the most loyal to their neighborhood."[62] High densities are necessary to sustain informal gathering places on neighborhood streets.

Professor of sociology Ray Oldenburg devoted a book—*The Great Good Place*—to that essential element of community life—the informal neighborhood gathering place—the pub, the coffee shop, the barber shop, the home away from home. Oldenburg observes:

> In their kind and number, there has been a marked decline in gathering places near enough to people's homes to afford the easy access and familiar faces necessary to a vital informal public life.…Without such places, the urban area fails to nourish the kinds of relationships and the diversity of human contact that are the essence of the city.[63]

The street itself—Sullivan Street—is one of the many gathering places in South Greenwich Village, a neighborhood of tenements and apartment buildings where lifelong resident Bobby Devito tells a reporter, "If I won the $294 million lottery I wouldn't move out of the neighborhood." Ninety-one-year-old Anna Maggio had lived proudly on Sullivan Street since her childhood when, in 1998, *New York Times* reporter Anthony Lappè profiled her and some of the neighborhood's other devoted residents. Erin Daniels, a newcomer from a St. Louis suburb, told Lappè, "People say hi to you and I actually know my neighbors." The newcomer Ms. Daniels and the old-timer Anna Maggio "share a love for their street," said reporter Lappè. He knows the feeling, for he too is a neighborhood resident, drawn to its "exciting array of cafes, restaurants, and bars…"[64]

New York City's high densities sustain all the amenities that enhance the daily lives of families for whom car ownership would be a financial burden. In her book *Chinatown: The Socioeconomic Potential of an Urban Enclave*, sociologist Min Zhou quotes a Mrs. Chen describing the benefits associated with high densities in her Manhattan neighborhood:

Living in Chinatown is just so convenient. We don't have to spend time on the subway train; my husband and I only walk a few blocks to work. It is also safer....Also, I can leave my kids next door at my neighbors'. If you lived elsewhere, even if there were other Chinese around, you could not possibly find a baby-sitter so close by...I can bring in fresh vegetables and food everyday after work. I feel life is much easier...[65]

If Eisner, Eisner, and Gallion, practitioners in southern California, had never experienced high-density life first-hand, ample documentation of its social efficacy was available when they disparaged it in 1993. In 1986, for example, Donald Rothblatt and Daniel Garr, professors of urban and regional planning at San Jose State University, reported that some categories of households are generally happier in apartment neighborhoods than in neighborhoods of detached houses. The professors measured social and psychological satisfaction in various settlement types and found that "higher density housing areas not only work better for unmarried women than do single family neighborhoods, but are also more rewarding environments for married women with small children."[66]

A Dubious "Density Equation"

Eisner, Eisner, and Gallion's sociologic concern for apartment dwellers is unmatched by an equal concern for nondrivers, a group shortchanged in the authors' automobile-oriented density equation: "The density equation must...embrace three practical elements: population in buildings, space for the movement of vehicles on streets, and parking space for the vehicles."[67] Vehicles account for two of three factors in this density equation, which fails to account for the relationship between density and transit feasibility. The issue of transit feasibility is fraught with social ramifications, e.g., the mobility of those too young, too old, too infirm, or too poor to drive cars.

Eisner, Eisner, and Gallion's tenement-era predecessors could advocate low-density living without advocating automobile-dependence; streetcars and subways were to be the vehicles of liberation from high-density neighborhoods. But to advocate low-density living in today's metropolis is to endorse automobile dependence, and the Eisners and Gallion do so not only implicitly but explicitly, extolling "the freedom of movement afforded by modern motor vehicles."[68] Nobody with credibility or clout advocates the revocation of the automobile option, but increasing numbers of planning practitioners, academics, and policymakers advocate a better balance among transportation modes. Our planners and policymakers have given us metropolitan regions in which automobiles are indispensable, even for city folk. Those who shape the metropolitan environment ought to reduce automobile dependence by creating genuine cities for the urbanites of the metropolis, cities in which walking and transit use are feasible and enjoyable.

HUD'S DENSITY AVERSION

"We've demolished a lot of really troubled public housing and are replacing it with new public housing that is less dense ..." said HUD Secretary Andrew Cuomo in 1997.[69] Federal and local housing officials are committed to the proposition that low-density housing is inherently superior to high-density housing, even in cities. The Department of Housing and Urban Development (HUD) has determined that highrise public housing is unfit for families, so highrises come crashing down in cities across the nation, to be replaced by lowrise housing. In the typical scenario the lowrise housing is also lower-density housing, even though public highrises do not constitute high densities but, rather, moderate densities. St. Louis's Pruitt-Igoe, which in 1972 set the precedent for the demolition of public highrises, was developed at a mere 48 units per acre, half the density of Boston's lowrise high-appeal Beacon Hill.[70] At 96th Street in Manhattan, where railroad tracks emerge from beneath Park Avenue, the Upper East Side gives way to Spanish Harlem, midrise luxury apartment buildings give way to highrise public housing, and densities drop off sharply.

Our national consternation over highrise public housing has blinded us to the deficiencies of lowrise public housing, which, it now appears, is as problematic as the highrises. In October 1997, Gladys McLaurien moved out of her highrise in Chicago's infamous Robert Taylor Homes, about to be demolished, into a freshly rehabilitated lowrise with a back porch. "But as McLaurien sought to reconstruct a life, she soon realized that she'd traded a CHA high-rise for a low-rise slum," reported the *Chicago Tribune* in a 1998 article about the housing authority's growing troubles with the lowrise housing that replaces highrises lost to the wrecking ball. "Her new apartment was burglarized within a week, and soon she had to move again."[71]

In September 1999, a year after the *Tribune* reported Gladys McLaurien's troubles, it reported Shanika Ellis's. Ms. Ellis relocated from a soon-to-be-demolished highrise in Henry Horner Homes to a nearby townhouse, one of 350 new units in the first phase of a development designed to replace the highrises. Under the front-page headline, "Old Problems Plague New Low-Rises," the *Tribune* reported:

> In the looming shadow of the gray, concrete high-rises of the Henry Horner Homes, blocks of white-trimmed town homes and red-brick, turreted row-houses have sprung up...But barely two years into the city's first large-scale public housing redevelopment project, one of those blocks—on Maypole Street—has become pocked with gang graffiti and boarded up and burnt out town homes. The Chicago Housing Authority blames gangs and some residents for trashing the dwellings.[72]

(The townhouses on Maypole Street afford easy access to the outdoors, but Ms. Ellis won't allow her daughter to play outside.)

If housing officials were surprised by this turn of events, they shouldn't have been. In 1996, HUD's Office of Policy Development and Research published the results of a nationwide survey of public housing residents, a survey that topples the long-established assumption that lowrise public housing is safer and more orderly than highrise public housing. That now-discredited assumption had gained credence in the 1980s and 1990s when the nation's media reported horrors in public highrises, most notably in Chicago where public housing occupies 11 of the nation's 15 poorest census tracts, according to 1990 census data. But the authors of HUD's 1996 survey and analysis note that "the crime-highrise nexus has not been systematically investigated and relies primarily on journalistic accounts...the existence of a crime-highrise connection is far from firmly established."[73] The analysis confirms conventional wisdom: highrise public housing is, in many cities, synonymous with crime and disorder. But the analysis also reveals that lowrise public housing is equally troubled, more so in some cases. Lowrise residents are more vulnerable to burglaries, for example, than highrise residents, and the "highest incidence of burglary" among large public housing authorities occurred in scattered-site housing, which consists mostly of "single-family homes and small multifamily buildings," according to the survey.[74]

Townhouses and lowrise apartments produced higher rates of complaint about gunshots and drug dealing than highrises did, and the same is true of complaints about disorderly conditions such as graffiti and "trashy yards." In many cities, scattered-site housing also produced higher rates of complaint about graffiti and trashy yards than highrises did, and nearly identical rates of complaint about gunshots and drug dealing. As highrises are demolished in Chicago, their tenants move to scattered-site units and engage in the same destructive behavior that led to the demise of their highrises. HUD's analysts concluded:

> Our findings suggest that townhouses and lowrise housing might be even more vulnerable [than highrises] to crime. From time to time, criminological research even casts doubt on the notion that big-city public housing is more criminogenic than private sector housing in the same neighborhoods...[75]

(HUD's analysis was based on a survey conducted in 1994 and was limited to family, as opposed to elderly, projects.)

There are good reasons to demolish much of the nation's highrise public housing, but density reduction is not among them. Highrises are not ideal for small children and their parents, who benefit from ready access to outdoor play areas, but this is not an argument for density reduction. Three-story garden apartments can be built at Pruitt-Igoe's former density in a configuration that highrise critics would approve for families with children, a configuration that leaves ample site area for playgrounds. Lowrise densities can be enhanced by mixing in some highrises for childless households. Highrise and lowrise apartment buildings coexist on New York City's high-density Roosevelt Island, where a mixed-income and variously aged population produces none of the chaos commonly associated in America with public housing.

Many public highrises are doomed because they deteriorated beyond economical repair after decades of burdensome federal mandates and local mismanagement; some lowrise housing is being demolished for the same reason. But well-managed public housing, highrise and low, is serving its purpose nicely in many cities even as HUD and local housing authorities triumphantly raze buildings across the nation in a campaign to eradicate 100,000 units.[76] HUD and local authorities are motivated largely by their highrises' reputation for disorder and crime. Like the housing critics of the tenement era, housing officials today blame buildings for the sins of their occupants.

SUBURBAN DREAMS

HUD's vision of the nation's cities as repositories of the very poor, for whom low densities are less troublesome than high densities, causes the agency to promote the suburbanization of cities. In July 1996, five months after HUD's Office of Policy Development and Research reported that lowrise public housing is no more wholesome or secure than highrise public housing, HUD announced a program to restore "families, neighborhood and life" to inner cities by earmarking $100 million of federal funds for the construction of 200 to 300 suburban-style houses in six to twelve blighted urban areas. Tenement critics who believed single houses to be more wholesome than tenements proposed to remove the poor to suburbs. HUD officials and their local accomplices propose to bring suburbs to the inner-city poor.[77]

Local officials embrace HUD's demolition and density-reduction schemes, and they share HUD's affinity for detached houses. In 1997, Minneapolis officials bought a crime-ridden apartment building in the Near North district (just two blocks from the Willard-Hay neighborhood) and ceremoniously razed the 10-unit building to make way for a modest single-detached house.

Why build suburban housing in the city? City officials realize that apartments and townhouses in all price categories rent and sell readily in today's metropolitan housing market. Curtis Johnson said, in 1996 when he was chairman of the Twin Cities regional planning agency—the Metropolitan Council—that "townhouses close to the urban center are the hottest thing around."[78] The market for apartments—condominium and rental—also thrives in U.S. metro areas including the Twin Cities. So why didn't Minneapolis officials combine their newly vacated lot with adjacent land under city ownership—16,000 square feet in all—and develop a half dozen townhouses or 18 apartments? Or better yet, why not acquire and raze some of the neighboring detached houses to make way for an even larger and denser development? Why settle for a detached house or two?

Because the Minneapolis City Council has decreed a reduction of housing densities in many of its residential areas, even near downtown. The council resolved in 1992 to "maintain the low density character of single-family neighborhoods," therefore each housing unit in the zoning district that governs their Near North site shall occupy no less than 5,000 square feet of land. The city's 16,000 square feet of near-downtown property therefore has the capacity for a maximum of three units, fewer than a third as many as existed on just half of that land before the summer of 1997.[79]

Perhaps the folks at city hall fear their new inner-city housing will follow precedent and filter down from moderate-income to low-income at-risk households. When that happens it is better to subject low-density housing to the process than high-density housing because low-density housing will concentrate fewer such households. Or perhaps the city's leaders are driven by the conviction that a wholesome suburban environ-ment will nurture in the distressed neighborhood's poor residents good habits and responsible citizenship. This attitude, after all, has a tradition dating back to the era of the tenement slum.

ADVICE ONLY PARTIALLY HEEDED

High residential densities foster the twin assets—neighborhood commerce and good transit—that minimize the automobile dependence of cities, but a high density does not, by itself, ensure a high level of vital-ity; rather it enables vitality. A state of vitality is possible only in the presence of a combination of physical attributes that begins with high density and includes the three additional conditions prescribed by Jane Jacobs in 1961: commingled land uses, small blocks, and variety in building ages and sizes.[80]

Urban policymakers now appreciate the acuity of Jacobs' vision. Commingled land uses are now considered essential to urban vitality, and neotraditional planners pursue this attribute even in outer suburbs. Small blocks are being restored to public housing sites from which streets were removed to create superblocks. And old buildings are revered and pro-tected today by national and local legislation. Jane Jacobs' urban fecun-dity is almost universally recognized today.

But Jacobs' advice is only partially heeded. Urban officials promote the construction of sizable housing developments exclusive of other land uses. They combine blocks into superblocks for suburb-style retail devel-opment. And they facilitate the demolition of old buildings, usually to make way for downtown parking garages. The failure to heed Jacobs' advice on mixed uses, small blocks, and old buildings is invariably rooted in a refusal to heed her advice about density:

• Housing-only redevelopment projects lack retail components because they are built at densities too low to support them. In Minneapolis, detached houses will be among the paltry 900 units sprawled across the Hollman site—a 100-acre redevelopment area just a stone's throw from downtown. This is a density too low to support walk-in retailing, so the sizable site will be single-use housing.

• Small blocks are combined into superblocks for supermarkets and strip centers because retailers need land enough for parking lots, as noted previously. Off-street parking is essential in the low-density environment where retail trade areas extend far beyond walking distance. City officials desperate for commercial development acquiesce to retailer's demands for parking lots.

• Old downtown buildings are sacrificed for parking garages because the neighborhoods surrounding downtown are too sparsely occupied to sustain good transit. If an old building has historical or sentimental value it will be spared, but Jacobs had in mind the economic importance of ordinary commercial buildings, old and not so old. Old low-rent buildings at the edge of downtown San Francisco help incubate high-tech companies today, contributing to the city's economic vitality.*

Urban neighborhoods that possess the attributes prescribed by Jane Jacobs continue to thrive four decades after the publication of her landmark book, while nonconforming neighborhoods have sunk further into despair. City officials, often goaded by national and state housing and transportation policies, suburbanize their decaying neighborhoods in an attempt to stabilize them, but this strategy prevents, or long forestalls, the restoration of vitality.

---

*South of Market's low-rent buildings have, for at least a couple of decades, attracted artists, many of whom found their way into the multimedia industry. This dynamic industry has led employment growth in a 10-square-block area dubbed "Multimedia Gulch," which held a total of 35,000 workers by the end of 1998. San Francisco's Planning Department acknowledges the contribution of low-rent buildings to an industry now worth billions of dollars to the city's economy: "South of Market has offered an ideal combination of resources for the development of the multimedia cluster....Its large warehouses provide appropriate spaces at low rent." (San Francisco Planning Department, "Commerce and Industry Issue Paper No. 1," July 1996; Brian C. Anderson and Matt Robinson, "Willie Brown Shows How Not to Run a City," *City Journal*, Autumn 1998, p. 63.)

2

Gray Zones, Green Zones, Gold Zones, and Pure City

*...after five or six hours of silence and solitude I want to step out my front door right in to the drama of life. And no other city delivers that as New York does...*WRITER RICHARD LOURIE[1]

The exuberant diversity associated with America's most densely populated city underlies the potential of all American cities, or at least that is the assumption under which America's urban leaders ought to lead. First of all, our political leaders ought to fully understand the several ways in which housing density affects the quality of life in urban neighborhoods. Such an understanding is advanced by a neighborhood typology of four classifications: gray zone, green zone, gold zone, and pure city.

GRAY ZONES

In 1968 *Time* magazine visited a Los Angeles neighborhood dominated by detached houses, and elucidated the correlation between the housing stock and civic disorder: "In the Los Angeles district of Watts, California's most notorious Slough of Despond, the orderly rows of one-story stucco houses reflect the sun in gay pastels."[2] Even earlier, Jane Jacobs had cited Los Angeles, which she described as "almost all suburban," to support her assertion—more surprising when she made it in 1961 than now—that low housing densities do not immunize cities from high crime rates and repellent streets:

Los Angeles stands so pre-eminent in crime that it is in a category by itself. And this is markedly true of crimes associated with personal attack, the crimes that make people fear the streets. The reasons for Los Angeles' high crime rates are undoubtedly complex, and at least in part obscure. But of this we can be sure: thinning out a city does not insure safety from crime and fear of crime.[3]

Smaller cities not commonly associated with urban grief have succumbed to the problems of big cities. Salt Lake City "seems like the perfect place to raise a family: safe, wholesome, serene," said the narrator of a 1996 TV report about a troubled mother who escaped a dangerous Chicago neighborhood with her two boys. But Salt Lake City didn't solve the family's problems. Their new home was a detached house on a woodsy Salt Lake City street in a neighborhood plagued by housing abandonment and gang misbehavior, a neighborhood that resembled Minneapolis' Willard-Hay neighborhood. In Minneapolis and Salt Lake City—two widely separated low-density American cities—one finds interchangeable detached houses on nearly identical streets in similar low-density neighborhoods, and one finds similar levels of urban disorder. In the closing scenes of the TV report, mother tells her younger boy that his older brother is in jail, arrested for a murder that occurred on the sidewalk in front of their detached house.[4]

Crime and disorder plague low-density neighborhoods in cities across America. The housing stock varies from city to city; in Philadelphia, Baltimore, and Washington, D.C., townhouses are abundantly represented in distressed neighborhoods. In Boston and in the small industrial cities along the Merrimack River, detached houses and townhouses share distressed neighborhoods with triple deckers. In New York City, some of the worst despair is found in once-vibrant neighborhoods in Harlem and the South Bronx, where tenements and townhouses have been abandoned and razed so prolifically that low-density neighborhoods remain in the shells of former high-density neighborhoods. But in most American cities from Buffalo to Los Angeles, including Detroit—synonymous with urban despair, Atlanta, Cleveland, Indianapolis, Kansas City, Minneapolis and St. Paul, Salt Lake City, Sacramento, Oakland, and scores of others, detached houses, duplexes, and small apartment buildings comprise the housing stock of distressed low-density neighborhoods—gray zones.

Low housing densities do not cause gray-zone distress, just as high densities did not cause the squalor of New York City's tenement slums, but in both cases housing density is an exacerbating factor. High densities in the tenement slums correlated with overcrowding, inadequate ventilation, and the accumulation of filth. Low densities in gray zones correlate with an absence of urban vitality. Urban vitality is demanded by urbanites in the metropolitan housing market, therefore urbanites reject gray zones, which are urban in location but suburban in physical character. Gray zones are rejected also by non-poor suburbanites who easily find better housing (with attached garages for example) in new suburbs than in old central-city neighborhoods. Disorderly streets repel both urbanites and suburbanites with the means to live elsewhere. Disreputable schools add to the reasons middle class urbanites and suburbanites reject housing in gray zones, which can only sink to the bottom of the metropolitan housing market.

Jane Jacobs referred to low-density neighborhoods in cities as "semisuburbs," which must be secluded from city life in order to remain viable and safe. Jacobs accurately predicted in 1961, when vast stretches of now-distressed urban America were still viable and safe, that low-density neighborhoods, unless isolated from city life, would become gray zones. Low-density neighborhoods, according to the prescient Jacobs, cannot ensure the safety of city streets, which need a constant presence of concerned citizens and attentive eyes. Researchers at the University of California, Berkeley, confirmed Jacobs' theory in 1968 when they reported a relationship between street crime and intensity of street activity. Most crime occurs within a "critical intensity zone," a pair of thresholds below which there are few potential victims on the street, and above which crime is deterred by the informal surveillance of the street's many occupants. Between the thresholds—inside the critical intensity zone—there is trouble.[5]

Jacobs contrasted street safety in Boston's high-density North End (net housing density in excess of 200 units per acre according to Jacobs) with the dangers in Boston's low-density Roxbury:

> Some city streets afford no opportunity to street barbarism. The streets of the North End of Boston are outstanding examples. They are probably as safe as any place on earth in this respect...the district's streets are...heavily and constantly used...Half a dozen times or so in the past three decades, says [a longtime resident-expert], would-be molesters have made an attempt at luring a child or, late at night, attacking a woman. In every such case the try was

thwarted by passers-by, by kibitzers from windows, or shopkeepers. Meantime, in the Elm Hill Avenue section of Roxbury, a part of inner Boston that is suburban in superficial character, street assaults and the ever present possibility of more street assaults with no kibitzers to protect the victims, induce prudent people to stay off the sidewalks at night. Not surprisingly, for this and other reasons that are related (dispiritedness and dullness), most of Roxbury has run down. It has become a place to leave.[6]

Roxbury

Jacobs characterized Boston's North End as "one of the city's healthiest areas" and noted that Roxbury, with a housing density "about a ninth" as high as the North End's, "has been steadily declining for a generation...."[7] Another generation after Jacobs recorded her observations, the North End remained vibrant and Roxbury had sunk even further into despair. In 1995, thirty-four years after Jacobs invoked Roxbury as Boston's district of deep despair, the Urban Land Institute's Jeff Minter had this to say about the area:

> To most people, mention of Boston's Roxbury neighborhood conjures up images of poverty, violence, crime, and decay...Roxbury's 59,000 residents struggle with a classic set of urban problems. Drug sales, crime and violence, limited job opportunities, and economic disinvestment have crippled the community....
>
> One-third of the population lives below the poverty line. Single-parent households with children under 18 years of age account for 65 percent of Roxbury's families . . . Although Roxbury contains only 5.8 percent of Boston's total housing stock, it is home to 22 percent of the city's vacant and boarded up properties.[8]

Minter goes on to prescribe a strategy for the revitalization of the neighborhood's commercial area, a strategy that envisions an increased level of pedestrian activity, which will suppress crime, especially at night. Such a strategy, according to Minter, entails the enhancement of residential densities: "The lack of housing particularly limits the development of restaurants and convenience businesses." High housing densities and middle-class purchasing power are necessary to support the commercial and cultural amenities that vitalize the streets of urban neighborhoods.

Millions of dollars in government and charitable funds have in the past decade helped Roxbury fill in some of its vacant land with new housing, but that housing is developed for a market too poor and at densities too low to lift the district out of its distress. (More about Roxbury in Chapter 9.)

As she did with Boston's high-vitality North End and its deflated Roxbury, Jacobs contrasted Philadelphia's vibrant Rittenhouse Square neighborhood with its "North Philadelphia slums." She contrasted Brooklyn's "most generally admired" Brooklyn Heights with its "tremendous expanses of failed or decaying…gray area." In San Francisco Jacobs contrasted "fashionable" Russian Hill and Nob Hill with its "chief slum problem" in the Western Addition (which was being cleared for redevelopment at the time Jacobs was writing).[9] In each case—Boston, Philadelphia, Brooklyn, and San Francisco—the high-vitality neighborhood had a population density at least double that of the "slum" or "gray area."

Jacobs noted that some high-vitality neighborhoods had suffered decline after the Depression, decline caused largely by the subdivision of townhouses into inferior multifamily buildings occupied by poor households; high density had become synonymous with crowding, just like in the tenement slums. But the high-density neighborhoods were able to "unslum" and "spontaneously upgrade" because of their innate appeal to urbanite households, many of whom bought townhouses and restored them to their original condition.[10] In low-density cities, Jacobs was unable to cite examples of high-vitality neighborhoods, but she found additional examples of gray zones that have endured these many years since she described them:

> In Oakland, California, the worst and most extensive slum problem is an area of some two hundred blocks of detached one- and two- family houses…Cleveland's worst slum problem is a square mile of much the same thing. Detroit is largely composed, today, of seemingly endless square miles of low-density failure.[11]

Gray Zones and Crime

Conspicuous physical defects—derelict commercial streets and inferior housing—interact with socioeconomic distress to repel middle-class households from gray zones. Gray zones suffer another, more subtle, physical defect: Their housing configurations facilitate the criminal activity that often accompanies poverty. Jane Jacobs described the ominous yards that surround public housing as "expanses of open land which are so hard to control in city life and produce so much vacuity and trouble."* That is also an apt description of the yards that surround detached houses in gray zones. The configurations of public housing and of gray-zone private housing leave too much space unattended, and too many escape routes for criminals.

Within a socioeconomically homogeneous area, the location that suffers the greatest crime problem is the one that "makes it easy for criminals to disappear after committing crimes," reports Anastasia Loukaitou-Sideris, associate professor of urban planning at the University of California-Los Angeles. Loukaitou-Sideris researched crime near bus stops in the vicinity of downtown Los Angeles and found "passages between buildings" to be among the "escape routes" that contribute to high rates of robbery and other crimes.[12] In *Fixing Broken Windows*, criminologist George Kelling and lawyer Catherine Coles recount the story of a high-crime neighborhood on Baltimore's west side where townhouses are interspersed with alleys and vacant lots, which provided escape routes to drug dealers. In order to curtail the drug dealers and their violent crime, neighborhood residents fenced off the gaps between houses. Kelling and Coles cite this as one of the measures responsible for a 56 percent reduction in violent crime in the neighborhood in the mid-1990s.[13]

Tightening control of urban space by blocking escape routes and eliminating access to unsupervised areas is an exercise in *situational crime prevention*, a term criminologists use to describe tactics that deter crime by reducing the opportunities and enlarging the risks associated with it.[14] Crime deterrence thus joins density and aesthetic considerations as prudent reasons to build attached rather than detached houses in urban neighborhoods. An unbroken wall of townhouses is not so penetrable as a row of detached houses, which is like a sieve unless surrounded by high unneighborly fences. (Few gray-zone landlords invest in fences.) Once a burglar gains access to the unsupervised space between or behind detached houses and duplexes, he finds side windows and back doors through which to gain entry. A traditional street-oriented townhouse provides only one accessible exposure with openings—windows and doors— whereas the typical detached house provides four such exposures.

---

* Jacobs added, "there must be a clear demarcation between what is public space and what is private space. Public and private spaces cannot ooze into each other as they typically do in suburban settings or in [public housing] projects." Jacobs proffered this theory in 1961, and in 1972 Oscar Newman amplified it in *Defensible Space: Crime Prevention Through Urban Design*. The theory is widely regarded today as a basic tenet of good urban design. (Jacobs' quotes from *The Death and Life of Great American Cities*, [New York: Random House, 1961], pp. 35, 215.)

The back and side yards and multiple exposures that elevate gray-zone houses' vulnerability to property crime fail to buffer them from violent crime. In 1995, when Minneapolis suffered a record level of violence, 64, or two-thirds, of the city's record-setting 97 murders occurred in the midst of detached houses. Of those 64 murders, 31 occurred at addresses occupied by detached houses; the other 33 occurred at addresses occupied by duplexes, small apartment buildings, commercial buildings, or other land uses, all located on blocks dominated by detached houses.[15] Sixty-five of the 97 murders occurred at residential addresses, and the distribution of those murder sites among the various housing types—detached houses, duplexes, and apartments—was similar to the citywide distribution of housing units among the various types.[16]

Some of the nation's lowest crime rates are found in its lowest-density cities, but not because low densities resist crime. The borders of our lowest-density cities encompass expansive land areas, enclosing freshly developed and still-developing sectors along with long-established neighborhoods—the entire metropolis. (Anchorage, Alaska, is coextensive with its metropolitan area—1,698 square miles.) The socioeconomic health of the fresh and still-developing "suburbs" suppress citywide crime rates. Lexington-Fayette, Kentucky, one of the nation's least densely populated cites, covers 285 square miles of land—almost as much as New York City (309 square miles), but Lexington-Fayette's population of 261,000 residents is less than 4 percent of New York City's population (8 million). In 1995 Lexington-Fayette was, unsurprisingly, one of the nation's 10 least crime-ridden cities, among 78 cities with populations of more than 200,000 residents; but New York City's crime rate was even lower, and it remained so in 1996, 1997, 1998, and 1999.[17]

The nation's low crime rate cities cover the spectrum of population densities, as do its high crime rate cities. In the first half of the 1990s, in the years before it plummeted, New York City's crime rate consistently ranked 40th or lower among the nation's most populous 78 cities—those with more than 200,000 residents. (The number of such cities fluctuates; it was 78 in 1994 according to U.S. Census Bureau estimates.) By 1995, New York City's rank had dropped to 73rd among the nation's 78 most populous cities. Atlanta's population density is only one-eighth that of New York City, but its 1999 crime rate was nearly three times as high, as was its rate of violent crime.

San Francisco is the nation's second most densely populated city, and its crime rate has throughout the 1990s ranked in the bottom half among the nation's large cities. San Francisco's population density is more than double that of nearby Oakland, but Oakland's crime rate was 32 percent higher, on average, throughout the 1990s. Oakland's rate of *violent* crime averaged 50 percent higher than San Francisco's in the 1990s.

Distressed low-density neighborhoods boost a city's crime rate and suppress its population density. By contrast, vibrant high-density neighborhoods suppress a city's crime rate while boosting it's population density. That's why New York City and San Francisco, the nation's two most densely populated cities, have crime rates lower than many of the least densely populated (Figure 2-1).

Figure 2-1. Crime rates/population densities—selected cities. Some of the nation's highest-density cities have some of its lowest crime rates. (1995 data for Oakland unavailable.)

Sources: Statistical Abstract of the United States, 1992–2000; U.S. Department of Justice, Crime in the United States 1999.

Gray Zones and Public Housing Rejects

Public housing is commonly associated with urban America's vilest social pathologies, but gray-zone private housing is equally implicated, more so in many cities.[18] Furthermore, gray-zone private housing will assume an expanding role in accommodating disruptive households as pressure mounts to restore civility to public housing. The Housing Act of 1937 was designed to help the working poor who had lost their jobs and homes during the Depression but, during the ensuing decades, federal mandates forced local authorities to turn their buildings over to the poorest of the poor, who turned out to be the most disruptive of the disruptive. Drug users and dealers plagued many buildings that weren't set aside for the elderly, but now local authorities are authorized by HUD to enforce stricter anti-drug policies, making it easier to exclude dealers and other criminals, through eviction if necessary.[19]

Market-rate housing in gray-zone neighborhoods—the bottom of the private housing market—is readily available to absorb public housing rejects. Moreover, the demolition of public housing increases the pressure on private housing to accommodate urban America's poorest households. Nationwide, HUD intends to replace 100,000 demolished units with as few as 40,000 and to increase the number of working-poor and moderate-income households in the units that remain. Those displaced by demolition and by new income guidelines will be transferred to the private housing market courtesy of the Section 8 tenant-based (voucher) program, which makes private housing available to "very-low-income renters" in HUD's parlance.[20]

The Section 8 voucher program houses 1.7 million households—more than are housed in conventional public housing. One-quarter of Section 8 housing units are detached houses and another two-fifths are in duplexes and small apartment buildings, those with fewer than 10 units. This private housing that is available to Section 8 renters is concentrated most heavily in central-city gray zones.[21]

GREEN ZONES

Low-density cities with some variety in neighborhood densities conform to the general pattern found in high-density cities: The highest-density neighborhoods are among the most appealing and affluent, while many low-density neighborhoods are crime-ridden and repellant—gray zones. In Oakland, for example, neighborhoods adjacent to Lake Merritt are of higher appeal and higher density than the gray-zone neighborhoods elsewhere in the city.

Some low-density neighborhoods in low-density cities have managed to elude the distress that decimates gray zones. Outer neighborhoods of many cities remain suburban in socioeconomic as well as physical condition, especially those with substantial inventories of post-World War II middle- and upper-middle-class houses. Attached garages and oversized lots are common in these neighborhoods, which are suburban except for jurisdictional circumstance. Jacobs predicted that these homogeneous neighborhoods would remain viable as long as they remain "secluded from city life," but city life and gray-zone status expand and corrode the retreating boundaries of many of these vulnerable areas.[22] Minneapolis' most northerly neighborhoods have the character of post-World War II middle-class suburbs, but a front of concentrated poverty has advanced toward them, and a 1993 homeowner survey revealed that, in these sub-urb-like neighborhoods, 37 to 50 percent of households with preschool children planned to move out of their suburban-style houses.[23] Disreputable schools are among the social factors that overpower a neighborhood's positive physical attributes.

Some low-density neighborhoods resist blight even though they are close to the center of the city; they do so by offering natural features and superior houses, which enable them to compete effectively with suburbs for non-poor households of the suburbanite persuasion, including households that can afford private schools. Bodies of water or wooded hills are the natural attractions of low-density high-appeal city neighborhoods— green zones. Green zones are the elite suburbs of the streetcar era, and because of their superior environs and housing they remain viable middle- and upper-income enclaves, suburban in character. Minneapolis' chain of lakes, for example, is encircled by a verdant ribbon of low-density high-appeal residential property. The one-family detached houses strung along this ribbon remain among the most valuable in the Twin Cities metropolitan area. University of Minnesota geographers John Adams and Barbara VanDrasek note the appeal of Minneapolis green-zone housing: "Fine houses facing the lakes sell in a few days for prices ten times the area's median family income, while house prices away from the water drop sharply block by block."[24]

Instead of lakes, Cincinnati's prosperous Clifton and Hyde Park green zones offer hilly terrain and winding streets. Clifton's housing stock includes 19th-century mansions on grounds that resemble great parks more than residential yards. Clifton was described in 1930 by the Countess of Chambrun, née Clara Longworth, as "the most fabulously beautiful paradise of a suburb in America."[25]

Green zones resist socioeconomic and physical degeneration, but other neighborhoods of similar density, similar proximity to downtown, and

even similar housing characteristics, but without benefit of natural amenities, have lost their middle-class and affluent residents to suburbs through
the process of invasion and succession. These neighborhoods have degenerated into gray zones. The boundaries between green zones and gray
zones have moved in a negative direction as formerly extensive green
zones have retreated toward their natural anchors. The lakes-area green
zones of Minneapolis receded toward the shorelines in the 1970s through
the mid-1990s as the city's gray zones expanded.[26]

The natural amenities that anchor green zones do not by themselves
guarantee green-zone appeal. Cincinnati's East End district suggests that
good housing stock—if not opulent, then at least charming—is also necessary. The East End is a strip of land extending from downtown
Cincinnati six miles eastward along an arc of the Ohio River. In spite of its
river prospect and its views of the downtown skyline, the East End is a
depopulated gray zone wherein most of the housing stock is either ordinary or rundown. The natural appeal of the East End attracts housing
developers, but effective community resistance to gentrification prevents
redevelopment on a large scale.[27]

Non-extensive enclaves of detached houses might avoid degeneration if
anchored by higher-density development such as a downtown, a university, or a high-density cluster of middle-class housing. Lockerbie Square
at the edge of downtown Indianapolis is a captivating 25-acre cobblestreet
enclave where 19th century houses coexist with newer townhouses, and
with condominium apartments retrofitted into an old factory.
Preservation Park at the edge of downtown Oakland is a smaller enclave
limited to detached houses, and it also stands out as an exemplary residential environment. The viability of these enclaves is bolstered by surrounding higher-density development. But extensive urban areas
dominated by pre-World War II detached houses and duplexes, removed
from natural features and higher-density development, have almost without exception degenerated into gray zones.

GOLD ZONES

High-density neighborhoods that avoid degeneration do so in essentially
the same way as stable low-density neighborhoods—by offering superior
amenities and fine housing. Natural features are among the amenities
offered by the nation's most appealing high-density neighborhoods.
Chicago's Gold Coast lies at the shoreline of Lake Michigan. New York's
Upper East Side and Upper West Side flank Central Park. Brooklyn

Heights offers the East River promenade and breathtaking views of the Lower Manhattan skyline. San Francisco's high hills—Russian and Nob—provide exceptional terrain, and views of the magnificent city and its bay.

But these high-density neighborhoods have something else to offer: urban vitality—the cultural and commercial assets that only highly concentrated populations can produce and sustain. Urban vitality is a naturally occurring feature of high-density neighborhoods. Although urban vitality is more abstract than a lake or a leafy hill, it is nonetheless a real contributor to the quality of urban life, a contributor without which neighborhood degeneration is more likely to occur. The nation's most appealing urban neighborhoods—gold zones—combine natural amenities with urban vitality.

Density and Affluence

The notoriously high housing densities of the tenement-era Lower East Side are matched today in two of New York City's most prestigious residential districts—the Upper East Side and, across Central Park, the Upper West Side.[28] The gross housing density in both districts is about 120 dwelling units per acre, and net densities in both districts average roughly 200 units per acre.[29] But, unlike the tenements, the buildings in these two districts are not crowded and they do not lack indoor plumbing; they include New York's most opulent apartments. Nine buildings on the Upper East Side have apartments averaging 15 or more rooms, and 8,000 to 20,000 square feet of floor area. (One of the East Side's apartments is a 12,000-square-foot unit in which the "grand salon" is aptly named: 78 feet long, occupying 2,800 square feet, with a 23-foot-high ceiling, an 18-foot-high fireplace, and six 20-foot-high windows. The newspaper heiress who paid $12 million for it in 1988 put it on the market for $35 million in 1996.)[30]

Extreme affluence isn't caused by high residential densities any more than extreme poverty was, but the nation's highest residential densities correlate with extreme affluence today just as they correlated with extreme poverty 100 years ago. (Passenger elevators produced the turnaround.) The law of supply and demand provides the simple explanation for today's correlation: In the nation's biggest cities, the most densely populated neighborhoods offer to a multitude of cultural and commercial amenities and social opportunities, as well as proximity to high-pay downtown jobs. Demand for housing in such neighborhoods outweighs supply, hence good housing is affordable primarily to the rich.

Beyond the simple supply-and-demand explanation, the nature of the housing stock in the nation's highest-density neighborhoods adds to their stability and appeal. Urban geographer Larry R. Ford credits large apartment buildings with maintaining the high status of the nation's most desirable urban neighborhoods. Ford avers that apartments in "large luxury apartment buildings," especially when congregated among other such buildings, "resist the forces of invasion and succession," the process of social, economic, and physical degeneration that occurs when affluent urban neighborhoods are invaded, and their populations succeeded, by less affluent populations.[31]

Ford cites these examples of affluent neighborhoods and high-status avenues bolstered by large luxury apartment buildings: Chicago's Gold Coast, San Francisco's Russian Hill, Washington's Connecticut Avenue, and New York City's Upper East Side and Central Park West—all high-density. Ford notes that "monumental apartment buildings such as the Dakota, the San Remo, and the Century have graced Central Park West for decades, and no changes are in sight."[32]

Change occurred, however, soon after Ford predicted the stability of Central Park West: prices rose dramatically in the mid-1990s. In September 1996, *New York* magazine's Christopher Mason reported that apartment prices had increased 31 percent in the previous two years, and that multimillion dollar sales had become common. One apartment sold for $3.2 million three days after it was listed. Mason quoted real estate broker Robby Brown, "Right now I could sell an apartment on Central Park West with 3,000 square feet and a terrace for 3 to 5 million bucks about fifteen times over. There just isn't enough inventory."[33] Real estate brokers attribute the spike in demand largely to the heightened vitality of the West Side—to the enlivening of streets by the recent addition of bookstores, gyms, cinemas, and restaurants to the district's long-established variety of cultural and commercial amenities.

Central Park West's notable apartment buildings are, like many such buildings in high-prestige neighborhoods, cooperatively owned (an arrangement that emerged in New York City around 1880) and effectively restricted by boards of directors to carefully screened potential buyers.[34] Hundreds of Manhattan co-ops accept only those applicants who can prove impeccable financial and social credentials and convince the board of an exemplary lifestyle. Among the San Remo's rejectees are singer-actress Madonna and fashion mogul Calvin Klein. (Klein went over to the Upper East Side where he bought a townhouse, in 1988, for $6.95 million; in August 1997, Madonna was reported to have paid more than $6 million for an 8,500-square-foot condominium loft on the top floor of a 12-story SoHo building.)[35] Admission to many of the co-ops on the east side of Central Park is even more daunting than on the west. A who's who list of East Side rejectees would include casino mogul Steve Wynn, heiress-fashion designer Gloria Vanderbuilt, former president Richard Nixon, conservative commentator Rush Limbaugh, entertainer Barbara Streisand, and financier Felix Rohatyn, whose resume includes the salvation of New York City from its financial crisis in the 1970s. A co-op at Park Avenue and 71st Street is rumored by brokers to exclude applicants with less than $50 million in assets.[36]

New York's Corcoran Real Estate Group compiled a list of New York's "top social buildings"—high-prestige co-ops with the most demanding admissions criteria. The list is 50 buildings long. Forty-eight are within the one and one-half square-mile area designated by New York City's planning department as Manhattan Community District 8—the Upper East Side—home to the most affluent postal zone in the United States (10021). And Corcoran's list is by no means inclusive of all Upper East Side co-ops in which apartments sell for millions of dollars, to say nothing of the district's many opulent condominiums and rental buildings.[37]

A large luxury apartment building creates its own critical mass of affluence, impenetrable to low-income households and resistant to change. A congregation of such buildings immunizes a neighborhood from the forces of urban decline even in times of severe social and economic stress. Park Avenue emerged as New York's most prestigious address before World War I and remained so through an economic depression.[38] And it remains so today in the late stages of a post-industrial economic revolution that has contributed powerfully to the devastation of other urban districts and whole cities.

PURE CITY

The rivers that circumscribe Manhattan, and the great park at the island's center explain much of the appeal of the Upper West Side and the Upper East Side; but many of Manhattan's thriving neighborhoods to the south are isolated from Central Park by Midtown, and from the Hudson and East rivers by major arterial roadways. The East Side's Murray Hill neighborhood, for example, is separated from Central Park by a mile of urban real estate that includes the Midtown business district, and the neighborhood is separated from the East River by a high-capacity roadway (FDR Drive) and by the United Nations complex. And yet the high-density 14-block heart of Murray Hill is nearly as affluent (indicating high appeal) as the average Upper East Side neighborhood. A high rate of transit commuting among the area's residents suggests that many live there for reasons other than the feasibility of walking to Midtown jobs.[39]

New York's spirited and popular SoHo is locked in the depths of Manhattan, isolated from nature by thousands of acres of surrounding urban landscape. Shops, galleries, restaurants, bars, bookstores, coffeehouses, historic architecture, a diverse population of residents and visitors, and fascinating adjacent neighborhoods are about all SoHo has to offer. In 1996, when *New York* magazine asked various notable New Yorkers what they like about their neighborhoods, SoHo artist Art Spiegelman responded with just eight words: "No parks, no supermarkets, no trees—pure city!"[40]

In voluptuous San Francisco, the flat and hard-edged South of Market district has been invaded by young and not-so-young professionals attracted to old lofts and new apartment buildings in an ambience roughly resembling SoHo's. As in SoHo, artists unwittingly primed South of Market for an invasion by more straitlaced urbanites. In Philadelphia, the Rittenhouse Square neighborhood lies adjacent to the Schuylkill River, but is isolated from it by rail yards and weedy terrain. This high-vitality, high-appeal, high-density neighborhood focuses inward on its small namesake park of only eight acres—less than one percent of Central Park's area.

The urban rather than the natural environment dominates neighborhoods such as these, and urban vitality—the proximate availability of multitudinous choices—is among their most appealing features. These neighborhoods demonstrate that urban vitality is more than just an abstract byproduct of high densities, it is a tangible neighborhood attraction.

Public housing represents densities in the range that encompasses SoHo and South of Market, but many public housing developments combine adverse social and economic conditions with an absence of proximate commercial buildings to prevent high levels of vitality. Commercial vitality is not necessarily incompatible with low-income neighborhoods, however, if their housing densities are not also low. Brooklyn's Williamsburg has a poverty rate in excess of 40 percent, but the neighborhood's townhouses and apartment buildings constitute a housing density about six times as high as that of Minneapolis' Willard-Hay neighborhood.[41] Williamsburg offers a broad range of retail and service businesses in its abundant supply of commercial buildings.

The Melrose neighborhood in the South Bronx provides another example of commercial vitality in the midst a poverty rate that exceeds 40 percent.[42] Melrose's commercial area, which is centered on 149th Street and 3rd Avenue and extends a couple of blocks in each of four directions, is alive with a hundred consumer businesses that draw people to the streets in considerable numbers, from inside and outside the neighborhood, on foot and on transit, to socialize as much as to shop (Figure 2-2). Much of the area's housing has been abandoned, but the occupied apartments, tenements, and townhouses within walking distance (a quarter mile) of the commercial streets constitute a density similar to that of

Figure 2-2. South Bronx commercial node (1998). The Melrose neighborhood in the South Bronx suffers a high rate of poverty, but moderate housing densities help sustain a lively commercial node at 149th Street and 3rd Avenue. Retailers are supported also by a subway station and some office buildings.

Williamsburg—about six times as high as Willard-Hay in Minneapolis.[43] Anchored by the traditional trio—supermarket, drugstore, and hardware store—the neighborhood's many small businesses include clothing and jewelry stores, fruit and vegetable markets, a meat market, a fish market, a flower shop, a variety of restaurants, and many other retail and service establishments of the types that have disappeared from the commercial streets of low-density neighborhoods like Willard-Hay.

The principal characteristics of the four neighborhood types discussed above can be summarized as follows:

• Gray Zone: Low-density, low-amenity urban neighborhood that has deteriorated physically and socioeconomically since the initial occupation of its housing stock. Gray zones are too low in density to sustain two essential elements of urban life: neighborhood retailing and good transit, thus they are suburban in character and their populations are automobile dependent. But gray-zone housing cannot compete effectively with newer suburban housing for non-poor households.

• Green Zone: Low-density high-amenity neighborhood capable of competing with suburbs for middle class and affluent households. Consequently the housing stock is well maintained, and much of it is upgraded by homeowners without resort to government-sponsored home-improvement programs. Natural features are the principal amenities of green zones.

• Gold Zone: Moderate- or high-density neighborhood that combines natural features and high vitality to produce very high appeal, which ensures a high level of housing maintenance and investment. The extravagant appeal of the nation's highest-density gold zones, such as New York City's Upper East Side and San Francisco's Russian Hill, limits them primarily to affluent households. This nation's highest-density gold zones are among the most prestigious neighborhoods in the world.

• Pure City: Moderate- or high-density neighborhood isolated from major natural features, thus it derives whatever physical appeal it possesses entirely from the urban environment. Moderate-density areas can be high in vitality and appeal unless they are plagued by adverse social and economic conditions, which are often imposed by government housing policy.

Many residential areas are hybrids that combine features of two or more generic types. Some gray zones, for example, include clusters of moderate-density housing, often public housing, and some green zones, such as

Cincinnati's Clifton neighborhood, include apartment buildings along their commercial streets. Clifton's Ludlow Street enhances the neighborhood with a full range of retail amenities, including a cinema, which detached-house densities cannot sustain. Similarly, dozens of apartment buildings and several townhouses surround Upton Avenue at the commercial heart of Linden Hills, a green-zone neighborhood in Minneapolis. Though not as urbane as Ludlow Street, Upton Avenue is exceptional among neighborhood commercial areas in Minneapolis because of the boost it gets from the moderate-density housing.

Clifton's and Linden Hills' moderate-density housing isn't extensive enough to support a high level of commercial vitality, but it fosters a level of vitality seldom if ever matched in the midst of detached houses alone.* Moderate-vitality commercial areas in green zones enhance the quality of life for neighborhood residents, and they attract shoppers from outside the neighborhood, for whom parking lots are generously provided. Gray-zone commercial areas repel rather than attract the middle class. The low-density housing adjacent to the typical gray-zone commercial street provides little boost to commercial viability. Devitalized West Broadway in Minneapolis' Willard-Hay neighborhood is flanked by a couple of small apartment buildings and a couple-dozen detached houses (some boarded up), in addition to its sparsely arranged commercial buildings. This bleak avenue has no power to attract outsiders to its remaining business establishments, or non-poor households to its adjacent neighborhoods.

THE SUBURBANIZATION OF LOT COVERAGE

Highrise buildings in public housing developments constitute moderate rather than high densities because they cover but a small fraction of their mostly empty sites, a condition characteristic of suburban buildings, but uncharacteristic of urban buildings in traditional high-density neighborhoods. While traditional urban buildings cover two-thirds or more of the land within their lot lines, suburban buildings typically cover less than a

---

*Upton Avenue in Linden Hills has but one grocery store—a co-op that functions, for many customers, as a mere dairy store because the food preferences of the mainstream are largely unaccommodated. The transportation preferences of the mainstream, however, are generously accommodated in the co-op's parking lot. Linden Hills' cluster of apartment buildings does not produce a flow of customers that can, by itself, sustain the commercial street, so automobile-bound customers must be accommodated. And neighborhood residents within walking distance of Upton Avenue make routine trips—in their cars—to grocery stores outside the neighborhood.

third. The buildings in Brooklyn's troubled Van Dyke public housing development cover only 17 percent of their lot.[44]

Prestigious apartment buildings throughout Manhattan cover more than half of their lots, proving the efficacy of high densities and high-percentage lot coverage. Nonetheless a prejudice against these attributes has persisted, even in cities, long past the tenement era when high lot-coverage ratios were implicated in the maladies of tenement districts. In 1960 the American Public Health Association (APHA) established standards for apartment densities that, when applied, yield buildings that are suburban rather than urban in their lot-coverage characteristics. The association's standards reflect apartment buildings that cover about one-third of their lots in the case of lowrise buildings, and even less in the case of taller buildings (Table 2-1). Public housing conforms to the density standards of the APHA.

Table 2-1. Density Standards for Multifamily Buildings

	Dwelling Units/Net Acre	
Building Height	Desirable	Maximum
3-story	40	45
6-story	65	75
9-story	75	85
13-story	85	95

Source: Committee on the Hygiene of Housing, American Public Health Association (1960), p. 39.

Zoning codes in most cities establish bulk limitations for apartment buildings that reflect the suburban densities promulgated by the APHA. In Minneapolis, for example, several multifamily zoning districts (R4) within a mile of downtown impose front and side yard requirements and bulk limitations that yield buildings more suburban than urban. A four-story building in these R4 districts is permitted to cover, at most, 38 percent of its lot, and even less for narrow or small lots. Such a low lot-coverage ratio ensures the availability of land to satisfy the city's off-street parking requirement.[45]

Lawn and parking pavement surround suburban apartment buildings, but land near the center of the metropolis should be sufficiently valuable that parking is relegated to basement garages; density and lot-coverage standards for urban apartment buildings should be set at levels much higher than the APHA's suburbanized standards. Urban-density buildings, properly designed, can comfortably cover more than half of a small lot (under a quarter acre), and they can cover two-thirds of a larger lot without impairing the health and comfort of their occupants.

The San Remo, the Dakota, the Majestic, the Century, the Beresford, the El Dorado, and many other Manhattan apartment buildings have two things in common: Their lot-coverage ratios exceed 60 percent and their apartments sell for millions of dollars (Figure 2-3). Because of their high lot-coverage ratios, Manhattan's renowned apartment buildings exceed the APHA's density standards by a wide margin. With 93 units on a site of 0.92 acres (101 units/acre), the Dakota, which covers two-thirds of its lot, exceeds the APHA's "maximum" density standard by 19 percent, and if its apartments were average rather than lordly in size its density would be triple the APHA standard. In spite of their deficiency in the eyes of the APHA, the opulent apartments in the buildings listed above routinely fetch more than $500 per square foot. These buildings benefit from Central Park exposures, but Manhattan's inland apartment buildings that are surrounded by other buildings cover equally high percentages of their lots. The legendary Ansonia covers 70 percent of its lot and its occupants, when they look out their windows, see not a great park but other build-

Figure 2-3. The Majestic and the Dakota: Two of Manhattan's prestigious apartment buildings that cover two-thirds or more of the area of their lots. Credit: Yann Athus-Bertrand/Altitude/Photo Researchers.

ings built tight to the sidewalk. The Ansonia houses 462 units on a one-acre site, therefore its density is 462 units per acre—more than quadruple the density deemed suitable by the APHA for a building of Ansonia's height—14 residential stories. Units in the Ansonia have sold for more than $2 million and they average more than $500 per square foot.[46]

The standards of the APHA might have been appropriate for the narrow tenement lots of 19th-century New York, only 25 feet wide by 100 feet deep. A tenement that covers 70 percent of such a lot exposes only 13 percent of its exterior wall area to the street, and another 13 percent to a small back yard. Since tenements were hemmed in on both sides by other tenements, most of their rooms were inadequately provided with outside light and air. Manhattan's prestigious apartment buildings occupy lots that are much larger. The San Remo, the Dakota, the Majestic, the Century, the Beresford, the El Dorado, and the Ansonia all occupy lots 200 feet wide—the entire width of a Manhattan block. Situated at the ends of blocks, these buildings expose three of their four exterior walls, i.e., 75 percent of their perimeters, to the daylight and fresh air of the street, compared to only 13 percent in the case of a tenement with a similar lot-coverage ratio.[47]

Building lots smaller than the full 200-foot width of a Manhattan block demand lower densities, but not so low as those recommended by the APHA. The richly ornate Alwyn Court apartments (near Carnegie Hall) occupy a corner lot—two street exposures and two alley exposures—less than one-third the size of the Dakota's lot, yet Alwyn Court covers about 75 percent of its lot and achieves a density of about 250 units per acre, triple the density deemed "desirable" by the APHA. The views from Alwyn Court's windows are of other urbane buildings across the street or alley, and Alwyn Court's residents apparently appreciate their homes, they tend to stay put. Only one of the building's 75 apartments was sold in 1999—a 1,590 square-foot unit that went for $775,000 ($487 per square foot), and, as of October 27, no sales in the year 2000.[48]

A lot as narrow as tenement lot cannot be developed as densely as a larger lot, but it can accommodate a much higher density than that promulgated by the APHA. A 25-foot by 100-foot lot can accommodate a 60-percent-lot-coverage building with one 1,200-square-foot apartment (plus elevator and stairs) on each of six floors. Each apartment would have, besides its street exposure, a rear exposure to an ample back yard. Such a building would constitute a density of 105 units per acre, exceeding the APHA's "maximum" density standard by 39 percent.

BUILDINGS THAT DEFINE STREETS

Boston's zoning code describes the public realm as "that aspect of the urban environment which is visible and accessible to the public, including both spaces and *the building walls which frame them*." (Emphasis added.) The principal space of the urban public realm is the street, as architecture critic Paul Goldberger explains: "The street is the building block of urban design and, by extension, of urban life; the city with vibrant street life is the city that works as a viable urban environment. It is the street, not the individual building, that is the key to making a city work as a piece of design, for the street is...the true room of the city."[49]

Apartment buildings (and other building types) that cover most of their lots not only produce densities appropriate to cities, they also define streets. Manhattan's legendary apartment buildings appear to fill their lots completely; their 30 percent, more or less, of open lot area is usually hidden from public view in an interior court, never revealed in a yard or parking lot situated between building and street. In addition to defining streets, street-wall commercial buildings present entries and display windows to pedestrians, enhancing their experience of the street. In the mutually beneficial relationship between urban street and urban building, the street provides the building with daylight and air. Windows in suburban buildings get daylight and outside air from the vacant space between building and street; in urban settings the street right-of-way provides light and air. It is often said that city streets use land more efficiently than suburban streets because city streets serve more functions; they carry not only private motor vehicles, but also transit vehicles and pedestrians. The provision of light and air is yet another duty performed by the urban street.

The European streetscape, universally admired today, had been rejected in the 1920s by notable European architects who promoted tower-in-the-park schemes, soon copied in America on public housing sites and later adapted to downtown redevelopment sites (tower-on-the-plaza). Fortunately, traditional urban form is again appreciated and the best of today's urban architecture embraces the street. Manhattan's exemplary Battery Park City, master-planned in 1979 and inspired by the streets and buildings of pre-war New York City, proves that new urban development needn't mimic post-war suburban development. (In a reversal, new suburban development mimics the traditional urban streetscape where neo-traditional planners and developers create fake main streets and street-hugging townhouses.)

DENSITY AND DIVERSITY

The residential buildings in prestigious high-density districts and neighborhoods, including the Upper East and Upper West sides, Brooklyn Heights, Rittenhouse Square, and Russian Hill, provide a rich variety of accommodations from single houses (townhouses usually) to highrise apartment buildings, and they accommodate households with widely varying incomes in close proximity. All income groups are well represented in the Upper West Side, where the poverty rate exceeds 12 percent (in 1990) and modest walk-ups share their blocks with park-view penthouses. The Upper East Side is more affluent, but its housing stock includes hundreds of old walk-up buildings and its poverty rate is just under six percent.[50]

In these high-density districts it is not uncommon for households of widely varied means to share a single apartment building. Apartments in the Ansonia sold for prices ranging from $180,000 to $2.35 million in 1999.[51] Neighborhoods dominated by single houses are more homogeneous. In these neighborhoods a house conspicuously out of scale or out of character with its neighbors lends a note of discord to the composition, which is why developers of suburban subdivisions vary their houses only superficially. Income diversity is agreeably accommodated in the housing of high-density districts, where apartment buildings provide only subtle clues as to the economic status of their inhabitants.

The income diversity of the nation's most appealing high-density neighborhoods abets a diversity in commercial establishments. Everything from discount clothing to fine art can be purchased where a high density provides markets for a wide range of goods in a compact area. Low-density districts have difficulty accommodating the commercial needs of a single economic class. Jane Jacobs noted in 1961 that the only effective economic demand that can exist in a low-density area is that of the majority.[52] In *A Man in Full*, Tom Wolfe described the low-density suburbs east of San Francisco Bay: "The only way you could tell you were leaving one community and entering another was when the franchises started repeating and you spotted another 7-Eleven, another Wendy's, another Costco, another Home Depot."[53] Low-density districts that sustain popular restaurants exert too little demand to sustain exotic restaurants; any such establishment depends almost totally on the patronage of outsiders arriving in cars. A high-density settlement will sustain a wider variety of restaurants than a low-density settlement of equal population, provided that tourism and business travel to both places are similar in magnitude.

The number of restaurants may be the same in both places, but the greater variety would accompany the higher density, for this reason:

Five neighborhoods in a low-density area might each have five restaurants, but there is a strong likelihood of duplication. Among the neighborhoods' combined inventory of 25 restaurants, several national chains would be represented, some with outlets in two or more neighborhoods. But if the populations of those five neighborhoods were congregated into a compact area they would eliminate some of the duplication, and they would substitute some specialized restaurants; if their restaurant inventory remained at 25, it would be more diverse. A sparsely settled neighborhood that sustains five restaurants will, by means of its residents' collective preference expressed with dollars, select the restaurants that the residents tacitly agree upon—the most popular, the lowest common denominator, the same restaurants chosen by adjacent sparsely settled neighborhoods.

Suburbs are therefore underrepresented by one-of-a-kind independent restaurants and overrepresented by national chain outlets, invariably located along major arterial roadways. Where densities are low, national chain restaurants with ethnic themes—restaurants built by investors rather than restaurateurs—substitute for the unique ethnic restaurants found mostly in cities. Suburbs in the Twin Cities metro-area are blessed with eight Olive Garden restaurants (Italian); the higher-density central cities have none. The metro area's five Chi-Chi's restaurants (Mexican) are all suburban as well.

Minneapolis and St. Paul, which contain about a quarter of their metro-area's population and households, contained half or more of the independent restaurants in most cuisine categories, including French, German, Japanese, Korean, Thai, Indian, Cuban, Middle-Eastern, Ethiopian, and Russian, according to a 1997 survey. By contrast, the eight full-service (as opposed to fast-food) national chain restaurants most abundantly represented in the Twin Cities area had established only 11 percent of their metro-area restaurants in the central cities, which, as mentioned above, contain about one-fourth of the metro area's population. Most national fast-food chains are also overrepresented in the suburbs.[54] (Upscale national chains with only one metro-area outlet, such as Morton's of Chicago and Ichiban, gravitate to downtown Minneapolis or the Mall of America.)

Duplication accounted for 16 percent of the restaurants in Minneapolis in 1997, compared to 33 percent in a representative sector of suburbia that includes inner and outer suburbs, a sector with an average population density much lower than that of Minneapolis. Minneapolis' neighborhoods sustained 103 differently named restaurants per 100,000 population, compared to 77 in the suburban sector, even though the total number of restaurants per 100,000 population was similar in both areas (Table 2-2).

Several factors contribute to Minneapolis' superior restaurant diversity, factors including ethnic and cultural influences and the availability of old low-rent commercial space. But Minneapolis' higher population density

Table 2-2. Population Density and Restaurant Diversity

	Minneapolis	Minneapolis Non-CBD (1)	Suburbs (2)
Resident Population (1996)	364,382	357,818	167,305
Land Area (sq. mi.)	54.7	53.6	84.2
Population Density (1996) (residents/sq. mi.)	**6,661**	**6,676**	**1,987**
No. of Restaurant Labels (3)	502	367	129
No. of Copies	94	72	62
No. of Restaurants (1997)	596	439	191
Copies as % of Total	**15.8**	**16.4**	**32.5**
Restaurants/100,000 population	163.6	122.7	114.2
Restaurant labels/100,000 pop.	137.8	102.6	77.1

General Notes: The following types of establishments are excluded: workplace cafeterias; bars that heat frozen pizzas and sandwiches rather than prepare food in house; establishments that offer only take-out and/or delivery service; establishments that impose a cover charge or minimum drink order for entertainment, such as striptease bars; concession stands and lunch counters at sports venues such as ice arenas, bowling alleys, and golf courses. (Golf course country clubs are included if their restaurants are open year-round.)

Numbered Notes:

(1) "Minneapolis Non-CBD" numbers exclude population, households, land area, and restaurants in downtown's census tracts 44, 45, 46, 53, and 54, which are primarily non-residential, and where most food establishments close before 6:00 p.m. Population deductions are based on 1990 census data.

(2) "Suburbs" are the four suburbs of the Metropolitan Council's 15th district, which is roughly equivalent to Minneapolis in geographic size and which includes inner and outer suburbs: Apple Valley, Burnsville, Eagan, and Mendota Heights.

(3) "Restaurant labels" counts chain or multiple-location restaurants only once regardless of the number of establishments of the same name in the area analyzed. Additional restaurants of the same name are called "copies."

Source for suburban restaurants: State of Minnesota Department of Environmental Health, list of Dakota County food service and lodging establishments dated 30 July 1997. Source for Minneapolis restaurants: Minneapolis Department of Environmental Health, list of food service establishments dated 14 August 1997.

is perhaps its strongest advantage, strong enough to more than offset the income advantage of the suburban sector.

A comparison between the restaurant inventories of Manhattan and Minneapolis would yield findings similar to the comparison between Minneapolis and its suburbs; Manhattan's high densities sustain a variety of restaurants unmatched in America. And what is true of restaurants is true of retailing in general: Among cities of equal population and affluence, the higher densities produce the greater diversity. Higher densities sustain a wider selection of specialized merchandise such as imported foods, rare books, foreign magazines, and art. "For centuries probably everyone who has thought about cities at all has noticed that there seems to be some connection between the concentration of people and the specialties they can support," said Jane Jacobs in 1961.[55]

THE CAPABILITY OF MAKING CULTURE

Higher densities sustain a wider selection of cultural amenities also, especially when the higher densities combine with affluence. The nation's greatest collection of design and visual arts institutions is situated in New York City's densely populated and affluent Upper East Side. The Metropolitan Museum of Art, the Whitney and Guggenheim museums, the Frick Collection, the Jewish Museum, the International Center of Photography, the Cooper Hewitt Museum, the National Academy of Design, and the Goethe Institute are collectively as strong a presence on the Upper East Side as the district's abundant commercial amenities; they enrich the district and the city immeasurably. It is not coincidental that these institutions, founded and anchored by New York's philanthropic rich, are situated along the city's most prestigious avenues.

The Upper East Side's arts institutions exist in synergy with the district's many art-related business establishments—galleries, dealers, restorers, frame makers, auction houses, and identification and registration services. New York City's Art and Design High School is situated at the lower edge of the Upper East Side.

Across Central Park, the New York State Theater, the Vivian Beaumont and Mitzi Newhouse theaters, the Metropolitan Opera House, Avery Fisher Hall, Alice Tully Hall, the Juilliard School, the School of American Ballet, the Library and Museum of the Performing Arts, the Film Society of Lincoln Center, the Chamber Music Society of Lincoln Center, the Lincoln Center Institute for the Arts in Education, and a multitude of rehearsal studios, dormitories, and support facilities constitute the nation's largest performing arts center, which every year attracts to its performances five million people, many of whom find their way onto the Upper West Side's sidewalks and into its shops and restaurants.[56] Lincoln Center attracts visitors from far beyond its neighborhood, but locals also devour the riches. New York journalist David Denby describes the Upper West Side crowd:

> They are intelligent and accomplished people, the striders-down-Broadway—lawyers, doctors, Wall Street workers high and low, students, musicians, theater people, professors and teachers, computer programmers, media executives and journalists, and I suspect that they consume more culture per capita than any other people in the world...[57]

Amidst the Upper West Side's consumers of culture are creators and promoters of culture. A strip of West Side land a half-mile wide and two miles long, which stretches from Midtown to the West 70s and encompasses Lincoln Center, Carnegie Hall, and the Broadway theater district, includes the workplaces and residences of musicians, actors, dancers, choreographers, and all manner of institutions and service establishments that nourish and facilitate their crafts. These include, in addition to the renowned institutions at Lincoln Center, the Fiorello LaGuardia High School of Performing Arts, several dance and opera companies, various music and dance instructors, acting instructors, theatrical agencies, musical-instrument repairers, costume makers, set designers, stage lighting consultants, and vendors of theatrical equipment, musical instruments, ballet shoes, and more.

Could these facilities and facilitators have materialized and thrived if New York's artists and patrons and public were spread out at suburban densities? In Orange County, California, the immense stone-clad Costa Mesa Performing Arts Center proves that cultural facilities can materialize today in car-dominated edge cities. But these suburban places lack the urban trait that Paul Goldberger calls "the capability of making culture." Unlike New York's cultural institutions situated in a dense concentration of talent, support services, and other cultural institutions, the culturally isolated Costa Mesa center "has spawned no community of artists and performers around it..." says Goldberger, who predicts that it never will.[58] New York City's Lincoln Center-Carnegie Hall-Times Square corridor is a cultural incubator where culture is created as well as consumed.

The culture that is created in the Los Angeles metropolis is the popular culture of the movie and television industries, which are more industrial than cultural or commercial in their land-use characteristics.* In spite of an immense pool of talent congregated in the metropolis to feed the entertainment industry, Los Angeles fails to produce a theater milieu equal to New York's in variety and stature. Arts and entertainment writer Neil Strauss notes the "lack of a cohesive arts audience" in Los Angeles, which he attributes to the "lack of a cohesive city." Todd Purdum, Los Angeles correspondent for the *New York Times,* describes a "special challenge" for theater in Los Angeles: "auditoriums are spread around a sprawling region with…little adjacent after-show night life…"[59]

High-intensity night life powerfully attracts creative people to lower Manhattan to live and to work. Farther north, Central Park separates the visual from the performing arts, but downtown they coexist in America's, if not the world's, most energetically creative neighborhoods. Greenwich Village, the East Village, SoHo, and Tribeca provide academies of instruction and opportunities for spontaneous creativity that could never coalesce where artists, institutions, supporting businesses, and patrons are widely dispersed. Proximity facilitates for artists the same kinds of information exchanges and intellectual cross-fertilizations that it facilitates for business people who deem it essential to situate themselves in the central business district. Manhattan's artistic districts attract ascending artists from around the world; "the influx of talent never stops," writes theater critic Frank Rich, noting the powerful magnetism of Manhattan's renowned theater companies.[60]

Manhattan's downtown districts are less affluent than its refined uptown districts, but downtown artists benefit from the wealth that trickles down, just as Broadway and uptown institutions benefit from the evolving talent and the cutting-edge creativity emanating from downtown. It was in downtown Manhattan, for example, that the musical *Rent* materialized, written and performed by downtown talent, first staged in the East Village. *Rent* became a smash Broadway hit in 1996, and then an export to theaters across America. The *New York Times* reported in December 1999, "Every year for the last five, Off Broadway has produced the Pulitzer Prize winning drama …" (including *Rent* in 1996).[61] The syn-

---

*Neil Strauss, arts and entertainment writer for the *New York Times*, reports that nonmainstream music "has trouble finding a home" in Los Angeles, but not in New York City. "Manhattan is a cultural capital…But Los Angeles is an industry town, pumping out audience-tested dreams…with the intention of pleasing the widest audience possible." Strauss notes that impaired mobility undermines the arts in Los Angeles: "On a busy weekend night, driving into Hollywood for a show can be an ordeal …"(Neil Strauss, "Knitting Factory Goes Hollywood," *New York Times*, 15 June 2000, p. B3)

ergy among Uptown and Downtown, East Side and West Side produces not only life-enhancing cultural vitality, but also profound economic benefit. An economic impact study revealed that New York City's cultural activities generated $9 billion in revenue in 1992.[62] It is no coincidence that North America's most culturally prolific dozen square miles is also its most densely populated.

CENTRAL-CITY DENSITY AND REGIONAL AFFLUENCE

The cultural, commercial, and intellectual vitality fostered by high densities generates robust economic activity, boosting the affluence of high-density cities. Manhattan's per-capita income was $58,000 in 1995, "by far the highest of any county in the United States," according to New York City's planning department. (Manhattan is a county, as well as a borough of New York City.) In the United States, high-density districts are often surrounded by low-density squalor, but the affluence generated by high densities does not entirely dissipate within the borders of high-density cities. New York City's planning department reported that "the [1995] per capita incomes of several suburban counties, including Westchester, Nassau, Fairfield, Bergen, and Morris, are…among the nation's highest, though far below Manhattan."[63] The nation's highest-density cities anchor its most affluent metropolitan areas, and low-density cities anchor the least affluent. In 1991, among the nation's 41 metropolitan areas with populations exceeding one million:

• Eight of the ten metro areas with the densest cores had average per-capita incomes higher than the national average; a ninth was average.

• Eight of the ten metropolitan areas with the most sparsely developed core cities had per-capita incomes lower than average.

• The nation's two densest urban cores were surrounded by its two most affluent metro areas, but they are at opposite corners of the nation. The New York City metropolis had the densest core city (23,701 people per square mile in 1990) and the highest level of affluence (134.5 percent of the national average per capita income in 1991). The San Francisco metropolis had the second most densely populated core city (15,502 people per square mile in 1990) and the second highest level of affluence (133.4 percent of the national average per capita income in 1991).

In the Northeast, the Midwest, the Northwest, and the South, the most affluent metropolitan area had the densest core city; the same is true in the heavily urbanized state of California. This general pattern held true in 1994 in metropolitan areas of more than one million residents, according to data compiled by the U.S. Bureau of Economic Analysis.[64]

The nation's most affluent metropolitan areas are among its most popu-lous, but core-city density is a better predictor of affluence than is metro-area population (Figure 2-4). The Los Angeles metropolis is more than twice as populous as the San Francisco Bay Area, but San Francisco's pop-ulation density is significantly higher, as is its metro area's level of afflu-ence. High-density districts not only generate economic activity, they attract affluence to their cities and regions from across the nation (and world). Urban vitality is a powerful attraction according to a 1997 Gallup poll that asked, "In which city would you most like to live?" New York City was the choice of a plurality of those polled; San Francisco was third, after Seattle, which was mistakenly perceived as the safest of the three. (A plurality of those polled wrongly believed New York City to be the nation's most dangerous city.)[65] New York's copious diversity of specialty retailers, restaurants, theaters, and museums—the byproducts of urban vitality—is of particular interest to households with substantial dispos-able income. Urban vitality is a force powerful enough to radiate afflu-ence, and to draw it from afar.

San Francisco's multimedia industry grew explosively in the 1980s and 1990s because "San Francisco offers qualities that multimedia firms value: proximity to creative people and quality of life…Multimedia profession-als…value the amenities of the city and gain value from their personal contacts here," according to the San Francisco Planning Department (which notes that the industry is "concentrated in dense bustling parts of the city").[66] San Francisco's "Multimedia Gulch" exists in synergy with Silicon Valley, which is largely indebted to San Francisco for the avail-ability of talent. San Francisco's talent reach is international. The planning department notes the city's magnetism for Japanese students and profes-sionals, and CBS *Evening News* profiled a Frenchman who gave up his Paris flat for an apartment on Telegraph Hill. He's a successful innovator in the computer industry and, like many other high-tech professionals, he prefers San Francisco to suburban Silicon Valley.[67]

"Young people and people with ideas and people who like the tumble and tide are attracted to Boston and San Francisco and Chicago and New York," says urban historian Kenneth Jackson. He was quoted in a *New York Times* article about the enduring appeal of America's precious few high-density high-amenity neighborhoods, including San Francisco's Pacific Heights, Boston's Beacon Hill, Philadelphia's Society Hill, and Chicago's Gold Coast, all of which continue to attract affluent households from near and far.[68]

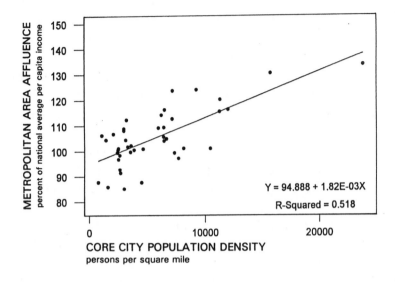

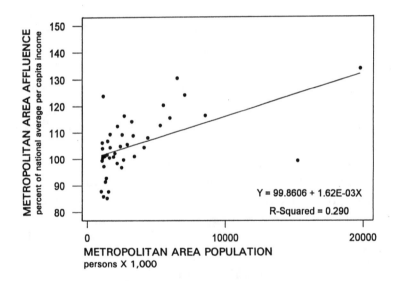

Figure 2-4. Regression plots: Metropolitan affluence. Metro-area affluence generally increases with core-city population density in the nation's 42 metro areas with more than one million residents, based on 1994 data. Core-city density is a better predictor of metro-area affluence than is metro-area population. (The correlation between metro-area affluence and core-city population is weak—not shown.)

Source of data: Statistical Abstract of the United States—1996, pp. 44, 355.

DENSITY AND TRAFFIC CONGESTION

The one and only rational apprehension about high urban densities today pertains to vehicular traffic congestion. High-density cities generate fewer vehicle trips per capita than automobile-dependent low-density cities, but the trips that are generated in high-density cities are concentrated in small areas. A good transit system allows central-city residents to avoid traffic congestion downtown, but neighborhood congestion erodes their quality of life. High-density residential neighborhoods, however, generate very little traffic.[69]

In New York City, vehicular traffic on most Upper East Side streets (as opposed to avenues) is surprisingly light considering the high ratio of households to street lanes. Traffic is light because most of the Upper East Side's east-west streets are purely local, terminating at the district's two natural boundaries: the East River and, less than a mile to the west, Central Park. Central Park's instigators intended to enhance the development potential of land in a largely underdeveloped area when they promoted the project in the 1850s, but they accomplished much more. Beyond providing a great natural landscape in the middle of the city, the park's creators enhanced the appeal of the adjacent districts in an important but perhaps unintended way: they created a massive barrier to through traffic. Of the Upper East Side's 38 east-west streets, 29 are blocked by the park, and the busiest of the through-park streets—Seventy-second Street—is closed to general traffic much of the time. Traffic on many of the Upper East Side's streets is therefore intermittent rather than constant, even during peak periods, and pedestrians cross at will, green light or red. The adverse effect of rush-hour traffic is minimized by the slow speeds at which it travels the narrow streets. At non-rush-hour times, moving vehicles are all but absent from many of the Upper East Side's streets.

The Upper East Side's north-south avenues are a different matter; wide and unending, they carry large volumes of outside traffic, much of it just passing through enroute from Midtown or Downtown to the world beyond Manhattan. From the standpoint of any particular Upper East Side neighborhood, almost all avenue traffic is through traffic from outside. When standing at most any street corner in Census Tract 126, for example, one sees few vehicles turning from avenues onto streets. The avenues of the Upper East Side are congested, but the localized, tranquil, east-west streets demonstrate that high traffic volumes are not an inherent trait of high-density neighborhoods.

Brooklyn Heights endures less through traffic than the neighborhoods of the Upper East Side because it is bounded on three of its four sides by obstructions—the East River on the west, Brooklyn Bridge abutments on the north, and Cadman Plaza and the Civic Center on the east. Brooklyn Heights is a traffic backwater fed mostly from the south, and through traffic from the south usually finds routes that are faster than neighborhood streets.[70] Even Brooklyn Heights' main commercial street—Montague Street—carries surprisingly little traffic considering its intensity of commercial activity. Montague Street is less than a half mile long, and it terminates at the East River. The quiet charm of Brooklyn Heights' residential streets and the rich variety of shops and restaurants along Montague Street make this high-density neighborhood (about 125 housing units per net acre) one of New York City's most appealing.

Another New York City neighborhood demonstrates that high-density housing, in the context of commercial vitality and good transit, generates virtually no vehicular traffic. Roosevelt Island's residential precinct is a high-density congregation of modern (post-1970) apartment buildings, ranging from lowrise to highrise, housing about 9,500 residents. The island is connected to the larger city by public transportation—subway, bus, and aerial tramway—and by a solitary narrow bridge (from Queens) that feeds private cars directly into a parking garage. Some cars, but not many, proceed into the neighborhood. Roosevelt Island is virtually free of traffic because its residents all live within walking distance of all the goods and services needed daily by the typical household. Just as important, all residents live within walking distance of good transit facilities that carry them to jobs and to specialized goods and services in the surrounding city. Almost completely free of moving vehicles most of the time, Main Street is as much a social as a commercial entity, where adults mingle while children (who grow up in apartment buildings) play.

Rivers, parks, and bridge abutments keep through traffic out of New York's high-density neighborhoods; steep hills keep it out of San Francisco's high-density Russian Hill, a prestigious neighborhood of many housing types, including highrise apartments. Through traffic is discouraged by the steep gradients of the neighborhood's streets. Russian Hill's main commercial street—Polk Street at the base of the hill—is an arduous trek for high-altitude residents in pursuit of convenience goods, but the neighborhood's high density sustains several commercial outposts—grocery stores, drugstores, restaurants, laundries, a shoe repair, and a hardware store. Thus the neighborhood's densely congregated residents needn't negotiate long stretches of steep sidewalk to get everyday goods and services, nor do they need to drive their cars.

New York City and San Francisco provide ample evidence that high-density residential neighborhoods generate little traffic from within, especially in the context of a high-density city well served by transit. High-density neighborhoods can avoid bothersome levels of vehicular traffic if they can find a way to exclude through traffic.

SIX TRAITS OF HIGH-DENSITY NEIGHBORHOODS

The densities of Manhattan, especially those of the Upper East Side, are extreme by American standards. But the extreme example of the Upper East Side illustrates the following facts about high housing densities:

1. They suppress automobile ownership and promote transit use and pedestrian activity.

2. They do not preclude peaceful tree-lined streets of low-rise apartment buildings and townhouses—the kind of urban environment that is universally appealing.

3. They foster safety and a sense of security, day and night.

4. They are found in places appealing enough to attract the nation's most affluent households.

5. They generate and sustain a rich diversity of commercial and cultural amenities, which attract affluent households to their region.

6. They do not generate high volumes of vehicular traffic.

HOW DENSE IS TOO DENSE?

Until its 1993 demolition, perhaps the highest-density residential district in the history of humanity, with housing densities nearly four times as high as Manhattan's highest-density census tract, existed in Hong Kong's Walled City of Kowloon. When its population peaked in the 1980s the Walled City housed 35,000 people on a piece of ground roughly 400 feet by 700 feet—the size of a pair of downtown blocks in most U.S. cities. The Walled City's 8,494 apartments on six and one-half acres constituted a net housing density of more than 1,300 housing units per acre.[71] Was that an excessive density?

The Walled City was an agglomeration of about 350 buildings, mostly slender, 10 to 14 stories high, limited by a height restriction imposed by nearby Kai Tak Airport. The city's buildings were packed together in a not-quite-rectangular pattern resembling a vertically extended tenement block. Several buildings on the periphery resembled stacks of birdcages because their balconies were enclosed floor to ceiling by metal grilles

(Figure 2-5). Lot coverages were often more than 100 percent; many buildings cantilevered, above the first floor, over the city's streets and alleys, turning them into dark, covered corridors. Jan Morris, the incisive chron-

Figure 2-5. Walled City of Kowloon—Hong Kong (demolished in 1993). The Walled City's net housing density exceeded 1,300 units per acre.
Source: Greg Girard and Ian Lambot, *City of Darkness: Life in Kowloon Walled City* (Haslemere, Surrey, England: Watermark Publications [UK] Limited, 1993.)

icler of cities, described the Walled City as "one congealed mass of masonry."[72]

When photographers Greg Girard and Ian Lambot learned of the impending demise of the Walled City, they spent four years documenting its people, its business establishments, and its architecture in a book called *City of Darkness*. Only a couple of the Walled City's buildings had elevators and, as was the case in New York's tenement slums, many rooms had no access to daylight and fresh air because their windows had been obstructed by newer buildings. Sixty percent of the city's apartments were about 250 square feet in size—half the size of a typical efficiency apartment.[73] Hundreds of businesses, including medical and dental clinics, made the city a self-contained and largely self-sufficient enclave.

The Walled City bore a reputation as a dangerous place following a 1950s era of uncontrolled vice, but after a government crackdown in 1967, criminal activity was confined mostly to drug use and property crimes, almost completely unattended by the violence that feeds America's collective fear of inner-city neighborhoods.[74] In its final decade, the Walled City's rate of serious crime was lower than in many other parts of Hong Kong.[75] The overall picture painted by the words and photographs in *City of Darkness* is one of industriousness and social harmony, attentive parents and thriving children; who can argue that high density is a defining element of urban squalor? The authors describe an underlying order in the enclave: "apart from the alleys there was remarkably little squalor. True, many factories were impossibly cramped...but an underlying order kept them running. And though without windows, many apartments were as clean and tidy as any similar abode in Hong Kong."[76]

When the Walled City was cleared for demolition in late 1992 an American firm was brought in to swing the wrecking ball. Many residents sternly resisted and sorely regretted the destruction of their community when its demolition began in April 1993. Many had lived there productively, contentedly, and in harmony with their neighbors. When the Walled City was demolished its former residents did not gather to cheer as did the residents of Philadelphia's Raymond Rosen public housing when a demolition crew worked there in 1995.[77]

The Walled City was demolished not because social conditions had become intolerable as they had in American public housing (where densities are one-twentieth as high), but because the colony's officials deemed its substandard construction unsafe.[78] The collapse of one building might have set off a chain reaction like a line of falling dominoes; a fire would have been even more catastrophic. The city's demise had everything to do with an absence of modern and safe building practices, and little if anything to do with the presence of the disease, poverty, and social chaos that plagued New York's tenement slums and, later, America's public housing. Many public-housing critics today, like the housing reformers in tenement-era New York, blame high densities for the social disorder that was largely absent from the Walled City in its final years.

Today one could design a viable housing development at Walled-City densities using highrise construction and modern building practices; viable, that is, provided a high level of civility and social harmony among the development's residents.* Any designer would be hard challenged, however, to concoct a playground with as much child-appeal as the Walled City's roofscape—a maze of parapets and offsets, a cacophony of nooks and crannies, access hatches, antenna groves, and stair-shed playhouses. Girard and Lambot's photographs depict energetic children playing on the rooftops, even riding bikes, under the attentive eyes of parents and grandparents lounging in the sun against a backdrop of spectacular views.[79]

OPTIMAL LAND UTILIZATION

Having glimpsed the Walled City, we can establish the definition of a term that will recur in this text: optimal utilization. Residential land in cities is optimally utilized when it is developed at densities sufficient to sustain the two essentials of urban life—good transit and robust neighborhood commercial streets. Such a density correlates strongly with good city form—buildings that form street walls. Freestanding houses are good enough for suburbs, but in cities they represent underutilization because they cannot sustain good transit and neighborhood retailing.

The Walled City represented overutilization of land in the context of its height limitation; its dwellings were packed together so tightly that many were deprived of access to outside light and air. Modern highrise buildings comprising similar densities are feasible, however, and would not necessarily constitute overutilization if located at the edge of a downtown where transit is concentrated and where many residents would walk to

---

*A 60-story tower on a 10-story pedestal, on a one-acre lot, would yield a density equal to that of the Walled City, given the following parameters: (1) The pedestal footprint is 0.7 acres, a 70 percent lot coverage. The pedestal has 41 apartments per floor, averaging 700 square feet. (2) The tower footprint is one-quarter acre, 25 percent of the lot area. The tower has 15 units per floor, averaging 675 square feet.

work. A state of overutilization exists where buildings are so tightly congregated that they deprive residents of sunlight, air, and views, or where the congregation produces intolerable levels of congestion on sidewalks and in transit facilities. But underutiliztion, rather than overutilization, is the curse of the American city.

The nation's most appealing neighborhoods are composed of townhouses and lowrise apartment buildings, a pedestrian-friendly condition known to planners and architects as *high-density lowrise*—optimal utilization exemplified by Boston's North End and Beacon Hill. The addition of some highrise apartment buildings, as in New York's Brooklyn Heights, Philadelphia's Rittenhouse Square, and San Francisco's Russian Hill, enhances the diversity of neighborhood retailing. Highrise housing does not usually push a neighborhood into a state of overutilization, although it might adulterate the character and appeal of a long established lowrise area. A neighborhood of highrise apartment buildings might constitute overutilization of land remote from downtown, but optimal utilization at the edge of downtown where transit is concentrated and jobs are within walking distance. The distance between a neighborhood and the central business district (CBD) is the prime factor in determining appropriate land utilization, for reasons discussed in Chapter 5.

America's cities remain grossly underutilized even as public investment promotes the expansion of suburbs. Underutilization is often the product of stagnation and abandonment, but it is just as often the product of the deliberate suburbanization of cities.

3

Irrational Decentralization

Sprawl is not a natural response to market forces, but a product of subsidies and other market imperfections. The costs of sprawl are borne by all of us.... REID EWING[1]

Peculiar political conditions yield a socially and environmentally deficient form of decentralization in the American metropolis, where land-use controls are fragmented among multitudinous competing jurisdictions—more than 50 in the typical metropolitan region.[2] Suburban jurisdictions compete with cities for development without which cities cannot revitalize, and our publicly funded transportation network gives suburbs the upper hand. The decentralization of the American metropolis is unplanned, indiscriminate, premature, and irrational. Metropolitan decentralization in the United States is harmful to the heart of the metropolis.

In their 1986 examination of urban decentralization, Donald Rothblatt and Daniel Garr cite three land-use categories routinely regarded by economists as inevitably and appropriately decentralized to the wide open spaces of suburbia: manufacturing, retail and service businesses, and housing.[3] The assertion that these land uses decentralize inevitably—inexorably—is a gross oversimplification at best. First, an important distinction is seldom made—the distinction between decentralization as a process of expansion from a saturated core, and decentralization as a process of abandonment of the core. (Here we use the terms *expansion* to denote the first condition and *de-centralization* to denote the second; the more general *decentralization* encompasses both meanings.) And second, each of these three land-use categories includes developments large-scale and small, high-density and low. A rational strategy for decentralization emerges from a consideration of these three land uses.

1. DECENTRALIZATION OF MANUFACTURING

Because manufacturing processes, generally, are obnoxious and land gluttonous, cities are better off without them.

American manufacturing was never much centralized in cities. The colonies were established to support English manufacturers, and America's first textile factory was built in a suburb of Salem in 1787. In the early decades of the 19th century, industrialists built textile mills in rural New England along streams and rivers that could be dammed to capture water power. These industrial satellites materialized within a day's journey of their mother cities—mercantile ports such as Boston and Providence—to which they were connected by railroads. The mother city was the center of commercial intelligence—the corporate control center that provided capital, marketing, wholesaling, and transportation infrastructure—port and railroads.[4]

The distinction between cities and industrial satellites blurred in the latter half of the 19th century as cities industrialized (thanks to steam engines and immigrant labor) and industrial outposts grew into small cities. Urban industry repelled non-poor households from the increasingly squalid vicinity of factories and from larger urban sectors to which air pollution broadcast the effects of industrialization. By the end of the 19th century, industrialization had provided the middle class with both the motivation and the transportation to join the upper class in its flight from cities' industrialized sectors.[5]

The Benefits of Urban De-industrialization

City air improved as petroleum supplanted coal to heat buildings and fuel locomotives. Where coal continued to power transit vehicles and industrial machines, it was through the intermediary of electricity. The social environment of the industrial city improved as unionization lifted the living conditions of factory workers. The physical and social environments of the American city should have improved for another reason as well: after a relatively brief period of intrusion, industry began to abandon cities.[6]

Industry is abandoning not only America's cities, but America. Of nine sectors of economic activity tracked by the U.S. Bureau of Labor Statistics, only agriculture and manufacturing experienced declining employment from 1970 to 1998, a period when total employment in the U.S. grew by 67 percent. By 1998 manufacturing accounted for only 16 percent of U.S. jobs, down from 26 percent in 1970.[7] Manufacturing jobs have disappeared from American cities since World War II at a rate faster than the rate at which they have disappeared nationally, indicating that manufacturers regard cities as unfavorable environments.[8]

The 19th-century New England model of industrial production, in which remote manufacturing satellites are managed from urban corporate headquarters, still holds; but the modern corporation's manufacturing satellites are globally rather than regionally dispersed (and still within a day's journey of headquarters). The American city has lost its competitive advantage as a place of industrial production, but this is not a bad thing for cities that retain their role as places from which industrial production is managed. The colonial port cities that industrialized in the 19th century and de-industrialized in the 20th retain their vital role as places from which industrial production is served by managers, bankers, lawyers, and advertisers. New York City lost 206,000 manufacturing jobs between 1953 and 1970, but gained 526,000 white-collar jobs. Philadelphia replaced 102,000 manufacturing jobs with 122,000 white-collar jobs in the same period, and Boston replaced 30,000 with 107,000.[9] Cities that originated as industrial satellites to be later abandoned by the industries that created them have suffered nearly to the point of extinction.

Pittsburgh's post-industrial transformation vividly illustrates the benefits of urban de-industrialization. The smoke and grime of steel mills and freight trains blackened the sky over downtown Pittsburgh so completely that, even as late as the 1940s, streetlights were kept burning day and night.[10] In 1943, the city's business and civic elite decided their flagging downtown was worthy of a more prosperous future than seemed imminent, so they schemed the de-industrialization of a triangular piece of land strategically located where the Allegheny and Monongahela rivers join to form the Ohio. The one-square-mile triangle was occupied by rail yards and industrial buildings in 1943, but in the next two decades it transformed into a post-industrial "Golden Triangle" of highrise office buildings, condominiums, hotels, and a riverfront park.[11] De-industrialization had removed downtown's smoky shroud to make way for this post-industrial renaissance.

Although the physical design of Pittsburgh's Golden Triangle leaves much to be desired, the transformation exemplifies the post-industrial evolution of the American city, which is once again a corporate center and not a production center. Alcoa, Westinghouse, U.S. Steel, and PPG Industries are just a few of the industrial giants controlled from post-industrial office towers in and adjacent to the Golden Triangle. The triangle's transformation from industrial production, warehousing, and transport to industrial corporate control reflects the reality of post-industrial America: Nearly half of the Pittsburgh region's workforce was employed in manufacturing in 1955; by 1987 the ratio was one in five.[12] Pittsburgh's business and civic leaders had positioned their downtown to exploit this new urban reality.

At mid-20th century, Pittsburgh was called "hell with the lid off," and derided by Frank Lloyd Wright, who advised, "Abandon it." In 1985, Rand McNally's *Places Rated Almanac* rated Pittsburgh as the nation's best place to live.[13] Waterfronts in Pittsburgh, as in many other cities, have been converted from shipping, warehousing, and manufacturing into parks and recreation sites. Abandoned railroad right-of-ways find new use as biking trails in post-industrial cities. Luxury condominiums take shape in obsolete industrial buildings, in a glove factory in Indianapolis, in grain silos in Minneapolis, in a steam plant in Toledo. This is not a trend of minor significance; some 5,000 rental and condominium apartments had been developed in Chicago's abandoned factories and warehouses by the spring of 1997.[14] Offices, stores, restaurants, theaters, interior furnishings showrooms, museums, and even a Presbyterian church occupy old industrial buildings today. These new uses are more compatible with cities—with concentrated populations—than the former industrial uses were.

Low-intensity Low-density Land Use

Some of industry's nasty byproducts, foul air for example, are diminished today by technological innovation and federal regulation, but others, such as a heavy traffic of obnoxious trucks, cannot be separated from industry. Industry should be de-centralized for an additional reason: it represents underutilization of city land. Modern factories and warehouses are occupied by fewer people—workers and customers—than office and retail buildings of equal size. Modern industry is, thus, a *low-intensity* land use. Furthermore, most modern factories are necessarily one-story buildings that require large sites for shipping, receiving, and storage; thus they are a *lower-density* land use than retailing and offices, which function nicely in multistory buildings. Low-intensity, low-density land uses have no place in the center of a properly evolved metropolis.

Urban Politics and the Retention of Industry

Premature decentralization of post-industrial jobs obliges urban politicians to cling to the economy of the industrial era. Suburbs in the

American metropolis outcompete cities for office buildings and the high-pay jobs they represent, while city land goes underutilized. Cities' inability to outcompete suburbs for post-industrial development leaves a void in the city's economy, and on city land abandoned by industry.

A few working-class neighborhoods (along Brooklyn's waterfront for example) retain a tenuous economic attachment to their industrial installations. However as the role of industry in the metropolitan economy flags, cities should lead rather than follow the march to a post-industrial economy. Industrial de-centralization is as economically inevitable and potentially beneficial today as agricultural de-centralization was in the past, and those urban leasers who doubt it should be aware of the agricultural precedent. From its beginnings until recently, agriculture was a city land use. Archaeologists in the 1960s dispelled the conventional wisdom that humans began to create permanent settlements only *after* the development of agriculture freed them from their nomadic ways. Now it is known that residents of the Neolithic towns of western Asia survived on food that was hunted and gathered rather than farmed, until they inadvertently invented farming in their towns.[15] Farming retained a foothold in towns and cities for several millennia; even in the early years of the 20th century, pigs were raised in the densest quarters of New York City. Farming was destined to de-centralize, however, to the rural environs of settlements as the economies of those settlements evolved.

Between 1870 and 1970, agricultural employment in the U.S. dropped from half the nation's workforce to less than 5 percent, while industrial employment steadily increased.[16] Now industrial production follows agricultural production not only in economic importance but in geographic location. In 1997, two hulking steel plants, one a mill and the other a processing factory, began production in the midst of farm fields a mile west of Delta, Ohio, a town whose population was 2,840 just before the steel industry arrived. Delta is located in rural Fulton County—some of the best farmland in Ohio.[17] If agriculture were today a present but diminishing sector of the urban economy, then political pressure would be mobilized to save and retrieve agricultural jobs, unless those jobs were being replaced by a larger number of high-pay post-agricultural jobs.

In pursuit of social and environmental benefits, the French National government launched a massive initiative in the 1960s to relocate factories from Paris to its environs, but America's political forces strive for the opposite.[18] Urban affairs writer Roberta Brandes Gratz tells us that Detroit "was so desperate to lure the auto giants back to downtown that in 1980 it leveled much of Poletown, what had once been one of its largest ethnic neighborhoods, to make way for a General Motors plant."[19] More recently, an industrial area less than two miles from downtown Detroit, only a couple of blocks from the Detroit River, attracts new industrial facilities thanks to its federal Empowerment Zone status.[20]

Minneapolis officials cheer an industrial expansion along the city's Mississippi riverfront as a provider of low-skill jobs. They're equally enthusiastic about an emerging industrial park developed with their assistance less than a mile from downtown; this is a welcome source of "new jobs for north Minneapolis residents," according to the mayor. The park is home to, among other industries, a marine supply and upholstery company that employs 27 people (as of October 1999) on its 1.3 acre site, only 21 employees per acre compared to hundreds per acre in the typical moderate-density office development. Cities across America establish industrial retention and expansion programs for the purpose of increasing job opportunities for disadvantaged residents.[21]

The de-centralization of agriculture was a pivotal event in the evolution of cities; the de-centralization of industry and warehousing is no less momentous. But, in the American metropolis, city politicians strive to gain and retain industry even as suburban politicians fervently and successfully pursue post-industrial development.*

Opportunity Cost—The Ford Plant

The Ford Motor Company's assembly plant in St. Paul, built in the 1920s and now among the oldest of Ford's 37 assembly plants in the United States, demonstrates the opportunity cost imposed by industry that remains in cities. Ranger pickups roll out of the St. Paul plant, a two-million-square-foot agglomeration situated atop a high verdant bluff of the Mississippi River within five miles of downtown St. Paul and six miles of

---

*Unique geographic or geologic conditions, like those found in New York Harbor, exempt some urban land from the rule that large industry no longer belongs in cities. After World War II, shipping de-centralized from Manhattan and Brooklyn to Newark, New Jersey, where land was more abundantly available for modern containerized cargo operations, which resemble large industrial sites in scale and in the nature of the transportation infrastructure necessary to serve them. But Newark's port is too shallow to accommodate today's mammoth deep-hull ships, and it is economically unfeasible to blast through the river-bottom bedrock to solve the problem. By rebuilding its port, Brooklyn can prevent its region from losing its vital shipping industry to other Atlantic regions. (Editorial, "A Tunnel to the Future," *New York Times*, 18 January 1997, p. 20.) Unlike shipping, most modern industry can be accommodated wherever reasonably flat land is available proximate to a high-capacity transportation infrastructure.

downtown Minneapolis. The plant doesn't pollute the skies over St. Paul, and it isn't surrounded by squalid worker housing. It lies at the edge of a middle-class neighborhood, and well paid workers arrive each day in their personal vehicles.

Ford's operation in St. Paul covers 138 acres—three times as much land as the one-story plant occupies—because the company needs vast areas of pavement to accommodate receiving, storage, and employee parking. Ford employs just under 2,000 workers on its 138 acres, which translates to about 15 workers per acre. A midrise office building comfortably sited on a solitary acre of land could easily accommodate 750 workers—50 times as many workers per acre as the Ford operation. Ford's St. Paul employees earned a combined $104 million in 1995, which translates to $754,000 per acre.[22] The midrise office building with 750 workers could easily generate a payroll of $25 million annually, 33 times the per-acre yield of the Ford plant.

Imagine Ford's 138 acres converted to residential, commercial, and recreational uses, each occupying one-third of the land. At a moderate density of 40 units per acre (net), the 46 residential acres would hold 1,840 units, which would considerably enhance the surrounding area's capacity to sustain retail and cultural amenities. This new residential development would be integrated with 46 acres of office and retail development (8 million square feet at an average floor area ratio of 4.0) and with 46 acres of Mississippi riverfront parkland.

Ford's 138 acres produced $1.51 million in property taxes in 1999, just a fraction of what our hypothetical mixed-use development would produce.[23] The residential component alone—one-third of the site—would yield at least $2 million annually, more than the Ford plant. Eight-million square feet of commercial development would add about $23 million annually; the total property tax yield might well exceed $25 million per year, compared to Ford's $1.51 million.

High Intensity, High Density Manufacturing

Industrial operations as varied as diamond cutting and necktie manufacturing employ as many people on a given amount of floor area as the typical office (high intensity). Moreover, they function smoothly without devoting land to shipping and receiving, and they thrive on upper floors of multistory commercial buildings (high density). Unlike most modern manufacturing operations, high-intensity high-density industry has a legitimate place in the post-industrial city.

Manhattan's SoHo district demonstrates how hazy the distinction between small-scale industry and some other categories of economic activity can be. SoHo's early artist-residents persuaded zoning officials that they were engaged in the manufacture of art and were therefore entitled to occupy SoHo's buildings zoned for industry. Some types of factory production differ from office production only superficially. Intellectual factors are a primary component of office production, but in offices, as in factories, a worker makes a living by adding value to input materials. While garment workers turn cloth into clothing, office workers turn paper into documents; in both cases there is a physical input and a physical output. High-intensity high-density industrial production is not incompatible with an urban commercial district, as long as obnoxious byproducts such as noise, odor, and toxins are absent or manageable.*

Small industrial land uses that serve the daily needs of central-city businesses and residents will remain in the city, as they should. Some of these small operations function best on ground floors, but they do so beneath the upper floors of multistory buildings, unlike modern one-story factories with their rooftops covered by mechanical apparatus. Printing companies at the edges of downtowns provide essential, and often impromptu, services to downtown firms; they will remain strategically located at the edge of downtown.[24] Neighborhood bakeries are manufacturers of bread and pastries to be sold fresh, on premises, to neighborhood residents. These, also, occupy the ground floors of multistory buildings in healthy urban neighborhoods.

But in many cities there are bakeries of another sort—commercial bakeries that resemble modern factories more than they resemble the neighborhood bakery—bakeries that manufacture sliced bread for a region's

---

*Jane Jacobs predicted in 1969 that future cities will produce more rather than fewer manufactured goods, but these goods will come out of small factories. Mass production, with its dependence on big land-gluttonous factories, will continue to de-centralize; but differentiated production, whereby manufacturers respond quickly to specialized markets (as printers do) will grow in importance, and cities are good incubators of differentiated production processes. (Jacobs, 1969, p. 245) Beer production provides a good example of this post-industrial order. Mass-market beer is mass produced today in huge modern exurban beer factories while many 19th century near-downtown breweries await demolition or adaptive reuse. Meanwhile, microbreweries emerge in trendy urban districts to serve more discriminating, or more status-conscious, tastes. Mass-market brewers increase their involvement in specialty beer production (acquiring microbreweries) because many of these are more profitable and faster growing than the traditional mass-market operations. (*Anheuser-Busch Annual Report* 1996, pp. 9-11)

supermarkets and hamburger buns for a region's fast-food restaurants. These single-story bread and bun factories devote considerable portions of their sites to trucking operations, and they do not belong in cities, at least not while demand for commercial space and multiple-unit residential development remains strong in the metropolis.

Devolution

The evolution of urban land to higher and better use is not irreversible in the troubled American city. Warehousing, in the form of parking lots and garages, replaces old office buildings, often historically and architecturally significant ones, in the American downtown (Figure 3-1). And agriculture, in the form of community gardens, replaces demolished housing in derelict inner-city neighborhoods.* Downtown parking lots and community gardens manifest urban devolution and devitalization. "In a healthy city there is a constant replacement of less intensive uses by more intensive uses," said Richard Ratcliff, professor of land economics at the University of Wisconsin.[25]

2. DECENTRALIZATION OF RETAIL AND SERVICE BUSINESSES

On October 24, 1998, Hudson's department store in downtown Detroit was imploded after standing for 87 years, and standing vacant for 15. In its 1950s heyday, the retail floors of the 25-story building hosted more than 100,000 shoppers a day. Hudson's demolition was preceded in 1978 by the demolition of Crowley's department store and in 1966 by the demolition of Kern's department store. The downtown stores were doomed by suburban malls built in the 1960s and later.[26]

Retailing was both centralized and dispersed in the American metropolis before World War II; department stores and specialty retailers were centered in the CBD, while grocery stores, pharmacies, hardware stores, and clothing stores were found both downtown and on neighborhood retail streets. Retailing in the post-war metropolis has not merely expanded to suburbia, but has truly de-centralized; more than 2,500 suburban shopping centers arose between 1945 and 1960, as retailers aban-

---

*In some cities with substantial inventories of derelict land, community gardening has evolved far beyond the rag-tag operations of the 1970s and 1980s: "A diverse array of innovative for-market city farming ventures are making their presence known, and pockets of support for city farming are found among local and higher-level government officials, community organizations, city residents, and local foundations in several cities," according to Professor Jerry Kaufman and senior lecturer Martin Bailkey, of the University of Wisconsin—Madison. (Lincoln Institute of Land Policy, *Land Lines*, January 2001.)

Figure 3-1. De-evolution in Minneapolis. Parking garages continue to replace old commercial buildings in American cities. In the heart of downtown Minneapolis, two midrise office buildings were demolished to make way for this garage, under construction in 1999.

doned cities. Rothblatt and Garr note that "the number of retail establishments declined precipitously in the central city as did the volume of sales" between 1954 and 1967. During that period, America's urban downtowns lost a third of their retail establishments.[27] The suburban shopping center eliminated most households' long-standing attachment to downtown, which until the 1960s was the retail focus not only for downtown workers, but also for the many neighborhood residents who routinely rode the streetcar to downtown's department stores and specialty shops.

Considerable public and private efforts to revive downtown retailing have produced embarrassing results. When downtown retailers in New Haven, Connecticut, were threatened by suburban competition in the 1950s, political and business leaders reacted with Chapel Square, a redevelopment scheme that replaced four blocks of 19th-century commercial buildings with three low-slung retail bunkers and an enormous parking garage, all interconnected by enclosed walkways. Malley's department store moved a couple of blocks from its long-established location to one of the bunkers, where it lasted less than a decade. Macy's occupied the bunker with the superior location, which it had won in its negotiations with city officials bent on gaining the retail giant. Macy's bailed out of Chapel Square in 1993. New Haven's redevelopment scheme could imitate, but couldn't outcompete, the seven suburban shopping centers—more than three million square feet of floor area—built in New Haven's suburbs between 1960 and 1973.[28] Malley's vacated bunker was recently demolished and replaced by a lawn, and Macy's blank-wall building remains empty. Chapel Square's third bunker houses a motley collection of discounted merchandise and abandoned shops.

In downtown Minneapolis, an opulent five-story retail center built in 1987 to much acclaim and great expectations was demolished a decade later, having failed to retain retail tenants; and this on a prime site on the Nicollet Mall—downtown's answer to growing competition from suburban shopping centers in the 1960s. Governor Rudy Perpich had blessed the new downtown center, named The Conservatory, at the grand opening festivities, and a few weeks later a local reporter enthused that the building "promises to bring the bloom back to Nicollet Mall's faded cheeks." The project's architect proudly claimed inspiration from Milan's Galleria, London's Regent Street, and Paris's Rue Ste-Honore, an expression of confidence that would prove overblown and naive in a city from which retailing was de-centralizing.[29]

Today the Nicollet Mall's inventory of vacant commercial space includes much of the retail space in a mixed-use monolith called "City Center." Donaldson's department store, which had established itself on Nicollet Avenue in 1881, moved into City Center as the anchoring tenant when the building opened in 1982. Donaldson's grand-opening celebration was kicked off by the Rockettes, flown in from the Big Apple for such a special occasion. A decade after the grand opening, Donaldson's was out, gone forever from Nicollet Avenue and downtown Minneapolis.

Within a year City Center found a new tenant—Montgomery Ward—to occupy the space vacated by Donaldson's. Ward's grand opening featured actor Ed Asner and a lot of optimism, but in 1997, only four years after signing its 10-year lease, the retailer announced that it would close the under-performing store, and five smaller stores followed Ward's out the door. In September 2000, much of City Center's retail space is occupied by office tenants, and about 25 percent is vacant. The co-owner of a prominent commercial real estate firm in downtown Minneapolis says, "I do not believe City Center is healthy…" Across the Nicollet Mall from City Center a more recent retail development called Gaviidae Common has lost many of its specialty shops and now its main tenant, which occupies three floors, is a bank.[30]

City Center's developer built a counterpart monolith called Town Square in downtown St. Paul, also in the early 1980s, and today most of Town Square's retail space is occupied by government agencies because, like City Center, Town Square lost its anchoring department store. Downtown St. Paul has two other mixed-use developments—the World Trade Center and Galtier Plaza—both celebrated as sparkplugs for downtown retailing when they opened in the 1980s, but now their retail space is mostly vacant or converted to office use. Dayton's department store "is about all that's left of retail in downtown St. Paul," according to real estate reporter Jim McCartney, and Dayton's is hanging on by a thread. The retail giant has built six stores (anchors to regional malls) in Twin Cities suburbs since the mid-1950s, but has decided to retrench in St. Paul—to convert retail space to other uses as it has already done in its flagship store in downtown Minneapolis. Two floors in the five-story St. Paul store will be rededicated to offices. The renovation will be funded largely by the city, which hopes to forestall the fate that has befallen Detroit, Kansas City, Baltimore, and the many other cities that no longer have a downtown department store. "Downtowns in general are risky markets for retailers," says McCartney.[31]

City politicians and downtown business leaders who strive to reinvigorate downtown retailing fight the unyielding forces of de-centralization. The average number of daily person-trips to downtowns Minneapolis and St. Paul for the purpose of shopping plummeted from 50,000 in 1949 to fewer than 20,000 in 1990, even though the metro-area population nearly doubled (Table 3-1). Retail vacancy rates in the downtowns of Minneapolis and St. Paul have improved, but not because retailers have rushed in; they have improved because retail space was removed from the market, the demolition of the Conservatory being the most notable example. Downtown St. Paul's retail vacancy rate exceeded 50 percent in

Table 3-1. Person Trips to the CBDs of Minneapolis and Saint Paul

Trip Purpose at CBD Destination	Average Weekday Arrivals			
	1949	1958	1970	1990
Work	129,099	129,123	127,199	122,700
Shop	50,704	54,363	26,897	19,500
All Other Purposes	133,389	128,626	115,772	125,000
Total	**313,192**	**312,112**	**269,868**	**267,200**

Source: Metropolitan Council, *1990 Travel Behavior Inventory Summary Report*, June 1994, Table 18.

1999, before the World Trade Center and Galtier Plaza were removed from the retail market.[32] Much of the occupied retail space in both downtowns is occupied by lunch vendors who open their doors only a few hours each weekday and keep them closed on weekends.

One might expect the highly visible growth of downtown office space to compensate for the diminution in the number of trips made specifically for shopping, but overall employment growth has been modest. The addition of new office space is counterbalanced by the demolition of old office buildings, and by declining employment in non-office sectors. In 1990 the number of trips into the downtowns of Minneapolis and St. Paul for work purposes was lower than the number of such trips in 1949.

The Decentralization of Entertainment

Downtown's formerly great movie palaces attracted patrons from the entire metropolis and beyond prior to the 1960s because they screened movies weeks before their release to lesser theaters, and all theaters outside of America's urban downtowns were decidedly lesser. Today the biggest and best movie houses are found in suburbs, and cities struggle to maintain a foothold in this sector of the entertainment industry. A renaissance in Broadway road shows prompted the rehabilitation of vacant theaters in some of America's downtowns, but the reborn theaters are dark many nights in a typical month, so they draw only a small fraction of the numbers drawn to downtown's entertainment milieu a few decades ago when a popular movie could fill a 4,000-seat theater several times a day.

In its golden years Detroit's entertainment district was Grand Circus Park, where eight extravagant theaters (in addition to others elsewhere downtown) offered more than 24,000 seats. Two—the Fox and the State—have been revived as performing arts venues, but the less fortunate Michigan was converted to a parking garage in 1978; others have been abandoned or demolished. The last functioning movie house in downtown Detroit—the center of a metropolis of 5.5 million—was a four-screen cineplex in Renaissance Center, and this closed in February 2001.[33]

More than 20 movie houses enlivened the streets of downtowns Minneapolis and St. Paul in 1955, but none do today. Downtown St. Paul's last remaining cinema—the four-screen Galtier—died in April 1999, ten days after the death of downtown Minneapolis' last remaining cinema—the six-screen Skyway.[34] The Skyway and Galtier cinemas were built in 1972 and 1985, respectively, in the heart of the metropolis, but they couldn't compete with suburban cinemas. The two cinema companies that shut down the Skyway and the Galtier continued to operate their combined inventory of 10 cinemas in the suburbs of the Twin Cities.*

More than 50 movie theaters were demolished or vacated in Minneapolis and St. Paul—downtowns and neighborhoods—between 1955 and 2000, while in the suburbs approximately 50 movie houses— more than 300 screens—were erected (most since 1970), and many more are planned or under construction. The mass de-centralization left only nine commercial movie houses with a total of 19 screens operating in the two cities. Detroit has fared even worse. In December 2000, the *Detroit News* reported, "Of the 100 or so neighborhood movie theaters that existed in Detroit prior to the coming of television, most are gone without a trace," and after Renaissance Center's cinema closed, the *New York Times* reported that Detroit "has only one movie theater." It wasn't the coming of television that killed the movies in Detroit; more than 400 screens in some 40 cinemas operate in the suburbs.[35] The urban movie theater, once a powerful promoter of street liveliness, nears extinction while the suburban cineplex proliferates, detached from the public realm by parking lots. Entertainment venues to which people once walked or rode transit are replaced, in the era of irrational decentralization, by venues to which people only drive.**

The Mall of America's cinemas, restaurants, and bars, and its celebrity appearances, charity extravaganzas, and various other happenings generate a steady flow of big crowds and immoderate media attention. Crowds and media descended on the mall in 1996 for Mary Tyler Moore's book signing appearance, an event that signaled the mall's new status as the agora of the metropolis. In the 1970s that was the status of downtown Minneapolis, the stage set for the popular television series that earned Mary a special place in the hearts of Minnesotans. Governor Arne Carlson joined Mary at the mall and proclaimed the day—October 19, 1996—to be

---

*In October 2000, ground was broken in downtown Minneapolis for a retail/entertainment complex that will include a cineplex, scheduled to open in the fall of 2002. City officials were desperate to return cinemas to a downtown where there is little market demand for them, so the officials committed a parking garage and $39 million in public money to the complex against the advice of the director of finance, who regards the deal as too risky. The project's development company reportedly will bring only $2.3 million of its own capital to the project. (Minneapolis City Council member Lisa McDonald, "Block E Development Could Leave City Taxpayers Holding the Bag," *Minneapolis Star Tribune*, 1 March 2000, p. A15.)

**Densely populated neighborhoods retain their cinemas. Twelve cinemas with about 35 screens are operating in Manhattan's Upper East Side—one and one-half square miles—in May 2001.

Mary Tyler Moore Day. In 1997, Miss America helped the mall celebrate its fifth birthday, and the governor was there again, proclaiming the day—August 11, 1997—to be Mall of America Day. In May 1999 Minnesota's colorful new governor—Jesse Ventura—chose the mall for his nationally reported book-signing appearance. In April 2001 the NCAA staged its basketball championship tournament in Minneapolis' downtown stadium, but the ancillary action was at the mall. "Final-Four fans are pouring into the Mall of America…all over the mall, it's like Christmas in April," said the narrator of a lengthy television report, which included side trips to mall-area hotels where fans had set up their headquarters.[36] The heart of the Twin Cities' retail and entertainment industries beat in downtown Minneapolis for a century, but after three decades of irrational decentralization the heart was transplanted to a second-ring suburb.

Principles of Rational Commercial Decentralization

As is the case with industrial activities, service and retail businesses should be geographically positioned according to their innate land appetites. Used car lots and repair garages epitomize low-intensity low-density land use, yet these are common on America's gray-zone commercial streets.* Central-city land should be too precious for commercial operations that employ few people and generate few customers per thousand square feet of building area. Central-city land should be too valuable for commercial operations that function efficiently only in one-story buildings flanked by pavement.

Specialization joins *intensity* and *density* as the factors that determine the suitability of commercial operations to the various metropolitan land

---

*Density is a quantifiable attribute of land development; intensity is less so but not altogether subjective. Building codes provide generalized summaries of land-use intensities in the form of "occupant load factors," used by building inspectors and architects to determine the number of emergency exits required to safely evacuate a building on fire. The *Uniform Building Code* specifies occupant load factors of five occupants per thousand square feet in a factory, 10 per thousand square feet in an office, and 33 per thousand square feet in a retail space. (Occupants are employees and customers, and anyone else who would normally be found in a building during its hours of operation.) Municipal zoning codes also recognize varying intensities of land use, and require the developer of a retail or office building to provide more parking spaces than the developer of a factory or warehouse of equal floor area. Zoning codes recognize, further, that central locations garner greater transit use than remote locations, thus the parking requirement for a single land-use category will vary with distance from the CBD.

parcels. The most generalized of retailing—convenience retailing—is appropriately expanded to locations that allow the typical suburban household to make a quick impromptu trip to buy a loaf of bread or a light bulb. Convenience stores, drug stores, and supermarkets are routine destinations that should be available in reasonable proximity to most metropolitan households.

Specialty businesses, on the other hand, should be centralized, unless they are necessarily land-gluttonous. On University Avenue in St. Paul there is a sizable parcel of land on which new and used Kenworth truck tractors are displayed, sold, and repaired—a business that is patronized by few households and patronized routinely by none. This establishment, though highly specialized, would be displaced to suburbia by more productive land uses in the rationally decentralized metropolis. Specialty retailers and service providers should remain centralized only if they meet the criteria outlined above for high-intensity high-density manufacturing, i.e., if they accommodate more than a few employees and customers per thousand square feet of floor area, if they prosper in multiple-story buildings, and if they require minimal land area for loading and unloading.

Specialized retailers such as rare book dealers and haute couture clothiers generate customer trips that are planned and infrequent rather than impromptu and routine, and the market area for these retailers extends to the edge of the metropolis and beyond. Specialized service providers also get their customers from a broad area. A custom photo-finishing lab, for example, serves photographers who travel considerable distances to do business with a favored technician. If located in the center of the metropolis, specialty retailers and service providers are accessible to the largest number of customers who can arrive conveniently on transit or on foot. Businesses that serve other businesses should remain centralized (unless land gluttonous) because the centralization of business is essential to the social and environmental health of the metropolis, a premise that will be proven in Chapter 4.

A Backward Land Rationalization

Economists who say service and retail businesses decentralize because suburbs offer a greater abundance of land have it backward: Businesses don't suburbanize because they need more land so much as they need more land because they suburbanize. Consumer businesses follow housing to suburbia, where low densities and segregated land uses create automobile-dependent populations, for whom businesses must provide parking lots. In the six-county Chicago metropolis, the amount of land devoted to commercial development increased by 74 percent between 1970 and 1990, while the area's population increased by only 4 percent. (In the same period, the amount of land occupied by residential development increased by 46 percent.)[37]

Businesses assume the density characteristics of their surroundings. Convenience stores in robust urban neighborhoods occupy ground-floor space in multistory buildings, which are surrounded by other buildings rather than parking lots because urban customers walk rather than drive. Convenience stores in low-density neighborhoods, both urban and suburban, are so completely dependent on drivers for patronage that they have merged with gas stations. Supermarkets in high-density neighborhoods occupy ground-floor space beneath apartments. The 55-story Trump Palace apartment building on Manhattan's Upper East Side leases much of its ground-floor and basement space to a supermarket (bakery and deli at ground level, packaged goods and produce in the basement, connected by escalator). The supermarkets at Trump Palace and elsewhere in Manhattan receive their goods off-hours at small loading docks, and they are unattended by parking lots because few customers arrive in cars. Customers who buy more than they want to carry can have their groceries delivered for a couple of bucks. Manhattan's high densities obviate the need for motorized delivery of groceries, pizzas, Chinese food, and small parcels; delivery personnel use pushcarts or bicycles to cover the short distances that accompany high densities.

Nearly all retail and service categories function nicely in multistory buildings. New cars are displayed and sold on the ground floors of downtown office buildings (inventories are stored elsewhere). A new 12-screen cineplex in Brooklyn Heights is a tower—a nine-story stack of cinemas (each with stadium seating).

Office Decentralization

Office buildings represent the metro area's densest land use, and one of its more intense; that segment of the service sector that does business in office buildings should, therefore, be centralized. Because of its intensity and density characteristics, a multistory office building is a metropolitan area's most powerful generator of routine trips. The centralization of such buildings will produce the metropolitan area's highest possible rate of transit use for work commutes. Transit represents the ultimate in metropolitan transportation efficiency because every transit system in the nation, outside of New York City, has excess capacity, while increasing numbers of metropolitan roadways are filled beyond capacity.[38] Decentralization of high-intensity high-density development feeds the automobile dependence of the metropolis.

Office buildings, unlike industrial buildings, have traditionally clustered in the center of the metropolis; the wide-ranging expansion of office space has occurred only in the past three decades. The nation's 50 largest CBDs contained 80 percent of their metro areas' office space in 1970, but suburbs had more office space than CBDs by the mid-1980s. By 1994, the CBDs share had fallen to 39 percent. Three-quarters of new office space occupied since 1970 have been in suburbs.[39]

In many of America's metropolitan areas, those with healthy downtowns, office space has not de-centralized since the 1960s so much as it has expanded beyond the edges of downtown. But the expansion is premature because so much downtown land has fallen into underutilization, devoted to automobile parking or left to languish. Many old downtown office buildings slowly decay because it is cheaper in the American metropolis, thanks to extravagant public investment in suburban infrastructure, to build new office space in suburbia than to upgrade old downtown buildings.

Downtown Detroit is a grim museum of vacated office buildings, many of them historically significant, standing amidst the parking lots and vacant land once occupied by yet more commercial buildings. Downtown's vacant office buildings include the David Broderick Tower—32 stories, the Kale's Building and the David Whitney Building—18 stories each, and at least a half-dozen others at 12 or more stories. Detroit's pitiful condition inspired writer and photographer Camilo Jose Vergera to propose that "a dozen city blocks of pre-Depression skyscrapers be stabilized and left standing as ruins: an American Acropolis. We could transform the nearly 100 troubled buildings into a grand national historic park of play and wonder."[40]

Downtown Detroit's functioning commercial office buildings contain about 13 million square feet of space, less than half the 27 million built since 1960 in just two of the city's suburbs—Troy and Southfield (accessible from interstate freeways).[41] Judging by downtown's acreage of parking lots and vacant land, and by its number and size of defunct buildings, it appears that office space has truly de-centralized—that more downtown space has been subtracted than added since 1960.

Suburban America's inventory of office buildings includes not only sleek highrises that compete directly with similar buildings in the CBD, but also many smaller wood-frame buildings—modern low-rent buildings that deflect demand from downtown's aged low-rent buildings. Downtown's old buildings, then, suffer high vacancy rates and, ultimately, demolition, which in some cases clears the way for new office towers. But too often demolition is prompted by parking demand. Parking lots and garages are more valuable than historic office buildings in the center of an irrationally decentralized automobile-dependent metropolis.

Ancillary to the decentralization of downtown office and retail space is the de-centralization of hotels, which, if centralized, provide accessible jobs to transit-dependent entry-level workers. Downtown Minneapolis lost nearly 600 hotel rooms between 1979 and 1989, while its metro area's suburbs gained about 10,000. At the end of 2000, downtown Minneapolis has 16 hotels with a combined total of 4,400 rooms—seven fewer hotels and 1,000 fewer rooms than in 1954 (net losses, which would be even greater if flophouses were counted). A six-mile stretch of Interstate 494, seven miles south of downtown, now has seven more hotels and 1,100 more rooms than downtown. The total for all of the Twin Cities' suburbs has grown to about 16,000 rooms.[42]

Metropolitan Detroit has more than 30,000 hotel rooms, of which about 2,800 remain downtown. The Cadillac was once the grandest hotel between Chicago and New York (Figure 3-2) but now its majestic entrances are boarded up, as are the Statler's and the Fort Shelby's. These three monumental hotels offered a combined 2,800 rooms in the downtown of the 1950s, as many rooms as exist today, and other hotels offered thousands more.[43]

Detroit epitomizes irrational decentralization, with its derelict and vacated office buildings and hotels in the center of a growing and thriving metropolis. In other cities the evidence of irrational decentralization is less dramatic but abundant. The presence of used car lots, boarded up commercial buildings, and single-story strip centers within two miles of downtown, and of hotels, office towers, and multistory regional malls a dozen miles from downtown evidences the irrationality of decentralization in the American metropolis.

Figure 3-2. Cadillac Hotel, Detroit. This is one of more than a dozen office buildings and hotels 12 stories and taller standing vacant in downtown Detroit in the summer of 2000.

3. DECENTRALIZATION OF HOUSING

In 1950 there were 26 cities in the United States with population counts in excess of 100,000 and population densities in excess of 10,000 inhabitants per square mile; in 2000 there are half as many. Detroit's population density in 1950 exceeded 13,000 per square mile, within reach of a level that might support some vitality today (San Francisco's density is about 16,600). But Detroit's density went in the wrong direction, declining to 6,900 persons per square mile according to the 2000 census count. The list of cities whose population densities dropped below 10,000 inhabitants per square mile sometime after 1950 includes Baltimore, Buffalo, Cleveland, Detroit, Pittsburgh, St. Louis, and Washington, D.C.

Detroit lost nearly 900,000 residents—49 percent of its population—between 1950 and 2000. The mass exodus from Detroit peaked in 1967 after rioting, prompted by a police raid on an illegal after-hours bar, left 43 people dead and nearly 2,000 injured. After that, Detroit's middle- and working-class households left en masse; 67,000 residents moved to the suburbs in the last five months of the year.[44] Detroit continued to lose about 2,600 residents a month, on average, in the 1970s, and the exodus has since slowed but never stopped. Detroit and Chicago lost the greatest number of residents in the post-war period, but St. Louis suffered the highest percentage loss, losing 59 percent of its population between 1950 and 2000.

In 1950, fifteen of the nation's 20 most populous cities were in the Northeast and Midwest, and all but one (New York City) of these 15 have fewer residents in 2000 than in 1950. The 15 cities have lost 21 percent of their combined 1950 population, and 10 of the 15 continued to lose population in the 1990s. Two cities among the group of 20 registered huge gains: Los Angeles, with much of its 469 square miles of land still developing, and Houston, which between 1950 and 1990 annexed its way from 160 to 540 square miles. Houston annexed so much undeveloped land between 1950 and 2000 that its population density declined even though its number of residents more than tripled. Generally, Northeastern and Midwestern cities with less than 100 square miles of land area have lost population in the post-war era, as their suburbs have grown dramatically (Table 3-2). The depopulation of cities has slowed since 1990, and even reversed in some cities, but this is a pale trend compared to the rapid growth of outer suburbs. Residential decentralization continues to be "by far the most dominant trend today," said demographics analyst Robert Puentes in March 2001.[45]

Table 3-2. De-centralization of Urban Population: 1950-2000

America's 20 most populous cities in 1950

	Core city population 1950 (X 1,000)	Population in remainder of metro area, 1950 (X 1,000)	Core City population change loss● gain○ 1950s 1960s 1970s 1980s 1990s	Population change, percent 1950-2000 Core city	Remainder of metro area
Northeast and Midwest					
New York City	7,892	5,020	●○●○○	1	74
Chicago	3,621	1,874	●●●●○	-20	187
Philadelphia	2,072	1,599	●●●●●	-27	124
Detroit	1,850	1,166	●●●●●	-49	199
Baltimore	950	387	●●●●●	-31	391
Cleveland	915	551	●●●●●	-48	222
Saint Louis	857	824	●●●●●	-59	174
Washington DC	802	662	●●●●●	-29	557
Boston	801	1,569	●●●○○	-26	80
Pittsburgh	677	1,536	●●●●●	-51	32
Milwaukee	637	234	○●●●●	-6	286
Buffalo	580	509	●●●●●	-49	72
Minneapolis	522	595	●●●●○	-27	335
Cincinnati	504	400	●●●●●	-34	229
Kansas City	457	357	○○●●○	-3	274
Sub-total: 15 cities	23,137	17,283	●●●●○	-21	151
South, West, & Southwest					
Los Angeles	1,970	2,398	○○○○○	88	262
San Francisco	775	1,466	●●●○○	0	195
Houston	596	211	○○○○○	228	954
New Orleans	570	115	○●●●●	-15	642
Seattle	468	265	○●●○○	20	599
Sub-total: 5 cities	4,379	4,455	○○○○○	71	302
Total: 20 cities	27,516	21,738	○●●●○	-6	182
Total: 18 cities* with less than 400 sq. mi. land area	24, 950	19,129	●●●●○	-19	163

* Los Angeles and Houston both have more than 400 square miles of land area.

General notes: "Remainder of metro area" includes sister cities, most of which experienced population decline since 1950; these include Newark, Camden, St. Paul, and East Saint Louis. Oakland and Kansas City, Kansas, gained slightly since 1950.

For year-2000, selected PMSAs rather than CMSAs are counted to exclude metro areas that are counted separately in 1950. New York City year-2000 metro population includes all PMSAs within the CMSA except Trenton NJ and adjacent counties, and PMSAs in Connecticut. Most MSAs have grown geographically since 1950, so some population growth is due to annexation of extant residents.

Sources of data: Census 2000 PHC-T-5, Ranking Tables for Incorporated Places; Census 2000 PHC-T-3, Ranking Tables for Metropolitan Areas; Statistical Abstract of the United States, various years since 1950.

De-centralization of Housing Units

Post-war population losses reflect an alleviation of crowding in some urban neighborhoods, and a diminishing number of people in the average household. Reductions in household size especially afflict cities, which are now considered by the middle class to be inappropriate environments for children. But uncrowding and smaller households do not account for the totality of cities' population losses; housing units have disappeared from cities too sparsely settled in the first place.* Urban renewal and freeway construction removed housing units from cities in the 1950s and 1960s, but more recently deterioration, abandonment, and demolition account for the losses. Detroit, St. Louis, Cleveland, Pittsburgh, and Buffalo, which lost 38 percent of their combined population between 1970 and 2000, lost 22 percent of their combined number of housing units in the same period. Eleven of the 15 Northeastern and Midwestern cities on Table 3-2 continued to lose housing units in the 1990s. (The exceptions were New York City, Boston, Chicago, and Kansas City.)[46]

Detroit's East Side is laced with boarded up, broken down, and burned-out houses. Boulevards are disposal sites for old scurvy mattresses, box springs, television sets, and smaller, less recognizable garbage. Weed lots are plentiful, some of them measured in acres rather than square feet. Occasionally one sees an abandoned house standing alone on a block, and some of Detroit's land has been abandoned long enough to have returned to a natural state (Figure 3-3). Urban affairs writer Chris Kelley notes that "vast parts of the city have reverted to prairie so lush that state game wardens export Detroit pheasants to the countryside to improve the rural gene pool."[47] Demolition permits in Detroit exceeded construction permits by nearly 42,000 in the 20-year period ending in 1993. The city had more than 15,000 derelict buildings in 1995, and more than 66,000 vacant lots. Detroit lost nearly 77,000 residents and 35,000 housing units in the 1990s.[48]

Detroit's situation had become so dire by the 1990s that Ombudsman Marie Farrell-Donaldson proposed a system of triage; she proposed that the city "mothball" its nearly abandoned neighborhoods and relocate residents to city-owned property elsewhere, then demolish all structures, fence off the leveled land, and suspend city services. This proposal, inspired by the downsizing strategies of corporate America, would allow the city to concentrate its scarce resources in neighborhoods of greater

---

* Immigrant families have reversed the trend toward smaller households in some cities. Minneapolis gained 14,000 residents but lost 4,000 housing units in the 1990s.

Figure 3-3. Burned out house on Lillibridge Avenue, Detroit (July 2000).
Housing abandonment, arson, and demolition have reduced some of Detroit's
neighborhoods to a rural density.

population.[49] Urban scholars forewarned in the 1990s that several other
cities are following Detroit's path to urban ruin, but simply are not yet as
far along.

Philadelphia lost 363,000 residents and more than 39,000 occupied housing units (net losses) in just two decades—from 1970 to 1990—and the
losses continued in the 1990s. In 2000, the city's inventory of abandoned
houses exceeds 30,000, and about 20,000 lots lie vacant according to city
officials.[50] Mark Alan Hughes, a senior fellow at the Brookings Center on
Urban and Metropolitan Policy, notes Philadelphia's staggering quantities of vacant land and vacated buildings and suggests that the city "right-
size" its land-use plan "to serve a much smaller population." One of
Hughes' strategies: make it easy for land owners to acquire adjacent lots
for parking. Philadelphia's suburbs have added far more housing units
than the city has lost.[51]

New York City lost more than 800,000 residents (net) in the decade of the
1970s, and in the same period 155,000 housing units were demolished and
another 99,000 were burned out, boarded-up, or simply abandoned.[52] In
some of the city's most distressed neighborhoods this cloud of housing
abandonment and demolition has a silver lining: Tenement windows

once darkened by adjacent tenements are now exposed to sun and breeze. But abandonment goes completely unredeemed in other cities, where housing densities were too low prior to abandonment. In Baltimore, 40,000 vacant rowhouses have "spread blight, crime, and despair across wide swathes" of the city according to *Baltimore Sun* reporter Jim Haner. New Orleans' scenic and popular sectors provide no clue that, elsewhere in the city, vast areas lie in a state of gross dereliction. Surrounding the city's touristed quarters are some 37,000 vacant housing units, 20 percent of the city's total.[53] The dramatic middle-class abandonment of St. Louis was followed by an equally dramatic desertion of neighborhoods. As in Detroit, vacant lots and abandoned buildings reduce some of St. Louis' neighborhoods to rural densities. The Pennsylvania Horticultural Society studied America's problem of urban housing abandonment in 1995 and concluded:

> Vacant land is a common sight in virtually every American city. Scattered among houses in residential areas, especially in distressed neighborhoods, small and large vacant, trash-filled lots contribute to an appearance of deterioration and blight...in contemporary American cities, vacant land is not simply a marginal or transitional phenomenon. The... forces that led to an exodus of people, businesses and wealth from urban centers have also elevated derelict land to a problem of major proportions.[54]

Land has become so worthless in some cities that it's hard to give it away. When the city of Providence, Rhode Island, put some of its estimated 4,000 abandoned properties on the market for 25 cents per frontage-foot ($12.50 for a 50-foot-wide lot) there were too few takers, so city officials dropped the price of a lot to one dollar. Even if the bargain lures buyers, revitalization is far from assured because city officials envision perpetual underutilization. Bill Floriani, the assistant director for project management in the city's real estate division explained, "The idea is to get rid of lots that just aren't being used and can be bought by neighbors for side yards, yards for children, vegetable gardens, and parking areas."[55] Officials in Baltimore can't lure buyers to many of the city's abandoned rowhouses, not even at $1 per unit, so the city demolishes the buildings at a rate of more than 1,000 per year. The *Philadelphia Inquirer* reported in September 2000 that "there is no market demand for most of [Philadelphia's] vacant land and buildings."[56]

Garbage collection is the only economically viable use for the vacuous land in some urban neighborhoods. Garbage haulers used vacant lots in

Boston's Roxbury neighborhood for sort-and-transfer operations in the 1980s, and on Chicago's West Side a block of vacant land became a huge illegal dump. Locals dubbed it "the mountain" when it reached a height of five stories and sprouted trees. The Associated Press reported in 1996 that prostitutes ply their trade in the hollows of the pile, and thieves evade cops on a trail through its crevices. One neighbor speculated, "There might be dead bodies up there."[57]

The Unnatural Causes of Irrational Housing De-centralization

Housing decentralization is inevitable in a growing metropolis with a fully developed core, but not in a metropolis with underutilized central-area land. America's metropolitan housing de-centralization is not the inevitable result of irresistible economic forces, but rather the calamitous result of political forces—federal housing and transportation policies. Rothblatt and Garr concluded that "suburban development has greatly been determined by decisions rendered in Washington, D.C."[58] Urban historian Kenneth Jackson cites, as one of several examples of federal promotion of housing de-centralization, the standards of the Federal Housing Administration (FHA), which specified lot size and setback minimums, favored houses over apartments, and discouraged loans in "crowded neighborhoods." These prejudices fueled an explosive growth of suburban houses. The FHA's various biases effectively wrote off much of urban America, including half of Detroit and one-third of Chicago.[59] As evidence of the FHA's "suburban favoritism" in its underwriting practices, Jackson cites the example of St. Louis:

> Of a sample of 241 new homes insured by FHA throughout metropolitan St. Louis between 1935 and 1939, a full 220 or 91 percent were located in suburbs. Moreover, more than half of these home buyers (131 of 241) had lived in the city immediately prior to their new home purchase. [The] FHA was helping to denude St. Louis of its middle-class residents . . .[60]

While the federal government paved the way for a large-scale middle-class occupation of suburbia, it also entrenched poverty in cities with a public housing program intended originally to provide decent housing for the working poor, but rededicated in the post-war years to the unemployed and the extremely poor. Public housing in American cities has since the 1950s exuded poverty and promoted socioeconomic decline in urban neighborhoods, pushing out the working class. Jackson summarized the role of the federal government in promoting irrational and premature decentralization:

> The result, if not the intent, of Washington programs has been to encourage decentralization. FHA and VA mortgage insurance, the highway system, the financing of sewers, the placement of public housing at the center of ghetto neighborhoods, and the locational decisions of federal agencies and the Department of Defense, to name only the most obvious examples, encouraged scattered development in the open countryside. While it was a national purpose to build subsidized highways and utilities outside of cities, it was not national policy to help cities repair and rebuild aging transit systems, bridges, streets, and water and sewer lines. Thus suburbanization was not an historical inevitability created by geography, technology, and culture, but rather the product of government policies.[61]

The unnatural forces of irrational decentralization produce housing abandonment and demolition not to make way for higher-density development, but to yield permanent underutilization.

The Decentralization of Political Power

Minneapolis Mayor Sharon Sayles Belton proudly admits that in her travels she promotes the Mall of America, which is located in Bloomington, a second-ring suburb south of Minneapolis. "As mayor of the City of Minneapolis," Belton said in 1997, "I very often join Mayor Coral Houle, who is mayor of [Bloomington], in promoting the Megamall."[62] For the same reason, St. Paul's Mayor Norm Coleman appeared in a television advertisement for the Mall of America. Like pigeons pecking for crumbs, the central-city mayors hope the mall's out-of-town visitors will drop some extra money during a downtown side trip.

Regional cooperation is an economic imperative in the integrated metropolitan economy, but the status of the central city has atrophied so deeply that its officials are often supplicants rather than leaders in metropolitan policy debates, underdogs in legislative battles, even those pertaining to land use within the city. Minnesota's legislature spurned its Minneapolis delegation in 2000 when it cleared the path for a junkyard owner to erect a giant metal shredder in Minneapolis on a bank of the Mississippi. Responding to neighborhood opposition, Minneapolis officials had denied a permit for the shredder, prompting a lawsuit by the junkyard owner, who took the further measure of lobbying state lawmakers. Some of these lawmakers proffered bills that would force the city to issue the required permits, and, sensing imminent defeat in the legislature, city officials settled the lawsuit. The junkyard owner won not only the right to proceed with the shredder, but also $8.75 million from city coffers (damages for the delay caused by earlier refusals to issue permits).[63]

Liability claims cost New York City $420 million in 1999, after a decade of dramatic increases. City officials seek from state lawmakers the kind of reforms enacted by most other states, but to no avail. "Year after year, city officials go to Albany seeking relief from fortune-hunting plaintiffs and year after year they're rebuffed," reported the *New York Times* in April 2000.[64] New York City contains 42 percent of its state's population, yet often finds itself at the mercy of an adversarial state government on issues of education, land use, and infrastructure. Most damaging to New York and other cities, state and federal transportation policies solidly favor the decentralization of infrastructure investment and the dominance of roadways. Political power in the nation's Capitol is systemically stacked in favor of roadways; eight rural states with a combined population less than three-quarters of New York City's population hold 16 seats in the U.S. Senate. Political power in the House of Representatives shifts from the Northeast to the Southwest and from cities to suburbs, whose populations grow thanks in large measure to federal transportation policies.

The 1992 national elections were the first in which more than half of voting age Americans lived in suburbs, but the political imbalance within metropolitan areas took hold much earlier, sometime in the early 1960s, when suburbs overtook cities as home to the majority of metro-area residents.[65] The growing imbalance in the distribution of population ensures that public investment in infrastructure will continue to flow to affluent suburbs while city land continues to stagnate. Minnesota State Representative Myron Orfield (representing a Minneapolis district) calls it "the push of concentrated poverty and the pull of concentrated resources."[66]

A February 1999 front-page headline of the *Chicago Tribune* encapsulates the problem: "Chicago Now 2nd City to Suburbs." Reporter Rick Pearson describes Mayor Richard Daley's defeat in a political battle over the siting of a third Chicago-area airport and notes that the original Mayor Daley was invincible on such matters because state and regional demographics had not yet turned against the city. Pearson describes the power shift:

> Back when Chicago's population outnumbered the suburbs, the city had the political leverage to turn its will into law....[but] Chicago's political clout, which started to fade with white flight from Chicago after World War II, had slipped away to the suburbs just as its population had.[67]

More than 40 percent Illinois' population lived in Chicago prior to World War II, while only 15 percent lived in suburban Cook County and the five surrounding counties. The 2000 census reveals that only 23 percent of Illinois' residents live in Chicago today, and 43 percent live in the Illinois portion of the surrounding metropolitan area. These demographic changes, according to Pearson, "point to the possibility of Chicago becoming politically isolated as government resources are poured into the suburbs in an attempt to keep up with demands for new schools and roads."[68]

Head counts alone do not explain the degree to which political power de-centralizes. Inferior socioeconomic conditions compel city officials to preoccupy themselves with social programs, while suburban politicians dominate issues of importance to the middle class. On the airport siting issue, Mayor Daley was thwarted by suburban state Senator James "Pate" Philip, called by Pearson "the region's most powerful suburban politician." Senator Philip bluntly defends his fervent and effective advocacy for his constituents: "I look at suburbanites as a [special] class of people. We're hard-working. We pay our bills. We're not on welfare. We don't take public aid. We're the power house of this state."[69]

THE SOCIAL CONSEQUENCES OF IRRATIONAL DECENTRALIZATION

Centralization of Poverty

The 10 most poverty-ridden census tracts in the Twin Cities metropolis are all in the core cities, seven in Minneapolis and three in St. Paul, according to 1990 census data. The two central cities contained 28 percent of their metro area's population and 60 percent of their metro area's residents living in poverty; the cities' combined poverty rate had increased 50 percent since 1980.[70] Two phenomena caused poverty rates in Minneapolis and St. Paul, and elsewhere in urban America, to rise as they did: an exodus of the non-poor and an influx of the poor. Both occurred simultaneously; the de-centralization of the middle class left a void that was filled, to the extent that it was filled, by an increase in the number of poor people, by birth and by in-migration.

As recently as 1970 the income profile of America's central cities was almost identical to that of the nation as a whole, but by 1993 the urban poverty rate had increased 50 percent, and in 1995 one in every five urban families lived in poverty, compared to fewer than one in every 10 suburban families (Figure 3-4). Poverty has spread to many of America's inner-ring suburbs, otherwise the contrast between urban and suburban poverty rates would be even more extreme. Unfortunately, this contemporary spread of poverty is more a process of expansion than of de-centralization; 73 percent of Minneapolis neighborhoods experienced an increased poverty rate between 1980 and 1990.[71]

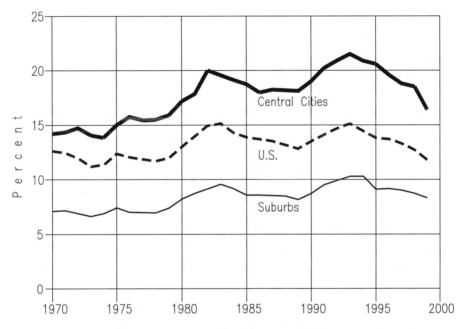

Figure 3-4. Poverty rates—city and suburb, 1970-1999. Poverty in America remains centralized in cities. Even as poverty spreads from cities to inner suburbs, the city rate remains double the suburban rate.
Sources for data: U.S. Department of Housing and Urban Development, The State of the Cities (June 1997), p. 33; U.S. Census Bureau, Poverty in the United States: 1999, p. viii.

Poverty in urban America deepened as it broadened. In the nation's largest 100 cities, the number of census tracts in extreme poverty—where at least 40 percent of residents are impoverished—nearly tripled in just 20 years, from 751 tracts in 1970 to 1,954 tracts in 1990 (Table 3-3a). The number of extreme-poverty tracts in Minneapolis and St. Paul nearly quintupled in that 20-year period, from six in 1970 to 29 in 1990.)[72]

Table 3-3a. Extreme Poverty in America's 100 Largest Cities, 1970-1990

	1970	1990
Number of census tracts in Extreme Poverty	751	1954
Extreme Poverty census tracts as percentage of all tracts in cities	6.0	13.7
Population in Extreme Poverty tracts (X 1,000)	2691	5496
Population as percentage of Cities' Population	5.2	10.7

Definition: An Extreme Poverty Census Tract is one in which at least 40 percent of residents are below the poverty threshold.

Source: Michael H. Schill and Susan M. Wachter, "The Spatial Bias of Federal Housing Law and Policy: Concentrated Poverty in Urban America," University of Pennsylvania Law Review, May 1995, p. 1285, See Table I on p. 1287 and Table II on p. 1288.

All of the nation's 25 largest cities experienced a decline in median family income between 1960 and 1990 as they exchanged middle-class families for poor. In the Northeast and Midwest, the 1996 median household income was 67 percent higher in suburbs than in cities, up from the 58 percent gap of 1989.[73] The economic status of the urban population improved in the 1990s according to poverty data, which show a steeper decline in the urban rate than in the suburban rate. But this masks a continuing decline in the relative economic condition of city residents, many of whom apparently exit poverty without ascending to the middle class. "The share of middle income households, of all ages, in cities is steadily declining...the share of high income households has declined as well," according to HUD's year-2000 *State of the Cities* report. Only low-income households—those in the bottom 20 percent nationally—increased their percentage of central city households in the 1990s.[74]

The De-Centralization of Fathers

The American city is, in HUD's assessment, "home to a disproportionate share of single-parent households—with all the additional social services such arrangements often entail."[75] In America it is suburbs, and not cities, that are synonymous with traditional families and traditional family values, which are synonymous with neighborhood tranquility.

The number of two-parent families with children increased by 1.3 million in America's suburbs between 1970 and 1990, while falling by 1.5 million in cities, and the exodus continued through the 1990s, according to a 1998 report by HUD.[76] Minneapolis and St. Paul contained 31 percent of their metropolitan area's total number of households in 1990, but only 18

Table 3-3b. Distressed Tracts in America's 100 Largest Cities, 1970-1990

	1970	1990
Number of Distressed census tracts	296	1850
Distressed census tracts As percentage of all tracts in cities	2.4	13.0
Population in Distressed census tracts (X 1,000)	1022	5704
Population as percentage of cities' population	1.7	11.1

Definition: A Distressed Census Tract is one in which the proportion of residents who are simultaneously below the poverty threshold, unemployed, receiving public assistance, and living in female-headed households falls at least one standard deviation above the 1980 average for all tracts.

Source: Michael H. Schill and Susan M. Wachter, "The Spatial Bias of Federal Housing Law and Policy: Concentrated Poverty in Urban America," University of Pennsylvania Law Review, May 1995, p. 1285, See Table I on p. 1287 and Table II on p. 1288.

percent of its married-couple families with children (after the number of such families declined 13 percent in the previous decade). The core cities housed a disproportionate 58 percent of their metro area's impoverished one-parent families (Figure 3-5). Married couples with children, nearly all of which are middle-class, constitute only 16 percent of the core cities' households in 1990, compared to 32 percent of their suburbs' households.[77]

Among the benefits associated with two-parent households are social benefits that accrue to neighborhoods. Households with fathers are most likely to produce the children who establish high academic standards in their schools. The U.S. Department of Education found in 1997 that, among children whose mothers are involved in their education, the addition of a father increases the likelihood of high academic performance, regardless of parents' income, education, race, or ethnicity. A high proportion of two-parent families in a neighborhood increases the level of parental involvement in neighborhood schools and in other institutions and affairs of the community. There is more parental time available in the two-parent family for activities that bring families to the public realm— trips to museums and movie houses. Two-parent households provide more adult role models and supervisors of children than an equal number of one-parent households. Oscar Newman found that high ratios of teenagers to adults produce high crime rates in urban settings.[78]

The poverty rate among female-headed families (80 percent of the nation's one-parent families) has for at least three decades hovered between 35 and 48 percent; whereas the rate for married-couple families

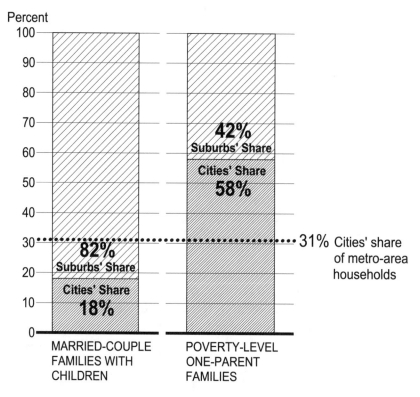

Figure 3-5. Distribution of families by marital and poverty status—Twin Cities metro area—1990. Minneapolis and Saint Paul house a disproportionately large number of poor single-parent families and a disproportionately small number of conventional families.
Source: Metropolitan Council, *Community Profiles: Housing, Population, and Households* (July 1993).

with children has never, in that time, exceeded 10.1 percent. (In 1999 the rates were 35.7 percent for the single-mother families and 6.3 percent for the married-couple families.) Only 23.4 percent of America's families with children were headed by an unmarried female in 1999, but 60.8 percent of poor families with children were, and the poverty rate among children in single-parent families is about five times higher than for children in two-parent families. (The correlation between poverty and single parenthood is stronger than the correlation between poverty and race; the difference in poverty rates between blacks and non-blacks is minor when controlling for marital status.)[79] The troublesome combination of fatherlessness and poverty has become perilously concentrated in the post-war inner city (Table 3-3b).

The Centralization of Crime

Neal Shine, publisher of the *Detroit Free Press*, explained that many of his city's children sleep in bathtubs because "the bullets won't penetrate the tubs as easily as their bedroom walls."[80] Children in the 1980s and '90s became frequent perpetrators as well as victims of urban crime. The eminent criminologist John J. DiIulio used the term "superpredator" to characterize juvenile criminals so impulsive and remorseless that they can "kill, rape, maim, without giving it a second thought." Superpredators, said DiIulio, are a byproduct of underclass neighborhoods: "We're talking about a group of kids who are growing up essentially fatherless, godless, and jobless, surrounded by deviant, delinquent, and criminal adults who basically encourage them through abuse, through neglect, to become criminal."*

Daniel Patrick Moynihan had warned in 1965 of the consequences to be expected from the rising tide of fatherlessness in American cities:

> From the wild Irish slums of the 19th century Eastern seaboard to the riot-torn suburbs of Los Angeles, there is one unmistakable lesson in American history: A community that allows a large number of young men to grow up in broken families, dominated by women, never acquiring any stable relationship to male authority, never acquiring any rational expectations about the future—that community asks for and gets chaos...[In such a society] crime, violence, unrest, unrestrained lashing out at the whole social structure—these are not only to be expected, they are very nearly inevitable.[81]

Seven years later, Moynihan's warning was corroborated by Oscar Newman, who found a strong correlation between "broken families" and high crime rates in public housing.[82] America's drug problem led William Bennett—President George Bush's drug czar—to public housing; he later reflected, "I saw very few men as tenant representatives. In the meetings I went to, the tenant councils were made up almost exclusively of women. For the most part, public housing projects in the United States are inhabited by women and children. Sometimes the only men around are bad ones."[83]

---

*DiIulio has joined George W. Bush's administration and recanted the undiplomatic language he used to describe underclass children, but the crux of his observations about the corrosiveness of the underclass environment is little disputed. (DiIulio quote from an interview on *CBS Evening News,* 9 April 1996. DiIulio and the Bush administration reported by Rebecca Carr, "DiIulio Driven by Values of his Boyhood," *Atlanta Journal-Constitution,* 8 April 2001, p. D5.)

Thirty years after Moynihan's warning, his assertions had been confirmed by educators, criminologists, sociologists, and psychologists. University of Minnesota psychology professor David T. Lykken found that boys raised in fatherless homes "are about seven times more likely to become delinquent...than are boys raised by both biological parents."[84] David Blankenhorn, author of *Fatherless America*, said in 1996:

> This trend of fatherlessness is the most harmful social trend of our generation. ...The presence or absence of a father in the home with a young man is the single most important determinant of whether or not that guy is going to end up in a jail cell. It's more important than skin color, or income, or where you live, or whether or not you've graduated from high school.[85]

Fatherless boys produce much of the chaos that repels middle-class families from cities, and fatherless girls produce the fatherless boys. Fatherless girls tend to emulate their mothers' practice of becoming pregnant while teenaged and unmarried. Kay S. Hymowitz studied the phenomenon in 1994 and concluded, "Fatherless girls are far more likely to begin sex early, to fall under the sway of swaggering, unreliable men, to become teen parents, and quite simply to accept single parenthood as a norm."[86]

Thirty years after Moynihan cautioned against rampant fatherlessness, the percentage of American families headed by a single parent had tripled and cities were most heavily burdened by the consequences.[87] Fatherlessness in urban America combines with poverty to reduce former middle-class and working-class neighborhoods to underclass neighborhoods, defined by the Urban Institute as concentrations of fatherless households immersed in poverty.[88] Underclass neighborhoods produce most of the unpleasantness associated with the inner city.

In his 1972 analysis of public housing, Oscar Newman reported that "public housing projects surrounded by other public housing have more crime in them than those surrounded by middle-income communities." Newman's observation that greater concentrations of poverty-level fatherless households produce not only more crime but also *higher crime rates* was confirmed in 1996 by researchers at HUD.[89] Areas where fatherlessness and poverty are combined and concentrated—underclass areas—turn many of their children into criminals, they breed crime.

The dominant culture in an underclass neighborhood embraces oppositional values and disseminates them to neighborhood children, who, if they adopt them, deliberately "do poorly in school, denigrate conventional employment, shun marriage, and raise children out of marriage," according to sociologists Douglas Massey and Nancy Denton. These children grow into adults who have little recourse to legitimate employment. Researchers at the Urban Institute concluded that the isolation and concentration of poor families exposes their children to "negative role models" who "subvert positive individual or family efforts."[90] An adolescent who would, in a middle-class neighborhood, find no barriers to civil behavior and few temptations toward uncivil behavior will, in an underclass neighborhood, find it tempting and useful to adopt the code of the street. William J. Wilson says that few families who live in close proximity to drug dealers in underclass neighborhoods come away unscathed.[91]

A six-year-old boy raised in a drug-infested neighborhood in the Bay Area city of Richmond, California, was charged in 1996 with attempted murder for beating an infant, fracturing his skull, leaving him with permanent brain damage—nearly dead. The young perpetrator was raised in house with his single mother and his ill-tempered grandmother. Grandma is a crack dealer according to her brother—a pensive and articulate old gentleman who tells a reporter:

> Every adult male member of my family has a police record for assault…Every male in my family—from 80 to 6—every one of us has at one point in our lives assaulted somebody. We have done GBI—great bodily injury—every male member in my family has shot or stabbed or assaulted somebody, including me.[92]

Members of families like these, families in which criminal behavior is intergenerational, account for 60 to 75 percent of all crime, according to a former Washington, D.C. corrections official.[93] And much of that crime is violent and powerfully repellent to families with the means to flee from its source.

Violent crime in America increased more than 500 percent from 1960 to 1990, and cities suffered the epidemic almost alone.[94] Extreme poverty is found in some of the nation's inner-ring suburbs and rural areas, but underclass neighborhoods and the crime they incubate are concentrated overwhelmingly in cities. Anthony Downs calculated that 75 percent of people who lived in "extreme poverty neighborhoods" in 1990 were central-city residents, but a higher 91 percent of people who lived in "underclass neighborhoods" were central-city residents. Pockets of poverty and fatherlessness in rural America produce crime rates nowhere near those of urban underclass neighborhoods.[95]

America's big cities got some good press in the latter half of the 1990s for dramatic reductions in violent crime, but urban rates continue to outstrip suburban rates by a wide margin. In America's cities with populations exceeding 250,000, the rate of violent crime, in incidents per 100,000 residents, was 1,125 in 1999 compared to 338 in suburbs, a ratio of 3.3 to 1.[96] Thus the urban:suburban ratio for rate of violent crime was substantially higher than the urban:suburban ratio for rate of poverty (Figure 3-6). That's because poverty in the city is concentrated and combined with adverse social conditions. As criminologist DiIulio said, "America does not have a crime problem; inner-city America does."[97]

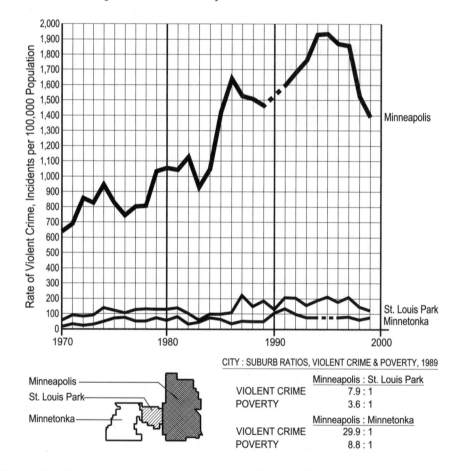

CITY : SUBURB RATIOS, VIOLENT CRIME & POVERTY, 1989

	Minneapolis : St. Louis Park
VIOLENT CRIME	7.9 : 1
POVERTY	3.6 : 1
	Minneapolis : Minnetonka
VIOLENT CRIME	29.9 : 1
POVERTY	8.8 : 1

Figure 3-6. Centralization of violent crime. Minneapolis-to-suburb ratios are higher for violent crime rates than for poverty rates because poverty is concentrated and combined with adverse social conditions in Minneapolis.
Source: U.S. Justice Department, Crime in the United States, 1970–1999.

Middle-class values. Leon Dash's astonishing chronicle of an underclass family in Washington, D.C., illuminates the insidious obstacles placed in the way of children so unfortunate as to be born into underclass families, and it confirms conventional wisdom about the importance of middle-class values in the lives of at-risk children. Rosa Lee, the namesake of Dash's 1996 book, heads a family beset by intergenerational poverty, drug addiction, criminal behavior, and incarceration, not unlike many of her neighbors. Among the life lessons Rosa Lee taught her children and grandchildren were a disregard for formal education and an indifference to the legal and moral consequences of petty theft, prostitution, and drug dealing. Rosa Lee's eldest daughter was, like Rosa Lee herself, 14 when she gave birth to her first child, and, again like Rosa Lee, that's when she dropped out of school. Rosa Lee involved her eleven-year-old grandson in her shoplifting sprees, and she recruited her five-year-old granddaughter to transport heroin.

Two of Rosa Lee's eight children escaped the underclass, two sons who shared something rare in neighborhoods of concentrated poverty and fatherlessness: exposure to middle-class life. One of the fortunate sons had taken a liking to a neighborhood girl whose parents worked for a living, so he was ashamed to be seen with his mother and siblings at the "welfare truck," which dispensed free food to welfare recipients. Later he acquired a middle-class friend who lived in a different world, one away from public housing, an orderly world in which meals were shared at the dining room table instead of the TV, for example. Rosa Lee's son was impressed; "I knew I wanted to live the way I was seeing them live," he explained to Mr. Dash.[98] The other of Rosa Lee's sons who exited the underclass did so under similar circumstances—shame at his mother's behavior and exposure to middle-class values. The two fortunate sons were helped in their teenage years by sensitive teachers and social workers, but their early exposure and reaction to middle-class values set them apart from their siblings and made them receptive to the help that was eventually offered.[99] Both escaped a way of life depraved beyond the imaginings of many among the middle class.

The Decentralization of Reputable Schools

"Lagging educational systems remain the single most important impediment facing cities in their attempt to keep middle-income residents," according to a 1999 report by HUD.[100] The *Philadelphia Inquirer's* annual "report card" on public schools reveals the magnitude of academic inferiority among city schools. The September 2000 report card evaluates public and charter schools in which at least 80 percent of fifth-graders took Pennsylvania's reading and math tests in 1999. That covers 168 schools in Philadelphia, and 154 of them—92 percent—produced test scores in the state's bottom quartile in both reading and math. Only one of the 168 urban elementary schools produced test scores in the top quartile in both subjects. In Minnesota, Minneapolis and St. Paul contain 13 percent of the state's population and 70 percent of its academically deficient elementary schools according to year-2000 test results. (Administrators blame non-English-speaking immigrants for their schools' dismal performances, but in Minneapolis, as perhaps in most urban districts, the lowest performing cohort is American-born English-speaking children who grow up in distressed neighborhoods.)[101]

The academic integrity of some of the nation's urban districts has become so conspicuously and embarrassingly inferior that federal and state authorities see fit to impose reform. Washington, D.C.'s elected school board was stripped of its powers by Congress, and Cleveland's by a federal judge. The State of Maryland seized control of Baltimore's schools in 1995, the same year the State of Illinois imposed reform on Chicago's schools, which had been declared the nation's worst by Secretary of Education William Bennett in 1987. In 1991, Wisconsin lawmakers funded vouchers to release 300 students from Milwaukee's failing public schools, sending them instead to non-religious private schools; and in 1995 the lawmakers expanded the program to include religious schools and thousands of students. In 1999, Michigan lawmakers stripped Detroit's elected school board of its power, and in 2000, the State of Missouri de-accredited Kansas City's public schools because they had flunked all 11 of Missouri's performance standards. At the turn of the millennium, school districts in Philadelphia, Los Angeles, Oakland, Buffalo, and New Orleans face the prospect of state intervention.[102]

Urban public schools are distracted from their exceedingly difficult academic mission by the social problems of poor and inadequately parented children, for whom schools now provide nutrition, medical and dental care, social and psychological counseling, and birth control services. These non-academic extras hold little appeal for middle-class parents who expect their children's schools to provide little more than a solid academic curriculum and the extracurricular basics—sports, music, theater—that they got from their schools. Suburban districts that remain focused on the traditional mission gain the children of the middle class.

With the exodus of the middle class, many urban schools are dominated by the children of the underclass. In his 1999 book, *Code of the Street*, sociologist Elijah Anderson reports that the "oppositional culture is well entrenched" in every one of the numerous elementary, middle, and high schools he observed in Philadelphia's areas of concentrated poverty.[103] *Minneapolis Star Tribune* columnist Syl Jones describes the "insidious barrier to achievement" erected by the oppositional culture in inner-city schools that are predominantly black:

> Black children who meet or exceed the academic standards in schools with significant black populations can expect to be threatened, ostracized, socially stigmatized and labeled "Oreos." These talented and often sensitive students can be severely traumatized by such labels and may even "dumb down" to gain peer acceptance.[104]

Within all races and economic classes, adolescence is a period of susceptibility to unwholesome peer pressure; in the underclass classroom, negative peer pressure robs poor children of middle-class futures. Elijah Anderson reported that four out of five first-grade students in a Philadelphia elementary school "are interested in the subject matter and eager to take instruction from the teachers—in effect, well disciplined." The remaining 20 percent demonstrate an oppositional influence. By the fourth grade, however, "about three quarters of the students have bought into the code of the street or the oppositional culture."[105] Veteran cop Paul Henry Johnson sees exactly the same phenomenon in Detroit: "Speaking to children in grade schools…[I find] most young men are interested in school…Then something happens. By the time they reach high school, they have lost their…enthusiasm. The streets become more enticing than education."[106]

Gangs, weapons, and violence join academic deficiency in persuading conscientious parents to withdraw their children from urban schools, if they have the means. In her nine years at Walton High School in the Bronx, Principal Nicola Genco "has seen three of her students killed and many others knifed or beaten," according to a 1999 report in the *New York Daily News*. Hoping to curb the violence, Genco and her dean of security conduct weekly "Peace Fest" meetings among 25 to 30 of the school's gang leaders according to the *Daily News* reporter, who adds, "The fact is, these gangs exist in every school in the city." And not just high school. An elementary school in Chicago formulated a dress code to keep gang colors out of the building, according to journalist Alex Kotlowitz, who reported also that "children as young as four or five at a neighborhood preschool program would arrive each day with their hats turned to the left, showing their allegiance to the Vice Lords, or to the right, for the Disciples."[107]

By the time 12 students and a teacher were murdered in a suburban Colorado high school in April 1999, urban schools had learned from experience how to curtail the deadliest violence, and it's a costly endeavor that diverts resources from academics. Detroit's school district budgeted about $11 million in 1999 for security, and school board members debate whether to spend more on academics or to increase the security budget. In September 1999, Detroit school board member Marvis Cofield declared, "We need more security officers,...wherever the money is in the budget, we need to move it to security."[108] At least 10 urban school systems in America have their own police force or security staff numbering in the 100s (e.g., 1,500 in Chicago and 800 in Miami).[109] City parents are burdened not only by the socially repellent conditions in their public schools, but also by the costs imposed by those conditions.

In the aftermath of the infamous Colorado shootings, school safety experts reassured suburbanites that their schools are safer than urban schools despite urban schools' metal detectors and security staffs.[110] Murders and other violence involving deadly weapons have abated, but sensational crime reports continue to illuminate the social deficits of urban schools. In St. Paul, in January 2000, a 16-year-old boy raped a 13-year-old girl in a public school stairwell. Later in the year three boys raped a 15-year-old girl in another St. Paul public school, and students' reactions worried the principal; many seemed neither surprised nor troubled by the incident.[111]

Sexual assault of students by students seems almost routine in New York City's outer boroughs. In June 2000, rampaging boys attacked at least seven girls, most of them 12 years old, on a middle-school playground in Brooklyn. Eleven days later, a pack of boys at a middle school in Queens held a 12-year-old girl upside down and groped her as they tried to strip her. Both attacks occurred while school was in session. During the second attack, some of the boys chanted "Puerto Rican Day Parade," apparently inspired by the gangs of rampaging youths who received national media attention when they sexually assaulted women and girls in Central Park a week earlier. In the first two weeks of October 2000, a 7-year-old boy was sodomized by two older boys on a Brooklyn school bus, and two 12-year-old girls were sexually molested by two 12-year-old boys on a Staten

Island school bus. In the spring of 2001, two boys—ages 10 and 11—were arrested for sodomy of a five-year-old girl in a Brooklyn elementary school, and an HIV-positive teacher was arrested for sodomy and sexual assault involving two boys—ages eight and nine—in his classroom in the Bronx. This was but one of the many incidents allegedly perpetrated by school faculty and staff. The *New York Times* reported that the spring's rash of sexual assaults "was far from an anomaly," and noted that the attacks occur in the city's schools at a rate four times the national average. Nearly one-quarter of the city's attacks are occurring at elementary schools.[112]

Urban teachers often suffer the predations of unruly students. During the 1999-2000 school year, Minneapolis officials recorded 371 student suspensions for attacks against teachers and other staff, about two attacks per school day. Teachers claim the number is much higher but administrators try to protect the image of their schools by discouraging the filing of assault reports. Lawmakers in Pennsylvania discovered massive underreporting of student violence against staff and classmates in Philadelphia's public schools for the same reason. City schools suffer teacher shortages because they can match neither the salaries nor the conditions offered by suburban districts.[113]

Metal detectors and onsite security personnel cannot stem the violence that surrounds many urban schools. On a single February day in 1996, elementary schools in Los Angeles and in St. Paul were besieged by gunfire from outside the building. In St. Paul, students dropped to the floor, as they had been trained to do, when they heard gunshots in the playground. In the Los Angeles incident, a teacher in a library was critically injured by a stray bullet fired from across the street; another bullet landed in a classroom full of students.[114] In 1997 a healthy and academically curious 15-year-old girl in Chicago went to school for the first time in her life. The girl's mother, who had fed and clothed the child well and schooled her at home, told authorities that it was out of fear for the child's safety that she didn't send her through the rough streets of their South Side neighborhood to school each day. Parents and students in Detroit were traumatized in the fall of 1999 by the rapes of eight girls on their way to or from school. In Queens, in October 2000, an 11-year-old boy walking home from school caught a bullet with his neck, one fired in a battle between the Latin Kings and another gang that calls itself Money Over Bitches. In South Central Los Angeles, school attendance increased dramatically after police and barricades were deployed to make the journey to school safer.[115]

Underclass neighborhoods and inner-city schools are potent repellents to middle-class families—those with both the inclination and the resources to live in decent neighborhoods. The exodus of the more affluent residents of underclass neighborhoods explains the deepening of urban poverty since the 1960s. The exodus of the more affluent residents of surrounding neighborhoods explains the broadening of urban poverty since the 1960s. When middle-class families flee the untenable conditions of the city they take their reputable schools with them. The Sierra Club reported in 1998 that 162 "physically adequate" schools closed in Minneapolis, St. Paul, and their inner suburbs between 1970 and 1990, while 78 new schools were built in outer suburbs.[116]

The Decentralization of Opportunity

In the 1980s, the percentage of American households without a car fell below the poverty rate. Twenty-three percent of welfare recipients in the central counties—Hennepin and Ramsey—of the Twin Cities area own a car.[117] Motor vehicles have become as indispensable in most city neighborhoods as they are in post-war suburbs because the irrational decentralization of the American metropolis all but immobilizes people who lack ready access to a personal vehicle. Fourteen percent of metro-area households in the United States are without vehicles, according to 1990 Census data, and within the 86 percent of households with cars, many individuals are prevented by age or physical condition from driving.[118]

"The lack of a good transit system...severely disadvantages the life chances of minority and low-income populations," according to urban geographer David C. Hodge, who notes a dramatic erosion of metropolitan accessibility since the wholesale decentralization of commerce from the transit focus of the metropolis began in the 1970s.[119] The welfare reform legislation of 1996 includes work requirements, but carless welfare recipients reach job training and jobs only with great difficulty today. "All the job training in the world won't mean a thing if you're not there to utilize it," said Rafael Ortega, Ramsey County Board member whose constituency includes St. Paul's East Side; "I'm talking about people in my district who can't see a bus if they stand on a 10-story building."[120] Many of the entry-level jobs available to welfare recipients are night-shift jobs and odd-hours jobs, but transit service in most American cities is meager even during peak periods. A 1999 survey of Minnesota's welfare workers revealed that inadequate access is, for 44 percent of recipients, the most formidable barrier to finding a job.[121]

New York Times reporter Robyn Meredith visited Detroit in 1998 and, in an article called "Jobs Out of Reach for Detroiters Without Wheels," described Dorothy Johnson's two-hour, two-bus trek from her city residence to her suburban job. Alice Newell's bus commute was equally long, until she quit her suburban job because the four-hour round trip extended her child-care expense so much that she couldn't afford to work.[122] Many of the entry-level jobs that have decentralized from the transit focus of the metropolis are in the hospitality industry, which employs tens of thousands in the typical metropolis of two million or more residents. A burgeoning new commercial thoroughfare called Elm Creek Boulevard in a developing suburb northwest of Minneapolis includes office and retail buildings, two hotels, and about 30 restaurants, but all these jobs are virtually inaccessible—more than two hours of travel time involving two bus transfers—for many of the residents of the distressed Near North district (which lies 12 roadway miles away).[123]

The decentralization of job opportunities is accompanied inevitably by the decentralization of post-high-school educational opportunities that prepare people for good jobs. For many decades the Minnesota School of Business occupied downtown Minneapolis buildings to which students rode the bus or walked from nearby dormitory housing. The institution moved to the suburbs in 1993 and distributed a glossy brochure to advertise that its new home "offers easy access to free parking, major freeways, shopping malls, and surrounding businesses." Today the Minnesota School of Business has three suburban campuses and none in Minneapolis or St. Paul. Another institution, still called the "Minneapolis Business College," is located in a suburb of St. Paul. At least two other Twin Cities business colleges—Rassmussen and Globe—moved from city to suburb in the 1990s, joined by the Medical Institute of Minnesota and the Brown Institute School of Broadcasting.[124] These joined such varied suburban institutions as the Academy of Accountancy, the Minnesota School of Professional Psychology, the Alfred Adler Institute of Psychotherapy, and many others. The State of Minnesota builds and expands community colleges at the outer edges of the Twin Cities metropolis where large tracts of rural land are available, a practice that contributes to the demand for housing and commercial development. These campuses are barely accessible by transit.

Access to education, jobs, and other necessities of everyday life is reasonably regarded as a right rather than a privilege. The Americans with

Disabilities Act is meant to improve disabled people's access to the nation's employment opportunities, educational institutions, public places, and commercial and cultural establishments. The act mandates the accessibility of buildings, and it also mandates the accessibility of transit. To meet the mandate, many transit agencies deploy special demand-response vehicles for disabled customers. But there is no mandate in America to accommodate the transportation needs of the millions of people denied access for lack of a car. Access can best be restored to the non-drivers of the metropolis by means of urban recentralization—restoration of downtown primacy in employment, rejuvenation of neighborhood commercial streets, and resumption of decent central-city transit service.

In the nation's few cities served by good public transportation and robust neighborhood commercial streets, low-income families are spared the financial burden of car ownership, a burden that in 1999 exceeded $6,000 annually.[125] Consider the transportation expenses of a hypothetical family of four in a high-vitality, transit-rich urban environment—let's say New York's Upper West Side. The family consists of an employed adult (we'll call him Ralph), a stay-at-home mom, and two kids. Ralph commutes to work each day on the subway, using a 30-day MetroCard that costs him $63. He and his family use transit for a family outing every weekend, to the Bronx Zoo, Yankee Stadium, Coney Island, Battery Park (they can walk to Central Park), or to Midtown during the holidays. Twice a month, on average, the family indulges in a taxi trip for a social visit or other purpose, at an average cost of $30 per round trip. Finally, once a year the family rents a car for a two-week vacation. In the Upper West Side, as in many other New York neighborhoods, people rent cars for vacations; rental agencies are within walking distance of most households in New York's high-density neighborhoods. Ralph's annual transportation cost adds up as follows:

Unlimited transit travel for Ralph:	$767
52 recreation/entertainment transit trips for Ralph's wife and kids @ $3.00 each per round trip	$468
24 taxicab round trips @ $30 (for miscellaneous purposes)	$720
One auto rental—two weeks for a family vacation, plus gasoline	$900
Total[126]	$2,855

Ralph's entire family spends $2,855 annually for a high level of mobility, well under half the average annual cost of owning and operating a car in America.[127] Ralph's Upper West Side family has, besides good transit, easy walking access to everyday needs and diversions—grocery stores and drug stores, and a broad variety of retail shops, doctors and dentists, restaurants, cinemas, and cultural institutions. Ralph's two kids can run family errands, and they can go to the movies or the local hangouts without begging for a ride. In low-density cities, as in post-war suburbs, people without cars are denied access to much of what the metropolis has to offer. This is the legacy of irrational decentralization.

The American impulse is not to reverse the process of irrational decentralization, but rather to feed the process and then to ameliorate the inevitable social distress by attempting to make car ownership universal. During the campaign season of 1996, Republicans offered a plan to help the working poor: repeal a federal gas tax increase that had been enacted in 1993. The Republican plan (a counter-proposal to a Democrat plan to increase the minimum wage) presupposed that all of the working poor drive cars, or it ignored those who do not (indirect benefit notwithstanding). Oklahoma Representative J.C. Watts envisions an America in which working-poor households own two cars. In his rejoinder to President Bill Clinton's 1997 State of the Union Address, the Republican Congressman noted that high interest rates are depriving some hard-working families of "money for a much-needed second car."[128]

Policymaking at the state and local levels is equally car-centric. The human service director for a suburbanizing county in the Twin Cities area foresaw transportation as one of the key impediments to a successful implementation of welfare reform, so he proposed a special accommodation to car-owning welfare recipients: "There should be flexibility in the welfare reform proposals to allow moneys to be used for emergency car repair." The Family Options program in Hennepin County enables welfare recipients to use welfare benefits for a down payment on a car.[129] The McKnight Foundation launched a program in the 1980s to help low-income women in the Twin Cities area buy and maintain cars. *Minneapolis Star Tribune* columnist Leanard Inskip credits the program with strengthening families.[130] What a sorry state of affairs that low-income families, even in cities, thrive only if they own cars.

Policies that advance automobile dependence are politically appealing in a nation where automobile ownership is so generalized that it extends to poverty-level households, a nation in which transit is so pitifully inadequate that it isn't regarded by the vast majority as suitable transportation. It is unsurprising in an overwhelmingly automobile dependent nation that liberals join conservatives in support of policies that undermine transit by encouraging automobile ownership.

When Republicans proposed the repeal of a gas tax during the 1996 election campaign, Democrats quickly joined them. In October 1999 New York's liberal Senator Charles E. Schumer called on the Clinton Administration to sell oil from the nation's Strategic Petroleum Reserve—a source for emergencies. The emergency that motivated Schumer was a two-bits-per-gallon increase in New York City's gasoline prices during the preceding six months. On September 21, 2000, presidential candidate Al Gore urged Clinton to tap the strategic reserve, and the president complied the next day. (Candidate George W. Bush had advised opening the Alaska wilderness to oil producers.)[131] If America's policymakers were interested in the social and environmental health of the metropolitan areas that house four out of five Americans, they would focus their quest for cheap motor fuel on rural folks and on truckers who haul goods that cannot be hauled efficiently by rail. As for the rest of us, we ought to be encouraged to ride.

The Extinction of a Cherished Lifestyle

The inner-city poor suffer the direst social consequences of irrational decentralization, but many among the middle and working classes also are deprived. Urban neighborhoods once cherished by their middle-class and working-class inhabitants are rendered uninhabitable, so these non-poor households are relegated to suburbs. Many suburbanites "buy...communities that they know are flawed," according to Philip Langdon, one of many critics of post-war suburbia; "they buy them because of the location, the quality of the local schools, or the price, even though they might prefer houses and communities very different from what the builders and developers are offering."[132]

A 1989 Gallup poll suggests that at least half of suburbanites would prefer to live elsewhere.[133] Nearly as many of the people surveyed indicated a preference for cities as for suburbs in 1989 in spite of all the problems that bedevil cities, and cities offer greater potential than suburbs to reproduce the attributes of the small town, the settlement type preferred by a plurality of the Gallup pollees.

The attributes of small-town life. Americans' strong preference for small-town life is based on the perceived presence of these attributes:

• Small towns foster a high degree of neighborliness—community of place coincides with communities of interest.

- Businesses are small and locally owned; proprietors and customers know and trust one another.
- Main street offers informal social gathering places within walking distance of most residents. These include the cafe where main-street merchants gather for coffee each day, and the pool hall or bowling alley where adolescents hang out on Saturdays and on weekday evenings.
- Long commutes and traffic congestion do not rob working adults of their time and comfort. Many merchants walk each day to their main-street stores.
- Children are safe, and adults are at ease, in the public realm.
- Children have an array of activities accessible to them without having to rely on an adult for transportation.
- Social cohesion and harmony permeate everyday life.
- Small-town life is affordable.

City neighborhood as small town. Neighborhoods resembling small towns are rare in the modern metropolis, although most small-town attributes were present in urban neighborhoods until the 1960s. Commercial streets in urban neighborhoods, for example, resembled small-town main street, according to Alan Ehrenhalt's description of the commercial street in St. Nick's Parish—a Chicago neighborhood—in the 1950s:

> Sixty-third and Kedzie had the standard equipment of neighborhood commerce: a Walgreens, a Kresge's, and a locally owned men's store facing each other on corner lots, with a shoe store, a sporting goods store, a candy store, a grocery, and a movie theater, all independent and locally owned, within a block or so....schoolchildren and housewives did their business there because it was familiar and comfortable...kids as young as five and six...trooped down to the store for a fresh loaf of bread.

> On Monday and Thursday nights, Sixty-third Street was crowded with knots of local residents who came out to window shop and make conversation, whether they intended to buy anything or not. Late shopping nights were a neighborhood social occasion, an important element of the word-of-mouth network. They were a mechanism for making contact not only with fellow shoppers but with the merchants who were neighborhood institutions themselves.

> The very act of shopping was embedded in the web of long-term relationships between customer and merchant . . .[134]

Neighborhood commercial streets are absent from post-war suburbia, and they have all but disappeared from degenerated central-city neighborhoods. Main street is identified today with small towns—it is part of the small-town allure. Even though the main streets in many small towns have eroded since the 1960s, Main Street remains a part of the idealized popular vision of the small town.

Public schools in traditional urban neighborhoods had much in common with their small-town counterparts according to Ronald P. Formisano's description of Boston's working-class neighborhoods in the 1950s and 1960s. Formisano described the role of sports teams in South Boston, Charlestown, and East Boston: "The sports teams of these schools commanded deep affection and passionate loyalty. Young men grew into middle age wearing their high school letter sweaters or team jackets."[135] Some of Boston's long-time residents refer to their neighborhoods as "towns."

All fundamental aspects of small-town life are consistent with healthy urban neighborhoods except one: the work commute. It is in the nature of the metropolitan economy that the workplace, for most employed adults, will be well beyond walking distance from home. (The reasons for this, and the ramifications, are discussed in Chapter 4.) The housing stock of small towns might seem incompatible with urban neighborhoods, but single-detached houses are by no means the only housing type in small towns. In the town of Henning, Minnesota (population less than 1,000), for example, some of main-street's merchants lived (in the 1960s) in apartments above their stores, and the doctor lived above his clinic. Apartments and townhouses are not uncommon in small towns.

If half or more of America's suburbanites are dissatisfied with their living environments, then the American system of creating neighborhoods is defective. If a plurality of Americans prefer small towns, then the attributes of small towns are worthy of emulating, and the effort should be focused on cities, where the attributes of small towns were only recently lost, rather than on post-war suburbs where, despite the best efforts of neotraditional planners, the attributes are unattainable.

THE ENVIRONMENTAL CONSEQUENCES OF IRRATIONAL DECENTRALIZATION

The False Promise of Environmental Policy

Public schools expanded their mission, in the 1980s, into the realm of environmental indoctrination. The ensuing curricula was surprisingly car-centric, even in urbanized states like New York, whose department of education produced a guidebook for high-school teachers declaring that the way to conserve transportation energy is to inflate a car's tires properly and to use its air conditioner sparingly. Transit isn't even mentioned.[136] It is with this same core assumption—universal automobile ownership and dependence—that national policymakers address the environmental consequences of irrational decentralization. Policymakers try to rectify the environmental hazards of automobile dependence more by taming the behavior of automobiles than by changing the practices of land developers.

The automobile, however, is proving difficult to tame. After the Environmental Protection Agency ordered 20 smoggy states to clean their air by adding methyl tertiary-butyl ether (MTBE) to their gasoline it was discovered that the additive, which causes cancer in test animals, was seeping into ground water and making people sick. More than half of the water supply in Santa Monica, California, was found to be contaminated with MTBE in 1999, and the EPA reversed its position. Researchers at California's Oak Crest Institute of Science reported in August 2000 that catalytic converters are producing massive volumes of ammonia, a catalyst in the formation of particulate pollutants that aggravate heart and lung diseases.[137]

The environmental gains rightfully attributed to cleaner burning fuels, catalytic converters, and fuel-efficiency standards have been largely canceled by increases in vehicle miles traveled (VMT). "Despite cleaner and more efficient cars...air quality in many metropolitan areas is worsening and raising concerns about public health...," according to a June 2000 report by HUD. The American Lung Association is concerned that ground-level ozone, a byproduct of vehicle exhaust, is inhibiting proper lung development in children. In the 10-year period ending in 1998, half the nation's largest 94 metropolitan areas (those with populations greater than 500,000) increased their number of days during which ozone levels were deemed unhealthy for children and people with asthma.[138] The air in metropolitan areas nationwide was found in 1998 to contain carcinogens that exceed established public-health benchmarks, and in 1999 the Minnesota Pollution Control Agency found that air pollution causes between four and eleven cancers per 100,000 people in the state. Vehicles are responsible for about half the air pollutants that poison human lungs.[139]

A consensus of informed opinion now recognizes global warming as a real rather than imagined phenomenon, but skepticism persists about the severity of the threat and the extent of human responsibility.

Environmental extremists' false alarms in the 1970s and '80s about an imminent depletion of oil and a looming overpopulation of the earth lend confidence to conservatives, who regard global climate as another sky that won't fall. Even if we imprudently dismiss climatic change as a phenomenon for which we bear no responsibility and over which we have no control, the list of undisputed environmental afflictions associated with vehicle emissions is long and grim.

Tailpipe emissions are merely the most direct of the automobile's myriad environmental atrocities; cars pollute indirectly by creating demand for petroleum. Drilling rigs, oil tankers, pipelines, refineries, and gas stations—everything between the pump at the oil field and the pump at the gas station—pollute air, land, and water. Tanker spills are almost common and, in the aggregate, much more damaging than the notorious Exxon *Valdez* incident. That one was merely the most irresistible to the news media because of its grand scale and newsworthy circumstance. (Referring to the captain of the Exxon *Valdez*, a Greenpeace ad said "it wasn't *his* driving that caused the Alaska oil spill, it was *yours*.") And tanker mishaps account for only a small fraction of the oil spilled during its maritime transport; most spilled oil enters the seas through routine operations such as loading and unloading, tank flushings, and wastewater discharge. Off-shore drilling dumps additional oil into the seas.[140]

On land, a pipeline operator in Wichita, Kansas, leaked three million gallons of crude oil, gasoline, and other petroleum products in 300 separate incidents in six states in the 1990s. The EPA blamed the leakage for fouling lakes, rivers, and the Gulf Coast shoreline, killing migratory birds and fish by the thousands. A pipeline fracture in Bellingham, Washington, dumped 229,000 gallons of gasoline into a park in June 1999, igniting a fireball and killing a fisherman and two 10-year-old boys.[141] A single refinery in Minnesota spilled an estimated million gallons of gasoline during the 1990s, and dumped additional pollutants into the Mississippi River. Refineries discharge air pollutants by the hundreds of thousands of tons annually, causing smog and triggering childhood asthma and cancer. Gasoline tanker trucks release hazardous pollutants into the air, and occasionally they spill their contents. (Sometimes they explode; one did in a collision in September 2000, killing a woman on Long Island. A similar accident killed a doctor in Yonkers, New York, in 1997.)[142] Gas stations contribute to the surface flow of nonpoint source contaminants, and to the seepage of contaminants (such as MTBE) into the ground water. In 1998 the commissioner of the Minnesota Pollution Control Agency reported that gasoline and diesel fuel leaked from underground storage tanks are "among the main pollutants of the state's ground water," and that there are 11,000 known leak sites in Minnesota. In the early 1990s some 500,000 of the nation's underground gasoline tanks were believed to be leaking.[143]

Alternate-fuel vehicles give us hope that the solution to the pollution problem is at hand and, therefore, it is unnecessary to fundamentally change the way we develop our metropolitan areas. But this is a false hope because, for decades to come, petroleum will continue to power nearly 100 percent of the nation's vehicles. Besides, vehicles pollute the environment in many ways aside from those related to petroleum.

Spent Tires and Other Junk

In August 1999, Ohio authorities advised people with respiratory problems to stay inside, behind closed doors and windows, because tires were burning. A tire dump 50 miles southeast of Toledo sent smoke plumes across four counties, and as far away as Columbus 70 miles to the south. The dump's estimated 18 million tires would burn for several days, the authorities warned. A tire dump in Texas burned for several weeks in 1995, costing the Environmental Protection Agency almost $4 million to extinguish.[144] Americans scrap more than 270 million tires each year on top of two to three billion already piled up. Twenty-five million tires lie in illegal dumps in New York State, where officials worry they will hatch mosquitoes that carry the West Nile virus, which kills people. Public health officials in Minnesota fear the rapidly spreading virus will come to the state via spent tires imported to the state's tire recycling plants.[145]

Americans retire more than 10 million cars and trucks each year, in junk-yards and dumps, along roadsides, and in the streets and vacant lots of America's derelict neighborhoods. Abandoned cars in Philadelphia numbered 40,000 in April 2000, when the city initiated a costly removal effort.[146] (Philadelphia is getting rid of its junk cars, but spent tires continue to litter many of the city's derelict neighborhoods.) Cars still in use promote the visual pollution—the car-oriented crudscapes—ubiquitous in metropolitan America. Cheap roadside strip-centers engulfed in bituminous replace natural and agricultural landscapes; parking lots and garages replace architectural gems in the nation's downtowns.

Land Gluttony

In the Twin Cities area, a 22 percent population growth from 1970 to 1990 was accompanied by a doubling of developed land area, even though the Twin Cities metropolis was under the planning directorship of the Metropolitan Council, which purportedly controls growth. Secretary of

Agriculture Dan Glickman reported in April 2000 that "we're seeing an acceleration of both prime farmland and prime forest land just evaporating and going into...development."[147] Much of this growth in metropolitan land consumption is attributable solely to vehicle access and storage. In the Minneapolis suburb of Apple Valley, a developer who builds 50,000 square feet of office space lays down 75,000 square feet of parking pavement in order to comply with the city's zoning code. The parking requirement for the same building in downtown Minneapolis is zero.[148]

In the San Francisco region, Rothblatt and Garr found that open space is "a major casualty of [sprawled] development pattern...the demand for [recreational] space and facilities far exceeds the supply." In the summer of 1999, CBS News reported that sports enthusiasts in Fairfax County, Virginia (in the Washington, D.C., metropolis), suffer a shortage of recreational space: "172,000 sports fans are desperate for a place to play, but here like elsewhere, the rush to build houses and businesses has left little open space.... In counties all across America, finding a diamond is rough." A front-page headline in the *Detroit News* announced, "Metro Suburbs Run Out of Places for Kids to Play." The April 2000 article cites Orion Township where "developers are snatching up tracts before the township can react."[149]

As is the case with other land uses, recreational land in the city is more productive than recreational land in the suburbs. The chain-of-lakes parkway in Minneapolis is heavily used, and the crowds are a big part of the attraction. Suburbanites shun their deserted parks and flock to the city's parks to be where the action is.[150] On Manhattan's west side, the Chelsea Piers offer a multilevel smorgasbord of recreational opportunity, including a four-tier driving range on the Hudson River. On Manhattan's east side, tennis courts are piled up four tiers high.

Killing Fields

Suburban webs of roads, parking lots, and drainage ditches divide virgin land into fragments, which, even if they remain undeveloped, lose their capacity to sustain the wildlife that once inhabited them. That's why biologist Michael Klemens refers to the pavement and fractured land at the edge of the metropolis as "killing fields."[151] Pavement kills also by conveying pollutants directly to water sources, preventing the natural purification process of percolation through the soil. Pollutants conveyed by pavement account for the pollution of approximately 40 percent of all waters analyzed by the Environmental Protection Agency in 1994. The

World Conservation Union counts metropolitan development as a major contributor to the recent and impending extinction of thousands of plant and animal species.[152]

Pavement inhibits rainwater infiltration into the soil, compelling public officials to build stormwater systems, stream diversions, channels, and dams, resulting in "hydrologic disruption" which kills habitat in and along streams and increases the severity of erosion and flooding. The Sierra Club blames floods for killing more than 800 Americans since 1990, and attributes many of the deaths to sprawl.[153] The "heat island effect" caused largely by pavement is blamed for raising urban temperatures to lethal levels; the phenomenon also exacerbates air pollution and increases demand for electricity to cool buildings. Pavement has replaced enough natural ground in Florida to disrupt the state's rain cycles; that's why desert-dry ground burned so profusely in the summer of 1998.[154]

With some 80 percent of the nation's population living in metropolitan areas, automobile use needn't be so pervasive and the automobile's contribution to the pollution of air, land, and water needn't be so vast. Policymakers ought to recognize land development practices rather than automobiles as the nation's true environmental culprits. Office development, for example, pollutes land, air, and water as surely as industrial development once did. Office buildings pollute by generating vehicle traffic. A downtown office building well served by transit pollutes far less than a suburban office building accessible only by car.

THE ECONOMIC COSTS OF IRRATIONAL DECENTRALIZATION

Damages caused by vehicle emissions cost Americans $10 billion annually. Traffic congestion costs $5 billion annually in lost time, fuel consumption, and vehicle operating costs, and that's just in one state—New Jersey. Infrastructure redundancies associated with sprawl cost Americans many billions of dollars each year.[155] Accidents, suicides, and criminal acts involving guns cost Americans $100 billion annually, a cost that can be attributed in large measure to the irrational decentralization that has turned viable urban neighborhoods into lethal underclass enclaves.[156] These are just a few of the many costs assigned by economists and academics to our flawed development practices.

We should acknowledge that some of these cost claims are suspect. Time "lost" in traffic congestion, for example, is becoming more productive thanks to cell phones and emerging computer technologies. Policymakers should pursue the recentralization agenda for social and environmental rather than economic reasons because pure economic reasoning might promote something less than the exuberant urban diversity illustrated by Jane Jacobs. The neighborhoods of greatest vitality might be economically cheaper (per household) than sprawl, but they probably are not as cheap as the semi-suburban middle-ground envisioned by many of the analysts who compare costs.[157] If urban vitality comes only at a cost premium, that premium is willingly borne by the affluent households without which cities cannot thrive; and metropolitan areas centered by stagnant cities cannot fulfill their social potential and they cannot much improve their environmental health.

Though it is impossible to pinpoint the economic costs of irrational decentralization, some generalities can be made. First, we pay an indeterminable but immense economic price for the social and environmental damage caused by irrational decentralization. Second, America's high rate of gasoline consumption exacerbates the trade deficit, which reached a record $33.3 billion in January 2001 as oil imports (25 percent of the deficit) rose to a record level.[158] Third, the military cost of protecting America's sources of oil is attributable in large measure to irrational decentralization.

THE MORAL CONSEQUENCES OF
IRRATIONAL DECENTRALIZATION

President Clinton unleashed warplanes and missiles against Iraq in December 1998 with a stern reminder, "When we must act in America's vital interests, we will do so."[159] Eight years earlier, President George H.W. Bush had warned the Iraqis that America would "take whatever steps are necessary to defend our...vital interests..."[160] The vital interests that Democrat and Republican presidents protect in the Arabian Gulf are oil and its unimpeded delivery.

The first Bush administration offered a range of considerations to explain its resolve in the gulf region, from Kuwaiti sovereignty to human compassion, even American jobs, but oil security was at the root: The administration feared Saddam Hussein would gain control of 40 percent of the world's oil if he continued past Kuwait to capture Saudi Arabia's ports. *Washington Post* reporter Rick Atkinson reported America's true military purpose: "Restoring the status quo in the Persian Gulf...permitted Americans to indulge their addiction to foreign petroleum with hardly a second thought."[161] The reluctance and frugality with which Washington intervenes in other foreign crises belie any claim of the primacy of humanitarian motives in the gulf.[162]

The secondary—humanitarian—goals of America's adventures in the Mideast are no doubt worthy, but if our immoderate oil appetite is at the root of our involvement in foreign carnage, or even a factor, then our policymakers are morally obligated to suppress the appetite and to leave no doubt as to the righteousness of America's motives.* A commodity over which lives are imperiled and lost should be regarded by a moral society as more precious than it is regarded in the United States. The eternal turmoil of the Mideast will not be eradicated by an American shift to energy-efficient development practices, but such a shift would minimize the importance of foreign oil in American life and foreign policy.

America's 1991 military victory over Iraq brought America's political leaders not only a renewed sense of national security but also a renewed sense of entitlement to the gulf region's resources. In June 2000, presidential candidate George W. Bush suggested that his father's military victory should be exploited as a source of leverage to impel Kuwait and Saudi Arabia to increase their oil output, thereby forcing America's gasoline prices down: "Ours is a nation that helped Kuwait and the Saudis. You'd think we had the capital to convince them to increase the crude supplies."[163]

Transportation, the centerpiece of America's petroleum dependence, accounts for about two-thirds of national consumption, and imports have risen from about one-third of consumption in the early 1970s to more than half today.[164] America's growing dependence on imported oil accompanies its migration to metropolitan areas, which offer the potential to dramatically reduce per-capita consumption. But the irrationally decentralized metropolis imposes automobile dependence on virtually its entire population. The difference between a rationally decentralized and an irrationally decentralized metropolis easily encompasses that margin

---

* As this goes to press, the U.S. prepares a response to the terrorist attack that destroyed the World Trade Center and killed thousands of its occupants (nearly all of whom used transit to get to work). The prime suspect is Osama bin Laden, who in 1998 declared a fatwa against the United States with the intent to eject our military from Islam's land of holy places—Saudi Arabia. America's leaders agree unanimously that a military campaign against terrorism is necessary, and Mideast experts warn that such a response is fraught with the potential to radicalize moderate Muslims. Absent from the debate is any proposal to eventually eliminate one of the underlying causes of Islamic resentment—America's military presence in the oil-rich environs of the Arabian Gulf. (Bin Laden's activities and motives are described by ABC News correspondent John Miller [who interviewed bin Laden] on *Charlie Rose*, broadcast 26 February 1999; and by John F. Burns and Craig Pyes, "Radical Islamic Network May Have Come to U.S.," *New York Times*, 31 December 1999, p. A16).

of consumption that binds us militarily to the world's most volatile region.[165]

The carnage associated with America's automobile dependence isn't limited to the Middle East. Pipeline explosions killed more than 2,000 Nigerians in the two-year period prior to August 2000. The scene of this bloodshed was the Niger Delta, one of the world's top oil producers. Most Nigerian crude oil finds its way into automobile gas tanks in the United States. The U.S. depends also on the oil of Angola, whose leaders, brutally indifferent to the suffering of the nation's desperately poor population, use their oil wealth to remain in power. "The United States needs Angola's oil and some American officials concede that this need dampens their willingness to chastise Angola or demand too much," reported the *New York Times* in September 2000.[166] The Texaco Oil Company fouled the rivers, forests, and wildlife of Ecuador's rain forest so egregiously that Amazonian Indians filed a lawsuit claiming environmental damage is so vast that it violates their human rights.[167]

Most Americans want their political and corporate leaders to do the right thing socially and environmentally, even at some personal expense. A 1997 poll by the Pew Center for the People and the Press found that 75 percent of those surveyed would pay five cents more per gallon of gas if they thought it would "significantly reduce global warming." When the hypothetical price increase was raised to 25 cents per gallon, a majority—60 percent—maintained their willingness to pay a premium. When American consumers learned in 1996 about exploitive labor practices in foreign clothing factories, many expressed a willingness to pay more for clothing produced in accordance with the legal standards that apply in America.[168] Political leadership is needed to channel Americans' social and environmental good will into public policy.

If guided by a strong and visionary political leadership, many Americans would consider a lifestyle of reduced automobile dependence; many would prefer such a lifestyle if it were available in the American metropolis. Reductions in petroleum consumption and dependence can be achieved painlessly: simply shift a few specific categories of land development away from far-flung suburban sites toward the center, and accompany that shift with a shift to a transportation policy more favorable to transit. These shifts would not eliminate the suburban option from America's metropolitan citizens; they would simply enhance the urban option.

Part

II

Metropolitan Recentralization

4

Recentralization of Commerce

Edge City is the crucible of America's urban future. JOEL GARREAU[1]

Suburban business concentrations replace "the old-fashioned Ozzie and Harriet commute from a conventional suburb to downtown" with a new-and-improved commute from suburb to suburb according to Joel Garreau, who lauds the new arrangement as an energy saver: "Edge City …is, on average, an improvement in per capita fuel efficiency over the old suburbia-downtown arrangement, since it moves everything closer to the homes of the middle class. That is why Edge City is the crucible of America's urban future."[2]

MONOCENTRICITY/POLYCENTRICITY/NONCENTRICITY

Garreau's proclamation of fuel efficiency was hardly original; several planners and academics had reached a similar conclusion in the 1970s, prompted by OPEC-induced gasoline shortages to consider how metropolitan development patterns affect transportation energy efficiency. No fewer than 10 studies, published in the five-year period from 1976 to 1981, concluded that polycentricity is superior to the other two generic patterns—monocentricity and sprawl (noncentricity)—in minimizing per-capita fuel consumption (Figure 4-1). Urban ecologist Valerie Haines revisited the issue in 1986 and sided with the polycentrists, explaining the theory behind her conclusion:

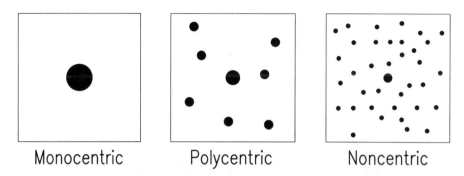

Monocentric   Polycentric   Noncentric

Figure 4-1. Three generic commercial development patterns. Polycentricity is widely regarded as the superior pattern because of its supposed energy efficiency.

> Multinucleation is the most energy-efficient urban form… By decreasing the spatial separation of urban functions, multinucleation allows the efficient use of transportation energy… Its spatial configuration allows clustering of land uses to reduce trip length for both nonwork and work trips without producing congestion.[3]

(Many metropolitan areas in America grew up bicentric—a dominant city and a smaller "sister city," each with a downtown. Polycentricity [multinucleation] refers to the development of multiple commercial concentrations in post-World War II suburbs. Garreau counted an average of 5.6 "edge cities" or "emerging edge cities" around the 36 core cities he surveyed, including eight around Detroit, and 11 around Houston.[4] Paired pre-war cities are considered monocentric in this discussion.)

In the late 1980s, while Garreau was poking around the suburbs researching *Edge City*, the Urban Land Institute was promoting high-density suburban development, claiming it reduces the amount of driving people do.[5] The purported energy efficiency of polycentricity has achieved the status of conventional planning wisdom, and regional planning agencies, including two of the nation's most highly evolved—Portland, Oregon's, Metro and Minneapolis-St. Paul's Metropolitan Council—have adopted multiple-centers growth strategies for the regions surrounding their underpopulated and underutilized core cities. The Metropolitan Council's 1992 vision statement, which cites energy efficiency as a fundamental goal, endorses the intensification of development around major suburban shopping malls in support of its multiple-centers strategy. Today the council pursues this polycentric vision by vigorously funding transportation projects in support of business concentrations in developing suburbs.[6] The suburban business concentration (SBC) is a mainstay of America's land development policy.

Events of the past two decades dispel the 1970s hysteria about petroleum shortages; innovations in exploration, production, transport, and resource management discredit the alarmists.[7] Nonetheless, transportation energy efficiency remains an important consideration in metropolitan development policy because energy efficiency, being inversely related to automobile dependence, is proxy for a host of other benefits—social and environmental. Furthermore, energy consumption is economically consequential for our petroleum importing nation. Therefore Garreau's claim warrants attention.

The energy-efficiency hypothesis adopted by Garreau and his predecessors was predicated on the assumption that suburban commercial development reduces suburbanites' driving distances to workplaces and shopping destinations, thereby reducing per-capita gasoline consumption. To support his assertion that "edge-city" development "moves everything closer to the homes of the middle class," Garreau cited the opinion of Alan Pisarski, author of *Commuting in America: A National Report on Commuting Patterns and Trends*:

> Typical commutes are becoming shorter, insists Alan Pisarski,… People typically took 21.7 minutes to get to work in 1980. The new Census number will probably be closer to twenty minutes, Pisarski believes. That is because of Edge City… jobs in edge city are closer to the homes of the middle class than at any time since World War II.[8]

Pisarski was wrong. The average commute time increased in the decade of the 1980s, from 21.7 minutes to 22.4 minutes, in the nation's largest 39 metropolitan areas—those with populations exceeding one million. (The average commute time increased in 35 of those 39 areas.)[9] And the increase was driven by the very factor upon which Garreau et.al. predicted its decrease, "a growing dispersal of workplaces in the suburbs," according to planners with the Federal Highway Administration.[10]

Average metropolitan commute distances, as well as commute times, have increased in the era of "edge city." Nationwide, the length of the average journey to work increased from 8.5 miles in 1983 to 11.6 miles in 1995 according to the Energy Information Administration, which concluded that "the locational changes of households and work have led to longer trip lengths…"[11] Average person-trip lengths have increased for shopping and other personal trip destinations as well. In only two of seven trip categories—*Work Related Business,* and *Social and Recreational*—did average trip lengths decrease between 1983 and 1995, and those decreases were only 7 percent and 8 percent, respectively. The average person-trip length for the work commute, which represents the largest share of vehicle travel, increased 36 percent in this period of prolific "edge city" development.[12] (Garreau should have used trip *distance* rather than trip *time* data to support his discredited claim that edge city "moves everything closer to the homes of the middle class." Trip times are affected by both distance and congestion.)

Commercial decentralization forces the typical metropolitan household to make more as well as longer routine trips.[13] In the Ozzie and Harriet days, a multitude of errands could be run from the downtown workplace, and a shopping trip to downtown or to the neighborhood commercial street was often a multipurpose trip. Unlike downtown workers, SBC workers drive to many of their routine destinations—to lunch, to the bank, to the post office. Even within many "edge cities," the distances among commercial destinations are long enough to encourage driving. For suburban workers with routine errands to run, a car is indispensable, but downtown's transit commuters conduct personal business on their feet today just as they did in the days of the "old-fashioned Ozzie and Harriet commute" to the CBD.

In the Twin Cities metro area, the cumulative effect of longer average trip distances and greater numbers of trips per capita was a 130 percent increase in vehicle miles traveled (VMT) between 1970 and 1990, when the population grew only 22 percent. Transportation researchers in the Twin Cities noted in 1994, "Longer trips caused by the spread of development added another 10 million miles of daily vehicle travel."[14] The trend continued through the 1990s. Citing 1995 data, the U.S. Department of Energy reported that "Americans continue to make more vehicle trips and drive more miles," and data from 1997 indicates that VMT growth outpaces population growth in America's metropolitan areas. (The nation's total VMT leveled off in 2000, according to the Federal Highway Administration, because of record gasoline prices and extreme weather.)[15]

Prior to the 1960s, the central city was the solidly dominant location of metropolitan jobs. In most if not all of our metropolitan areas, the vast majority of households was clustered within a five-mile radius of those jobs. Three decades later, the average commuter was driving about twice that distance in spite of widespread business decentralization, much of it in the form of SBC development.

EXPANDING UNIVERSE

Garreau's assertion that "edge cities" move businesses closer to the homes of the middle class is partially true, but it is more false than true. Business decentralization—polycentric or noncentric—moves jobs away from the majority of homes in the metropolis in a way explained by simple geometry: in a metropolis in which commerce is decentralizing, businesses move outward, closer to new suburban households as Garreau noted, but no single business moves closer to all households. At the same time a business moves closer to some households, it moves farther away from others. When a business moves away from the center of a universe of uniformly distributed households, its distance from the majority of those households increases. Only if a business moves closer to the center does it move closer to a majority of households. As business reporter Jay Hancock wrote in the *Baltimore Sun*, "geometric logic shows that hanging a shingle in the hub of a dispersed economy gives an employer access to the highest number of potential workers."[16]

The post-war expansion of the business universe of the Twin Cities metropolis led planners in 1994 to a conclusion clearly at odds with Garreau's: "Even though jobs are following homes to the suburbs, the average distances between places is increasing. This is mirrored most directly in the average distance of a daily trip, which has increased by 21 percent [from 1970 to 1990]."[17]

THE FUTILE PURSUIT OF SELF-CONTAINMENT

Robert Cervero, professor of city planning at the University of California, Berkeley, analyzed commuting patterns in the San Francisco Bay Area and found the fundamental flaw in the reasoning of the polycentrists. Cervero examined Bay Area municipalities' levels of self containment, a property he defines as follows: "Self-containment refers to achieving a built form that allows people to live, work, shop, and recreate within a community…"[18] If a predominantly residential suburb could achieve self-containment, then the travel distances for its residents' routine trips would be reduced and transportation energy would be saved. This is apparently what Garreau had in mind when he wrote that edge city "moves everything closer to the homes of the middle class." He assumed that an SBC would endow its host suburb with a measure of self-containment by making jobs and goods and services available locally, thus reducing driving distances and producing energy savings. Edge cities, Garreau apparently believed, would allow suburbanites to live much of their lives in economically (if not socially) self-contained enclaves.

Cervero tested this hypothesis by determining the levels of self-containment in the San Francisco Bay area's 23 largest municipalities, on the basis of 1980 and 1990 work commutes. Cervero compared the number of internal (within the municipality) commutes to the number of external (from home in one municipality to work in another) commutes for each municipality. He then assigned an "independence index" to each municipality based on a simple formula: a municipality's independence index equals its percentage of internal work commutes divided by its percentage of external work commutes; the higher the index, the more self contained, or "independent," the municipality.[19] Localities designated by Garreau as "edge cities" are among the least independent in the Bay Area according to Cervero's analysis.

Five of the seven Bay Area communities characterized by Garreau as "edge cities" were found by Cervero to be among the 12 cities with an independence index under 0.25, indicating a low level of internal commuting (Table 4-1). A sixth Garreau-designated "edge city" is the "San Jose-central Silicon Valley area." Cervero found the municipality of San Jose to have a relatively high independence index of 0.60, the fourth highest of the twenty-three municipalities he analyzed. But is San Jose an "edge city?"

Garreau dismisses the city of San Jose as "part of an Edge City," and he includes the following in his definition of edge city: "Edge City is any place that… was nothing like 'city' as recently as thirty years ago. Then, it was just bedrooms, if not cow pastures. This incarnation is brand new."[20] But San Jose was founded in 1777 and had a 1960 (pre-"edge-city" by Garreau's definition) population in excess of 200,000.[21] San Jose's CBD, firmly established early in the 20th century, includes pre-World War II office towers and at least one remaining pre-war high-rise hotel. The fact that San Jose's downtown office inventory grew rapidly after 1960 does not distinguish it from other American cities. Robert Cervero characterizes San Jose as a "central city," along with San Francisco and Oakland, and the U.S. Department of Transportation agrees, designating San Francisco, Oakland, and San Jose as the core cities of Bay Area.[22]

Aside from its status as a city rather than "part of an Edge City," San Jose is situated 50 miles away from San Francisco, the Bay Area's dominant business center. Therefore, San Jose had established an independent urban economy before becoming intertwined in the larger Bay Area met-

Table 4-1. Self-Containment Among 23 Bay Area Municipalities

	City	Independence Index (1990)
	San Francisco	1.23
	Santa Rosa .	0.74
b	Napa	0.70
r	San Jose+	0.60
b	Fairfield	0.48
	Berkeley	0.44
	Oakland	0.42
r	Vallejo	0.40
r	Alameda	0.37
	Palo Alto	0.32
	Fremont	0.26
"low level of internal commuting"		*<0.25*
	Hayward	0.24
b	**Pleasanton+**	0.24
b	**Concord**	0.24
	Sunnyvale+	0.21
b	**San Mateo+**	0.21
	Santa Clara	0.19
	Walnut Creek	0.19
	San Leandro	0.19
*b	Redwood City	0.19
b	Richmond	0.18
b	Mountain View	0.13
*	Daly City	0.07

Bold text indicates municipalities designated "edge city" by Garreau.

b = balanced between jobs and housing—within .15 in 1990.
r = predominantly residential
+ = Garreau adds suffix "area"

* Garreau's Bay Area Emerging Edge Cities:
  Pleasant Hill BART area
  Redwood City area
  Daly City Area
  San Rafael

Source: Robert Cervero, "Jobs-Housing Balance Revisited," *Journal of the American Planning Association* 62, no. 4 (Autumn 1996), p. 497.

ropolitan economy. San Jose's substantially independent economy is responsible for its high independence index. If Garreau had been more careful with his designations, he would have excluded central San Jose from his list of "edge cities." And if Robert Cervero had separately analyzed the business areas outside of downtown San Jose, he would, in all likelihood, have found them to have followed the pattern of very low self-containment that is typical among the suburban Bay Area communities that he analyzed.

One of Garreau's Bay Area edge cities—the Bishop Ranch area—was excluded from Cervero's analysis because it is not among the Bay Area's largest 23 municipalities. If we disregard San Jose and the Bishop Ranch area, and limit our discussion to those five Bay Area localities that were properly designated by Garreau as edge cities and then later analyzed by Cervero, we can say that all five—100 percent—were clustered in the bottom half of Cervero's list, which ranks municipalities in order of independence. All five edge cities were among the municipalities Cervero found to have an independence index under 0.25 in 1990. Cervero assigned his lowest independence index to Daley City—one of Garreau's edge cities. Among the five localities properly designated by Garreau as edge cities according to his own definition, and then analyzed by Cervero, more than four times as many commuters crossed municipal boundaries each workday as remained inside.[23] Cervero reported that these low levels of independence among the Bay Area's edge cities adversely affect commute distances in the Bay Area:

> Cities with independence indexes under 0.25 (low internal commuting) averaged nearly two more vehicle miles per worker (in one direction) than did cities with indexes above 0.50 (high internal commuting). Summed over all workers for some 300 work days per year, this difference amounts to over 800 million more vehicle miles of commuting annually in these noncontained cities as compared to self-contained cities.[24]

The epitome of the edge city phenomenon is the Bay Area municipality of Pleasanton, a predominantly residential suburb into which 26,000 jobs moved between 1980 and 1990.[25] (Garreau included the "Dublin/Pleasanton area" in his list of edge cities.) One would expect, having read Garreau, that many, if not most, of these new jobs would be filled by Pleasanton residents commuting short distances. But that is not what Cervero found in Pleasanton. Instead, he found "a greatly expanded commute shed" in which "four times as many people commute in and out of the city each day as within."[26] While the share of mid-range commutes (11 to 15 miles) into Pleasanton remained constant during the six-year period ending in 1993, the share of commutes shorter than 11 miles decreased and the share of commutes longer than 15 miles increased. The share of very short commutes—five miles or less—fell from 32 percent to 23 percent over the six-year period, and the share of very long commutes—21 miles and longer—increased five percentage points so that, by the end of 1993, those longest of commutes accounted for 34 percent of the total, making up the plurality of all commutes into Pleasanton. By the end of 1993, the average commute distance for Pleasanton workers was 18.8 miles, or 31 percent higher than the Bay Area average of 14.4 miles. Few of Pleasanton's new edge-city jobs have been filled by its resident population.[27]

Professor Cervero found that even if the numbers of jobs and employed residents were fairly evenly matched—balanced—in a particular suburban community, it does not follow that the community is self-contained; it does not follow that the residents of that community work at and patronize that community's businesses:

> The association between balance and self-containment in the Bay Area is fairly weak.... The fact that the correlation fell close to zero in 1990 suggests that the link between balance and self-containment was far weaker at the end of the decade than at the beginning.[28]... achieving a numerical balance of jobs and housing, in and of itself, is unlikely to yield many dividends.[29]

Commercial decentralization in all of its forms exacerbates automobile dependence and its consequences, but the polycentric "edge cities" form of decentralization advocated by Garreau appears to be the worst offender. The typical "edge-city" is, by Garreau's definition, a suburban business concentration, a place with "more jobs than bedrooms."[30] Such a place, according to Cervero, "averaged more commute vehicle miles per worker" because of "slightly longer distance commutes."[31] Cervero's analysis disproves the polycentrists' apparent assumption that edge-city jobs will be matched to and occupied by residents of the surrounding area, that edge-city retailers will be matched to the shopping preferences of surrounding consumers, that edge-city health-care establishments, if any, will be matched to the preferences and afflictions of the surrounding population.

Hamburger Trips

Within the expanding universe of metropolitan business sites, why haven't those in suburbia generated self-containment? Why haven't residents chosen to work, shop, socialize, and get medical attention at the locations closest to their homes? What explains the failure of Garreau's thesis to hold up to scrutiny?

The answers are readily understood by anyone who functions in the modern metropolis: only a fraction of our routine trips are to destinations for which proximity is the decisive factor. A trip to a fast-food restaurant is an example of the limited number of trips that are influenced primarily by proximity. The products, prices, and service offered by any particular Burger King restaurant are identical or nearly identical to the products, prices, and service offered by all other Burger Kings in the same metropolitan area, so Burger King patrons have no reason to travel farther than the nearest outlet; proximity is the decisive factor in determining which one to patronize. This principle applies not only to chain restaurants, but also to chain retail outlets and to gas stations and convenience stores; it applies to few other trip destinations.

Most trips are more specialized than hamburger trips. Most people do not choose doctors and dentists on the basis of proximity. Nor do they abandon friends, relatives, and business associates when they move from one household or job location to another. Nor do they shop for clothing and specialty items only at the stores nearest their homes. A decade before Garreau published *Edge City*, researchers in New York found that "travel time, in itself, is not a prime determinant of households' shopping choices..."[32] People travel to the Mall of America in Bloomington, Minnesota, from as far away as Japan for the primary purpose of shopping. Suburbanites do their specialty shopping in regional malls, which for most households are several miles away—a greater distance than separated most suburbanites from downtown in the Ozzie and Harriet days.

The Work Commute

A key deficiency in the polycentrists' reasoning is revealed by a consideration of the work commute, which is important because it is a routine trip that creates peaks in daily traffic volume, thereby burdening roadways and influencing decisions about infrastructure investment.[33] The emergence of a new SBC will reduce the length of the work commute only if it causes workers and their workplaces to move closer together, and that can happen only if the new SBC causes one of the following relocations:

   • A suburbanite's employer relocates his business to a new SBC nearer the suburbanite's home, or
   • the suburbanite gets a new job in a new SBC near his home, or
   • the suburbanite gets a new job in a new SBC distant from his home, and then relocates to a dwelling near that SBC, or
   • the suburbanite's employer moves his business a new SBC distant from the suburbanite's home; then the suburbanite relocates to a nearby dwelling.

The first of these scenarios—employer relocation to an SBC nearer an employee's home—would benefit that one proximate employee, or maybe a few, but other employees would face longer commutes. The typical business does not make a relocation decision based on a survey of employees' places of residence. Any sizable business that made the attempt would find that its employees' households are scattered throughout the metropolis.

If businesses will not or cannot relocate toward their employees' homes, will the typical worker change jobs in order to work in an SBC close to home? Unless that SBC has a massive employment base, it is unlikely that more than a very small fraction of neighboring residents will find jobs there. Someone seeking employment in a fast-food restaurant might keep his job search close to home because fast-food jobs are somewhat interchangeable, but seekers of more specialized jobs are forced to de-emphasize proximity as a factor in the job search. Business decentralization has changed the geography of employment opportunity so that the ever-broadening metropolitan area, or at least a large sector of it, rather than the CBD, represents the job market for most metropolitan job seekers. That is why Cervero found that Bay Area municipalities "rely heavily on each other for importing and exporting labor."[34]

Only by causing workers to change their place of residence can SBC development realistically be expected to minimize distances between workers and their jobs. If SBCs reduce commuting distances, they do so not by bringing jobs closer to workers *per se*, but by providing more job locations in which workers can find employment, and toward which they can subsequently move if job-home proximity is important to them. At first glance it seems plausible that this process of co-location will transpire, eventually, in metropolitan areas. In addition to job changers, newcomers to the workforce who find employment in an SBC might seek residence nearby. All in all, SBC development might be expected to reduce average commute distances over time.

But commute-distance data suggest that workers are not moving close to their suburban jobs. At least five factors mitigate against the effectiveness of the co-location process as a reducer of commute distances: multiple-worker households, flexible labor force, employment churning, jobs-housing imbalance, and jobs-housing mismatch:

1. *Multiple-worker households:* Seventy percent of commuting households have two or more workers, according to a 1996 report by the Eno Transportation Foundation.[35] The likelihood that two workers from a single household will find employment in the same SBC is remote; most suburban two-earner households will generate at least one work commute to another community. (Half of suburban families had at least one worker employed in the central city in the mid-1990s.)[36] The same principle applies to multiple-job workers; six percent of U.S. workers held two jobs in 1998.[37] Many of these workers, no doubt, traveled considerable distances from one job to the other.

2. *Flexible labor force:* Contract workers and temporaries, increasingly represented in the American workforce, commute to several different business locations each year. The nation's flexible labor force contains as many as one-fourth of all U.S. workers according to U.S. Department of Transportation estimates.[38] (Temporary employment increased almost 250 percent between 1982 and 1993, while total employment grew only 20 percent.)[39]

Moreover, many full-time employees are not pinned to a solitary workplace. Sales people make the rounds of several businesses in the course of a routine day, roaming far and wide in the decentralized metropolis, beginning or ending the workday far from home. Construction workers begin and end their days in various locations in the course of a year; in the decentralized metropolis, these locations are dispersed. For mobile workers, proximity of residence to an employer's headquarters does not translate to short daily commute distances, especially in a metropolis in which businesses are widely scattered.

3. *Employment churning:* Workers who find employment in an SBC and then succeed in finding nearby housing will experience a significant time gap between those two events. If suitable housing is available near an SBC for all of its workers, and if all of those workers relocate to that housing, each worker will experience some temporary locational mismatch; people do not move from one dwelling to another with instantaneous ease. In the aggregate, these temporary locational mismatches would produce substantial outside commuting given the job-mobility of today's workforce.[40]

4. *Jobs-housing imbalance:* The number of jobs in most suburban communities is not well balanced with the number of housing units. The supply of housing near many SBCs is inadequate for the SBC's workforce. Cervero observed a trend toward numerical jobs-housing balance among some of the Bay Area communities he analyzed, but not appreciably so among job-surplus localities (Garreau's "edge cities").[41]

5. *Jobs-housing mismatch:* Even where the number of housing units is balanced with the number of jobs in a suburban area, the housing units are not necessarily occupied by the area's workers. The cost of the housing, for example, is not always matched to the incomes produced by the area's jobs.

Jobs-Housing Imbalance and Mismatch

Jobs became numerically well balanced with housing in the Bay area municipality of Pleasanton during the 1980s, after officials enacted an ordinance meant to reduce traffic congestion and commute distances by balancing the two land uses. But Pleasanton's housing was too costly for most of its workforce; consequently, Pleasanton's workers were driving longer-than-average distances to work. Cervero noted, "although it evolved into one of the Bay Area's most balanced communities during the 1980s, most workers live elsewhere and most residents work elsewhere."[42]

Pleasanton's efforts to balance jobs with housing, and other similar efforts elsewhere in California, have failed to achieve their goals because numerical balance has not produced self-containment; a municipality's workers too seldom occupy its housing.[43] Anthony Downs, the eminent authority on metropolitan development issues, doubts the potential effectiveness of environmentally motivated policies aimed at improving jobs-housing balance.[44] Nonetheless, the quest for suburban jobs-housing balance motivates public officials to encourage the continuing decentralization of the metropolis. Jim Solem, former chief administrator for the Twin Cities' Metropolitan Council, advocated "balanced growth between jobs and housing…to get people closer to work."[45] Planners and policymakers use the imbalance in various suburbs as a rationale for promoting further development of the land use that is in shorter supply.

If self-containment among suburban communities improves with time, the improvement is slow, and the benefits are offset by new imbalances in newly developing areas. Levels of self-containment have remained low in suburban Bay Area communities, even in long-established communities where market forces have had ample time to increase those levels. Some Bay Area communities "inched" toward a higher level of self-containment in the 1980s, according to Robert Cervero, but those communities started and ended the decade at low levels.[46]

If Garreau believed that an adjustment period would be necessary to achieve self-containment in his "edge cities," he didn't say how long that period would be. In fact Garreau didn't mention that such an adjustment period might be needed. Professor Cervero's research suggests that the self-containment of many or most edge cities will not improve with time; in the Bay Area, "imbalances generally worsened in job-surplus cities."[47] By 1993 Pleasanton had had several years, following a substantial infusion of jobs resulting in near numerical balance, to show signs of self-containment: reduced commute distances and VMT. But the commuting trend lines were moving rapidly in the opposite direction as of 1993.[48]

The expectation that most of the workers in a particular SBC will occupy housing in the same area is reasonable only if government officials dictate not only the quantities of jobs and housing units to be developed in that area, but also the cost of the housing units. Therefore, jobs-housing balance will remain elusive unless land development is immaculately planned and controlled. But therein lies a conundrum. Garreau's praise for edge cities includes the observation that they are a product of our free-market system of land development.[49] One cannot immaculately engineer development patterns and housing costs within such a system. If planners and policymakers could subvert the free market and immaculately engineer development patterns in pursuit of jobs-housing balance and self-containment, they would first of all reverse the direction of residential growth and direct it away from the edge of the metropolis back to the underutilized land surrounding downtown, where the surplus of jobs is greatest. Then, just as businesses followed households into the suburbs, business recentralization would follow residential recentralization—the end of edge-city proliferation.

The Devaluation of Jobs-Housing Proximity

If job-home proximity is important to employed suburbanites, that proximity is difficult to attain in the modern metropolis because business decentralization reduces the feasibility of proximity for many, if not most, metropolitan households. A two-earner household would be more strongly attached to an employment center that employs both workers than to a center that employs only one; business decentralization reduces the likelihood that both workers will have a common work destination. A flexible-job household cannot be strongly attached to any location in a decentralized metropolis. A job-mobile worker might have a strong attachment to a commercial area if all of the jobs in his or her occupation were concentrated in that area, but not if those job opportunities were scattered far and wide.

For multiple-job households, flexible-job-location households, and job-mobile households, any attempt to locate residence near employment is futile in a decentralized metropolis; business decentralization thus causes many households to de-emphasize work location as a factor in the household location decision. Most metropolitan households will attempt to live in the same broad sector of the metropolis, but not necessarily in the same community, in which they work. The greater the degree to which jobs are scattered throughout a metropolitan area the more irrational it is for job-mobile workers to try to live near their workplaces. The business decentralization advocated by Garreau as a way to bring jobs closer to middle-class homes produces the opposite effect by causing households to accept longer commutes as a price worth paying for residential stability.

Only 26 percent of U.S. residents cited "convenience to job" as the reason they chose their present neighborhood, according to the American Housing Survey for the United States in 1995.[50] Cell phones have made long commutes more tolerable to many suburbanites, and onboard computers with voice-recognition software will soon increase the productivity of drivers who commute long distances. Besides, some suburbanites regard the drive to work as a source of pleasure. In 1966, researchers found that one-third of commuters in the Ithaca, New York, area who routinely drive to work enjoy the drive and consider a long commute to be one of the rewards of suburban life.[51] This suggests that a sizable fraction of commuters would be unmoved by policymakers' initiatives to bring the workplace into closer proximity to the suburban home.

In the Bay Area's fast-growing Solano County, the percentage of employed residents who commuted to jobs in another county more than tripled between 1960 and 1990, from 11.8 percent to 38.6 percent.[52] Nationwide, the number of workers who commuted to jobs outside their home counties increased by 206 percent between 1960 and 1990 while the national workforce increased by 78 percent.[53] Business decentralization has made home-to-workplace proximity a subordinate factor in metro-area residents' search for employment and housing.

BUSINESS TO BUSINESS TRIPS

An architectural firm is visited routinely by structural engineers, mechanical engineers, electrical engineers, building contractors, representatives of building products manufacturers, and the usual assortment of folks who sell office supplies and fix copy machines. The firm thus imposes hundreds of VMT on its metropolis every week unless it shares a business concentration with most of the businesses with which it routinely inter-acts. An architectural firm with a diverse practice will collaborate with more than one structural engineering firm and more than one mechanical engineering firm over the course of a year, thus the architectural firm will generate routine business-to-business automobile trips unless it is sur-rounded by a multiplicity of engineering firms. Multiply this phenome-non by a multitude of business types and business relationships and it becomes evident that only a massive but compact business concentration can eliminate most routine business-to-business car trips. Thus far in America, only the CBD is massive yet compact enough to fit the bill.

In the CBD, business-to-business trips are made on sidewalks and in building elevators rather than automobiles. Downtown couriers use bicy-cles instead of cars. The higher the percentage of metro-area businesses concentrated in the CBD, the fewer vehicle miles traveled for business purposes.

SUCKING UP FREESTANDING TOWNS

The notion that the municipalities within a growing metropolitan area would become increasingly balanced and self-contained over time defies the most fundamental characteristic of the metropolitan economy. The U.S. Office of Management and Budget defines a metropolitan area gen-erally as a core city and those surrounding communities with which it has a high degree of economic and social integration.[54] Metropolitan-area expansion signals a broadening, not a shrinking, of interdependence among communities. Metropolitan economic expansion is a powerful force, powerful enough to suck formerly-independent municipalities (small freestanding towns) into a unitary field of economic interdepend-ence, powerful enough to turn free-standing towns into suburbs. Metropolitan-area expansion captures freestanding towns and makes them less independent of the larger metropolitan economy.

Freestanding towns some 15 miles away from the center of a typical American metropolis began the decade of the 1960s in pretty much the same way as towns of equivalent population a hundred miles away. Local merchants ran main-street businesses that served the local population and surrounding farmers. The local population worked mostly in the local economy, and they shopped, visited the doctor and dentist, and went to the movies on main street. With the numerical and spatial expan-sion of the metropolitan population, the farmland surrounding these free-standing towns was converted to housing for households attached by employment to the metropolitan economy; the buyers of the new houses were more likely to work in the central city than in a business along nearby main street.

The freestanding town's expanding population attracted new commercial development, but not to main street. New shopping strips sprouted on arterial roads a few miles away from main street and pulled shoppers in from the new subdivisions surrounding the town. Those new shopping strips also lured many of the town's longtime residents away from old main-street businesses. The new residents of the formerly freestanding town outnumbered the longtime local population within a decade of the first subdivision, and the new residents continued to work at their former jobs, visit their former doctors and dentists, worship at their former churches, socialize with their old friends, shop at their former shopping malls, all outside the municipality of their new residence. The new residents' routine trip destinations were far-flung; new neighbors worked and played and worshipped in different and widely dispersed communities. The metropolitan area, not just the home community, is the everyday realm of the modern suburbanite.

Rosemount, Minnesota, 18 miles (straight-line distance) south of downtown Minneapolis, was in 1960 a small town with a typical small-town main street and a population of 2,012. By 1970, Rosemount's population had more than doubled, and in 2000 its population was more than seven times the 1960 level.[55] Housing subdivisions stand on the former farm fields that surround Rosemount, and modern commercial development is scattered along the area's main roads. Meanwhile, outstate Minnesota towns that had a 1960 population similar to that of Rosemount have experienced little or no population or economic growth; many have experienced population declines since the 1960s.

When Rosemount built a community center for its expanding population in the late 1980s, it got its architect from Minneapolis, its engineers from St. Paul, and its facility manager from Shoreview, a suburb at the opposite end of the metropolis. Increasing interdependence, not independence, among municipalities in an expanding metropolis is the natural order of the metropolitan economy. The notion that a modern suburb can achieve self-containment is naive, but that is the notion upon which is constructed the myth of "edge-city" energy efficiency.

THE EXCEPTIONAL CENTER

As he researched travel patterns in the Bay Area, Robert Cervero found an exception to the rule that metropolitan communities exhibit low levels of self-containment. His indices of self-containment for Bay Area communities reveal the dominant community—San Francisco—to be conspicuously more self-contained than the others; San Francisco was the only Bay Area community with more internal (within the municipality) than external (from one municipality to another) work trips. Cervero found that four out of five employed residents of San Francisco worked in their home city in 1990.[56] All other communities in the Bay Area ranked far behind San Francisco in self-containment; only about a third of Bay Area workers outside San Francisco worked in their home community in 1990. As Cervero noted, "The only Bay Area city that can lay genuine claim to being self-contained is San Francisco itself."[57]

Santa Rosa, Napa, and San Jose ranked second, third, and fourth behind San Francisco. These three cities are most distant from San Francisco, all some 50 miles or more away, and are therefore most likely to have established independent economies and jobs-housing balance prior to falling into San Francisco's sphere of economic influence.[58]

San Francisco's high level of self-containment evidences the importance of a critical mass of employment in a city. If an attractive and amenity-rich city contains a substantial share of its metro area's jobs, then that city is better able than a suburb, with a smaller number of jobs, to attract and retain local workers as residents. The city accommodates a high level of job mobility within a compact geographic area. Multiple-job households, flexible-job households, and job-mobile households that value both home-to-work proximity and residential stability are most likely to find both in a locality with a large and spatially concentrated pool of employment opportunities. A large number of employment options allows workers to change jobs without changing the general location of their workplace, a situation that adds to the advantage of central-city living.

San Francisco holds the plurality of jobs—about 20 percent in 1990—among all the municipalities in the vast Bay Area metropolis. (San Jose, the runner-up, held about 12 percent in 1990.) The edge city of Walnut Creek held less than 2 percent of the Bay Area's jobs.[59] San Francisco held nearly 12 times as many jobs as Walnut Creek in 1990, therefore the chance of job availability for a randomly selected worker is 12 times greater in San Francisco than in Walnut Creek. In the Ozzie and Harriet era, the CBD contained the lion's share of metropolitan jobs in most job categories, so the CBD and its surrounding neighborhoods constituted a self-contained city. Healthy central cities remain substantially self-contained, but no edge city has the critical mass of jobs and the broad range of housing necessary to attract and anchor a substantial population of resident workers.

SPRAWL GENERATORS

Commercial decentralization hasn't prevented a lengthening of average metropolitan trip distances, but distances would grow also in a monocentric metropolis with an expanding field of residential development. Some might argue that commercial decentralization has constrained the growth of routine trip distances and that monocentricity would have produced greater increases in trip distances than polycentricity produced. But such an argument fails to recognize how commercial decentralization influences residential decentralization.

Commercial decentralization, whether polycentric or noncentric, vastly increases the range of residential decentralization, which is largely responsible for longer average trip distances. Even though job location has diminished as a factor in metropolitan households' location decisions, it nonetheless remains a factor. But the vastly dispersed and enlarged metropolis and its abundant network of highways has caused workers to alter their concept of job-home proximity and to accept commutes of much greater distance. Many metropolitan workers are willing to commute a half hour or longer to their jobs, and suburban roadway development has increased the distance that can be traveled in that time, at least on roads not yet congested—roads at the periphery of the metropolis. The average speed of the American metropolitan commute has steadily increased in the past two decades, largely because of faster speeds on uncongested roads at the periphery.[60]

Who's driving the fastest rush-hour commuting speeds? Simple logic tells us that the commuters who live and work farthest from the center of the metropolis enjoy the speed advantage. Substantial commercial development—polycentric and noncentric—in second- and third-ring suburbs has created an employment base large enough to spawn residential development far beyond those suburbs. For example, prolific commercial development in the suburbs south of Minneapolis (specifically, the second- and third-ring suburbs situated in a zone eight to twenty miles south of downtown) has created a critical mass of employment capable of generating demand for housing 40 miles south of downtown.[61] The rush-hour commute to downtown from the vicinity of Northfield, a town 40 miles south of downtown, takes an hour or more, long enough to discourage large numbers of downtown workers from settling in the new subdivisions around Northfield. But the commute from Northfield to any of a half-dozen second- and third-ring suburbs, which together provide a substantial employment base, is a half-hour or less, a reasonable commute. Hence substantial commercial development over a large suburban area is capable of attracting workers to a broad and expanding sector of the metropolis, especially to the leading edge of expansion, thereby increasing the range of residential sprawl. Even though an SBC cannot usually attract its workers to nearby housing, a substantial collection of SBCs and scattered businesses is potent in attracting workers to housing on the frontier of the metropolis where roadways are least congested. That is how suburban commercial development boosts the range of residential sprawl.

The *Urban Transportation Monitor* reported in 1995, "the nation's 20 fastest growing counties are all beyond traditional suburbs, accelerating the dispersal of urban life into communities where it is more difficult to constrain travel."[62] Suburban commercial development, edge cities and otherwise, powerfully promotes far-flung residential sprawl, which triggers yet more commercial decentralization.

In the Twin Cities metropolis, work trips with nondowntown destinations are about as long, on average, as work trips with downtown destinations (9.3 miles for commutes with downtown Minneapolis or downtown St. Paul destinations in 1990; 9.2 miles for all metro-area commutes).[63] If virtually all of the metropolitan area's jobs had located in the downtowns, then the average commute distance would likely be shorter because the downtowns would exert a strong magnetic force on households wishing to avoid long commute times. In the absence of commercial decentralization, most households would try to locate within 30 minutes, during rush-hour, of downtown; this would powerfully constrain commute distances and sprawl. (Sixty-one percent commuters in the nation's largest 39 metropolitan areas spent less than a half-hour getting to their jobs in 1990.)[64]

Housing in the monocentric metropolis would be closer to downtown because more land would be available for it. Thousands of acres of suburban land occupied by shopping malls, office developments, and their vast parking lots would instead be available for housing, diminishing the extent of residential sprawl and reducing average distances between suburban households and downtown. (If suburban commercial floor area were located in central cities instead, that floor area wouldn't necessarily displace housing; it could occupy underutilized land.) The leading edge of sprawl is producing the longest average trip distances today, so a reduction in the extent of sprawl would shorten the longest commutes in the metropolis.[65]

Monocentricity would further constrain sprawl by increasing demand for housing of higher density. Apartments and townhouses located near downtown allow workers to minimize their commute times. This higher-density housing would support better transit, without which roadways to a single work destination would become intolerably congested.

THE TRANSIT FACTOR

To support his declaration that "Edge City development is, on average, an improvement in per capita fuel efficiency over the old suburbia-downtown arrangement," Garreau cited Alan Pisarski's prediction of reduced automobile commute times, which did not materialize. Even if reductions in average commute times (and distances) had occurred, the reductions wouldn't prove better transportation energy efficiency. Rates of energy consumption might increase in a metro area where declines in average trip times and distances are accompanied by declines in transit use. Garreau's dubious energy-efficiency assertion ignores the vital role of transit in reducing VMT. Even if polycentric commercial development delivered shorter average trip distances than monocentricity, monocentricity would still consume less transportation energy because it is a better promoter of transit ridership.

Transit ridership held steady from 1969 to 1995 as America's number of households increased 58 percent and household VMT soared 167 percent. Daily VMT per driver increased from 20.6 to 32.1 during this period. The average number of occupants per vehicle has steadily declined since the 1960s because commercial decentralization in any form reduces the likelihood that neighbors will commute to a common work location.[66] Policymakers try in vain to entice commuters into carpools, they hope to decrease trip distances, and, before the 1990s proliferation of gas-guzzling sport-utility vehicles, they cheered increases in automobile fuel efficiency. This focus on the automobile distracts policymakers from the more important challenge, that of reducing the automobile's share of metropolitan travel. The most efficacious way to achieve a per-capita energy reduction in a metropolitan area, even in the context of rising affluence, is to reduce per capita VMT by increasing transit ridership—to switch drivers to riders for routine trips.

Commercial decentralization thwarts the efficiency and viability of transit, and that is a greater impairment to the energy efficiency of a metropolis than is an increase in routine driving distances. The preceding discussion about self-containment and automobile trip distances only scratches the surface of the deficiency of Garreau's energy-efficiency hypothesis.

Transit and Energy Efficiency

The American Public Transit Association has calculated that, on average, a single person commuting via transit instead of driving alone will save 200 gallons of gasoline a year, and a 10 percent nationwide increase in transit ridership would save 135 million gallons a year.[67] Residents of the Houston metropolis were using about 70 percent more gasoline per capita than residents of the New York City metropolis in the 1980s because the Houston area workforce was commuting in automobiles at a rate nearly double that of the New York City area. Houston's CBD holds only one-quarter of its metro area's office space, compared to New York City's two-thirds (Table 4-2).[68] The polycentric and noncentric (sprawled) commercial development that dominates the Houston metropolis renders it incapable of providing the high level of transit service that is available in the New York area.

Table 4-2. Gasoline Consumption, Automobile Commuting, and Office Decentralization in Selected U.S. Metropolitan Areas, 1980

Metropolitan Area	Gasoline Use Per Capita, Gallons	Share of Population Commuting to Work by Automobile	CBD Share of Metro Area Office Space
New York	323	64 percent	67 percent
Chicago	353	76	63
San Francisco	424	78	60
Denver	462	88	39
Houston	546	94	25

Source: Lester R. Brown and Jodi L. Jacobson, Worldwatch Paper 77, *The Future of Urbanization: Facing the Ecological and Economic Constraints* (Washington D.C.: Worldwatch Institute, 1987), p. 18, Table 4, citing Newman and Kenworthy, 1986. CBD share of office space is estimated, based on 1992 data from *Statistical Abstract of the United States 1993*, Table 1250.

"The primary market for transit services, in cities of any size, tends to be the residents of the central city of the metropolitan area, traveling to jobs also located in the central city," according to the Transportation Research Board of the National Research Council.[69] Extreme roadway congestion and costly promotional campaigns by transit agencies have failed to revive transit ridership to the levels that prevailed prior to the rampant decentralization of work destinations.[70] By 1990, only 5.1 percent of the nation's work commutes were on transit, down from 6.2 percent in 1980 and 12.6 percent in 1960. (Rates of transit use are even lower for non-work trips.)[71]

Two-thirds of all jobs created in the decade of the 1970s were created in suburbs, and the trend has since accelerated. Consequently, suburb-to-suburb commutes are now the largest fraction of metro-area work trips, constituting 39.5 percent of all such trips in 1990 (Figure 4-2). The suburb-to-city commute of the Ozzie and Harriet days had fallen to 17 percent by 1990, less than half the suburb-to-suburb share. (Within-city commutes accounted for 27 percent in 1990, down from 31 percent in 1980.)[72] This loss of focus in the nation's commuting patterns is powerfully detrimental to transit ridership, which has sunk as low as it has because commercial decentralization—the dispersal of transit destinations—is inimical to the delivery of good transit service. With commercial decentralization, the commute least amenable to transit replaces the commute most amenable. Commercial decentralization—the decentralization of transit destinations—is more potent than residential decentralization in damaging the viability of transit.

Mode Choice Rationale

A typical suburbanite with a suburban job gets into her car each day without leaving her house and she drives to a suburban office building where she parks free of charge within one or two hundred feet of the entrance. Her commute time from the garage door of her house to the front door of her office building might be less than 15 minutes. Transit use, involving long walks and long waits, would be irrational. This is true also for a city resident with a suburban job.

No wonder that in 1990 only 1.2 percent of all commute trips that began and ended in suburbs were transit commutes. Suburban residents who commute to central-city jobs use transit at a rate nearly five times as high as for those who commute to suburban jobs. In fact, the rate of transit use among suburbanites working in cities was, in 1990, higher than the rate among city residents working in suburbs, suggesting that the trip destination more strongly influences the rate of transit use than does the trip origin, and proving that commercial centrality is vital. By 1990, suburbs had overtaken central cities as the destination for a majority of metro-area commutes; nonetheless, only 13.7 percent of all metro-area transit commutes were to suburban workplaces, compared to 75.2 percent to work-

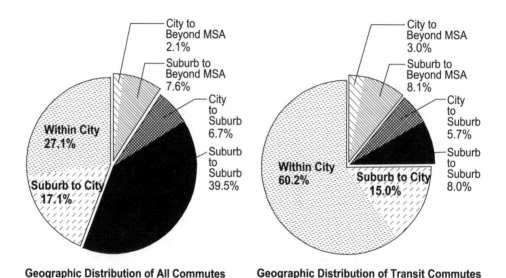

Geographic Distribution of All Commutes   **Geographic Distribution of Transit Commutes**

Figure 4-2. Geographic distribution of metropolitan work commutes, 1990. Central-city workplaces generate a disproportionately high share of metropolitan transit commutes.

Notes: Graphs are based on commuting data for 33 Metropolitan Statistical Areas (MSA's) with 1980 populations exceeding one million. Trips to "Outside MSA" are to exurbs and beyond. Some such trips are to cities, especially in the Northeast where commuter rail and bus lines deliver passengers to cities in adjacent MSA's. This explains transit's relatively high share of these commutes. The absolute number of these transit commutes, however, is less than 1 percent of the total number of work commutes.

Source of data: Transportation Research Board, Transit Cooperative Research Program of the National Research Council, *TCRP Report 27—Building Transit Ridership: An Exploration of Transit's Market Share and the Public Policies that Influence It* (Washington, D.C.: National Academy Press, 1997) p. 19, Table 13.

places in cities (Figure 4-2). (About 11 percent of transit commutes were to destinations beyond the metro area, including cities in adjacent metro areas.)

By 1990, more than twice as many suburbanites in the workforce were commuting to suburban workplaces as to city workplaces, a situation that would please the polycentrists. Suburb-to-suburb (intra- and inter-suburb) commuters had become the largest segment of the commuting market.[73] But, as noted above, only 1.2 percent of suburb-to-suburb work trips were transit trips; the worst transit market now accounts for the largest share of America's metropolitan work trips thanks to widespread commercial decentralization. Transit's share of commutes to suburban destinations has decreased rather than increased during the contemporary era of edge city development.

When Garreau surmised that edge cities represent energy efficiency, he was comparing a bad situation—edge city development—to one he perceived as worse: "the old suburbia-downtown arrangement." But the old suburbia-downtown arrangement was better, not worse. Filled-to-capacity park-ride lots at BART stations in the San Francisco region, and at Metro stations in the Washington, D.C. region, demonstrate the ongoing viability of the old suburb-to-downtown transit arrangement. The expense and inconvenience of downtown parking (traffic congestion is also a contributor) motivates many suburbanites to get out of their cars and into transit vehicles.

The points of trip *origin* were exploded by suburban residential development, especially since WWII, but suburban commercial development, including SBC development, has for the past three decades dispersed the points of trip *destination*, with dire consequences for transit. Transit researchers in Houston studied three business concentrations outside the CBD and found, in 1987, that "CBD workers are five times more likely to use transit than workers in other activity centers" even when their trip distances are similar. And researchers in the San Francisco Bay Area found that among several thousand office workers who were transferred from downtown San Francisco to three suburban office campuses, transit ridership plummeted from 58 percent to 3 percent.[74]

Where Transit Works

Transit ridership is maximized where a transit agency can deliver good service, and good service is viable only in the presence of a particular set of land-use characteristics, characteristics undermined by commercial decentralization in any form. In their landmark study of transit viability, transit planners Boris Pushkarev and Jeffrey Zupan examined the effects of various land-use variables on transit ridership and found the size and density of the CBD to be the dominant factor. (The extent and density of surrounding residential areas, and the proximity of those residential areas to the CBD, are the other key land-use variables.) Pushkarev and Zupan concluded, "The higher the density of a downtown and the larger its size, the more it will shift travel from auto to transit."[75]

Pushkarev and Zupan's analysis was published in 1977, and their central conclusion was confirmed in 1996 by a comprehensive research program conducted by the Transportation Research Board of the National Research Council. The council reported that an increase in CBD employment produces an increase in transit ridership, while, "job decentralization, either in polycentric regions or in dispersed patterns, results in less use of transit for all trip purposes."[76] A sincere attempt to increase a metropolitan area's rate of transit ridership would focus on shifting commercial development from suburbs to downtown.

Downtown's Inherent Transit Advantage

Downtown's share of jobs has plummeted in the past three decades, and SBC competition motivates downtown business and political leaders to increase their parking inventories. Nonetheless, downtown remains the best transit generator. Robert Cervero studied the travel habits of people who live near the stations of the Bay Area Rapid Transit (BART) regional rail system and found that the dominant downtown on the system produces far higher rates of ridership than the SBCs:

> If someone living near a Bay Area rail station owns one car, works in San Francisco, and has to pay for parking, there is nearly an 80 percent likelihood that the person will commute via rail transit.... For secondary urban centers like Oakland and Berkeley where commercial parking rates are typically charged, there is around a 35 percent chance the person will commute by BART. For all other destinations, (where often workers park free), on average only 4 percent of the commute trips by station-area residents will be by rail.[77]

Might there be a way to achieve high rates of transit ridership in the context of continuing SBC development? Perhaps the downtown transit advantage is superficial. Maybe the advantage would disappear if downtown weren't the solitary business concentration on which transit routes are focused, in which parking space is in short supply; maybe downtown's advantage would disappear if it weren't the only transit-oriented destination in the metropolis. If an increased rate of transit ridership is an important goal, why not simply transform SBCs into transit-oriented destinations? Transit routes can be added, bus routes easily so; and parking could be regulated or taxed regionwide. Metro, the regional government for the Portland, Oregon, area, regards parking policy as a regional planning tool, and planners elsewhere have proposed parking taxes as a means to reduce roadway congestion.[78] If a substantial parking tax could be imposed on SBCs, the cost of parking might be equalized throughout the metropolis, eliminating downtown's unique position as the only business concentration in which people pay to park their cars.

With the addition of transit routes and the elimination of free parking, SBCs might be transformed into transit-oriented destinations. Would polycentric development then generate the same rate of transit ridership as monocentric development, proving that downtown's transit advantage is superficial and that polycentric development is fundamentally consistent with transportation energy efficiency?

The operating practices of commercial airlines provide the answer: A commercial airline establishes a hub-and-spoke route system because that is more cost-efficient (profitable) than a system of direct connections between every airport and every other airport on the airline's itinerary. A small airline operating out of a hub can serve, for example, nine other cities with nine links. If that airline were to establish direct connections among all 10 cities on its itinerary, it would need to operate 45 links, many of which would be unprofitable.

The traditional radial transit system—a hub-and-spoke system—is more cost-efficient than a system of multiple direct connections could possibly be. If a transit agency were able to operate with unlimited resources it could establish direct connections among all communities and business concentrations in the polycentric metropolis, but to do so with limited resources would stretch service so thin as to suppress ridership. Transit agencies, like airlines, must allocate their resources strategically, so the concept of providing direct transit routes among all the localities in a metropolis can be dismissed as unrealistic. Therefore, most localities served by a metropolitan transit agency will be connected to each other by indirect routes, routes involving at least one transfer, and the transfer is the inherent weakness of the hub-and-spoke system.[79]

Hub-and-spoke configurations are cost efficient, but they are less effective in garnering passengers than a no-transfer system of direct links would be if such a system were economically viable. Air travelers prefer direct flights and, when offered the choice, pay a premium to avoid a change of plane. Some air travelers pay a very high premium—the cost of owning and operating a private aircraft—in order to gain the flexibility that a hub-and-spoke airline cannot provide. Ground travelers pay a premium for flexibility as well, in much greater numbers than air travelers; nearly 90 percent of the nation's metropolitan households own or have access to at least one motor vehicle.[80] Consequently, most metropolitan travelers can make direct trips from any locality to any other in the metropolitan area. A transit agency might provide good service from some points to some others, and thereby compete effectively with private vehicles on some routes, but an efficient transit agency is forced to interconnect many points through a hub, and transit suffers a competitive disadvantage on two-link routes connected by a hub.

A hub is a point of transfer, and transfers deter ridership because they force riders to endure a second cycle of walking and waiting—the transit equivalent of a change-of-plane.* Transit planners consider walking and waiting time, or "out-of-vehicle" time, to be two to three times as burdensome as in-vehicle time, so that a transit trip with two 10-minute links and a 10-minute transfer period—a half-hour trip—is psychologically the equivalent of a single-link trip of 40 to 50 minutes.[81] Most transit customers avoid a transfer only if their destination is at the hub or en route to it. Therefore, destinations at the transit system's hub generate the highest rates of ridership among choice (as opposed to captive) passengers. This would be true even if parking costs at nonhub destinations were identical to those at the hub.

In a monocentric metropolis served by a radial hub-and-spoke transit configuration, all transit trips to business destinations are single-link trips to the CBD hub—the location of all businesses.[82] In a polycentric metropolis served by any reasonably cost-efficient transit configuration, many transit trips to routine destinations require a transfer (Figure 4-3). The monocentric pattern is, therefore, a fundamentally superior promoter of transit use.

---

*Real estate consultant Diane R. Suchman advises housing developers, "Access to public transportation should be considered, as well as whether transit routes provide direct service to employment centers or require one or more transfers." (Diane R. Suchman and Margaret B. Sowell, *Developing Infill Housing in Inner-City Neighborhoods: Opportunities and Strategies* [Washington, D.C.: Urban Land Institute, 1997], p. 40).

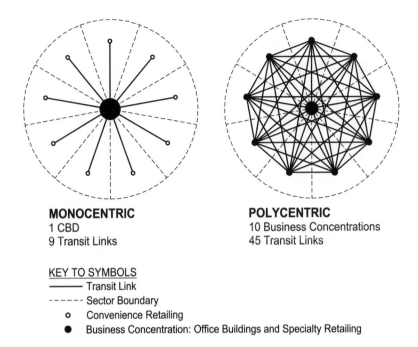

MONOCENTRIC
1 CBD
9 Transit Links

POLYCENTRIC
10 Business Concentrations
45 Transit Links

KEY TO SYMBOLS
——— Transit Link
------ Sector Boundary
  o   Convenience Retailing
  ●   Business Concentration: Office Buildings and Specialty Retailing

Figure 4-3. Monocentric and polycentric transit patterns. In the monocentric pattern, nine residential sectors are connected directly to a CBD by nine transit links. In the polycentric pattern, a business concentration is added in each sector, and 45 links are required to directly connect each sector to the CBD and all outside business concentrations. Transfers or lengthy journeys, which discourage ridership, can be prevented in the polycentric pattern only by connecting all sectors directly to all business concentrations.

Downtown's transit advantage is weaker in a city with a spatially extensive downtown than in a city with a compact downtown employing the same number of commuters, but the downtown advantage is never entirely absent. Expansive downtowns impose a transfer upon downtown workers whose workplaces are remote from their transit stops. Expansive downtowns thereby put many of their businesses in a position equivalent to that of the typical SBC—outside the reach of many of the region's direct transit routes. But the transfer and second leg of a downtown journey are quicker and less burdensome than those of an SBC journey. Scores of transit routes, which sparsely cover the periphery of a metropolis, converge on the downtown hub in a dense web of multiple routes on closely spaced streets, so the downtown transfer to a downtown destination involves only a brief walk (or no walk in some cases) and a brief wait. A typical SBC lacks the critical mass necessary to justify such frequent transit service. An SBC might be better served if it were designated as a transit hub, but the airline analogy tells us that not all SBCs can be hubs.

In some expansive downtowns, transit demand is sufficiently high to justify distributors on separate right-of-ways. Denver's mile-long CBD is served by the Sixteenth Street Transit Mall, where passengers disembark from the region's transit lines to be shuttled to their office buildings on free-fare buses that run every two to three minutes. Miami's spread-out downtown is connected by Metromover, an elevated automated people mover to which transit users transfer quickly and easily from Metrorail. Metromover runs every five minutes during the day, more frequently during peak periods, shuttling workers from Metrorail's Government Center station to the extremities of the extensive downtown.

When downtown workers transfer to a second transit vehicle, the journey to their final destination is a short one; downtown distances are shorter than metropolitan distances. Denver's transit mall extends just a half mile in each direction from the light rail line that feeds it. Miami's Metromover covers a strip of land two miles long, one mile in each direction from the Government Center, where it picks up Metrorail riders. The distances between downtown transit hubs and SBCs are, of course, much longer. Two of the largest SBCs in the Twin Cities metro area, both in the southwest quadrant, are 9 and 11 bus-route miles away from downtown Minneapolis, and those SBCs are 17 miles from each other, so neither would be a more strategically located transit hub than downtown.[83]

Although the transfer to a workplace on the periphery of an extensive downtown adds time and inconvenience to a transit trip, the intra-downtown trip is faster than a trip to an SBC, and the transfer is normally less burdensome. Therefore, the monocentric pattern is a fundamentally superior promoter of transit use even where the downtown hub is expansive enough to necessitate a transit transfer.

Robert Cervero tells us that metropolitan-area travel demand is shaped by economic connections among all communities and business concentrations in the metropolis; all substantial business sites will be connected by travel patterns to each other and to all residential sectors. Any SBC that is not directly connected to all sectors will generate a lower rate of transit use than the CBD. By extension, unless every metropolitan community is directly connected by transit to all SBCs, polycentric development will produce a lower rate of transit ridership than monocentric development.

Rates of transit use are affected by many factors in addition to commercial development patterns, factors that include residential development patterns, quality of transit service, parking availability, roadway congestion, gasoline prices, and safety concerns. But when all factors other than commercial development patterns are discounted, monocentric commercial development emerges as the fundamentally superior transit promoter. Every square foot of commercial space that is developed in the CBD rather than in an SBC increases the potential if not the actual rate of transit ridership in its metropolitan area. The lower the suburbs' share of commercial space, the higher the metropolitan rate of transit ridership because monocentric development has a fundamental, not just a superficial, advantage over polycentric development in promoting transit use.

The SBC's Contribution to the Decentralization of Transit

The Metropolitan Council of the Twin Cities area advocates "the expansion and intensification of existing major job concentrations...that have more than 3,000 jobs and job densities that allow transit service to function effectively."[84] Some 20 concentrations of 3,000 or more jobs exist farther than six miles away from the nearest CBD (and the council's definition of transit effectiveness is more generous for these suburban areas than for cities). *

---

*The Twin Cities area transit agency—Metro Transit—monitors its transit system for the purpose of identifying poorly performing routes. Routes on which subsidies exceed predetermined thresholds are reviewed for service cutbacks, fare increases, or elimination. Metro Transit's subsidy thresholds for "suburban local" routes were more than double the agency's thresholds for "urban local" routes in 1999. Based on this double standard, 74 percent of suburban local routes were deemed financially healthy, compared to only 70 percent of urban local routes.

University of Washington geographer David Hodge notes a *counter-equitable subsidy flow* in the Seattle metropolis, where subsidies support suburban service most generously, at least on a per-passenger basis: "absolute per-passenger subsidy is lowest near the Seattle central business district and the University of Washington, and gets progressively higher toward the service area periphery..." Because many central-city routes are more productive than suburban routes, central city passengers, including those in low-income neighborhoods, subsidize suburban passengers in the fare box. (Twin Cities area performance thresholds noted in Metropolitan Council, *Transit Redesign 1996*, p. iv-2-9, and *1999 Transit System Performance Audit*, p. 7-17; 1999 threshold information provided by Lynn Wallace, Metro Transit, 31 May 2001. Counter-equitable subsidy flow in Seattle reported by David C. Hodge, "My Fair Share," in *The Geography of Urban Transportation*, 2nd Edition, Susan Hanson, ed. [New York: Guilford, 1995], pp. 365-69.)

Although a suburban job concentration cannot generate as high a rate of transit use as a CBD, it can outperform widely scattered (noncentric) commercial development. The SBC, invariably situated along a major roadway, has location and critical mass in its favor. Therefore, in spite of the fact that polycentric commercial development erodes the former and potential rate of metro-area transit use, public officials promote polycentric development and SBC expansion.

Consistent with its advocacy of commercial decentralization, the Metropolitan Council adopted a "Vision for Transit" that formally promotes the decentralization of transit resources. The council's vision includes suburban hubs connected not only to the CBDs, but also to each other.[85] As of 1997, the council had identified 14 suburban transit hubs— shopping centers and office concentrations—on which to focus transit service. (The council identified only five central-city hubs.)[86] The council's transit arm has established several suburban circumferential routes connecting suburban business developments to each other but not to a CBD.

In 1996, Metropolitan Seattle's transit agency implemented its Transit Development Plan, which replaces a downtown-centered hub-and-spoke system with a multiple-center system that includes new suburb-to-suburb routes.[87] St. Louis' transit agency noted in its *Fiscal 2000 Annual Report* that "travel patterns are shifting from a downtown to a multi-centered orientation...business centers are scattered throughout [the] 3,600 square mile service area." The transit agency therefore defines its mission as "getting... workers to these centers." SBC development motivates transit agencies to decentralize transit service to a greater degree than residential suburbanization ever did.

In the first half of the 20th century, interurban rail lines reached a dozen or more miles from major downtowns to residential areas and small-town main streets, but these and other suburban routes traditionally emanated from the CBD and served central-city neighborhoods en route to the suburbs. Today, however, intersuburban circumferential routes that connect SBCs to each other completely ignore CBDs and central city neighborhoods. The practice of circumventing downtown isn't new; old crosstown routes bypass downtown, but some of these central-area routes have been discontinued as new suburban circumferentials are added. For example, old Minneapolis Route 3, which once connected Willard-Hay to its easterly neighborhoods, has been discontinued, and Route 590 has been added, traveling Interstate 494 from Eden Prairie (shopping) Center to the Mall of America, seven miles south of downtown Minneapolis. The route's nearly empty buses are sustained by a subsidy of $5.86 per ride because farebox revenues are far from adequate, according to a January 2000 report in the *Minneapolis Star Tribune.*[88]

Transportation planner Alan Black notes that, nationwide, these inter-suburban circumferential routes are a costly and dubious enterprise: "Because of the dispersion of suburban trip ends, most circumferential bus routes carry few passengers at a high cost per passenger. Transit authorities may experiment with such routes, but... they are inefficient in comparison with central city routes."[89] While SBCs generate more transit trips than scattered smaller business sites, they cannot generate the high levels of ridership that the CBD can. [90]

Transit agencies in the United States operate perpetually in the red, so they cannot maintain high levels of service in cities as they chase commercial and residential development farther and farther into suburbs. Streetcars ran every minute on many of Minneapolis' routes from the 1920s until sometime after World War II, but transit service in the city has diminished so drastically since that time that transit is hardly an option for car owners.* In 1996 the Minneapolis Planning Department reported transit decentralization's effect on central-city service:

> When a transit agency is forced to reduce service, it often faces the choice of eliminating service in an outlying area or reducing the frequency of service in the Core. Understandably, the choice is often to reduce service frequency in the Core. The effect of this over the years, especially since 1977, has been to erode service in the Core to the point that it is... not a quality option for the choice rider and an increasingly discouraging choice for the captive rider.[91]

Thus the pursuit of the suburban transit market carries a high monetary cost and a higher opportunity cost. All primary segments of the transit commuting market—city-to-city, suburb-to-city, city-to-suburb, and sub-

---

*Many city residents can attest that poor service deters transit use. I resolved in 1998 to ride the bus from my southwest Minneapolis residence to my downtown workplace whenever practical, but my enthusiasm for the experiment soon waned. Unlike suburbanites riding express buses on HOV freeway lanes, my bus-mates and I traveled slower than the speed of cars, not only stuck in traffic but also stopping at dozens of bus stops, taking 20 minutes longer than a car to reach downtown. In winter mornings I waited at an unsheltered bus stop, often longer than 10 minutes. At the end of the day I endured longer waits—longer than 20 minutes sometimes. It would have been necessary to leave the office before 5:00 p.m. to avoid this idle time at the downtown bus stop, which is too dark and cold in the winter to pass the time reading. Soon I was driving more often than riding.

urb-suburb—have lost market share as service has responded to commercial and residential decentralization.[92]

Intersuburban circumferential routes operate on the outskirts of European cities, but they do so without jeopardizing central-city service. A circumferential light rail line opened outside of Paris in 1992 to connect the suburbs of St. Denis and Bobigny, but these are dense inner suburbs only one mile north of the boundary of Paris, a city that exists in a state of optimal land utilization. As transit service expands in Paris' suburbs, it expands in Paris also. A new Metro line opened in central Paris in 1998.[93]

America's SBCs are promoted as more energy efficient than small commercial sites scattered broadly like a shotgun blast over a vast suburban area. But the scattered sites are less successful at luring transit resources away from the central city; therefore the scattered sites perhaps represent greater energy efficiency than SBCs even if they generate fewer bus trips. Transit decentralization and the attendant reductions in central-city service have contributed to reduced rates of transit ridership and increased rates of auto ownership in the central city. Therefore, it can be said that transit decentralization spoils good transit markets to serve bad transit markets.

If downtowns offered two jobs to two-worker households, and if neighborhood commercial streets offered a full range of commercial amenities—everything from grocery stores to cinemas—and if streetcars still ran on one-minute intervals, central-city neighborhoods would have higher rates of transit ridership and lower rates of automobile ownership. Households with downtown work destinations own fewer cars, on average, than households with suburban work destinations, holding income and neighborhood density constant.[94] Transit's potential to reduce automobile ownership exists primarily if not solely in central cities, and this potential should be exploited.

Commercial decentralization reduces central-city rates of transit ridership and diminishes the competitive position of the city relative to suburbs, which encourages further decentralization. Transit agencies feed this cycle when they decentralize their resources. Good transit is an asset to a city and its neighborhoods; when this asset is diminished, the city's competitive position suffers.[95]

THE NEARLY INFINITE CAPACITY OF THE CENTRAL CITY

It isn't for central-city land shortages that commercial development proliferates in suburbia. Each of America's 65 most populous cities—those with 250,000 or more residents—has a downtown with the capacity for 50 million to 100 million square feet of office and retail space, but only a quarter of these cities have downtown inventories in excess of 20 million square feet.[96] The typical downtown could absorb tens of millions of additional square feet of commercial space at moderate densities without sacrificing architecturally and historically significant buildings or other old buildings that lend character and texture. When a CBD reaches a state of optimal utilization, then it will be appropriate to decentralize commercial development to a nearby transit oriented satellite, such as Paris' La Défense. Today, in all but a few metro areas in the United States, it is premature to develop suburban satellites.

Parisian land was optimally utilized, and the region's rate of transit ridership far surpassed that of any American metropolis, when the modern office towers of La Défense were planned. La Défense and other suburban office developments were built to spare historic Paris from Manhattanization at a time of tremendous pressure to convert historic sectors of the city into American-style CBDs.[97] Paris' central commercial area—its optimally-utilized 10 inner *arrondissements*—nine square miles—contained more than 100-million square feet of commercial, institutional, and cultural floor area as La Défense's office towers were rising. (La Défense, which contained about 20 million square feet of office space in 1990, is nicknamed by the French "Manhattan sur Seine.")[98] New commercial development needn't take historic buildings in the American downtown, where underutilized land is abundant.

America's urban downtowns are in pretty decent shape according to Joel Garreau's assessment: "for all the moaning about the plight of cities, there is really only one major American downtown that has gone to hell in a handbasket, and that is Detroit."[99] This, of course, is a just a rationalization for the promotion of suburban commercial development. All of America's urban downtowns are blighted with parking lots and garages, and all are flanked if not surrounded by a wasteland of obsolete buildings and vacant lots—a "zone of discard" in the words of urban geographer Larry Ford. Outside of downtown, the commercial streets in all of America's distressed neighborhoods are riddled with abandoned buildings and vacant lots (Figure 4-4). A congressional subcommittee reported in 1980 that "the average city has 25 percent of its land vacant" and the percentage probably hasn't changed much. In 1989, Portland, Oregon's, inventory of vacant and underdeveloped land was found to be sufficient to absorb nine times as much development as was projected two decades

Figure 4-4. Halsted Avenue, Chicago (June 2000). Derelict neighborhood commercial streets like this are found within a few miles of downtown in virtually all American cities.

out.[100] The American metropolis decentralizes prematurely, spinning commercial development off to distant suburbs as the core stagnates in underutilization.

Minneapolis is above average among American cities in its land utilization; nonetheless this city has enough grossly underutilized land to comfortably accommodate as much retail and commercial office space as exists in its entire metropolitan area—about 125 million square feet.[101] In other words, the metro area's commercial space could be doubled—more than 50 year's growth—without any further suburban development.

Minneapolis' Central district—downtown and five surrounding neighborhoods—covers 5½ square miles, about half of which was categorized as "undeveloped and unused" by the Minneapolis Planning Department in 1992.[102] Perhaps 50 acres within Minneapolis' CBD have been developed with new office and hotel towers since the planning department's 1992 inventory; outside of downtown, in the city's great zone of discard, the land that has been developed at all has been developed at suburban density. Therefore, approximately 1,800 acres of land in the Central district are ripe for urbane development. If one-quarter of those 1,800 acres were developed as commercial space at a modest floor area ratio (FAR) of 3.8, then 75 million square feet of commercial space would be added in the Central district. (FAR would be higher than 3.8 downtown and lower in the remainder of the Central district; 3.8 is an average.) In this scenario, downtown Minneapolis' density might resemble that of downtown San Francisco, with about 60 million square feet of commercial space; density in the remainder of the Central district would be much lower.

Outside the Central district, Minneapolis has eight primary commercial corridors (in addition to lesser commercial streets) that offer about 16 linear miles of grossly underutilized land: one-story commercial buildings, parking pavement, detached houses, and other manifestations of land value distortion. Ten principal intersections along these primary corridors should be developed as major commercial nodes, each with an average of two million square feet of commercial area (four blocks defining the intersection developed at an average FAR of about 4.0). That adds 20 million square feet. An additional 10 million square feet could be spread out along these corridors, mostly on the first floors of mixed-use buildings.

One of Minneapolis primary commercial corridors is University Avenue, the main link in a chain of three avenues that connect the downtowns of Minneapolis and St. Paul. University Avenue should be developed as an extension of the CBD, lined with midrise and highrise office buildings and served by a subway, like Wilshire Boulevard in Los Angeles. (Many cities have an avenue that stands out as a logical extension of the CBD, such as Woodward Avenue in Detroit and Central Avenue in Phoenix.) University Avenue should be the Twin Cities' premier boulevard, the real and symbolic connection between two great revitalized downtowns, a retail/entertainment extravaganza bolstered by high-density housing, a thoroughfare to rival the grand boulevards of Europe. University Avenue, however, evolves in a different direction—strip malls, fast-food restaurants, and discount department stores, all one-story and all surrounded by parking pavement. They have recently joined the avenue's old car lots, gas stations, industrial buildings, and detached houses. If developed as a CBD extension, University Avenue would accommodate eight million square feet of new commercial space along the one-mile segment between the University of Minnesota and the St. Paul border. (An additional five-mile segment in St. Paul extends to the state capitol at the edge of downtown.)

In an era of de-industrialization, Minneapolis' 1,845 industrial acres offer enormous additional capacity. Develop just 10 percent of the industrial acreage at an average FAR of 1.5 and you add 12 million square feet to increase the total to 125 million square feet of new commercial floor area with only a ripple in the city's skyline (Table 4-3). To look at commercial capacity in more general terms, Minneapolis has 3,057 acres of commercial land according to the planning department's 1992 inventory; this represents 133 million square feet of commercial floor area at an average FAR of 1.0, but the land is developed at an average FAR of perhaps 0.25. Minneapolis' capacity to absorb development is equaled in St. Paul, therefore the two core cities could absorb more than a century's worth of their metropolitan area's commercial development at the current robust growth rate.

Table 4-3. Minneapolis' Capacity to Absorb Commercial Development

	Redevelopment Land Area (acres)	Average FAR	Added Floor Area (sq. ft.)
Central district (5.5 sq. mi.)	450	3.8	75,000,000
Non-CBD commercial nodes	115	4.0	20,000,000
Non-CBD commercial avenues	500	0.5	10,000,000
University Avenue (one mile)	48	3.8	8,000,000
De-industrialized land	185	1.5	12,000,000
TOTALS	1,300	2.2	125,000,000

Source for land areas: Minneapolis Planning Department, *State of the City 2000* (January 2001), p. 42.

APPROPRIATE DECENTRALIZATION

Commercial decentralization is appropriate and necessary in mature cities with optimally utilized cores. Lower Manhattan existed in a state of overutilization (it was crowded beyond the capacity of its infrastructure) when a new subway accelerated the pace of decentralization in 1904, transforming Midtown into the dominant commercial center.[103] The distance between Wall Street and 42nd Street is only 3½ miles, precisely the distance that separates Paris's centrally located First Arrondissement from La Défense.

Midtown is connected to the downtown financial district by three subway lines and four bus routes, and the First Arrondissement is connected to La Défense by two rail transit lines—a local Metro line and a regional RER line. In both cities, the streets between the business concentrations are lined with high-density commercial and residential development. Proximity, high-density development, and high-capacity transit unify the annex core with the fully-utilized original core in both of these cities—each pair functions almost as single core.

Toronto's recent growth follows the examples set by Paris and New York: A pair of modern high-density office and residential developments called "regional commerce centres" lie two and three miles north of

Figure 4-5. Regional Commerce Centre, Toronto. This concentration of high-density commercial and residential development is anchored by the subway station at Eglinton Avenue and Yonge Street, three miles north of downtown. Another centre is anchored by the subway station at St. Clair and Yonge, two miles north of downtown. Retail shops, restaurants, and cinemas are found in these centers.

downtown, above Yonge Street subway stations (Figure 4-5). New York, Paris, and Toronto offer examples of controlled, transit-oriented commercial sub-centers tightly bound by proximity and by transit to the original commercial centers. In these transit rich cities, transit is a viable alternative to the automobile for business trips between business concentrations.

SUMMARY— MONOCENTRICITY/POLYCENTRICITY/NONCENTRICITY

Polycentric commercial decentralization has replaced an inherently transit-efficient single-hub land-use pattern with an inherently transit-inefficient multiple-hub pattern. In the process it has converted riders to drivers. Polycentric development, which has failed to move "everything closer to the homes of the middle class," also has failed to reverse the post-World War II decline in transit ridership. Polycentric development does not represent "an improvement in per capita fuel efficiency over the old suburbia-downtown arrangement" as Joel Garreau imagined. Edge city is not "the crucible of America's urban future."

Policymakers interested in energy efficiency and in the social and environmental benefits associated with low levels of automobile dependence will aim to centralize rather than decentralize commercial development, to redirect it to underutilized core cities. As transportation planner Alan Black said in 1995:

> It is clear that in a centralized, high-density city... people will make shorter trips, and some trips will be on foot. Further, there will be more transit travel because these conditions make transit service more efficient and economical. Both of these factors will cause less automobile travel, which will reduce air pollution and energy use. This is one reason why gasoline consumption per capita is lower in foreign cities than in U.S. Cities.[104]

Population growth accounts for very little of America's increase in vehicle miles of travel according to the U.S. Department of Transportation; the agency attributes as much as 87 percent of the increase in driving to factors influenced by sprawled development patterns (Figure 4-6). Commercial decentralization, whether polycentric or noncentric, is a primary culprit because it undermines transit and boosts the range of residential sprawl.

The polycentrists were wrong to assume that polycentric development saves energy by moving "everything closer to the homes of the middle class." And they were negligent when they ignored the role of transit in metropolitan energy efficiency, to say nothing of its role in the social and environmental health of the metropolis. Until the hundreds of acres of unused and underused commercial and industrial land in the typical American city are put to good use, it is premature of public officials to promote or to abet the continuing decentralization of commerce in the American metropolis.

Federal, state, and regional policymakers truly interested in abating metropolitan automobile dependence will pursue this one objective more vigorously than any other: the recentralization of commerce.

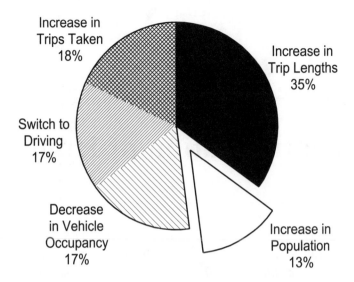

Figure 4-6. Factors contributing to the growth in driving. Household VMT increased 41 percent between 1983 and 1990, while the number of households increased 9 percent. As much as 87 percent of the increased driving was caused by factors influenced by sprawl, according to the U.S. Department of Transportation.

Source: Graphic is from the U.S. Department of Transportation, Federal Transit Administration, *Travel Behavior Issues in the 90s*, (July 1992), p. 14. Growth of households and household VMT reported by U.S. Department of Transportation, Federal Highway Administration, *Summary of Travel Trends: 1995 Nationwide Personal Transportation Survey—Draft* (January 8, 1999), p. 7.

5

Recentralization of Housing

Say the options are to double residential density...within one mile of a downtown...or at a distance of 10 miles from it. In the first case, public transit trips per capita in the affected area will increase seventeen times as much *as in the second case.* REGIONAL PLAN ASSOCIATION[1]

The average suburban household generates 24 percent more vehicle miles of travel (VMT) than the average central-city household.[2] Suburbanites' greater affluence affords them more leisure and vacation driving, but the primary reason suburbanites drive more is that they make more trips each week, and many of their routine trips are longer. In 1990, automobile commuters who lived in developing suburbs surrounding the Twin Cities traveled 23 percent farther to work each day than automobile commuters who lived in Minneapolis and St. Paul. Suburbanites' average nonwork trip was longer as well.[3]

In the Twin Cities metropolis, 93 percent of employed residents in suburbanizing Dakota County own cars, compared to 65 percent of employed residents in Minneapolis and St. Paul, and affluence does not completely explain the difference.[4] Households in Minneapolis and St. Paul own fewer cars than their suburban counterparts of equal income; this is true across the spectrum of income levels.[5] Outer suburbia—America's state of the art in metropolitan development—captures an increasing share of households and drives up metropolitan rates of automobile ownership and dependence.

THE CENTRAL-CITY TRANSIT ADVANTAGE

Only 2.5 percent of suburban workers commuted to their jobs on transit in 1989, representing a steady downward trend, down from 4.6 percent in 1977. Transit's share of all suburban travel nationwide had sunk to 1.3 percent by 1990 because suburbanites use transit for a negligible number of their nonwork trips.[6]

Commuters in high-density cities use transit at higher rates than commuters in low-density cities, but commuters in all cities use transit at higher rates than their suburban counterparts. In the Twin Cities metropolitan area, 12.5 percent of central-city employed residents routinely commuted to work on transit in 1990, compared to only 2.6 percent of suburban workers. In the Portland, Oregon, metropolitan area, 11.3 percent of central-city workers used transit compared to 3.4 percent of suburban workers.[7] The rate of transit use for all trip purposes—work and otherwise—among residents of Minneapolis and St. Paul in 1990 was six times that of residents of developed suburbs, and 14 times that of residents of developing suburbs. Nearly 80 percent of all transit travel in the Twin Cities metro area occurred within the central cities in 1990, even though they contained only 28 percent of the metro area's population.[8]

JOBS-HOUSING BALANCE AND SELF-CONTAINMENT

Any serious attempt to reduce per capita VMT and derive the accompanying social and environmental benefits must begin with a strategy of moving businesses and households closer together—to improve jobs-housing balance, but the strategy can succeed only if focused on the center of the metropolis. Ratios of imbalance are highest in exclusively residential suburbs, but in real numbers, imbalance is nowhere as extreme as in central cities, where the number of jobs grossly outweighs the number of employed residents. In San Francisco, for example, there were 144,000 more jobs than employed residents in 1995, for a ratio of 1.38 jobs for every employed resident. Minneapolis had a higher ratio of 1.46 jobs for each employed resident, and a surplus of about 91,000 jobs. Even after decades of transit-eroding business decentralization, downtowns remain dense employment concentrations to which many, if not most, workers commute from suburbs.[9]

The commuting burden imposed on a city by jobs-housing imbalance is exacerbated by jobs-housing mismatch. Some of a city's employed residents work outside the city, i.e., they are not matched to the city's jobs. Therefore the number of commuters entering a city each day is equal to the city's number of surplus jobs *plus* the city's number of employed residents who leave the city to work each day. In 1995, 94,000 San Francisco residents worked outside their city, to which one would add the city's 144,000 surplus jobs, for a total of 238,000 commuters into the city each day.[10]

A city would minimize commuter travel if it could achieve a numerical balance between its jobs and its housing, and if it could match its jobs to its residents. A city could do both if it were able to selectively export jobs and/or selectively import employed households, but only by selectively importing households will a city improve its fiscal condition, political stature, downtown liveliness, and neighborhood vitality. And what's good for the city is good for the metropolis. The metropolis would realize a reduction in average vehicle miles per commute if the city were able to outcompete its suburbs for employed households, especially those employed in the CBD. If central-city housing growth outweighed suburban growth substantially, metropolitan areas would experience reductions in per-capita VMT not only for work trips but for most categories of travel.

A metropolitan area can dramatically reduce its per-capita VMT if its core city can achieve jobs-housing balance accompanied by self-containment (see Chapter 4). In order to achieve self-containment by means of adding households (rather than relinquishing jobs), cities must concentrate large numbers of households within the limited areas inside their borders. Therefore a self-contained city is by definition a densely populated city, which sustains robust neighborhood retailing—a natural feature of self-containment. A substantially self-contained city is one in which most residents work within a few miles, and shop within a few blocks, of their homes.

In order to maximize their levels of self-containment, cities must do more than simply increase their raw numbers of housing units; they must increase their numbers of high-quality housing units that will appeal to middle- and upper-income households, including families with children, who occupy the high-pay jobs concentrated in the CBD. These high-quality housing units must be built at high densities because affluent households of the urbanite persuasion will not be lured to cities and neighborhoods that lack the cultural and commercial amenities that only high densities can sustain. Households of the suburbanite persuasion should not be targeted in a strategy to improve jobs-housing balance and self-containment in the city because accommodation of those households consumes too much land. Cities will never achieve absolute self-containment, but they will come closest to the goal by targeting the urbanite rather than the suburbanite segment of the housing market. The present magnitude of the jobs-housing imbalance is so large that cities must strive for greater quantities of new households than suburban densities will accommodate.

New downtown housing cannot by itself fulfill the housing requirements of a city that strives to maximize its level of self-containment. Downtown housing has proliferated in American cities in the past three decades, and there is room for much more as industrial land is decommissioned for new use. But the neighborhoods surrounding downtown also must increase their numbers of downtown workers because there isn't enough land area in and adjacent to downtown. The effort to repopulate cities necessarily involves families with children—a major component of the downtown workforce—and most parents demand lower densities than are appropriate for downtown sites. Urban land economics dictate that downtown and adjacent-to-downtown housing will be in apartment buildings, mostly high-rise buildings, which dissuade parents. Toronto officials, for example, have no delusion that families with children will be attracted to their downtown's burgeoning Bay Street Corridor, which they describe as "a high density neighborhood for population comprised primarily of non-family households and family households without children."[11]

Urban residential densities—high densities in and adjacent to downtown and moderate densities in outlying neighborhoods—will maximize the number and variety of housing units available to accommodate the full range of household types—from singles to traditional families with children—in close proximity to their jobs. Residents of urban-density neighborhoods will walk and use transit not only to reach their workplaces, but also to get to stores, restaurants, and cinemas on their reinvigorated commercial streets.

Planners in Toronto recognize that non-poor residents of transit-rich, pedestrian-friendly, urban-density neighborhoods will not give up their cars altogether, but they will use them less often, and many two-adult households will survive with just one car. As noted in Chapter 1, residential densities high enough to support good transit and neighborhood retailing suppress rates of automobile ownership.

STRATEGIC ALLOCATION OF HIGH-DENSITY HOUSING

Planners, policymakers, and academics advocate higher housing densities in suburbs for a variety of reasons these days, including self-containment of suburban communities. But it is infinitely more important to increase housing densities in our central cities because they hold the greatest potential to reduce the social and environmental harm caused by metropolitan automobile dependence. A residential area will produce a high rate of transit ridership only if provided with a high quality of transit service, defined most elementally as *closely spaced routes* and *short headways* (short time intervals between vehicles, i.e. frequent service). Closely spaced routes and short headways are provided more economically close to the CBD than farther away.

The traditional transit route pattern still holds in the American metropolis, where route spacing exceeds a mile in outlying areas and gradually decreases with better proximity to the CBD. The route configuration in Buffalo, New York, where several radial streets are superimposed on the rectangular grid, loosely resembles a spider web in which the cells decrease in size as they converge on the center (Figure 5-1). The center of the metropolis offers the shortest walking distances to bus stops.

The traditional transit route pattern also offers shorter headways to households near the CBD. As scores of transit routes approach a CBD from all directions they converge on select streets. Headways on the CBD side of a point of convergence are only a fraction as long as headways on the far side. In the southwest sector of Minneapolis, three downtown-bound bus routes converge on Hennepin Avenue at a point two miles from downtown, therefore headways within two miles of downtown are one-third as long, on average, as they are beyond the point of convergence. At their outermost reaches into suburbia, these three routes diverge into six branches, the extremities of which offer as few as 10 downtown-bound buses per weekday, compared to 171 buses on the portion of Hennepin Avenue that is within two miles of downtown. Headways on some of the suburban extremities exceed one hour throughout most of the day, compared to 10-minute non-peak headways on Hennepin Avenue.[12]

Because the traditional transit route pattern provides the best service close to the CBD, transit ridership can be maximized by maximizing the number of households close to the CBD. The traditional urban density gradient, in which household density increases as proximity to the CBD improves, maximizes the number of households situated close to a tran-

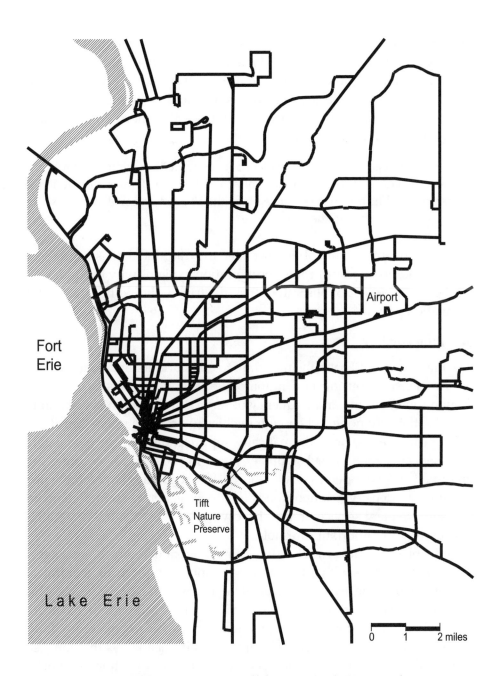

Figure 5-1. Transit Route Pattern in Buffalo, New York. Varying distances between transit routes reveal the location of downtown Buffalo.

Source for route pattern: Niagara Frontier Transportation Authority, "Metro Map," 1994.

sit route. Thus transit will realize its maximum potential in the center of a metropolitan area where the traditional density gradient coexists with the traditional transit route pattern. Transit analysts Boris Pushkarev and Jeffrey Zupan examined the issue of residential density distribution and found that density enhancement is dramatically more effective near downtown than distant from it:

> Say the options are to double residential density…either within one mile of a downtown of 10 million square feet or at a distance of 10 miles from it. In the first case, public transit trips per capita in the affected area will increase *seventeen times as much* as in the second case.[13]

The fundamental compatibility between the traditional density gradient and the traditional transit route configuration explains why the underutilized core of the metropolis, rather than the fringe, should be targeted for population growth.

Schedule Anxiety

Proximity to the CBD, vitally important to transit ridership, is squandered on low-density housing and automobile-dependent households. Even though route spacing and frequency of service are better in cities than in suburbs, they are not good enough in cities to promote much transit use among car owners, or to dramatically suppress rates of car ownership. Route spacing remains substantially intact in most cities, as routes are preserved and extended to serve suburbs. But headways have lengthened because low-density neighborhoods no longer generate enough demand to justify frequent service. In fact, headways on many central-city routes now exceed an important threshold.

Transit planners discern a headway threshold above which passengers concern themselves with schedules; they cannot simply walk to a transit stop and expect the arrival of a transit vehicle within a few minutes. This "schedule-anxiety" threshold was traditionally assumed to be a 20-minute headway (10-minute average wait), however recent studies indicate that today's transit users are impatient with headways that long, so the schedule-anxiety threshold has moved in the direction of shorter headways.[14] Transit routes that offer headways shorter than the schedule-anxiety threshold are significantly advantaged in attracting riders. Parisians, for example, know that their Metro train will arrive within two or three minutes, so they do not concern themselves with schedules or worry that if they miss one train they will have to endure a long wait for the next. Short waiting times greatly enhance the appeal of transit, but headways in this nation's low-density cities have grown longer since the 1950s, and routes that once provided service well within the schedule-anxiety threshold now impose the penalty of a long wait upon passengers who fail to consult schedules. The necessity of knowing transit schedules, and planning around them, exacerbates the inconvenience of transit and weakens its competitive position relative to driving.

Frequent service depends upon high housing densities because low densities produce inadequate farebox revenue, forcing public subsidies beyond acceptable limits. The Institute of Transportation Engineers has calculated that net housing densities of eight units per acre (detached-house densities) can sustain only two buses per hour, or 30-minute headways—well beyond the schedule-anxiety threshold. A level of service considered by transit planners to be "frequent" requires net housing densities of 15 or more units per acre, well above the densities of most neighborhoods in low-density cities (cities of fewer than 7,500 residents per square mile).[15]

Minneapolis' Willard-Hay neighborhood, and some other low-density neighborhoods within a few miles of the CBD, are served by buses that run on 30-minute, or longer, headways throughout much of the day. San Francisco's neighborhoods of townhouses and small apartment buildings, more than twice the density of Minneapolis' neighborhoods on average, are served by light rail trains that run within the schedule-anxiety threshold all day: every 12 minutes during daytime non-peak periods and six-minute intervals at peak periods.[16] The rate of transit commuting for San Francisco residents is more than double the rate for Minneapolis residents, largely because the San Franciscans needn't concern themselves with schedules and long waits.[17]

Transit planners in Toronto, another city with good transit sustained by residential densities more than double those of most U.S. cities, have formulated a simple rule-of-thumb to quantify the relationship between population density and transit sustainability: At 2,000 people per square kilometer (5,180 per square mile) transit cannot compete effectively with the automobile; at 4,000 people per square kilometer (10,360 per square mile) transit is a viable alternative to the automobile, although a public subsidy is required; and at 6,000 people per square kilometer (15,540 per square mile) transit has the potential to pay for itself given good management and a competitive labor environment. The Toronto planners observed that as densities fall below 3,000 people per square kilometer

(7,770 per square mile), automobile use and gasoline consumption increase dramatically.[18] Only 12 of our nation's 67 cities with more than 250,000 residents in 2000 have densities above this threshold of 7,770 people per square mile.

Transit analysts have determined that cutting headways by half increases ridership by 24 to 77 percent, depending on the initial headway, but service frequency in low-density cities has decreased rather than increased.[19] Underfunded transit agencies cannot increase service frequency to neighborhoods of stagnant or declining population levels. Low population densities produce low rates of transit use, and low rates of transit use cause transit agencies to reduce service, which discourages transit use all the more.

DENSITY INVERSION

Until the 1960s, the American metropolitan landscape was typified by a densely developed city surrounded by sprawled suburbs of detached one-family houses, but suburbs have become more densely populated and cities have thinned out. The traditional density gradient—low outer densities gradually building up to a peak at the center—reflected the transit dependence of pre-automobile cities. Widespread use of motor vehicles in the 1920s allowed businesses and workers to separate themselves from the city center, but the general shape of the density gradient remained intact until the 1960s. In the freeway era, the pre-industrial pattern of density distribution was inverted as commerce suburbanized in high concentrations, and suburban housing developed at higher densities than in many central-city neighborhoods.[20]

The traditional density gradient still holds in the most general sense, but it is increasingly adulterated by widely dispersed pockets of high-density suburban development, and by large areas of central-city underutilization and abandonment. This random and chaotic distribution of residential densities, characterized by suburban apartments and townhouses surrounding central-city detached houses, is referred to here as *density inversion*.

In Los Angeles County, more than half of suburbanites now live in areas with greater overall population densities than those of Los Angeles.[21] Apartment buildings and townhouses—urban housing types—proliferate in suburbs today even as many cities increase their supplies of detached houses. More than half of the nation's apartment buildings with more than 10 units were located outside of central cities by 1980. Low-density Atlanta had only 37 percent of its metro area's inventory of 10-plus-unit apartment buildings in 1980, down from 91 percent in 1960; St. Louis experienced a decline of similar magnitude.[22] Minneapolis' affluent inner suburb—Edina—issued building permits for 6,975 housing units in multi-unit buildings from 1970 through 1999, more than four times as many as for detached houses. The proliferation of apartments and town-houses extends to the outer suburbs that are least able to produce transit passengers regardless of housing density. More than half of the housing units in Burnsville, an outer suburb south of Minneapolis, are in multiple-unit buildings; 59 percent of the units built from 1970 through 1999 are in multiple-unit buildings. In Maplewood, a developing suburb of St. Paul, 48 percent of units built in that period are in multiple-unit buildings.[23]

Meanwhile, central cities protect their low-density zoning and promote the construction of one-unit detached houses. Minneapolis and St. Paul, combined, issued building permits for 6,410 detached houses from 1970 through 1999. The land hogs now comprise 44 percent of Minneapolis' housing units and consume 77 percent of the city's residential land.[24] Today's urban landscape is one of cities too sparsely populated and sub-urbs too densely populated.

Rational Residential Density Distribution

A metropolitan citizenry interested in minimizing land consumption, automobile dependence, and immobility among non-drivers will sort out its low-density, moderate-density, and high-density residential develop-ments and distribute them in a rational pattern. Rational residential den-sity distribution is a simple matter of allocating various housing types to the locations where they best serve the social and environmental well-being of the metropolis, i.e., where they can produce metropolitan bene-fits. For each of the several housing types found in the American metropolis, a potential metropolitan benefit accompanies a unique and inherent occupant benefit. *Occupant* and *metropolitan* benefits of various housing types include the following:

Detached house on large (multi-acre) lot:
   Occupant benefit: the ultimate in privacy and seclusion in a natural or agricultural setting.
   Metropolitan benefit: Land remains in its natural state, or in agricultural use, and exerts minimal demand on infrastructure and government serv-ices. Large-lot areas unserved by public utilities represent a reserve of land for future higher-density development in a growing metropolis.

Detached house on standard lot:
Occupant benefit: private ground space, opportunity to engage in gardening and lawn maintenance.
Metropolitan benefit: represents a large stock of owner-occupied housing, which is good for neighborhood stability. (This in not an inherent advantage of single houses; all housing types can be owned. Detached houses make up the highest percentage of owned housing units.)

Townhouse:
Occupant benefit: private ground space with minimal maintenance requirements.
Metropolitan benefit: consumes only a moderate amount of land per household; constitutes a housing density that supports moderate levels of transit service and neighborhood retailing, thereby discouraging automobile use.

Apartment:
Occupant benefit: virtually no property maintenance; highrises provide panoramic views; apartment buildings accommodate smaller, less costly units than are feasible in the form of attached or detached houses.
Metropolitan benefit: consumes a minimal amount of land per household; constitutes a housing density that supports a high level of transit service and neighborhood retailing, thereby minimizing automobile use and maximizing access for automobile-deprived people.

When urban housing types—townhouses and apartments—are developed in suburbs, the inherent occupant benefits are fully realized, but the potential metropolitan benefits are realized only partially, if at all. Many suburban townhouses and apartment buildings stand in the midst of parking pavement and low-density development, isolated in areas that will never see decent transit service or neighborhood retailing. The occupants of these buildings are as automobile-dependent as their detached-house neighbors. In a Twin Cities developing suburb called Inver Grove Heights, a mixed-use development of commercial buildings, detached houses, townhouses, and apartments began to materialize in the mid-1990s adjacent to a new highway interchange. The development, called Arbor Pointe, is bordered by a road on which transit buses occasionally stop, but the apartments and townhouses will be separated from those buses by fields of detached houses. (Figure 5-2). The master plan for the 450-acre site disregards the available transit route because planners know

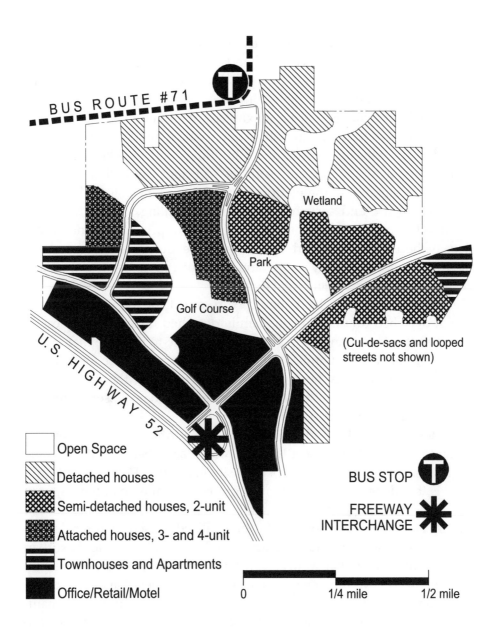

Figure 5-2. Land-use plan for Arbor Pointe, Inver Grove Heights. Arbor Pointe's planners ignored the area's only bus route when they plotted commercial land uses and housing densities. This was not an oversight; buses visit the bus stop infrequently—only 11 buses per weekday. Occupants of the development's apartments and townhouses will be as automobile-dependent as occupants of its detached houses.

Source for land-use arrangement: BRW, "Arbor Pointe Master Plan" (March 1993)

that residents will seldom if ever use it. Many of Arbor Pointe's town-houses are now built and occupied, and they will generate no pedestrian traffic to the bus stop, judging by the abundance of driveways and the scarcity of sidewalks in the development.

Metropolitan benefits will be maximized if urban-density housing is developed close to the metropolitan core, where good transit service is provided cost-effectively. Apartment buildings and townhouses should be regarded as unique urban resources—precious assets that should be carefully positioned in the metropolis to exploit their potential to maxi-mize transit use and sustain neighborhood retailing. Only when cities reach a state of optimal land utilization is it appropriate to extend urban-density housing into suburbia. Then will be the time to expand the metropolis, not randomly and chaotically but rationally, in a way that ensures continuing transit orientation.

Meanwhile, suburban land should be reserved for those who wish to live in detached houses. The one-family detached house is firmly estab-lished as the American ideal, and it is unrealistic to imagine that a high percentage of affluent families will abdicate their preference for it. To the extent this low-density housing must be included in the metropolitan housing mix, it belongs at the outer edge, leaving room closer to the cen-ter for housing of higher density.

(The terms city and suburb are used here as shorthand for *close to the cen-ter* and *farther from the center*; the legal boundaries between the two are irrelevant to the plotting of proper density gradients. The pertinent prin-ciple is that densities should follow a gradient from high at the center to low at the outer edge of the metropolis.)

There are a few exceptions to this generalized prescription for density distribution in and around American cities. First, suburban and exurban freestanding towns that were established before they were absorbed by suburbanization would benefit from a limited number of apartments and townhouses for elderly longtime residents who no longer wish to main-tain their detached houses and lawns. Second, downtowns should be con-nected to airports by rail transit, flanked along the way by high-density or moderate-density development. Third, many central cities would do well to maintain some of their residential green zones—grand old neigh-borhoods of substantial houses situated on or near natural features. If the redevelopment of a green zone to a higher density would necessarily destroy large numbers of mature trees in areas that resemble parks more than subdivisions, then such redevelopment should be considered cautiously. Green zones, unlike gray zones, yield property-tax revenues that more than pay their way.

Green zones, however, hold the greatest potential to attract the most affluent of the metro-area's households, and in many areas that potential should be exploited. Grand mansions once lined Fifth Avenue adjacent to New York City's Central Park, but most were replaced by apartment buildings in a natural process of urban evolution. Today, Fifth Avenue's apartments house affluent residents in large numbers, residents without whom the district's commercial and cultural richness could not be sustained.

Suburban-density Urban Housing

Urban neighborhoods are underpopulated today because reverence for low densities drives housing policy in cities as it should only in suburbs. City officials envision the perpetual maintenance, if not the growth, of their excessive inventories of detached houses, housing that made planning sense a half century ago but does no longer. Today this housing is trapped between post-war suburbs and post-industrial downtowns, hogging precious land needed for apartments and townhouses for the downtown workforce. The land in the neighborhoods surrounding downtown is needed to improve jobs-housing balance and self-containment in the city.

City officials accommodate the low-density preferences of current and prospective residents in ways both passive and active. Passively they allow detached-house zoning to live on. A single detached house on an R-1 lot in Minneapolis consumes twice as much land as a townhouse and 12 times as much land as an apartment unit in a three-story building (at urban ground-coverage rates). Therefore, each single house on an R-1 lot displaces one to eleven potential additional households. These additional households would improve transit service and neighborhood retailing by elevating demand. Actively, city officials fund maintenance and rehab programs for existing detached houses, and they promote the construction of new detached houses. Detached houses represent an obsolete low-intensity land use that city officials should banish to suburbia.

The University of Minnesota is only one mile from downtown Minneapolis, but between them lies a neighborhood oversupplied with detached houses and duplexes. In 1993 the five city council members who constitute the operating committee of the Minneapolis Community Development Agency (MCDA) approved the following plan for the neighborhood: Build four detached one-unit houses at a cost of $567,282, on top of $485,000 already spent for land, demolition, and relocation. Then sell the houses for prices ranging from $85,000 to $98,000, for a net loss of $692,782.[25] This is how desperately city officials strive to retain low densities where they least belong.

At a 1999 conference entitled "Growing Smart in Minnesota," Minneapolis City Council member Lisa McDonald proffered a tactic for strengthening the state's core cities: Encourage owner-occupants of detached houses to upgrade them and stay put, rather than sell and move to better houses in the suburbs. The councilmember recommended a plan book devoted to enlarging and upgrading existing bungalows, Cape Cods, and ramblers. Thus the Minneapolis official used the podium at a "smart growth" conference—a forum focused on reducing metropolitan automobile dependence—to unwittingly promote the continuing automobile dependence of her city.[26]

The federal government enables, if not encourages, city officials to maintain low residential densities. Federal programs such as Community Development Block Grants (CDBG) and Home Ownership Made Easy (HOME) channel funds into cities' affordable housing initiatives, many of which focus on the renovation of existing houses. Minneapolis' Consolidated Plan for fiscal year 1999 earmarks $810,000 in HOME funds "for the treatment of 15-20 vacant, three- and four-bedroom single-family homes in need of renovation..."[27]

Policymakers and developers who accede to consumer demand for suburban housing in cities, and to demand for urban housing in suburbs, impose enormous social and environmental costs on their metropolitan regions. Consumer demand for urban-density housing in suburbs is driven largely by adverse social conditions in the city. Demand for suburban-density housing in the city is driven by a predilection for a hybrid settlement that includes the virtues of both city and country. Critics of modern suburbs impugn suburbanites for trying to reap the benefits of urban life in a rural homestead, but the city resident who insists on having it both ways—city living and country housing—inflicts the greater social and environmental harm.

The city dweller of the suburbanite persuasion prevents proper redevelopment of central land, thereby forcing into suburbanization those who *are* amenable to an urban lifestyle. The proliferation of urban housing types in suburbia evidences considerable market demand for urban life. Many suburban apartment buildings are surrounded not by bucolic landscapes but by other apartment buildings, parking lots, and commercial development; many high-priced suburban apartments provide their affluent occupants with views of adjacent apartment buildings and town-houses rather than lakes and woods. The residents of these apartments represent a market for apartments in decent central-city neighborhoods.

Middle-class urbanites are forced into suburban apartments and town-houses by the city's symbiotic combination of social distress, disreputable schools, low-density zoning, and scarcity of suitable apartments and townhouses. The apartments and townhouses in high-appeal urban neighborhoods are too costly for moderate-income folks because demand exceeds supply. An influx of middle-income households into new urban-density housing in rejuvenated gray zones would go a long way toward rectifying jobs-housing imbalance and relieving inner-city social distress; but such an influx is prevented by the low-density zoning that is bolstered by a misplaced preference for suburban housing.

This misplaced preference drives city officials not only to preserve detached houses, but also to increase their supply, and even to replace higher density housing with the land hogs. Pittsburgh's historic Manchester neighborhood, just across the Allegheny River from down-town, was still occupied by 19th century townhouses in the early 1970s, even though many were abandoned after the 1968 race riots hastened the depopulation of the neighborhood. Realizing that the middle class was fleeing to detached suburban houses, city officials and neighborhood activists adopted a strategy of imitation. More than 400 brick townhouses were demolished to make room for a quarter as many detached houses. Longtime Manchester resident Stanley Lowe, who helped coordinate the misguided redevelopment, recalled with regret, "we decided to build suburbia in the inner city."[28]

In Minneapolis, the Minneapolis Community Development Agency (MCDA) acquires and clears derelict property and installs infrastructure for nonprofit housing developers, who build detached houses on the reconditioned land. One such venture yields a near-downtown subdivision named Lyn Park, whose promoters' unabashed pursuit of suburban-ites is revealed in a sales brochure:

> Lyn Park is…a new residential neighborhood with many of the amenities of a suburban development. Thus, at Lyn Park you can enjoy the convenience of living within walking distance of downtown and the benefits of the suburban lifestyle. Such benefits include living on cul-de-sac streets; having a larger than average city lot; your own driveway with 2 car attached garage and lots of backyard space.[29]

Lyn Park lies at the edge of Minneapolis' Near North district, barely beyond the morning shadows of downtown office towers. Double-wide garage doors dominate the subdivision's split-level houses, situated on curvilinear streets and cul-de-sacs—the standard issue of post-war suburbs (Figure 5-3). But in the heart of the city, Lyn Park represents a gross and tragic underutilization of land. West Broadway Avenue, the devitalized commercial street of the Near North district, is but a block away from the northern edge of Lyn Park. The city neglected an opportunity to endow Near North with a housing development that would support the revitalization of West Broadway. The 41 acres of land devoted to Lyn Park's 129 houses should accommodate 10 to 20 times as many households.

A rail-transit corridor is another location for which high-density housing is the only appropriate housing, but the route of a planned rail-transit link between downtown Minneapolis and the airport is bordered by new detached houses, upon which city officials lavish public resources. Minneapolis officials paid $450,000 for a 23-acre strip of land along Hiawatha Avenue—the future transit corridor—and then developed a dozen detached houses with the expectation that their investment would spark the development of dozens of additional detached houses on the strategically located land. Officials established a standard lot size of nearly 6,000 square feet in order to compete effectively with suburbs for detached-house buyers. As was the case in Lyn Park, the officials' decision to compete with suburbs on suburbs' terms was conscious; the city's project coordinator was quoted by the *Minneapolis Star Tribune*: "Many of our buyers have been out in the suburbs looking. They come here, and they want to see the same thing."[30]

The pursuit of suburbanites by city officials is a nationwide phenomenon. In Cleveland, an eight-acre riot-scarred piece of land has been converted to a middle-class minisuburb called Renaissance Place, with city subsidies for street improvements and a new cul-de-sac. The development's eight acres are devoted to only 20 housing units—detached houses. Among the project's instigators were suburbanites who wanted to continue their lifestyle closer to downtown Cleveland.[31] The city of Detroit intends to convert a derelict neighborhood into a new development of 400 suburb-style houses, at considerable public expense. Detroit tested this concept in the early 1990s, replacing a piece of a distressed neighborhood with an upscale development called Victoria Park—100 suburb-style houses on curvy new streets and cul-de-sacs. The City of Oakland helps a nonprofit developer build Bayport Village—a

5-3a. Suburban apartment buildings in Edina, Minnesota. The Durham (foreground) and the Yorktown Continental are situated near townhouses and additional apartment buildings.

5-3b. Lyn Park in Minneapolis. This "Suburb in the City" was developed with the assistance of the City of Minneapolis.

Figure 5-3. Density Inversion. The apartment buildings in the top photograph are located eight miles south of downtown Minneapolis. Lyn Park is just one mile from downtown Minneapolis.

superblock occupied by 71 detached houses just a half mile from downtown. The city of Los Angeles and the federal government help finance Santa Ana Pines, an emerging development of 114 detached houses in Watts.[32]

In addition to their minisuburbs, city agencies and nonprofit developers build individual detached houses—infill houses—in scattered locations, mostly in distressed neighborhoods. In Cleveland, a nonprofit called Mount Pleasant Now Development Corporation recently built 50 detached houses at dispersed locations, on vacant lots provided by the city, which also offers property-tax abatements to buyers. The houses were financed by a combination of city and state funds. The New Homes for Chicago program, begun in 1990, builds single-detached houses on that city's vacant land, and in November 1999, Mayor Richard Daley announced a $100 million commitment to a new program—HomeStart—which is expected to produce more than 600 single-family homes on city-owned vacant lots throughout the city.[33] In Minneapolis, the Greater Minneapolis Metropolitan Housing Corporation (GMMHC), a nonprofit developer that works in partnership with the MCDA, boasted in its 1996 Annual Report: "GMMHC has built and sold 909 new or rehabilitated single family houses over the past 26 years." All of these houses are in "the inner city." The developer had pledged in 1995 to pick up its pace, announcing a goal of building 100 new single-detached houses annually for the ensuing five years.[34] (Figure 5-4.)

A housing policy predicated on proper density distribution would seek to redevelop distressed neighborhoods not with detached houses but with moderate-density housing, including townhouses and apartments for middle-class families with children. It is unreasonable to assume that these conventional families overwhelmingly favor suburbs because of some inherent affinity for low residential densities; it is doubtful that childbirth converts people of the urbanite persuasion into people of the suburbanite persuasion. It is more likely that childbirth deflects an urbanite family's housing search away from cities, where disorderly neighborhoods and disreputable schools accompany much of the housing stock. Housing in safe neighborhoods with good schools is more plentiful and affordable in suburbs than in cities, where townhouses in high-vitality neighborhoods are costly specialty items. Childbirth redirects a family's priorities away from an urban lifestyle, toward safe streets and good schools. If these qualities were available in high-vitality urban neighborhoods, in which townhouses were priced competitively with suburban detached houses, the urban neighborhoods would compete effectively.

Figure 5-4. Inner-city sprawl (2000). These new infill houses just one mile northwest of downtown Minneapolis are typical of the detached houses built and renovated by the Greater Minneapolis Metropolitan Housing Corporation.

320,000 NEW HOUSEHOLDS

Density enhancement in American cities is hindered by federal and state policies that ensure suburbs an ever-increasing capacity to absorb housing. The federal government requires metropolitan planning organizations (MPOs) to judiciously plan the investment of federal transportation funds. The planning organizations, typically created by state legislatures and appointed by governors, base their transportation planning decisions on trend-based forecasts, a practice that ensures the continuing flow of infrastructure and households to developing suburbs. (Critics of the practice call it "predict and provide.")

The Northeastern Illinois Planning Commission, responsible for coordinating growth in the Chicago region, forecasts rapid growth for the suburbs and slow growth for the underutilized city, whose population density is only three-quarters as high as San Francisco's. Chicago lost more than 600,000 inhabitants in the 24-year period from 1970 to 1994, and the planning organization forecasts that it will take an equal period of time to regain just half that number. The planning organization allocates only 10 percent of the region's growth to Chicago.[35]

In the Twin Cities metropolis, development is shaped by the Metropolitan Council, which forecast an increase of 320,000 households in its metro area in the 25-year period from 1995 to 2020. A paltry 6 percent of those households will end up in the underutilized central cities, according to the council's planning.[36] In an attempt to improve the efficiency of metropolitan development, the council encourages developing suburbs to increase their housing densities.

Minneapolis and St. Paul hold the region's greatest potential to reduce per capita automobile dependence, and to produce the environmental and social benefits that enlightened planners and officials strive to attain. But the central cities are regarded as fully developed, as though they have virtually no land available for expansion of the housing supply. City officials who maintain low-density zoning and abet the production of suburb-style housing near their downtowns force state and regional officials to rely on the advancing fringes of the metropolis to accommodate new households, including apartment dwellers.*

An Exemplary North American City

The underutilized core cities of Minneapolis and St. Paul could absorb 100 percent of their metro area's 25-year growth—all 320,000 households— and still end up with an overall population density lower than that of an exemplary North American city—San Francisco. San Francisco's high and moderate housing densities, which sustain neighborhood commerce and good transit throughout most of the city, should be emulated by low-density cities in growing metropolitan areas, cities such as Minneapolis and St. Paul and scores of others.

San Francisco's undeniable appeal is widely recognized from afar and much appreciated by locals. The late San Francisco journalist Herb Caen told the story of a San Francisco native who died and went to heaven, looked around and said "It's not bad, but it ain't San Francisco." Visitors from the world over admire, and natives appreciate, San Francisco's colorful neighborhoods—North Beach, Chinatown, Nob Hill—and its inclined street-walls of century-old architecture. The city's flatter, more

---

*Minneapolis and St. Paul willingly comply with the Metropolitan Council's anemic growth plans for the central cities. In 1999 the City of Minneapolis enacted a new zoning code that maintains the city's low neighborhood densities. In the same year, St. Paul's city council set a 10-year goal of adding a paltry 300 to 400 housing units annually, or only 3,000 to 4,000 units in the decade. (St. Paul housing goal noted by Kevin Duchschere, "St. Paul Approves Housing Guidelines," *Minneapolis Star Tribune*, 23 March 2000, p. B3.)

remote, less visited neighborhoods—Richmond, Sunset, and Parkside—also provide vitality and visual appeal to their residents. Few cities in the Americas equal San Francisco in overall quality of life, and no American city outside the New York City region equals San Francisco in residential density.

San Francisco's overall housing density is appropriate for American cities even though it produces somewhat lower levels of transit use than New York City's higher density. In the five boroughs of New York City, single houses—attached and detached—account for less than 15 percent of the housing inventory, compared to 32 percent in San Francisco.[37] Cities must include a substantial number of one-unit houses—townhouses—in their inventories for reasons of demographics and economy: city neighborhoods and public schools need an infusion of middle-class families with children—families that demand one-unit houses. And the utilities under existing streets in detached-house neighborhoods will economically handle only a doubling or tripling of housing density. Therefore, a strategy of density enhancement for American cities must include townhouses, including some two-flat and three-flat townhouses, replacing detached houses and duplexes on many streets; and the strategy must include apartment buildings of various sizes on and near neighborhood commercial streets. A density-enhancement strategy for America's devitalized cities should envision neighborhood densities and housing types common in San Francisco.

San Francisco's population density of 16,632 people per square mile (in 2000) is more than double that of most U.S. cities, as is its citywide housing density of about 7,420 units per square mile.[38] San Francisco's effective densities are even higher. Its effective population density is about 18,000 persons per square mile, nearly identical to the population density (in 1996) of another exemplary North American city—Toronto—which like San Francisco is renowned for its middle-class livability. San Francisco's effective citywide housing density is more than 8,000 housing units per square mile. These higher effective densities are derived by deducting from San Francisco's density factors 6 ½ square miles of land—14 percent of the city's total—in Potrero and South Bayshore. This area includes the recently decommissioned Hunter's Point Navy ship repair yard and other industrial land that will be converted to post-industrial use, including housing. That portion of San Francisco that is already developed to a state of substantial completion has a gross housing density that exceeds 8,000 units per square mile, and densities are on the rise even in these substantially completed areas.[39]

San Francisco's housing is distributed among a rich variety of neighborhoods, and a rich variety of housing types within many of those neighborhoods. The housing stock of Russian Hill, Nob Hill, and Pacific Heights consists of townhouses, flats, and a rich variety of apartment buildings—lowrise, midrise, and highrise, old and new, some elegant, some plain. An occasional freestanding mansion offers a yard full of lush flora. Sunset and Parkside are extensive lowrise neighborhoods of townhouses, flats, and small apartment buildings (Figure 5-5). San Francisco's census tracts range in density from 103 housing units per gross acre at the base of Nob Hill, to four units per gross acre in the Twin Peaks green-zone neighborhood.[40] Much of the city's lowest-density housing is found in its most distressed areas.

Figure 5-5. Sunset neighborhood, San Francisco. Townhouses and flats in the Sunset neighborhood yield housing densities three times as high as detached-house densities. Sunset's moderate densities support rail transit and neighborhood retailing, which contribute to the neighborhood's high appeal.

Residential densities in San Francisco's most appealing neighborhoods—Russian Hill, Nob Hill, and Pacific Heights—are triple the densities of the city's outer neighborhoods such as Richmond and Sunset. But these moderate-density neighborhoods of townhouses, flats, and small apartment buildings support good transit and neighborhood retailing, they attract and retain non-poor households, and they remain above the fray of urban decline. Richmond and Sunset, where houses fetch prices above the metro-area median, demonstrate that San Francisco's high appeal can be attributed to more than its hilly terrain and bay views.[41]

San Francisco's urban densities support one of the nation's finest transit systems, with closely spaced routes and frequent service provided by 16 trolley bus routes, 54 diesel bus routes, and three rail modes—light rail, streetcar, and cable car. (Caltrain and BART bring regional service—rapid rail and commuter rail—into the city.) Transit planner Alan Black notes that San Francisco's dense web of transit routes prompts residents to "travel anywhere in the city by transit, even though car ownership is high."[42] In 1998, the *San Francisco Examiner* reported a common bond among city residents—transit use: "An ethnically and culturally diverse population shares a common experience: a ride home on Muni after a hard day's work…"[43] Nearly half of San Francisco residents who also work in San Francisco use transit to get to their jobs, triple the national rate at which central city residents use transit to get to jobs in their home city. Transit would get an even higher share of commutes in San Francisco if nearly 15 percent of the city's resident workers didn't walk or bike to their jobs.[44]

San Francisco's moderate and high densities sustain the city's vitality, which contributes to its high appeal. San Francisco's appeal is evidenced by its housing costs—higher than those in surrounding suburbs, an unusual situation among cities in the United States. The median price for a three-bedroom house in San Francisco was $311,240 in 1997, compared to the Bay Area median of $266,180.[45] The *San Francisco Examiner* surveyed 700 city residents in 1998, and reported that "most respondents have happily resided in their neighborhoods for an average of 12 years and don't want to move."[46]

The low-density cities of Richmond and Oakland are stuck with the Bay Area's expansive gray zones, similar to the gray zones of Minneapolis, St. Paul, and other low-density cities. The population level and land area of Oakland are almost the same as those of Minneapolis, therefore the two cities' population densities are nearly identical—7,121 inhabitants per square mile in Oakland in 2000, and 6,969 in Minneapolis. (St. Paul's population density is 5,438 inhabitants per square mile in 2000.)[47] As is the case in Oakland, Minneapolis and St. Paul's highest-density neighborhoods are among their most appealing.

A relative absence of serious crime elevates San Francisco's quality of life above that of most cities. Minneapolis crime rates were higher than San Francisco's in 1999 across the board—for every index crime tracked by the FBI; Minneapolis' crime rates more closely resemble Oakland's than San Francisco's. Minneapolis' overall crime rate was 3 percent higher than Oakland's in 1999, and 51 percent higher than San Francisco's. Minneapolis' rate of violent crime was 10 percent lower than Oakland's in 1999 and 60 percent higher than San Francisco's. These 1999 relationships among crime rates are not anomalous, they are consistent with those of the decade's earlier years.[48]

San Francisco's densities reflect a cityscape of shoulder-to-shoulder commercial and residential buildings that form richly articulated street-walls, much appreciated by residents and public officials, who are intent on preventing the street erosion inflicted on other cities by automobile dependence.[49] San Francisco's neighborhoods will not succumb to the kind of suburbanization that has defiled cities of lower density. As a general proposition, cities with overall population densities lower than San Francisco's are underutilized and ripe for density enhancement. The Twin Cities metropolitan area is representative of scores of U.S. metro areas in which housing of all types continues to proliferate in suburbs as central-city neighborhoods stagnate in underutilization.

A 50-Year Plan for Density Enhancement

Let's say, hypothetically, that the elected leadership of Minneapolis and St. Paul advised the Metropolitan Council that the core cities are ready to participate meaningfully in the accommodation of their region's population growth. Then the Metropolitan Council, if guided by a sense of social and environmental altruism (another hypothetical), might agree to exert its power to curtail the expansion of suburban capacity in order to redirect growth to the center. Minneapolis and St. Paul might then offer to absorb virtually all, rather than a paltry 6 percent, of the 260,000 housing units that the Metropolitan Council has predicted will be added to the metropolis between the years 2000 and 2020. This would nearly double the cities' year-2000 housing densities. Nonetheless, the cities would reach the year 2020 with a combined gross density substantially less than San Francisco's. If the Twin Cities absorbed the entirety of their metro-area's growth in households until the year 2020, then their combined density would increase from 2,778 to 5,200 housing units per square mile, which is 70 percent of San Francisco's actual density (7,420 units per square mile), and only 65 percent of the livelier city's effective density (8,000 units per square mile).[50] The Twin Cities' housing densities are so very low that 20 years of metro-area population growth cannot boost densities to San Francisco levels.

The Metropolitan Council estimates that about two-thirds of the housing units to be built in its jurisdiction over the next 20 years will be single houses. Therefore, the two core cities would grossly inflate their inventories of single houses if they were to absorb the totality of their metro area's housing growth. They would absorb too many houses to achieve a San Francisco density, even if all the houses were townhouses. The ongoing demand for single houses dictates that some population growth must be directed to developing suburbs.

Minneapolis and St. Paul would reach a higher state of land utilization and vitality by relinquishing most new single houses to suburbs and holding out for 50 years' growth in demand for apartments. Twenty years' worth of apartments is not enough; density enhancement is a long-term proposition that city officials should commence immediately. With their vision extending to the year 2050, officials in Minneapolis and St. Paul might formulate a program of density enhancement with the following key provisions:

1. The central cities will absorb at least 90 percent of the metro-area's new apartment units between the years 2000 and 2050. (The remainder of apartment units would go to freestanding towns captured into the expanding metropolis. There the apartments would accommodate longtime residents wishing to retire to low-maintenance housing without leaving town.)

2. The central cities will absorb one-third of the metro area's new single houses between the years 2000 and 2050. All new central-city houses will be townhouses.

3. In order to make room for new apartments and townhouses during the 50-year period, the central cities will, by means of zoning revisions and development incentives, encourage the demolition of 70 percent of their detached houses, virtually all of their duplexes, and about 20 percent of their existing apartment units—the ones in small, derelict, low-density buildings.

If demand for new housing were to continue through the year 2050 at the rate forecast by the Metropolitan Council for the years 2000 through 2020, then the central cities would avail themselves of more than 200,000 new apartment units under this program of density enhancement. The combined housing density of Minneapolis and St. Paul would grow from about 2,780 units per square mile in the year 2000 to about 6,170 units per square mile in the year 2050 (Table 5-1). The central cities' housing density would be, in the year 2050, eighty-three percent as high as San Francisco's current density. The average net housing density for the two cities would increase from 12 to 25 units per acre, from a density that supports "intermediate" bus service to a density that supports "frequent" service according to transit planners.[51] Furthermore, these higher densities would substantially increase the feasibility of rail transit with short headways in the central cities. These enhanced central-city densities would support good transit by more than doubling the number of households within easy reach of it.

Single houses—attached and detached—would constitute 45 percent of the central cities' housing units in the year 2050, down slightly from approximately 49 percent in 2000; but 87 percent of all single houses would be attached in 2050. Forty thousand existing detached houses, mostly in green zones, would escape the purge of the land hogs, at least for a time. Additional detached houses (and some townhouses) would be purged after the year 2050 as the cities continue to evolve. Continuing evolution would bring also the continuing demolition of low-density (low lot coverage) apartment buildings to make way for apartment buildings of greater density, if not greater height.

Under this 50-year program of density enhancement, 522,000 new central-city housing units (366,000 added units plus 156,000 replacement units) would carry the $1 billion cost of demolishing 156,000 existing units, including 96,000 detached houses. That translates to about $2,000 per new housing unit.[52] Given the depressed value of real estate in gray zones, where redevelopment would occur most prolifically, average land costs for the new units would be less than the prevailing per-unit cost for raw land and new infrastructure in developing suburbs.[53]

Arrested Evolution

Under the density-enhancement scenario outlined above, 1,920 one-family detached houses would succumb to demolition crews in Minneapolis and St. Paul every year, a rate of demolition that would alarm neighborhood activists and affordable-housing advocates. But 1,920 units are only 1.4 percent of the two cities' bloated inventory of approximately 136,000 detached houses in the year 2000. In Minneapolis alone, 14,289 detached houses—18.4 percent of the city's inventory—were considered substandard by the inspections department in 1999.[54] Much of the housing stock

Table 5-1a. Minneapolis-Saint Paul Density Enhancement—Inventories

Housing Type	Estimated Inventory year 2000	%	Minus demo- litions	Units re- maining in 2050	New units 2000 to 2050	Inventory year 2050	%	Net Add
Det. House	136,000	45	96,000	40,000	0	40,000	6	-96,000
Townhouse	12,000	4	0	12,000	248,000	260,000	39	248,000
Duplex	37,000	12	37,000	0	40,000	40,000	6	3,000
Apartment	115,000	38	23,000	92,000	234,000	326,000	49	211,000
Total	300,000	100	156,000	144,000	522,000	666,000	100	366,000
Gross density units/sq. mi.	2,778					6,167		
Average Net density Units/acre	12.2					24.7		

Note: This density enhancement scenario assumes that Minneapolis and Saint Paul's combined residential land area will increase by 2,500 acres, from about 24,500 to about 27,000. In Minneapolis in 1992, 7,538 acres were counted in the commercial, industrial, and "unused" categories; it is assumed at least 1,250 acres of this land will accommodate new housing or mixed-use development that includes housing, and that a similar quantity is available in St. Paul. Commercial property on neighborhood commercial streets, for example, will gain apartments above ground-floor commercial space.

Sources for year 2000 housing inventory estimates: Metropolitan Council, *Community Profiles*, July 1993; Metropolitan Council, Residential Building Permits, 1991 through 1999; Minneapolis Planning Department, *State of the City 1999*, p. 8.
Source for growth forecast: Metropolitan Council, "Preliminary Forecasts of Population, Households and Employment," March 1997.

Table 5-1b. Minneapolis-Saint Paul Density Enhancement —Average Net Densities in the year 2050

Housing type	Number of units	Land consumed (acres)	Average net density (units/acre)
Detached house	40,000	5,510	7.3
Townhouse	260,000	16,414	15.8
Duplex	40,000	1,263	31.7
Apartment: low-rise	190,000	3,276	58.0
Apartment: mid-rise	60,000	300	200.0
Apartment: high-rise	76,000	237	321.0
Totals	666,000	27,000	**24.7**

Notes: (1) Most duplex units are flats in townhouses. (2) Low-rise apartments' average density assumes the average building has 3 residential floors at 50 percent lot coverage. The relatively low density reflects the retention of many existing buildings. (3) Mid-rise apartments' average density assumes the average building is 9 stories high at 60 percent lot coverage. Most mid-rise buildings would be new with higher lot coverage and density-to-height ratios than other building types.

of America's central cities is obsolete, a factor in neighborhood distress. Obsolete housing must be removed to clear the way for a higher level of land utilization.

Healthy urban neighborhoods constantly evolve; buildings are upgraded to retain their utility and appeal, and sometimes old structures are adapted to new uses. These superficial forms of evolution are welcomed by city officials and residents, but a more substantial form of evolution, morphological evolution from suburban to urban densities, is widely resisted. This more dramatic form of evolution is necessary to revitalize gray-zone neighborhoods, which materialized at densities too low to sustain urban vitality today. These neighborhoods must evolve to a higher level of land utilization in order to revitalize.

In many high-vitality neighborhoods, conspicuous evidence of a prior state of lower utilization can still be found. In Boston's North End, for example, the Paul Revere house remains three centuries after it was built, preserved for its historical significance, to reveal the lower densities that once characterized the neighborhood (Figure 5-6). Revere's two-story wooden house lost its original neighbors and stands alone today among four- and five-story tenements and apartment buildings with ground-floor shops, most built in the late 19th century. Had the North End retained its late 17th-century density, it might survive today as an artifact for the amusement of tourists, but it lives on as more than that. It lives on as a vibrant neighborhood because it upgraded its density to a level that sustains the essential ingredients of functioning urban neighborhoods.

Also in Boston, Beacon Hill evolved from a neighborhood of freestanding mansions and wooden houses, early in the 19th century, to the high-density low-rise neighborhood of red brick apartments and townhouses so much admired today. Only a few of the many freestanding mansions and wooden houses that once occupied Beacon Hill survive.[55] Only a few of the 19th-century townhouses that once lined Park Avenue on Manhattan's Upper East Side survive; most were replaced during three distinct periods of evolution during which progressively larger apartment buildings appeared. Park Avenue's evolution culminated in the 1920s with the construction of elegant apartments in 12-story to 16-story buildings, in perfect scale with the broad landscaped boulevard.[56]

The process of morphological evolution reshapes neighborhoods in Vancouver, British Columbia, where nearly 50,000 new households were accommodated between 1971 and 1991, a period of urban depopulation in America. Stately old houses have been sacrificed so that housing den-

Figure 5-6. Paul Revere house, Boston. The two-story wooden house and its five-story neighbors portray the evolution of the North End.

sities can be tripled and quadrupled, a process that allows the Vancouver region to grow without overwhelming its population and its landscape with the cancer of automobile dependence.[57] Vancouver, a city both dynamic and beautiful, evolves toward higher densities because social and environmental concerns trump sentimentality.

Cities and their various districts and neighborhoods evolve or waste away. Conspicuous and dramatic evolution, such as the development of office towers on derelict industrial sites, has revived urban economies; the development of high-density housing on underutilized gray-zone land is no less necessary to revive neighborhood vitality. Detached houses in a gray zone represent a land use no less obsolete than a coal yard on a downtown waterfront. Gray-zone neighborhoods once functioned as complete and largely self-contained entities, but remain neighborhoods only in name because they have failed to evolve in response to new economic and social realities that dictate higher densities to sustain the essential elements of urban life.

Minneapolis officials in the 1920s planned and zoned for a future population of more than one million, a magnitude of population that would sustain the essential elements of urban life that have since wasted away. Seventy years later the city houses a third as many residents as once envisioned by visionaries who wrongly assumed their city's neighborhoods would evolve. Zoning revisions subsequent to the 1920s prevented densities from reaching the anticipated levels.[58]

The Dilution of Poverty

The preceding density-enhancement exercise for Minneapolis and St. Paul demonstrates the capacity of low-density cities to absorb decades of their metropolitan areas' growth in apartments and townhouses, thereby increasing jobs-housing balance, neighborhood vitality, and transit feasibility in the cities. Urban density enhancement would enlarge the metropolitan area's fraction of households that have access, by means of transit or shoe leather, to jobs, retail establishments, and cultural destinations.

Redirecting population growth to cities would produce another important social benefit: the dilution of central-city poverty. Most if not all of America's central cities have higher poverty rates than their surrounding suburbs, so a redirection of population growth into cities would reduce those cities' poverty rates, provided that the rate among the city's newcomers is commensurate with the metro-area's existing rate rather than the city's. Cities' overall rates of poverty would be diluted even though their numbers of poor people would increase somewhat. The 1990 poverty rate for Minneapolis and St. Paul, for example, was 18 percent, and for the metropolitan area it was 8 percent.[59] If the two cities were to double their populations, and if the poverty rate among the central cities' newcomers were to match the metro-area's current 8 percent rate, then the central cities would reduce their combined poverty rate from 18 to 13 percent.

The Salvation of Farmland and the Creation of Urbanity

Central-city density enhancement entails not the removal of forest and farm, but the removal of obsolete central-city houses, to make way for new households in the growing metropolis. Density enhancement envisions not the construction of new suburban infrastructure but the optimization of underutilized urban infrastructure. The 50-year scenario outlined for the Twin Cities would deflect more than 300,000 new households from suburbs to cities (Figure 5-7). About 250,000 of those households are assigned by the Metropolitan Council to land heretofore undeveloped, according to the council's trend based forecasts extended to the year 2050. Those households would consume more than 100 square miles of undeveloped land, and create a market for schools and commercial development that would consume scores of additional square miles. Those households would, in developing suburbs, add monumentally to demand for roadway capacity and other public resources.[60]

The replacement of obsolete inner-city housing by higher-density housing would shift property appreciation from farmland to gray-zone land whose value is artificially suppressed by obsolete zoning classifications and by housing policy that concentrates social distress in cities. Property appreciation would bring the tax revenues that would finance the public amenities that attract and retain the middle class. The most important dividend of density enhancement would be the creation of urbanity where it doesn't exist today. Metropolitan areas with millions of residents ought to be centered by real cities.

THE SPRAWL ARGUMENT

Low-density suburban development exacerbates sprawl, the argument goes, and forces the metropolitan boundary farther afield. Advocates of density inversion would control sprawl by promoting apartments and townhouses, and smaller detached-house lots, in developing suburbs. This proposition presupposes that cities rest in a state of optimal land uti-

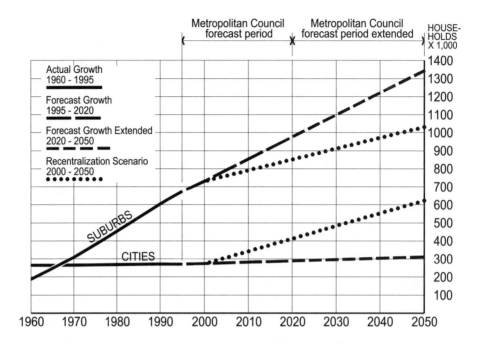

Figure 5-7. Household growth forecast for the Twin Cities area. The Metropolitan Council's trend-based forecast allocates to suburbs 94 percent of the growth in the number of metropolitan households. Dotted lines correspond to the density-enhancement scenario described in the text, which would increase housing density in Minneapolis and Saint Paul to a level that sustains neighborhood commerce and good transit.

Note: The Metropolitan Council has forecast that 13,000 households per year will be added to the metropolitan area in the years 2000 to 2020. That translates to about 13,650 housing units per year, factoring in vacancies and non-household housing units.

lization, unable to absorb much population growth, therefore it is necessary to zone developing suburbs for higher densities in order to restrain the forces of sprawl.

When suburbs are zoned for higher densities and made accessible by new infrastructure, their capacity to absorb population growth is increased, and potential demand for housing in the city is correspondingly decreased. Apartments and townhouses are inherently urban housing types; their availability in suburbs diverts a large segment of the metropolitan housing market from cities. Population growth is not occurring rapidly enough in most metropolitan areas, especially those with the most severely distressed cities, to sustain substantial suburban growth and urban revitalization simultaneously. Promoters of higher suburban densities disregard this simple and crucial fact.

Promoters of higher suburban housing densities overestimate their power to reduce sprawl. Where automobile dependence reigns, every housing unit, even a townhouse or apartment, creates demand for pavement in many locations—supermarket, shopping center, school, church, exercise club, barber shop, restaurant, and on and on, not to mention all the roadway pavement needed to connect the housing unit to all the parking pavement. Only in cities can significant reductions in per-capita parking acreage be achieved. Advocates of higher densities should focus their efforts on cities rather than suburbs.

The most effective way to curtail sprawl is to implement a program of urban neighborhood renewal on a massive scale, and to shift investment in transportation infrastructure from suburbs to cities. Focus middle-class housing subsidies and incentives on cities as well. In a metropolis without growth boundaries and infrastructure discipline, the core city must compete all the more effectively for high-density residential development, and the promotion of apartments and townhouses in suburbia does not help cities' competitive position. Nor does a city's protective attitude toward its deteriorating stock of obsolete detached houses.

THE FALSE PROMISE OF NEOTRADITIONAL PLANNING

Urban-density suburban development has many champions among planners, politicians, academics, and newspaper editorialists, who contend that the higher densities promote transit use, walking, and even "community." In other words, these proponents of density inversion seek for suburbs the traditional but increasingly scarce attributes of cities.

Advocates of higher suburban densities concern themselves, naturally, with suburbs yet to be shaped, but these are the outermost suburbs where higher densities are least likely to promote transit use and neighborhood retailing, and most likely to increase metropolitan per-capita VMT. As noted previously, average distances for routine trips increase with distance from core-city downtowns. Advocates of higher suburban densities overestimate the power of apartment buildings and townhouses to reduce automobile dependence in a suburban context.

Today's preeminent advocates of suburban urbanity are the promoters of neotraditional planning, alternately referred to as New Urbanism or

Traditional Neighborhood Development. Inspired by the conviction that post-war suburbia is unwholesomely automobile dependent, neotraditional planning rejects the principle of separation of home and business. New and improved suburbs—higher density, mixed-use suburbs—should accommodate business places in close proximity to apartments, townhouses, and detached houses with neighborly front porches on compact lots. Then, allegedly, fewer suburbanites will drive to their working, shopping, and social destinations. Neotraditional communities purportedly enable metropolitan society to drive less and socialize more.

Judging by the expansive parking lots at the retail developments in Kentlands, an acclaimed neotraditional community 15 miles north of Washington, D.C., neotraditionalists fail miserably to curtail automobile dependence (Figure 5-8). Kentlands' planners might argue that Kentlands Square shopping center needs its vast parking lot because, as a regional center, it must accommodate the cars of outsiders, but many locals can walk. But many or most of Kentlands' residents live beyond practical walking distance of Kentlands Square and other retail developments, and

Figure 5-8. The ugly truth about neo-traditional suburbs. This is but a small fraction of the vast parking lot at Kentlands Square shopping center.

since the shopping centers in Kentlands generously accommodate cars, many or most local residents no doubt choose to drive. If the regional shopping center of the Kentlands area had been built *outside* Kentlands, then all customers from Kentlands would drive to it in their cars, and because it was built *inside* Kentlands, outsiders arrive in their cars. Automobile dependence is the stark reality of post-war suburbs, neotraditional and otherwise.

The fact that some Kentlands residents can walk to shopping destinations hardly distinguishes the neotraditional suburb from many other post-war suburbs. In Edina, a suburb southwest of Minneapolis, Southdale shopping center is surrounded not only by fast-food restaurants and auto repair shops, but also by several apartment buildings within easy walking distance. All of this post-war development was built as a matter of course long before the neotraditional movement captured the attention of journalists and policymakers, long before there was such a thing as a neotraditional movement. Neotraditionalism is more style than substance.

Michael Southworth, chairman of the University of California planning department, analyzed Kentlands and another acclaimed neotraditional community—Laguna West, 12 miles south of downtown Sacramento—and he concluded that they are "piecemeal efforts...little more than old suburbs in new styles."[61] Southworth found that "neither of the developments achieves the ease of access to retail and office uses, mix of housing types, pedestrian access to daily needs, and overall connectedness found in many small towns or in the early-twentieth-century streetcar suburbs that the neotraditional models emulate...There is little urbanity in the New Urbanism." Southworth says, "like other suburbs, the neotraditional models are essentially anti-urban,...and they exclude much of what it takes to make metropolitan regions work."[62]

Neotraditionalists' efforts to create urban virtues in suburbs divert resources, intellectual energy, and middle-class households from distressed cities. Insofar as households disenchanted with standard suburban subdivisions represent the target market for neotraditional suburbs, neotraditionalists compete with cities for market share. And, diabolically, they compete on the claim that their developments are environmentally healthful.[63] The neotraditionalists cannot, in their neosuburbs, come close to matching cities' capacity to extract metropolitan benefits from urban-density housing.

If the "new urbanists" were any kind of urbanists at all they wouldn't promote the urbanization of suburbs while our urban centers stagnate in underutilization. Those who profess concern for the social and environmental health of the metropolis while cultivating new suburban markets for their architectural and planning practices ought to focus their efforts on deteriorating inner suburbs and existing exurban towns rather than greenfield suburban land. The deteriorating inner suburbs should be reconditioned for, among others, people who insist on living in detached houses close to the urban core. This will include people displaced from their detached houses in the properly evolving city. And the existing main streets of free-standing exurban towns about to be engulfed in suburbanization should be strengthened by new higher-density housing within easy walking distance. Inner suburbs and freestanding towns need and deserve the attention of urbanists.

Gross Misallocation of Resources

Measurable reductions in automobile use will occur only in a compact mixed-use development with enough housing for at least 10,000 residents—the critical mass required to sustain basic neighborhood retailing. The development's housing—apartments and townhouses—would have to be arranged in a dense settlement so that each household is within walking distance of commercial amenities and transit. In order to facilitate convenient patterns of pedestrian movement, public right-of-ways would have to be generously distributed in a fine-grained pattern; blocks would be smaller than the superblocks characteristic of suburban development. Parking would have to be restricted mostly to underground garages; surface lots and garages dilute residential and commercial densities and lengthen walking distances, to say nothing of their deleterious effect on the appeal of the pedestrian environment. Few residents would work in this new community unless its employment base were vast. Local residents would work elsewhere and few would use transit because service would be infrequent and it wouldn't directly serve all the various work destinations to which the community's employed residents travel each day. That problem could be solved only by focusing a new network of transit routes on the new community.

In other words, only a populous, dense, urbane, transit-rich community would measurably mitigate automobile dependence in a developing suburb, and such a community represents a diversion of resources from underutilized cities, where the investment would produce higher rates of transit use and walking. Those who advocate high densities for the developing suburbs that surround low-density cities are promoting an increase in automobile dependence and per-capita VMT in the metropolis, unless they promote suburban development that is denser and more urbane than central-city development, in which case they promote a gross misallocation of resources.

LOCATIONAL-CHOICE ADVOCACY

Neotraditional planners envision mixed-income but predominantly middle-class suburban communities; another faction of the density inversion chorus concerns itself entirely with the housing opportunities of low-income households. Many affluent suburbs exclude these households with zoning codes that mandate large lots for detached houses, and multi-unit housing is excluded altogether from many sectors of developing suburbia. Advocates blame this exclusionary zoning for keeping low-pay jobs, increasingly available in developing suburbs and increasingly unavailable in the inner city, out of the reach of poor households trapped in urban neighborhoods. Build low-cost housing, including apartments and townhouses, in developing suburbs where jobs are being created most rapidly, and the balance between low-pay jobs and low-cost housing will improve, say the advocates. Unemployed inner-city parents would gain access not only to suburban housing and jobs, but also to better schools for their children.

New low-cost housing is necessarily higher in density and lower in quality than many suburbanites welcome into their realms, but locational-choice advocates, metropolitan planning agencies, newspaper editorialists, courts of law, and owners of suburban businesses that depend on low-skill labor, all badger developing suburbs into easing their large-lot zoning requirements and increasing their supplies of low-cost urban-density housing. In the Twin Cities area for example, a locational-choice advocacy group headed by former St. Paul Mayor (and former HUD assistant secretary) George Latimer urged the Metropolitan Council—the Twin Cities' metropolitan planning agency—to push for higher residential densities in developing suburbs in order to accommodate new low-cost housing.[64] None of these opponents of exclusionary zoning proposes that developing suburbs shall restrict their new urban-density housing to poor households, thus they would open the floodgates for developers of increasingly popular high-cost townhouses and condominiums, the housing most sorely needed in cities. Nor do the advocates propose the construction of dormitory housing in the shadows of suburban industrial plants to which workers would walk every day; they envision housing well integrated into suburban communities, housing from which employed residents would drive or take the bus to work. But people who drive to work have some flexibility in their place of residence, and people who bus to work will find better service in developed suburbs than in developing suburbs where service is not well established.

To advocate the construction of new low-cost urban-density housing in developing suburbs is to implicitly or explicitly advocate the further diversion of scarce transit resources to those suburbs. Wealthy large-lot homeowners have no need for transit but many poor households cannot get along without it, which is why locational-choice advocate Barbara Lukermann of the University of Minnesota's Humphrey Institute admonished that "we should be doing a better job of providing transit services…" to the suburban sites of low-cost housing.[65]

Advocates largely ignore the existing abundant supply of modest suburban housing that could be made available to low-income households more economically than units in new buildings. Existing housing scattered throughout the metropolis is an overlooked resource, according to the Twin Cities North Metro Mayors Association, which surveyed the region's housing inventory in 1996 and concluded that, "the region's older housing supply is by far its largest source of affordable housing. It is almost impossible to build new units today at the same affordability levels as the older housing supply."[66]

West Ridge

The year before that report by the North Metro Mayors Association was issued, the Minnesota legislature passed, and the governor signed, the Metropolitan Livable Communities Act (MLCA). This act offers public money to Twin Cities-area municipalities willing to adopt various "livability" goals intended to increase the area's supply of low-cost housing and to reduce automobile dependence. Most suburbs have signed on to the program and many have agreed to increase their residential densities in order to comply.

The legislation established five publicly funded demonstration projects, the most ambitious of which is West Ridge in the recently developed suburb of Minnetonka, west of Minneapolis. West Ridge is an exercise in locational choice combined with neotraditional planning—a development consisting of 392 housing units—apartments and townhouses—and more than a quarter-million square feet of retail space. A small fraction of West Ridge's housing units are reserved for low- and moderate-income households, about which more in Chapter 7. West Ridge is richly rewarded by the public for its contribution to density inversion in the name of housing affordability.

Judging by West Ridge, the MLCA's purported intent to reduce automobile dependence is a sham. West Ridge's 392 units are inadequate to sustain walking-distance convenience retailing, and the development is hemmed in by a freeway, some scattered small office buildings, and a neighborhood of detached houses, so it unlikely to grow to a size and density that will sustain pedestrian-oriented convenience retailing. The development's commercial component is a collection of major chain specialty stores in three large buildings surrounded by parking lots. Residents can walk to these businesses, but few will routinely, for they cannot buy groceries or toothpaste or aspirin at any of these establishments; they can buy computers, golf clubs, and big-screen TVs. Chain restaurants also are included in the commercial mix, and all commercial buildings are oriented to a freeway frontage road and well buffered from each other and from the new housing by parking pavement and loading zones. When residents walk to stores and restaurants from their apartments and townhouses they will walk across parking lots, or they walk lengthy circuitous routes.

Residents can walk to the bus stop too, less than a half mile away at the edge of the freeway, but the shortest route for many is through parking lots and past loading docks. It is safe to predict that only downtown-bound workers will use transit, and only for their work commutes. But downtown-bound workers who are amenable to transit use and to apartment and townhouse living in a mixed-use environment should be housed in the city, not in an outer suburb, especially when public subsidy is involved. On the whole, the residents of West Ridge will be as automobile-dependent as the residents of the neighboring detached houses. And West Ridge's commercial establishments will get approximately 100 percent of their patronage from people arriving in cars.

The townhouses at West Ridge are inspired by those in old New York: street-oriented, narrow and tall—three stories—with high stoops, more urbane in their design than most of the housing built in Minneapolis since World War II. Residents of West Ridge's townhouses, and of many of its high-priced condominium apartments, look out their windows to see other buildings. This is the housing market that cities need to exploit, but housing policy at all levels satisfies the demand for this housing in suburbs too much and in cities too little.

All of the clamoring and badgering by locational-choice advocates in the Twin Cities prompted legislation that helps developing suburbs provide the kind of housing sorely needed in the central cities, where it would do more social and environmental good. For Minneapolis and St. Paul, and their aging inner suburbs, the MLCA includes a provision meant to preserve detached houses in deteriorating neighborhoods.[67] Meanwhile, at suburban West Ridge, 63 detached houses were demolished to make way for the higher-density development.

THE VACANCY CHAIN

If locational-choice advocates were at all interested in the welfare of cities they would relinquish their preoccupation with new housing in developing suburbs and focus instead on existing suburban housing. Some first-ring suburbs are overburdened already with poor households, but not all; and many second-ring suburbs have modest houses within reasonable driving distance of outer suburban jobs. Nondrivers would find better transit service in developed suburbs than in developing suburbs; modest apartment buildings on or near commercialized arterial streets with long-established bus routes are not rare in first-ring and second-ring suburbs. It would be little or no more difficult, and likely easier, to establish transit connections between these existing buildings and suburban low-pay jobs than to establish connections from new housing in the more sparsely developed outer suburbs.

The challenge for policymakers interested in urban revitalization and in suburban housing opportunities for the poor is to reverse the direction of the vacancy chain, to turn it toward the center. Up until now, non-poor households have moved farther and farther away from the center of the metropolis, leaving their aging houses behind for poorer households. Now it is time to create our metropolitan areas' best housing opportunities in rejuvenated city neighborhoods capable of luring a wide range of suburban households of the urbanite persuasion, including middle-class families connected by employment to the CBD, and empty-nesters ready to relinquish their detached houses for new apartments within walking distance of art museums and reclaimed waterfronts. As non-poor suburbanites move toward the center they will leave their aging houses and apartments to poorer households including many from central-city neighborhoods. Urban gentrification has already brought some suburban households back to the city, but just a minute fraction of the number to be hoped for.

The vast majority of low-income households in urban America are accommodated in private housing, most of which has filtered down from middle-class households to successively lower-income households. During the housing shortage of the post-World War II era, the federal government adopted filtering as a deliberate component its low-income housing strategy. The Federal National Mortgage Association's Section 221(d)(3) program increased the supply of low-cost housing not by promoting the construction of it, but rather by stimulating the construction of higher cost housing, thereby freeing up older housing for lower-income households.[68] The application of state and federal housing resources to middle-income housing in cities, rather than to low-income housing in suburbs, would free up aging suburban housing for low-income households while revitalizing city neighborhoods with an essential influx of middle-class households.

The socioeconomic deterioration that now extends into many inner suburbs could be alleviated if the detached houses in those suburbs were acquired and upgraded by city residents with a penchant for detached-house living. Many such residents eschew modern suburban subdivisions, but the detached-house neighborhoods in many inner suburbs resemble the detached-house neighborhoods of their host cities. A flow of middle-class households from detached houses in the city to detached houses in declining inner suburbs would free up city land for redevelopment at appropriate densities while simultaneously upgrading the socioeconomic condition of the inner suburbs.

BANANA

Developers of suburban housing use the acronym BANANA (Build Absolutely Nothing Anywhere Near Anyone) to describe the attitudes of many homeowners in developing suburbs. These homeowners cherish big yards, wide open spaces, and uncongested streets and roads. Residents of Orland Park, a developing suburb southwest of Chicago, objected in 1998 to a proposed six-house subdivision because the five-acre site was too small; the municipality's comprehensive plan mandates a minimum lot size of one acre. In nearby Homer Township, residents resisted the annexation threats of the adjacent municipality of Lockport, which envisions higher residential densities than allowed under Homer Township's land-use plan. Lockport would increase the average density from one dwelling unit per acre to 2.5 dwelling units per acre.[69] Voters in Shorewood, Minnesota, a developing suburb 12 miles west of

Minneapolis, elected a mayor in 1996 who had campaigned on a promise to maintain low densities.[70] In the Twin Cities developing suburb of Woodbury, Minnesota's fastest growing municipality in the late 1990s, citizens protested a comprehensive plan formulated to cut the rate of housing construction by half. Growth under the plan, even though cut in half, would still be too rapid according to the protesters.[71] In November 1998, 240 local and state initiatives to curb development appeared on ballots nationwide, and 72 percent of them passed.[72]

A majority of Americans oppose new housing of higher density in their neighborhoods, according to a 1999 survey by the National Association of Home Builders. This attitude, which prevails throughout metropolitan America, should be disregarded in cities and respected in suburbs. Suburban communities of detached houses are especially vehement in their organized opposition to developers who threaten them with townhouses and apartments, the housing types that the proponents of density inversion would impose on them.[73] Most suburbanites are uninterested in the urbanization of their environs, preferring to avoid the traffic problems and the loss of privacy that ensue.

The outer fringes of the metropolis operate most efficiently with low-density development, specifically with expensive houses on large lots, because such houses generate more than enough property tax revenue to pay for the local government services they consume. Houses valued at less than $165,000 (1996 dollars) generally consume more in services than they produce in tax revenue, according to officials of a Twin Cities developing suburb.[74] As is the case with density, ground coverage should decrease as distance to the CBD increases. If development—house and pavement—were restricted to a given percentage of lot area, say 20 percent maximum, then the builder of a large house with a tennis court would need an extra large lot, most of which would remain in a natural state.

Suburban growth benefits the owners of suburban businesses, and the owners and developers of suburban land, but it is not usually appreciated by the run-of-the-mill suburban homeowner. Planners in fast-growing St. Croix County, Wisconsin, surveyed county residents on growth policy in 1996, but first they categorized the residents according to occupation and interest: government officials, environmentalists, farmers, developers, and the general public. Farmers (landowners) were evenly divided on the question of whether growth was occurring too fast; developers were the only group that strongly supported continuing growth at a fast pace.[75]

LET SUBURBS BE SUBURBS

Once-vibrant commercial avenues in low-density cities increasingly resemble suburban strips. At the same time, policymakers prescribe for suburbs the attributes traditionally associated with cities. Social critics lament the blurring of distinctions among America's various regions—the same chain restaurants, hotels, and retail outlets, and the same architectural styles in housing and commercial development are now found throughout the nation. Likewise, the distinctions between city and suburb are increasingly blurred, a situation with consequences more dire than mere aesthetic disorientation.

Now that the American city is substantially suburbanized, neotraditionalist planners demand the urbanization of suburbs. The neotraditionalists are emboldened by a strong sense of moral and intellectual superiority, bordering on outright contempt for post-war suburbs and their inhabitants. In his 1996 book, *Home from Nowhere*, writer James Howard Kunstler impugns not only suburban subdivisions but also the "subnormal developers" who build them and the "subnormal home buyers" who populate them. Kunstler recounts a conversation he had with some notable proponents of New Urbanism, including Peter Calthorpe, who offered a theory about the flawed design of post-war suburbs. Calthorpe theorized, according to Kunstler, that America's post-war suburbs were designed and developed by war heroes who had returned to America only to suffer mind-deadening lives of perpetual corporate boredom. Family life consisted of mundane parental routines that were insufficiently fulfilling for the returned war adventurers, so they turned to alcohol:

> A whole generation of heroes slipped into a permanent semicoma, soothing their boredom and anomie with heavy doses of hard liquor—their beloved martinis—and living out the rest of their days in an alcoholic fog. This, Calthorpe said, explained why the world they built for us—the suburban sprawl universe—was so incoherent, brutal, ugly, and depressing: *they didn't care about what they were building. They were drunk most of the time, in a stupor.*
> (italics in original)

"These theories admittedly veer into burlesque," writes Kunstler, "but there is still much to admire in them."[76] Kunstler suggests that post-war suburban life turns teenagers into potheads; referring to his teenage acquaintances in suburban Long Island, he wrote, "By puberty they had entered a kind of coma. There was so little for them to do.... Since they had no public gathering places, teens congregated in furtive little holes—bedrooms and basements—to smoke pot."[77] Philip Langdon, another promoter of neotraditional suburbs, proclaims: "A modern suburb is an instrument for making people stupid."[78] The deficiencies and alleged deficiencies of America's post-war suburbs are documented in literature that dates back at least to 1956 when John Keats blamed suburban subdivisions for destroying the individuality of their inhabitants. Suburban developments, according to Keats, are "conceived in error, nurtured by greed, corroding everything they touch."[79] In 1957 the *Chicago Daily News* blamed "new suburban development" for turning boys into "little sissies."[80]

Hate not and pity not the suburbanite. "Everyone loves to hate the suburbs except for the people who live there," observed Iver Peterson, writing for the *New York Times* in December 1999. Peterson reports the emergence of a new wave of literature in which "academic revisionists are reporting that suburbia, far from crushing lives, has had a liberating effect on residents...They have found that the sense of community can be as strong on a suburban block as it is in a small town." Peterson cites historians, professors of planning, and authorities on American culture who characterize today's familiar litany of criticism as cliché unsupported by research and contradicted by evidence.[81]

Just one recent example of contradictory evidence: In the summer of 1998 a violent storm damaged some houses in a sprawling new subdivision in Woodbury, a developing suburb east of St. Paul, so the temporarily homeless occupants banded together for mutual assistance and support. Catastrophe binds disparate and mutually unfamiliar people together, but the storm wasn't responsible for the social cohesion of the Woodbury families; they had formed strong bonds of friendship soon after they moved into their new suburban houses.[82]

Underutilized cities would benefit if those who make and influence policy would let suburbs be suburbs, as constituted in the post-war decade and as desired by many suburbanites: low-density tracts of one-family houses. Then perhaps cities could once again become cities. If the growing middle-class demand for apartments and townhouses proximate to commercial amenities cannot be met in suburbs, then the urbanites of the metropolis will have to look to revitalized cities to satisfy their housing preferences. If policymakers insist on bestowing upon suburbs the virtues of cities, then they should emulate the southern European example of high-density suburbs tightly bound to fully utilized core cities by proximity and by transit. Consideration of such a paradigm might force policymakers to realize the magnitude of central-area underutilization, and to realize that it makes sense to first bestow upon cities the virtues of cities.

Locational-choice advocates excoriate the large-lot exclusionary zoning of affluent developing suburbs, when the low-density exclusionary zoning enforced by cities is the real problem. New Urbanists fret about the single-use sprawls of porchless detached houses in post-war subdivisions, when the city's commercially devitalized neighborhoods of obsolete houses more urgently need whatever intellectual energy and public resources are available in the metropolis. The absence of traditional downtowns in post-war suburbs is a minor social problem in America. The absence of front porches on suburban houses does not cause social and economic distress, as does the absence of middle-class families in the inner city. Better to recapture the lost essence of the traditional neighborhood in cities than to try to create it anew in suburbs. The enhancement of suburbs subverts cities' prospects of regaining the middle class.

The increasing availability of apartments and entertainment establishments in suburbs undermines cities' ability to compete even for those households long associated with urban lifestyles. David Varady and Jeffrey Raffel, professors of planning and public administration, researched cities' competitive positions in their metro areas and concluded, "the dispersion of multi-family housing and entertainment spots to the suburbs has increased the attraction of 'nontraditional households' such as singles, couples without children, and gays to suburban areas."[83] Housing opportunities for these households are now more abundant in many suburbs than in their low-density host cities.

Sparsely populated land generates less demand, per square mile, for commercial development and public facilities than densely developed land. Sparsely populated suburban land generates fewer if not shorter automobile trips per square mile. Sparsely populated suburban land generates little demand for transit resources. Pockets of high suburban densities motivate transit agencies to decentralize their transit resources to serve transit-averse suburbs at the expense of potentially transit-efficient cities. In April 2000, the Twin Cities Metropolitan Council approved a four-year, $165 million plan, which, according to the *Minneapolis Star Tribune*, "signals their intentions for the region. The emphasis was on making buses a more attractive option for suburbanites…" The council is especially generous to developing suburbs that have built or planned according to the council's precepts for metropolitan growth, i.e., outer suburbs that facilitate the development of apartments, townhouses, and business concentrations.[84]

High-density suburban development enlarges the capacity of outlying land to absorb households and all that they demand. Unless a metropolitan area's suburban capacity is limited by legal mandate to a finite number of households, high suburban densities undermine cities more than low suburban densities. But advocates of higher suburban densities do not stipulate that the higher densities shall be accompanied by a strict limitation on the capacity of the suburban realm to absorb metropolitan growth. Nor do the advocates stipulate that low-density neighborhoods in underutilized cities shall be densed up first. They don't stipulate that higher-density development should occur only where transit service is firmly established. They don't suggest that undeveloped suburban land should be held in reserve to absorb higher-density development in the future, along transit lines, after central cities are repopulated and revitalized; advocates of density inversion advocate in the present tense. Locational-choice advocates do not stipulate that apartments and townhouses in outer suburbs shall be limited to poor households so that middle-class seekers of apartments and townhouses will have to consider the city.*

Higher-density suburban development should occur only along fixed transit routes—mostly rail transit routes—emanating from optimally utilized cities. Unlike the historic core of the transit-rich European metropolis, the American city is not yet fully developed. Promoters of higher-density suburbs in the U.S. do not stipulate the attributes of European urbanization as a prerequisite.

THE MARKET FOR URBAN NEIGHBORHOODS

Housing preference surveys, including one by the National Association of Home Builders, consistently indicate that about 80 percent of the market prefers detached houses to townhouses and apartments, but these surveys do not factor in the greater neighborhood amenity to be expected in a healthy, high-density urban setting. Professor Robert Cervero found

---

*In *Suburban Nation*, Andres Duany, et.al. (2000) acknowledge that "urban infill" sites should be assigned a higher priority for development than suburban greenfields (p. 145); but then they lay out a rationale for developing suburban greenfields now (p. 185). Moreover, they praise low central-city densities. They proudly claim some of the credit for the construction of 81 detached houses in Cleveland (p.136) and they object to cities "raising their zoning capacity" (p. 173). Most troubling, they dismiss urban neighborhoods as unfit for middle-class families: "revitalization efforts should not focus unduly on bringing families back to the inner city. In truth, many urban neighborhoods do quite well in the absence of children." (p. 172)

greater acceptance of higher densities when he factored neighborhood amenity into his housing preference survey in the San Francisco Bay Area. Cervero tested the potential market for urban-density housing by measuring Bay Area residents' reactions to four neighborhoods, one of detached houses, one of townhouses, one of smaller townhouses, and one of apartments. Greater numbers of retail stores came with increasing housing density, a reasonable real-world expectation; and, as a compensation for a shortage of private outdoor space, the two neighborhoods of highest density included public parks. Cervero simulated a walk through each of the four neighborhoods using computer-generated images composed of digitized photographs. The simulations were designed to isolate housing type and neighborhood amenity as the only variables (architectural style, for example, was the same in all neighborhoods).

A majority of participants—58.2 percent—chose the detached-house neighborhood as their favorite, but more than 40 percent chose a more urbane environment. (The townhouse neighborhoods were favored by 22.4 percent, and 19.4 percent favored the apartment neighborhood.)[85] It is reasonable to conclude that in a metropolitan area with two million residents, at least 25 percent—500,000—would prefer to live in a neighborhood of apartments, townhouses, and commercial vitality, flanked by other such neighborhoods, all of which combine to support good transit and a lively downtown. Many metropolitan residents who prefer detached houses live in apartments and townhouses out of financial necessity. There is a substantial market for urbane housing and cities should pursue this market to the exclusion of all others. The creation of urban environments where they are absent but attainable—in the centers of populous metropolitan areas—would not only provide housing opportunities for urbanites, it would also produce important and far-reaching social and environmental benefits.

The post-war proliferation of suburban apartments and townhouses reflects substantial demand for housing traditionally associated with cities. A simple redirection of residential densities would restore to our metropolitan areas the option to live a socially and environmentally agreeable lifestyle, an option that has disappeared from most American cities.

LIFESTYLE RAMIFICATIONS

The density redistribution proposed here would revitalize cities—neighborhoods and downtowns—and it would bring all the social and envi-

ronmental benefits associated with reduced rates of automobile dependence. Density redistribution would dilute central-city poverty. For all
these benefits, the lifestyle concessions would be insignificant for most of
the metropolitan population. Assuming that social order, good schools,
and commercial recentralization would accompany the recentralization of
multiple-unit middle-class housing, a residential density redistribution
such as that proposed here would impose these lifestyle changes on metropolitan residents:

1. Many single-house occupants would do without side yards because a
higher fraction of single houses would be townhouses. Townhouse occupants would have private rear yards and small front gardens, and they
would be freed of many of the maintenance chores associated with
detached houses.

2. Commute times would increase somewhat for some workers who
switch from automobiles to transit. But they would get much if not all of
that time back; they would spend less time gassing up and servicing their
cars, and they would read the newspaper or a book on the way to work.
Some downtown workers who need a car occasionally for business
would nonetheless commute by transit because some of their coworkers
would commute in company cars that would be pooled for business use.

3. Many two-adult households would survive nicely with one rather
than two cars. These households would recapture the hundreds of hours
that it takes each year to earn the money to own, operate, and maintain
each car. Many households would revert to the situation prevalent in the
"recreational auto era" of this century's early decades, when cars were
used by city residents for weekend outings and recreational purposes
rather than for routine daily transportation.[86]

4. People would pay for parking at more of their destinations. For example, a transit-averse suburbanite who wishes to partake in the urban experience of seeing a movie and then walking to an Italian restaurant other
than the Olive Garden would drive toward the center of the metropolis,
perhaps to a community commercial street, and park in a discreetly-sited
parking garage. The garage would be used during the day by patrons of
the area's retail businesses, and during the evening by patrons of the
area's restaurants and cinemas. Most patrons of these establishments
would arrive on foot or on transit, but others would drive and park, and
they would pay a nominal fee for the privilege.

The cost of housing is higher in high-vitality cities than in low-vitality
cities, but, as noted in Chapter 2, incomes are higher also, and the cost of

car ownership can be eliminated or reduced in high-vitality cities. Tragically, concerns about housing costs dampen the pursuit of vitality. The editor of a Minneapolis community newspaper opined, "we don't want to be a San Francisco, where the only people who can live in the city itself are the wealthy—or the homeless."[87]

The editor exaggerates. Housing costs in San Francisco's famous neighborhoods are astronomical compared to costs in Minneapolis, but more than 100,000 San Francisco units are affordable to middle-class folks. Average and median housing costs are higher in San Francisco than in Minneapolis, but the livelier city probably has more units affordable to the middle class, for the livelier city has twice as many units as Minneapolis (on less land area).[88]

It is true that San Francisco offers less house for the dollar than Minneapolis does; this is because San Francisco's valuable land spikes housing costs. An effective way to suppress a city's cost of housing is to suppress its land value, and that is done by maintaining low densities, thereby suppressing vitality. The rich are attracted to only two kinds of metropolitan living environment: secluded suburbs and high-vitality cities; that is why housing costs are high in high-vitality cities. It is grossly irresponsible for city leaders to shun the rich.

Rather than suppress housing values, city governments should enhance densities in order to accommodate an influx of middle-class and rich folks alike. Middle-class people who want more house than they can afford in the city will find it in suburbs where land is less precious. No one who appreciates real cities would disagree with this proposition: It is better to live *near* a high-vitality city than to live *in* a low-vitality city.

As a matter of fact, revitalization by means of recentralization (the only means) should suppress housing costs for a period of decades. Costs are high where demand for housing is strong relative to supply, and land is the big variable in cost extremes. Upzoning in the city would, with a pen stroke, flood the market with enough land for hundreds of thousands of housing units. This would suppress the cost of housing until most of the upzoned land is absorbed. Revitalization would eventually bring higher land values, but the per-unit cost of land would be held in check as long as a generous supply of upzoned land is available for new housing. Low-density cities hold considerable power, by means of upzoning, to suppress their metropolitan area's land values.

SUMMARY

On November 12, 1999, the Minneapolis City Council adopted a new zoning code formulated to perpetuate low residential densities in the city's neighborhoods. Less than five months later, the Metropolitan Council agreed to expand the supply of outer suburban land available for residential development. Ted Mondale, the Metropolitan Council's chairman, urges higher densities on the expanded supply of suburban land.[89]

The failure to allocate metropolitan development geographically according to density is at the root of the urban transportation crisis. Chaotic density distribution in the American metropolis is evidenced by suburban apartments and townhouses dependent on a web of roadways that carry few transit vehicles, and by central-city detached houses that produce little demand for transit. Transit feasibility is the most tragic casualty of chaotic density distribution. Nonetheless, apartment and townhouse development proliferates throughout suburbia while city officials guard the sanctity of detached houses and low-density zoning in their near-downtown neighborhoods. The attitude that cities are fully developed—filled to capacity—is not unrealistic in view of the political condition of cities.

Our metro areas are rich in housing opportunities for those with an affinity for gardening and landscaping and automobile ownership, and poor in opportunities for those who seek a more urbane lifestyle. City residents increasingly live a lifestyle marked by automobile dependence—a suburban lifestyle. The urban lifestyle is the most socially beneficial and environmentally benign lifestyle available in the metropolis, but in America that lifestyle remains available only to the residents of a handful of neighborhoods in a few cities.

Two concerted density-related policy objectives are required to achieve significant and enduring urban revitalization: First, federal, state, and regional governments must curtail infrastructure and transportation investment that promotes any but very-low-density development in suburbs, and they must maintain these policies until cities are repopulated and revitalized. And second, cities must adopt zoning and development policies to promote the repopulation of their neighborhoods by middle-class households in high- and moderate-density housing. In support of these policies, property taxes should be reformulated to penalize low central-area densities and high outer densities. The hearts of our metropolitan areas will remain cities in name only until these policies are seriously pursued.

6

Recentralization of Transportation Infrastructure

The history of the struggle over transportation at all geographic scales is filled with the obvious recognition that the location of transportation affects the accumulation of...wealth. URBAN GEOGRAPHER DAVID C. HODGE[1]

Minnesota's liberal senator beamed like a proud father as he cut the ribbon with a giant pair of ceremonial scissors. With that gesture Senator Paul Wellstone, joined by an equally ebullient Jim Ramstad—Minnesota's Republican U.S. Representative—opened a floodgate through which jobs and middle-class families would flow into the rural hinterland south of the Twin Cities. On that special day in October 1995, the sylvan land around the town of Shakopee, fifteen miles southwest of downtown Minneapolis, was primed for large-scale development by the opening of the new Bloomington Ferry Bridge, built at a cost of $138 million, $100 million of it from the federal government. The mile-long bridge extends the range of metropolitan decentralization into an area long secluded from the Twin Cities by the Minnesota River, a natural barrier that had "really stymied growth," according to a Shakopee official.[2]

Prior to the October 1995 ribbon-cutting ceremony, Shakopee and surrounding Scott County had been connected to the metropolis by a low-capacity bridge set close to the water line, prone to flooding. The new bridge is much more than a loftier replacement. With six lanes, 120 feet wide, the new bridge is a virtual freeway projected to carry 60,000 vehicles a day, triple the number on the two-lane bridge it replaced. But it would make no sense to connect a high-capacity bridge to a low-capacity road, so the feeder road was widened, and new interchanges and access roads were built. The new bridge is but one link in the metropolitan area's growing web of high-capacity suburban roadways.

Shakopee's assistant administrator reported that developers' inquiries "skyrocketed" as the bridge neared completion, and he added, "we certainly expect a surge in economic activity in every sector." At the time of the bridge's inauguration, the editor of the *Minnesota Real Estate Journal* enthused, "The significance of the opening of the Bloomington Ferry Bridge is big…The opening of the bridge should attract more residential development followed by industrial, office and retail."[3] The director of Shakopee's Chamber of Commerce exclaimed, "the boom is coming."[4] By 1998, the Shakopee area was among the metro-area leaders in residential and retail growth (Figure 6-1) and in 1999 the U.S. Census Bureau reported that the municipality of Savage, adjacent to Shakopee and just a half mile from the new bridge's interchange, is Minnesota's second-fastest growing municipality.[5]

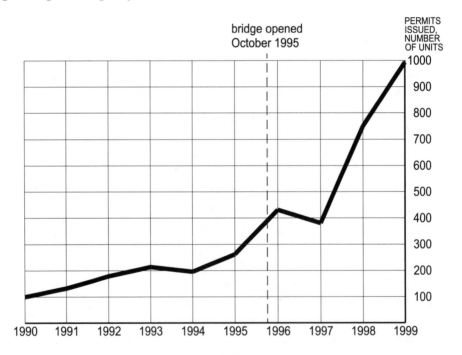

Figure 6-1. Trend in Residential Construction in Shakopee, Minnesota. The construction of the Bloomington Ferry Bridge brought a dramatic increase in the rate at which residential building permits are issued in Shakopee.

Source of data: Metropolitan Council, *Regional Population, Household, and Construction Trends* (April 1999) and Residential Building Permits Issued in the Twin Cities Metropolitan Area (1995–1999)

Access is everything to land speculators and developers. "Obviously, without access, you can't sell it or build on it or do anything with it," said Arizona state senator Rusty Bowers, pleading for roadway access to some land outside Phoenix.[6] The Realtors' mantra *location, location, location* translates *access, access, access*, and suburban access is generously enlarged by state departments of transportation (more aptly called "highway departments" until the 1980s). The potent synergy among departments of transportation, federal highway money, suburban municipal and county officials, and private land developers feeds the growth of suburbs and abets the stagnation of cities.

PRIMING ACTIONS AND CHAIN REACTIONS

Hezekiah Pierrepont's farmland in Brooklyn was inaccessible to the masses who worked in the densely congregated commercial buildings of lower Manhattan, until 1818. That's when Robert Fulton's steam ferries began transporting passengers across the East River every day. The ferry service that transformed Pierrepont's farm into a suburb was not a fortuitous turn of events with which Pierrepont was uninvolved; the landowner was a major investor in the venture.[7]

Similar events played out on the other side of the continent about a half century later. A report in the December 12, 1876, edition of the *Oakland Daily Evening Tribune* explains why three of Oakland's land barons founded the Broadway & Piedmont streetcar line:

> This was a private enterprise projected by Walter Blair and Samuel and Montgomery Howe solely to give access to their landed property and to enhance the value of the property along the line. The increase in the value of property along the line as well as the high volume of sales which has accompanied the new line has proved the wisdom of the enterprise.[8]

The tactic had become routine by 1920, the year Oris and Mantis Van Sweringen completed the extension of a railroad line they had purchased solely to improve access to their 4,000 acres just east of Cleveland. Within 10 years of completing their rail connection, the two brothers increased the population of their exclusive residential development called Shaker Village (now Shaker Heights) from 1,600 to 18,000. On the developing outskirts of Boston, Atlanta, Minneapolis, Los Angeles, and cities across America, landowners created their own access and thereby raised the value of their land. As Kenneth T. Jackson notes in his history of American suburbanization, "Transit tycoons were less interested in the nickels in the fare box than they were in their personal land development schemes."[9]

In America today it is the public rather than private sector that endows suburban land with the accessibility that multiplies its value; it is the public sector that determines the patterns of access that shape the patterns of land use. The shape of the metropolis is influenced by internal and external factors that include economic and demographic conditions and geographic and geologic features. But none of these is more powerful than the political factors that determine the nature and location of infrastructure investment. Mountains are tunneled and rivers are bridged where political will is marshaled. The opening of the Bloomington Ferry Bridge prompted this observation by the editor of the *Minnesota Real Estate Journal:* "Population growth in the Twin Cities is not constricted by natural boundaries."[10]

The most influential of infrastructure investments, known to planners as priming actions, trigger chain reactions of subsequent development—both public and private.[11] Throughout America's history, transportation priming actions—seaports in the 18th century, railroads in the 19th, and roadways in the 20th—have shaped land development. The priming action that most profoundly affects the form of the post-war metropolis is the federally-sponsored metropolitan freeway, which has become the backbone of metropolitan transportation, spawning adjacent roadway construction and opening vast new land areas to high-volume access. "The maturing freeway system was the primary force that turned the metropolis inside out after 1970, because it eliminated the region wide centrality advantage of the central city's CBD," according to urban geographer Peter O. Muller.[12]

In a most conspicuous example of the phenomenon, Chicago's CBD lost the corporate headquarters of Sears Roebuck and Company in 1992 when the organization moved from its landmark tower to new digs in the Schaumburg agglomeration at the intersection of Interstates 90 and 290, twenty-four miles northwest of the Loop. Schaumburg Township was a small village settlement, distant from important trade routes, prior to the coming of the freeways. Eight miles south of downtown Minneapolis, a new corporate headquarters is about to replace Wally McCarthy's Oldsmobile dealership at the intersection of Interstates 494 and 35. McCarthy calls this land "the best location in the state of Minnesota."[13] Toronto's planning commissioner David Gurin calls America's federal freeway dollars "cataclysmic money." Gurin was a transportation official in the U.S. before he assumed his post in Toronto, and he blames "10-cent dollars from Washington" for the fact that American cities deteriorated while Canadian cities flourished.[14]

By 1995, our national government had funded more than 12,000 miles of interstate within metropolitan areas. These freeways set off chain reactions of suburban real estate development and demand for additional tens of thousands of miles of highway and roadway, all to feed yet more suburban real estate development.[15] Interstate 494 accelerated the pace of suburban expansion south of Minneapolis and St. Paul when it was completed in the mid-1980s, and in 1995 a spokesman for the Minnesota Department of Transportation explained that this freeway-induced suburban expansion is what prompted his agency to build a new highway extension and interchange that had just opened in suburban Inver Grove Heights: "as suburban sprawl spread, more access became necessary."[16] Not only did the new highway project improve access to extant households and businesses, it triggered a new wave of land development.

Today a development called Arbor Pointe partially engulfs the new interchange. When complete, Arbor Pointe will include a half million square feet of commercial space and 1,250 housing units on the front line of suburbanization, on land that was rural before it was ripened for development by the new highway extension and interchange. Arbor Pointe will inevitably be followed by additional development: "Development follows transportation, and we are looking forward to more development in the area," said Bill Lucking, representing Inver Grove Heights business people who had eagerly awaited completion of the new highway project.[17] All this new development will contribute to demand for yet more transportation investment. That's how the American system of metropolitan decentralization cycles forward; roadway investment triggers land development, which then justifies further roadway investment.

Mode imbalance

Interstate freeways account for more than half of all high-speed, limited-access, multiple-lane roadways, known as freeways or expressways, in America's metropolitan areas. The total mileage of such roadways is about 23,000. By contrast, metropolitan America has, at the turn of the millennium, only 4,400 miles of rail-transit route (including 3,150 miles of commuter rail) for a ratio of more than five miles of metropolitan freeway to every mile of rail-transit route. Even with 45 miles of MARTA rail in place, the ratio of freeway to rail-transit miles in Atlanta's seven-county metropolis is six to one.[18]

Rails and roads are better balanced in and around European and Canadian cities, most of which have been spared the circumferential freeways of America's big cities. In the Vancouver metropolitan area, where freeways terminate far outside the CBD, the ratio of freeway miles to rail transit miles is three to one. In Metropolitan Toronto, the ratio of freeway miles to rail transit miles is less than one to one. (Toronto's ratio would be even lower if its dozens of miles of streetcar route were included. The streetcar mileage is excluded here because, functionally, Toronto's streetcars resemble bus transit.)[19]

Urban highways are transit corridors too, they carry buses. In the American metropolis, however, bus riders account for a negligible fraction of highway travelers. The Twin Cities area's busiest freeway—Interstate 35W—carries 11,000 transit passengers a day in more than 300 buses, according a report issued by Minnesota Department of Transportation in support of an expansion project. But those 11,000 transit passengers represent less than 4 percent of the number of people transported in private vehicles each day.[20] Departments of transportation do not plan metropolitan roadways as transit routes. High-occupancy-vehicle (HOV) lanes are typically available to cars carrying as few as two occupants. Metropolitan roadways are planned for, built for, and overwhelmingly used by private vehicles; transit use is incidental and negligible.

Since the inception of federal transit funding in 1964 (forty-eight years after the inception of highway funding), highways have consistently received a disproportionately large share of the dollars, four out of five in 1990. ISTEA (1991) and its successor TEA-21 (1998) earmark more than 80 percent of their multi year appropriations for roads and bridges and less than 20 percent for transit.* These funding priorities would make sense if

---

*A portion of ISTEA's and TEA-21's funds are transferable from road projects to transit, but a study by the Brookings Institution concluded: "On average, states have used only about a tenth of [flexible] funds available to them." (Robert Puentes, "Flexible Funding for Transit: Who Uses It?" Brookings Institution, May 2000; TEA-21 appropriation noted by James Dao, "$200 Billion Bill for Public Works Passed by Congress," *New York Times*, 23 May 1998, p. 1.) TEA-21's 19 percent transit authorization might seem generous in light of transit's paltry ridership levels: "Transit services appear to account for less than 3 percent of the total metropolitan area passenger miles," according to a 1997 report commissioned by the Federal Transit Administration. (Charles River Associates, Transportation Research Board of the National Research Council, TCRP Report 27: Building Transit Ridership: An Exploration of Transit's Market Share and the Public Policies that Influence It [Washington, D.C.: National Academy Press, 1997], p. 28.)

America were still a rural nation, but 80 percent of the population now lives in metropolitan areas, therefore a transit commitment of less than 20 percent represents the federal government's indifference to the social health of cities and the environmental health of metropolitan areas. U.S. Representative Robert Livingston, as chairman of the House Appropriations Committee, said of TEA-21, "Our priority was to build highways."[21]

RECENTRALIZATION OF TRANSPORTATION INFRASTRUCTURE

A new focus for priming actions is needed to redress the imbalance between roads and rails in the American metropolis. A recentralization of transportation infrastructure is needed to stimulate the recentralization of commerce and high-density housing, without which cities will not revitalize. Rail investment, however, is not the panacea that some of its promoters imagine. Promoters proclaim rail's power to reign in urban sprawl and to mitigate automobile dependence, but the far-flung decentralization of the American metropolis began before streetcar systems were dismantled. Moreover, the decentralization of commerce and high-density housing continues unabated in metropolitan areas that have built new rail systems since 1970, and cities long served by rail transit have nonetheless decentralized to conform to the whims of the automobile. New York City's region is largely automobile dependent, with more roadway miles per capita than the Los Angeles region.[22] Toronto is cited as the North American city with an exemplary transit system—a well-integrated network of subways, streetcars, and regional rail. But Toronto's outer suburbs have begun to develop in the manner of developing suburbs in the United States. Nevertheless, a properly configured rail system is an essential ingredient in the transportation mix of a metropolitan area.

The Nature of Today's Transit Challenge

New York's first subway line was a response to intolerable congestion on the streets of Lower Manhattan, but the subway's mission went beyond congestion relief. New York's subway visionaries set out to change land-use patterns, to redistribute residential densities, to thin out Lower Manhattan by spreading its over-concentrated population to undeveloped and underdeveloped land in Upper Manhattan and the outer boroughs. The subway accomplished the mission; farmland and dirt roads were transformed almost immediately into "subway suburbs," and Lower Manhattan was reprieved.[23] Only a high-capacity transit system had the power to transform the New York cityscape so radically and so quickly.

Post-World War II rail transit investment also seeks to relieve traffic congestion and to influence land-use patterns, but new-generation systems seek to do that by *reconcentrating* rather than *deconcentrating* metropolitan real estate development. The present goal is more elusive than that faced by New York's subway visionaries. They opened a valve through which the confined masses surged, having built like steam in a pressure cooker; today's transit planners seek to gather up the widely dissipating vapors of metropolitan sprawl. To say that urban revitalization depends upon rail transit is not to say that rail transit assures revitalization. No rail transit system can, by itself, counteract the powerful forces of irrational metropolitan decentralization.

Rail transit, however, is essential to metropolitan recentralization because it has greater power than roadway transit to influence the distribution of businesses and households. To the extent that it shifts business development from suburbs to the CBD, rail transit increases the number of jobs to which transit, both rail and bus, provides a viable means of commuting. And rail facilitates high residential densities in the neighborhoods surrounding the CBD. Rail transit is an ingredient without which cities cannot achieve and sustain commercial and residential densities sufficiently high to support vitality.

The Natural Inferiority of Buses

Rail transit is superior to roadway transit as a force for revitalization for at least four reasons:
1. Buses are stigmatized, rail transit is not.
2. Rail offers better service.
3. Rail operates more efficiently.
4. Rail provides greater capacity.

1. Buses are stigmatized.
Rail transit can outperform buses (sometimes called "loser cruisers") in delivering workers to their downtown workplaces because bus-averse car owners, of which there are multitudes in the United States, are not so averse to rail transit. "Trains are sexy, buses are not," argued a transportation commissioner in Los Angeles during the debate over the city's proposed rail transit system. In *Edge City*, Joel Garreau quotes an anonymous senior transit official: "Show me a man over thirty who regularly takes the bus, and I will show you a life failure."[24]

Office workers, shoppers, residents, and hotel guests in Washington, D.C., believe, by a wide margin, that the city's Metro system is clean and reliable and that the city's buses are not, according to a 1989 survey. This view was shared by respondents who used neither rail nor bus transit regularly, indicating that rail has a greater potential than buses to convert drivers to riders.[25] Transit officials in four other cities—Atlanta, Miami, Portland, and San Diego—that have inaugurated new-generation (post-1970) rail systems reported to the Texas Transportation Institute that their constituents regard rail as more dependable, comfortable, and attractive than buses. These perceptions do affect travel behavior according to other surveys, which reveal that rail transit is more successful than buses at enticing car owners to ride. Three-quarters of Sacramento's light rail riders have access to a car, compared to less than half of its bus riders. Surveys reveal also that transit users are willing to walk substantially longer distances to a light rail station than to a bus stop.[26]

Fred Hansen, director of Oregon's Department of Environmental Quality, says, "People who would never get on a bus will get on MAX" (Portland's light rail system). A 1987 study credits MAX with attracting 6,500 new transit riders in its first year of operation. People ride Max for nonwork trips, and even for pleasure: "MAX has almost as many riders on Saturdays as...on weekdays," according to Portland transit officials.[27] Out-of-towners disinclined to board a bus will readily use rail transit; two steel tracks engraved in the street are "an easily understood connection" to the CBD, according to the authors of a 1996 analysis sponsored by the Federal Transit Administration.[28]

Some bus operators recognize the lowly status of their vehicles and camouflage them to resemble trolleys. City agencies and downtown business organizations in cities nationwide sponsor fake trolleys to generate interest in downtown and its businesses. Apparently the sponsors believe that people will board the vehicles under the delusion that they are not actually boarding a bus.

2. *Rail offers better service.*

A single car with a solo occupant, waiting at an intersection to make a turn, can delay a fully loaded bus. Buses in motion travel at the speed of congestion-bound cars, but buses are often stationary, loading and unloading passengers. Minneapolis residents can drive from the edge of the city to downtown Minneapolis in half the time it takes a bus. In Manhattan, pedestrians outpace buses on some route segments during peak traffic periods.

A rail system with an exclusive right-of-way offers faster service. Most light rail vehicles operate on separate right-of-ways along considerable portions of their routes, and some get priority at traffic lights where they share streets with cars. A bus running on an exclusive right-of-way—a transitway or busway—rivals the running speed of light rail, but few if any such arrangements match rail's overall speed, which is boosted by faster passenger boardings. Rapid rail is rapid because passengers walk from the platform onto the car without negotiating steps; moreover, rail passengers have more and wider doorways through which to board. New York City's old subway cars have three doors, each four feet wide, through which passengers board. Newer longer cars have four four-foot doors.

Bus passengers line up single-file when the bus arrives, and one at a time they climb through the narrow front door and up the steps to pay their fares. Some fumble for change and some interrogate the driver for route information as the bus idles, as seated passengers watch the traffic light cycle through its colors. Bus boardings are often tedious and protracted processions, one of the reasons transit buses are the most unpopular form of mechanized human transport in the world.

Transit buses, some of which travel on HOV freeway lanes, transported their passengers at a national average speed of 13 miles per hour in 1997, compared to 14.4 miles per hour for light rail vehicles. Heavy rail, alternately called rapid rail, traveled at the faster average speed of 20.7 miles per hour because the trains travel entirely on exclusive right-of-ways, and because passengers board and exit quickly.[29] Rail vehicles supplement greater speed with greater comfort—a smoother ride. Old rail cars rock and sway, but they don't rattle the bones like buses do. New-generation rail vehicles are smooth as silk. The rail ride is also quieter, with the exception of old subway systems that squeal when trains negotiate an arc in the track. Collisions add to the discomfort of a ride, and buses produce higher rates of collision than rail vehicles.

3. *Rail operates more efficiently.*

Rail transit, both heavy and light, operates at a lower cost per passenger trip than bus transit. (Commuter rail costs the most to operate per passenger trip.) Operating costs per passenger trip were $2.12 for buses in 1997, compared to $1.82 for light rail and $1.43 for heavy rail, and rail's advantage has been increasing. Operating costs per passenger mile also were lower for light rail than for buses, 47 cents versus 54 cents nationwide in 1997, despite the fact that most light rail systems were new and still developing ridership. Rapid-rail systems performed best—29 cents per passenger mile. Multimodal transit agencies have reported that rail fares cover a higher fraction of operating costs than bus fares—66 percent versus 44 percent in San Diego.[30] With rationally planned routes and better utilization rates, rail's advantage is potentially much greater.

Rail systems lend themselves to automation, which dramatically reduces operating costs while improving service. In Canada, Vancouver's Skytrain (opened in 1986) is fully automated; both its trains and its stations operate without personnel. Automation allows Vancouver's transit agency to operate Skytrain on five-minute headways throughout the day.[31] Thus far in the United States, only a few fixed-guideway systems— downtown and airport people movers—are automated, but there is a potential to retrofit heavy rail systems. Paris's transit agency, RAPT, opened its first automated line in 1998, and plans to eventually automate the entire Metro system.[32] Manually operated rail-transit vehicles will someday be as quaint as manually operated passenger elevators.

4. *Rail has greater capacity.*

The capacity of a rapid-rail line is more than double that of a bus route (and 18 times that of automobiles on a single lane of freeway) according to transit planners' observations in American cities. Washington, D.C.'s Metro system carried nearly 200,000 people in a two-hour period on July 4, 1990. The New York City subway carried 65,430 passengers over a single track (53rd Street tunnel under the East River) in a one-hour period in 1991. That is the capacity of 900 buses fully loaded, with standees—a crowded bus every four seconds over a lane of roadway.[33] Larger vehicles and multiple-vehicle trains account for rail transit's greater capacity, but another factor is at play, especially for rapid rail: Rail vehicles board more passengers in a given amount of time. New York City's subways dwell at their stations about 10 to 20 seconds, during which time scores of passengers board and disembark. Buses dwell just as long to board a few passengers.

Rail Transit as a Shaper of Development

Because of its superior appeal, service, efficiency, and capacity, rail transit has a greater ability than roadway transit to discipline metropolitan density gradients and land-use patterns. The world's rail-transit systems remain tenaciously focused on central business districts, and transit agencies cannot readily manipulate rail routes to serve the process of random commercial and residential decentralization. As the Regional Plan Association observed in 1991, "Rail transit represents...to developers and employers an investment in fixed facilities that will be in place for the long term."[34] Transportation planners in New York concluded that rail transit "forces a focus on land use and development...Bus systems are usually followers of development, while rail systems shape development."[35]

Rail transit's effect on the shape of the metropolis was unambiguous before rails were overpowered by roads. Urban geographer James E. Vance, Jr. describes rail's contribution to compact downtowns:

> It is hard to imagine the central business district in its halcyon days without the contemporaneous development of the trolley, and then of rapid transit. This association of shopping with transit development is well demonstrated by the impact of rapid transit on cities. Boston's Tremont Street and Washington Street subways fixed the heart of the shopping district, concentrating the location of department stores in a fairly tight clustering at the intersection of the two true rapid transit lines at Washington and Summer-Winter streets. This process [was also] at work in other large cities.[36]

Rail transit is an absent or minor component in the transportation infrastructure of most American cities, but where it is present it influences the location of commercial development. Merchants in downtown Portland, Oregon, reported increased volumes of weekend foot traffic and higher sales after MAX began operating in 1986. Within 16 years of the day in 1979 when Oregon's Governor Victor Atiyeh recommended funding for MAX, $1.23 billion worth of development had materialized along its route. About $1.1 billion—88 percent—of that development occurred in downtown Portland and in the adjacent Lloyd District.[37] The "Tijuana Trolley" is credited by Gordon Fielding, a transportation analyst at the University of California, with assisting in the transformation of downtown San Diego from a "marginal place" to a thriving urban center. After the light rail line opened in 1981, downtown San Diego enlivened with new shopping centers and hotels, more than 3,000 housing units, and the reclaimed Gaslamp District—formerly a skid-row.[38]

A downtown served by rail accommodates more workers per acre than a downtown deprived of rail, for two interrelated reasons. First, a rail route delivers more passengers per hour than a bus route. Second, rail's greater capacity and greater ability to attract passengers reduces a downtown's burden of providing parking facilities, freeing up land for office and retail development and maximizing the number of jobs within walking distance of downtown transit stations. Rail transit reduces automobile dependence for business-to-business trips by maximizing the number of businesses within walking distance of one another.

Office development in San Francisco reaches its highest density at the northeast end of Market Street, a transit river fed by many streams: five light rail lines, a streetcar line, about 15 bus routes, and three lines of the Bay Area Rapid Transit system (BART). "It is unlikely that 28 million square feet of office space built [in downtown San Francisco] since BART's 1973 opening could have been accommodated without a regional rail network," according to a 20-year impact study of BART. Many rail-deprived downtowns also experienced significant growth during the same period, however that growth was accompanied by prolific development of parking facilities. The BART impact study concludes: "BART has allowed downtown San Francisco to continue to grow and maintain its primacy in the urban hierarchy."[39]

Other big American cities have maintained strong and growing CBDs by investing in new rail systems, expansions, and modernizations in the post-World War II era, according to a 1996 report sponsored by the Federal Transit Administration: "In Boston, Philadelphia, and Washington, D.C., growth in the CBDs clearly would not have been possible in the absence of large, well-developed rail transit systems capable of delivering a majority of workers by transit every day."[40]

Toronto's subway routes are visible on the skyline, as ridges of modern midrise and highrise buildings. Many of Toronto's apartment buildings are lined up along rail routes, with the densest concentration at the intersection of the Yonge Street and Bloor Street subway lines. The Yonge Street line, opened in 1954, is credited by planners with igniting a development explosion along its route. Toronto-area developers are more attracted to rail routes than to bus routes, according to a transit official: "Our developers tell us we can't get them to develop an area with private capital along a bus route that could be taken out tomorrow. They want to see the tracks."[41] Toronto demonstrates, as U.S. cities cannot, the power of rail transit to shape land development in the context of effective metropolitan land-use management.

Decentralization of parking is, for CBDs, a primary benefit of new-generation regional rail systems, which allow the number of jobs in a CBD to grow faster than the number of parking spaces. Ridership levels are highest in systems that serve large downtowns with high ratios of jobs to parking spaces. BART brings tens of thousands of suburbanites into downtown San Francisco each day without their cars, which they leave at home or in BART's park-ride lots and garages. Downtown San Francisco accommodates the cars of only about 20 percent of its workers. By contrast, downtown Minneapolis, deprived of rail and littered with parking garages, accommodates the cars of half its workers.[42] BART and local rail lines are responsible for the bay city's lower parking ratio, and, by extension, its superior aesthetic appeal.

Rail Neighborhoods

Rail transit not only allows downtown's commercial growth to outpace parking growth, it also supports high-density neighborhoods sufficiently appealing to attract well-paid CBD workers. Rail transit and high residential densities are mutually supportive; high residential densities, if extensive enough, support high-quality frequent-service rail transit, which helps make high densities livable.

Nearly every high-density high-appeal neighborhood in America is adjacent to a downtown or is connected to one by rail transit, or both. Some of the nation's finest urban neighborhoods are proximate to one end of an extensive downtown, and connected by rail transit to the other end. Boston's Back Bay is flanked by Boylston Street's office buildings, and is connected to the more distant government and financial districts by the Green Line of the city's rail system. Philadelphia's Rittenhouse Square neighborhood flanks the office district west of City Hall, and is connected by rail to Market Street East.

Great urban neighborhoods that are beyond walking distance of the CBD but connected by rail include Carnegie Hill and the other prestigious high-density neighborhoods in the northerly two-thirds of Manhattan's Upper East Side. In Brooklyn, the exemplary Brooklyn Heights is separated from Manhattan's financial district by the East River, but the two are connected by three subway lines. (The financial district is just one stop away from Brooklyn Heights on all three lines, and Midtown is just 20 minutes away by IRT express.) In San Francisco, the affluent Laffayette Park neighborhood (in Pacific Heights) includes the city's highest-density census tract west of Van Ness Avenue. This tract, which resembles Russian Hill in density and housing mix, lies adjacent to the cable-car terminus for the California Street line, which carries local commuters to the financial district at the other end of the line. Cable cars appear to function as a mere tourist amusement, lacking the speed to perform serious transit duty, but speed is a minor factor because routes are short. It takes about 15 minutes to travel the length of the California Street line, and the fact that the cable car system's most frequent service is scheduled on that line during morning and evening rush hours attests to the significance of local commuting.[43]

Rail transit is an asset to any residential neighborhood and is a necessity to a high-density neighborhood that isn't adjacent to downtown. A good transit connection to the CBD enhances the appeal of an urban neighborhood, especially among CBD workers, because rail transit is, in an urban context, the best substitute for proximity. The Transportation Research Board reported in 1996 that a rail-transit station in a desirable neighborhood increases residential property values, and New York City's planning department reported in 1997 that "housing prices are beginning to rise rapidly in high-amenity neighborhoods either within Manhattan or with good subway access to Manhattan."[44] If rail transit elevates the appeal of an urban neighborhood, then it is an indispensable agent for revitalization—a facilitator of higher densities and a magnet for households employed in high-pay CBD jobs.

Residential densities sufficient to sustain high quality rail transit also sustain vibrant neighborhood retail streets. The combination of transit and neighborhood retailing provides a household the opportunity to live unencumbered by automobile dependence; rail transit, therefore, suppresses automobile ownership. A well-planned rail-transit system, in combination with the high residential densities that it fosters, can reduce automobile dependence and revitalize neighborhoods.

Rail Transit as a Priming Action for Neighborhood Revitalization.

There are four kinds of neighborhood (non-CBD) commercial street in American cities: vibrant, marginal, underdeveloped, and derelict. The linear mileage in the last two categories outnumbers the linear mileage in the first two categories by a ratio of at least ten to one. It's a safe guess that half of all the linear mileage of vibrant neighborhood commercial street in America exists in Manhattan, Brooklyn, and San Francisco. In other cities, the extent of vibrant neighborhood commercial street is measured in feet rather than miles. America's underdeveloped and derelict neighborhood commercial streets desperately need the boost that only rail transit and higher surrounding residential densities can provide.

In the days when rail transit dominated urban transportation it attracted commercial development not only to its downtown focus but also to neighborhoods. Many formerly lively neighborhood commercial streets are former streetcar routes. In Brooklyn and in the Bronx, pre-war high-rise office buildings are found adjacent to subway stations. Rail's power to channel growth is much weaker today, diluted by extensive webs of roadway, but the power is not altogether absent. Rail transit retains some power to attract commercial development not only to downtown but to outer station areas according to research sponsored by the Federal Transit Administration, published in 1996. The power is greatest in the Washington, D.C., region, where land development is guided by land-use controls that are more effectively coordinated with transit development than elsewhere in the nation.[45] Rail transit's power to attract development to non-CBD stations should be directed to the central area that holds the greatest potential to reduce automobile dependence, the area that so desperately needs revitalization.

Rail transit alone does not ensure revitalization, as is evident in every American city with a system. Parking pavement surrounds the MetroLink station in the heart of East St. Louis; detached houses and vacant land surround MARTA's Ashby station just a mile from downtown Atlanta. Main Street in Buffalo, New York, is a new-generation rail corridor, and a corridor of gross underutilization. Nonetheless, rail transit can be a catalyst for neighborhood revitalization by helping to attract middle-class residents and by channeling those residents onto the commercial street. Chicago's Woodstock Institute found rail transit to be a factor in the superior condition of commercial streets in some of Chicago's modest-income neighborhoods such as North Uptown-South Edgewater, where "small convenience, and in some cases, larger shopper's goods stores cluster around [rail transit] stations, putting them near the path of a good deal of pedestrian traffic."[46] In Brooklyn, retail stores thrive beneath elevated train stations, but storefronts a few blocks away are permanently shuttered.

The revitalizing potential of a new rail system is untested in inner-city America. New-generation systems devote too few resources to the effort. The few new-generation stations that have materialized in America's inner-city neighborhoods are more often accompanied by park-ride lots than by the aggressive rezoning and redevelopment efforts required to attract middle-class households to high-density housing. Transit is first an instrument of transportation, not revitalization, but rail transit holds considerable potential to increase ridership by elevating the appeal of central-city neighborhoods. Rail-transit stations add value to residential land in desirable neighborhoods; apartments and townhouses within a quarter-mile of a transit station generally fetch higher rents and sales prices than comparable housing farther away.[47] A gray-zone neighborhood primed by rail transit and repopulated with middle-class households will see the resurrection of its commercial street.

AUTOMOBILE-ORIENTED TRANSIT

"The New York subway system came into existence through sheer force of need," says Robert Kiley, the former chairman of New York City's Metropolitan Transportation Authority.[48] That force of need was exerted by densely populated neighborhoods. In metropolitan America today, depopulated central-city neighborhoods exert insufficient demand for high-capacity transit. Suburban politicians who are instrumental in transit funding are most interested in roadway congestion, so congested suburban roads have supplanted densely populated urban neighborhoods as the force of need behind rail investment. The federal government's share of funding is contingent on the efforts of metropolitan planning organizations (MPOs), whose natural inclination it is to facilitate the continuing flow of households to growing suburbs. To an MPO, rail transit represents a way to grow the suburbs without growing congestion.

Transportation investment decisions are complicated by competition among counties and municipalities, which are disinclined to participate in the funding of a regional transit system if they feel shortchanged by its route configuration. System planners are often forced to exploit the cost savings associated with existing rail lines and roadway right-of-ways. So goes the planning of post-1970 (new-generation) rail transit; political factors and short-term economies, rather than sound planning principles, determine the route configurations of new-generation systems.[49] The resulting sub-optimal route configurations produce disappointing levels of ridership on many systems and, more tragically, they belittle rail's potential to influence development patterns for the social and environmental good of the city and its environs.

Political realities and false economies produce regional rail systems that bypass distressed central neighborhoods as they stretch far into suburbia, catering to park-ride passengers—mostly downtown workers opting to avoid the cost and inconvenience of downtown parking. Some suburban passengers arrive at their stations in buses, but most arrive in cars; therefore new-generation transit stations are more often surrounded by park-ride lots than by the kind of high-density development that grew around stations prior to World War II.[50] New-generation stations spawn parking pavement rather than architecture.

Surrogate Highways

Until the 1960s, capital investment in rail transit was justified by its direct user benefits—improved service and shorter trip times for passengers— but the increasingly apparent evils of automobile dependence caused a change in objective. In the 1960s, policymakers began to promote rail for its ability to constrain air pollution and sprawl, to relieve roadway congestion, to preserve neighborhoods in the path of proposed freeways, and to strengthen the position of stagnating downtowns. Petroleum conservation joined these concerns in the years following the 1973 OPEC oil embargo; however this consideration faded along with the nation's memory of the crisis.

America's new-generation rail paradigm is in large measure a reaction to the freeway revolt launched in the 1960s by environmentalists and residents of urban neighborhoods threatened by proposed freeways. The revolt forced the cancellation of several urban segments of the interstate freeway system; consequently, the federal government established a provision in the 1973 Highway Act that allows states to transfer federal funds from canceled interstate freeways to transit projects.[51] The freeway revolt focused on the means but not the mission; the freeway's mission of improving access to growing suburbs was not impugned, the means of improving access was. Freeways were rejected as environmentally and socially destructive, but rail transit, a symbol of enlightened urban transportation policy, was embraced as an environmentally benign means of achieving the same mission that is normally assigned to freeways. "Light rail transit" became a mantra of urban environmentalists, who seem unaware that the smoggy Los Angeles metropolis owes its dispersed development pattern to a network of regional rail lines built early in the 20th century.[52]

Portland, Oregon's, light rail system is a freeway substitute that owes its existence to the freeway revolt. In the mid-1970s era of urban freeway proliferation, the Oregon Department of Transportation was preparing to penetrate Portland's east side with the Mount Hood Freeway, but forceful opposition by local officials and neighborhood residents persuaded Oregon's governor to convene a task force of state, regional, and local officials to consider the merits of a transit substitution. The task force decided in favor of transit, effectively killing the Mount Hood Freeway scheme and freeing up much of its federal funding for a new transit system.

At the time of the Mount Hood Freeway debate, the Banfield Freeway, which connects downtown Portland to the suburbanizing town of Gresham 12 miles to the east, was so congested that it held top-priority status for roadway improvements. Gresham was the fastest-growing suburb in the region at the time, and more roadway capacity was needed to accommodate her growth. The Mount Hood Freeway, had it been politically viable, would have relieved the congested Banfield Freeway, but that was not to be. So Oregon's officials decided to piggyback the canceled freeway's stand-in—the new rail-transit line—onto a Banfield Freeway expansion. The Banfield Freeway would provide an economical right-of-way for much of the new rail line's route.

A Banfield Supercorridor—rail transit combined with an upgraded freeway—emerged as the legacy of the annulled Mount Hood Freeway plan. Portland's initial light rail line is a substitute for a canceled freeway and a supplement to an existing freeway, with which it shares not only its right-of-way but also its mission of improving access to the growing suburbs east of Portland.[53]

Many new-generation rail systems, besides Portland's MAX, follow metropolitan highways, demonstrating new-generation rail's true mission. In metropolitan Washington, D.C., Metro's Orange Line follows Interstate 66 some fifteen miles west to Vienna, Virginia. In metropolitan Atlanta, MARTA's southern route follows U.S. Highway 29 and its northern route follows Georgia State Highway 400. New-generation routes in the Baltimore, Miami, Dallas, Los Angeles, San Diego, and San Francisco metro areas follow freeways or highways for considerable distances. The ultimate in automobile-oriented transit is found northeast of Sacramento, where the Watt/Interstate 80 line of the new light rail system gets its name from the interstate with which it shares some of its route. Three transit stops along the Interstate 80 segment of the route are surrounded by park-ride pavement and hemmed in between east-bound and west-bound lanes of the freeway.

Critics of roadway-dominated transportation infrastructure advocate a better balance between modes—between roadways and rail transit. But rail investment that ignores central-city neighborhoods so that it can better serve outlying areas fails to redress the more fundamental imbalance in metropolitan transportation—the imbalance between centralizing and decentralizing infrastructure.

Misguided Motivation

Regionwide political support is needed to fund rail transit today, so promoters must win the hearts of many who will seldom if ever ride a proposed system, and the key to their hearts is roadway congestion. Harvard Professor John Meyer had predicted that Bay Area voters who would never ride BART would nonetheless vote to increase their property taxes to build it, "because they hope that it will attract other drivers off the

road."[54] Roadway congestion has emerged as the overwhelmingly dominant motivation to plan, fund, and build rail transit systems in the Unites
States.

In the Twin Cities metropolis, where only 2.5 percent of all trips are
made on transit, the chairman of the Metropolitan Council regards transit as a "congestion-relieving tool," and his sponsor, Governor Jesse
Ventura, cites roadway congestion as the reason to fund rail transit. The
majority leader of Minnesota's state senate opposes the governor's rail
plan because the proposed route follows a mere highway rather than a
congested freeway. The Republican majority leader demanded, "Put light
rail [routes] where cars travel! Put 'em on [Interstates] 35 and 94! Put 'em
where cars travel! That's where light rail has to be."[55] Policymakers of
every political complexion concern themselves with the convenience of
drivers. Transit is merely a tool to abet that convenience.

The distinction in primary intent is important; a transit system designed
primarily for the convenience of drivers takes on a configuration much
different from a system designed to reduce automobile dependence by
revitalizing and repopulating the core of the metropolis. Rail-transit lines
that follow roadways far into suburbia are designed to relieve congestion
on those roadways, or to prevent congestion from reaching intolerable
levels as the suburbs grow. Centralized transit, which ignores congestion
on suburban roadways, is a necessary accompaniment to the recentralization of households and commerce—the only effective way to reduce
metropolitan automobile dependence. Urban recentralization and revitalization, and reductions in metropolitan automobile dependence, will
occur only in metro areas where driving is, for a substantial share of the
population, less convenient than transit.

REACH

Paris' Metro epitomizes centralized neighborhood-oriented rail transit; it
leaves not a single square mile of the city unserved, with the exception of
the great parks—Bois de Boulogne and Bois de Vincennes—outside the
boulevard peripherique (ring road). Metro was developed as a purely local
system by Parisians who jealously opposed suburban expansion. (Most of
Metro's 14 lines have leaked out beyond the *boulevard peripherique*, but not
far, since the first line opened in 1900.)

Metro has 130 miles of route, but its longest reach—a straight-line meas-
urement from the system' most centrally located station (Châtelet) to its
most distant station (Créteil-Préfecture)—is only 7½ miles. The average

new-generation system in the United States reaches more than 10 miles with less than 30 miles of route. Paris's Metro devotes its 130 miles of route almost entirely to the central city, where its 14 lines form a dense web on which trains provide frequent service.[56]

New York's subway system, with 230 miles of route on 22 lines, reaches 15 miles from Grand Central Terminal to Mott Avenue in Far Rockaway (Queens). But unlike far-reaching new-generation systems in the United States, New York's long lines serve high-density development. Brooklyn's highest-density census tract—113 housing units per gross acre (in 1990)—is located at the Ocean Parkway station, a 12-mile straight-line distance from Grand Central.[57]

Washington, D.C.'s new Metro has fewer than half as many route miles as New York City's subway, yet it reaches just as far—15 miles. Like nearly all new-generation systems, Metro reaches far into suburbia at the expense of central-city service. Three-mile distances between routes are common within the boundaries of Washington, D.C.—within a five-mile distance, approximately, of the Metro Center station. Within a five-mile distance of New York's Grand Central Terminal, only a single strip of the city's land is so sparsely covered by subway routes—a strip of land in Queens occupied largely by cemeteries. But Washington, D.C.'s Metro is generous to its core city by comparison to other new-generation systems. Metro is the only new-generation system with more than 25 miles of route within a five-mile radius of the most centrally located station. Most new-generation systems have a dozen or fewer miles of route within a five-mile radius of their center-point stations.

The nation's most centralized rail-transit system outside New York City is San Francisco's Muni light rail system, an upgraded network of old streetcar lines. (Muni light rail, like other upgraded streetcar systems, is not counted here as a new-generation system.) Muni's five light rail lines cover 26 miles of route, 38 miles if overlapping route segments are counted separately, yet the system reaches less than seven miles from its Powell Street station in the downtown retail district. Muni's rail lines do not leave the city.

Elsewhere in California, the San Diego Trolley, completed in 1981 to be America's first new-generation light rail line, reaches twice as far as Muni. The trolley's initial line reaches 14 miles with just 16 miles of route. San Diego's second light rail line reaches 14 miles in a different direction, (to Santee), with 20 miles of route. Portland, Oregon's, acclaimed Metropolitan Area Express (MAX) reaches 12½ miles with its 15-mile

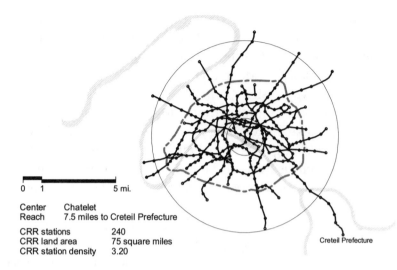

Center Chatelet
Reach 7.5 miles to Creteil Prefecture

CRR stations 240
CRR land area 75 square miles
CRR station density 3.20

Creteil Prefecture

Figure 6-2a. Centralized rail transit—Paris Metro

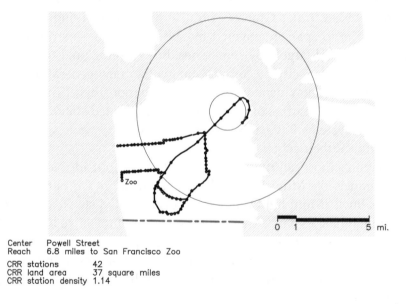

Zoo

Center Powell Street
Reach 6.8 miles to San Francisco Zoo

CRR stations 42
CRR land area 37 square miles
CRR station density 1.14

Figure 6-2b. Centralized rail transit—San Francisco MUNI

inaugural line, from the heart of downtown Portland eastward to the growing suburb of Gresham. MAX's second line, completed in 1998, reaches 15 miles westward to Hillsboro, with 18 miles of route. New-generation rail systems in the U.S. are stretched too thin to serve more than a few central neighborhoods. (See Figures 6-2a through 6-2e for selected system reach diagrams.)

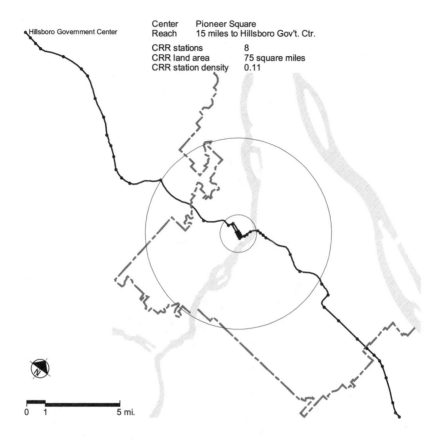

Figure 6-2c. Decentralized rail transit—Portland MAX

STATION DENSITY

The most basic measure of a rail system's quality of service to the central neighborhoods in its metropolis is the number of stations it devotes to those neighborhoods; the larger the number of strategically sited stations, the larger the number of existing and future households within walking distance of rail. If a rail system serves its central area well, that central area will have a high station density. The 20 arrondissements that make up the Ville de Paris—the city of Paris—have 6.8 Metro stations per square mile, a higher density of rail-transit stations than any other city in the western world.

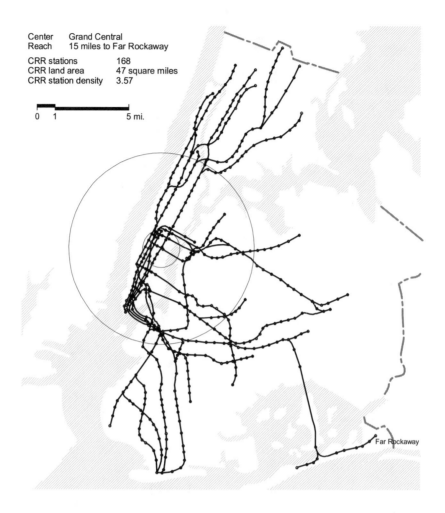

Center Grand Central
Reach 15 miles to Far Rockaway

CRR stations 168
CRR land area 47 square miles
CRR station density 3.57

0 1 5 mi.

Far Rockaway

Figure 6-2d. Centralized rail transit—New York City subway

Paris's web of 14 Metro lines, plus a couple of branch lines, blankets the city so thoroughly that perhaps 90 percent of all residential, commercial, and institutional buildings in the twenty arrondissements are within a quarter mile of a station. Paris's few neighborhoods not well served by Metro are served instead by RER—the regional rail system that is well integrated with Metro. A gap in Paris's network of rail transit routes usually signals the presence of a low-demand land use such as a park, cemetery, industrial area, or railroad yard. Paris's exemplary rail system is sustained by high density—approximately 57,000 people per square mile

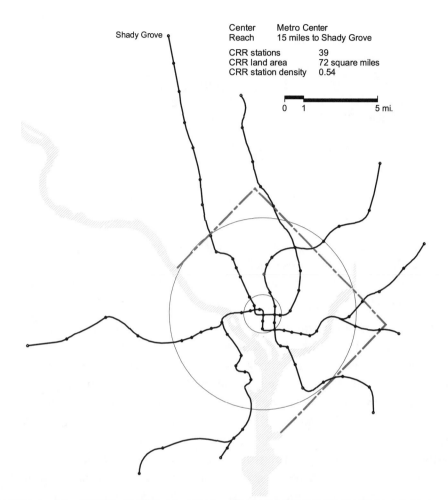

Figure 6-2e. Decentralized rail transit— Washington, D.C. Metro

within the *boulevard peripherique*—a population density comparable to Manhattan's. The island of Manhattan has a station density of 4.6 subway stations per square mile, and the American cities served exclusively by new-generation rail systems all have station densities well below 1.0.

A transit system's quality of service to the central neighborhoods in its metropolis can be most accurately assessed by counting the number of stations inside the central area but outside the downtown nucleus, which is composed largely of non-residential land uses. The downtown nucleus covers one to three square miles in the typical metropolis, but we can simplify station-density calculations by generalizing that the nucleus covers

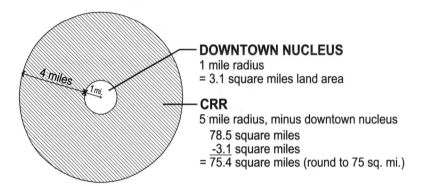

DOWNTOWN NUCLEUS
1 mile radius
= 3.1 square miles land area

CRR
5 mile radius, minus downtown nucleus
   78.5 square miles
   <u>-3.1</u> square miles
= 75.4 square miles (round to 75 sq. mi.)

Figure 6-3. Central Residential Ring (CRR). The CRR represents the metropolitan area's best transit market. It consists of 75.4 square miles (rounded to 75) of mostly residential land surrounding the downtown nucleus of 3.1 square miles.

three square miles, defined by a circle with a one-mile radius. (Much of the residential land within that three-square-mile circle is within walking distance of the heart of downtown, and the rest is well served by the multitude of transit routes that converge in the downtown area.) If a circle with a five-mile radius is drawn concentric with the one-mile-radius circle, a ring of land 75 square miles in area is defined, outside the one-mile radius and inside the five-mile radius (Figure 6-3). This ring of land, which excludes the downtown nucleus, encompasses residential neighborhoods and their supporting parks, schools, and commercial streets, plus some institutional and industrial land uses. Since this ring of land is primarily residential (and becoming more so in the post-industrial era), it is appropriate to call it the metropolitan area's central residential ring (CRR).

The CRR, if developed at densities appropriate to the center of a metropolis, is highly dependent on transit, so every sector should be connected to the CBD by rail. A system that provides decent coverage to most of its central neighborhoods will have a CRR station density of at least one station per square mile. Washington, D.C.'s Metro—the most centralized of America's new-generation systems—provides a station density of only 0.5 stations per square mile in the CRR. (Washington, D.C.'s Metro Center station is taken as the center-point of the CRR.) Paris and New York have CRR station densities of 3.2 and 3.6 respectively. (Station densities for selected rail systems are illustrated in Figures 6-2a through 6-2e.)

Like other new-generation systems, Washington, D.C.'s Metro serves its downtown area reasonably well, devoting 10 stations to the three-square-mile nucleus, but Metro devotes only 39 stations to the 72 square miles of land in the CRR. (The Potomac River, as well as the downtown nucleus, is excluded from the CRR land area.) As low as it is, Metro's CRR station density of 0.5 stations per square mile is higher than that of other new-generation systems because it has more routes emanating from its central hub. One of Metro's routes terminates at the center of the system and four other routes pass through the center, creating a total of nine spokes. Most other new-generation systems, striving for suburban reach rather than central-area coverage, have only one or two spokes—long spokes—emanating from their hubs.

As 2001 begins, new-generation rail lines are operating in 19 American cities that had no rail transit three decades ago, except perhaps a commuter line or a tourist trolley. Five of these are downtown loops or other minuscule lines; 14 connect the CBD to outlying neighborhoods, but the neighborhoods within five miles of the CBD are badly served. Denver, St. Louis, and Salt Lake City each have fewer than eight stations and station densities lower than 0.10 within the CRR. Only three new-generation cities—San Diego, Miami, and Washington, D.C.—have CRR station densities higher than 0.25 stations per square mile. New-generation systems contribute little if anything to the re-population of depopulated central-city neighborhoods.

Most new-generation systems in the United States are little more than a shuttle service between suburban park-ride lots and the CBD. These regional systems do little or nothing to advance the vital cause of bringing suburbanites to the city not only to work but to live.

DUCKS

Are new-generation systems the beginnings of inchoate larger systems that will eventually serve their central areas well? The current impulse is to expand new-generation systems by adding new far-reaching lines, or by extending existing lines farther into suburbia. St. Louis' Metrolink provides only seven stations in the 75-square-mile CRR, but a branch and an extension, both in construction, will lengthen the system's reach and add 12 stations beyond the CRR. No stations will be added inside the CRR. Four branches that will add 46 miles of route to the San Diego Trolley are in various stages of planning, design, and construction; only one of the planned 30 stations will be inside the CRR. Extensions entirely beyond the CRR were completed in Atlanta and Los Angeles in 2000, and extensions entirely or largely beyond the CRR are planned for Dallas and Sacramento.[58]

Can new-generation systems be centralized by adding stations to the central portions of far-reaching lines? To do so would undermine the investment already made in the more distant stations. The two tasks of hauling some passengers short distances and other passengers long distances are at fundamental odds with one another, yet most new-generation systems are meant to do just that. Highly evolved rail transit keeps local service separate and distinct from regional service. The two types of service overlap and interconnect, as in the Paris region where local lines (Metro) extend a short distance into the suburbs and regional lines (RER and SNCF) serve several stations within Paris. Metro, RER, and SNCF lines are well integrated, interconnecting at several principal stations in Paris and its near suburbs, but they remain separate systems with distinct specialties.

New York City's subway, with its 15-mile reach, combines short-distance and longer-distance service, but it does so in a unique way: it dedicates separate tracks to express trains. The subway is actually two systems, local and express, which share tunnels and right-of-ways; therefore longer-distance service does not interfere with local service, and vice versa. San Francisco's nine Muni rail lines (including three cable-car lines) provide short-distance local service to San Francisco residents, while BART—the Bay Area's regional system—specializes in long-distance service, serving only eight stations in San Francisco. Four of those eight stations are located in downtown's Market Street transit tunnel, where BART passengers can transfer to Muni, and vice versa.

Local service is kept distinct from suburban service for two important reasons. First, long-distance regional trains cannot attract suburban passengers very effectively unless they avoid the extended travel time that would be imposed by a multitude of closely-spaced central-area stops. Consequently, regional rail, where it is distinct from local rail, serves few stations in the central city. The Long Island Railroad's commuter trains serve 134 stations, only one of which is in its destination borough—Manhattan.[59]

Most new-generation systems resemble regional systems insofar as their central-area stations are few and far between. On some far-reaching new-generation routes, stations within the CRR are spaced a mile or more apart. Stations along Portland's MAX line to Gresham are spaced an average of one mile apart along an eight-mile segment, half of which is inside the CRR. Even so, MAX takes 45 minutes during rush hour to travel the 15-mile length of its Gresham line.[60] Greshamites would be discouraged from using MAX if their trip time was protracted by closely spaced stations in the central area. (Central-area station's on Max's new westward line are spaced farther apart than on the Gresham line.)

Rush-hour trip times for San Francisco's five local Muni routes, from route extremities to the middle of the CBD, range from 30 to 40 minutes, almost as long as MAX's maximum trip time, even though Muni vehicles travel only half the distance.[61] Muni vehicles devote their travel time to scores of closely spaced stops in central-city neighborhoods. Local systems serve central-city neighborhoods much better than regional systems can.

The second reason to separate suburban from local service is to enable efficient scheduling. Suburban trains run less frequently than local trains because of lower suburban demand throughout the day. The contrast between peak and off-peak demand is more pronounced at suburban stations than at central stations because suburban stations specialize in serving downtown's day-job commuters. BART's North Concord/Colma line offers five-minute service intervals (headways) during peak periods, and so do three of San Francisco's local light rail lines. But the local lines offer off-peak headways shorter than BART's.[62] It is prohibitively costly to run trains to distant low-demand stations on frequent intervals throughout the day, so rail transit specialization affords cost-efficient optimization of service. High central-area densities are needed to support specialized transit systems such as those in San Francisco, Paris, and New York.

Singular rail systems that try to perform both local and suburban duty are like "ducks," those amphibious tourist vehicles found in some of America's recreational areas. Designed to traverse both land and water, ducks traverse neither very well. Likewise, city-suburban rail systems cannot serve both the city and its suburbs very well. New-generation rail combines local and suburban service into a thin hybrid that acknowledges the political power of suburbs and the political emaciation of cities, whose neighborhoods are too sparsely populated and too underrepresented by CBD workers to warrant investment in rail. Inspired by suburban roadway congestion rather than central-city underutilization, new-generation systems leapfrog depopulated city neighborhoods in order to speed park-ride commuters to their CBD jobs.

THE SUPERIOR PERFORMANCE OF LOCAL RAIL

In 1988 the Congressional Budget Office reported the wastefulness of rail-transit funding:

> New federally assisted transit systems have not added to mass transit; instead, they have replaced flexible bus routes with costly fixed-route service to a few downtown areas,…transit fleets in general are greatly underused, and the new transit systems have for the most part added to costs and to unused capacity without attracting riders from cars.[63]

With a few exceptions, new-generation rail systems have failed to measure up to ridership expectations, and to remove significant numbers of auto drivers from their cars. In the San Francisco region, BART attracted less than half the number of daily passengers, in its first two years, that transportation planners had predicted. It took BART more than two decades to achieve the ridership level predicted for its first year, and that level of ridership was finally achieved because the Bay Area's population and employment levels had risen substantially in those 20 years. BART improved upon bus's capacity to deliver suburbanites to Bay Area downtowns, but the system has exerted only a minor impact on Bay Area travel habits—mainly the conversion of some bus passengers to train passengers.[64]

Portland's MAX, the backbone of the region's much touted land-use/transportation strategy, was promoted and built on the proposition that it would increase transit use and reduce automobile dependence. But in 1994, after MAX had been in operation for eight years, Portland journalist Gordon Oliver reported, "despite huge investments in transit, the automobile is becoming more—not less—important in the region."[65] In 1997, preservationist urbanists Richard Moe and Carter Wilkie sadly noted, "Portland's hard-earned urbanity is eroding."[66]

In 1998, nineteen years after MARTA began operating its regional heavy rail system, metropolitan Atlanta joined Houston (which has no rail system) in the second-worst of the EPA's clean-air categories. Only Los Angeles occupied a more onerous category. A reason for Atlanta's air problems: even after massive federal and state investment in MARTA rail, the typical driver in the region drives more miles each day than his counterpart in any other metropolis in the United States.[67] MARTA's far-reaching lines reinforce decentralization. MARTA isn't necessarily counterproductive to the air quality situation, or even ineffective; if investment in rail had gone to roads instead, Atlanta's air would probably be worse. And a more localized rail system wouldn't by itself solve Atlanta's air problems; the New York City region is also an EPA nonattainment area. But a more localized system, in conjunction with the central-area density enhancement that it supports, would convert more drivers to riders, and it would produce more passengers who walk rather than drive to the station.

Centralized rail systems are inherently more productive than regional rail systems in terms of passengers per route mile. Rail-transit productivity is maximized where service is concentrated close to the core and bolstered by high-density development.[68] Among factors that positively affect transit ridership, proximity of residential-area stations to the CBD is second in importance only to the employment population of the CBD.[69] A report published in 1996 by the Transportation Research Board of the National Research Council demonstrates that where all factors other than

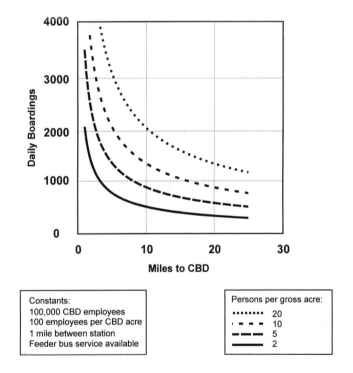

Constants:
100,000 CBD employees
100 employees per CBD acre
1 mile between station
Feeder bus service available

Persons per gross acre:
········· 20
· ▬ ▬ ▬ 10
▬ ▬ ▬ 5
▬▬▬ 2

Figure 6-4. Transit use and proximity to the CBD. Residential density and proximity to the CBD affect rates of transit ridership on the nation's light rail systems. As distance from the CDB increases, transit use falls off.

Source: Parsons Brinckerhoff Quade & Douglas, Inc., Transit Cooperative Research Program of the National Research Council, TCRP Report 16: Transit and Urban Form (Washington, D.C.: National Academy Press, 1997) Volume 1, Part II, p. 30, Figure 7.

Table 6-1. Rail Transit System Comparisons

	One-way route miles	Reach Miles	CRR station density, stations/ square mile	Center station	Passenger trips, millions/year	Passenger trips per route mile, millions/year
New-Gen. Rapid Rail						
Atlanta	45.0	13.0	15/75=**0.20**	Five Points	83.8	1.95
Baltimore	15.0	11.5	5/70=**0.07**	Lexington	13.6	0.91
Los Angeles	16.5	10.5	9/75=**0.12**	Metro Center	19.6	1.96
Miami	20.5	9.5	10/36=**0.28**	Govt. Center	14.1	0.69
Washington, D.C.	103.0	15.0	39/72=**0.54**	Metro Center	163.3	1.73
Averages	*40.0*	*11.9*	*78/328=0.24*		*58.9*	*1.61*
New-Gen. Light Rail						
Baltimore	30.0	15.0	10/70=**0.14**	Lexington	8.7	0.29
Buffalo	6.2	5.7	7/43=**0.16**	Church	6.5	1.05
Dallas	20.0	6.5	10/75=**0.13**	Akard	11.4	0.57
Denver	14.0	11.5	7/75=**0.09**	Transit Mall	9.1	0.65
Los Angeles/	29.0	13.0	5/75=**0.07**	Metro Center	25.7	0.63
Long Beach	12.0	11.0	3/40=**0.08**	5th Street	Incl. in L.A.	Incl. in L.A.
Portland	33.0	15.0	8/75=**0.11**	Pioneer Sq.	21.2	0.64
Sacramento	20.5	10.0	11/75=**0.15**	Capitol	8.7	0.42
Saint Louis	34.5	16.0	7/75=**0.09**	8th & Pine	14.1	0.83
Salt Lake City	15.0	13.0	3/50=**0.06**	City Center	6.2	0.41
San Diego	46.5	14.5	19/48=**0.40**	Civic Center	27.0	0.58
San Jose	33.5	10.5	11/75=**0.15**	S. Clara	7.9	0.25
Averages	*24.5*	*11.8*	*98/776=0.13*		*12.2*	*0.53*
Centralized Systems						
Paris Metro	130.0	7.5	240/75=**3.20**	Chatelet	1,157.0	8.90
New York Subway	230.5	15.0	168/47=**3.57**	Grand Centr.	1,285.8	5.58
San Francisco Muni	26.0	6.8	42/37=**1.14**	Powell St.	37.2	1.43

Table 6-1 Notes: "New-generation" systems listed here are those opened after 1970 in cities that, at the time of their new system's inauguration, had no operational rail transit except perhaps a tourist trolley or a commuter line. Upgraded systems such as San Francisco's MUNI are not counted here as new-generation. Downtown loops or people movers such as those in Memphis and Detroit are excluded.

For cities served by more than one rail transit system, data pertain only to the primary local system.

Route mileage and station density data are based on systems as configured on May 20, 2001; extensions/stations under construction are not included.

Passenger trips are for fiscal year 2000 except the following: Denver, which is a post-Mineral Avenue extension estimate based on information from Denver RTD 19 February 2001; Salt Lake City, where TRAX began operation in mid-FY2000, ridership is calendar year 2000 estimate based on daily, Saturday, and Sunday averages received from UTA, February 27, 2001; New York City—1999; Paris—1998; San Francisco—FY1995 prior to operation of F streetcar.

Route mileage for the purpose of calculating annual passenger trips per route mile

distance between a light rail station and the CBD are held constant, *stations near the CBD produce more passengers than stations farther away.* Station boardings increase exponentially as distances between stations and the CBD decrease. Generally, each doubling of the station-to-CBD distance will reduce the number of station boardings by one-third (Figure 6-4).[70]

In metropolitan areas with separate local and regional rail systems, the local systems are more productive by far. New York's subway produces 10 times as many passengers per route mile as the Long Island Railroad's commuter rail network. San Francisco's Muni local light rail routes produce about twice as many passengers per mile of route as BART.[71]

SAN FRANCISCO'S ALMOST OPTIMAL RAIL SYSTEM

Not one of the new-generation light rail systems indicated in Table 6-1 carries as many passengers each year as San Francisco's Muni, not even the San Diego Trolley with nearly twice as many miles of route. In fact San Francisco's local light rail system carries about three times as many passengers per route mile as the average among America's new-generation light rail systems. Muni light rail owes its superior performance to the

are as listed in the table except as follows: Atlanta—43.0 (mileage prior to opening of 2-mile North Springs extension, which was completed after FY2000); Los Angeles' rapid rail—10.0 (mileage prior to opening of 6.5-mile North Hollywood extension at the end of FY2000; Washington DC—94.5 (the average of route mileage before and after the 2.5-mile infill extension between U Street and Fort Trotten was completed in mid-FY2000); St. Louis—17 (mileage prior to opening of College Station extension; San Jose—31.5 (mileage prior to opening of Milpitas extension).

Route and reach mileage longer than 10 miles are rounded to 0.5.

Deducts from CRR (besides downtown nucleus) include bodies of water wider than one-half mile and the land areas beyond them (except Washington DC, where land beyond the Potomac is served by Metro); Wasatch Cache National Forest and, because it lies largely in the CRR, Salt Lake City International Airport are deducted from Salt Lake City CRR

Passenger trips are "boardings" except for some multi-route systems such as Paris Metro, on which ridership is measured in "journeys," which include linked trips.

Several cities have some stations that serve two or more lines. In most such cities, including Paris, a multi-line transfer station is typically indicated as a single station, while in New York City, some transfer points are indicated as multiple individual stations. (Some of New York City's transfer points are logically considered multiple stations because the various platforms are quite distant from one another.) This situation can be interpreted as exaggerating New York City's station density relative to Paris's.

Sources: Tony Pattison, ed., Jane's Urban Transport Systems 2000-2001 (Alexandria, VA: Jane's Information Group, 2000), and various transit agencies. Where scaled transit agency maps were not available, Rand McNally maps were used. Some Rand McNally maps did not indicate recently completed routes or extensions and their sta-

supportive residential densities along its routes and to four attributes without which rail transit can achieve only a trace of its potential: closely spaced routes and stations, fast downtown travel, routing for bi-directional flow, and reinforcement of neighborhood commercial streets.

1. *Closely Spaced Routes and Stations*

Muni's five light rail lines are former streetcar routes that continue to serve moderate-density neighborhoods in San Francisco's southwest quadrant. The Sunset and Parkside neighborhoods, stretching westward to the Pacific Ocean from Twin Peaks in the middle of the city, are served by the Judah and the Taraval lines, which are parallel to each other and about 1¼ miles apart. Residential densities are highest along or near the routes, so nearly all residents in the two neighborhoods live within a half mile of rail transit, and most live much closer. Transit stops are closely spaced along the lines, typically about 1,000 feet—three short blocks—apart. Crosstown and radial bus routes intersect the two rail lines so that a transit customer living a half mile from a rail route can either walk to the rail station or take a short bus ride with a free transfer, assured that the wait at the rail station will usually be a short one. (A BART corridor, a Caltrain corridor, a streetcar line, and three cable-car routes serve much of San Francisco's land area not served by light rail, and additional rail corridors are planned for residential districts served only by buses.)[72]

2. *Fast downtown service*

Downtown is where buses, and even some rail-transit vehicles, bog down to an excruciatingly slow pace, but Muni's light rail system is designed to move its vehicles swiftly through downtown. Muni's light rail vehicles (LRVs) travel their downtown segment in the Market Street transit tunnel, thereby avoiding the delays associated with downtown traffic. (Before reaching the downtown tunnel, the Judah Street line submerges into a tunnel at Buena Vista Park, and the Taraval line submerges under Twin Peaks, avoiding the trip time that would otherwise be added by the challenging topography. Sunset and Parkside residents, some of whom live as far from downtown as is possible within San Francisco's boundaries, are thus provided quick and comfortable transportation to the heart of the CBD.)

Muni's five light rail lines are actually branches of the single line that travels under Market Street, an arrangement that allows the system to cover a lot of residential terrain with minimal investment in the costly but essential tunnel. The tunnel hastens service not only by avoiding downtown traffic, but also by facilitating quick boarding at busy downtown stations; Muni light rail takes on the characteristics of rapid rail in the tunnel. The separate right-of-way provided by the tunnel elevates Muni's old trolley lines to the status of modern rail transit.

3. *Routing for bi-directional flow*

All five of Muni's light rail lines terminate in downtown San Francisco, and four of the lines terminate, at their outer ends, at or near nonresidential land uses. The Taraval line terminates at the San Francisco Zoo, and three other lines—J, K, and M—terminate at or near the City College of San Francisco. The M line also serves San Francisco State University a short distance from its termination near City College. Good transit connections to these destinations enlarge the universe of people attracted to the neighborhoods along the routes.

Although Muni's non-CBD rail destinations draw only a small fraction of the number of riders drawn to the CBD, the non-downtown destinations do provide some measure of bi-directional demand. Where the CBD is a transit system's only destination, the system runs at half capacity during peak periods because vehicles run full in one direction and empty in the other. High-density nonresidential destinations at both ends of a route promote transit efficiency by fostering ridership in both directions simultaneously. High-density nonresidential land uses—universities, medical centers, commercial concentrations—at the non-downtown extremities of a centralized transit system represent a compact, controlled, transit-oriented form of polycentricity that promotes transit efficiency, even though it doesn't produce the highest possible number of riders, as monocentricity does. Not all of a metropolitan region's high-density nonresidential development fits or belongs in the CBD; that which does not is best located at the non-CBD ends of centralized rail-transit routes.

4. *Reinforcement of neighborhood commercial streets*

San Francisco's light rail lines travel the main streets in their neighborhoods, streets of commercial development and peak neighborhood density (Figure 6-5). That arrangement minimizes automobile use by maximizing the number of households within walking distance of two basic ingredients of urban life: transit and neighborhood commerce. When transit and neighborhood retailing share the same course, transit commuters can pick up convenience goods on the way home from work, eliminating a common reason to drive. Moreover, commercial development along the length of a transit route promotes bi-directional flow.

Local Rail Optimization

San Francisco's peninsular situation precludes just one aspect of rail sys-

Figure 6-5. Localized rail transit, N-Ocean Beach line on Judah Street in the Sunset neighborhood, San Francisco. Muni's modern LRVs run on old trolley lines, serving closely spaced stops on neighborhood commercial streets. Approaching downtown, they submerge into a tunnel to avoid heavy traffic.

tem optimization. All of Muni's routes terminate in the CBD rather than continue past it; San Francisco Bay prevents continuation. If Muni's routes could continue on land on the other side of the CBD, they could be twice as long, while reaching no farther from the CBD. Lengthy rail lines draw more passengers than short lines, although the increase in ridership diminishes as distance from the CBD increases. For a system with a given number of route miles, long lines are more cost-efficient than a larger number of short lines, up to a point.[73] An optimal route configuration has long lines but short reach.

Such a route configuration might consist of a downtown tunnel shared by three or four lines, beneath a corridor of peak-density development. Beyond the downtown tunnel, the three or four lines would subdivide into six or eight spokes. Each spoke would consist of six to eight miles of route, reaching about five miles from the central station. (Street patterns dictate that six to eight miles of route are normally required to reach five miles, not all streets are straight-line radials from the CBD.) Some spokes would branch out to provide dense coverage to densely developed sectors of the city. Some spokes would intercept suburban commuters at the edge of the city, holding parking and congestion at bay (Figure 6-6). Such a localized configuration, accompanied by appropriate residential densities, will be more powerful than regional rail in recentralizing business according to urban geographer James Vance, citing 1940s Boston: "rapid transit moving over a fairly short distance was the greatest force in con-

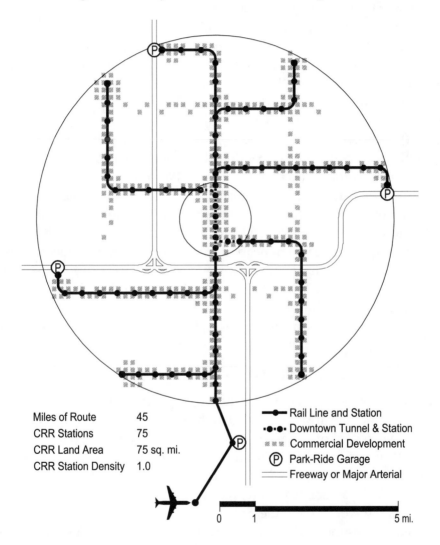

Miles of Route	45	
CRR Stations	75	
CRR Land Area	75 sq. mi.	
CRR Station Density	1.0	

Legend:
- Rail Line and Station
- Downtown Tunnel & Station
- Commercial Development
- (P) Park-Ride Garage
- Freeway or Major Arterial

0 1   5 mi.

Figure 6-6. Centralized rail transit. Four lines form eight spokes routed along commercial streets in this hypothetical configuration. The longest reach is to the airport; all other lines terminate within the CRR.

centrating retailing."[74]

Eventually, after the local rail system reaches maturity, city land would reach a state of optimal utilization. By that time the park-ride garages at route extremities will have been replaced by high-density commercial and residential buildings whose occupants use transit or park discreetly underground. The decentralization-of-parking function would then be taken over by a new regional rail system.

Just one line in an optimized local rail system would extend more than five miles from downtown in the typical American city—the one to the airport. Phoenix, a desert city, calls its airport Sky Harbor, a reminder that the airport has eclipsed the water port as gateway to the metropolis. Railroad terminals functioned as gateways in the first half of the 20th century but they also have lost their importance, except in the northeast. Union Station in St. Louis hosted as many as 100,000 passengers a day in its peak years, but Amtrak abandoned the grand depot and its counterparts in many other cities in the 1970s and 1980s after passenger volumes had withered.[75] Today, for long-distance business travelers and tourists, the point of entry into the metropolis is remote from the traditional heart.

Downtown's gateway role can be revived by making downtown-bound transit the quickest, easiest, cheapest, and most comfortable means of exit from an airport terminal. Such an arrangement is necessary to restore to the American downtown its former status as the unrivaled focus of the metropolis. The vital airport connection can't wait for the development of regional rail; it must be a part of the local system, which would be the initial system in a rationally planned metropolis.

TRANSIT-ORIENTED DECENTRALIZATION

Transit researchers in the San Francisco, Philadelphia, and Washington, D.C., metropolitan areas concluded in the late 1970s that regional rail systems have contributed to the decentralization of metropolitan households. Planners in the San Francisco Bay Area credit BART's trans-bay route with helping to make Contra Costa the region's fastest-suburbanizing county.[76] The trans-bay route freed up roadway capacity by replacing buses that traveled over the San Francisco-Oakland Bay Bridge; this relieved congestion and reduced travel times for cars. BART also converted drivers to riders more effectively than buses, freeing up more capacity.[77]

New-generation regional rail promotes residential decentralization not only by freeing up roadway capacity for suburban commuters, but also by attracting transit commuters to suburban station-area housing, including growing numbers of townhouses and apartments. Washington, D.C.'s Metro, the nation's most productive new-generation system, has created a market for thousands of suburban apartment units, including many in luxury highrise buildings built after Metro began operating. While Metro's suburban stations attracted new housing, the central city lost households and population.[78]

An analysis of BART's impact on Bay Area land-use patterns, conducted 20 years after BART was completed in 1973, concludes that the most significant post-BART difference in the land-use patterns of suburban station areas has been the addition of apartment buildings—at least 2,000 units—many of which are commanding rent premiums.[79] In Portland, Oregon, Tri-Met credited MAX with creating demand for more than 1,100 suburban apartment units along the Gresham line within a decade of its opening, and the agency proclaimed that "higher density projects are now in the pipeline and may portend a trend."[80]

New apartment buildings in suburban station areas draw their residents from the limited pool of middle-class people employed downtown and amenable to a lifestyle of apartment living and habitual transit use. Half of the employed residents of the 1,800 apartments near BART's Pleasant Hill station commute to jobs in downtown San Francisco or Oakland, compared to 10 percent of employed residents from the wider Pleasant Hill area. "Some developers are starting to realize that a number of downtown workers, many of whom are young professionals earning good wages, are attracted to rail-based housing," reports Robert Cervero.[81]

Middle-class households employed in the CBD and amenable to apartment living and transit use are desperately needed to revitalize cities, but advocates for decentralization have adopted regional rail transit as a central component of their agenda. Neotraditional planner Andy Kunz claims, "With a good train system in place and pedestrian-friendly towns at the stations, it is feasible to live without a car." By "towns" he means "new" as well as old.[82] (Kunz writes for *The Town Paper*, a publication that promotes neotraditional suburbs. Real estate agents trying to sell houses in those suburbs hand out copies to potential customers.)

Transit-oriented decentralization, in its various forms, fails to deliver on its promise of reducing suburban automobile dependence to any meaningful degree; it fails on at least three counts. First, suburban stations have been unsuccessful in attracting the critical mass of high-density commercial development that would enable station-area residents to walk to their jobs. Second, suburban station-area residents use their cars for non-work trips. Third, suburban station-area workers—those who work in the few commercial buildings that have materialized near suburban stations—commute in their cars.

1. *Decentralized transit fails to reduce suburban automobile dependence because few suburban stations attract high-density commercial development.*

BART, completed in 1974, was expected to channel suburban growth into densely developed nodes along transit corridors. But after 25 years of operation, only a few of BART's suburban stations have attracted anywhere near as much commercial development as envisioned and intended by the system's planners. Some suburban municipalities shun the envisioned densities; several communities along BARTs suburban routes downzoned their station-area land in the 1980s, fearing that high-density development would increase traffic congestion. This is a well-founded fear, and a rail-transit station only exacerbates the problem when it attracts drivers to its park-ride lot. Robert Cervero and John Landis reported in 1995 that commercial growth in Bay Area suburbs has largely ignored BART stations and has occurred along freeways instead.[83]

MARTA rapid rail is failing to shift commercial development from highways to rail routes in the Atlanta metropolis, according to urban geographers Ronald Mitchelson and James Wheeler:

> In general, the MARTA rapid rail lines are not going to connect with those parts of the metropolitan area that are growing most rapidly, the suburban downtowns. The present and proposed routes were selected before it was realized that those suburban downtowns would emerge on such a gigantic scale.[84]

Miami's new rapid-rail system joins BART and MARTA in failing to shift more than a negligible share of suburban commercial growth to transit stations. The nation's light rail systems also have failed to supplant roadways as the prime determinants of commercial development patterns in suburbia.[85]

The nation's only new-generation rail system to attract substantial commercial development to more than a few of its suburban stations is Washington, D.C.'s, Metrorail, which is unmatched elsewhere because of unique circumstances, including strong county governments that embraced the concept of transit-oriented polycentricity and planned for it during a 1960s period of rapid suburban growth. Aside from a few exceptions in the Washington, D.C., region, suburban stations have failed to attract enough high-density commercial development to enable more than a few station-area residents to walk to station-area jobs.[86]

2. *Decentralized transit fails to reduce suburban automobile dependence because* *suburban station-area residents use their cars for non-work trips.*

Commercial and residential buildings are tightly congregated around transit stations in traditional urban neighborhoods. But at the few suburban new-generation stations that have attracted development, buildings are dispersed and densities are diluted by parking lots and garages, which extend walking distances and prevent the high densities associated with traditional neighborhoods. Large blocks, broad busy streets and roads, and banal architecture add to the unpleasantness of the typical suburban station-area environment. In the automobile-oriented environment of the suburban transit station, it is easier to drive than walk, even to destinations that are within walking distance of the station.

Twenty-five years after the first new-generation rail system began operating in the United States, only a couple of the approximately 150 suburban station areas remotely resemble the kind of environment in which people would prefer walking to driving. Station-area housing attracts residents who use transit to get to workplaces in the CBD, but most of those residents depend on their cars for access to other of life's destinations. Robert Cervero analyzed travel behavior in the suburban Lafayette station area on BART's Concord line and found that 96 percent of non-work trips are by automobile, compared to two percent on transit and two percent on foot or bicycle.[87]

3. *Decentralized transit fails to reduce suburban automobile dependence because station-area workers commute in their cars.*

Office buildings have materialized near a few suburban transit stations, but only a small fraction of the workers who commute to these office buildings each day do so on transit. Referring to suburban business sites, Robert Cervero tells us that "employees in transit supportive areas were generally as dependent on their cars to get to work as those working in more auto-oriented sites." Less than five percent of the workers who commute to the office buildings clustered around rail-transit stations in Bethesda, Maryland, and Walnut Creek, California, arrive on transit, compared to more than half the commuters to San Francisco's CBD.[88]

Commercial buildings in suburban station areas fail to produce high rates of transit commuting because they generously accommodate automobiles. Eleven miles north of downtown Atlanta, MARTA's Dunwoody station is sandwiched between two big parking garages, beyond which lie hundreds of sprawled retail buildings and office towers that have grown like weeds along Interstate 285 and its intersecting roads (Figure 6-7). A few commercial buildings are within walking distance of the station, but who wouldn't drive to these destinations, each of which has its own park-

Figure 6-7. Automobile-oriented transit—MARTA. In the few places where suburban stations and office buildings co-locate, both surround themselves with parking lots or garages. Most suburban stations are mere park-ride transfer points. (MARTA's Dunwoody station 11 miles north of downtown Atlanta is shown here)

ing lot or garage? In the San Francisco Bay Area, three of BART's suburban station areas—Walnut Creek, Pleasant Hill, and Concord—have attracted commercial development that is somewhat more tightly congregated around the stations than at Dunwoody. But here too it is irrational of an automobile owner to commute on transit. Automobile commuters to the commercial buildings near BART's suburban stations determine their own schedules and park near (or in) their buildings, but rail commuters must get themselves to a BART station, wait for a train and, upon arriving at their work destinations, hike across BART's huge park-ride lot. The apparent purpose of BART's suburban stations is not to deliver commuters to nearby office buildings, but rather to transfer them from their cars to trains headed for a downtown in which parking is inconvenient and costly.

In *Transit Villages in the 21st Century*, Robert Cervero observed, "Islands of transit-oriented development in a sea of freeway-oriented suburbs will do little to change fundamental commuting habits."[89]

One-route Towns

Among Joel Garreau's misstatements in *Edge City* is this: "A train station invariably results in a knot of dense development."[90] This is the basis for Garreau's dream that the typical edge city, if served up with a transit station, will dense up to provide a more pedestrian-friendly environment. Unlike Toronto's close-to-the-core Regional Commerce Centres, the edge cities to which Garreau would allocate train stations are separated from the nearest CBD by thousands of acres of underutilized land. And unlike Toronto's Regional Commerce Centres, Garreau's edge cities are situated on highways and freeways, the source of edge city sustenance, rail station or no rail station. Garreau acknowledges that the introduction of a rail station in an edge city will convert few automobile commuters to rail commuters; the transit station is merely a device to enhance the appeal of edge-city land, according to Garreau's reasoning. But other transit-oriented polycentrists imagine that regional rail will reshape metropolitan development and wean more than a few suburbanites from their automobiles. Proponents of transit-oriented development (TOD) imagine that residents of TODs will commute to their jobs on transit and walk to their other routine destinations.

Planners and developers cannot create a true transit-oriented suburban station area—one that fosters walking and transit use more than driving—unless they create a sizable, urbane, high-density community—a true urban environment, which, as noted in Chapter 5, represents a gross misallocation of metropolitan resources in the context of central-city underutilization. The creation of a true urban environment is an appropriate endeavor for a central-city station area, or for a suburban station area in a growing metropolis with a fully developed core city, but not for the suburbs of an underdeveloped city.

The suburban TOD, even if developed as a true urban environment, can never dissuade automobile use as effectively as a real urban neighborhood because the TOD is anchored by a single rail line; it's a one-route town even if its rail station is fed by feeder buses from surrounding residential areas. The real urban neighborhood, being closer to the CBD, is better served by transit. Proximity to the CBD ensures a higher density of transit routes, a higher frequency of service, superior transit access to universities and other non-CBD employment concentrations, and shorter travel times for most trips. Real urban neighborhoods hold the greater potential to discourage not only automobile use but also automobile ownership.

Robert Cervero tells us that suburban TOD's cannot fundamentally change commuting habits unless they exist in a "transit metropolis." If any metropolis in the United States can be characterized as a "transit metropolis," it would be the New York City metropolis—the only metropolitan area in America where more than a quarter of all commuters commute by transit. Twenty-seven percent of commuters in the New York City metropolis commuted by transit in 1990, compared to 13 percent in metropolitan Chicago—the runner-up. Less than five percent of commuters use transit in most of America's metropolitan areas. The New York metropolis accounted for 37 percent of all of America's transit trips in 1990. America's only transit metropolis is, by no coincidence, anchored to America's only transit city.[91]

The Inherent Automobile Dependence of Suburban Transit Users

Chris Bushell, editor of the annual worldwide transit survey, *Jane's Urban Transport Systems*, reported in 1998, "Just a couple of hours' off-peak travel around [London's] suburbs reveals near-empty trains running past or even through vast new housing developments and shopping complexes..."[92] Suburban station-area housing produces even fewer nonwork transit trips in America than in England, it is safe to say. Most suburban rail commuters live beyond walking-distance of the nearest station, so, even for the work trip, they depend on their cars, which they deposit in the park-ride lots that surround suburban stations. In 1997, Robert Cervero reported, "currently, over 80 percent of suburban Bay Area residents who ride BART reach stations by private automobile." Most of the remainder ride feeder buses to stations; a small fraction of suburban passengers walk to BART stations. All of BART's suburban stations have park-ride lots, which accommodate 30,000 cars.[93]

Regional rail does not reduce the number of car trips made by park-and-ride and by kiss-and-ride passengers, it only reduces the length of the automobile segment of their work trip. Since most suburban transit commuters begin their commutes in their cars, and since negligible numbers of suburbanites use transit for non-work trips, regional rail does next to nothing to alleviate the automobile dependence of its suburban customers.

A rail system that fails to remove commuters from their cars altogether falls far short of rail's potential. Any economic justification for rail transit diminishes or disappears unless rail transit replaces some of the production of roadways and cars; regional systems merely supplement the production. A cost-benefit analysis by the Minnesota Department of Transportation reveals that the Twin Cities public will get 42 cents worth of benefit for every dollar spent on the region's first light rail line, which awaits funding. Charles Lave, an economist from the University of California, Irvine, analyzed the energy costs and savings associated with the Bay Area's BART system, and concluded that BART will take more than 500 years to repay its initial energy investment—the consumption of energy that went into building the system. [94] Extravagant public spending on rail systems is justified only where it allows reductions not only in public spending on roadways, but also in private spending on personal vehicles. Regional rail systems, unlike centralized systems, do little or nothing to suppress automobile ownership.

FEEDING THE INSATIABLE APPETITE FOR ROADWAY

"See that traffic jam? As governor, I'll issue construction bonds, double the number of road projects, and get us all moving again..." This was Democratic candidate Mark Dayton's promise during the 1998 election campaign. Dayton's voice was accompanied by an aerial view of a congested freeway interchange.[95]

Rail transit's revitalizing power will be neutralized by metropolitan roadway development unless policymakers surrender their predisposition to satisfy the escalating demands of suburbanites mired daily in traffic congestion. Buffalo's local rail line was built on the promise that it would redirect growth to a floundering downtown, but the objective was sabotaged by New York's Department of Transportation, which expanded the suburban highway network even as the rail system was in planning and construction.[96] The relentless demand for an ever-increasing inventory of suburban pavement was articulated in 1996 by William R. Eager, president of a transportation planning firm in Seattle, Washington:

> New roads that fill up with traffic are an indication of the need for them. Their use makes it possible to improve service to current travelers and reduce congestion elsewhere. The problem is that rarely are there enough improvements to accommodate traffic growth...[97]

This doctrine has dominated metropolitan transportation planning in the United States for half a century. The Metropolitan Council of the Twin Cities adopted the doctrine in its 1986 *Metropolitan Development and Investment Framework:* "new [roadway] construction will be necessary when traffic volumes approach design capacities. . ."[98]

Planners at long last comprehend the principle of insatiable demand: Roadway development in growing metropolitan areas merely creates demand for additional roadway development. This lesson has been available for more than half a century; it was demonstrated in the New York City area well before the era of metropolitan freeways. When construction began on the Triborough Bridge in 1929, officials promised an end to Long Island's severe traffic congestion, but soon after the bridge opened in 1936, Long Island parkways bogged down in perhaps the biggest traffic jams in the region's history. In order to relieve the new congestion, master road builder Robert Moses immediately built the Bronx-Whitestone Bridge and opened it less than three years after he opened the Triborough. Somehow the Bronx-Whitestone immediately filled to capacity without relieving the other congested bridges that connect Long Island to the rest of the world. The six million vehicles carried by the Bronx-Whitestone in its first full year of operation were added trips, and the new bridge was as congested as the others.[99]

The Triborough and Bronx-Whitestone bridges long ago evidenced the malignancy of roadway investment in the American metropolis, where land-use controls are fragmented among competing jurisdictions. In that context, roadway projects facilitate the decentralization of destinations so that transit becomes increasingly useless and driving becomes increasingly necessary. America's post-war metropolitan roadways converted transit-oriented populations into automobile-dependent populations, and new roadway lanes deepen the dependency. In attempting to satisfy demand in growing metropolitan regions, roadway builders create additional demand (which planners call induced demand).

These truths have become increasingly evident. The same Metropolitan Council that in 1986 endorsed endless roadway construction in the Twin Cities area finally saw the light a decade later, a decade of unabated commercial decentralization and the attendant intensification of traffic congestion. In 1996 the council admitted, "The region cannot build its way out of congestion; adding lane capacity, while reducing congestion in the short term, only increases roadway access that, in turn, encourages additional decentralization of development."[100]

Roadway construction has not abated in the Twin Cities area. As elsewhere in the nation, investment shifts from the construction of new roadways to the expansion and upgrading of existing roadways. The anticipated effect of a typical capacity-enhancement project—a highway bypass—is described in the *Minneapolis Star Tribune*: "The [project] is expected to spur housing and commercial development in [suburban] Scott County because the road improvements will make the center of the metro area so much easier to reach."[101]

Capacity enhancements contribute to increased VMT, which in the 1990s combined with declining fuel efficiency to produce record levels of gasoline consumption, which in turn produced record levels of gas tax revenue, which produced record levels of roadway spending, which encourages further increases in VMT. In Minnesota, roadway spending increased from $348 million in fiscal year 1995 to $506 million in fiscal year 1999, with a majority of the money going to the Twin Cities metropolitan area, where capacity enhancements dominate the spending.[102] And roadway spending is not limited to gas tax revenues. In 2000, Minnesota enacted a transportation appropriation, over and above the routine annual appropriation of about a half billion dollars, that earmarks $177 million for metro-area roads and only $5 million for transit. Most of the appropriation will come from the state's general fund. The transportation act outlines the goal of its metro roadway commitment: "$177,000,000 is for state trunk highway improvements within the seven-county metropolitan area primarily for the purpose of improving traffic flow and expanding highway capacity by eliminating traffic bottlenecks."[103]

The Safety Pretext

To justify their costly improvement of a congested highway interchange in a suburb of St. Louis, officials invoke driver safety, an emotionally invincible argument for the urgency of capacity enhancements on metropolitan roadways.[104] Minnesota's Department of Transportation cites safety concerns to justify its $100 million plan to decongest one of the busiest segments of freeway in the Twin Cities region.[105]

The nation's metropolitan segments of interstate are, in fact, far safer than its rural highways, on which nearly 100 people are killed each day. Metropolitan interstates have a fatality rate about one-sixth that of local rural roads, and many of the fatalities that occur on rural roads can be prevented by minor improvements in alignment or visibility.[106] But rural America, like urban America, has lost political power to suburban America.

Departments of transportation ought to shift their safety related spending to rural America where its byproduct—capacity enhancement—is benign. As for metropolitan America, nearly all roadway accidents are minor accidents involving no serious injury or loss of life. The chance of a serious roadway accident is so remote in metropolitan America that motorists are unconcerned. What concerns them is congestion and delays. Minor traffic accidents cause delays; those delays rather than safety concerns motivate transportation officials to improve roadways. If transportation policymakers were truly concerned about personal safety, they would stop building roads and start laying rails because rail vehicles produce a fraction of the number of deaths per million passenger miles that automobiles produce.[107] The blood of a million dead and injured motorists stains the hands of those responsible for our grossly unbalanced, roadway-dominated transportation infrastructure.

The Transit/HOV Pretext

Beyond the safety pretext, two others are dubiously invoked to justify roadway capacity-enhancement—the "transit/HOV pretext" and the "benevolent neighbor" pretext. The transit/HOV pretext goes like this: In order to abate the growth of freeway congestion in growing metropolitan areas, we must encourage transit use and car-pooling, which we can do by adding roadway capacity. In her appeal for more roadway spending in the Twin Cities area, Carol Molnau, chairwoman of Minnesota's House Transportation Committee, argued that "the backbone of the [transit] system ...is the bus system [which needs] roads to drive on. There's no other way..."[108] Faced with growing congestion on Atlanta-area freeways, Georgia's Department of Transportation has, since 1994, added 60 miles of HOV lane (open to cars with as few as two occupants) at a cost of $41 million, much of it from the federal government.[109]

If a new HOV lane is successful—if it fills with car-poolers and buses—then it is even more efficient than an open-access lane in feeding suburban growth. And if an HOV lane is unsuccessful, i.e., underused, then it is susceptible to conversion to solo-driver traffic. Transportation officials in San Diego sell the excess capacity on their underused HOV lanes to single-occupant drivers willing to pay a fee. Popular opposition to underused car-pool lanes in New Jersey inspired politicians to open them to all drivers. Thus "high-occupancy-vehicle" lanes, which are two-occupant-vehicle lanes in most metro areas, are susceptible to becoming any-occupancy-vehicle lanes.[110] One way or another, HOV lanes expand roadway capacity.

Houston's buses operate on the nation's most extensive network of HOV lanes, which carry mostly private vehicles. A 1996 analysis of American transit systems finds Houston's all-bus system to be ideally suited to a dispersed and sprawled metropolitan region: "Houston area residents value the suburban lifestyle and the advantages of the automobile...If the transit system has had any affect on urban form, it has been to support the dispersed pattern of living."[111] Roadway congestion costs the average Houston area resident nearly 50 percent more in wasted time and fuel than it costs the average New York City area resident. On October 7, 1999, Houston officially surpassed Los Angeles as the smoggiest city in the United States.[112]

Restricted lanes have a place in metropolitan America, but not for personal vehicles. If policymakers wish to reign in the forces of decentralization and sprawl, they will recognize congestion as a positive force so long as it doesn't interfere with transit, emergencies, or commerce. Restricted-access lanes should be reserved for buses, emergency vehicles, and commercial trucks. Manufacturing and warehousing are, in the rationally decentralized metropolis, suburban and exurban enterprises, while households and retailers are concentrated in the central area. The efficient distribution of goods in such a metropolitan configuration depends upon uncongested routes for commercial trucks.

The Benevolent Neighbor Pretext

Perhaps the most disingenuous pretext for increasing suburban roadway capacity is one proffered by suburban growth advocates who pretend concern for the central city. Minnesota state representative Ken Wolf, representing Burnsville, a developing suburb south of Minneapolis, exercised the pretext in 1996 in support of an expansion proposal for Interstate 35, the congested freeway that links his suburb to Minneapolis. Faced with central-city opposition to the expansion, Representative Wolf offered some brotherly advice:

> The problem here is simple. Minneapolis must decide whether it wants economic development and growth downtown—or not. If it does, access must be provided. If access is denied, downtown will continue to deteriorate. Without suburban support the sports franchises will leave, jobs will leave and mobile Minneapolis residents will follow…the issue is simple-economic vitality or deterioration. The choice is up to Minneapolis.[113]

Minneapolis officials (who favored light rail over freeway expansion) and downtown business people were well aware of the representative's point about the importance of access. City officials and merchants across the nation supported the initial metropolitan segments of the interstate system believing that the freeways would deliver suburban customers to downtown businesses. But freeways are two-way streets, as the representative unwittingly remarked when he warned of the impending flight of sports franchises, jobs, and residents.

For their part, city policymakers interested in city vitality ought to remember that the best way to disarm the marauding benevolent neighbors is to increase the population density and purchasing power of the city. City officials must do what they can to shift political power, and the infrastructure investment that follows it, away from developing suburbs, back to cities.

Capacity Enhancement Technology

Federal environmental legislation has forced transportation officials in some areas to enhance roadway capacity by means other than paving. Now federal and state funding is abundantly available for capacity enhancement by means of traffic management and technological innovation. In-vehicle navigation computers will soon be ubiquitous. The FCC dedicated part of the radio spectrum to the technology in 1999, so the day when most drivers are guided by radio signals to the least congested roads is near at hand.[114]

This and much more are part of the U.S. Department of Transportation's *Intelligent Transportation System*, which will someday include an automated highway system (AHS), a high-tech solution to the most annoying aspect of congestion: slow speeds. AHS will allow closely spaced vehicles to move safely at high speeds.[115] These generously funded programs aim to expand the capacity of metropolitan roadways in a way that is more cost-effective than the construction of new lanes. But the effect is the same; both the construction of new pavement and the technological optimization of existing pavement expand the capacity of developing suburbs to absorb households and businesses.

Customers of the nation's biggest subway system—in New York City—descend to the sweltering fetid platforms without a clue as to when their train will arrive. They can only hope they won't be delayed a half hour by a mechanical malfunction or some other mysterious occurrence. In America, public riches and technological innovation are devoted to drivers while transit systems operate essentially the way they did a century ago.

CONGESTION IS GOOD

In the East Bay sub-region of the San Francisco area, just two transportation arteries—road and rail—carry more than 140,000 commuters from East Bay residences to their San Francisco jobs. The San Francisco-Oakland Bay Bridge and the BART tunnel beneath the bay are the only connections, except for lengthy circuitous routes and a low-capacity ferry service. Congestion on the Bay Bridge produces the region's longest commute times (105 minutes in 1992), compelling commuters to ride BART.

A majority of East Bay commuters have determined that driving is the inferior means of commuting because it is slower than BART (even after BART relieved congestion on the Bay Bridge). Parking costs also contribute to a CBD-bound commuter's decision to use transit, but the fact that the Bay Area's longest commute time corresponds with the Bay Area's highest rate of transit use indicates the power of congestion to influence travel behavior.[116] Bay Bridge congestion produces environmental benefits for San Francisco and the entire Bay Area.

The Planning Department of the City and County of San Francisco recognizes the positive role of traffic congestion: "Congestion is a means of controlling traffic growth…"[117] In 1973, San Francisco officials adopted a "Transit First" policy, which entails not only the provision of high-quality transit, but also the curtailment of accommodations to the automobile. This policy has guided the city in the unprecedented direction of decreasing its roadway capacity. When the Embarcadero and Central freeways were damaged in the earthquake of 1989, the city decided that the damaged and razed portions should not be replaced. Nearly all of the substantial growth in commuter travel to and from San Francisco's CBD since the city adopted its "Transit First" policy has been accommodated on transit.[118]

Policymakers who are serious about increasing transit's share of metropolitan travel will pursue "transit first" policies on a metropolitan scale and, accordingly, they will recognize the need to curtail the expansion of roadway capacity. "Policies that focus on making private vehicle use less attractive are likely to spur transit ridership to a more marked extent than those that make transit more attractive," according to a 1997 report sponsored by the Transportation Research Board.[119] When we get serious about increasing transit's role in metropolitan travel we will, to a large extent, replace rather than supplement roadway funding with transit funding.

Transportation researchers Peter Newman and Jeffrey Kenworthy found, in 1989, that congestion can produce fuel efficiency. Uncongested areas produce high rates of automobile use, and even though individual vehicles get better gasoline mileage on uncongested roads, the preponderance of private vehicles makes uncongested areas more energy-gluttonous than areas where congestion is severe enough to force commuters into transit vehicles.[120] Congestion serves a positive function where it discourages driving and encourages riding, thereby ameliorating the imbalance between the two modes.

Congestion as a Push Factor

In America's urban regions, where core cities are underutilized, the combination of roadway congestion and localized rail transit has the power to compel many suburbanites who commute to the CBD not just to switch from car to transit, but to go a step further, to seek housing in revitalizing central neighborhoods closer to their jobs. Planners in Vancouver regard congestion as an "ally" that helps fuel an explosive growth in central-area housing. [121]

Congestion can influence the locations of businesses as well as households. William Wheaton, professor of economics at the Massachusetts Institute of Technology, has determined that intensifying congestion on suburban roadways might eliminate the competitive advantage that suburban businesses hold over CBD businesses. CBD businesses are at a competitive disadvantage, says Wheaton, because travel times to the CBD workplace are longer than to the suburban workplace due to such factors as downtown congestion, traffic lights, and greater walking distances from parking to workplace. Also, downtown parking is costly. Those employed in the CBD, therefore, demand more pay from their employers because, consciously or subconsciously, they factor greater travel time and parking costs into their consideration of a CBD job. These CBD-suburb wage differentials motivate firms to decentralize. Wheaton surmises that the CBD's competitive disadvantage can be reversed by transit improvements to the CBD accompanied by intensifying suburban congestion: "The best prospect for many inner cities may be to wait until commuting within the suburbs becomes as onerous as commuting to the CBD."[122]

Traffic congestion has already reached a level that threatens the expansion of some of the nation's suburban business concentrations. Congestion impelled the Hewlett-Packard corporation to reconsider its expansion plans in the Perimeter Mall business concentration 11 miles north of downtown Atlanta; and in North Carolina, executives at Glaxo-Wellcome and at Cisco Systems warned Governor Jim Hunt that they could not expand their companies' offices in Research Triangle Park—a large SBC in the Raleigh-Durham metropolis—unless something is done to relieve traffic congestion.[123] In 1999, the *Atlanta Journal-Constitution* reported that "access to inexpensive land for development, which has spurred suburban growth, is being threatened by nightmarish traffic."[124] This is congestion's highest calling—to influence not only travel behavior, but also the location decisions of businesses and households. A recentralized transportation infrastructure is needed to ensure that these businesses and households will be pulled in rather than pushed out.

Compact Cties

The strategy of controlling decentralization by curtailing roadway investment is far from radical and far from original; it was proffered two decades ago, in the aftermath of the petroleum shortages of the 1970s, by a subcommittee of the U.S. House of Representatives' Committee on Banking, Finance, and Urban Affairs. The Subcommittee on the City issued a program of policy recommendations in 1980 called *Compact Cities: Energy Saving Strategies for the Eighties*. Among the recommendations: "State governments should help conserve the central business districts of their cities by withholding capital expenditure in aid of suburban malls and other developments that could undermine existing commercial centers." By "capital expenditure," the subcommittee meant roadway investment: "Highways, beltways, exit ramps, and access roads, all built at taxpayer expense, literally pave the way to the shopping centers."[125]

America's policymakers have soundly rejected this and other principles championed by the subcommittee. In the mid-1980s, for example, Minnesota's legislators committed $50 million to the roadway improvements that make the Mall of America accessible.[126] But it appears the subcommittee's principles may have found a voice. Rocketing levels of air pollution and roadway congestion in the Atlanta metropolis prompted Georgia's governor and legislature to create the Georgia Regional Transportation Authority (Greta) in 1999. Greta's chairman has warned that his powerful organization will deny road-access permits to developers who propose regional malls in locations not well served by transit.[127] If this philosophy doesn't cause the further decentralization of transit, Greta might demonstrate an effective new direction in land-use control.

BEYOND POLYCENTRICITY

Proponents of our market-oriented system of metropolitan land development reject the concept of centralized planning, arguing that private land markets best determine which land uses and densities belong in any particular location. The market is sensitive and responsive to the preferences of consumers and business owners, and the many jurisdictions within a metropolis are more acutely attuned to the preferences of consumers and businesses than central authorities could ever be. Proponents trust that the unconcerted actions of many participants coalesce naturally, even if mysteriously, into a land-use pattern that reflects not only the most efficient distribution of economic activity, but also the collective will of the consumer population. The unfortunate side effects of the market-oriented system are not so serious as to warrant government intervention, say the proponents of American suburbanization. Besides, interventions can only be ineffectual because decentralization and the decline of core cities are unavoidable in the post-industrial era. Few if any proponents of unfettered land markets object to the centralized intervention that feeds suburbanization—roadway funding.

In *Edge City*, Joel Garreau endorses the malignant combination of free land markets and roadway-dominated transportation infrastructure; he correctly credits these factors with producing the kind of land development he advocates:

> The system of individual transportation we Americans have devised, of course, is the finest method of moving the most people and freight in the most directions at the most times ever devised by the mind of man. At its center is the automobile and the hard-surfaced, all-weather road. Place these dreams in a market system that is responsive to what people feel is rational to trade off in time and money, and what you get is Edge City.[128]

But it now appears this statement is disproved. It turns out that Garreau's "market system" is moving our metropolitan areas beyond the polycentric pattern of decentralization observed and advocated by Garreau, and toward a more dispersed pattern, according to Peter Gordon and Harry Richardson, professors of planning and economics at the University of Southern California, Los Angeles. Gordon and Richardson have concluded that American urbanization is evolving "beyond polycentricity," beyond a pattern of multiple business concentrations or "edge cities." Gordon and Richardson's research in the Los Angeles area—the quintessential polycentric metropolis—shows that discernible commercial centers—edge cities—are being eclipsed in economic importance by commercial development that is thinly dispersed—spread thin over the broad suburban landscape, like post-war housing. (This pattern of widely dispersed individual businesses and small business clusters is referred to here as noncentric development.)

Major business centers in the Los Angeles metropolis employed only 12 percent of the region's workers in 1990, down from 19 percent in 1970, and Gordon and Richardson noted that "...the trend of a declining...proportion of jobs in subcenters, however defined, has continued."[129] And in the Dallas-Fort Worth area, researchers have identified numerous small clusters of business development, which are proliferating and becoming more powerful economically than the larger "edge-city" concentrations.

Gordon and Richardson concluded, "just as urban researchers are beginning to devote considerable attention to the phenomenon of polycentricity, the world is perhaps moving beyond it."[130]

"Edge City is the crucible of America's urban future," says Garreau, but edge cities are in their embryonic stage of development, "works in progress" that need a bit more time to evolve, to reach their potential as great and fulfilling places.[131] If this is so, isn't the future of edge city worth protecting from the natural forces of the market system? Isn't the unfulfilled potential of "the crucible of America's urban future" worth promoting by means of government intervention? "Only, I came to believe, if we come to see it all as sacred—the land on which we build as sacred as the land we leave untouched—will we break through to higher ground and reunite our fragmented universe. That is precisely how and where we can help save our world."[132] With this hyperbole Garreau tells us that the survival of the world is at stake. One can reasonably assume, then, that Garreau would condone government intervention in support of the metropolitan development pattern that he judges to represent our very survival.

There is a particular pattern of urbanization that is worth promoting by means of government intervention, but that pattern is not the polycentric pattern advocated by Garreau, not yet anyway, not for cities in the United States. The pattern of urbanization that is worth promoting for social and environmental reasons is the old monocentric pattern, modified to conform to the post-industrial economy—post-industrial monocentrism. Central-city land is grossly underutilized and our enormous investment in the infrastructure that feeds suburbanization is premature, and destructive to core cities.

Priming Actions in the Ile-de-France

Garreau cites, as evidence of the inevitability of polycentricity, the worldwide emergence of the phenomenon, including six "edge cities" surrounding the great flourishing city of Paris.[133] Five of the six are *villes nouvelle*—new towns—established by the French national government, and one is La Défense, the modern office subcenter just $1\frac{1}{2}$ miles west of the city, also a manifestation of centralized planning.

Garreau overlooks a pair of vitally important factors that differentiate American edge cities from their counterparts in the Paris region: The new developments surrounding Paris are connected to the host city by rail transit; and Paris, unlike our cities, exists in a state of optimal land utilization. Garreau defends his enthusiasm for edge-city proliferation with the implication that nearly all American cities exist in a state of optimal utilization: "For all the moaning about the plight of the cities, there is really only one major American downtown that has gone to hell in a handbasket, and that is Detroit." Garreau belittles the rail factor too; he advocates rail transit as a mere semi-functional embellishment: "the vast majority of all people will continue to arrive at . . . a rail-served Edge City by car. Even in a building directly over the tracks, 90 percent of all office workers will demand parking. But so what?" [134]

Rail service to La Défense and to the new towns surrounding Paris is much more than an embellishment. La Défense, one of nine "suburban growth poles" established by the French government to channel post-industrial growth, is a transportation hub at the confluence four rail lines—Metro, RER, SNCF, and the new Trans-Val-de-Seine light rail line. (Eighteen bus routes also feed the hub.) The RER line that connects La Défense to the heart of Paris is so heavily used that Paris's transit authority recently opened a new Metro line to relieve it. [135]

The five new towns, farther from Paris than La Défense, were established to absorb population growth and industrial decentralization. They also are connected to Paris by rail transit—by a network of 41 regional rail lines, which, in the Paris region of about nine million suburbanites, accommodates roughly 900 million passenger journeys annually. (Hundreds of public and private suburban bus routes transport additional hundreds of millions of passengers annually.) This rate of suburban ridership dwarfs the rates in America's most transit-oriented metropolitan areas. [136]

Reverence for the core city, rather than indifference, inspired France's post-industrial vision for the growth of the Paris metropolis. In the early 1960s, Paul Delouvrier, the state-appointed chief executive for the District of the Paris Region, developed a regional plan with twin objectives: to preserve the region's natural and agricultural land, and to protect the heart of Paris from intensifying development pressure. La Défense, with some 20 million square feet of office space, is the manifestation of reverence for a historic city threatened by an impending onslaught of office towers. The banal office tower in Montparnasse, out of character and out of scale with the fine fabric of its Parisian environs, had warned the French in the 1950s to divert post-industrial development away from established neighborhoods, toward underused land just beyond the city boundary. To attract development to La Défense, the French built a massive and complex infrastructure, the backbone of which is rail transit. The state's investment at La Défense was protected by its participation in planning the region, a role that mitigates competition among local jurisdictions.[137]

Premature Polycentricity

By citing the examples of La Défense and the five *villes nouvelle* outside Paris, Garreau highlights the social and environmental deficiencies of the American polycentricity he advocates. But Garreau's advocacy is close to the mark in one respect—polycentricity has greater social and environmental potential than noncentricity. Suburban business concentrations are more easily and efficiently connected to their core cities by transit than are widely dispersed business locations. Disciplined, transit-oriented, polycentric decentralization is right for metropolitan areas in which the core city has reached a state of optimal land utilization. But the advocacy of such a form of polycentricity requires the repudiation of roadway-dominated transportation investment because, as noted above, our over-extensive and widely dispersed webs of roadway are moving us in the direction of noncentricity.

Only after our core cities have reached a state of optimal land utilization is it appropriate to resume public investment that feeds the decentralization of commerce and high-density housing. And when that time comes, infrastructure investment must create an orderly, socially beneficial, and environmentally benign form of decentralization rather than the chaotic decentralization that characterizes the American metropolis.

Perhaps the kindest assessment that can be rendered upon Garreau's advocacy of polycentricity is that it is ahead of its time—50 years ahead, for that is how long it will take most cities in the United States, if conditions are favorable, to reach a state of optimal land utilization.

Part

III

Poverty and Politics

7

Decentralization of Poverty

Married-couple families have virtually disappeared in many communities, especially in big cities. TOMMY THOMPSON, U.S. SECRETARY OF HEALTH AND HUMAN SERVICES[1]

Urban revitalization is an unattainable dream if cities are unable or unwilling to compete with suburbs for the middle class, and not just middle-class singles or middle-class empty nesters, but middle-class families with children. Cities can't compete unless they provide orderly neighborhoods, and public schools attuned to the aspirations middle-class parents hold for their kids. The proliferation of apartments and townhouses in suburbs, and the extravagant appeal of townhouses in Manhattan, Brooklyn, and Boston demonstrate a strong middle-class market for higher-density housing, a natural market for cities if only their schools and social conditions could be elevated to the standards that prevail in suburbs.

Middle-class parents write off city neighborhoods and whole cities; central-city policymakers seem to have written off middle-class families, being more attentive to the housing needs of the poor. Conventional middle-class families, however, are the most important segment of the metropolitan housing market. The nation's percentage of single-parent families tripled between 1960 and 1991, but middle-class conventional families—married couples with children—remain the backbone of American society, "the bedrock of a stable community," according to HUD.[2] Conventional families account for about a quarter of all the nation's households, outnumbering single-parent families by a ratio of nearly three to one. And almost all conventional families are middle class, earning four times as much, on average, as the never-married mothers over-represented in gray zones.[3] Conventional families are the most economically and politically powerful cohort in the nation, and they demand good housing and exemplary schools in decent neighborhoods.

Socioeconomically distressed households congregate in cities by reason of public policy. It is therefore appropriate to redirect public policy to the dilution of poverty and the restoration of middle-class habitability in distressed urban neighborhoods.

FOUR REASONS TO DILUTE POVERTY

The Jewish Triangle in Brooklyn's Williamsburg proves, as do some big-city Chinatowns, that concentrated poverty in a high-density environment does not necessarily produce the kind of disorder that triggers flight among those who can afford to flee. Conventional families congregated among other conventional families, even if poor, are unlikely to produce populations of youths and young adults who destroy communities. Sociologist George Kranzler describes the poor but tradition-bound Hasidic Jews in Brooklyn's Williamsburg, where the rate of poverty exceeds 40 percent, and where the rate of juvenile delinquency is lower than in pre-World War II days:

> Large families crowd into small apartments. The head of the household earns a low income…Yet, most are far from the spirit of defeatism that fills the poverty-ridden ghetto areas around Williamsburg. They display few of the common indicators of crime and filth, of the drug-ridden dwellings so prevalent in New York's slums.[4]

The poverty-ridden but socially healthy neighborhood is the exception in urban America because concentrated poverty is usually accompanied by high rates of unemployment and fatherlessness, the combination that produces chaos.

Until recently it might have been possible in America to limit a neighborhood's number of poor fatherless families—at-risk families—by means of housing discrimination based on family composition. But the Fair Housing Amendments Act of 1988 stripped from private-market landlords the same discretionary powers that were stripped, disastrously, from public housing authorities in the 1960s and later. The 1988 act adds familial status—the marital status of the head of a household and the composition of his or her family—to the list of factors that must be overlooked by landlords. Many state and local jurisdictions add public assistance status to the list of conditions that landlords must disregard. Thus a landlord with a three-bedroom house can no longer favor a married couple with two toddlers over a welfare-dependent single mother with two teenage boys, even if the neighborhood is already overburdened with similar at-risk households.

Although at-risk households congregated in cities long before the 1988 housing act took effect, the act represents an additional obstacle in the path of neighborhood revitalization. Cities are disadvantaged because they have large and concentrated stocks of housing that is suitable for and affordable to at-risk households. Nearly three-fourths of the housing affordable to very-low-income families in the Twin Cities metropolis is located in the two central cities.[5] Much of this housing exists in the form of rental houses, which are for many households with children more desirable than apartments, and more available. Gray zones have abundant supplies of rental housing that is appropriate for, affordable to, and available to at-risk households.

With the signing of the Fair Housing Amendments Act of 1988, a distressed neighborhood can decentralize its at-risk households, and prevent recentralization, only by upgrading or replacing much of its housing stock so that it is no longer affordable to large numbers of low-income households. Gray-zone neighborhoods should be redeveloped not only at higher densities, but also with a preponderance of higher-cost higher-quality housing that will long resist the forces of invasion and succession.

Why should the poor and at-risk households that populate gray zones be subjected to an invasion by the middle class, which, after all, abandoned these neighborhoods? The middle class was, in large measure, induced by government policy to abandon them, as noted in Chapter 3, and now it is necessary to transform distressed neighborhoods into predominantly middle-class neighborhoods in order to rectify the social and environmental damage wrought by today's geographic distribution of metropolitan poverty. There is room for poor households in the revitalized city, but not for concentrations of at-risk households. It is not necessary to eliminate poverty from neighborhoods so much as to dilute it and, to the extent possible, disperse at-risk households in order to encourage an influx of the middle class.

The economic power of the middle class is required to sustain cultural and commercial diversity, and to improve public services for all residents. Middle-class students are needed to restore prestige to urban public schools. Where tax revenues are scarce, public library hours are cut back and park maintenance suffers, as does street and sidewalk cleanliness. A city's cost of police protection rises about five percent with each percentage-point increase in the city's poverty rate, and other municipal costs follow a similar pattern.[6] All city residents suffer the consequences of fiscal stress that accompany high poverty rates.

Beyond these general social and economic considerations, there are four distinct reasons, related to physical development, that policymakers should target their housing priorities on the middle class instead of the poor and the at-risk:

1. High-density housing, the first requisite to revitalization, is incompatible with socioeconomic poverty.

2. Transit ridership is undermined by the centralization of at-risk households.

3. Downtown revitalization is stymied by the centralization of at-risk households.

4. The urban public realm is undermined by the centralization of at-risk households.

1. High-density housing is incompatible with socioeconomic poverty.

A 23-month-old boy fell to his death from the sixth-floor window of his Minneapolis highrise in September 1998. The boy's mother was joined by her neighbors and by a neighborhood activist in blaming the building's management for the tragedy; they alleged that the building's manager had ignored requests to fix an insect screen that had become dislodged from the window. Apparently they considered the insect screen to be a safety device, and they considered the requests for repair to be a transfer of responsibility for the child's welfare.

Some low-income households depend on the near-constant involvement of landlords and government agencies in their lives, which is why a Boston developer says his mixed-income housing developments "require more care and feeding than the average."* Higher-income households, generally, have the resources to take matters into their own hands and

---

* J. S. Fuerst, a housing scholar and retired professor of social work, avers that the Chicago Housing Authority, if it wishes to stabilize its properties, needs to "clear out 25 percent of the tenants, or else take them all on, but put in the counseling, the psychiatry, the social services, the health care, the security and maintenance . . ." (M.W. Newman, "When the CHA Homes Were Camelot," *Chicago Tribune*, 21 June 2000, p. 1.) Boston developer Joseph Corcoran is quoted by Diane R. Suchman and Margaret Sowell in *Developing Infill Housing in Inner-City Neighborhoods: Opportunities and Strategies* (Washington, D.C.: Urban Land Institute, 1997), p. 63.

avert threatening situations. Middle-class parents unable to constantly supervise their small children can choose housing devoid of obvious danger, or they can modify housing units to suit their circumstances.*

Joan Campbell, the city council representative for the neighborhood where the little boy fell, impugned the high density of the HUD-financed apartment complex: "There's so many people in such a small space."[7] City officials who see low-density housing as the only rational choice for low-income households will not increase densities in the neighborhoods most in need of the revitalization that only higher densities can produce.

Mayor Ed Rendell's Philadelphia was acclaimed as a city in renaissance in the 1990s, but the city's most troubled neighborhoods stayed the path of decline—population loss, housing abandonment, and decay. The social and physical wretchedness of these rowhouse neighborhoods caused city leaders to imagine lower rather than higher housing densities, as Buzz Bissinger reports in *A Prayer for the City*: "There was no longer any point in trying to save or rehabilitate blighted housing, acre after acre of the city was being leveled. Now the hope was that one day a less dense, more suburban style of housing could be built on this land."[8] Nobody in Philadelphia or elsewhere in urban America advocates high housing densities for impoverished populations. The nonprofit developer of a detached-house subdivision less than one mile from downtown Minneapolis cites socioeconomic distress to rationalize the low density: "Once the location with its social and economic factors is understood, this low-density land use becomes a most resourceful use of this land. This fact becomes most important when we consider the record of high density housing in inner-city neighborhoods."[9]

The social mission of housing the poor has impelled officials to suburbanize cities since the 1930s, when the New York City Housing Authority, assisted by the New Deal's Public Works Administration, leveled 10 city blocks of street-wall buildings to make way for Williamsburg Houses—four superblocks of buildings that reject the street and cover less than a third of their Brooklyn site (Figure 7-1).[10] The suburbanization of lot coverage remains a defining characteristic of public housing development.

---

*In *The Hidden War*, an examination of public housing in Chicago by Susan J. Popkin, et.al., a tenant in her early thirties explained that her child was burned by a hot pipe in her apartment because the housing authority's maintenance crew failed to act: "I'd complain, complain, complain. One day I'm in the kitchen cooking something…I hear my son, 'Ma!' When I went back…all his skin was wrapped around the [pipe]. Third degree burn…You see them pipes? They're supposed to be covered up. They're not covered up." (p. 145)

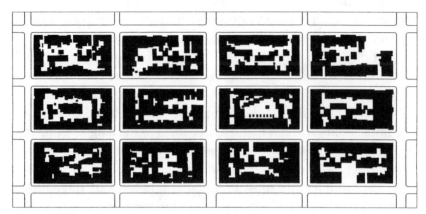

Site of Williamsburg Houses prior to demolition

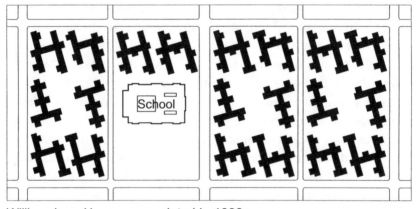

Williamsburg Houses, completed in 1938

Figure 7-1. The suburbanization of the city on behalf of the poor. Brooklyn's Williamsburg houses obliterated hundreds of buildings on 10 city blocks to make way for 20 buildings on four superblocks. The original high-percentage-lot-coverage buildings defined streets; Williamsburg Houses, which cover less than one-third of their net site area, shun the streets.
Williamsburg Houses design by the firm of Shreve, Lamb and Harmon; Richard H. Shreve, principal in charge, William Lescase, chief designer. (Richard Plunz, *A History of Housing in New York City* [New York: Columbia University Press, 1990], p. 217)

HUD's campaign of public housing rehabilitation and demolition/replacement offers an opportunity to urbanize density and lot coverage, but the opportunity is routinely rebuffed. HUD's campaign is funded largely by the agency's HOPE VI program, which aims to relieve concentrations of poverty and to integrate public housing into the fabric of the community. Most units in the new mixed-income communities will be dedicated to public-housing-eligible families and other low-income households, and densities will remain far too low for central-city land. In most cases, densities already too low are being reduced. In Atlanta, Techwood/Howell's 1,195 low-density units are being replaced by 900. In Baltimore, Lafayette Courts' 807 moderate-density units have been replaced by 338. The consent decree that mandates the redevelopment of Chicago's moderate-density Henry Horner Homes stipulates that it shall be converted to a neighborhood of "low-density homes."[11]

The impulse to reduce residential densities also afflicts the private housing stock of low-income neighborhoods, where city officials and nonprofit developers replace derelict apartments and townhouses with detached houses. Densities are reduced even where pitifully low in the first place—in detached-house neighborhoods where demolition produces bigger yards for the houses that remain. Derelict houses that represent precious opportunity for higher-density redevelopment are preserved for the sake of housing affordability and upgraded with public funds.[12] On top of all that, city officials impose suburb-style retail developments on the devitalized commercial streets of gray zones. These blank-wall buildings and their vast parking lots are welcomed in neighborhoods long deprived of commercial amenities, but affluent residents of real urban neighborhoods would never allow them.

Beyond the general proposition that high housing densities are incompatible with poverty, there is a practical reason to avoid high densities for poor populations, especially families with children: High-density housing provides less dwelling unit per dollar than low-density housing. Corridors, stairs, elevators, and other common facilities in apartment buildings elevate the cost, per square foot, of individual units. Building codes dictate costly construction—fireproofing and soundproofing—for common walls between units, and codes dictate costlier exterior wall construction for buildings close together than for buildings far apart, a lesson learned in the 19th century era of great fires. The most economical midrise apartment buildings cost 10 to 15 percent more to build, per square foot, than the most economical lowrise buildings, and the most economical highrise buildings cost 50 percent more to build than the most economical lowrises.[13] (Public housing highrises were built notoriously cheaply for the most part, and many were built in the 1950s and earlier, when building codes were less stringent.) Parking in the high-density environment is consigned to underground garages, and these are more costly than the surface lots invariably found on low-income apartment sites. For housing units of equal size and amenity, construction costs increase as density increases. The high cost of high-density construction is offset by land economies in healthy urban neighborhoods, but land is cheap in distressed neighborhoods. Officials in Philadelphia reason that, with a fixed budget, they can redevelop more of their vast acreage of derelict land at low density than they can at moderate or high density.[14]

The cheapest of new housing units—mobile homes—are commonly associated with rural areas and downscale suburbs, but the genre invades cities thanks to a federal demonstration program—the *Urban Design Project*—assisted by the Manufactured Housing Institute (MHI), whose member firms install "manufactured housing units" in five American cities. The program "will . . . help the traditionally rural manufactured housing industry to reach a better understanding of how housing is delivered in urban environments," according to a former HUD official.[15] Mobile homes appeal to urban policymakers because they cost half the median construction cost of site-built houses. The MHI would point out that the developments needn't look like inner-city trailer parks; on a site in Oakland, individual units are enhanced with site-built garages and false fronts that resemble shallow-pitch roofs.

One-story houses with shallow-pitch roofs are entirely inappropriate for the urban environment, but they proliferate in America's urban gray zones (Figure 7-2). Separated from each other by lawn and air, the new houses are strictly suburban—pitiable alternatives to the streetwalls of stone and brick townhouses and apartment buildings of great neighborhoods. Even cities with rich traditions of urbane architecture—New York, Boston, Philadelphia—are invaded by detached and semidetached houses clad in cheap lightweight siding, but never in affluent neighborhoods, only in poor. In Philadelphia, over the objection of preservationists, semidetached houses invade the distressed Cecil B. Moore neighborhood where streets were once lined with three-story masonry townhouses. One factor more than any other explains the growing numbers of these houses in America's distressed neighborhoods—affordability. Affordable housing and new urbane residential architecture are two

Figure 7-2. Low-cost housing—Detroit (2000). The most economical of new housing units are too low in density, and aesthetically inappropriate, for cities.

different things. Cities and their neighborhoods are more than social entities; they are physical entities that should long outlast their ephemeral inhabitants. It is inconsistent to demand the preservation of great historic buildings and districts while abiding low aesthetic standards for today's buildings. Aesthetic issues are a legitimate concern for those responsible for the future of our cities.

New houses and renewed neighborhoods will eventually age, and some will fall on hard times, but high-quality high-appeal housing attracts gentrifiers to declining neighborhoods. Phillip Clay cites Boston's South End as the classic example of a neighborhood that attracted gentrifiers after its period of decline: "Boston's South End…is filled with street after street of well-constructed nineteenth-century townhouses with detailed architectural rendering and elegant amenities and fixtures."[16] Turn-of-the-century townhouses on Manhattan's Upper West Side had been subdivided into rooming houses by the 1960s, but in the 1970s they were snatched up by gentrifiers in spite of the conspicuous presence of drug dealers nearby. An 1887 five-story brownstone on West 71st Street that had been cut up into apartments was restored to single-house status and sold for more than $4 million in 1996. High-quality residential buildings in high-density urban neighborhoods are blue-chip investments. "High densities can generate enough value for a project to carry quality materials, great on-site amenities, and a nice contribution to neighborhood infrastructure," says Larry Beasely, co-director of planning in Vancouver, B.C. [17]

2. The centralization of at-risk households undermines transit ridership

Insofar as the middle class constitutes a large fraction of the downtown workforce, and insofar as transit operates most efficiently where it links downtown to its proximate neighborhoods, downtown's middle-class workforce should be accommodated near its workplace. Transit analysts Boris Pushkarev and Jeffrey Zupan found the middle class to be the richest target in a strategy of boosting transit use by increasing housing densities: "The reduction in auto trips (and total trips) per person and the increase in transit trips with higher densities is most pronounced among middle-income households."[18] Unless middle-class households are accommodated at high densities in close proximity to downtown jobs, most will continue to drive to work.

Once settled near downtown, the middle-class will use transit only if vehicles and stations feel safe. "Crime and fear of crime…prevent people from using public transportation," reported Anastasia Loukaitou-Sideris, associate professor of urban planning at the University of California-Los Angeles. Loukaitou-Sideris based her conclusion on her research in Los Angeles, where high rates of transit crime are found, unsurprisingly, in low-income areas rife with "signs of incivility" such as graffiti, litter, and vandalism.[19] Even in transit-dependent New York City, ridership rises and falls in response to real and perceived threats to safety. When ridership falls, service eventually follows. The operators of the San Diego Trolley reduced the system's hours of operation after ridership fell 17 percent from 1992 to 1994. The decline in ridership was attributed to crime.[20] The middle class avoids the streets of distressed neighborhoods; its avoidance of public transportation is in some measure attributable to the same concerns.

While transit customers were exposed to increasing levels of everyday disorder—slashed bus seats, graffiti, litter, and raucous youths—during the 1980s and '90s, non-customers were exposed to sensational news of crime. The killers of Brian Watkins, the Utah tourist slain on a subway platform in New York City, brought international infamy to the subway system, as did the homeless man who stabbed a six-year-old girl with a hypodermic needle on a subway train and then refused to be tested for H.I.V. A man lost his legs and a woman lost her life when shoved in front of oncoming subway trains in two separate incidents, nationally reported, both in New York City in the first four months of 1999.[21] And in April 2000, a mother was robbed on a Queens subway platform by a man holding a pistol to her toddler's head.

National reports of incidents like these give the general impression that transit has become as dangerous as the inner city, an impression reinforced throughout the nation by reports of transit crime perhaps less sensational than New York's but close to home. In Minneapolis in 1997, a woman was shot in the head by a 16-year-old boy as he exited a bus at a gray-zone bus stop; he didn't like the way she looked at him. In August 2000 at a downtown Minneapolis bus stop, a man killed another man by pushing him off the bus.[22] Atrocities like these reassure automobile commuters that transit avoidance is prudent (notwithstanding the fact that accident rates are higher in cars); and transit commuters who avoid violence are nonetheless exposed to disorderly conditions and disruptive behavior on transit vehicles and at transit stops.[23] Downtown's entertainment milieu is especially disadvantaged by the real and perceived dangers associated with nighttime transit use. When the patrons of restaurants, bars, and cinemas decide to drive rather than ride, they choose destinations with convenient parking, bad news for downtown.

Rail transit boosts the value of station-area land, unless disorderly passengers make their presence known. Passenger behavior undermines the value of rail transit in places like Atlanta's Lenox Square, where "rowdy" passengers who arrive on MARTA repel affluent shoppers, according to journalist Tamar Jacoby.[24] Disorderly passengers jeopardize potential development at some of San Diego's light-rail station areas. The manager of La Mesa Village Plaza—a modern mixed-use development on the Trolley's Orange Line—reported that the presence of the trolley's disorderly riders raised his security, maintenance, and repair costs above those of similar developments located away from transit. The manager calculated that these added costs outweigh the value added by the rail station. As Robert Cervero notes, "transit's ridership has been drawn disproportionately from the inner-city poor," and some among this cohort have not only suppressed ridership, they have made developers wary of station areas.

In the San Francisco Bay Area, BART should have immediately sparked a development boom along its shortest and most urbanized route—the Richmond corridor that connects San Francisco to Oakland, Berkeley, and Richmond. BART, however, has produced fewer land-use changes on the Richmond corridor, with all its underutilized urban land, than on others in the East Bay according to Cervero, who adds:

> The greatest disappointment along the Richmond corridor has been at the Richmond station itself. When BART arrived, city officials had high hopes it would trigger a building boom because of the area's...large inventory of vacant land. But...little has changed around the Richmond station over the past 20 years despite efforts by the city's redevelopment authority to entice new investment through various incentive programs. A depressed economy, urban blight, and increased crime have suppressed development.[25]

Some of BART's suburban stations have done very well in attracting upscale apartments and residents. The 892-unit Park Regency—the largest and densest (72 units per acre) apartment building at the Pleasant Hill BART station—is occupied largely by professionals, many of them previous residents of Bay Area cities. "Park Regency's tenant mix is heavily weighed toward...people who want to get away from the crime and hassle of city life, but still have an easy commute via BART," reports Michael Bernick, co-director of the National Transit Access Center at the University of California, Berkeley.[26]

If disorderly people jeopardize redevelopment at inner-city transit stations and force housing demand to suburban stations, then these people must be so convincingly outnumbered that they are rarely noticed at any given station area or along any given route. They are rarely if ever noticed at suburban commuter-train stations or on the commuter trains in which middle-class suburbanites en route to their downtown jobs bypass inner-city neighborhoods. (The same can be said for buses that travel HOV freeway lanes.) Commuter trains are the most comfortable form of transit in America; a passenger is unlikely to encounter anything more disturbing than a nearby cell-phone conversations. (And commuter trains are America's most heavily subsidized form of rail transit on a per-passenger basis.)[27]

Because of its superior speed and physical comfort, rail transit has greater potential than bus transit to convert drivers to riders, but the psychological comfort of rail transit can be inferior to that of the meager bus. Manhattan's avenues are never deserted, so its bus stops feel safer late at night than its ominous subway platforms. Moreover, bus stops are more easily escaped than subway platforms. Late at night when transit vehicles are nearly empty, vulnerable bus passengers feel reassured by the presence of the driver, whereas subway passengers feel captive and unprotected. Some of New York's transit users, and probably many, consider the subway off-limits past 9:00 or 10:00 at night. It isn't just fear of crime that deters discretionary late-night ridership, but also an unwillingness to put up with the vagrants and beggars who become so conspicuous in the relative absence of ordinary folks.

Rail transit will someday be automated; it already is in Vancouver and in some downtowns and airports in the United States. Transit will be faster and more efficient when manually operated transit vehicles are as quaint and obsolete as manually operated passenger elevators. But we learned in public housing that automated passenger elevators can be dangerous places. Transit might be equally dangerous without on-board personnel to discourage mischief. Automation is vital to the future of transit, but the benefits will be largely neutralized if transit agencies are forced to staff their vehicles with security personnel. The benefits of automation will be altogether unrealized where safety considerations prevent transit agencies from automating in the first place. Centralized rail transit is necessary for the social and environmental good of the metropolis, but it cannot achieve its potential where disorderly people are centralized also. Transit will reach its greatest potential only where transit resources and middle-class households are both centralized.

3. Downtown revitalization is prevented by centralization of at-risk households

Two business executives were shot and killed on the plaza of the Five Points MARTA station in downtown Atlanta in the summer of 1991 (and a third was wounded) by a gunman who lived in a neighborhood just outside of downtown. In the two years that followed, Rich's flagship department store, two of Atlanta's largest banks, and other smaller businesses vacated their longtime homes in Five Points.[28]

Actually, these businesses had made their decision to flee before the day of the murders, and many other businesses had already evacuated—at least 15 buildings, up to 10 stories high, were vacant in Five Points. A month prior to the double murder, one of Atlanta's prominent real estate brokers had warned city officials that Five Points will continue to bleed unless its street criminals and vagrants are banished. Another real estate broker advised that the stench of urine in some of the area's lobbies isn't popular with potential tenants.[29]

Crime and fear of crime contributed to the slow and steady abandonment of commercial buildings in downtown Atlanta. In Chicago's Loop, crime and fear of crime took its toll in a slightly different way: Crime and fear of crime impelled Chicago officials to acquire a block of historic buildings for demolition even though many were still occupied and viable. Situated between Marshall Field's and the Civic Center, Block 37's buildings housed a rich variety of businesses—small professional offices, grocery and specialty food stores, clothing stores, an assortment of restaurants and bars, a cinema, a pool hall, a coin and stamp shop, a shoe store, a caramel-corn stand, a comic book store, a tailor, a violin maker, and many more. Most of the block's buildings were architecturally significant, nominated, to no avail, by the Landmarks Preservation Council of Illinois for protection from demolition crews. Clarence Darrow once practiced law in the block's Unity Building, an 1892 skyscraper.

The demolition of Block 37 began with a ceremony on October 17, 1989, when Mayor Richard M. Daley surveyed the doomed buildings and declared, "We take a giant step forward today to rebuild our central business district."[30] Block 37's old buildings had got in the way of progress, but not because the underlying land was needed for new buildings; the block remained vacant more than a decade. Block 37 impeded progress by threatening the comfort of middle-class office workers, who were needed to populate the Loop's modern office towers—Chicago's foothold in the post-industrial economy.

The urban critic Ross Miller explained that Mayor Daley "singled out blocks like 37 not because they failed economically, but paradoxically because they were succeeding..."[31] It was the nature of the success that was problematic: "The downtown's retail clientele was composed increasingly of those who used to shop the thriving ghetto retail shops," but once the ghetto's commercial streets were devitalized by depopulation, race riots, and urban renewal, "those who patronized [their] shops had no choice but to travel to the Loop." Included in this clientele was a "disorderly population of...teenagers" lured to downtown's sidewalks, video arcades, and action-adventure movies. Police Sergeant Greg Couchrene from the Loop Tactical Unit pointed toward Block 37 and said "that whole strip is neutral ground for gang bangers. It's where they strut their stuff. They go in that arcade, blow their last quarter, then rob somebody for 'L' fare home." The sergeant was unsentimental about the impending demise of the historic buildings on Block 37, "It's no loss as far as I'm concerned." He called the demolition "crime prevention with a wrecking ball."[32]

If Chicago's "disorderly population" hadn't brought crime and fear of crime to the Loop, there is a strong likelihood that Block 37's historic buildings would still be standing and an impending redevelopment would go to some of the underdeveloped land a few blocks to the west. Crime and fear of crime cost the heart of downtown Minneapolis a block of once lively bars and restaurants. These were on Hennepin Avenue, downtown's once bustling entertainment strip, but the block was razed in 1988 and remained a parking lot for 12 years.* Crime and fear of crime roused New York City officials to rebuild Times Square. The new Disneyfied version will be more homogenized and inert than the old.** Crime and fear of crime killed Underground Atlanta in the 1970s, and stifled the success of the complex in the 1990s after it had been rebuilt at inordinate public expense.

Middle-class flight from the neighborhoods surrounding downtown bled the market that sustained downtown's retail and entertainment busi-

---

*A much maligned redevelopment scheme for the Hennepin Avenue block was narrowly approved by city officials in June 2000, getting strong support from officials who had been on the city council that voted to raze the block in the 1980s. These officials (one of them now the mayor) were perhaps embarrassed by the block's enduring status as a parking lot. The approved plan grossly shortchanges the potential of the site on at least four counts: (1) The site is just one block from the 100% corner of downtown Minneapolis but will be developed at a floor area ratio of only 4:1. (2) The approved design fails to restore the continuity of a streetwall of historic warehouse buildings on one of the bordering streets—First Avenue. (3) The approved design is an internalized whole-block building that pretends, with facade fakery, to be several buildings. Ralph Rapson, the dean of Twin Cities architects, characterized the design as a "terrible, terrible mistake." (4) The development plan is financially risky according to the city's director of finance, who opposed the deal, which involves an inordinate commitment by the city: a parking garage and about 30 percent of the cost of the development, compared to less than 3 percent, reportedly, in developers' equity. (Ralph Rapson quote from Rochelle Olson, "Despite Critics, Block E Advances," *Minneapolis Star Tribune,* 16 May 2000, p. B1. See also Dan Wascoe Jr., "Minneapolis Property Taxes Could Soar, Finance Chief Warns," *Minneapolis Star Tribune,* 24 March 2000, p. 1; Lisa McDonald, "Block E Development Could Leave City Taxpayers Holding the Bag," *Minneapolis Star Tribune,* 1 March 2000, p. A15.)

**Robert A.M. Stern, architect to the Disney organization, answers critics of the "sanitized" 42nd Street by pointing out that, prior to renewal, the street had become vacuous. Only the muggers remained, says Stern, and even they abandoned the street because there was nobody left to mug. (Robert Stern's comments at American Institute of Architects—New York State, Convention 2000, 23 September 2000, Brooklyn, New York.)

nesses, and it contributed to devitalization in another, more subtle, way. As socioeconomically deprived households replaced the middle class, tax revenues became increasingly scarce but increasingly needed. This situation elevated official enthusiasm for downtown redevelopment, including the replacement of buildings that yielded modest tax revenues with buildings that promised greater tax revenues. With whole-block redevelopment projects covering large areas of downtown, the potential for traditional day-and-night vitality was lost. New homogenized downtowns lack the visual, social, and economic texture that is found only where building sizes and rents vary widely. Ross Miller said of the rebuilt Chicago Loop, "hundreds of businesses and organizations...would be lost to the city forever. There would be no place for them in a homogeneous downtown of great towers and [high] rents."[33]

New concert halls and revived theaters bring some folks back to some downtowns, but not the masses who just four decades ago shopped in the best and biggest stores, dined in the finest restaurants, imbibed in the fanciest bars, and escaped the daily grind in the grandest cinemas in the metropolis. Downtown was splendid enough for a special occasion and accessible enough for an evening stroll and a Coney Island hot dog. Nothing in today's city or suburb compares with the richness of the pre-1970s downtown entertainment strip.

If the masses are drawn downtown today for nonwork purposes it is to a new stadium or arena. These facilities have the power to shift some of a metro area's entertainment spending from suburb to city, but they don't belong downtown, not the gargantuan stadiums anyway. It is a sign of downtown devitalization that stadiums are so coveted by city officials. Stadiums are idle most hours of the week, and invariably they attract massive parking lots and garages, even Yankee Stadium in the Bronx, at the intersection of two subway lines. That's why stadiums belong in places like the Bronx, well removed from downtown yet inside the city, which thus benefits from any associated economic development and entertainment spending. At the edge of a city, a stadium's parking garage can double as a park-ride facility for the outer terminus of a rail-transit line. This arrangement decentralizes the parking of downtown commuters while maintaining the centrality of the transit system.

City officials covet downtown stadiums and arenas because the depopulated and automobile-dependent neighborhoods surrounding America's downtowns no longer produce the quantities of non-poor people necessary to support downtown vitality. The neighborhoods surrounding downtown no longer sustain high-quality transit without which downtown stores, restaurants, and cinemas are less accessible, for want of free and convenient parking, than their more distant suburban counterparts. America's downtown retailers, even those in downtowns with stadiums, can no longer realistically hope to compete with suburban malls, not even for the patronage of city residents. Downtown Toronto's shops, restaurants, theaters, and cinemas teem with residents as well as visitors because most of the city's neighborhoods are affluent or solidly middle class, and well connected to downtown by transit. Most of the region's sizable concentrations of low-income, subsidized, and public housing are situated in North York, East York, and Scarborough, five miles or farther from downtown.[34]

"The willingness to make trips falls off sharply with distance. As a result trips to a downtown...will be found in very large numbers only from fairly close proximity to that downtown," according to transit analysts Pushkarev and Zupan, who refer to this phenomenon as "distance decay."[35] Distance decay especially affects nonwork transit trips, including shopping and entertainment trips. Consequently, the neighborhoods surrounding a downtown must be repopulated at higher densities with a more affluent population, and they must be provided with good transit, if ever downtown is to reach its potential. A non-poor population surrounding a downtown enhances the prospects for downtown revitalization.

4. The urban public realm is undermined by the centralization of at-risk households

Distressed neighborhoods in Chicago, St. Louis, and Dayton, Ohio, have fought against crime by blocking streets, converting through-streets into dead ends—inner-city versions of the suburban cul-de-sac. The inner-city cul-de-sac aims to reduce the flow of vehicles carrying johns, drug buyers, and fleeing wrong-doers. (Pedestrian access is unimpeded.) The technique is effective and gaining the attention of city officials nationwide. As noted in Chapter 2, natural barriers to through-traffic enhance the quality of life in high-density neighborhoods, but the inner-city cul-de-sac is demarcated by a thin artificial barrier—a gate or a curb or a row of bollards—that reminds residents and informs outsiders that this is a troubled neighborhood, one from which the welcome mat has been removed. And the thin barrier frustrates neighborhood residents who are forced to unlock gates or drive circuitous routes to get to routine destinations.[36] Taxi drivers navigate gated neighborhoods with difficulty. America's great urban neighborhoods are ungated.

Commercial streets and transit stations are primary assets in high-vitality neighborhoods, but these assets become liabilities in neighborhoods where at-risk households are concentrated. A commercial street's contribution to a civil neighborhood is larger than mere convenience; the street's businesses foster social interaction, according to Marlys McPherson and Glenn Silloway, researchers at the Minnesota Crime Prevention Center: "Commercial centers function socially as parts of neighborhoods and have effects on neighborhood attachments ...the centers can strengthen ties to the neighborhood."[37]

But the commercial street in a distressed neighborhood is a liability, avoided by outsiders and by many neighborhood residents. Commercial streets overburdened with liquor stores, check-cashing joints, boarded-up buildings, scabby parking lots, graffiti, loiterers, drug dealers, and prostitutes hurt their neighborhoods and "reinforce a cycle of decline," according to McPherson and Silloway.[38] Public parks, also, are assets in middle-class neighborhoods and liabilities in neighborhoods overrepresented by at-risk households, and the cost of park maintenance and safety is highest in neighborhoods where tax proceeds are lowest. Robert Moses's biographer Robert Caro noted the difficulty of providing parks for the residents of New York's slums: "Because you couldn't afford to keep a full-time supervisor on duty in every vest-pocket park, those small parks located in slums quickly became filled with rubbish and winos." When a new vest-pocket park called Piazza d'Italia was dedicated in downtown New Orleans in 1978, *Progressive Architecture* magazine called it "an ensemble of unqualified pleasure and delight [that] fills its beholders with feelings of happiness, romance, joy, and love." Twenty-two years later, the park is an open-air flophouse, an ensemble of weeds and broken marble. Sociologist Elijah Anderson notes that Vernon Park, located in a distressed part of Philadelphia's Germantown neighborhood, suffers "the carelessness and even vandalism of some of the people who like to gather there." As director of the Street Life Project in New York City, William H. Whyte (author of *The Social Life of Small Urban Spaces*) discovered that ordinary folks and "undesirables" repel each other from urban public places.[39] It is necessary, therefore, to create neighborhoods in which "undesirables" are never more than a minuscule fraction of the population.

Vandalism and crime impel public officials to deaden the public realm with dreary buildings, like Harlem's Intermediate School 201, a fortress built windowless to save the dollars and prevent the dangers associated with broken windows. In Chicago, a new library near the Cabrini-Green public housing site is, for fear of vandalism, a windowless bunker, unlike the new and generously glazed branch in the more sedate Archer Heights neighborhood. Vandalism and crime discourage America's public officials from providing public amenities taken for granted in European cities. The high tech self-cleaning public toilets manufactured in Europe are attractive enough to be welcomed on the classiest boulevards of Paris, but America's urban officials deploy them sparingly if they deploy them at all. "There have been concerns about the toilets being magnets for homeless people, drug users, and prostitutes...proposals often have been shot down because of concerns about crime," reported the *New York Times*. In Los Angeles, "the concern has focused on downtown ...[which encompasses] a 50-square-block zone filled with cheap hotels and shelters for the homeless." [40]

When middle-class Americans withdrew from cities and from the public realm, they created as a substitute the extravagant private realm of the shopping mall. Mall developers spare no expense in their efforts to attract the middle class; city officials should exert equal efforts on behalf of the public realm of distressed neighborhoods. City leaders should visualize streets and boulevards no less extravagant than the great boulevards of Paris and Barcelona, but such a vision is inconsistent with cities abandoned and shunned by the non-poor population. The tax base of a substantial middle-class and affluent population is required to develop and maintain a first-rate public realm, which benefits poor and non-poor residents alike.

CHINATOWN

It is neither necessary nor desirable to repopulate cities entirely with non-poor residents. The availability of low-cost housing gives American cities some of their most vibrant districts—Williamsburg in Brooklyn, Adams-Morgan in Washington, D.C., Chinatowns in San Francisco and New York City. Min Zhou's socioeconomic profile of New York City's Chinatown characterizes the neighborhood as a dynamic economic enclave—a miniature Hong Kong—where "immigrants can make their American dream come true." [41] Restaurants and shops are the most visible of Chinatown's enterprises, but thriving businesses in the FIRE sector of the economy are also found there. In smaller cities, long-derelict neighborhood commercial streets show signs of life as Asian and Latino immigrants establish businesses in low-rent buildings. Low-rent districts are the most alluring or the most repelling of city neighborhoods, depending upon social conditions and their physical manifestations.

Among the factors contributing to the lively commercial streets near some of the nation's universities is income diversity. The streets of San Francisco's Haight-Ashbury and Manhattan's East Village are lively enough to attract affluent outsiders to the company of impoverished students and artists. Writer John Weir described the mix in New York's gentrifying East Village:

> The East Village is one of the few places in New York where poor people and rich people, self-proclaimed failures and ashamed sellouts, drug addicts, vegetarians, anarchists, and skinhead supremacists, Puerto Rican landladies and sixties leftovers and anxious militant queers can, however tentatively, get along. Or at least live on the same block.[42]

Mixed-income districts like the East Village and Chinatown are among America's great places, but they attract few middle-class families with children—the population most desperately needed to repopulate urban gray zones. Besides, most gray zones lack the potential to revitalize in the form of an East Village or a Chinatown because their commercial streets are too vacuous, and new commercial development exacts rents too high for the numerous small independent businesses that energize the liveliest of neighborhoods. But gray zones are well suited, by virtue of their strategic locations, to revitalize into middle-class neighborhoods for the downtown workforce, neighborhoods capable of sustaining commercial streets along which many buildings are necessarily new. It is appropriate, therefore, to redevelop gray zones into moderate-density predominantly middle-class neighborhoods with high-density commercial streets.

There is ample room in the post-industrial city for many among the working poor and the employable poor, but a revitalized city is not first and foremost a provider of housing to the poorest households in the metropolis. A revitalized city is resilient enough to accommodate low-income households in a proportion commensurate with the metropolitan area's proportion of such households. Unless poor and at-risk households are dispersed and shared with suburbs, cities cannot attract and retain the non-poor families without which there will be no revitalization, only stabilization.

The administrators of Chicago's Gautreaux program, which provided suburban housing opportunities to public housing residents, adopted a strategy of relocating only a tightly controlled number of at-risk house-holds to any one suburban community because, the administrators rea-soned, the program would remain politically viable only if "receiving" neighborhoods were virtually unaffected by the introduction of at-risk households.[43] If more than a few at-risk households are deemed detrimental to a middle-class suburban neighborhood, then it must be assumed that a middle-class city neighborhood deserves similar consideration.

THE UNWELCOME POOR (AND MIDDLE CLASS)

Households unable to afford detached houses on large lots are excluded from many affluent suburbs by zoning provisions. This form of exclusion is not prohibited by the Fair Housing Act of 1968 or the Fair Housing Amendments Act of 1988, which ban housing discrimination if it's based on race, gender, religion, physical disability, or familial status, but not if it's based on economic status. HUD outlined its position as follows: "[HUD] has determined not to publish rules regarding issues relating to local government exercise of police powers in the areas of land use and zoning."[44]

In the absence of a federal affordable-housing mandate, advocates of locational choice for low-income households have persuaded some state legislatures and courts to force-feed low-income households to non-poor communities, including affluent developing suburbs. Under Massachusetts' "anti-snob zoning law," suburban communities in which less than ten percent of the total housing stock is "affordable" can no longer enforce zoning ordinances that have the effect of excluding afford-able housing. Courts in New York and New Jersey also have directed suburban communities to provide housing opportunities to low-income households.[45]

Exclusive suburbs in the Twin Cities metropolis are moved by legislated incentives, rather than mandates, to open their doors to low-income households; still many suburban communities remain beyond financial reach. In metro areas nationwide, advocates push for the mandatory inclusion of low-income households, but the usual force-feed approach is fraught with deficiency, and it is most unpromising as a force for urban revitalization. Before considering a strategy more beneficial to cities, it is helpful to understand the nature of the challenge and the inadequacy of the standard prescriptions. First of all, it is helpful to understand the rational basis for resistance to the force-feed approach. When force-feed advocates tell us that households of varying socioeconomic backgrounds are fundamentally compatible as neighbors, they are being somewhat truthful and maybe even generally truthful, but not entirely truthful, and affluent suburbanites will not willingly abide the wishful thinking of the advocates.

A Man in His Shirt Sleeves

"Most people tend to move where they can afford to live, among people who are like themselves," says Michael Weiss, author of *The Clustering of America: A Portrait of the Nation's 40 Neighborhood Types—Their Values, Lifestyles and Eccentricities*.[46] Self-segregation is found even within populations that might be assumed quite homogeneous, as this excerpt from a report by the New York City Planning Department explains:

> The Chinese population of New York City have defined their own standards for location, i.e., if you are unskilled and have limited education, you live in Chinatown, Manhattan. If you are a Chinese professional who has achieved, you live in Flushing; if you are young, studying and on your way up, you live in Borough Park.[47]

This natural tendency of many Americans to settle into socioeconomically homogeneous enclaves is defied by the force-feed approach to poverty dispersal.[48] Advocates chastise exclusionary suburbanites, characterizing their rejection of low-income households as evidence of moral deficiency. Charges of racism are liberally bandied and enthusiastically reported by a conflict-oriented and race-hyperconscious news media. The pontificating advocates deny the reality that stress and friction are probable where socioeconomically homogeneous enclaves are invaded.

The poor are not the only victims of exclusionary attitudes in metropolitan America; the middle class is unwelcome in enclaves of the rich. In Heathrow, Florida, rich homeowners insisted that the developer of an adjacent subdivision of middle-class houses build a brick wall and a separate vehicular entrance to keep the middle-class intruders at bay. Often a household's acceptability is determined not by economic status per se, but by outward signals of class. A millionaire professor of civil engineering in Huntington Beach, California, was shunned and sued by neighbors for refusing to clean up her embarrassingly sloppy house and yard. An upper-middle-class condominium in Haverhill, Massachusetts, banishes from its driveways the blue-collar icon—the pick-up truck.[49] No matter who drives them, pick-ups and campers are flotsam in the eyes of affluent homeowners who invest fortunes in landscaping. Middle-class homeowners who tolerate pick-ups and campers on driveways are disturbed by junk cars in back yards.

Vehicles are an everyday factor in neighborhood disorder. Parking pavements surrounding low-rent apartments are oil-stained from do-it-yourself vehicle maintenance and repair; building managers discourage the practice to little avail. Minneapolis City Council member Alice Rainville ignited a furor during a council debate about low-income housing when she impugned some of the occupants: "They can pull an engine out of a car, but they can't figure out how to mow the lawn."[50]

Exclusionary attitudes are not irrational. John P. Marquand conveyed this in his 1936 book about George Apley, the upright Bostonian whose father bought a house in the South End, a neighborhood of "fine [bowfront] mansions with dark walnut doors and beautiful woodwork." The senior Apley made a hasty decision to flee from this elegance, repelled by his neighbor's offensive behavior. George described the moment of his father's disillusionment: "'Thunderation,' father said, 'there is a man in his shirt sleeves on those steps.'" The next day George's father sold his house to move to a better neighborhood. The senior Apley's "unfailing foresight" paid off, for the South End became "a region of rooming houses and worse."[51]

The Apleys were fictional, but their Brahmin constitution and their Boston were authentic. As long ago as the 1920s, socioeconomic conditions were recognized as more powerful than physical conditions in affecting neighborhood property values.[52] Socioeconomic condition manifests itself in property maintenance (the dilapidated housing stock of many gray zones includes large and formerly elegant houses) and property maintenance is not a minor issue for many homeowners. In New Orleans a man shot and killed a woman with whom he had been feuding about lawn maintenance.[53]

The significance of homeownership as a factor in property maintenance couldn't be more evident than it is at some of Chicago's public housing sites. At Stateway Gardens on the south side, yards are strewn with litter, which in all likelihood didn't blow in from off site.[54] Alex Kotlowitz, in his book *There Are No Children Here*, describes conditions on the grounds of Chicago's Henry Horner Homes: "soiled diapers dumped in the grass" and, near a building entry, "the unmistakable smell of urine."* Sanitation and orderliness in these public housing developments are much inferior to conditions in neighborhoods like Willard-Hay in Minneapolis, where incomes are modest but the rate of homeownership is relatively high. Homeownership rates are lowest, of course, among the poorest of the poor.

Heterogeneity and Social Conflict

In their study of neighborhood crime prevention, sociologist Stephanie Greenberg and planner William Rohe conclude that socioeconomic heterogeneity brings not only conflicting standards of property maintenance but also conflicting standards of public behavior, thereby producing stressful relationships among neighbors in "transitional" neighborhoods:

> It is difficult to establish agreed-upon norms for public behavior in these areas because different classes, lifestyles, and family types typically have different conceptions of the appropriate use of public space, and, hence, of desirable and undesirable public behaviors. More importantly, these conceptions may be not only different but also in conflict.[55]

This reality plays out in a new suburb-style retail development that buffers Chicago's Cabrini Green public housing from the more affluent neighborhood to the north. The retail development includes a supermarket—Dominick's—where Cabrini residents rub shoulders with their more affluent neighbors. In June 2000, *Chicago Tribune* columnist Mary Schmich reported, "Occasionally problems flare. Sometimes [middle-class] customers seem unnerved by more boisterous customers from Cabrini."

Special measures are required to ensure Dominick's success, according to Schmich: "When it opened a year and a half ago, the store's success was hardly guaranteed. Would [the area's affluent residents] patronize the new supermarket? Sure they would. If you gave them ample parking...If

---

*Kotlowitz also notes that an entry canopy serves "as a landing place for junk thrown from the upper floors—a black vinyl car seat, a baby bottle, Coca-Cola bottles, a suitcase, shoes of various sizes..." (Alex Kotlowitz, *There Are No Children Here*, pp. 45, 121) In *The Hidden War: Crime and the Tragedy of Public Housing in Chicago*, Susan J. Popkin and her co-authors describe "dirt and debris" and "trash from apartment windows" on the grounds of Chicago's housing projects (pp. 95, 143); as well as "trash and junk" inside and outside buildings (pp. 95, 135, 163). Also: "As in Rockwell [Gardens], the hallways [in Henry Horner Homes] often reeked of human waste as well as garbage." (p. 95) It's not that filth accumulates for lack of maintenance; the authors quote a resident of Henry Horner Homes, "The janitors...come in the morning and they do clean up. But over the weekends, the janitors don't do anything on weekends. Then everything is a mess on Mondays." (p. 123)

you drove panhandlers off the lot. If you gave them five security guards instead of the usual one...." (Schmich also reported some potentially violent conflict at Dominick's: "Not long ago, members of two rival gangs bumped into each other while shopping; security was called.")[56]

In a 1997 report to the New York City Council, Thomas McMahon, Larian Angelo, and John Mollenkopf conclude that conflicting standards of public behavior are determined primarily by economic status:

> A shared economic position often promotes the shared goals and values that create a framework for an unspoken code of acceptable behavior. This accepted code of behavior reduces social tension and allows a city to rely on custom rather than law to regulate daily activities. When the economic experience of groups diverge sharply, this code breaks down and social frictions are exacerbated.[57]

The behavior-income nexus rings true among conservatives, who argue that character flaws give rise to irresponsible behavior, which in turn gives rise to poverty. But not inevitably; many low-income households, and even some low-income enclaves, maintain high levels of civic order. Few would dispute, however, that crime in America is most commonly found among low-income populations. The war on poverty was a reaction to rising crime rates coupled to the presupposition that there exists an "intimate relationship between poverty and crime."[58] David Rusk, the former mayor of Albuquerque, theorizes that stress is what links poverty to crime:

> As poverty increases [within a neighborhood], the interaction between stressed families also increases, particularly as stable middle-class families move away. Once...the concentration of poverty reaches a critical level, a chain reaction begins in the community: crime and delinquency rise, alcoholism and drug addiction increase, schools fall into decline, neighborhoods deteriorate, unemployment and welfare dependency increase, and social meltdown begins.[59]

Rusk's theory ignores the high-poverty neighborhoods in which uncivil behavior is the rare exception. Sociologist Elijah Anderson and the eminent planner Phillip Clay attribute varying standards of behavior to social and cultural rather than economic factors. Anderson distinguishes between low-income "decent" people and low-income "street" people; in a neighborhood dominated by decent people, residents are "civil and respectful to one another," while in a neighborhood dominated by street people, "public decency gets little respect."* Clay uses the terms "civil class" and "uncivil class" and notes that "anyone, regardless of income or occupation, can be a member of either class."[60]

Whatever the causes of uncivil behavior, the consequences devastate communities. Kelling and Coles describe an incident in which a single invasive household destroyed the tranquility of a quiet stable neighborhood:

> In the summer of 1994, in New Haven, Connecticut, two...women and their four children moved from a housing development to a quiet residential neighborhood...Soon after...the two women had a birthday party for one of their brothers. The party grew loud and moved outdoors, with music resonating from speakers placed in the yard. The family next door...called police three times starting at 10:30 p.m.: The police came to the house shortly after midnight. After the police left once, and later returned, a major conflagration ensued with ten officers injured, ten citizens arrested, and someone at the party throwing a radio through the window of the next-door neighbor...The community had been seriously frayed by these incidents...[61]

Intolerably loud music wasn't the only noise that followed the uncivil-class newcomers into their new neighborhood, "A lingering dispute from the housing development followed the women to their new home, erupting into violence when someone fired seventeen shots into the next-door neighbor's house, believing it to be the new residents' home."[62]

"Some poor people live problematically...they may live noisily with limited regard for neighbors," said Howell Baum, professor of urban studies and planning at the University of Maryland. He was referring to the low-income renters in a vulnerable neighborhood in Southeast Baltimore, a neighborhood where disruptive behaviors disproportionately found among the poor threaten a more sedate lifestyle long taken for granted by the neighborhood's working-class homeowners.[63]

Unattended Children and Criminal Youths

Noisy living and disregard for neighbors is often associated with badly

---

*"The culture of decency is characterized by close extended families, low incomes but financial stability, deep religious values, a work ethic and desire to get ahead, the value of treating people right, and a strong disapproval of drug use, violence, and teenage pregnancy. The street represents hipness, status based on one's appearance, and contempt for conventional values and behavior, which are easily discredited because of their association with whites. These behaviors can include doing well in school, being civil to others, and speaking standard English." (Elijah Anderson, *Code of the Street: Decency, Violence, and the Moral Life of the Inner City* [New York: W.W. Norton, 1999], p. 287)

parented children. Referring to the conversion of public housing projects to mixed-income developments, real estate consultants Diane Suchman and Margaret Sowell (both formerly with HUD) warn would-be developers, "Many existing residents can be expected to have problems and will need help with...housekeeping and parenting skills..."[64] Oscar Newman's examination of public housing provoked his observation that "children of low-income families are generally unattended. The rule system for expected behavior is often minimal and sporadically enforced."[65] Jim Tarbell, an advocate for Cincinnati's poor and homeless, came to the painful conclusion that some of his poor neighbors were "sloppy people" who "threw garbage out of windows, played loud music night and day, got drunk in the street, and let small children roam the streets unattended."[66] (Tarbell lost patience with "sloppy people" when he realized they hinder the prospects of the civil-class poor.)

Unattended children are an obnoxious presence where poor fatherless families are congregated, as journalist Buzz Bissinger observed in Philadelphia. In *A Prayer for the City*, Bissinger tells the story of Linda and Jon Morrison, a young middle-class couple who in 1990 bought an "irresistible...three-story row house" just a quarter-mile from South Street—Philadelphia's exuberantly lively neighborhood commercial street. The first night in their new home, the couple was awakened at 2:00 a.m. by screams in the alley that separated them from a Section 8 apartment complex inhabited largely by single mothers and their children. Night after night the noise continued and time after time the Morrisons called the police, to no avail. In desperation the Morrisons went to the source, "They tried asking the parents to supervise their children, to keep them from screaming and yelling at all hours of the night, but more often than not they were met by bemused half stares, as if such a request were not only impossible to comply with but comical. The screams and yells continued."[67]

Linda Morrison gave birth to the couple's first child in August 1991. Eleven months later they fled to the suburbs. Jon and Linda, childless, tolerated the disorder, and even the occasional violence, that afflicted their neighborhood; tolerance was part of the cost of their modest house within walking distance of the Italian Market, dozens of restaurants, and the myriad shops that line South Street. But the couple's affinity for an urban lifestyle was overpowered by parental instinct.[68]

The inability or unwillingness of poor single mothers to control their kids brought social chaos to the housing projects of South Boston in the

1970s and 1980s. This is told in Michael Patrick MacDonald's autobiography, rife with tales of drug abuse, crime, and premature death by murder and suicide. The South Boston projects of MacDonald's youth epitomized the "wild Irish slums" invoked by Daniel Patrick Moynihan when he warned against the rising tide of fatherlessness in urban America.[69]

Public disorder is perhaps more strongly correlated to age than economic status; solidly middle-class neighborhoods are hardly immune to the occasional raucous party, blaring stereo, or recklessly driven car. But socioeconomically deprived neighborhoods, especially those with large numbers of teenagers, are most productive of street crime and violence. Oscar Newman reported in 1972 that among public housing projects, the more teenagers the more crime. (Newman noted that the combination of numerous teenagers and numerous elderly adults produces the highest crime rates.) Of the "low-income criminal" Newman said, "he and his crimes are the most obnoxious to society."[70]

Rational Resistance

Although the poverty-crime nexus is not absolute, the correlation between high poverty rates and high crime rates is strong in American cities. Those individuals characterized by Phillip Clay as belonging to the "uncivil class" come disproportionately from households immersed in poverty, hence, middle-class and affluent homeowners behave rationally when they resist the encroachment of low-income and, especially, at-risk households. Yet their resistance is impugned as classism, if not racism—character flaws that should be punished. The imposition of low-income households on exclusionary neighborhoods is a punishment that fits the crime in the mind of the locational-choice advocate, who exempts no community from the obligation to house the poor. The modern liberal's obsession with diversity and inclusiveness feeds the attitude that all neighborhoods should be economically diverse and inclusive of their metro area's low-income and poverty-level households.

This 1999 letter to the editor of the *Minneapolis Star Tribune* illustrates the corrosive effect of seemingly petty behavioral deficiencies visited upon a middle-class neighborhood by a locational-choice initiative:

> Within six months of moving to Minnetonka [a suburb west of Minneapolis], we were notified by the city that an affordable housing townhome complex was proposed adjacent to our property. Three single-family homes with established landscaping would be moved in the process—what we thought would be part of our quiet suburban neighborhood. Despite neighborhood opposition, the project went forward.

And now we are left to listen to four-letter words routinely screamed by older children and teenagers, and harsh parental discipline heard through open windows. We have to monitor our property for kids playing in our garden and yard who leave litter behind. We have been harassed by older kids living in that complex, and our daughter is terrified that they will kill our cat, as promised.

The manager of the complex was very sincere in wanting to hear about any issues we have. But is it realistic to have to report profanities and other offensive behavior every time they occur? We chose this neighborhood because it is private, quiet and established, yet now we live with a very unsettling feeling.

The issues I have are not those related to the concept of "affordable" housing…the issues have to do with those in positions of leadership deciding what is "the greatest good" while we have to live with the effects. Our neighborhood has taken on a different character, yet it isn't "affordable" for us to move for a while. (Ginny Mathews, Minnetonka, letter to the editor of the *Minneapolis Star Tribune*, 20 May 1999, p. A20)

A DIVERSION OF HOUSING RESOURCES

In 1993, HUD Secretary Henry Cisneros said that one of the highest priorities of his urban strategy was to "press the case for …the *production* of affordable housing…"(Emphasis added.) Housing advocate Peter Dreier urges HUD to apply housing funds to *new* housing in affluent suburban areas. A housing advocacy group led by former St. Paul mayor George Latimer urges Minnesota legislators to subsidize the *construction* of suburban housing, suggesting subsidies of up to $90,000 (1997 dollars) for *new* townhouses. Hennepin County attorney Mike Freeman, while campaigning for the Minnesota governor's office in 1997, called for the *construction* of affordable housing in the affluent developing suburbs around the Twin Cities. Metropolitan regionalists David Rusk and Myron Orfield push their *new*-affordable-housing-in-affluent-suburbs agenda nationwide.[71] This is a basic tenet of locational-choice advocacy: Low-cost suburban housing will be *new* housing rather than aging middle-class housing, which has traditionally accommodated the overwhelming majority of poor households in American cities.

Any new housing—even "affordable" housing—that complies with building codes is superior to most of the dilapidated and obsolete, but still occupied, housing in America's urban gray zones. American cities desperately need an infusion of new housing, especially higher-density middle-income housing, but housing advocates persuade policymakers to dedicate public money to new housing in developing suburbs.

The Metropolitan Livable Communities Act

In 1994, a Minnesota legislator introduced a locational-choice bill designed to reduce the sales tax on construction materials used for new affordable housing, and to develop a pilot project in Eden Prairie, a well-to-do developing suburb southwest of Minneapolis. That bill was vetoed by Governor Arne Carlson, but the Metropolitan Livable Communities Act (MLCA), which provides financial incentives for new suburban low-cost housing, was signed into law in 1995. (The bill was crafted by Ted Mondale, a suburban state senator who later assumed the chair of the Metropolitan Council.)[72]

Minnesota's MLCA demonstrates the power of locational-choice initiatives to undermine urban revitalization by diverting housing resources away from cities. The act, exceedingly generous in its definition of "affordable," parcels out public funds to suburbs that accommodate the development of housing for people far above the poverty threshold. For owner-occupied housing, the MLCA's threshold of affordability is defined as "affordable to families at 80 percent of [metro-area] median income." These families could afford houses priced at $120,000 in 1996—the program's first full year of operation—when seven of Minneapolis' nine predominantly residential districts had median house values below $120,000. Citywide, the median sale price for houses was only $81,000 in 1996, and the median was less than $50,000 in the Near North district.[73]

For rental housing, the MLCA's affordability threshold is set at 50 percent of the metropolitan area's median household income, but several distressed neighborhoods in Minneapolis have median household incomes less than 50 percent of the metro-area median. More than half the households in these neighborhoods cannot afford the new suburban apartments eligible for state subsidy under the MLCA. The median rent for the full universe of Minneapolis' rental apartments was lower in 1996 than the MLCA's affordability threshold for efficiency apartments. [74]

As noted in Chapter 5, the MLCA funded five pilot projects including a suburban development called West Ridge, which was chosen because some of its housing units are affordable according to the MLCA's criteria. Aside from 126 apartments for the elderly, six of West Ridge's 64 rental units were earmarked for families relocated from a Minneapolis public housing development evacuated for demolition. Another 14 were set aside for households with incomes 50 percent of the metro-area median, but those 14 command higher rents than a majority of apartments of equivalent size in Minneapolis.[75] Prices for West Ridge's 104 owner-occupied townhouses, about half of which were completed and occupied in 1996, started at $94,000—well above the Minneapolis median house price—and extended up to $160,000 (Table 7-1).[76] Nonetheless, 24 of West Ridge's townhouses qualified for Minnesota Housing Finance Agency funding to assist first-time homebuyers. West Ridge's 98 condominium apartments, priced from $189,000 to more than $500,000, got no direct public funding, but they share West Ridge's infrastructure and site development, which were financed in part with MLCA funds. (West Ridge's townhouses are a buffer between the condominiums and the apartments, Figure 7-3.)

Aside from its 126 apartments for senior citizens, West Ridge contains 266 housing units—apartments and townhouses. All told, only six of those 266 units are affordable to poverty-level households, compared to 178 units that will be owned and occupied by affluent and solidly middle-class households, households that are desperately needed in Minneapolis neighborhoods. As gray zones decayed in Minneapolis, nearly $1 million in MLCA money, plus additional housing money from the Minnesota Housing Finance Agency and from HUD, helped build public infrastructure and urban-density housing in a developing suburb.

THE DIVERSION OF HUMAN RESOURCES

Locational-choice initiatives divert three categories of human resources from cities to developing suburbs: the *non-poor*, the *aspiring poor*, and the *elderly*.

The Non-poor

The universe of low-income households covers a broad socioeconomic spectrum, with at-risk households at one extreme, working-poor families in the middle, and, at the other extreme, entry-level college-educated professionals, well above the poverty threshold, soon to form affluent two-earner households. Locational-choice advocates are promiscuous with their compassion, urging suburban housing subsidies for the entire spectrum. The Livable Communities Housing Task Force, headed by former St. Paul Mayor George Latimer, urged Minnesota policymakers to subsidize new suburban housing for households earning up to $27,300 annually (in 1996). That's the income of entry-level accounting, advertising,

Table 7-1. MLCA's Misdirection of Housing Resources—West Ridge

West Ridge Owner-Occupied Units

Type of Unit	Number of Units	1996 Price Range		
Townhouses, first-time homebuyer	24	$94,000		
Townhouses, market rate	80	110,000	to	160,000
Condominium apartments	98	189,000	to	520,000
Total number of units	202			

Minneapolis median house value in 1996:   **$81,000**
Percent of West Ridge ownership units priced above Minneapolis median: **100**

West Ridge Rental Units (excluding elderly component)

Type of Unit	Number of Units	1997 Price Range		
Public housing replacement units	6	(subsidized)		
Units reserved for households at 50% of median income	14	$511	to	710
Remainder of units	44	600	to	852
Total number of units	64			

Minneapolis median rent 1997:   **$485**
Percentage of West Ridge rental units priced above Minneapolis median: **91**

Notes:

1. The first of West Ridge's owner-occupied units—both townhouses and apartments—were completed in 1996. The first of West Ridge's rental units were completed in 1997. Most municipalities set their MLCA housing goals in 1996. (Goetz and Mardock, 1998, p. 9)

2. Minneapolis' 1996 median house value—$81,000—is the average of 1st quarter 1996 and 1st quarter 1997 medians. (Minneapolis Planning Department, State of the City 1997)

3. Twenty-four of West Ridge's townhouses qualified for the State of Minnesota's first-time home buyer program because they were priced below $95,000. (City of Minnetonka, West Ridge Market, undated project description, received 9/11/96)

4. The most expensive of West Ridge's condominium apartments completed in 1996 sold for $400,000. The developer planned to price some units in subsequent buildings for $520,000 or more.

5. West Ridge's rental rates for non-subsidized units are higher than the corresponding Minneapolis median for each apartment type—one bedroom, two-bedroom, and three-bedroom.

6. Minneapolis 1997 median rent—$485—is the average of 1st half 1997 and 1st half 1998 medians. (Minneapolis Planning Department, State of the City 1998, p. 19).

7. Six rental units at West Ridge are replacement units for public housing demolished in Minneapolis. (City of Minnetonka, West Ridge Market)

8. West Ridge rental prices from City of Minnetonka, West Ridge Market; developers' promotional literature; and telephone discussion with Metropolitan Council's Linda Moloacious, 11 September 1996.

Figure 7-3. The fruits of Minnesota's Metropolitan Livable Communities Act.
MLCA funding helped build upscale West Ridge, where condominium
apartments in the background building sold for more than three times the
metro area's median house value. West Ridge is located in Minnetonka, an
affluent suburb of Minneapolis.

and banking professionals, young college graduates beginning their
career-ladder climb. Many locational-choice initiatives, including the
Twin Cities' Livable Communities Act, target the whole spectrum of low-
and moderate-income households, rather than the most troubled
extreme.[77]

The MLCA targets a population that is more affluent than of a majority
of residents in Minneapolis' distressed neighborhoods. Since extreme
poverty is accompanied by disproportionate levels of incivility, the
MLCA will do little or nothing to decamp the most uncivil of the inner-
city population to suburbia. Instead, the program will suburbanize
socioeconomically robust households willing to buy into a predominantly
middle-class community of townhouses and apartments. These households are underrepresented in cities and indispensable to the process of
revitalization; it's a shame they are consigned by public policy to developing suburbs. A locational-choice strategy with urban revitalization as a

goal would devote its resources to the inner city's concentrations of at-risk households, but urban revitalization is low on the agenda of locational-choice advocates, if it is on the agenda at all.

The economically rising young adults who are lured to West Ridge from the cities of Minneapolis and St. Paul, which offer few modestly-priced townhouses in desirable neighborhoods, are lost to the suburbs forever, according to Herbert Gans, who found that suburban immigrants from cities tend to remain forever in suburbs.[78] When these young households are ready to move up to higher priced housing, they typically seek and find it in their suburban sectors. If Gans is correct, it is best to parcel out citizens to suburbs with considerable care.

For the City of Minneapolis, the MLCA funded a demonstration project on a derelict stretch of East Lake Street, where the city envisions nine single-room apartments slated to rent for $290 per month in an obsolete two-story commercial building. Minneapolis' demonstration project demonstrates the willingness of the city to accommodate the poor in strategic locations at inappropriately low densities.*

The Aspiring Poor

Chicago's Gautreaux program targeted poverty-level families, as opposed to low- and moderate-income households, for relocation from city to suburb. The narrowly focused program was developed in response to a 1976 Supreme Court consent decree in a lawsuit filed against HUD by public housing tenants, who had charged the agency with discriminatingly assigning black households to public housing.[79] Under the Gautreaux program, some of Chicago's public housing residents, and some families on Chicago's public housing waiting list as of 1981, received Section 8 housing certificates with which many rented suburban apartments in widely dispersed existing buildings for the same amount of money they had been paying to rent apartments in public housing. (Some Gautreaux participants were rehoused in low-income central-city neighborhoods to provide a control population for an evaluation of the benefits of suburban residence.)

---

*Housing is just one component of the Minneapolis project; the funding application lists an additional objective: "develop successful...businesses and...ultimately provide good-paying jobs for area residents. (City of Minneapolis, MLCA Demonstration Account, Pilot Project Application, 21 February 1996) The applicants apparently regard the neighborhood as perpetually disconnected from the lucrative downtown economy just 1½ miles away.

In 1995, nearly two decades after the Gautreaux consent decree, Professor James E. Rosenbaum of Northwestern University reported positive outcomes for suburban participants. More than 5,000 families had participated in the program from its 1976 inaugural year to 1994, and the families who moved to suburbs fared better than those who relocated to other housing in the inner city. The suburbanized adults were more likely to be employed and their children were academically outperforming their central-city counterparts at all levels, including college admissions. The success of Gautreaux inspired the federal Moving to Opportunity (MTO) program, implemented to test the Gautreaux principles in five U.S. cities.[80]

The Gautreaux program would likely have failed if its administrators hadn't carefully chosen the suburb-bound participants and left the most troublesome families in the city. The program targeted at-risk households—single mothers receiving Aid to Families with Dependent Children, but within that universe of households, only those likely to produce positive outcomes were chosen for suburban relocation. For starters, families with more than three children were excluded. Families with a qualifying number of children were eligible only if fiscally responsible: good credit rating, enough money on hand for a security deposit and first month's rent, and no large debts that might interfere with timely payment of rent in the future. Also, families considered likely to cause property damage were denied the suburban opportunity. This policy of discrimination weeded out many of public housing's "most needy" families, according to Rosenbaum, but this was necessary to ensure success:

> If [the most needy] do not know how to take care of apartments, or if they have violent family members or visitors, then property damage will be likely. Not only will these circumstances lead to eviction, but even one such eviction can give the program a bad reputation, leading many landlords to avoid taking any more program participants. . . the program must select people who can meet the expectations of the private [housing market]: regular rent payment and lack of property destruction....[81]

Many public housing tenants "cannot handle the rigors of the program, the costs, or the behavioral norms required," according to Rosenbaum. Susan Popkin and her colleagues concur, based on their sociological examination of Chicago's public housing in the 1990s: Programs modeled after Gautreaux "may have little relevance for today's much more troubled [public housing] population...the majority of families who came through the program never moved; those who succeeded—and were therefore represented in the research—were the most determined and motivated."[82]

Gautreaux and its successor programs focus on *people* rather than *place*, designed to rescue families trapped in dysfunctional neighborhoods rather than to revitalize those neighborhoods. The distinction is succinctly framed by Minneapolis' Neighborhood Planning for Community Revitalization program, an advocate of locational choice:

> the dispersal of affordable housing . . . should not be undertaken to relieve the burden of central-city neighborhoods, but rather to enhance the educational and employment opportunities available to lower-income people and to provide families with a wider range of communities to choose from when they make housing decisions.[83]

Although the socioeconomic-remediation and poverty-dispersal aspects of locational choice are complimentary, the emphasis on people rather than place bodes ill for the revitalization of cities. The Gautreaux program improved the lives of many people; in that respect it was successful and deemed worthy of emulation. HUD Secretary Henry Cisneros argued the case for emulation in 1996 with people rather than place in mind: "When people are given the opportunity to live near jobs and near schools, quality schools...we see dramatic changes in their life circumstances...Almost every indicator of progress rises as people are exposed to good jobs and the best educational opportunities."[84]

Gautreaux-inspired programs are never promoted this ardently for their potential effect on place. A place-focused program of poverty dispersal would disperse the poor in order to prep a neighborhood—a place—for an influx of the middle class. This aspect of the Gautreaux program was never evaluated because it was not an objective; in fact Gautreaux's formula for success was at odds with such an objective. The Gautreaux program succeeded because it creamed public housing's most promising tenants off the top and moved them to suburbs, while keeping public housing's most troubled families in the city. A place-focused program of urban revitalization would do exactly the opposite.

The Gautreaux program fell short not only qualitatively but also quantitatively. In a 20-year period the program moved perhaps 12,000 to 15,000 individuals to suburbs, a paltry number considering Chicago's poverty-level population numbered more than 600,000 in 1990. Urban Institute data from 1990 indicate that more than 350,000 poor people would have to be moved out of Chicago in order to achieve an even distribution of the poor throughout the metropolis. As a matter of fact, poverty spread like wildfire in Chicago during the Gautreaux years: The city's number of census tracts with a poverty rate of 20 percent or higher doubled between 1970 and 1990, and the number of tracts with concentrated poverty (40 percent or higher poverty rate) more than quadrupled. (Some tracts had a poverty rate of 100 percent in 1990).[85] Meanwhile the Gautreaux program was moving only a fraction of one percent of the city's poor people to the suburbs in its average year.

Rosenbaum reported that the architects of Gautreaux deliberately chose not to relocate the maximum possible number of families, but to limit the scope of the program in order to ensure success.[86] Success was claimed by decamping only the aspiring poor.

The Elderly

Elderly people are among the precious human resources targeted by locational-choice advocates, some of whom espouse the construction of new suburban housing for retirees. The housing inventory at West Ridge includes 126 apartments for senior citizens, financed in part by HUD. Meanwhile the number of senior citizens in Minneapolis has plummeted in the past two decades because the city is overstocked with old high-maintenance detached houses, many of them in environments ill-suited to vulnerable people.[87]

Retirees are invaluable to cities because they participate generously in the day-to-day business of running a neighborhood, volunteering at schools, libraries, and at election polling places. They support neighborhood merchants loyally, especially when they stop driving. And, most important, they help keep cities secure by populating neighborhoods during the daytime hours when most adults are at work. Public policy that encourages the further exodus of retirees from cities undermines cities' prospects for revitalization.

Cheap Labor

From the ranks of the non-poor and the aspiring poor come the entry-level workers for whom urban and suburban businesses compete. The advocacy group led by Former St. Paul Mayor George Latimer cited an estimate that nearly 100,000 jobs paying less than $10.50 an hour will be created in Twin Cities suburbs in a 15-year period beginning in 1996. The specter of so many workers inappropriately housed incites the advocates to demand massive public subsidies and higher-density zoning for suburban housing. Business owners in developing suburbs, who experience worker shortages so severe they organize job fairs to recruit inner-city labor, are the natural allies of locational-choice advocates. In Maryland, Montgomery County's Moderately Priced Dwelling Unit Ordinance is in large measure a suburban economic development initiative.[88]

Among the businesses in developing suburbs that need low-cost labor are many that decentralize prematurely from cities—specialty retailers, cinemas, restaurants, and hotels. Only those public officials who disavow all concern for the well-being of cities would wish to provide these businesses with nearby sources of cheap labor at considerable public expense. Policymakers interested in the well-being of cities and their metropolitan areas will concern themselves first and foremost with the shortage of middle-income housing near downtown jobs. As the middle class recentralizes, businesses and entry-level jobs will follow, allowing city residents (and many suburbanites) to find employment accessible by transit.

Locational-choice advocates specifically endorse the premature decentralization of commerce and, in so doing, they promote the most socially and environmentally destructive force in the American metropolis—automobile dependence.*

City businesses need every available advantage in their competition for economic development, including an ample labor force. Some firms in Minneapolis cite a shortage of labor as the reason they consider a move to the suburbs.[89] Therefore, the banishment of employed and employable city residents should be undertaken with greater care than is exercised by locational-choice advocates.

LIBERALS, CONSERVATIVES, AND THE ENTRENCHMENT OF POVERTY

Minnesota state representative Myron Orfield, representing a Minneapolis district, notes that neither conservatives nor liberals are much interested in repopulating cities with non-poor residents:

---

*There is a way to get city workers to suburban jobs without subsidizing suburban housing or imposing additional burdens on transit systems: Business owners are at liberty to provide transportation. Suburban restaurant owners in the New York City region send vans into the city daily to pick up waiters and cooks; this is a cost of doing business.

Liberals concentrate on bringing in outside resources to promote enrichment programs in the city, conservatives on cutting off government funds and reg-ulations and letting the discipline of necessity restore order. Although they agree on little else, both major approaches attempt to solve the core problems in place by turning disadvantaged residents into more successful (and more middle-class) people. However, neither strategy…contemplates efforts to bring back the middle class or persuade young, stable families to settle in the older parts of the region where poverty is concentrated.[90]

At the federal level, conservatives appear more amenable than liberals to a middle-class repopulation of cities. A bill passed in 1997 by the U.S. House of Representatives, sponsored by Rick Lazio, (R-N.Y.), would have reduced by half the number of extremely poor tenants in the nation's pub-lic housing.[91] But HUD Secretary Andrew Cuomo resisted the measure, insisting that public housing remain available to the most disadvantaged households in the nation's metropolitan areas. Cuomo favored an upgrading of the economic status of public housing populations, but not such a radical upgrading as proposed by House Republicans. Cuomo envisioned cities that continue to house disproportionate numbers of their metro area's poorest, often unemployed, residents: "While the Clinton Administration supports bringing more working poor families into public housing, the House bill goes to far …"[92] Under the leadership of Cuomo's predecessor, Henry Cisneros, HUD had rejected a plan by the Chicago Housing Authority (CHA) to substantially increase the number of working families in the Cabrini-Green public housing development. The CHA proposed to convert the development from a poverty trap into a mixed-income development, but HUD objected to the high level of gen-trification envisioned in the local authority's plan.[93]

Conservative and liberal politicians at all levels of government agree that America's poor belong in cities, and so the politicians generously fund housing programs that keep them there. In August 1996, New Jersey's Republican Governor Christine Todd Whitman mounted a bull-dozer in Camden, just across the Delaware River from downtown Philadelphia, to assist with the demolition of a city block's worth of dilap-idated and abandoned townhouses. The 1880s brick houses (among more than 3,000 abandoned houses in Camden as of August 1996) were cleared to make way for new low-cost housing. Camden's Mayor Arnold Webster and the conservative Whitman were politically incompatible on plenty of issues, but both could agree that low-cost housing was the appropriate use for central-city land a stone's throw from downtown Philadelphia. (Camden's administration filed for bankruptcy protection in July 1999.)[94]

The process is repeated in Baltimore, where hundreds of dilapidated townhouses a couple miles from downtown are bulldozed to make way for new housing—housing for low-income households.

A Faustian Bargain

Mayors are saying that "urban America's biggest challenge of late is prosperity," according to a June 2000 report in the *New York Times*: "The mayors complained about...too many well-off people moving back to the city...driving up prices."[95] This reversal of the forces of decay should please city officials, who ought to understand why central-city land should be the most coveted in the metropolis rather than the most worthless, which much of it has become. The dilution and redistribution of poverty is, ostensibly, a goal of urban elected officials, but when prompted by market forces rather than their own frail intervention, the officials resist. Virtually all American cities house their metropolitan area's poorest households, so an upward trend in the socioeconomic condition of the urban population should be not only welcomed but vigorously pursued.

Urban policymakers lack the motivation, if not the resources, to meaningfully disperse poverty to the other side of the municipal boundary. City council members and legislators elected in predominantly poor wards or districts "have a vested interest in expanding the number of low-income constituents," according to Anthony Downs.[96] Planning professor Peter Salins credits a natural alliance between urban liberals and suburban conservatives for keeping poverty entrenched in cities:

> What American urban policy really amounts to is a kind of Faustian bargain struck by the leaders of the cities and the residents of the expanding suburbs: the cities agree to serve increasingly as the poorhouses of the metropolitan community, as long as the suburbanites—with Washington and the state capitals acting as brokers and intermediaries—underwrite the extra costs this role imposes.[97]

Boston

Boston, in the late 1980s, housed about 20 percent of its metropolitan area's population and about 40 percent of its poor population, a situation that exacerbated the city's fiscal crisis and diminished its capacity to administer basic services. Yet the impulse to further entrench poverty in the city was systemic, involving not only the federal government and the state of Massachusetts, but also the city of Boston, its charitable organizations, and some of its corporations.

Boston's populist Mayor Ray Flynn had been elected to his first term in 1983 with the support of the city's "housing activists," a term that usually means "promoters of the construction and rehabilitation of housing for poor people." Under Flynn, Boston was subjected to perhaps the nation's most aggressive policies aimed at providing housing for the poor. A housing advocate—Peter Dreier—was appointed director of housing for Boston's Housing and Redevelopent Authority in 1984. Dreier described the profusion of conditions favorable to the entrenchment of poverty in Boston:

> This set of conditions—a sympathetic state and local government, a supportive business and philanthropic community, a network of capable community-based developers and technical experts, and a politically adept housing activist movement—was probably optimal for maximizing resources and addressing the housing needs of those not well served by the private market place.[98]

Boston's housing officials focused their efforts on the creation of additional housing for a population already overrepresented in the city. If suburbs fail to relieve a perceived shortage in their metro area's supply of low-cost housing, then it behooves the city to take up the slack without hesitation, or so goes the logic of the urban housing activist. Housing director Dreier lamented, "City resources (even with the state's support and some federal funds) could not build enough new low-income housing to accommodate . . . demand."[99]

Boston was visited in the 1980s by a reversal of population loss, a declining poverty rate, rising property values, and market-rate housing development, but, for Dreier, this good news signaled a troubling trend, one to be resisted:

> the city's legal and economic resources were simply too limited to counter the forces of the private…housing markets… . Developers continued to speculate on private land… .The city's zoning laws and its inclusionary efforts slowed down the pace of speculation, but they could not stop speculators from buying and selling land and buildings.[100]

Real estate speculation and market-rate housing development are anathema to urban housing advocates such as Dreier, who disdains gentrification: "Boston's efforts served primarily as a holding action, a 'finger in the dike,' to slow down the tide of gentrification..."

Dreier heralds the housing policy established under the Flynn administration as "perhaps the most progressive housing policy of any major American city." That policy ensures the ongoing construction of low-cost housing by forcing downtown developers to fund it. That policy requires developers of market-rate housing to set units aside for low income residents, and it includes "strong tenants' rights laws, protecting renters from rising rents, evictions, condo conversions, and the loss of rooming houses."[101] If Boston's poverty rate ever declines to less than double its metro-area's rate, it will not be for a lack of official efforts to keep poverty entrenched in the city.

The Twin Cities

In the 1980s the state of Minnesota imposed a one-for-one housing replacement statute on Minneapolis, St. Paul, and Duluth, designed to prevent losses of low-income housing in redevelopment projects. The statute was authored by a Minneapolis representative. When the state legislature voted to repeal the statute in 1995 (out of concern about concentrated poverty) opposition came from central-city lawmakers, including those representing areas most often affected by the requirement. Before the legislature voted to repeal the replacement statute, the Minneapolis City Council debated the issue and voted not to lobby for repeal. Rebuffed by the state legislature, the Minneapolis City Council has taken matters into its own hands and adopted its own "no net loss" policy.[102]

Minnesota's city officials vigilantly protect all but the most hopelessly dilapidated of their low-cost housing. St. Paul officials decided in 1998 to buy seven decaying apartment buildings and turn them over to a non-profit housing group in order to maintain low rents. The owner of the buildings was about to sell to a developer who planned to renovate and raise rents. And in Minneapolis, in 1999, Minneapolis Mayor Sharon Sayles Belton announced, "Efforts are under way to prevent hundreds of subsidized units from converting to market rate."[103]

Among the low-cost units that Minneapolis officials resolve to retain are the 49 rooms in the Fairmont Hotel in downtown Minneapolis, a building that inspired this description by *Star Tribune* reporter Kevin Diaz after he toured the premises in 1999:

Once you get past the hotel lobby, the first thing that gets you is the stench: Some 50 years of accumulated urine in the wood, the carpets, the walls. Bare bulbs light the hallways, which occupy three floors above a Hennepin Avenue porno shop. A note posted on the third-floor washroom warns that the person who's been defecating in the tub better quit or risk getting thrown out on the street.[104]

Diaz reported that a developer wants to convert the rotting Fairmont into an upscale boutique hotel like those in San Francisco, but to the Minneapolis City Council, the Fairmont is an indispensable bastion in the sacred crusade against homelessness.

Local officials strive not only to maintain the low-cost housing that over-burdens their cities, they strive to expand the supply. Core-city legislators claim entitlement to a disproportionate share of state and federal funding for low-income housing. Minneapolis and St. Paul legislators jealously guard the proceeds of Minnesota's Housing Trust Fund, and they aggressively pursue federal tax credits for low-income housing, credits that are disproportionately allocated to the central cities. A suburban legislator convincingly blames his central-city colleagues for perpetuating poverty in their cities.[105]

The city of St. Paul suffers a poverty rate double that of its metropolitan area, but in 1999 the city council voted unanimously to enact a housing plan that will devote city money to the creation of additional low-income housing units. Under the plan, 10 percent of housing to be built during the first decade of the new millennium will be devoted to households earning 50 percent or less of the metro-area's median, and another 10 percent will be devoted to even poorer households—those earning only 30 percent, or less, of the metro-area median.[106] (Remember that the Metropolitan Livable Communities Act commits state money to new suburban housing affordable to households earning 80 percent of the metro-area median.)

"Minneapolis is taking concrete action to...increase the supply of affordable housing," said Mayor Sayles Belton in her 1999 State of the City address. (In her subsequent two state-of-the-city addresses the mayor mentioned "affordable housing" 23 times with nary a mention of "middle-class housing" or middle-class retention or middle-class anything.) In December 1999 the Minneapolis City Council and mayor approved a budget that increases the city's financial commitment to low-income housing by about 50 percent and funds the increase with the heftiest property-tax hike permitted by state law. On top of that, "we're asking the legislature for additional resources," said the mayor.[107] The executive director of the Minneapolis Community Development Agency boasted, "I would challenge anyone to find a more aggressive program in investing in affordable housing...than what is happening in Minneapolis." To the suggestion that affordable housing is a regional problem that the city of Minneapolis cannot solve alone, city council member Jim Niland responded that Minneapolis must take the lead. Council member Lisa McDonald promises a commitment to affordable housing even stronger than Sayles Belton's. McDonald and other challengers to the incumbent mayor have made affordable housing a hot issue in the election campaign of 2001.[108]

Minneapolis officials expand their commitment to low-cost housing even though the city's housing costs are among the lowest in the metropolitan area. With its chain of lakes, its Mississippi waterfront, and its CBD, Minneapolis' land values should be the highest in the region and its house prices should reflect this, but the median price for houses in the city is far below the suburban median, and the city's apartment rents are lower as well. Many of the metropolitan area's costliest apartments are in downtown Minneapolis and along the city's lake shores; nonetheless, the city's average rents, for most unit sizes, are lower than the suburban averages.[109] The city's averages are suppressed by low-rent apartments in gray zones. Minneapolis' low-cost housing stock accommodates a disproportionate number of low-income households and suppresses the city's economic power (Figure 7-4).

Minneapolis officials, like their counterparts in St. Paul, target their low-cost housing agenda on the poorest of the poor. The Minneapolis City Council resolved in 1998 to increase the production of housing for extremely-low-income households—households with incomes at or below 30 percent of the metro-area median. (The city's Affordable Housing Task Force recommended that 70 percent of this affordable housing be dedicated to families with children.) Minneapolis has lost 100,000 middle-class residents since 1960 (net loss), nonetheless the city's leaders focus their housing efforts on the retention of the poor.[110]

It's not that Minneapolis' public leaders are unaware of the consequences of concentrated poverty; like urban liberals everywhere they devoutly believe that the consequences of concentrated poverty can be averted by programs of social remediation. The city council's low-income-housing resolution therefore stipulates, "The [Affordable

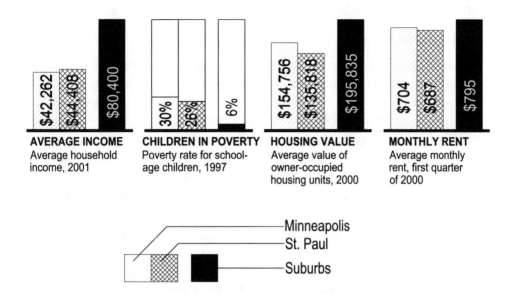

AVERAGE INCOME
Average household
income, 2001

CHILDREN IN POVERTY
Poverty rate for school-
age children, 1997

HOUSING VALUE
Average value of
owner-occupied
housing units, 2000

MONTHLY RENT
Average monthly
rent, first quarter
of 2000

Minneapolis
St. Paul
Suburbs

Figure 7-4. Economic indicators—Minneapolis, St. Paul, and suburbs. City officials pursue a housing agenda that will maintain the economic disadvantage of their cities. (Suburban data are for suburbs in the seven-county metro area.)

Note: The rental disparity between cities and suburbs is likely greater than indicated above because data are compiled on the basis of buildings of at least 12 units, according to David Browner of Apartment Search, Minneapolis, 25 October 2000. Therefore, the data exclude the small substandard apartment buildings found in abundance in the cities' gray zones. In Minneapolis, for example, 11.4 percent of apartment units are in buildings with three or four units, and 47.5 percent of these units are deemed substandard by the Minneapolis Planning Department. (State of the City 2000, pp. 12, 18.)

Sources for data:

Average income: Editor and Publisher Market Guide, 77th Edition, Housing, Income, Education, and E&P Indices, pp. IV 46-47.

Children in poverty: U.S. Census Bureau, Small Area Income and Poverty Estimates, 1997 School District FTP Files, Minnesota.

Owner-occupied housing values: Minneapolis Area Association of Realtors, Year 2000 Home Sales as Reported by MLS Participants.

Monthly rent: Apartment Search Profiles (Edina, MN) Quarterly Review, 1st Quarter 2000.

Housing] Task Force shall work with Hennepin County to recommend strategies for early intervention to support ...families at risk..."[111]

Inhospitable Suburbs

While city officials and housing activists eagerly accommodate poor and at-risk households, suburbanites do not. Many developing suburbs discourage, or prohibit by means of zoning mandates, the development of low-cost housing; and fully-developed suburbs strive to keep poverty at a distance. Baltimore's inner-ring suburbs vigorously opposed their metro area's participation in HUD's five-city locational-choice demonstration project—Moving to Opportunity. This suburban opposition was instrumental in persuading Congress to cancel the program after the first round.[112]

Poverty in Minneapolis marches northward from the afflicted neighborhoods of the Near North district, but the suburb of Brooklyn Center, just north of the border, defends itself against impending encroachment. Brooklyn Center officials decided in 1996 to spend millions of dollars to buy and demolish up to 26 deteriorating houses on their side of the Minneapolis border. The officials intend to replace the substandard houses with a greenway buffer and some new houses, which will sell for prices comfortably higher than the metro-area median, and more than double the median value of houses in the Minneapolis neighborhood against which Brooklyn Center feels compelled to protect itself. Brooklyn Center's city manager explained, "The stability of that neighborhood . . . and the protection of property values is very important."[113]

In another suburb north of Minneapolis—Brooklyn Park—municipal officials decided to spend more than $4 million to acquire and demolish a 306-unit low-income apartment complex that is blamed for a decline in nearby property values. The suburb's special projects planner, Stacie Kvilvang, is unapologetic in her response to the criticism of housing advocates: "They're looking at it from a regional perspective. We're looking at it from a local perspective."[114]

Mayor Sharon Sayles Belton Holding up Her End of the Faustian Bargain

Minneapolis Mayor Sayles Belton acknowledges and fully accepts the stark reality that suburban officials are little obsessed with the needs of the poor, and that the MLCA's locational-choice effort is little focused on the most troubled and troublesome households in her city. The mayor

readily accepts her city's role as host to the area's most socially and economically disadvantaged households. In 1996 she articulated her vision:
Minneapolis will remain a staging area for the administration of social
services to the region's disadvantaged population:

> These hard-to-employ people are not going to be the first ones who have the
> opportunity to take advantage of the affordable housing that is being built in
> the suburbs. These are the people who are going to continue to live in the city
> of Minneapolis, who are going to look for affordable rental units, and, maybe
> if we impact significantly...they might be eligible for home ownership, but
> only in the housing units that are going to be built that have values of about
> $50,000. Those are not the...affordable housing units that are being built in the
> region; and we ought to come to grips with that. What's the message? The
> message is that those [who] are the most poor will continue to live in the core
> city, and we are going to continue to need additional resources if we are going
> to help those people to become self-sufficient and contribute to the vitality of
> our community.... Those folks who are less attractive [will remain in
> Minneapolis]. I'm O.K. with that...I respect the fact that as a mayor of a core
> city I'm always going to have our region's poorest people...I've come to grips
> with this idea of creaming that's going to occur, and accept that, as long as I
> can get the resources...[115]

The mayor espouses the centralization of poverty resources rather than
the decentralization of poverty. Additional resources will allow the poorest of the poor to remain in the city to sustain an entrenched social-serv-
ices establishment. Additional resources are desired not only for social
services, education, and job training, but also for transit that will deliver
inner-city residents to suburban jobs. The reverse commute, part of the
mayor's comprehensive vision of socioeconomic remediation, gives her
constituents access to low-skill jobs in suburbs—usually in developing
suburbs not yet well served by transit—while retaining their inner-city
residency. The mayor does not propose to upgrade her city's housing
stock so that inner-city residents holding low-pay suburban jobs might be
displaced to suburban housing, to be replaced by suburbanites holding
higher-paying downtown jobs—the old switcheroo. Instead of that,
Mayor Sayles Belton advocates the decentralization of transit in order to
maintain the centralization of poverty.

Mark Alan Hughes, a policy analyst at Philadelphia's Public/Private
Ventures, notes that big-city mayors and legislative representatives are
unlikely to endorse any meaningful campaign to disperse the constituency that elected them:

Big-city politicians would, under a successful dispersal campaign, only lose or decrease the...constituents that have helped elect mayors and congressional representatives... . Even longtime advocates of Gautreaux in Chicago recognize the political limits to implementation of the strategy beyond the few thousand who now participate.[116]

VULNERABLE NEIGHBORHOODS AND AFFLUENT ENCLAVES

A fundamental deficiency of the force-feed approach to poverty dispersal is that it often targets non-poor neighborhoods in the city. In 1995, Minneapolis settled a discrimination lawsuit with an agreement (the Hollman consent decree) to deconcentrate its public housing, and shortly thereafter Mayor Sayles Belton proposed a set of housing principles intended to disperse public housing tenants and other low-income households throughout the city. The principles were opposed by council members representing wards targeted to be on the receiving end of the deal.[117] Their concerns appear to have been validated by the namesake of the consent decree under which public housing tenants were de-concentrated: In 1999 the *Minneapolis Star Tribune* reported that Lucy Mae Hollman is living in a scattered-site public housing unit well removed from her former home, and now she is in conflict with her new neighbors, some of whom complain repeatedly about disturbances emanating from her property.[118]

A handful of marginal neighborhoods in Chicago bear the brunt of an exodus from public housing that falls to the wrecking ball; a resident of one such neighborhood complained, "It's as if the gates of Hell ...opened and these people were let out." The circumstances are similar in a working-class neighborhood in South Philadelphia, and so is the complaint: "kids are up all night...out in the street yelling [obscenities]. It's like they're trying to find the worst people."[119] Housing advocates demand many more low-cost units than are needed to accommodate households displaced from public housing; city officials who acquiesce to those demands have little choice but to increase the numbers of low-cost units in marginal neighborhoods—vulnerable neighborhoods not already oversupplied with low-cost housing and not already filled to capacity by middle-class and affluent households.

The most dynamic urban neighborhoods are those with housing for a wide range of incomes, but cities should promote a wide range of housing preferences by allowing housing markets to produce some economically segregated enclaves as well. Most of the nation's largest 100 cities have 20 or more square miles of land area devoted to residential neighborhoods. Within that land area there is room for some middle class and affluent enclaves. Cities should include not only income diversity within most neighborhoods, but also a diversity of neighborhoods.

Minneapolis is about to lose one of its longtime corporations—Allianz Life North America—to a lavish new headquarters closer to the chief executive's home in an affluent suburb west of the city. This kind of move—toward the chief executive—is not uncommon among American businesses, and it will cost Minneapolis 550 jobs. Cities must exploit their potential to attract business owners and corporate decision makers to high-cost housing in central neighborhoods, a potential amply demonstrated in New York, Boston, and San Francisco. Affluent residential enclaves affect business location decisions not only by attracting business owners, but also by elevating purchasing power and demand for the specialty retailing that is lost too often to suburbs.

Rich residents benefit cities profoundly with their prestige, social leadership, and philanthropy. Zachary Fisher, for example, served on the boards of Carnegie Hall and the Metropolitan Opera, and he demonstrated that the founding of great urban institutions is not a thing of the distant past. With a $25 million gift and a determined effort, the Manhattan resident converted a west-side Manhattan pier into the Intrepid Sea-Air-Space museum, which receives more than half a million visitors a year, including thousands of children who come for physics and history lessons and vocational training, and for the after-school programs of the Intrepid's cadet corps.[120]

In order to attract the rich, cities must allow and encourage the development and expansion of affluent enclaves. Until cities no longer house inordinate numbers of low-income households, the pursuit of income diversity should focus on the gentrification of distressed neighborhoods rather than the introduction of poverty to middle-class neighborhoods. Officials in low-density cities should focus on redevelopment at higher densities with higher-cost housing as a way to dilute poverty; they should strive to attract middle-class and affluent households to poor city neighborhoods rather than to shunt the poor from one neighborhood to another. City officials should in no way jeopardize land values in non-poor neighborhoods; to the contrary, they should strive only to increase them.

Unfortunately, many of those who control or influence the fate of cities care little about land values; some disdain the rich and their landed riches. *Millionaires, billionaires, the rich*—these are terms of derision in the mouths of urban liberals, as in, "The rich get housing that is cheap and sometimes even free." This pronouncement is the work of urban affairs professor John Adams, citing tax deductions for mortgage interest.[121] The middle class joins the rich in their exploitation of the tax code, thus the property wealth of the rich and the middle class is ill-gained and if that wealth is eroded by the imposition of housing for low-income households, then the cause of social justice is doubly advanced. Moreover, if property values deteriorate, that is the fault not of low-income newcomers but of middle-class incumbents: "Local residents…choose the future they want. They determine the market response, expectations of decline, and other effects…of subsidized housing on America's neighborhoods," according to housing advocates in New York.* This refusal to acknowledge the correlation between congregations of at-risk families and neighborhood disruption is endemic to housing advocates, as is an indifference to the housing market's response to adverse social conditions.

In a capitalist democracy the wealthiest households enjoy the best cars, clothes, houses, and neighborhoods, but locational-choice theory dictates that prestigious neighborhoods ought to be exempted from the list of things that only money can buy. This doctrine is fueled by the leftist presumption that wealth in America lands on the wrong side of oppressive economic relationships. Ann Douglas, a professor of English literature at Columbia University, proclaims, "People whose gains are someone else's losses prefer to live away from the people who are losing."[122] True to the faith, Minneapolis' Affordable Housing Task Force insists that "all residents should have actual opportunities to live anywhere in the region, in

---

* The New York advocates produced one of several recent studies that purportedly demonstrate stability in real estate markets near subsidized housing. (Other studies indicate property value erosion.) The analysis covers seven scattered-site public housing (SSPH) projects totaling 200 units that were built in middle-class neighborhoods in Yonkers, New York, in response to a 1985 court order. Analysts measured the effects on receiving neighborhoods and concluded that property values, generally, were not adversely affected by the imposition of SSPH. But scattered throughout the analysts' report were several allusions to the interventions and conditions necessary to mitigate the impact feared by residents: Tenants were selectively chosen, and they participated in counseling before and after they occupied the SSPH; police were especially vigilant where SSPH was sited; buildings were well designed; buildings were well managed; and individual projects were small—14 to 48 units each (the authors concluded that smaller is better). In spite of all that, the analysts acknowledged "anecdotal evidence from owners and real estate professionals that homes within a block of the sites were selling slowly and at discounted prices." (Xavier de Souza Briggs, Joe Darden, and Angela Aidala, "In the Wake of Desegregation," *Journal of the American Planning Association* 65, no. 1 [Winter 1999], pp. 33-45.)

any city, county, or neighborhood."[123] These sanctimonious ideologies are unthreatening to the most affluent of suburbanites, the ones rich enough to afford isolated estates or gated and guarded communities. That can be done at the developing fringe, but not in the cities that need every advantage in the competition for affluent households.

CHAPTER

8

Recentralization of Affluence

One reason Paris has so few problems is that the type of people who make problems can't afford to live in Paris...A FRENCH URBAN PLANNER[1]

In order to appreciate the unfulfilled potential of American cities, it is necessary to reconsider of the roles of city and suburb in housing poor and non-poor households. It is difficult in America to imagine inner cities safer and more affluent than their surrounding suburbs, but that is the paradigm in many places outside the United States, places admired by many Americans for their exemplary transit systems and their inviting streets and parks.

The most prestigious residential districts of Rome, Barcelona, Vienna, and Amsterdam are near the central business district, and the poor are consigned to suburbia. In Sweden, suburbs were established as repositories for low-income housing. Beginning in 1904, Stockholm's government began to buy thousands of acres of land on the periphery to house the working class. In Germany, Holland, and France, the pattern was similar.[2] Journalist Alex Marshall explored cities and their suburbs throughout Europe in 1994, and reported high levels of satisfaction with urban living among the middle class: "In Barcelona . . . I met all kinds of ordinary people who lived in the center and intended to stay there."[3]

WHY PARIS WORKS

In the Ile-de-France—the Paris metropolitan region—the poor reside in suburbs, while aristocrats and conventional middle-class families occupy La Ville de Paris—the core city. The French national government, which has for decades controlled land and infrastructure development in the Ile-

342

de-France, has allowed the private housing market to operate nearly unimpeded in most Parisian neighborhoods. Once-opulent neighborhoods at the center of Paris had been converted during the industrial revolution into working-class quarters; by the 1960s, however, the economic status of these neighborhoods reversed again as business executives, young couples, and intellectuals seeking an urbane lifestyle discovered the dense neighborhoods and moved in, driving up housing prices and displacing low-skill workers. Along with gentrification, or *embourgeoisement*, came the resources to effect physical improvements including the preservation of historic buildings. Even the eastern arrondissements, Paris' last outpost of the inner-city working class, yield to the pressures of gentrification. H.V. Savitch, professor of urban affairs at the State University of New York, noted in 1988 that "Paris is a city where there is an ever diminishing stock of low-cost housing…"[4]

The government built housing in three of Paris's outer arrondissements to maintain a working-class (as opposed to welfare class) presence in Paris, but it has done little else to impede the natural forces of gentrification. In fact, the French national government has facilitated, if not encouraged, gentrification. Charles De Gaulle's conservative national government reasoned in the 1960s that the gentrification of Paris would diffuse the power of the leftists in the region. To make room for gentrification, the poor were removed to new housing developments in the suburbs.[5]

In a *New York Times Magazine* article called "Why Paris Works," Paris correspondent Steven Greenhouse reported that "affluent families are rushing not to flee for the suburbs, but to buy apartments in Paris's choicest neighborhoods and to send their children to public schools."[6] The public resources of America's cities are increasingly devoted to social services from which the middle class derives only indirect benefit, if any at all. Parisians' tax revenues are devoted largely to maintaining the city's splendid public realm, which benefits all Parisians. Streets and parks are maintained to standards unequaled in urban American. Paris's century-old Metro stations are much cleaner than America's pre-war stations, and trains run on 80-second intervals during peak periods. The quality and cleanliness of transit demonstrates as well as anything the government's dedication to making Paris work.

Public schools in Paris are the most prestigious in the region, attracting rather than repelling affluent families. Greenhouse quotes a Parisian executive who moved his family from suburb to city not only for the city's superior public schools, but also for its superior cultural opportunities:

"Life for children is more interesting and lively in Paris, with the movies, museums, theaters and concerts, than it is in the suburbs."

And life in Paris is safe. "The roughest parts of Paris seem no more dangerous than the safest parts of many American cities," Greenhouse says, adding that Paris's remaining low-income enclaves are troubled by purse snatchings and burglaries rather than violent crime. Greenhouse cites Paris's 1991 murder rate: 3.6 murders per 100,000 population when the rate in this nation's capitol was 80 murders per 100,000.[7]

Unlike decaying American cities, Paris is "improving with age," according to Greenhouse, who concludes, "While many Americans shun their own cities as if they were places suffering from the plague, Paris is a city with which countless people still have a passionate love affair."

Suburban Slums

A highrise building in a public housing development in Courneuve, a suburb north of Paris, was demolished in 1986. Like many of its American counterparts, it was built in the 1950s, occupied by a poverty-level socially disjointed population, and overcome by squalor. Unlike its American counterparts, it was built well beyond the city boundary. Courneuve is one of the suburbs north of Paris where the region's cheapest housing is found, accompanied by the worst social problems.[8]

This nation's public housing might have conformed to the Paris paradigm if a close advisor to President Franklin D. Roosevelt had had his way. As the president was contemplating the idea, unconventional in America, of federal involvement in the production of housing for low-income families, Rexford Guy Tugwell, head of the president's Resettlement Administration, advised him to build the public housing outside the cities, in wholesome brand-new settlements. Roosevelt was inclined to go along with the suburban solution, but the production of public housing became intertwined with slum clearance, so cities became the subjects of the ensuing program.[9] It is ironic that Tugwell, who disliked cities, proposed an approach to low-income housing that, if followed, would have led American cities and their suburbs to different destinies.

HOUSING POLICY FOR REVITALIZATION

A strategy for the revitalization, as opposed to stabilization, of America's cities entails a bipartite housing policy, a policy aimed at enhancing the density and socioeconomic condition of urban neighborhoods, while allowing suburban housing to filter down to lower-income households.

1. *Enhancement of density and socioeconomic condition in cities*

At the end of 1998, the Minneapolis Community Development Agency announced a $1.8 million program to encourage the rehabilitation of distressed houses in distressed neighborhoods with grants of up to $17,000 for participating homeowners. This was piled on top of other city programs with similar goals, such as the Neighborhood Revitalization Program and the federally funded Single Family HOME Program. Earlier in the year, Minnesota state representative Jean Wagenius, representing a Minneapolis district, proposed a state incentive designed to encourage owner-occupants of dilapidated detached houses to upgrade their properties. Eligible homeowners would be enticed by a 10-year exemption from property taxes, but the exemption would apply only to substandard houses in "marginal neighborhoods" in Minneapolis, St. Paul, and Duluth. A St. Paul legislator who supported the bill (which was enacted) noted that his district includes many houses that would benefit from the program—houses valued below $20,000.[10]

Dilapidated detached houses in central cities should be bulldozed rather than bolstered at public expense. Programs to salvage these houses impede the natural process of urban evolution. If urban policymakers wish to financially assist the low-income owners of inner-city detached houses, they ought to upzone their land and prime it with a new transit infrastructure. Then the low-income owners would be richly rewarded by developers with visions of higher-density higher-status enclaves. But, tragically for cities, urban politicians regard obsolete houses as assets— affordable housing for the constituency that empowers them.

The central goal of urban housing policy should be the conversion of low-density poverty-saturated inner-city gray zones into moderate- and high-density neighborhoods populated primarily by middle-income households.* Households employed in the CBD and amenable to apartment and townhouse living are the logical focus of such a strategy. Urban housing subsidies must be redirected from the poor to the middle class.

---

*Even on most public housing sites, densities should be increased rather than decreased. Sites should be urbanized with new streetwall buildings and the housing should be gentrified. With higher densities, a greater number of middle-class gentrifiers could be accommodated, and the more middle-class newcomers, the lower the percentage of low-income incumbents. For middle-class viability, incumbents would have to be as carefully screened as the Gautreaux program's suburb-bound tenants. Public housing is a tough nut to crack, however, because any attempt to meaningfully gentrify a project will likely be met with a legal challenge and a court order to accommodate an unwieldy number of incumbent tenants on or near the site.

Housing subsidies for the middle class violate basic principles of social justice, according to the precepts of "equity planning," championed by city officials since the early 1970s. Equity planners oppose efforts to fund middle-class housing, maintaining that the subsidies should go only to the poor, a tenet that, as applied thus far, entrenches poverty in cities. But the concept of subsidizing the construction of middle-class housing in cities is neither radical nor original. Cities in the United States have used property-tax abatements, below-market-rate loans, and land grants to stimulate the construction and rehabilitation of many thousands of middle-class housing units. Chicago's HomeStart program, launched at the end of 1999, will provide land and construction financing for houses that will sell for as much as $300,000.[11] As noted in Chapter 5, however, HomeStart and many other middle-class programs devote their resources to housing too low in density. And most middle-class housing programs aim at the lower end of the middle-class spectrum.

In North America, Canadian cities have led the way in housing programs for the middle class. Montreal's housing initiatives have created 25,000 middle-income units on city-owned land, much of which is sold to developers at below-market prices.[12] Non-poor families seeking adequate housing in American cities have too few choices according to David Varady and Jeffrey Raffel. In the Cleveland metro area, for example, only 4 percent of housing units priced at or above the metro-area median are in the city, a situation that is "driving suburbanization."[13]

Therefore the backbone of an honest effort to revitalize, as opposed to stabilize, a gray-zone neighborhood must be the replacement of obsolete housing with better housing, at higher densities, appropriate for the downtown workforce. Many suburbanites who work downtown appreciate the innate attributes of suburban living, but many others prefer a more urbane environment. In the Cincinnati region, Varady and Raffel found that proximity to stores was deemed "important" or "very important" to 44 percent of suburban respondents, while only 38 percent expressed the same appreciation for large lots.[14] The city is best positioned to exploit the growing market for urban housing in an urban setting, housing appropriate for affluent downtown professionals.

Manhattan's Battery Park City offers a lesson in the creation, from scratch, of a non-poor urban enclave. Battery Park City was conceived as a mixed-income community in 1969, but a proposed low-cost housing component was eliminated in order to make the project financially viable. (New York officials decided that the development's financial success would finance low-income housing elsewhere in the city.) It wasn't until

1998, when more than 4,000 units were in place and occupied by residents with a median household income of $110,000, that the first modest-income units were introduced. These are in two so-called 80-20 buildings whose developers get low-interest financing for allocating 20 percent of their units to carefully selected individuals and families earning 50 percent or less of New York City's median income ($17,150 income limit for a single person in 1997). When the two 80-20 buildings are occupied, Battery Park City's modest-income households will account for less than 3 percent of the total.[15]

2. *Filtering down of suburban housing*
The irrational decentralization that shapes the American metropolis has damaged cities profoundly, but it yields two byproducts—suburban transit routes and moderately priced suburban housing—that should now be exploited for the benefit of cities. Transit decentralization provides low-income suburbanites with access to jobs, better access than is available in many underserved neighborhoods in the inner-city. And the explosive post-war growth of moderately priced suburban housing leaves a plentiful supply of units available to filter down to lower-income households. As Paris gentrified in the post-industrial era, the French government built new suburban housing for low-income households. American suburbs already have ample stocks of housing suitable for low-income households.

Policymakers interested in both the dispersal of poverty and the revitalization of cities will resist advocates' demands for *new* suburban housing and look instead to the vast stock of *existing* suburban housing, only a minuscule fraction of which would house half of a typical city's poverty-level households. The Twin Cities metro area has a poverty rate about half that of the two core cities. Suburban and urban poverty rates could be equalized, according to 1990 census data, by moving roughly 26,000 poverty-level households from city to suburb, to be replaced by nonpoor households. Those 26,000 poverty-level households represent just 4 percent of the suburbs' 605,000 households (in 1990) and a similar percentage of suburban housing units not already occupied by poor households.[16] (If the growth in suburban housing units has outpaced the growth in central-city poverty over the past decade, then the percentage of suburban units that would be affected has declined.) The process of poverty dispersal would span a couple of decades as new housing is built in the cities to absorb middle-class households, therefore an almost negligible fraction of suburban housing units would be involved each year.

In most metro areas a vast suburban land area is available to absorb poverty-level households. In the Twin Cities area, suburban housing is scattered over a developed land area six times as large as the land area of the core cities, abundant territory over which to deconcentrate poverty, over which to spread it thin.

The process of poverty dispersal should be driven not so much by the forces of class resentment as by the forces of private housing markets. Poverty has already leaked out of most cities into inner suburbs, and if private housing markets were left alone the process would spread to scattered locations in second- and third-ring suburbs. Much additional suburban housing would filter down to lower-income households if left to market forces, but that housing is propped up by government programs designed to maintain middle-class livability.

Existing housing in Twin Cities suburbs is propped up by the Minnesota Housing Finance Agency (MHFA). One of the programs administered by the agency in the 1990s was the "Neighborhood Preservation Loan Program," which stabilized declining suburban neighborhoods with rehabilitation loans. One of the program's beneficiaries was a declining neighborhood in the second-ring suburb of Bloomington, where money was lent at below-market-rate interest to improve owner-occupied houses, as well as neighborhood infrastructure. The agency provided 345 low-interest fix-up loans to suburban homeowners in 2000.[17]

HUD sends housing rehabilitation funds to cities and suburbs in the form of Community Development Block Grants (CDBG) and HOME program funds. Although most of this money lands in cities and inner suburbs, much is available to socioeconomically robust middle and outer suburbs. In the Twin Cities area in 1994 and 1995, about $5 million in CDBG and HOME funds went to second-ring and developing suburbs. (Nearly $20 million went to the cities, much of it to bolster the value of housing that should be replaced.)[18]

Federal funds also prop up the value of suburban houses near airports. The Federal Aviation Administration provides about 80 percent of the funding to soundproof some 7,000 houses under the flight paths of the Twin Cities international airport. The funding, which averaged more than $42,000 per house in 2000, reaches houses not only in Minneapolis and its adjacent suburbs, but also in second-ring and developing suburbs.[19] These houses were not uninhabitable prior to the soundproofing program; many in the suburbs were built, bought, and occupied by middle-class households fairly recently, thus they represent a future source of decent low-income housing. Yet public resources are devoted to delaying the time when these houses will filter down to lower-income households. The federal government also funds states' homeownership programs, which bolster demand for existing suburban housing, forestalling the day when it will filter down to poor households.[20]

Programs like these exempt suburbs from the forces of invasion and succession that have devastated central cities, and, in so doing, they keep poverty entrenched in cities. State and federal housing programs that benefit suburbs should be narrowly focused on those first-ring suburbs that are already overburdened by low-income households. Programs designed to prolong the lives of obsolete inner-city houses also should be refocused on overburdened first-ring suburbs so that the inner-city houses can die a natural death to be replaced by housing appropriate to cities. Socieconomically deteriorating inner suburbs should eventually be revitalized by higher-density renewal, but not until the core city has reached a state of optimal utilization.

Aging suburban detached houses are suitable for the many low-income households disinclined to relinquish their automobile habit. These households would gravitate to suburban neighborhoods of detached houses as revitalizing cities become less accommodating of them. It is reasonable to assume that many automobile-dependent low-income households would prefer single detached houses to townhouses or apartments, which are typically envisioned by locational-choice advocates who espouse new housing. Aged houses appeal to many house buyers because they provide opportunities to add value through sweat equity, opportunities unavailable in the new apartments and townhouses envisioned by the advocates.

The carless poor could be accommodated in modest and aging suburban houses and apartments near long-established transit routes in the first- and second-ring suburbs of most cities. Inasmuch as transit is better established in developed suburbs than in developing suburbs, and inasmuch as transit focuses on the CBD, the occupants of these houses and apartments would be more readily available, as employees and customers, to established businesses in the CBD than to new businesses in developing suburbs. Locational-choice initiatives (and reverse commute schemes) that feed the decentralization of commerce do more social harm than good.

Programs, such as Gautreaux, that rely on existing suburban housing have the advantage of political pragmatism, according to Kale Williams, professor in applied ethics at Loyola University in Chicago:

Neighborhoods that would be quick to resist new construction of publicly- or even privately-sponsored subsidized housing have not been troubled by the quiet move of individual families from some of Chicago's poorest and most distressed neighborhoods, one-by-one, to existing apartments available for rent in the private market.[21]

Existing suburban housing is largely ignored by nonprofit housing organizations, which use government and foundation funding to acquire and rehabilitate, and sometimes construct, central-city housing for rent-subsidized households.[22] Nonprofits should focus exclusively on strategically located suburban housing—existing housing—for at-risk households. The benefactors of nonprofit housing organizations should insist that their funds be used to acquire widely scattered and strategically located suburban housing for the essential purpose of dispersing at-risk households. Much of this housing is isolated from neighborhoods of homeowners, and located in healthy school districts; thus it represents an ideal source of housing for at-risk households. Nonprofits are notorious for squandering fortunes to upgrade the decrepit inner-city housing they acquire. They could more economically purchase existing suburban housing in habitable condition. The decentralization of at-risk households is compatible with the current trend toward the decentralization of social services.

Some poor inner-city households that are offered an opportunity to move to the suburbs by Gautreaux-like programs decline because they value the social arrangements of their neighborhoods, and they lack the mobility to visit friends if separated from them. At-risk households, therefore, must be provided with sufficient incentives, such as transit subsidies and reduced rents (higher rent subsidies) in suburban locations to entice them to accept widely scattered living arrangements. Transit agencies increasingly serve low-density developing suburbs with costly demand-response arrangements. This kind of service should be, in some areas, available and affordable to the suburban poor.

If accompanied by the recentralization of commerce and transportation infrastructure, the decentralization of poverty would improve the mobility of suburbanized low-income households because the *suburban residents of a centralized metropolis* get better transit service than the *urban residents of a decentralized metropolis*. In 13 of the nation's 20 most populous metropolitan areas, the longest commute times are endured by the inhabitants of low-income inner-city neighborhoods. The transit-dependent residents of these neighborhoods depend upon slow-moving buses that run infrequently, especially during off-peak hours.[23]

Millions of Parisian suburbanites enjoy good rail-transit access to the center of Paris, whence they reach any of the city's destinations quickly and easily on Metro. In the decentralized American metropolis, transit-dependent suburbanites and city residents alike reach important commercial and cultural destinations with great difficulty. A transit-dependent resident of the Willard-Hay neighborhood northwest of downtown Minneapolis might wish to visit the Minneapolis Institute of Arts—the city's major art museum—on a Saturday afternoon. But he might be discouraged by his bus system's long headways and downtown transfer, which stretch the four-mile trip into a journey of 45 minutes or more, each way. Transit in the centralized metropolis, even in its suburbs, is much more accommodating.

All programs considered, our system of metropolitan housing subsidization thwarts urban revitalization by

1. creating new suburban apartments and townhouses, but not for the poorest of metro-area households,
2. prolonging the existence of obsolete housing in the central city, and
3. preventing existing middle-class suburban housing from filtering down to the poorest of metro-area households.

These three categories of housing initiatives should be replaced with three others designed to foster revitalization. A housing policy consistent with the goal of urban revitalization would

1. subsidize new middle-income housing in cities,
2. acquire existing strategically located suburban housing to be made available to housing voucher recipients, and
3. focus housing rehabilitation funds on poverty-saturated inner suburbs and on high-density housing in the city.

Subsidization of middle-income housing in cities would, if extensive enough, trigger a reversal in the direction of the vacancy chain, causing existing suburban housing to filter down to low-income households as the middle-class masses flow into cities. As noted in Chapter 5, a federal housing program was designed in the post-war era to increase the supply of low-income housing by expanding the supply of middle-income housing. This is an appropriate strategy for the revitalization of cities and the concomitant dispersal of poverty to suburbs. The Gautreaux program demonstrates the effectiveness of suburban living in improving the employment and educational prospects of the poor, and it demonstrates that suburban housing needn't be new in order to achieve the purpose.

THE SUBURBANIZATION OF IMMIGRANT COMMUNITIES

Urban politicians unwilling to vigorously pursue middle-class retention welcome immigrants as politically unthreatening replacements—a safe alternative to continuing depopulation and deterioration. America has traditionally hosted immigrant populations in urban "ethnic" neighborhoods where individuals and families assimilate and eventually disperse to the suburbs, but this pattern is changing. The inner city no longer holds a monopoly as the initial point of settlement for immigrant communities.

In the Twin Cities, a community of recent Liberian immigrants straddles the municipal boundaries between Minneapolis and two of its northerly suburbs. The Liberians' business and trade organization is headquartered in one of the suburbs, Brooklyn Park.[24] Elsewhere in America, various immigrant communities are totally suburban. Little Saigon, reportedly the world's largest Vietnamese community outside of Vietnam, is centered in Westminster, an Orange County suburb bisected by Interstate 405, twenty miles southeast of Los Angeles. Little Saigon's thriving main street—Bolsa Avenue—is thoroughly suburban in physical character, an eight-lane bituminous artery lined with retail strip centers and subdivisions of one-story detached houses (Figure 8-1). But the street is more urban than suburban in its social character. The sidewalks bordering the street are actually used, shared by pedestrians, bicycle riders, and people waiting at bus stops. The retail array consists of Chinese and Vietnamese businesses; universally recognizable chain stores and restaurants are absent. Little Saigon is no longer exceptional; two studies published in 1999 reveal an increasing tendency among immigrants to settle initially in suburbs.[25]

This may spoil the romanticized image many urban liberals hold of immigrants, but it's true: immigrants drive cars. Nicollet Avenue, Minneapolis' multicultural main street, is congested more with vehicles than pedestrians as people of Asian descent flock to the avenue's restaurants and grocery stores. The nations from which immigrants are emigrating have joined the automobile age. Today's immigrant neighborhood hardly resembles the Lower East Side of a century ago,

Figure 8-1. The suburbanization of immigration—Little Saigon. This is one of many Vietnamese strip centers on Bolsa Avenue—main street for the Vietnamese community in Westminster, a suburb of Los Angeles.

where immigrant populations were tightly congregated among the retailers and settlement houses that served them. In Minneapolis, the Hmong American Services Center and Hmong Senior Health Care, Inc. are 28 blocks and a bus transfer away from each other, on the south side of the city, and the Hmong Community Alliance Church is in Brooklyn Park, a suburb north of the city.

It's a pleasure to see and experience immigrant businesses in the walking environment of the city, and the city should provide the physical, economic and regulatory atmosphere in which small businesses—immigrant-owned and otherwise—can thrive and outcompete their suburban counterparts. For immigrants and natives who are voluntarily or involuntarily deprived of a car, the city should provide access to all the necessities and pleasures of daily life. But urban politicians should no longer regard immigrants as replacement fodder for departing middle-class natives, nor should they exploit the immigrant population as an excuse to enlarge the city's inventory of low-cost housing, not unless they can guarantee that social privation will not accompany economic disadvantage. After all, the socioeconomic poverty of the city is a factor in the suburbanization of immigration.[26]

Urban politicians ought to remember that America's most vibrant immigrant communities are housed in neighborhoods where private-market housing predominates, where high densities sustain more than a few businesses, and where natural rather than political forces determine who belongs and who doesn't. It's easy enough to recognize socially healthy immigrant communities where they exist, and to leave them unscathed by housing policy. Beyond that, unless urban politicians figure out how to create a socially robust immigrant community from scratch, they ought not use the immigrant population as an excuse to entrench poverty.*

RURAL VALUES

Locational-choice initiatives should focus on existing housing in suburbs and beyond. Among the populations of America's rural towns are many aging residents stuck in big old two-story houses, often burdensome and difficult to maintain. Many of these residents would prefer smaller zero-maintenance accommodations with no stairs to climb, close to the stores on main street. Locational-choice programs should be integrated with rural housing programs to offer these elderly residents new apartments and townhouses if they will leave their larger houses to at-risk city families who would benefit from middle-class schools and small-town life. Federal and state governments should fund infrastructure development for new industry in small towns that agree to accommodate a few urban housing-voucher recipients as part of the bargain.

If suburban Gautreaux participants fare better than their inner-city counterparts, it is likely that at-risk families would do better also in small towns, especially where jobs are available. Since the late 1960s, the rural poor have escaped poverty at increasing rates, while rates of poverty-exit among the urban poor have declined. In the mid-1980s, the rural poor were escaping poverty at a 30 percent rate, compared to 20 percent for the urban poor. And, in the present era of welfare reform, rural counties are reducing welfare caseloads faster than urban counties.[27] Journalist Kay Hymowitz studied the problem of teen pregnancy and noted, "in rural states like Maine, Montana, and Idaho, the out-of-wedlock birth rate among African-Americans is low, not because there is less poverty but

---

*Ramsey County Commissioner Janice Rettman, for example, invokes immigrants in her opposition to the economic upgrading of distressed neighborhoods in St. Paul: "Frogtown, the lower East Side and parts of the West Side have always been a place for immigrants who need affordable housing . . . we will guard against gentrification." (Steve Brandt and Mary Lynn Smith, "For Cities, Big Home Price Gains," *Minneapolis Star Tribune*, 4 March 2001, p. B1.)

because traditional, mainstream norms hold sway."[28] For the children of poverty-level households, small-town schools would likely provide better opportunities than inner-city schools. At-risk families might benefit profoundly if offered small-town housing before their children reach school age.

Rural living has long been regarded as a panacea for troubled and at-risk inner-city children. Nineteenth-century charitable organizations in New York City and Chicago decamped troubled kids to the countryside where they were more likely to prosper. Tens of thousands of New York City kids were sent by the Children's Aid Society to farms in New York State and in the Midwest, where they learned the habits of responsible adults. Some were merely exploited as farm labor in the early years of the program, but most fared very well, including many who eventually became business executives and high public officials.[29]

New York City still sends at-risk kids to the countryside, kids like Perry Robinson, whose future in Mott Haven, a notorious neighborhood in the South Bronx, was uncertain at best before he visited the Minnesota countryside. In the mid-1980s, when he was 10 or 11, Perry was sent with a group of New York City's at-risk kids to a youth camp near Moose Lake, Minnesota—population 1,400. The countryside and the lakes lifted Perry's spirits, so he returned in the ensuing summers. When he went to Minnesota "he was like a flower . . . he would bloom," said Jesus Ramos, his Bronx social worker, "and within a week of when he would come back, he'd close down. He was very withdrawn. He'd not even give you eye contact."

When he was 15, Perry was invited by a Moose Lake farm family to spend the summer, and the next year they invited him back not only for the summer but for the duration of his high school career. He didn't hesitate to accept. At his new high school he played on the baseball team, sang in the choir, and made friends easily. In 1996, he became the first of his mother's five children to graduate, even though he was the youngest. He planned to remain in Minnesota after graduation to attend college.[30]

THE GENTRIFICATION OF PUBLIC EDUCATION

Real estate advisors Diane Suchman and Margaret Sowell cite "urban school systems, which are perceived as ineffective (and even unsafe)," to support this assessment of the potential market for inner-city housing: "well researched market analyses predict that the market for residential units will include few households with school-age children, and these analyses recommend targeting childless singles and couples, empty nesters, and elderly households."[31] In promoting the urbanization of suburbs, neotraditional planner Andres Duany and his colleagues advise planners and developers that urban revitalization efforts "should not focus unduly on bringing families back to the inner city. In truth, many urban neighborhoods do quite well in the absence of children."[32] Middle-class families with children are too large a segment of the metropolitan housing market, and too socially valuable, to write off.

Court-imposed busing accelerated middle-class flight, and a return to neighborhood schools is a first step in restoring middle-class dominance to urban school districts. Middle-class and affluent parents in New York City "turned mediocre and even failing neighborhood schools into popular ones, where test scores are rising and students feel safe," according to an October 2000 report in the *New York Times*, referring to elementary and middle schools. Now, as their kids approach high-school age, these parents lobby for a reinstatement of neighborhood high schools. Middle-class parents groups in Cleveland, Omaha, and other cities also have organized to reinstate neighborhood high schools. (These devoted parents, many of them black and Hispanic, face the inevitable accusations of racism.)[33] Invoking the "learning gap," civil rights activists plead the case for school integration as though middle-class students are mere fodder to enhance the prospects of poor black and Hispanic students.[34]

Even after the disastrous lessons of court-ordered busing, outside forces continue to impose destructive policies on urban public schools. As the 2000 school term approached, New York State's education commissioner dictated that the most qualified teachers hired by New York City's public schools be assigned to the system's worst schools, an edict upheld in court. The schools chancellor reported in October 2000 that the policy cost his system more than 1,200 certified teachers, all of whom withdrew from the application and hiring process after learning of their impending assignments. These teachers were desperately needed to fill shortages in the city's public schools.[35]

Varady and Raffel identify the "two-worlds dichotomy" of metropolitan schools as a nearly insurmountable force that impels middle-class families with children to reject cities.[36] Urban schools represent an educational ethic alien to middle-class parents of every race, parents who doubt that educators can simultaneously serve the best interests of their children and of disadvantaged, poorly prepared children. As Sara Mosley wrote in 1997, "no one in the history of American education has ever succeeded in fashioning a big-city school system that works for all children."[37] Advocates for underachieving children demand that the finite resources of urban school districts be focused on the underachievers. New York City schools chancellor Rudy Crew was credited with significantly improving the performance of his district's schools and students after he assumed control in 1995, but advocates for the poor demanded changes in Crew's strategy when hopelessly disadvantaged students continued to perform poorly. "Our members feel like this is a middle-class agenda and that it's not serving our kids," said Helaine Doran, a director of Brooklyn's chapter of ACORN.[38]

Community activists like Doran are often joined by the education bureaucracy in resisting middle-class norms of education. A "rich man's" curriculum is what a superintendent in Baltimore's failing public school system called a program that dramatically improved academic achievement in one of its elementary schools. Rather than build on the program's striking success, Baltimore school officials "resisted it to the death" says Robert Embry, whose Abell Foundation provided funding for the experiment.[39]

Today, the achievement disparity between middle-class white and poor black students preoccupies urban educators, who stress the importance of "closing the gap," implying that high achievers are as much a problem as low achiever. Following a national trend, Minneapolis schools superintendent Carol Johnson has launched a race-conscious plan that concentrates resources on African-American, Hispanic, and American Indian students. (This was part of a political payoff to black activists who had supported the district's most recent bond referendum.) Anticipating criticism from white and Asian parents, the superintendent said, "of course we care about all the kids. But..." The Manhattan Institute's Heather Mac Donald writes that the urban education bureaucracy has come to believe that "the only way to improve the low-achieving schools is to pull down the high achievers, an agenda inimical to the middle class."[40]

"Three years ago, one of New York City's most adventurous school districts set out to tackle a nagging problem: the...disparity between the test scores of white middle-class students and their poorer black and Hispanic counterparts," according to an April 2000 report in the *New York Times*. As part of the solution, the district adopted a "constructivist" math curriculum (called "whole math" until the trendy "whole language" was academically discredited) which values "reasonable" answers over single correct answers to math questions. Nearly 200 university mathematicians and scholars denounced key elements of the curriculum in 1999, warning of "serious mathematical shortcomings." Math professors found many of the curriculum's programs to be one to two years behind grade level, aimed at underachievers, unlikely to prepare students for college-level instruction. The *New York Times* reported widespread dissent among middle-class parents, convinced by their children's assignments and experiences that constructivist math is a "dumbing down" of mathematics education.[41]

Middle-class parents (of all races) have seen an increasing dedication of resources to programs of no interest to high achievers.[42] Baltimore's district has spent $1 million to train its staff in Afrocentrism, meant to improve the performance of underachieving black students by elevating their self-esteem. The Abell Foundation's Robert Embry noted that the program "was put in without any evidence of its working—without any evidence expected." The Baltimore district spent $5,873 per pupil in 1996, almost as much as Maryland's statewide average, but produced dismal results because too much money went to a bloated bureaucracy and to "dubious social programs," according to a 1997 exposé in *Time* magazine.[43] The district's schools had become "academically bankrupt," in the words of Robert Schiller, who was called in to reform the system.

The purported beneficiaries of the today's urban education agenda are the most tragic victims, deprived of the options available to the middle class. Thomas Sowell laments that the youths growing up today in his old Harlem neighborhood are unlikely to assume the kinds of successful and illustrious careers that freed him and many of his former schoolmates from economic poverty. Sowell counts public schools among the instruments of his success: "What the school we went to gave us was more precious than gold. It was an education. That was what schools did in those days...nobody gave us condoms or chirped about 'diversity.' And nobody would tolerate our speaking anything in school but the king's English."[44]

The perception that urban school boards and administrators focus excessively on racial diversity, social issues, birth control, and discipline problems at the expense of academic achievement is a big factor in middle-class parents' rejection of urban schools.[45] Parent Michelle Ambroggio registered her resentment of Detroit's education policy in 1997 in a letter to the *Detroit Free Press*:

I do not send my children to school to gain an appreciation, understanding and tolerance of others, or to unite a community…I do send my children to a small, local, private school to gain an excellent academic appreciation of reading, writing and arithmetic. After subjecting my children to the public school system for kindergarten through fifth grade, I realized my tax dollars were not providing the quality academic education I had experienced during my scholastic career. Do I resent my tax dollars going to support a system more concerned with political correctness than the academic achievements of all its students? A resounding yes.[46]

"When did a school's priority become teaching values and diversity instead of reading and math?" A parent posed this question to the *Minneapolis Star Tribune* after the paper printed a report critical of suburbanites who, being less interested in racial diversity than in traditional education, reject city schools.[47] "I want my children to go to school with children like them. Children with values, respect for adults, discipline; with a family that cares about them and sacrifices for them," wrote the parent, "I don't care [where] the families are from…Is that racist?" The writer was defending her and her husband's choice to live in a suburban neighborhood with reputable schools: "We studied the school districts and test scores, and moved within walking distance of good elementary and junior high schools." Suburban and rural school districts monopolize the top-10 list of Minnesota districts ranked by test scores for math and reading; Minneapolis and St. Paul occupy the bottom-10 list.[48] The rational educational choices routinely made by middle-class parents will not be easily revoked, not by media pontificators, urban politicians, or education bureaucrats. Urban schools will have to compete with suburban schools on the basis of academic merit.

Urban schools need to improve their social as well as academic environment in order to compete. A 1997 incident reported in the *New York Times* illustrates how far social policy and student behavior have strayed, in the urban public school, from the mainstream norm: "Four teen-agers were arrested and charged with gang-raping a 14-year-old girl…Investigators said that before the attack on April 16 at August Martin High School [in Queens]…two of the suspects went to a counselor's office for condoms."[49] Former Secretary of Education William Bennett cites the urban education bureaucracy's "hostility to middle-class values" as a factor in the inferior education and dim future of the inner-city child.[50]

Metropolitan-wide school desegregation, by class and race, would provide some hope of improving the climate of urban schools and neutralizing the suburban hold on middle-class families. School desegregation can be achieved by means of housing desegregation or metro-wide busing. Busing, however, is a discredited and flagging endeavor that diverts resources from academics; besides, metro-wide busing programs have failed to change conventional families' preference for suburbs. Mandatory busing of school children contributed to the demise of many city neighborhoods, but has little power to revive them.[51] Metro-wide housing desegregation is the best bet for disadvantaged children, but government housing policy hinders more than helps that cause. Segregation by income is tantamount to segregation by race in metropolitan America, thus racial integration of housing cannot occur unless poor and non-poor households are geographically redistributed.

Urban school systems will not reach parity with their suburban counterparts unless cities repopulate themselves extensively with middle-class families. The decentralization of poverty would improve the educational prospects of children who leave the city and children who stay behind, but that's not enough; the recentralization of middle-class families also is needed to infuse urban districts with the economic and social resources necessary to win the prestige now associated with suburban schools. Until that prestige is restored, middle-class families with children will have little inclination to choose cities and their public schools. Disreputable schools will impede the recentralization of the middle class even where good housing opportunities are offered.

And that is the predicament, the Catch 22. In order to attract conventional middle-class families to distressed city neighborhoods, the schools in those neighborhoods must first be populated predominantly by middle-class students.[52] Perhaps an evolutionary upgrading of the socioeconomic composition of neighborhood schools is possible. If so it would begin with the isolation of disruptive students, but inasmuch as these students usually come from at-risk households, and inasmuch as at-risk urban households are disproportionately black and Hispanic, this issue is racialized. Some civil rights advocates and school officials assume that disproportionate numbers of black and Hispanic students are disciplined, expelled, and isolated in remedial classes because of racial discrimination rather than differential behavior and ability. Disciplinary policies are then racialized to the detriment of the academic environment.[53] Journalists Brian C. Anderson and Matt Robinson reported in 1998 that San Francisco, which retains a higher percentage of middle-class families than other big cities, is nonetheless vulnerable to the racialization of urban education: "Racial vigilance permeates the entire school system. The San Francisco Unified School District, for example, has sought to limit the number of blacks and Latinos suspended or kicked out of its schools. The district's false assumption, that only racism can explain the greater number of black and Hispanic students expelled, sends exactly the wrong message to unruly minority kids."[54]

The racialization of urban education extends to academic issues as well. Several members of San Francisco's board of education invoked a claim of discrimination in an attempt (unsuccessfully) to block California's requirement that teachers prove themselves to be in possession of tenth-grade-level reading and math skills.[55] Civil rights advocates demand proportional representation in elite classes and schools regardless of academic merit, alienating parents of academically qualified but racially disqualified students.[56]

These race-conscious practices point to an urgent need to retrieve the growing numbers of middle-class black families who flee cities (for the same reasons that white families do). These families would populate city schools with high-performing black students, a situation that would diffuse the racialization of urban education policy. Locational-choice advocates are motivated in part by racial considerations; if race-conscious housing programs have a place in America, then those programs should be designed to entice middle-class black families with children to city housing and public schools. The middle-class repopulation of cities offers the best hope for the advancement of integration in metropolitan housing and schools; it represents the best hope for socioeconomically deprived children. As Varady and Raffel conclude, "Middle-class children are [a] resource, there are few of them in most cities to go around because of the attraction of suburban schools. Therefore, city school administrators need to be concerned about attracting sufficient numbers of middle-class students to…insure that…schools serve their original purpose for middle-class as well as poorer families."[57]

The Gautreaux program demonstrates that disadvantaged students benefit when immersed in a middle-class academic environment, but urban school districts alienate middle-class parents and thereby prevent integration by class and race. Integration of a city's housing would bring the integration of its public schools, but the entrenchment of poverty causes urban educators to deemphasize the academic aspirations of the middle class, which powerfully discourages integration. Thus housing integration is prevented by the policies of educators who should be most interested in achieving it.

A MORAL OBLIGATION

Poverty is power in urban politics, so it is largely up to higher levels of government to redistribute poverty in our metropolitan areas. Insofar as state and federal policies and court decisions have concentrated poverty in America's cities, and insofar as concentrations of poverty breed crime and ruin schools, state and federal governments bear responsibility for a great deal of urban crime and academic failure. State and federal governments are therefore obligated to eliminate the urban-suburban differential in crime rates and in school quality by means not heretofore seriously considered—the redistribution of at-risk households on a meaningful scale. Conservatives would combat crime with tougher law enforcement; liberals would rely on social programs. Conservatives would employ vouchers to rescue urban kids from failing schools; liberals would tweak the status quo. The problems of crime and school failure can be solved fundamentally and permanently only by destroying underclass neighborhoods—America's breeders of crime and destroyers of schools. This is accomplished by dispersing America's concentrations of at-risk households and priming the liberated neighborhoods for an influx of middle-class families. After decades of policy emphasis on the centralization of poverty, state and federal governments are morally obligated to rectify the damage they have visited upon cities.

Part

IV

The Gray Zone

CHAPTER

9

Defending the Gray Zone

We have developed a civic culture in which prestige more often goes to those who prevent the city from developing than to those who enable it.
DANIEL PATRICK MOYNIHAN[1]

DEFINING VITALITY DOWN

The word *vitality* denotes vigor, animation, a state of being lively, not just alive. Vitality is "exuberant diversity," to use Jane Jacobs' words.[2] Neighborhood *revitalization*, then, should mean the restoration of vitality lost, but city officials and neighborhood activists have stripped the hackneyed phrase of its literal definition. Activists in the Roxbury district—Boston's grand exemplar of urban decay—claimed "comprehensive community revitalization" for a community that retains hardly a trace of its 1950s liveliness.[3] The activists pursue an agenda designed to prevent true revitalization. In Minneapolis, the Neighborhood Revitalization Program is, in reality, a *neighborhood stabilization-by-means-of-suburbanization* program that maintains low-density housing and funds inner-city strip centers. Invoking phrases like urban vitality and neighborhood revitalization, officials and activists pursue nothing more than social and economic viability—the bare capacity to survive, and in the pursuit they rob their cities of the potential for true revitalization.

The word vitality denotes the power of endurance, but more than three decades of government intervention have produced inner-city neighborhoods that can endure only as long as the intervention continues. Massive public and philanthropic investments in social services, housing programs, and economic development initiatives have failed to launch inner-city neighborhoods on a trajectory of self-sufficiency, let alone vitality. More than three decades after the Model Cities program began the direct flow of federal dollars into city neighborhoods, blight is broader and deeper, and the power of endurance is long gone from the thousands of neighborhoods in perpetual need of government funds, services, programs, and interventions. Neighborhood activists who invoke the phrase "neighborhood revitalization" are most interested in the endurance of the flow of public money.

America's urban neighborhoods have sunk so deep that officials and activists would be content to return them to the condition they were in 30 years ago, when they were wearing down but not yet repellent. Highly evolved neighborhoods better and livelier than ever before are beyond the imaginations of those in control, judging by their words and deeds. Incremental neighborhood improvement might seem the logical route to creating truly revitalized neighborhoods, but the incremental approach pursued by officials and activists merely entrenches conditions that will prevent or long defer revitalization.

The multitudinous "revitalization" programs sponsored ceaselessly by charitable organizations and by national, state, and local government agencies are programs not of physical renewal but of social remediation, intended not to rebuild physical communities so much as to rebuild the lives of the individuals living in those communities. "We are reclaiming the inner city for the people who live here," says Mary Keefe, associate director of St. Joseph's Hope Community, a poverty-focused nonprofit organization that acquires and rehabilitates obsolete houses on Portland Avenue, less than a mile south of downtown Minneapolis.[4] Portland Avenue is a long and wide thoroughfare—a potential rail-transit route—that originates downtown; that stretch of the avenue within two miles of downtown should be lined with midrise and highrise apartment buildings constituting a housing density 10 times as high as the grossly inadequate density entrenched by the nonprofit. Higher densities would allow many of "the people who live here" to remain while also accommodating newcomers—middle-income downtown workers—but the Hope Community entrenches poverty and underutilization, and prevents revitalization.

Housing improvement programs targeted on distressed neighborhoods usually "do little to improve the socioeconomic status of the neighborhood's residents or the quality of its housing stock," according to Harvard economists John Kain and William Apgar, Jr., who based this conclusion on their analysis of several Chicago neighborhoods.[5] In 1998, the *Minneapolis Star Tribune* analyzed Minneapolis' Neighborhood Revitalization Program (NRP), which spends much of its funding on housing, and found "no statistically significant correlation between where NRP investments were made and where home prices were rising."[6] Housing deterioration has outpaced housing remediation in many of the nation's gray zones because city officials and neighborhood activists attack symptoms rather than root causes.

The most ambitious of housing programs targeted on distressed neighborhoods aim to attract modest numbers of moderate-income households to new housing—usually detached houses—but the motivating impulse is to improve the prospects of incumbent residents. In his 1999 book, *Inside Game, Outside Game*, David Rusk offers some examples of long-deteriorating neighborhoods that have begun to ascend, but the modest gains in population, income, and property values grossly shortchange the great potential of central land. Gains often lag behind metro-area gains and are attributable more to outside economic forces and private market activity than to the interventions of housing programs.[7]

The private real estate market could do in a few years what government and charity have failed to do in more than three decades, if only government would lead in the right direction. Concentrated socioeconomic poverty is the root cause of urban neighborhood distress, which is remedied by diluting the concentration with a substantial infusion of new housing for new middle-class households—urban renewal and gentrification. But the word gentrification burns like an obscenity in the ears of neighborhood activists.

THE NATURAL ORDER OF THE POST-INDUSTRIAL CITY

Gentrification is the natural order of the post-industrial American city. Only through zoning prohibitions, historic preservation restrictions, and anti-gentrification edicts are many city neighborhoods prevented from swelling with middle-class households. San Francisco's notoriously seedy (and high-density) Tenderloin, for example, glitters with cafes and delis and with new and renovated market-rate apartment buildings, but the city's ordinance to preserve low-cost housing prevents rapid and total gentrification.[8] Lesser neighborhoods in lesser cities would easily attract middle-class households if liberated from the twin forces that prevent revitalization—housing advocacy and low-density zoning. Distressed neighborhoods need greater affluence and higher densities in order to revitalize, but activists defend their turf against both of these essential ingredients of revitalization.

DEFENDING THE GRAY ZONE AGAINST HIGHER DENSITIES

Gray-zone revitalization entails the replacement of obsolete low-density housing with higher quality housing developed at densities appropriate to precious land near the economic heart of the metropolis. But this involves substantial physical change, which is resolutely opposed by neighborhood activists and nonprofit housing developers. These defenders of the gray zone embrace superficial change—improvement of the existing low-density housing stock—while they resist the morphological evolution from suburban to urban housing densities (see Chapter 5). The defenders visualize neighborhoods in which incumbent residents inhabit housing that is, for the most part, existing but improved at considerable public and philanthropic expense.

The defenders' agenda is supported in city halls nationwide. In Minneapolis, the Neighborhood Revitalization Program is a powerful force against revitalization, fostering superficial change and preventing the evolution necessary to revitalize obsolete neighborhoods. The program's participating neighborhood organizations, empowered and funded by the city, determine their own "revitalization" strategies and formulate and execute their own plans. Neighborhood organizations in gray zones prolong underutilization by devoting public resources to the rehabilitation of obsolete detached houses and to the construction of new detached houses. In 1997, after six years of NRP operations, Minneapolis officials boasted that the program had improved 815 single-family detached houses, and built another 30.[9]

Minneapolis' Phillips neighborhood, where St. Joseph's Hope Community entrenches underutilization, is a high-crime gray zone at the edge of downtown, overloaded with substandard housing and ripe for high-density redevelopment. But the Phillips NRP plan calls for the maintenance of the neighborhood's low housing density—less than 10 units per gross acre.[10] In considering housing densities, neighborhood leaders in Phillips determined that their strategic location at the edge of downtown is of no particular consequence, and the city of Minneapolis acquiesces.

A 1996 report on the NRP notes that "communities are focused on lowering housing densities..." Thirty-three percent of neighborhood plans submitted to the city of Minneapolis as part of the NRP process adopted the objective of downzoning some of their land.[11] Demolitions are greeted as opportunities to reduce density, as a community organizer in Minneapolis explains: "If you want…larger lots, it doesn't make sense to rehabilitate three homes…It's better to tear down one of the homes and give more yard space to the other two."[12]

The Essence of Urbanity

The neighborhood activists who promote the maintenance of obsolete houses apparently believe that the essence of an urban neighborhood is its housing stock. The essence of a typical post-war *suburban* neighborhood is its housing stock because that's all there is, isolated from other land uses. But the essence of an urban neighborhood—the characteristic that distinguishes it from other settlement types—is urban vitality—the proximate availability of everyday goods and services and diversions, and of good transit connections to all else that the city has to offer. Houses combine with yards and streets to create a suburban neighborhood; housing combines with commerce, informal gathering places, transit, and streets that carry pedestrians as well as vehicles to create an urban neighborhood. All of these elements combine to produce urban vitality—the soul of an urban neighborhood. Housing is merely outerwear. Aged and obsolete detached houses are ragged and outmoded outer garments that should be replaced.

The Minneapolis Planning Commission concurs with the view that a neighborhood's defining and sanctifying attribute is its housing stock, even if it is obsolete and no longer capable of sustaining urban vitality. As noted in Chapter 1, the commission asserted in its 2000 comprehensive plan that the city's neighborhood commercial streets have an "oversupply of commercial space" in the aftermath of population loss, income decline, and competition from suburban malls. Boarded storefronts on derelict commercial streets motivate the city's planners to ponder other uses for empty commercial buildings, rather than to increase housing densities as necessary to sustain commercial vitality.

In preparing its comprehensive plan, the planning commission vigorously solicited citizen participation in a process that became laden with neighborhood activists, as these affairs usually are. Participatory planning doctrine dictates that planning officials follow rather than lead, and the process in Minneapolis produced a plan dedicated to the preservation of the city's low-density housing stock, composed disproportionately of detached houses. The department thus declared in its 2000 comprehensive plan that "Minneapolis will maintain the...unique character of the city's housing stock, thus maintaining the character of the vast majority of residential blocks in the city." To do this is to "maintain areas that are predominantly developed with single and two family structures... Rehabilitation is preferred...over demolition."[13]

Even the worst of the city's houses would be spared, according to one of the planning department's housing objectives: "Encourage renovation and investment in boarded and condemned housing." And public funds would be devoted to the effort: "Ensure that [the Minneapolis Community Development Agency's] grants and programs are designed to encourage rehabilitation and renovation that reflects the traditional architectural character of residential areas..."[14] Consistent with that, the MCDA's executive director has declared that his agency will strive to rehabilitate rather than demolish the houses it acquires, typically the most decrepit of the city's board-ups, lost by owners who fail to pay their property tax. (In their efforts to entrench low densities in gray zones, cities are generously assisted by HUD, which helps fund the rehabilitation of boarded-up detached houses.)[15] Cleveland's housing network, an umbrella organization of 13 neighborhood nonprofit housing developers, has restored more than 1,000 dilapidated and abandoned houses for low-income families. Cincinnati's Housing Blueprint of 1989 noted the city's nearly 7,000 substandard houses and called for public funding to rehabilitate 1,000 of them annually.[16]

It is seldom for historical or architectural significance that gray-zone housing is preserved. Of the 7,700 detached houses and duplexes (5,881 single houses and 1,819 duplexes in 1994) in Minneapolis's Near North district, only 11 have been marked for preservation by the Minneapolis City Council, and only one of those 7,700 buildings is listed on the National Register of Historic Places.[17] Most of the city's gray-zone houses are modest, plain, run down, and far from worthy of the near-downtown land they occupy.

Few gray zones reflect the unique heritage or housing stock of a particular city or region. The gray zones in Minneapolis resemble the gray zones in Buffalo, New York, and in Oakland, California, and in dozens of cities in between (Figure 9-1a-c). Nor do gray-zone houses represent family tradition, passed on from generation to generation. Their value is strictly utilitarian.

Ever vigilant against density enhancement, gray-zone activists suppress their cities' already stunted housing goals. Cincinnati's high-potential

East End, bordering the Ohio River and extending eastward from downtown, is controlled by urbaphobic neighborhood organizations that considered a modest renewal plan by the city too aggressive. The city's renewal plan of 1989 called for the retention of all existing housing in the East End as a measure to minimize displacement, and it called for the construction of only 1,370 new housing units. But the East End Area Council rejected the plan and, in 1991, proffered its own vision—Recipe for Success—advocating densities even lower than those proposed by the city, and specifying that a majority of new dwellings shall be in one- and two-family houses.[18]

Even Boston, a city with North America's most appealing high-density lowrise neighborhoods, cannot escape activists' compulsion to suburbanize their surroundings. Jane Jacobs exampled Boston's Roxbury as one of the nation's notorious urban wrecks in 1961, and in the ensuing years things only got worse as Roxbury continued to lose residents and retailers (Table 9-1). But the Dudley Street Neighborhood Initiative (DSNI), a neighborhood housing and social services organization representing the Dudley Street neighborhood in the middle of the depopulated and decayed Roxbury district, established semi-suburban housing densities in a "revitalization" plan for its 500-acre turf just two miles south of the commercial heart of Boston.[19] DSNI disregards its neighborhood's best architectural precedents—townhouses and lowrise apartment buildings clad in masonry, shoulder-to-shoulder, similar in character to the housing in Boston's great neighborhoods. Instead of that, the organization builds semi-detached houses (Figure 9-2).

Table 9-1. Commercial Devitalization in the Heart of Roxbury, Boston

Commercial Street	Number of Businesses				
	1950	1960	1970	1980	1993
Dudley Street	129	79	49	26	32
Blue Hill Avenue	210	150	74	47	28
Total	339	229	123	73	60

Note: Commercial inventories are for the prime commercial streets on the land controlled since 1985 by the Dudley Street Neighborhood Initiative. Dudley Street inventory is for the segment from Warren Street to Alexander Street. Blue Hill Avenue inventory is for the segment from Dudley Street to Quincy Street. 1993 inventory is approximate.

Source: Peter Medoff and Holly Sklar, *Streets of Hope* (Boston: South End Press, 1994), p. 14.

9-1a. Buffalo. Boarded-up house in the Southampton/Jefferson area, East Buffalo.

9-1b. Minneapolis. Boarded-up house in the Phillips neighborhood, South Minneapolis.

9-1c. Oakland. Boarded-up house on Chester Street, West Oakland.

Figure 9-1. Derelict houses, various cities—1999. It isn't to preserve a unique local resource that gray-zone defenders protect obsolete housing. Gray zones and their houses are uniformly common in cities nationwide.

DSNI's new low-density housing will do little to revive the area's depleted commercial streets. More than 40 percent of the meager supply of retail square footage in DSNI's neighborhood was devoted to automobile service and parts businesses in the early 1990s, but DSNI embraced rather than rejected this deficiency; the organization's plan suggests exploring the feasibility of an auto repair park.[20] Having decided to maintain and entrench suburban residential densities in their neighborhoods, neighborhood defenders and city officials have no realistic choices for their commercial streets but to suburbanize them or do nothing at all.

Gray zones cannot revitalize unless they are released from their low-density zoning classifications, but in the present era of politically powerful neighborhood organizations, prospects for up-zoning are nil because neighborhood activists are strongly influential in zoning decisions. In Louisville, Kentucky, a city with a 2000 population density of only 4,126 people per square mile, aldermen invoked neighborhood preferences when they resisted the increased central-city densities proposed in a countywide land-use plan called Cornerstone 2020. The plan suggested

9-2a. New infill housing in Roxbury. Semi-detached houses (two units side-by-side) have materialized throughout the heart of Roxbury, thanks to the efforts of DSNI.

9-2b. Old townhouses in Roxbury. Old townhouses and flats on Cottage Street, in the middle of DSNI's turf, resemble those in Boston's great neighborhoods.

Figure 9-2. The suburbanization of a distressed Boston neighborhood (1998). The Dudley Street Neighborhood Initiative (DSNI) suburbanizes a potentially great urban neighborhood. DSNI's operatives were apparently uninspired by the historic townhouses and flats in Boston's great neighborhoods and in their own neighborhood.

higher housing densities in the urban core as a way to alleviate the environmental stress caused by automobile dependence, but a committee of Louisville aldermen offered an amendment aimed at preserving single-family zoning in their neighborhoods. One alderman argued that neighborhoods in his ward have fought to downzone in order to restrict the construction of apartments. The *Louisville Courier-Journal* reported that the committee of central-city aldermen complained that "the plan gives too much emphasis to the environment and not enough to the automobile."[21]

Why Suburbanize?

Why, oh why, do neighborhood activists and city officials pursue housing densities too low to sustain urban life? No doubt many are suburbanites at heart and value big lawns and gardens. In distressed neighborhoods, the activists' social mission dictates a focus on affordable housing, which generally means existing low-density housing rather than new higher-density housing.

Activists determine the city's planning agenda because city planning departments, from which physical development leadership should emanate, are increasingly immersed in equity planning, more oriented to a social mission than to traditional physical planning. The social mission of equity planning demands, in part, that planners relinquish their leadership roles and follow the whims of neighborhood activists. Equity planners join neighborhood activists in their dogmatic opposition to gentrification; the planners must then oppose high densities, which they realize are incompatible with poverty.

There is another reason, practical rather than ideological, that planners avoid the measures necessary to revitalize cities: the pursuit of revitalization is more strenuous than the maintenance of the status quo. Revitalization entails a more daunting array of physical planning issues, some of which are beyond the scope of the contemporary planning focus—the neighborhood. Creativity, discipline, and determination are necessary to synthesize the several indispensable elements of a revitalization plan. Centralized rail transit, for example, is requisite to the development of high-density middle-class housing on a broad scale. Strong political leadership is necessary to pull all the affected factions together in a coordinated effort. It is easier to suburbanize.

DEFENDING THE GRAY ZONE AGAINST GREATER AFFLUENCE

Seven-year-old Dantrell Davis was shot in the face as his mom walked him to Chicago's Jenner Elementary School in 1992. The bullet killed him. School officials later threatened to close the school because police had been unable to stop the frequent gun battles at a Cabrini-Green highrise across the street, a building known as a den of gang iniquity. In the spring of 1997, gunshots within range of Jenner became almost a daily occurrence, and in the autumn of that year gunshots were exchanged between two highrises—the gang highrise and another—that engulf the school. During a day of sporadic gunfire that autumn, Jenner students looked out the windows and witnessed the shooting of a man in the parking lot of the gang highrise. (The Chicago Housing Authority has since begun the evacuation of the gang highrise.)

Cabrini-Green's first big moment of national infamy came in 1981 when newsmen followed Mayor Jane Byrne to one of the compound's buildings. The mayor had moved in for three weeks, accompanied by cops and bodyguards, to restore order after 11 people were killed and 37 wounded in a two-month period.

Disrespect for the law is accompanied by a powerful resentment of lawmen at Cabrini. A confrontation between dozens of cops and hundreds of Cabrini residents erupted in March 1997, triggered by a drug arrest to which many residents apparently objected. The cop making the arrest was confronted by a crowd and fired his gun, accidentally in a struggle with a protester according to the police, deliberately and unprovoked according to residents. In any event, the cop's bullet wounded a resident and a melee ensued, eventually involving hundreds of Cabrini residents and dozens of Chicago and CHA police. The cops exchanged gunfire with one or more snipers in a Cabrini highrise. Violent conflict between cops and Cabrini residents has been almost routine since 1970, when snipers in one of Cabrini's buildings shot and killed two cops walking across a yard.

"The last 24 hours had been kind to Cabrini-Green," reported the *Chicago Tribune* on June 1, 1997. "There was an arrest for strong-armed robbery, for purse snatching, for criminal sexual abuse, for aggregated battery, for burglary, for pickpocketing, for three counts of theft…But no shootings…so that would be a quiet night." Mayhem is so common at Cabrini-Green that its absence would be oddly conspicuous. Murder is unexceptional at the complex. The latest to make the news as this is written in June 2000: A 15-year-old girl is shot dead in front of a Cabrini-Green building at the end of April, and a 13-year-old boy is charged. This murder of a child by a child at Cabrini warranted only a page-3 story in the *Chicago Tribune's* Metro section. (The Tribune's report notes that Cabrini's level of violence has increased lately and that elderly tenants fear leaving their rooms.)[22]

It was in the stairwell of a Cabrini-Green highrise that the nine-year-old girl who became known as Girl X was deposited by a sexual predator after he beat her nearly to death. As he assaulted her, the tormentor choked the child to silence her screams, then he threw her to the floor and stepped on her throat, then he emptied a can of insecticide into her mouth to destroy the evidence of his deviance, then he scrawled gang graffiti on her body, and he dumped her, blind and unconscious, in the stairwell and left her for dead. Most Americans would agree that Cabrini-Green, a public housing development for families, is a less-than-wholesome environment for children. Signs above building entries advise, ENTRY REQUIRES PASSING THROUGH A METAL DETECTOR. Fatherlessness, teen pregnancy, poverty, and unemployment are the norm. Only 7 percent of residents were employed in 1998. In 1993, the Winfield Moody Health Center at the edge of Cabrini-Green began administering prenatal treatment to three girls who had been clients there since their own births, 10 years earlier.

Before it was thinned out in the latter years of the 1990s, Cabrini-Green was arguably the rottenest hellhole in the history of urban America. Nonetheless, housing activists have opposed the dismantling of Cabrini-Green and the dispersal of its poverty-ridden population.[23]

Deconcentrating Poverty

Where poverty is concentrated, it can be diluted in any of three ways:

1. Demolish buildings selectively to displace the households of lowest income.

2. Increase residential densities to accommodate an influx of non-poor households.

3. Gentrify buildings to replace low-income households with higher-income households.

Neighborhood activists and housing advocates routinely oppose any meaningful implementation of any of these tactics. In response to a discrimination lawsuit, HUD and the City of Minneapolis agreed, in 1995, to deconcentrate poverty from the city's north-side gray zone by demolishing a cluster of four public housing projects, dispersing the tenants, and developing replacement housing for a mixed-income population. Throughout the process, activists opposed the measures necessary to achieve the intent of the settlement:

1. Activists demonstrated against the impending demolition of some of the doomed buildings in June 1999, insisting that low-income housing is precious, having decided that concentrated poverty is not a serious problem.

2. As the city planned to reduce housing density from *low* to *very low,* activists lobbied for an *extremely low* density—just six to 10 units per net acre—for a redevelopment site less than a mile from downtown Minneapolis.

3. Activists insisted that at least half of all replacement units, rather than one-quarter as planned by the city, be dedicated to low-income households. [24]

The activists who oppose measures necessary to revitalize neighborhoods are most active these days in public housing developments, but they're active also in distressed neighborhoods of low-density private-market housing—gray zones. It is in these gray zones that the potential for revitalization should be greatest because land is controlled by individuals and city development agencies rather than HUD and local housing authorities.

Gentrification and Anti-gentrification

Citing evidence from New York City, urban affairs writer Roberta Brandes Gratz tells us that the physical and socioeconomic ascension of a gray zone might proceed unimpeded by resident resistance (activist resistance is another matter) provided that most of the low-income residents are assured a place in the renewed neighborhood:

> Middle-income people do not...resist moving into a neighborhood that has a low-income, racially mixed population already in place. Conversely, in-place, low-income residents don't resent higher-income newcomer—in fact, they welcome them—so long as their own continuance there is not threatened. [25]

Unless a neighborhood is largely abandoned, higher densities are needed to accommodate a middle-class influx that doesn't displace incumbents. Middle-class parents, less adventurous than the stereotypical gentrifiers, would reject the gentrifying neighborhood unless surrounded by large numbers of their own kind, and this entails a density upgrade of a magnitude sure to be opposed by activists. Activists in many low-income neighborhoods would oppose another component of housing policy that would tame the apprehensions of middle-class parents: a program designed to help significant numbers of disruptive and at-risk families find housing outside the city. The political liberalism rampant in distressed neighborhoods rejects the notion that at-risk families, even where concentrated, pose a threat to neighborhood civility and tranquility. Neighborhood incivility is rooted in the social and economic injustice that is endemic to white racists and their capitalism, according to the cant of the urban leftist. Social and economic injustice is exacerbated by government's supposed stinginess in funding neighborhood social programs; these factors are responsible for neighborhood distress say the activists who represent or claim to represent the nation's most distressed neighborhoods.

Urban liberals reject terms such as *underclass* and *at-risk*, terms that implicitly "blame the victim" for the sins of an oppressive mainstream society. Mimi Abramovitz, professor of social policy at Hunter College in New York City, refers disdainfully to Daniel Patrick Moynihan's warning about the consequences of epidemic fatherlessness, and asserts that "society blames women for the failed policies of business and the state."[26] Peter Medoff, former DSNI executive director, acknowledged the disproportionate fatherlessness and poverty in the severely distressed Dudley Street neighborhood he represented: "Over half of Dudley's children live in households headed by women, and over half of those families live below the official poverty line."[27] Medoff faulted liberalism's usual culprit—racism—for the sorry condition of his neighborhood. Dudley is submerged in poverty, according to Medoff, because policymakers tolerate discrimination, and they scapegoat single mothers: "Instead of rooting out discrimination and implementing the kind of family supports common in numerous countries, many policy makers are busily blaming women for their disproportionate poverty."[28]

Consistent with this view, Medoff (who wrote that poverty is caused by "the economic system") argued that higher AFDC payments are necessary to relieve neighborhood stress; he did not argue that an infusion of middle-class two-parent families would be helpful. The deficient parents overrepresented in urban America's distressed neighborhoods are exonerated by urban liberals who invoke, as Medoff did, the old proverb, "it takes a village to raise a child."[29]

Having absolved poor fatherless families of any responsibility for the repellent nature of the inner city, activists believe their neighborhoods need middle-class two-parent families like a fish needs a bicycle. The activist agenda is shaped by the belief that distressed neighborhoods will be resurrected not by an infusion of middle-class values but by an ascendance of social and economic justice, as defined by the activists. And the activists define social and economic justice in a way that relieves them of any responsibility to exercise prudent stewardship over their turf. As their neighborhoods lie submerged in despair, even after public and philanthropic fortunes have been squandered on dubious housing programs and social agendas, activists unabashedly continue to demand more public subsidies, insisting that outsiders—racist capitalists and the policymakers they control—are wholly responsible for the sorry condition of their neighborhoods.

Gentrification is Genocide!

A New York City man screamed "gentrification is genocide!" and then he pledged to "fight in the streets" to prevent the construction of condominium apartments on the Lower East Side.[30] This scene unfolded at a city council hearing in August 1997, convened to discuss the fate of several hundred city-owned vacant lots, many of them converted to gardens, on the city's derelict blocks. The activist was one of an unruly crowd agitated because their city's administration had the audacity to propose that some of its vacant land be used for condominiums instead of agriculture. The city would have met less resistance if it had proposed to build housing for the poorest of the poor.

Gentrification is an evil of capitalist housing markets, which banish the poor to the streets, according to Rutgers University's Neil Smith: "Gentrification and homelessness in the . . . city are a microcosm of a new global order etched by the rapacity of capital." Gentrification causes displacement, which causes homelessness, according to Smith, who declared in 1992, without citing evidence: "'The homeless' are more accurately described as 'the evicted.'"[31] Smith conjures an image of working-class masses forced onto the streets by the cruel onslaught of gentrification, but the reality is much different.

Urban geographer Brian Berry analyzed gentrification in American cities and found that the process typically affects neighborhoods with high vacancy rates and abandonment.[32] An analysis by John Kain and William Apgar reveals that the displacement of low-income households from gentrifying neighborhoods is not so cataclysmic as housing activists claim. Many renters in the path of gentrification would move voluntarily, or be evicted, regardless of gentrification. Forty percent of all rental households in socioeconomically distressed urban neighborhoods are likely to move in any given year, for which reason Myron Orfield refers to these neighborhoods as "transient places." Gentrification is a gradual process, according to Kain and Apgar, which "alters neighborhood socioeconomic composition primarily by changing the pool of in-migrants rather than by accelerating the departure of residents."[33]

Kain and Apgar's analysis of low-income Chicago neighborhoods led them to the conclusion that a failure to upgrade the socioeconomic condition of a distressed neighborhood creates a greater hardship than does gentrification: "Many low-income central-city neighborhoods that are not upgraded experience rapid deterioration, arson, and abandonment, changes that are at least as likely as revitalization to displace households …the alternative to displacement through upgrading may be displacement through deterioration."[34]

Cincinnati's Over-the-Rhine has a housing stock worth preserving, unlike the typical American gray zone, but the neighborhood lost nearly 3,000 units, mostly to demolition and arson, between 1970 and 1990 as its defenders warded off the natural forces of gentrification (Table 9-2). The defenders opposed, and succeeded in stalling, the neighborhood's listing on the National Register of Historic Places, a source of funds not only for preservation but also for low-income housing. The defenders feared that designation as a historic district would encourage private investment and drive up rents for some of the neighborhood's housing.[35]

Table 9-2. Deterioration of Population and Housing in Over-the-Rhine

	1970	1980	1990	
Total population	16,363	12,355	9,572	
Number of dwelling units	8,515	7,312	5,655	
No. of occupied dwelling units	6,658	5,558	4,200	(estimated)
No. of assisted occupied units	0	1,900	2,500	(estimated)
% of occupied units assisted	0	34	60	

Source: Zane L. Miller and Bruce Tucker, *Changing Plans for America's Inner Cities: Cincinnati's Over-the-Rhine and Twentieth-Century Urbanism* (Columbus: Ohio State University, 1998), p. 161.

THE FIRST LINE OF DEFENSE: SOCIAL OWNERSHIP OF LAND

The Marxist perspective on urban housing markets might be harmless enough if ignored by policymakers, but it is not. New York City

Councilwoman Miriam Friedlander echoed Neil Smith's sentiments when she denounced a Lower East Side revitalization plan as "just a front for gentrification" and claimed that "the real people who will profit from this housing are the developers who renovate it."[36] The Marxist perspective is adopted by gray zones' nonprofit housing developers, among whom "there's a disdain for private business," according to Eric Wieffering, senior editor at *Corporate Report Minnesota*. Wieffering quotes Alan Arthur, the executive director of Minneapolis' nonprofit Central Community Housing Trust: "I am totally opposed to people using real estate as an investment tool."[37] In Boston, DSNI director Ro Whittington voiced a similar sentiment: "we're not going to support people who come to make money off of housing."[38]

DSNI's turf is in Roxbury's Dudley Street neighborhood, where the organization's leadership sought to hold back a "tide of speculation and gentrification." To achieve this they endeavored (with considerable success) to "gain control of the land in order to stop outside developers." DSNI's 1987 "revitalization plan" includes among its guiding principles, "community action and legislation targeting speculative real estate brokers and developers." The philosophy was articulated by DSNI president Ché Madyun: "We warn speculators…you are not welcome here."[39]

DSNI's strategy of removing its turf from private housing markets was abetted by the City of Boston, which owned more than half of the numerous vacant lots in the heart of Dudley. The city sold this land for $1 to DSNI's perpetual community land trust; then, in an action unprecedented in the nation, Boston officials granted DSNI the power of eminent domain, a power the organization would use to acquire the abundant supply of privately held vacant land in the heart of its neighborhood. (DSNI's land acquisition was consistent with the precepts of the Association of Neighborhood Housing Developers, which promotes the "social ownership" of land.) By the early 1990s, DSNI had established dominance over the land market in its neighborhood and set out to develop its heavily subsidized low-density, low-income housing.[40]

A community organizer in Cincinnati preached that neighborhood organizations must "own the dirt" in order to protect themselves from landlords and homeowners seeking profits. Over-the-Rhine's Community Council pursued land control with zeal and, in the early 1980s, named its new community development corporation Owning the Realty, Inc.[41] Activists in super-potential areas like Boston's Roxbury and Cincinnati's Over-the-Rhine know full well that the unimpeded forces of private land development would claim their turf in short order. Land control is therefore an essential tactic in the struggle to prevent an influx of the non-poor.

DEFENDING THE SYSTEM

Another way to control land development, besides owning the realty, is to erect institutional barriers to private developers. Nonprofit housing developers in Minneapolis exploit a privileged relationship with city hall in order to monopolize gray-zone housing development, which consists, as usual, of the construction and rehabilitation of houses and small apartment buildings for low-income households. City officials are beholden to the politically influential neighborhood organizations that spawned the nonprofits, and, in many cases, their own political careers. Minneapolis City Council President Jackie Cherryhomes had been the development director of a north-side nonprofit developer, one that has been richly endowed with government grants since Cherryhomes rose to city hall. Steve Cramer, executive director of the Minneapolis Community Development Agency, was formerly the head of Project for Pride in Living, one of the city's prolific nonprofit housing developers.[42] *Corporate Report's* Eric Wieffering explains the power that has accrued to nonprofits in Minneapolis:

> Neighborhood nonprofit developers have exclusive territorial rights…the barriers to a for-profit developer are so high as to be almost insurmountable. For one thing, they must get neighborhood approval for their project. If that neighborhood…has its own nonprofit developer, the reception is usually icy…It is a system that virtually chases private owners out of the market and then rewards nonprofit developers.[43]

Wieffering calls Minneapolis' cabal of nonprofits "an entrenched bureaucracy of holier-than-thou empire builders who share a profound sense of entitlement."[44] In Brooklyn, the leadership of the nonprofit Bedford-Stuyvesant Restoration Corporation is accused of being "unwilling to endorse any proposal that does not give Restoration joint ownership," according to a May 2000 report in the *New York Times*. The powerful organization is seen by many today as an "impediment to progress, an entrenched and sluggish bureaucracy instead of a spark plug for local entrepreneurs." Conceived in 1966 in a Brooklyn neighborhood that remains distressed 34 years later, Restoration is the progenitor of the nation's community development corporations, which number in the thousands today.[45]

THE HOUSING MISSIONARIES

Alan Arthur, the aforementioned executive director of a Minneapolis non-profit housing developer, explained his organization's mission: "This is an endeavor to provide as much affordable housing as we can."[46] The mission statement of a St. Paul nonprofit illustrates nonprofits' subservience to neighborhood activists: "CommonBond Communities creates opportunities for people to improve their lives by providing affordable housing *guided by community and resident leaders.*"[47] (Emphasis added.)

Neighborhood activists' exclusionary attitudes do not extend to the low-income population, therefore nonprofit developers assume the task of increasing the supplies of affordable housing in neighborhoods already overburdened. In their 1998 book about the tragic and unnecessary degeneration of Cincinnati's Over-the-Rhine neighborhood, historians Zane Miller and Bruce Tucker report that Over-the-Rhine's Community Council "wanted to provide low-income housing in Over-the-Rhine not only for current residents but also for other low-income people who might want to move into the neighborhood." Accordingly, the council's Housing Committee hatched a plan in 1983 formulated to "increase the number of low-income dwelling units," and, at the same time, to "keep out more prosperous people ..."[48]

The pattern is similar in Roxbury, where DSNI stands vigilant against gentrification, but welcomes low-income outsiders into its new subsidized housing. Insisting upon perpetual affordability, DSNI established a community land trust and land lease arrangement to preserve the affordability of its housing units when sold to future owners.[49]

Neighborhood activists and nonprofit developers operate under the conviction that the nation's supply of affordable units is short and shrinking. Dilapidated housing, including public housing, falls to the wrecking ball, and subsidized units built in the 1970s under the Section 8 new construction program are being converted to market-rate units. The advocates don't mention the filter-down process, the traditional provider of low-cost units. On balance, to be sure, there is a constricted supply of decent housing units affordable to "extremely low income" households, and on that basis the advocates insist that the forces of gentrification shall be tightly circumscribed and subsidies shall flow to the production of low-cost housing.

If the nation's supply of decent affordable housing is inadequate, the problem is probably not as severe as the advocates claim, and not so severe that overburdened neighborhoods should expand their burden. The advocates' inflated assessment of the housing shortage, and their political tactics, are inspired by the deceptive homeless advocacy of the 1980s, which portrayed the nation's homeless people as blue-collar victims of industrial dislocations and housing shortages. This widespread myth was perpetrated by media-savvy advocates, whose detractors were far less interesting to journalists. Among the rejoinders to the advocates' inflated claims was this, written by Alice Baum and Donald Burns after many years of service to homeless people:

> Newspapers, magazines, books, and television programs reported stories of homeless two-parent rust-belt families temporarily down on their luck or of homeless individuals who had recently been laid off from permanent employment...None of these descriptions bore any resemblance to the people we knew. Nor were they consistent with the emerging research, which documented that up to 85 percent of all homeless adults suffer from chronic alcoholism, drug addiction, mental illness, or some combination of the three.[50]

The homeless advocates' adoption of the housing-shortage ploy was a strategic decision—a deliberate deception—ratified in the 1980s, as the *New York Times* explains:

> To win public sympathy, advocates oversimplified homelessness. "There was a discussion that went on among us all," said Marsha A. Martin, who served on the board of the Coalition for the Homeless. "Do you market it as a problem of shelter, or do you tell people about alcoholism, drug addiction, mental illness, concerns about child abuse?" The problem was "marketed" as soluble with the simple provision of housing. In one television report, [homeless advocate Robert] Hayes walked through Harlem saying the solution was simple: "In three words, housing, housing, housing."[51]

No matter how many decent low-cost housing units are available in a metropolitan area, many families and individuals will remain stuck at the margins of the housing market. Aside from the relatively few afflicted with mental illness, alcoholism, and drug addiction, many rental applicants with histories of criminal activity, property destruction, eviction, or bad credit seek housing, private and public, with difficulty. In the nation's cities, vacancy rates are highest among the cheapest housing units. Vacancy rates in Minneapolis' two most distressed residential districts are nearly double the citywide average. While these high rates reflect higher-than-average percentages of substandard units, and low neighborhood appeal (a condition not remedied by opposition to gentrification), they also reveal that low-cost housing is far from unavailable, even if far from luxurious. The Minneapolis Planning Department reported in 1999 that the city's distressed neighborhoods have higher-than-average vacancy rates in part because many of their units "do not offer modern amenities desired by today's younger renters."[52]

In asserting the severity of the low-cost housing shortage, advocates adopt these two precepts:

1. A low-income household is entitled to a housing unit that is little if any inferior in size and in quality to the average unit occupied by a middle-class household with the same number of people. Modern standards of privacy dictate that low-income families with more than one or two children will no longer live in the crowded conditions that accompanied poverty in the past. (HUD defines crowding as "more than one person per room.")

2. A low-income household should spend no more than 30 percent its income for housing.

Advocates' inflated assessment of the housing shortage is a product of the simultaneous application of the quality standard and the cost standard. For example, the narrator of a 1997 documentary about affordable housing in the Twin Cities indicated that the current average rents for two- and three-bedroom apartments in the metropolitan area were $621 and $841 respectively, implying that these monthly rents were required to obtain average or decent apartments. Then the narrator explained that for *low-income* people, these *average* rents would absorb more than 30 percent of income.[53] The Minneapolis Affordable Housing Task Force, composed disproportionately of housing advocates and nonprofit housing developers, proposed an affordable-housing budget which assumes that the average production cost for affordable units will be the same as the metro-area median value for single-family houses. Nonprofit housing developers routinely spend far more than the per-unit median to develop their low-income units.[54] Even though many low-income households are consigned to sub-optimal housing, few are afflicted with the threat of imminent homelessness, as the advocates claim.

Mass homelessness looms as a threat, but hunger is already pervasive, the hunger of children no less, say the housing advocates. In the introductory paragraph of its report to the mayor and city council, the Minneapolis Affordable Housing Task Force avers, "Children are going without enough food because their families cannot afford both food and rent."[55] But the task force offers no evidence that a housing shortage causes child hunger in Minneapolis. Public and philanthropic food programs—food stamps, food shelves, and prepared-food programs—make food so abundantly available to Minneapolis' poor parents that if children are going without enough food it is because of gross parental neglect. The U.S. Conference of Mayors' *Status Report on Hunger and Homelessness in American Cities* lists Minneapolis as one of the many cities in which "food assistance facilities" provide an adequate supply of nutritionally balanced food and turn no one away.[56] A Ramsey County child-protection worker blames child malnutrition on the misdirected spending priorities of their parents, many of whom spend too much on material goods, entertainment, and beauty services, and not enough on their children's needs. Referring to her current caseload of clients, the child protection worker said, "food is the least of their problems...they don't know how to budget and they don't want to budget."[57]

The sociologist Elijah Anderson offers a similar observation in his 1999 book, *Code of the Street: Decency, Violence, and the Moral Life of the Inner City*: Some parents "have a limited understanding of priorities and consequences, and so frustrations mount over bills, food, and, at times, liquor, cigarettes, and drugs." Anderson observed "status-oriented behavior" among the inner city's teenage mothers, who "spend inordinately large sums" to feed their status hunger. Some of the available money is spent on children, reports Anderson, but not always responsibly: "The young mother often feels the need to dress her baby in the latest and most expensive clothes that fit (rather than a size larger, which baby can grow into): a fifty-dollar sweater for a three-month-old or forty-dollar Reebok sneakers for a six-month old...The teenage mother derives status from her baby." One of Anderson's informants told him, "they sometimes do more to more to clothe the baby than to feed the baby."[58]

The Minneapolis Affordable Housing Task Force claims also that the city's ill-housed children suffer "compromised school achievement" because of the low-cost housing scarcity.* The task force makes no mention of the adverse affects of a dearth of middle-class pupils in Minneapolis schools. Middle-class schools in middle-class neighbor-

---

*As was the case with child nutrition, the task force ignored the role of parental deficiency in children's education. Parental non-involvement is a critical factor in the poor performance of Minneapolis Public School students according to *A Report on the Minneapolis Public Schools 2000*, issued jointly by the Minneapolis Public Schools, the Minneapolis Foundation, and the Greater Minneapolis Chamber of Commerce.

hoods are the best antidote for the inferior achievement of inner-city students, according to the evidence of Chicago's Gautreaux program.

As noted in Chapter 8, an abundant existing supply of modest and aging-but-sound housing units in the nation's suburbs would become available to low-income households if housing policy focused on the large-scale production of middle-class housing in cities—a mechanism for the dispersal of poverty and an essential ingredient of revitalization.

THE ENTRENCHMENT OF CONCENTRATED POVERTY

Convinced of a cataclysmic shortage of decent low-cost housing, and bent on a mission to solve the problem unilaterally if necessary, nonprofit housing developers produce and preserve subsidized housing in the overburdened neighborhoods that produce the least political resistance (Figure 9-3).[59] Nonprofits' housing initiatives include, besides the production and rehabilitation of low-cost detached houses, the acquisition, rehabilitation, and management of low-rent apartment buildings. A 1996 survey of apartment buildings acquired and rehabilitated by Minneapolis nonprofits finds that "these projects are located in the poorest neighborhoods in the city," and "very low income households are overrepresented among the project site tenants…70.9 percent have incomes below 50 percent of the area median."[60]

A typical example of a nonprofit housing initiative: a Minneapolis nonprofit called Project for Pride in Living dumped $207,000 into the 1983 acquisition and rehabilitation of a crummy two-story fourplex just $1\frac{1}{2}$ miles from downtown Minneapolis, in the Near North gray zone. The initiative hasn't triggered any new development in the area; 16 years after the acquisition, vacant lots lie fallow across the street. The estimated market value of the nonprofit's building had sunk to $96,000 by 1999, when it produced only $1,286 in property taxes.[61] The fourplex should have been demolished, along with its neighboring wooden houses, to make way for urban development.

Occasionally a nonprofit developer gets its hands on an apartment building worth saving, a building with some potential to eventually attract non-poor households to a derelict neighborhood. To a nonprofit housing developer such a building represents an opportunity to entrench poverty rather than disperse it. And occasionally a nonprofit developer gets its hands on a building worth saving in a gentrifying neighborhood, a neighborhood with considerable potential to alleviate the city's inordinate poverty burden. A St. Paul nonprofit called CommonBond

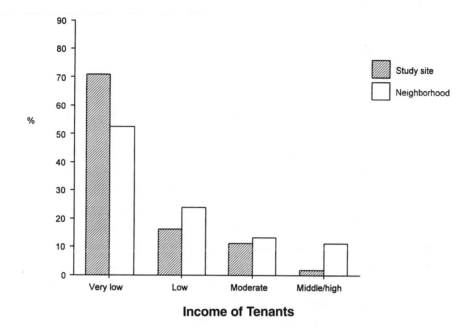

Income of Tenants

Figure 9-3. Nonprofit housing developers and poverty entrenchment.
Nonprofit housing developers ply their trade in low-income neighborhoods
and dedicate their buildings to low-income tenants.
Source: Edward Goetz, Hin Kim Lam, and Anne Heitlinger, *There Goes the Neighborhood?*
(Minneapolis: Center for Urban and Regional Affairs, 1996), Figure 6, p. 72.
Notes:
1. The graphic reflects a study of 23 subsidized multi-unit building acquired or constructed in
   Minneapolis by nonprofit housing developers. The authors of the study selected buildings with
   the intent to "maximize the variation on geography (we included both north and south side
   projects), size of the project (number of units), age of the development, type of subsidy (i.e.,
   Section 8 rental subsidy or building subsidy), rent levels, income mix of tenants, and type of
   building management …" (p. 17)
2. The authors define "very low" income as income 40 percent of median or lower (p. 75).
3. The authors note a higher rate of public assistance dependence among the tenants of the
   nonprofits' buildings (p. 73).

Communities got its hands on a bunch of high-potential apartment buildings in the high-potential Cathedral Hill neighborhood, invested enough
money in the buildings to make them marketable to middle-class households, and then loaded them up with low-income families.

The Cathedral Hill neighborhood overlooking downtown St. Paul is better positioned than any other in the city to attract middle-class urbanites
to the vicinity of some 55,000 jobs in the downtown and in the state capi-

tol complex, both at the neighborhood's edge. Cathedral Hill is a potential gold zone whose assets include, besides altitude and proximity to downtown, some of the city's finest old apartment buildings and townhouses. Unsurprisingly then, the socioeconomically marginal neighborhood sporadically gentrifies in spite of substantial public investment in low-income housing.

Ever vigilant against the natural forces of gentrification, CommonBond Communities entrenches poverty in Cathedral Hill—in the neighborhood's census tract 340 to be precise—where the poverty rate exceeds 40 percent according to 1990 census data. In 1998, CommonBond won an $8.2 million deal to remodel an urbane complex of seven aging apartment buildings that could easily attract middle-class households, especially with the millions spent on remodeling. It wasn't to prevent displacement that the nonprofit dedicated the units to low-income households; the buildings' occupied units were emptied for construction crews. Opponents of the deal warned against the concentration of low-income tenants, but neighborhood groups backed the nonprofit, and then the St. Paul City Council approved the deal, turned the city-owned buildings over to the nonprofit, and authorized more than a half-million dollars in financial assistance, in addition to earlier commitments. The cost per remodeled unit in CommonBond Communities' Cathedral Hill apartments was about $135,000, more than the 1998 median price for single-family detached houses in the Twin Cities metropolis.[62]

Cathedral Hill's importance to St. Paul is profound. The gentrifying neighborhood lies between downtown and one of the city's persistently depressed gray zones, into which the revitalization process would spread if strengthened rather than weakened by public investment. The unimpeded gentrification of Cathedral Hill would trigger a wave of commercial revitalization strong enough to enhance the appeal of adjacent residential land, thereby boosting the prospects for the spread of revitalization. The city's low-performing public schools and their disadvantaged students would benefit if activists and officials pursued middle-class families as ardently as they pursue low-income families.

Fortunately, nonprofits are less active in high-potential areas like Cathedral Hill than in lower-potential gray zones where, by some measure, the organizations exert a positive force. Some of the best buildings in some of the worst neighborhoods are the ones rehabilitated by nonprofits. These buildings provide decent low-income housing and, with their exteriors improved, they upgrade the image of a derelict area. Occasionally a nonprofit upgrades the economic condition of a depressed area by developing housing that will attract households slightly more affluent than the area's average. In the absence of a gray-zone revitalization plan and commitment by the city, the stabilization efforts of the nonprofits can be seen as a good thing.

But if results are measured against potential, then the efforts of the nonprofits must be seen as harmful. In concert with city officials, nonprofits systemically prevent revitalization when they maintain low densities and entrench poverty.* Nonprofits' extravagant waste of public and philanthropic money drives up the cost, and maybe even preempts the possibility, of true revitalization. Once developed, nonprofits' low-cost housing fails to sustain itself and sucks fortunes out of public and philanthropic treasuries. Even greater than the direct public costs are the opportunity costs—the unrealized potential tax revenue—imposed by the maintenance of underutilization. All of the resources devoted to the entrenchment of poverty are desperately needed instead to prime gray-zone land for private-market revitalization.

UNDER THE ACTIVISTS' THUMB: CITY HALL

The stunted vision emanating from city hall is far-sighted compared to the near blindness of neighborhood organizations, which see no farther than a neighborhood's boundaries. The organizations pursue economic self-containment at the neighborhood level (about which more later) and they exert a downward pressure on their cities' already modest housing goals. In Boston's long-distressed Roxbury district, DSNI rejected the city's criteria for the affordability of low-income housing and opted for even lower income thresholds for the new housing it developed.[63] Besides promoting densities too low to sustain vitality, DSNI develops subsidized

---

*In *Comeback Cities*, a glowing assessment of nonprofit housing developers and their neighborhoods, author Paul Grogan says, "The point is not that poverty has been abolished, or will be, nor is it that cities can or should return to the full glory of their wealthier past." Grogan, who for 13 years headed a national organization that supports local nonprofit developers, envisions cities as places populated primarily and perpetually by people of low and modest income: "Even after the revitalization of poor and blighted neighborhoods, very wide income disparities between city and suburbs will probably persist indefinitely." This is fine with Grogan so long as crime is reduced and schools are improved (by means other than a middle-class influx). Grogan hopes also that retailers will return to distressed neighborhoods, but the low-density housing he admires will support only the suburbanized version of retailing. (Paul S. Grogan and Tony Proscio, *Comeback Cities: A Blueprint for Neighborhood Revival* [Boulder, Colorado: Westview Press, 2000], pp. 7, 55.)

housing that perpetuates Roxbury's burden of accommodating the poorest households in the Boston metropolis.

Perhaps DSNI's antipathy toward gentrification motivates the organization to build housing that will not attract gentrifiers in the future. Gentrifiers are attracted to houses of architectural distinction in commercially robust neighborhoods, which DSNI's development practices preclude. DSNI follows the lead of neighborhood housing activists who, in the late 1960s, opposed mixed-income development in the South End and advocated, instead, maximum efforts and expenditures on behalf of the poor.[64]

The liberals in city hall are moderate compared to many of the leftist activists who influence housing policy. Officials in Cincinnati "cannot promote market-rate housing too actively," according to David Varady and Jeffrey Raffel, for fear of agitating neighborhood activists.[65] Cincinnati is remarkable for its untapped potential. If market forces were unleashed it would soon rival San Francisco as a world-renowned city of hilly terrain and thriving high- and moderate-density neighborhoods. But the politics of poverty imprison Cincinnati's super-potential neighborhoods in a state of gross underutilization. Two such neighborhoods are the East End and Over-the-Rhine. In Cincinnati's East End, situated on the bank of the Ohio River, the East End Area Council rejected the city's 1989 mixed-income housing plan and countered with its own "Recipe for Success" focused on low-income housing. The neighborhood organization rejected a provision in the city's strategy that would have required redevelopment to pay for itself through increased tax revenue, and it rewarded its first new housing development to a nonprofit developer.[66] As long as neighborhood activists control housing development in the East End, it will not achieve its great gold-zone potential.

If left to market forces and prudent public policy, Cincinnati's Over-the-Rhine district would soon become as well known as Boston's North End and New Orleans' French Quarter for its superb 19th century residential-commercial environment. Like Philadelphia's Rittenhouse Square and Boston's Beacon Hill, Over-the-Rhine is adjacent to its city's downtown, enabling it to attract a sizable segment of the workforce if reclaimed by the middle class. The district's high-density lowrise collection of small-scale red-brick commercial and residential buildings merits inclusion on the National Register of Historic Places, unlike the detached houses of typical gray zones. But Over-the-Rhine's neighborhood activists, with the acquiescence of city officials, seized control of the neighborhood, presided over its continued depopulation, and turned it into a "permanent low-income…ghetto—a stagnant, decaying reservation for the poor at the doorstep to downtown," in the words of an official who dissented almost alone. In April 2001, Over-the-Rhine hosted America's first urban race riots of the new millennium, an event that enlarged the neighborhood's colossal inventory of boarded buildings. Cincinnati councilman Jim Tarbell seemed unsurprised that Over-the-Rhine should succumb to anarchy: "That's one of the biggest dope-dealing dens and dysfunctional environments that we have in this city…It's absolutely the most frightening environment that we have in Cincinnati today." [67]

Over-the-Rhine' tragic era of activist control began in the early 1960s. Historians Zane Miller and Bruce Tucker tell us that by 1962,

> Cincinnati's social work administrators had established the principles of community organizing for neighborhood autonomy as the linchpin of their social welfare programs and had identified Over-the-Rhine as one of the city's neediest neighborhoods…Not surprisingly, such an identification attracted community organizers to Over-the-Rhine.[68]

Cincinnati's planners had formulated a revitalization plan for downtown and its environs in 1964, a plan that envisioned Over-the-Rhine as a cosmopolitan neighborhood of mixed land uses and rehabbed historic buildings populated by middle-class and affluent folks who would walk to their downtown jobs. But the burgeoning activist movement stifled city hall's vision and proffered one of its own: A neighborhood of and for low-income residents who would, under the activist's tutelage, determine their neighborhood's future. The activists won the support of city officials who sympathized with people threatened by displacement; other Cincinnati neighborhoods had recently been cleared for freeway construction and urban renewal, and the displacement issue loomed large.[69] Activists thus gained permanent control of the neighborhood.

The activists deliberately entrenched poverty. Over-the-Rhine's number of subsidized housing units increased from zero in 1960 to about 2,500—60 percent of the neighborhood's total number of occupied units—in 1990.[70] Miller and Tucker describe the effect of nearly three decades of community control:

> Over-the-Rhine's population [was] about 30,000 in 1960. A decade later that number had shrunk by half…In 1990, census takers counted just 9,752 people in Over-the-Rhine…By then, too, more than a quarter of the neighborhood's apartments stood vacant and the area's median household income was just $5,000, well below the figure for the city, $21,006.

These impoverished people lived in the city's most crime-ridden turf, a territory haunted by pimps, drug pushers, prostitutes, thieves, and muggers. Over-the-Rhine also accounted for more than its share of the city's domestic violence cases, street fights, and murders. For the most part, criminals picked on their neighbors.[71]

Urban housing advocates are not unaware of the problems associated with concentrated poverty in American cities; Norman Krumholz, a staunch proponent of equity planning, refers to the "delinquency, drugs, graffiti, and the mountain of other problems that are present in neighborhoods of concentrated poverty."[72] The advocates evidently believe that social remediation rather than deconcentration is the solution to these problems.

If liberated from the grips of activists, Cincinnati's Over-the-Rhine and East End would contribute profoundly to the repopulation and revitalization of Cincinnati. The two areas had a combined population of 12,000 in 1990, but they could accommodate 50,000 comfortably in townhouses and lowrise apartments. Many of the middle-class newcomers would walk or ride transit to downtown jobs.

In their 1995 book, *Selling Cities*, Varady and Raffel outline the several benefits associated with a return of the middle class to cities, but city officials, often under the influence of neighborhood activists, resist meaningful efforts. From their examination of urban housing programs nationwide from the mid-1960s to the mid-1990s, Varady and Raffel conclude, "Our review shows that virtually all the plans that have been prepared, regardless of the auspices, focus exclusively on low-income housing needs."[73]

MISREPRESENTATION AND EXPLOITATION

The small parks in Baltimore's distressed Highland Park community had sunk to a derelict and dangerous condition by the 1980s, so the National Park Service provided a grant with which to improve some of the parks and, by logical extension, the living conditions of surrounding residents. As a condition of its grant, the Park Service required resident participation in the planning, reconstruction, and maintenance of the eight parks selected. This participatory reclamation process would be monitored for its effectiveness, and a positive outcome would set a new direction in the restoration of order and safety to urban neighborhood parks. The program was a pilot that, if successful, would improve Baltimore and other cities by converting neighborhood liabilities to assets.

Resident participation was channeled through established neighborhood organizations, a seemingly logical tactic, but the organizations proved to be the program's fatal weakness. First of all, the organizations failed to garner true resident participation; few residents even knew of the project long after it was funded. Some neighborhood leaders were less interested in the parks than in their own political and financial futures, according to Sidney Brower, a professor in the School of Social Work and Community Planning at the University of Maryland. Representatives of two neighborhood organizations didn't much consider the program's conceptual objective; they were preoccupied with the questions of who would be hired and how much would they would be paid. "The project went off course," according to Brower, "a good deal of energy that could have gone into furthering the purposes of the grant was funneled off into …social services, and into the struggle for political power."[74]

If altruism rather than avarice guides most neighborhood organizations and activists, they nonetheless operate in comfortable isolation from the residents they supposedly represent. William Rohe and Lauren Gates reported that many neighborhood groups are dominated by a single faction unrepresentative of the attitudes and interests of the larger community.[75] The small groups that turn out for neighborhood meetings are "susceptible to manipulation," according to Susan Fainstein and Clifford Hirst, two planners who observed the Neighborhood Revitalization Program in Minneapolis and concluded, "The informality and limited membership of neighborhood organizations allow a small, determined number of people to take control with little trouble."[76]

Homeowners are usually unsympathetic to the activists' poverty agenda, so the activists target renters for participation in neighborhood planning.* The pursuit of renters, however, is seldom productive. "In

---

*Marginal neighborhoods in which homeowners are well represented in planning activities are more likely than low-income neighborhoods to thwart housing activists. Nonprofit housing developers encountered homeowner resistance in some of Minneapolis' marginal neighborhoods, where the homeowners organized under the auspices of the NRP and accused the nonprofits of trying to control neighborhood organizations to promote their housing agenda. The homeowners also accused the nonprofits of wasting public money and exploiting their privileged relationship with city hall in an attempt to dominate the NRP. In response to the homeowners' resistance to subsidized housing, the nonprofits have greedily tried to shield NRP funds from the preferences of homeowners. It seems the activist-friendly NRP process has, in marginal neighborhoods, betrayed the traditional activists and their nonprofit brethren by accommodating the involvement of non-poor homeowners, who oppose the traditional activists' housing agenda. (Edward G. Goetz, Hin Kin Lam, and Anne

those neighborhoods where steering committees made valiant efforts to attract renters, their participation remained low," said Fainstein and Hirst, based on their NRP observations. A neighborhood planner involved in the NRP process lamented, "Getting renters involved is difficult. Try and try, and they don't come. To demand that they come is utopian. What should we do? Pay them to come?"[77]

Howell S. Baum, a professor of planning and urban studies at the University of Maryland, observed a similar phenomenon in a gentrifying sector of Baltimore, where a core group of organizers solicited participation in a community planning effort, sending invitations to more than 50 neighborhood organizations and individuals. "When they found that their list was predominantly white and working-class or middle-class, they targeted public housing tenant associations and minority group organizations." That effort produced disappointing results.[78] Political non-participation among distressed populations is a persistent source of consternation for urban liberals; distressed neighborhoods are "transient places with minimal voter turnout, where it is difficult to develop a sense of community," according to Myron Orfield.[79]

Boston's Roxbury district is sufficiently large and distressed to have incubated several poverty-focused neighborhood organizations, and to have attracted outside organizations, all of which compete for power and resources. ACORN, for example, was drawn to Roxbury, where it competed with DSNI for publicly owned land on which to develop low-cost housing.[80] According to a 1994 report by the Urban Land Institute (compiled by a panel of professionals highly accomplished in real estate planning, development, and finance), none of these fragmented organizations is perceived by the residents of the area (or by the other organizations) as representing the community.[81]

Neighborhood meetings in Roxbury, as elsewhere, are usually poorly attended, a situation undaunting to DSNI's former executive director Medoff, who rationalized, "True inclusive participation does not just mean large numbers turning out at meetings…you can set up a structure that's representative and still have basically one or two people running the show." DSNI's founding activists had called their inaugural commu-

Heitlinger, *There Goes the Neighborhood?* [Minneapolis: Neighborhood Planning for Community Revitalization and the Center for Urban and Regional Affairs, 1996], p. 10) Hennepin County Commissioner Mark Stenglein calls the Minneapolis Neighborhood Revitalization Program "an employment agency for neighborhood activists." (Steve Brandt and Rochelle Olson, "Adding a Wild Card to Mayor's Race," *Minneapolis Star Tribune*, 16 July 2001, p. B1.)

nity meeting in February 1985 to recruit support for a cause they had already established: "This meeting will be geared to building on the consensus already achieved, to bringing more people in."[82] Community organizers in distressed neighborhoods are less successful at organizing residents than at organizing organizations to serve their own agenda.

Saviors

"Why do I do what I do? It's the transformation of individual souls..." said a St. Paul housing advocate named Caty Royce, who claims she was born with a sense of social justice.[83] Royce is a college-educated white woman raised and privately educated in the affluent suburbs of the Twin Cities before going on to college and the Peace Corps. Today she self-righteously serves her own political agenda, according to St. Paul Mayor Norm Coleman's top aide.

"Liberals were usually the ones working on social problems, and they...tended to see blacks as the persistent dependent and their own white selves as provider," writes Michael Patrick MacDonald in *All Souls*, his 1999 account of a distressed Boston neighborhood.[84] In Baltimore, the leaders of the community planning processes observed by Professor Howell Baum were "middle-class white liberals" who felt morally superior and "tried to speak for everyone." The self-anointed leaders discouraged participation by working-class whites who did not share their liberal views.[85]

In their expose of neighborhood activism in Cincinnati, historians Miller and Tucker profile the typical neighborhood activist as a college-educated white male from a middle-class background. (In Boston, DSNI's former executive director Medoff fit this characterization.) These activists derive their power from the disaffection of residents in urban America's most distressed neighborhoods, where poverty rates are highest, homeownership rates are lowest, and the politics of resentment and entitlement are most effective. Miller and Tucker document a "demoralized and functionally...illiterate people under the control and manipulation of a . . . misguided group of soft-hearted, hard-headed, white middle-class dropouts."[86]

Cincinnati's most effective exploiter was Buddy Gray, a white man who grew up middle class and attended Purdue University, where he protested the war in Vietnam. Gray dropped out after two years, and in the 1970s he moved to Over-the-Rhine. There he sheltered street alcoholics and fell in with a community organizer who trained him in confrontational activism. Gray now described himself as a "hard-nosed radical, a street fighter for street people."[87]

In the early 1980s, Gray gained control of Over-the-Rhine's Community Council and its Planning Task Force, a position of inordinate power in the era of neighborhood empowerment. Gray "played upon city council's commitment to neighborhood autonomy to secure in 1985 a plan for the neighborhood that took as its top priority the protection and enlargement of the neighborhood's stock of low-income housing," according to Miller and Tucker. The historians add that this 1985 plan was the product of Gray's exclusionary vision for Over-the-Rhine: "Gray...committed [the Community Council] to the idea of racial and socioeconomic separatism."[88]

Gray and his faction sought to exclude non-poor people from Over-the-Rhine for the usual reason—fear of displacement—and for another reason as well: incompatibility of lifestyles. Middle-income people would object to the conduct of many of the incumbent residents, especially the derelicts who wandered around Gray's shelter. Therefore the Gray faction endeavored to establish Over-the-Rhine as an exclusive enclave for the poor and their self-appointed leaders. The endeavor was successful, according to Miller and Tucker: "Gray and his allies...held to and realized a vision of an Over-the-Rhine dominated by an ideologically homogeneous people—themselves and the mostly black, low-income people they had chosen to represent and reside among."[89]

Why did Cincinnati's elected officials go along with this madness? Because their deference to neighborhood autonomy was nearly total, and they recognized Gray as Over-the-Rhine's legitimate leader. The elected officials were encouraged by their appointees and bureaucrats. The planning director, for example, "sided almost from the outset with Gray," according to Miller and Tucker, and the city manager accommodated Gray in making low-income housing the top development priority for Over-the-Rhine.[90] Myron Orfield lends insight in his 1997 book, *Metropolitics*, wherein he notes that some city policymakers "want to preserve the status quo of racial segregation and concentrated poverty for political...reasons" (even though most black residents would prefer to live in integrated neighborhoods).[91]

To further understand the city's acquiescence to Gray, an advocate for the homeless, it helps to remember the pervasive sentimentalization of homelessness in the time of Gray's leadership. (See Baum and Burns' *Nation in Denial: The Truth About Homelessness* and Myron Magnet's *The*

Dream and the Nightmare: The Sixties' Legacy to the Underclass for exposés of the deceit, hypocrisy, and naiveté surrounding homeless advocacy, and see Kelling and Cole's *Fixing Broken Windows: Restoring Order & Reducing Crime in Our Communities* for a discussion about the physical, social, and economic damage wrought by a homeless policy driven by misinformation and sentimentality.) Miller and Tucker note that many in city government "saw Gray as a charitable humanitarian friend of the homeless rather than as a builder of the second ghetto, a champion of poverty and social and civic fecklessness as life-style choices."[92]

Gray was murdered in 1996 by one of the homeless men he had housed and befriended, but not before his stewardship over the neighborhood produced immeasurable and lasting damage. Gray's murder was one of 1,452 incidents of murder, rape, and robbery in Over-the-Rhine in 1996.[93]

THE CALAMITOUS LEGACY OF URBAN RENEWAL

The empowerment of modern-day neighborhood activists was provoked by the federally funded urban renewal debacles of the 1950s and 1960s, which treated healthy neighborhoods more as chattel than as social organisms. Urban Renewal (and freeway construction) eviscerated socially robust working-class neighborhoods. Slum clearance was an objective of the federally funded programs, but renewal projects often wiped out housing that was highly valued by its occupants, who were heartlessly banished to worse housing in alien neighborhoods.

Local renewal agencies pledged to elicit citizen participation in order to qualify for federal funds, but requirements were ill-defined and political sophistication among neighborhood organizations was yet to come. Renewal agencies encountered escalating opposition from new organizations and coalitions of grassroots protest groups according to urban geographer Paul Knox:

> By the 1960s the baby-boom generation, with its rebellious counterculture of iconoclastic politics and a collectivist approach to the public interest, was coming into young adulthood...In Boston's South End, white activist ministers, poverty program employees, African American social workers, Puerto Rican community organizers and ideologically motivated young white professionals and college students joined together in opposition to the Boston Redevelopment Authority. A similar mix of militant activists emerged in...nearly every city that had an urban renewal program.[94]

Thus the atrocities of urban renewal ignited a new kind of militant activism and neighborhood empowerment "strong enough to change the dynamic of urban politics," according to Knox. (In 1969 Norman Mailer, as candidate for mayor of New York City, adopted the slogan "Power to the Neighborhoods.")[95]

At its best, neighborhood empowerment gives neighborhoods some control of their destinies and promotes grassroots involvement in the affairs of the city, but the sanctification of neighborhoods also undermines the ability of city officials to act in the interest of the larger polity. Allen Jacobs and Donald Appleyard, longtime advocates for a revitalized public realm, wrote in 1987 that the neighborhood movement "can be purely defensive, parochial, and self-serving. A city should be more than a warring collection of interest groups, classes, and neighborhoods; it should breed a commitment to a larger whole." Historians Miller and Tucker note that Over-the-Rhine's neighborhood activists saw the city as a "balkanized collection of mutually suspicious and competitive local enclaves."[96]

Federally funded urban renewal not only destroyed neighborhoods worth saving, it spawned an apparatus that prevents the revitalization of neighborhoods in need of renewal. The concept of renewal was condemned for the deficiencies of the execution, and the era in which robust neighborhoods were destroyed by government agencies has been supplanted by an era in which devitalized neighborhoods are successfully defended, by poverty-obsessed activists, from renewal that is sorely needed. The leftist activists who seized the neighborhood development agenda stigmatized physical redevelopment and embraced social remediation, which, on balance, can claim no greater success than the old urban renewal. That is why there are few appealing urban neighborhoods in America today.

THE BILLIONS OF DOLLARS THAT MADE THINGS WORSE

It should be acknowledged here that one of America's few appealing urban neighborhoods owes much of its appeal to neighborhood activists: New York City's historic Brooklyn Heights has survived the modern ambitions of developers thanks to neighborhood residents who persuaded city hall to landmark the neighborhood in 1965. This was a single-issue cause with a concisely defined objective dear to the hearts of many residents. Neighborhood empowerment as constituted today grew from, or was imposed by, a different impulse, a sweeping ideological yearning by nationally influential social engineers (characterized by Daniel Patrick

Moynihan as "condescending and naïve") to redistribute both wealth and power from the establishment to the people, specifically the poor. But the instigators of empowerment—elites from such places as Columbia University, the Ford Foundation, and the White House who in the 1960s engineered the federal government's Community Action Programs— faced a dilemma: pure neighborhood empowerment must be, as in Brooklyn Heights, conceived and nurtured in the neighborhood. Deception was therefore necessary, as Moynihan reported: "The need for outside intervention to appear locally initiated was always in view. That there was an element of deception in this posture—that it was altogether deception—should not be doubted."[97]

The federal government's initial and continuing role in neighborhood empowerment explains the uniformity of purpose among neighborhood organizations in distressed urban neighborhoods nationwide. It began with President Lyndon Johnson's war on poverty, whose Community Action Programs channeled federal funds directly to neighborhoods in pursuit of "maximum feasible participation" by the poor. Neighborhood organizations that were spawned or legitimized in pursuit of maximum feasible participation adhered to the mission dictated by their federal sponsors, a mission "radicalized" by mid-level functionaries, according to Moynihan. A few years after the federal government began to empower distressed neighborhoods, Senator Robert Kennedy's anti-poverty agenda produced in New York City the Bedford-Stuyvesant Restoration Corporation, progenitor to at least 2,000 nonprofit Community Development Corporations (CDCs) whose poverty-focused coffers are fattened by the federal government.* The Community Reinvestment Act of 1977 was a "definitive factor in the spread and increasing influence of CDCs," according to Louis Winnick, vice chairman of the Institute of Public Administration. The National Affordable Housing Act of 1990 requires cities receiving HOME program housing funds to allocate 15 per-cent to CDCs, and the act authorizes additional money for technical assis-tance to nonprofits. HUD's 203(k) program guarantees bank loans to nonprofits for the production of affordable housing.[98]

Giant liberal foundations helped the federal government broadcast poverty-focused neighborhood empowerment all across urban America.

---

*Howard Husock, director of the Case Program at Harvard's Kennedy School of Government, says "CDCs are bad for cities…they threaten to keep the poor frozen in poverty and cities forever frozen as warehouses for the eternally poor." (Howard Husock, "Don't Let the CDCs Fool You," *City Journal*, Summer 2001, p. 68.)

In a *City Journal* article entitled "The Billions of Dollars That Made Things Worse," Heather Mac Donald explains how foundations that once built great urban institutions—universities, medical schools, libraries—changed ideologically after their founders' philanthropic fortunes became too much to manage and were turned over to experts. "Eventually this transfer of control yielded the paradox of funds made by laissez-faire capitalists being used for the advocacy of a welfare state," according to Mac Donald. The Ford Foundation, instrumental in the development of the federal government's Community Action Programs (and bountifully generous to DSNI's misguided housing program) was but one of several large foundations that went radical in the 1960s. Robert Schrank, a former Communist and a former program officer at the Ford Foundation, referred to the "anti-capitalist orientation" of his Ford colleagues and said "people were influenced by the horror stories we Marxists had put out about the capitalist system." In 1968, Carnegie Foundation president Alan Pifer exhorted his comrades in the foundation world to support "aggressive new community organizations which...the comfortable stratum of American life would consider disturbing and perhaps even dangerous."[99] The leftist tilt of the foundations influenced the ideological orientation of their client neighborhood organizations, which continue to attract leftist or left-leaning activists decades after the war on poverty was lost.

In establishing its community action agencies, the Ford Foundation "invented a new level of American government" and initiated "nothing less than institutional change in the operation and control of American cities," according to Moynihan. Ford established demonstration agencies in Boston, Philadelphia, New Haven, and Oakland to serve and empower the inner-city poor, and in its zeal to see the agencies replicated nationally at federal expense, the foundation ignored reports that the demonstrations were failures. Ford's community action agencies were reincarnated by the Johnson administration as Community Action Programs (CAPs), whose primary yield seemed to be ethnic hostility and "public disorder...sanctioned, induced, or led by middle-class liberal-radicals," according to Moynihan. Beneficiaries of the program's federal funding included Chicago gangs and a program director in Newark who urged blacks to arm themselves before the 1967 riots. The Syracuse, New York, CAP published a manual declaring "no ends are accomplished without the use of force." (Syracuse CAP employees applied $7 million of their $8 million federal grant to their own salaries.) Community action bureaucrats in Washington endorsed the "power of rioting" as a "very real power and possibility" and, as the late-1960s period of urban riots drew to a close, a study sponsored by the Metropolitan Applied Research Center implicated community action: "The community action phase of the antipoverty programs…has contributed significantly to the fuel of urban conflagration." Community action "increased the power of demagogues and added to the restlessness, the alienation, and the sense of hopelessness of the deprived," added the study.[100]

Community action was but one of the several corrosive urban enterprises jointly engineered and funded by the Ford Foundation and various agencies of government. New York City and the federal government joined Ford in a 1960s program called Mobilization for Youth, whose intellectual leader was a Columbia University professor who "moved fairly rapidly from the effort to integrate the poor into the system to an effort to use the poor to bring [the system] down," according to Moynihan.[101] The program organized blacks and Puerto Ricans into separate regiments in a battle against the system, but soon they were battling each other. Mobilization for Youth thus fractured the Lower East Side community that it sought to unite.

In the name of neighborhood empowerment, the Ford Foundation funded a program in a Brooklyn ghetto meant to turn control of schools over to parents, but militantly anti-Semitic black activists, who were supported by fewer than a third of the schools' parents, seized control. (The Ford Foundation generously supported the activists.) The eight schools embroiled in the program were soon overcome not only by vandalism and chaos but by "separatist hatred" and "poisonous levels of black anger and vituperation," according to Tamar Jacoby, author of *Someone Else's House: America's Unfinished Struggle for Integration*.[102] In 1968, one year into the program, conflict between the program's separatist leaders and the schools' Jewish teachers was so intense that Mayor John Lindsay, a staunch supporter of the program, convened a panel to root out the cause. The mayor's panel reported, "The countless incidents, leaflets, epithets, and the like in this school controversy reveal a bigotry from black extremists that is open, undisguised, [and] nearly physical in its intensity…" The intensity did become physical when students, incited by a militant black teacher, attacked white teachers. (Many white teachers were fired because of their race.) The program's leaders were removed by New York City's board of education, but not before they provoked a "spiral of hatred" that would poison race relations for years to come.[103]

The leadership of the Brooklyn schools program had indoctrinated its poverty-stricken black students more in resentment and militancy than in academic skills. One of the many black youths inspired by the program's leaders is today a widely recognized racial provocateur. Because of its immediate impact and its enduring aftermath, Tamar Jacoby counts this Ford-funded disaster as one of the landmark events that derailed America's journey toward racial harmony.[104] McGeorge Bundy—the Ford Foundation's unrepentant leader—dismissed the disaster as an unfortunate "disruption" that would not deter him: "If private foundations cannot assist experiments, their unique role will be impaired."[105]

Community action agencies, Mobilization for Youth, and the Brooklyn schools debacle are just a few of the several flamboyant failures perpetrated on cities by the Ford foundation. In 1977, Henry Ford II quit his namesake foundation's board in disgust. He wrote in his resignation letter, "The foundation is a creature of capitalism, a statement that, I'm sure, would be shocking to many professional staff people in the field of philanthropy."[106] Citing the Ford Foundation and several others, Heather Mac Donald concluded, "the impulse toward the activism that over the past 30 years has led the great liberal foundations to do much more harm than good remains overwhelming…Once an agent of social good, those powerful institutions have become a political battering ram targeted at American society…The results, from the 1960s onward, have been devastating."[107]

Liberal foundations remain the primary funders of the urban housing movement, made up of local housing activists and national advocacy groups, such as the National Low-Income Housing Coalition and the National Coalition for the Homeless.[108] The Ford Foundation, whose fortune is rooted in the production of automobiles, unwittingly feeds America's automobile habit by funding nonprofits whose housing initiatives keep middle-class suburbanites separated from downtown employment, shopping, and entertainment destinations. DSNI's land grab in Boston was bankrolled by the Ford Foundation, which provided a $2 million, 1 percent loan with which DSNI paid for the land it acquired through eminent domain.[109]

DSNI's administrative operations also were extravagantly funded by foundations. In 1993 DSNI had a staff of 12, plus interns, and an operating budget of more than $840,000 (aside from land acquisition and construction funds). Medoff acknowledged his and his colleagues' indebtedness to their generous benefactors: "With adequate funding from

Riley, the Boston Foundation, the Hyams Foundation, and others, DSNI…didn't think cheap when it came to hiring consultants or paying staff salaries…"[110] And the DSNI operatives so adequately funded by liberal foundations are, of course, ideologically compatible with foundation liberalism. Executive director Gus Newport (hired in 1989 to replace the departing Medoff) was hailed by Medoff as a "social justice activist" with a "radical reputation," and deputy director Sue Beaton had been the development director of a homeless shelter. Ros Everdall, hired in 1988 as organizing director, especially impressed Medoff with credentials that glowingly qualify her as a DSNI operative:

> Everdell, a White woman with a masters in community economic development, had many years of organizing experience in New York and Boston around economic justice, food and hunger, welfare rights and women's issues. Before joining DSNI she staffed the Boston Rainbow Coalition and was the Northeast regional coordinator for the Jesse Jackson Campaign for President.[111]

Middle-class flight to suburbia is in some measure a flight from the alien social agenda of community activists and the liberal foundations that fund them. "The 'community leaders' favored by foundations do not represent the community; they represent the activists," according to Mac Donald.[112]

THE FEMINIZATION OF URBAN POLICY

"New York became great in no small part because of what it built," wrote Michael Tomasky, but "we've come to believe that we can't build things anymore." An era of great physical creativity "was replaced by a welfare-state liberalism that took money out of capital projects and put it into social-service programs."[113] Redistributive spending (public assistance, social services, health, and housing) rose from 25.8 percent to 35.8 percent of New York City's budget in the decade of the 1960s, while spending for infrastructure and transportation fell by half. The change in spending priorities was even larger in some other cities.[114] Referring to New York City's spending reorientation, Fred Siegel, a history professor at Cooper Union, said, "More and more, the economic life of the city revolves around the custodial care of the underclass…You have a growing industry with a vested interest in human failure."[115]

New York City is, at the turn of the millennium, slowly repopulating and reviving its appreciation for public works. Other cities facilitate physical development funded mostly by federal, state, and county governments:

rail transit, waterfront parks, and sports arenas. But local funds and planning efforts are disproportionately devoted to neighborhood organizations and to the poverty agenda. Traditional city planning—physical
planning—is of little interest to neighborhood activists.

Over-the-Rhine's neighborhood activists gained responsibility for planning in their neighborhood, but so obsessed were they with social issues
and affordable housing that they couldn't come close to meeting their
deadline to produce a physical plan. Those present at the poorly attended
meetings were disinterested in physical development issues such as land
use, infrastructure, and market-rate housing. The task force became
known as "Stevens' Folly," after planning director Herbert Stevens, who
was sympathetic to the activists' self-constricted planning agenda. As the
task force dawdled, the neighborhood was "self-destructing," according
to property owners, who cited the neighborhood's declining population
and its increasing rates of demolition, arson, vagrancy, theft, rape, and
murder.[116]

Neighborhood activism is a path to political power in American cities
today, and city halls are filled with former activists more sympathetic to
the social agenda than to the physical agenda. Many of those in city hall
validate Daniel Patrick Moynihan's prediction that the federal government's radicalized Community Action Programs would "influence...the
personal and ideological formation of a significant number of urban political leaders."[117] The price paid for the political ascendance of neighborhood activists and their organizations is the political emaciation of cities,
now reduced to near impotence in legislative debates about metropolitan
development issues vital to urban prosperity. Cities' political stature had
just begun to wane in the early 1960s when Jane Jacobs warned of the
social consequences of maintaining low residential densities. Thereafter,
neighborhoods in the custody of activists stagnated and deteriorated, and
the public realm fell into disrepair while the middle class fled to the suburbs with the political power necessary to affect the shape of metropolitan development.

The urban officials who stood by and watched the depopulation of cities
apparently didn't much appreciate the economic assets they were losing,
even though the loss threatened their social agenda. Their social efforts
only intensified, consuming escalating shares of municipal budgets, driving up taxes, and jeopardizing services important to the middle class. In
the 1960s, as city halls began to fill with politicians rooted in leftist
activism, the middle class dissipated, transit atrophied, and city officials

preoccupied themselves with sociology. Minnesota state representative Myron Orfield, representing a non-poor Minneapolis district, noted that the core cities of the Twin Cities metro area have been "strikingly absent" from debates about physical development in their metropolis.[118]

Minneapolis Mayor Donald Fraser exemplified the feminization of urban policy in 1992 when, as president of the National League of Cities, he encouraged a policy focus on families and children.[119] That same year, the Metropolitan Council of the Twin Cities area released a draft of its 20-year vision for metropolitan development, a vision big on suburban development and myopic on urban development. In response to the council's solicitation of feedback from the public and its representatives, Mayor Fraser did not plead for a reversal in the direction of infrastructure investment; if he was alarmed about the continuing exodus of middle class households and commerce, he didn't let on. Instead, the mayor of Minneapolis produced a sociological dissertation about families, children, social services, and, of course, community: "My interest centers on the question of community, and the delivery of social services."[120]

Cities' worst social nightmare—the exodus of the middle class—is a cataclysmic reality. Urban politicians' standardized strategies for the socioeconomic remediation of the remaining distressed populations have a long history of failure. Minnesota's former Attorney General Skip Humphrey, son of the late Hubert Humphrey and not himself a conservative, bluntly admitted in 1997 that the "remediation of human lives is expensive and it doesn't work very well."[121] At about the same time, former mayor (and former congressman) Donald Fraser reflected on his legacy of social programs as he addressed a conference of community social workers, and he admitted, "We have not yet seen the progress…we all were hoping to see."[122]

"Cities are thoroughly physical places," wrote Jane Jacobs, and physical-development initiatives, more than social programs and socialist housing initiatives, are needed to revitalize them.[123]

MIDDLE-CLASS DISPLACEMENT

Housing activists' brutal disregard for the middle class is illuminated by the rhetoric of displacement, a word liberally invoked, but seldom in reference to the middle class. Middle-class flight is in large measure middle-class displacement from neighborhoods assaulted by physical and social deterioration, but this doesn't seem to concern housing activists, who oppose its reversal—gentrification. Activists exaggerate the extent of low-income displacement caused by gentrification, as noted earlier, and they disregard the middle-class displacement caused by the failure to revitalize neighborhoods.

Hundreds of acres of derelict South Bronx land that was deserted in the 1960s and 1970s have been reclaimed thanks to a billion public dollars of housing investment, but local activists have criticized the city's involvement where new housing is targeted on middle- and moderate-income, rather than low-income, households. The South Bronx renaissance has given working-class residents the option to stay put rather than flee as soon as they can afford to. Upwardly mobile residents can finally believe that their neighborhood is emerging from the depths of squalor, and now they can move up to better housing without leaving the neighborhood. The new housing attracts outsiders as well, including middle-class former residents who were displaced in the 1970s by skyrocketing crime rates.[124]

Housing activists would argue that middle-class residents who leave distressed neighborhoods are acting voluntarily, unlike the poor, who are displaced coercively by gentrification. But crime and the threat of crime in a distressed neighborhood are no less coercive than an eviction notice in a gentrifying neighborhood. In gentrifying neighborhoods, most homeowners, regardless of income, have options that are absent from stagnant and declining neighborhoods. They have the option to stay put. They have the option to upgrade their dwellings; to do so in a stagnant or declining neighborhood is to risk their investment. High rates of incumbent upgrading in gentrifying neighborhoods demonstrate that gentrification restores confidence to homeowners of all incomes, and improves their living conditions.

Low-income renters have fewer options than homeowners, but if displacement is visited upon them humanely, with ample notice, relocation assistance, and good replacement housing, it is hardly as cruel as activists characterize it to inherently be. In the context of revitalization, intra-neighborhood displacement represents a substantial quality-of-life improvement for low-income renters.

In distressed neighborhoods that fail to gentrify, the residents who are displaced "voluntarily" are those most economically advantaged. They are succeeded by poorer households, the focus of nonprofit housing developers. This explains why poverty has deepened and broadened in our cities, and why gentrification is an essential component of revitalization.

RESIDENTIAL IMMOBILITY

Urban America is afflicted with a condition as insidious as displacement, and that is displacement's opposite—immobility. Many low-income renters would leave their gray-zone neighborhoods if they could afford to, and many longtime homeowners are shackled to property once stable but now so depreciated that they can't recoup the equity necessary to buy into a decent neighborhood. When neighborhoods deteriorate they drag a lot of homeowners down with them.

Myron Orfield noted in 1997 that, in Minneapolis, "residential property around the expanding poverty core lost from 15 to 25 percent of its value over a five-year period," while housing values in exclusive suburbs soared.[125] In August 1996, in the aftermath of two well-publicized murders on Minneapolis' Newton Avenue in the Near North gray zone, a Twin Cities news crew reported that a single-family detached house, one that appeared on the television screen to be in decent condition, had just sold for $10,000.[126] The scene was less than two miles from the greatest business district between the Great Lakes and the Rocky Mountains, some of the Upper Midwest's most worthless real-estate lies within two miles of its most valuable.

In the winter of 2000 the city of Minneapolis was selling residential lots 1½ miles from downtown, in the Near North gray zone, for as little 99 cents per square foot. Land sold for more than four times as much—$4.35 per square foot—in Boston's Back Bay more than a century ago.[127] The valuable Back Bay land was, at the time, the same distance from Boston's commercial center as Minneapolis' cheap land is from downtown Minneapolis today. But the Back Bay was developing in a manner appropriate to its location, with high-density housing for a non-poor population. (Back Bay land is no doubt worth hundreds of dollars per square foot today).

Urban housing activists are more troubled by increasing property values than by declining values, but gray-zone homeowners are egregiously cheated by property depreciation in neighborhoods that fail to revitalize. In metropolitan America, the property value appreciation associated with population growth is forced, by city officials and neighborhood activists, to developing suburbs.

Much of the devalued land in gray zones is owned by low-income homeowners who can ill afford the consequences of neighborhood deterioration. Robert Rector of the Heritage Foundation reported that, in 1989, 38 percent of poor people in the United States lived in owner-occupied houses; many of these houses are in the inner city.[128] Many of the home-owners afflicted by property depreciation are the purported beneficiaries of urban liberalism: low-income African Americans. According to 1990 Census data, nearly 1,000 housing units in Minneapolis and St. Paul were occupied by elderly black homeowners who had lived in their houses long enough to have paid off their mortgage loans, virtually all of them within three vast gray zones.[129] Most of these longtime homeowners did-n't buy into high-crime neighborhoods but were eventually engulfed in them. These homeowners were robbed of the lifestyle options and mobil-ity enjoyed by homeowners in good neighborhoods, where appreciated property values represent substantial retirement nest eggs. Anti-gentrifi-cation sentiments combine with local zoning codes and federal trans-portation and housing policies to needlessly suppress the intrinsic value of gray-zone land. This is a grave but untold injustice to inner-city home-owners who can little afford the corrosive effects of urban housing activism.[130]

ECONOMIC INSULARITY

The anti-gentrification rhetoric and behavior of gray-zone activists reveal a siege mentality and a deep distrust of outsiders, or at least of non-poor outsiders. DSNI's welcome mat extends to low-income outsiders on the waiting list for affordable housing, but it extends little further. Outside planners and developers are especially shunned, except as consultants under DSNI's direct control. DSNI president Ché Madyun said proudly, "the city wanted to come in and give us a hand but we said no."[131] While DSNI demanded Boston taxpayers' money, it rejected the city's planning input.

The city had formulated a plan for the neighborhood that recognized the power of the post-industrial economy, a plan that included office build-ings and hotels, but neighborhood activists rejected the city's vision because the modern commercial buildings would be owned and con-trolled by outside investors. The city's vision was therefore extinguished and the post-industrial investment flowed, most likely, to Boston's ever-accommodating suburbs. The urban renewal debacles of the 1950s and 1960s give neighborhood residents good reason to be wary of outside planners, but not to shut out the outside economy. Nonetheless, neigh-borhood development organizations strive for economic self-contain-ment—neighborhood jobs for neighborhood residents.

Neighborhood activists cling to the industrial economy in the post-industrial era, fondly remembering a time when city residents worked at living-wage jobs close to home. In St. Paul's distressed Frogtown neighborhood, activist Denise Harris nostalgically recalls that "people...worked in the neighborhood" a few decades ago when the Frogtown foundry was still operating, when railroad companies repaired their equipment in nearby shops, when neighborhood businesses provided jobs in abundance.[132] Activists trace the fall of urban neighborhoods to neighborhood de-industrialization, which some interpret as a capitalist denunciation of the inner city and its population. The activists then strive to recreate the neighborhood-based industrial economy on their own terms.

Hoping to reduce unemployment and welfare dependence in their neighborhood, the Frogtown Action Alliance, a nonprofit neighborhood organization, built a factory. The endeavor was funded by the City of St. Paul, the State of Minnesota, and a Twin Cities foundation in the belief that the factory's low-skill jobs (the manufacturing of puzzles) would help neighborhood residents escape welfare. The neighborhood's city council representative enthusiastically welcomed the venture: "It's a business, and it's in the neighborhood and that's beautiful."[133] The executive director of the area's planning council was optimistic that the puzzle factory and other pending industrial development would revive the neighborhood by creating jobs.

Fifty thousand jobs already exist within a mile of Frogtown, in downtown St. Paul and in the state capitol complex adjacent to the neighborhood. Most workers commute to these jobs alone in their automobiles, creating demand for the parking lots and garages that adulterate the downtown environment.[134] Frogtown's greatest potential is to attract suburban automobile commuters to the city, as residents who walk and ride transit to their nearby jobs. Frogtown's economic development strategy should focus on the post-industrial economy, on office, retail, and entertainment development along University Avenue—the neighborhood's grossly underutilized main thoroughfare. The inner-city poor and unemployed are best served by the recentralization of post-industrial jobs and middle-class households; industrial-era economic self-containment at the neighborhood level is no longer a viable proposition. The Frogtown puzzle factory closed after five months, during which "only a few puzzles were made by five employees," reported the *Minneapolis Star Tribune* in September 2000.[135]

As neighborhood activists strive to recreate industrial-era jobs-housing proximity, their insularity causes them to alienate the outside businesses that might wish to relocate or expand, for business rather than social reasons, to a strategic location in the inner city, close to the CBD. Michael E. Porter, professor of business administration at Harvard Business School, notes that some businesses interested in locating in inner-city Boston "decided against it because of demands to…cede control of hiring and training to community-based organizations." (Activist also have demanded that businesses build playgrounds and fund scholarships.) Porter notes that these demands are counterproductive: "Such demands on existing and potential businesses rarely help the community, instead, they drive businesses—and jobs—to other locations."[136]

Businesses are wary of ceding hiring control to socially motivated organizations for good reason: The quality of the inner-city work force has deteriorated. Referring to the workforce at Dominick's supermarket across the street from Cabrini-Green, *Chicago Tribune* reporter Mary Schmich writes, "Almost all the employees live…in Cabrini. Some have never worked. Some decide work's not worth their while for $5.65 an hour. Too many don't show up when they should."[137] Disproportionate levels of absenteeism, false injury claims, and drug use among the inner-city work force inhibit market-driven business development, according to Porter, who cites also bad work attitudes that contribute to "poor relations between labor and management." Some inner-city workers perceive businesses as "exploitive," a notion engendered by "the antibusiness attitudes held by community leaders and social activists."[138]

When business rejects the inner city, neighborhood organizations are left to their own devices, but most of the economic development projects initiated by neighborhood organizations fall short of minimal expectations, according to Porter:

> While there have been a few notable successes, the vast majority of businesses owned or managed by [community-based organizations (CBOs)] have been failures. Most CBOs lack the skills, attitudes, and incentives to advise, lend to, or operate substantial businesses. They were able to muster low-income housing development, in which there were major public subsidies…But…CBOs simply can't compete with existing private sector institutions.[139]

Porter notes the futility of "trying to cure the inner city's problems by perpetually increasing social investment and hoping for economic activity to follow." He is pessimistic about the prospects of business development in neighborhoods led by people "who have devoted years to social causes and who view profit and business in general with suspicion."[140]

SYNERGY

Andres Duany and Elizabeth Plater-Zyberk, leaders of the neotraditional planning movement, acknowledge the sorry condition of America's cities, and then they explain that neighborhood activism forces planners and developers to ply their trade in developing suburbs: "While it is the first rule of regional planning to concentrate growth in existing urban centers, many factors conspire against doing so, including…neighborhood politics [and] opposition to gentrification."[141] Writer James Howard Kunstler, who has written two books in praise of neotraditional suburbs, agrees with Duany and Plater-Zyberk, citing the case of the aborted Atlantic Center in Brooklyn.

Conceived in the mid-1980s, Atlantic Center was a plan to convert 24 acres of barren wasteland into an urbane development consisting of 688 housing units and about three million square feet of office and retail space. The housing was to be lowrise, inspired by the area's historic brownstones, and the commercial component was to be dominated by a pair of 24-story office towers built on top of a transit hub and flanked by a landscaped public square. The plan won the support of Mayor Ed Koch and others in city hall who were alarmed by an exodus of back-office jobs to the suburbs of Long Island, Westchester County, and New Jersey. Atlantic Center aimed to accommodate more than a few households and post-industrial jobs in a development appropriate to its location at the edge of downtown Brooklyn, at the confluence of subway lines, bus routes, and commuter rail.

But the project was killed by activists. A neighborhood group filed a lawsuit against the development claiming the densities were too high and the new housing (some of which was to be reserved for low-income households) would trigger gentrification. The lawsuit was dismissed after three years—enough time to kill the deal.[142] The neighborhood has since got the kind of commercial environment sure to repel affluent households—a blank-wall retail bunker (Figure 9-4). Standing in a prominent position near the bunker is a sheet metal shack rusty and bent and smeared with graffiti—this is the neighborhood's subway entrance, which was to be swallowed by the office development and replaced with one better suited to such an important site.

In a book titled *Developing Infill Housing in Inner-City Neighborhoods: Opportunities and Strategies*, Diane Suchman warns prospective developers, "When any infill development is proposed for an [inner-city] neighborhood, existing residents may object, even if the development will improve the neighborhood."[143] (Suchman should have been more specific: "neighborhood *activists* may object…") Suchman advises developers faced with neighborhood opposition to go elsewhere; the avoidance of politically hostile neighborhoods "enables the developer to focus time, money, and energy on developing the project, rather than fighting political battles."

Figure 9-4. The legacy of neighborhood activism in Brooklyn (April 2000). Atlantic Commons, this retail bunker at the edge of downtown Brooklyn, occupies some of the land on which activists prevented development more appropriate to the site.

Much of the development unwelcome in urban neighborhoods ends up in the suburbs emerging at the fringe of the metropolis. Housing developers in the Twin Cities area have urged the Metropolitan Council to extend infrastructure to the rural fringe, and "council members and staff promised to do what they could," according to a February 2000 report in the *Minneapolis Star Tribune*. The argument that persuades the council is the housing-cost argument: a scarcity of developable land is driving up the cost of new housing. The price of suburban land has doubled in most areas, and quadrupled in some, since 1996 according to a local developer. This situation not only drives up housing costs in the metropolitan area, it hyper-extends sprawl by driving developers and home buyers to relatively cheap land in the counties beyond the traditionally defined metropolis.[144]

The synergy between suburban real-estate speculators and gray-zone defenders (who scorn real-estate speculators) couldn't be purer: The defenders shun high-density housing and middle-class households, forcing middle-class urbanites to pursue their lifestyle in suburbs. In turn, the suburban speculators, with the help of metropolitan planning organizations and state highway departments, remove development pressure from cities, allowing the defenders to pursue their exclusionary agenda with impunity. The defenders of low densities in cities relegate high-density housing to suburbs, where automobile dependence reigns regardless of housing density. Gray-zone defenders share responsibility for the disastrous environmental and social consequences of automobile dependence, which permeates the metropolis—suburb and city.

A city's leaders must make a fundamental choice in dealing with their gray zones: they must choose either a social agenda or a physical agenda. The social agenda entails the preservation of gray zones as staging areas for the delivery of social services, and the physical agenda entails the conversion of gray zones into high-vitality city neighborhoods. In making this choice, leaders should remember that the physical agenda, if conceived and executed properly, will produce important social benefits. By converting low-density low-income neighborhoods into higher-density predominantly middle-class neighborhoods, policymakers improve the educational prospects of remaining poor children, they repopulate neighborhoods with employed adult role models, they expand the tax base to better support municipal services, they elevate purchasing power to support neighborhood retailing for the convenience of non-drivers, they improve transit service, and they improve downtown's competitive position relative to suburbs, thereby increasing the number of jobs accessible to central-city non-drivers. The social agenda has produced the opposite result on every count, and that is why cities have suffered socioeconomic deterioration since the defenders of gray zones assumed power in the 1960s.

Gray-zone revitalization is, by definition, density enhancement accompanied by gentrification. All that is good for cities—lively downtowns, good transit, prestigious schools, safe streets, political relevance, and revitalized neighborhood commerce—can be attained only with an infusion of middle-class households into the central city, which requires higher housing densities and a welcoming attitude. Density enhancement and gentrification are a combination without which urban neighborhoods will not revitalize.

CHAPTER

10

Liberating the Gray Zone

...we will transmit this city not only not less, but greater, better and more beautiful than it was transmitted to us....OATH OF THE ATHENS[1]

To liberals, the inner city is the sanctified domain of oppressed populations and the activists who claim to represent them. To conservatives, like columnist Katherine Kersten, the inner city is the devil's domain, as evil as the sins associated with it: "Religion [is] a key variable in recovering from alcohol and drug addiction, *escaping the inner city*, preserving marriages and staying out of prison." (Emphasis added.)[2] Politically off-limits, the inner city perpetually stagnates. For the social and environmental good of the metropolis, the inner city must be brought into play. The first step is to expose the great potential of this precious land at the heart of the metropolis.

THE DORMANT VALUE OF NEAR-DOWNTOWN LAND

Endemic to urban liberalism is an assumption of urban dependence upon, and entitlement to, the assets of suburbanites. Civil rights leaders insist that suburban schools educate urban children. City officials insist that suburban taxpayers enlarge city coffers. David Rusk, the former mayor of Albuquerque, prescribes an "outside game"—a litany of policy initiatives formulated to solve city problems with suburban resources; the transfer of tax revenues from affluent suburbs to poor cities is a prime component of Rusk's agenda. Among those who would endorse the outside game are gray-zone defenders bent on a social policy that prevents the recentralization of middle-class households. Others advocate the outside game because they cannot or will not envision a recentralized metropolis. Rusk, for example, lauds the suburbanization of Charlotte Street in the South Bronx as a "remarkable achievement," and he advocates higher-density housing in the suburbs that surround low-density cities.[3]

Because of their strategic locations and unique physical assets, cities hold considerable potential to go it alone, to attract substantial metropolitan wealth to the territory within their borders. Vancouver has seen fit to exploit its innate property wealth for the social and environmental good of the metropolis, according to a 1996 report by the Transportation Research Board:

> It is not uncommon to find standard building lots in the City of Vancouver (50 x 120 feet) selling for $1 million CAD (1995 value). Much of the high cost associated with such properties are driven by the location of the lot within the central city.... Such high prices have been an encouragement to the construction of high-rise apartment buildings and condominiums...[4]

The aggregate market value of all the residential property in Minneapolis in 1999 was $12 billion. If the city had developed at the densities suggested in Chapter 5, and if the average value of the city's housing were in line with suburban values, then the market value of Minneapolis' residential land would be around $33 billion (1999 dollars).[5] In other words, some $21 billion in real estate value lies fallow, suppressed by the city's obsolete zoning and by its elected officials' compulsion to provide a disproportionate share of the metropolitan area's low-cost housing. The great potential value of the city's central land is displaced to developing suburbs more accommodating of middle-class growth.

A $21 billion increase in residential real estate value represents a tax revenue of more than $300 million annually—enough, when combined with the added commercial tax base of the recentralized city, to build and upgrade parks, schools, and libraries, and to build and operate a localized rail transit system to serve the properly urbanized neighborhoods.[6]

Twenty-one billion dollars in real estate value and all the tax revenue that it would generate are the opportunity costs that accompany the real costs of the myriad housing programs that perpetuate the underutilization of Minneapolis' neighborhoods. Moreover, the enormous social and environmental costs of suburban expansion are attributable to city officials' refusal to open up their turf to a middle-class influx. The exclusionary attitudes of city officials and neighborhood activists are the root cause of monumental social and environmental distress that reaches far beyond the borders of the city.

GOOD RENEWAL

Because Urban Renewal is synonymous with neighborhood carnage, it is easy to assume that nothing good came of the federally funded programs; but at least one exemplary project materialized in the 1950s and '60s, proving that the concept of urban renewal is sound, even if many individual projects were ill conceived. Before its renewal, Philadelphia's Society Hill was a neighborhood of derelict housing and dilapidated industrial buildings. The neighborhood park—Washington Square—had been taken over by "perverts," according to Jane Jacobs.[7] The renewal regime, launched in 1956, rehabilitated the neighborhood's townhouses and converted its underutilized industrial land to high-density housing for affluent newcomers.

The first phase of renewal focused on boosting the socioeconomic status of the neighborhood dramatically in order to assure potential developers and residents that investment in the neighborhood would be sound. Toward that end, Mayor Richardson Dilworth moved to new quarters in Society Hill in the first year of the renewal program. Soon to follow were Henry Miller Watts Jr., former board chairman of the New York Stock Exchange, and C. Jared Ingersoll, a multimillionaire lawyer and former president of the Philadelphia Museum of Art. Ingersoll vacated an elite suburb to rehabilitate a Society Hill townhouse, whose pre-rehab condition he described:

> My wife and I...bought from the Redevelopment Authority a lovely old house built in the early eighteenth century which had gone completely to rack and ruin. The filth was beyond belief, the fleas were such and the stench was such that you couldn't stay in the house about ten or fifteen minutes...There were two dead cats found in the bathtub.[8]

Society Hill's pioneering gentrifiers, many of them civic leaders, got the attention of Philadelphia's news media and thereby made their confidence in the neighborhood's future known to the public. Once Society Hill's future was secured, the architects of renewal began to accommodate larger numbers of incumbent residents, including residents displaced in the first phase.

The renewal program for Society Hill was not without flaws. Commercial land uses were not well integrated with residential, and the neighborhood's most visible new buildings—I. M. Pei's trio of luxury highrises—stand in stark contrast with the neighborhood's historic architecture. But at least that architecture survives, renewed and much respected by the designers of most of the neighborhood's new buildings. Society Hill is recognized by planners and urban geographers as a textbook example of good urban redevelopment.[9]

Unlike Society Hill, today's run-of-the-mill gray zone has little worth salvaging. The typical gray zone's detached houses represent an inappropriate housing type for the center of a metropolis, and most of them lack any claim to historical or architectural significance. In Minneapolis' Willard-Hay neighborhood, for example, none of the 2,100 detached houses is listed on the National Register of Historic Places, and only two are recognized by the city's Historic Preservation Commission as "historic resources."[10] For such a neighborhood, Battery Park City, created from scratch, is an appropriate model for redevelopment. The street patterns in Willard-Hay and similar neighborhoods are firmly established, and some of the schools, parks, churches, and commercial buildings are worthy of preservation, but most of the housing stock is obsolete. The housing and the public spaces in Battery Park City evidence how much we have learned since the renewal misadventures of the 1950s and 1960s, and the planning principles embodied in Battery Park City can be adapted to different environments, and the adapted principles can be codified in zoning legislation.

A COMMUNITY BUILT FROM SCRATCH

Paul Bauknight Jr., a Twin Cities architect with professional experience in some of Minneapolis' distressed neighborhoods, expounds the political obstacle to massive renewal of gray-zone neighborhoods:

> We don't go bulldozing entire neighborhoods...you can't recreate a neighborhood...The people who live there have a connection to it. If someone comes in, tears it down and puts up all new houses, it's not the same anymore. Neighborhoods grow and evolve, they don't just happen.[11]

Bauknight overstates the case somewhat; communities are rebuilt under dire circumstances. Valmeyer, Illinois, was swamped by the great Mississippi River flood of 1993, so its 900 residents rebuilt their town on a site two miles away from the original (and 400 feet higher). The original town was physically flawed—it lay in a flood plain—so it was abandoned after the floodwaters destroyed 90 percent of its buildings. Federal and state governments were generous in the rebuilding effort, contributing $35 million to build new infrastructure and public buildings. By 1996 the social landscape of the community began to emerge; that was the year of the rebuilt town's first school prom, its first garage sale, and the ringing of its first church bell. To its residents, New Valmeyer was becoming home soon after its construction.[12]

Gray-zone communities are destroyed not by natural disaster, but by forces no less harsh. Jonathan Barnett notes that inner-city neighborhoods are destroyed by "disaster in slow motion."[13] If long-established communities can successfully rebuild after falling to natural disaster, then obsolete gray-zone neighborhoods, ravaged by the destructive and unnatural forces of social and economic disaster, can be replaced by sustainable new neighborhoods. And the renewal of a city's gray zones would span decades rather than months, not such a traumatic disruption. The federal government should be as helpful in rebuilding gray zones as it was in rebuilding Valmeyer.

The reconstruction of Valmeyer on a new site represents a new federal response to flood damage, a response since repeated elsewhere. Previous federal policy was to rebuild levees and dams, but that approach failed to correct the underlying problem. So too does the standard urban policy of propping up gray-zone neighborhoods while ignoring their underlying fundamental flaws.

THREE STRATEGIES

Today's standard strategy for gray-zone stabilization in the United States can be characterized as community-based socioeconomic remediation. Community-based organizations pursue housing and economic development initiatives financed by charitable foundations and government agencies, intended to improve the social and economic condition of the extant resident population.

Another strategy, advocated by Harvard professor Michael Porter, would replace the emphasis on social remediation with an emphasis on private-sector economic development, as noted in the previous chapter. Porter believes that a "sustainable economic base can be created in the inner city, but only as it has been created elsewhere: through private, for-profit initiatives and investment based on economic self-interest and genuine competitive advantage—not through artificial inducements, charity, or government mandates."[14]

The inner city should exploit its strategic advantages—its near-downtown location, unmet local market demand, and substantial numbers of employable-but-unemployed residents. These assets provide inner cities with the potential to compete effectively with suburbs for job-creating business development, according to Porter.

But the goal of Porter's strategy is the same as that of socially oriented community organizations—the socioeconomic improvement of incumbent inner-city residents. This is a narrow goal. A more comprehensive vision for inner-city neighborhoods is re-population—a massive influx of middle-class newcomers who would, incidentally, elevate the prospects of incumbent residents, especially in the context of business recentralization. Revitalization rather than stabilization is the focus of this third strategy, which would produce metro-wide benefits associated with reductions in automobile dependence.

The third strategy is a comprehensive vision that adopts Porter's two fundamental premises: Socially focused programs fail to revitalize gray zones, and private-sector economic development is a necessary ingredient in inner-city revitalization. Most importantly, the third strategy embodies Porter's assertion, "Inner cities are located in what should be economically valuable areas."[15] It is the high potential value of near-CBD land that lends viability to the third strategy for inner-city revitalization. The third strategy exploits the gray zone's enormous potential to serve the best interests not only of the city but of the metropolitan region.

In liberal as well as conservative national and state regimes, the American middle class manages to retain most of the proceeds of taxation for its own purposes, as evidenced by an unremitting flow of public investment into suburban schools, parks, community facilities, and transportation infrastructure. Light-rail transit, a mainstay of metropolitan progressives, bypasses inner-city neighborhoods to serve middle-class suburbs. Central-city neighborhoods will never achieve their potential as great living environments as long as they exclude the middle class. Efforts to convert the extant inner-city population into a middle-class population by means of social remediation are not succeeding at a respectable scale and speed, if they are succeeding at all. If these remedial efforts are succeeding, they're not enough; existing densities are far too low. The revitalization agenda requires a massive influx of newcomers from the solid middle of the middle class.

BLUEPRINT FOR RENEWAL

For the social and environmental good of the city and its metropolis, a city's leaders should facilitate the conversion of *green zones* to *gold zones*, and they should aggressively pursue the more daunting task—the conversion of *gray zones* to *pure city* neighborhoods (see Chapter 2). Green zones would become gold zones naturally and almost spontaneously if the land were rezoned for urban densities. The more daunting task of converting gray zones to pure city involves a four-part regimen of physical development:

1. Create middle- and upper-income housing at moderate and high densities.

2. Revitalize neighborhood commercial streets by means of urban rather than suburban development.

3. Build a new centralized transit infrastructure.

4. Create a new public realm designed to attract the middle class.

1. Housing

In order to create (or to revive) a pedestrian-oriented commercial street, it is necessary to create a market within walking distance by increasing residential densities to a level that retailers recognize as capable of sustaining their stores with foot-traffic alone.

Critical mass is essential. A smattering of moderate- and high-density housing in a sea of low-density housing will not provide enough units in close proximity to the commercial street. East Franklin Avenue, the mile-long commercial street of Minneapolis' Seward neighborhood, has dozens of apartment buildings, including four highrises, within a block of it. But the street is commercially deprived with only 1.1 consumer businesses, on average, per block face, compared to 10 businesses per block face on the lively Montague Street in Brooklyn Heights. (Average block-face lengths are nearly identical on the two streets.) The high-density housing flanking East Franklin Avenue is sporadic rather than extensive, and nearby land is low-density, mostly detached houses.[16]

Generally, more than 10,000 housing units in a compact area—320 acres more or less—are required to sustain a lively commercial array with a cinema. The Seward neighborhood has about 4,000 units on some 500 acres. (Brooklyn Heights has more than 10,000 units on less than 200 acres.) Scattered developments of moderate- and high-density housing in several American downtowns have failed to generate street vitality because the housing is not extensive enough. Commercial vitality is not recognized as an accompaniment to high housing densities in most American cities because critical mass is absent.

Unfortunately, the typical American city begins the 21st century with a housing density so low that it cannot, in a 50-year period, achieve an average net density higher than 25 units per acre, not even if 90 percent of the metropolitan area's new apartments and townhouses are built in the city (as suggested in Chapter 5). An average net density of 25 units per acre is about twice the current average in cities like Cleveland,

Minneapolis, and Oakland, but only half the density needed to put 10,000 housing units in an area so compact that most residents will walk routinely to the commercial street. Therefore a *target-neighborhoods* growth strategy emerges as an alternate to the *whole-city* strategy envisioned in Chapter 5. Rather than distribute housing growth throughout the city as envisioned by the whole-city strategy, the target-neighborhoods strategy would concentrate growth in select neighborhoods. This strategy would yield some exemplary high-density neighborhoods, especially if the fortunate targeted neighborhoods are adjacent to one another, creating a great critical mass of high and moderate density housing in a single sector of the city.

But the target-neighborhoods strategy fails to capture as many middle-class families with children as the whole-city strategy because fewer single houses (townhouses) can be accommodated in the higher-density mix of the targeted neighborhoods. The whole-city strategy spreads moderate housing densities throughout the city and allocates to the city not only tens of thousands of new apartments, but also tens of thousands of new townhouses. The target-neighborhoods strategy allocates too many new housing units to suburbs, unless the market preference for houses is largely replaced by a preference for apartments. Thus the target-neighborhoods strategy is, for the city, a slower-growth strategy, which results in higher localized densities but a lower overall density. The whole-city strategy captures for the central area much of the metropolitan area's growth in one-unit houses, and it targets all of the city's underutilized land. Low-density cities can achieve only moderate overall densities in their fifty-year outlook, but moderate densities sustain a respectable level of transit service and neighborhood retailing, as many of the outlying neighborhoods in San Francisco and Toronto prove.

The whole-city strategy is a good start; it will produce robust if not exuberant neighborhood commercial streets if densities are properly distributed throughout the city and within each neighborhood. The city's highest-density housing would be developed in and around downtown in order to maximize the number of walking commutes. Transit travel would be encouraged by high downtown densities because downtown has the best transit connections to the city's non-downtown destinations. High densities would occur also along waterfronts, which hold the power to attract substantial numbers of middle- and upper-income households to midrise and highrise apartment buildings. Runner-up densities would be situated out in the neighborhoods, at the intersections of major transit/commercial streets; these intersections would develop in a manner similar to Toronto's Regional Commerce Centres.

At the neighborhood level, the highest densities would gravitate to the primary transit/commercial street, as they already do in Seward and many other neighborhoods. The density gradient for the run-of-the-mill neighborhood would include these additional characteristics:

• The peak-density housing that lines the primary commercial/transit street is developed at a density of 50 units per net acre, on average, in a half-mile-wide zone centered on the street, i.e., a zone wherein all land is within a quarter-mile of the primary street (Figures 10-1 and 10-2). Most of the housing in this zone is in lowrise apartment buildings, but some midrise and highrise buildings are developed at strategic locations. Nearly half the land in this peak-density zone is occupied by housing and by mixed-use buildings that include housing.

• Because peak-density housing lines the primary street, half the neighborhood's households are situated within one-quarter mile—walking distance—of it.

• Density trails off to an average of about 14 units per net acre in the zone farther than one-half mile from the primary street. This is a density that accommodates the new townhouses, and a few exemplary existing detached houses, necessary to attract middle-class families with children. (This lowest-density zone would have a higher average density than Minneapolis' current citywide average of 13 units per net acre.)

• Intermediate densities of about 20 units per net acre occupy the land between the peak-density zone and the low-density zone. These transitional densities boost the viability of commercial outposts (grocery stores, laundries, cafes) and secondary transit routes in the areas beyond easy walking distance of the primary street. (Intermediate densities sometimes follow secondary commercial/transit streets; where they do, they extend farther than one-half mile from the primary street.)

The concept of neighborhood density gradient seems too obvious to warrant much discussion, but those with custody of precious urban land sometimes disregard the concept, if they are aware of it. In March 2000, Minneapolis' elected leaders enthusiastically endorsed a Near Northside redevelopment plan that distributes various housing types—detached houses, townhouses, and small apartment buildings—without regard to their proximity to Glenwood Avenue—the neighborhood's primary commercial/transit street (Figure 10-3a). The master plan envisions more than

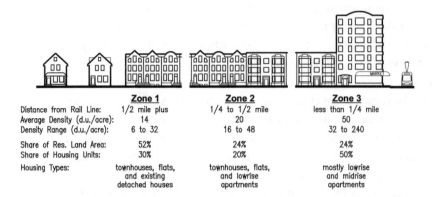

	Zone 1	Zone 2	Zone 3
Distance from Rail Line:	1/2 mile plus	1/4 to 1/2 mile	less than 1/4 mile
Average Density (d.u./acre):	14	20	50
Density Range (d.u./acre):	6 to 32	16 to 48	32 to 240
Share of Res. Land Area:	52%	24%	24%
Share of Housing Units:	30%	20%	50%
Housing Types:	townhouses, flats, and existing detached houses	townhouses, flats, and lowrise apartments	mostly lowrise and midrise apartments

Figure 10-1. Neighborhood Density Gradient—net residential densities.
This density gradient supports rail transit and neighborhood commerce. It is based on the following assumptions:

• About 45 percent of neighborhood land area is devoted to housing, including commercial/residential mix.
• Transit configuration is as indicated in Figure 6-6, in which 48 percent of CRR land is within ½ mile of a rail route.
• The average net residential density for the neighborhood is 24 units/acre, slightly lower than for the city as a whole; the city average is spiked by high net densities in select locations, including downtown.

(Existing average net density in Minneapolis, citywide, is 13 units per acre.)

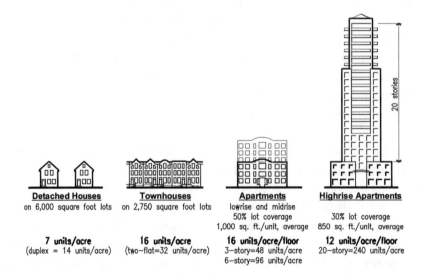

Figure 10-2. Representative residential building types and their net densities.

130 detached houses and townhouses within one-quarter mile of Glenwood Avenue. (All detached houses and townhouses south of Olson Memorial Highway in Figure 10-3a are within a quarter mile of Glenwood.) The redevelopment schematic illustrated in Figure 10-3b acknowledges the importance of Glenwood Avenue, and the site's proximity to downtown.

The great variety of localized conditions within a typical urban neighborhood prevents strict adherence to the density formula depicted in Figure 10-1, but general adherence is seldom if ever unfeasible. In Minneapolis' Willard-Hay neighborhood, for example, two exceptional detached houses occupy adjacent lots on a block situated within a half mile of West Broadway—Willard-Hay's primary commercial/transit street. Figure 10-4 illustrates a redevelopment plan in which the block's density is increased to the level suggested in Figure 10-1 without sacrificing the exceptional detached houses.

The hierarchy of neighborhood housing densities recognizes varying block dimensions and street widths. Streets parallel to the long axis of a city block are usually narrower than the streets perpendicular to the long axis, and the lower densities should line the narrower streets. In the intermediate zone of an urbanizing neighborhood, for example, townhouses would line the narrow streets parallel to the long axis of the block, and apartment buildings would occupy ends of blocks, bordering the wider streets. This is the typical arrangement in Manhattan.

Most of the brownstones that line Manhattan's narrow streets are unadulterated by garage doors, which is to say that the brownstones lack garages, for there are no alleys to provide vehicle access. City blocks with alleys afford an opportunity to add garages to townhouses without adulterating the street frontage with garage doors and curb cuts. With the addition of second-story apartments, detached garages accessible from the alley become carriage houses, which enhance security by providing surveillance of the alley. Taken one step further, detached alley-access garages become attached garages when linked to their host townhouses in the manner indicated in Figure 10-5. Houses of this concept offer the best of both worlds: elegant street frontages unadulterated by garage doors, and attached garages—an important feature in a competitive housing market. (In highly evolved cities, townhouses don't need garages to attract affluent buyers. Owners of multimillion dollar townhouses in Manhattan feel lucky when they find a parking space on the street in front of their house.)[17]

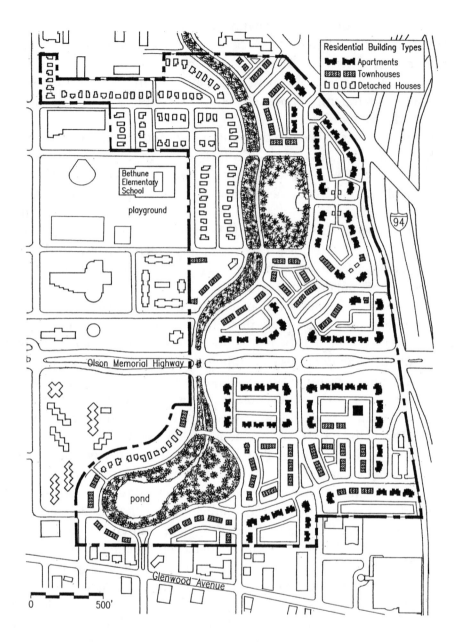

Residential Building Types
- Apartments
- Townhouses
- Detached Houses

Bethune Elementary School

playground

94

Olson Memorial Highway

pond

Glenwood Avenue

0   500'

Figure 10-3a. Hollman site, Minneapolis. For a clean-slate redevelopment site in Minneapolis' Near Northside, city officials enthusiastically endorsed a master plan that ignores the principles of proper metropolitan and neighborhood density distribution. The plan envisions a net density of only 15 dwelling units per acre* on a site located just a half mile from downtown, and in its distribution of housing types it disregards the neighborhood's primary commercial/transit street—Glenwood Avenue.

* Block interiors, devoted to parking and lawn for residents of the block, are counted as residential land in calculating the net density of 15 units per acre; alleys are counted as public right-of-way, consistent with net-density calculations for traditional city blocks.

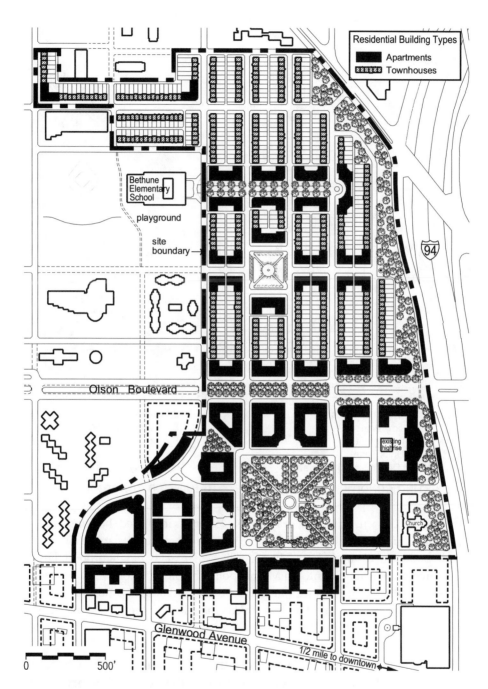

Figure 10-3b. Urbanized vision of the Hollman site. The capacity of the near-downtown site is at least 4,000 units (65 units per net acre) plus 100,000 square feet of ground-floor retail space. This density can be achieved even if all new buildings are lowrise. Distribution of housing types and pattern of pedestrian access recognize the importance of Glenwood Avenue—the neighborhood's primary commercial/transit street. The plan builds upon the neighborhood's existing street pattern.

Sources of information, figure 10-3a: Minneapolis GIS Department, aerial photographs 51B, 51D, and 52B; McCormack Baron & Legacy Management, Urban Design Associates, and SRF Consulting Group, Inc., Near Northside Draft Masterplan (March 2000), figures 26 and 65; Dan Wascoe Jr., et.al., "Hollman Site Redevelopment Proposal OK'd," Minneapolis Star Tribune, 25 March 2000, p. B1.

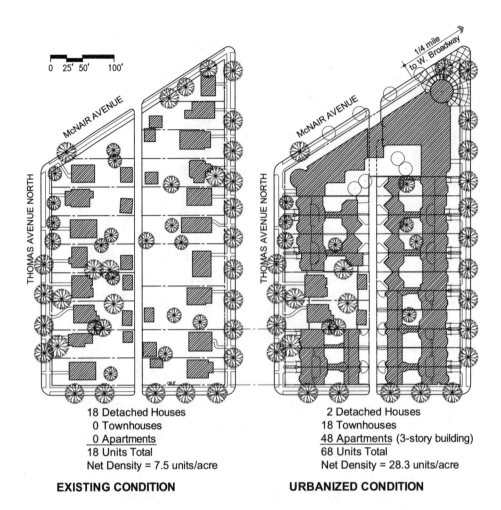

18 Detached Houses
0 Townhouses
0 Apartments
18 Units Total
Net Density = 7.5 units/acre

EXISTING CONDITION

2 Detached Houses
18 Townhouses
48 Apartments (3-story building)
68 Units Total
Net Density = 28.3 units/acre

URBANIZED CONDITION

Figure 10-4. Urbanization of a gray zone. Density is increased, housing is upgraded, burglar access is reduced, and most front-yard trees are retained in this hypothetical example from Minneapolis Willard-Hay neighborhood. Less than three miles from downtown Minneapolis, the block is zoned for detached houses on 5,000 square-foot (minimum) lots. The "urbanized condition" indicates townhouse lots that are two-thirds the width of the typical detached-house lot. Two exceptional detached houses are retained.

"It is through the townhouse that the ethos of urbanism demonstrates its strength and its potential," writes Paul Goldberger in the forward to architect Alexander Gorlin's book about this resurgent housing type.[18] Goldberger isn't referring to the multi-unit "townhome" developments increasingly found in suburbs (and cities), but rather to the individual townhouses, old and new, that line the streets of America's most appeal-

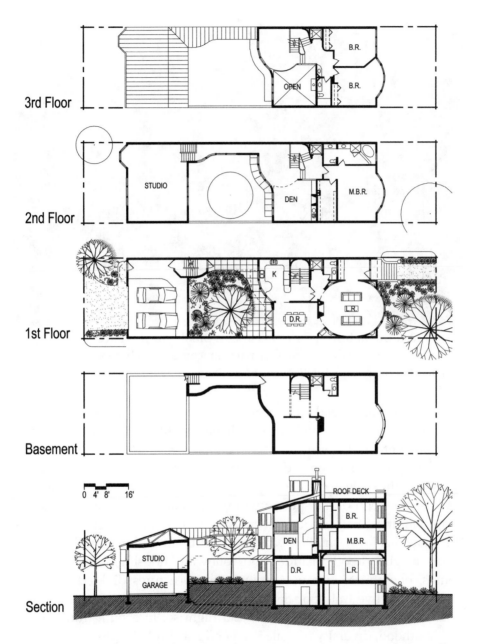

3rd Floor

2nd Floor

1st Floor

Basement

Section

0 4' 8' 16'

Figure 10-5. Townhouse Design. This design by Etienne Montebello illustrates one of many ways to attach an alley-access garage to a townhouse. Occupied space above the garage lends a measure of security to the alley. The lot is the same size as the townhouse lots indicated in Figure 10-4.

Figure 10-6. Union Street, Carroll Gardens, Brooklyn. This street of brownstones reveals the potential visual character of detached-house neighborhoods with mature front-yard trees.

ing urban neighborhoods. The economics of urban land development dictate that some new townhouses will be repetitive units in multi-unit developments, but these do not represent the ideal for urban streets. Urban neighborhoods need diversity of scale in residential development, starting at the scale of the carriage house and individual townhouse.

At the other end of the spectrum of residential scale lie the large apartment buildings that provide density, critical mass, and occupant amenities unavailable in smaller buildings. Thus an architecturally diverse urban neighborhood includes the following housing types: carriage houses, one-unit townhouses, townhouse structures divided into flats (from two to five full-floor flats per building), and apartment buildings small and large, lowrise, midrise, and highrise. In a built-from-scratch neighborhood, diversity of scale is a good substitute for diversity of age. Some of urban America's most appealing residential districts were built up over a short span of time.

The slums of Philadelphia and Baltimore prove that sizable tracts of townhouses are as vulnerable to decay as sizable tracts of detached houses, therefore the lowest-density zone needs special amenity: recreational opportunity and verdant tranquility. The lowest-density zone is where parks and parkways large enough for running and Rollerblading should be built. (Promenades and parks along high-density waterfront development should offer similar opportunities.) The lowest-density zone is where exemplary detached houses are preserved, and where the biggest and finest townhouses are built.

The residential blocks in most cities are big enough to accommodate new townhouses without sacrificing existing front-yard trees. Therefore, the blocks cleared of detached houses to make way for townhouses and flats would resemble some of the prestigious blocks in Carroll Gardens, Brooklyn, where sizable front yards accommodate mature trees (Figure 10-6). (Existing blocks would be subdivided into narrower lots without changing the front-to-back dimension of lots.) Small private parks such as Louisburg Square in Boston and Gramercy Park in Manhattan would help maintain the allure of the lowest-density zone.

The number of housing units—the critical mass—required to sustain neighborhood vitality varies, depending on the size and shape of the neighborhood in question, the density and density gradient within the neighborhood, the density and extent of adjacent residential neighborhoods, and the number of occupants in nearby commercial buildings. In the absence of density and critical mass, a neighborhood's commercial establishments can survive only if they attract large volumes of outsiders arriving in transit vehicles or automobiles. In low-density cities they will arrive in automobiles, which retailers are compelled to accommodate in off-street parking lots, same as the retailers in post-war suburbs.

2. Commercial Streets

Three mixed-use buildings—residential/commercial—were built on the commercial streets of three separate residential districts in Minneapolis circa the 1980s. All three are designed essentially as such buildings should be: multiple floors of apartments atop ground-level retail space, built tight to the property line at the street. All three buildings provide easy pedestrian access to the retail space, by means of generous display windows and a highly visible entrance for each retailer. In this respect, the three buildings replicate their predecessors of a century ago.

But the old urbanism doesn't work very well today, and the modern mixed-use buildings do not enliven their streets with retailers as the developers and the city envisioned. After years of underperformance and vacancy, the buildings' retail space is occupied mostly by social service agencies and non-retail businesses, including government tenants that have stepped in to fill the embarrassing retail void. A community clinic operated by the Hennepin County Medical Center occupies nearly all of the retail space in one of the buildings. The clinic locks its doors on weekends and at 4:30 p.m. on weekdays, and even during its truncated business hours it shutters many of its big display windows with venetian blinds.[19] From across the street, the venetian blinds look like white paper taped over the windows of vacant space. The residential densities that surround the mixed-use buildings are too low to sustain pedestrian-oriented retailing.

The city's new suburb-style retail developments are more successful in attracting and sustaining retailers because customers' cars are generously accommodated. Fast-food restaurants with drive-through windows and discount department stores with no windows at all do quite well in city and suburb, and this is the kind of retail development city officials impose on gray-zone commercial arteries because this is the kind of retail environment best sustained by low residential densities. Neotraditional planners and developers, acknowledging the evils of automobile dependence, endeavor to create pedestrian-oriented environments in suburbs where only cosmetic approaches are feasible. What a shame city officials won't produce genuine pedestrian-oriented environments. City hall's predilection for low residential densities precludes the kind of commercial development that promotes walking.

Once residential densities are brought up to a level that sustains urban rather than suburban commercial development, these principles of revitalization can be applied to the neighborhood commercial street:

• Retain old street-wall commercial buildings of appropriate condition and height. With low rents, old buildings house the independent shops and restaurants that lend charm and encourage strolling and window shopping. Old buildings promote diversity of businesses because they are most affordable to own, and independent business owners who also own their premises are least vulnerable to displacement by national chains.[20] Building codes and regulations can be relaxed without compromising occupant safety so that old buildings can be upgraded and occupied economically. Some old buildings, however, are inappropriate to a thriving urban commercial street. Generally, retain three-story buildings, demolish one-story buildings, and judge two-story buildings on their functional and architectural merit.

• Establish zoning mandates and incentives that will yield street walls of commercial/residential buildings with closely spaced entrances and generous display windows. The broad (75 feet or wider) primary commercial streets found in most residential districts should be defined by buildings averaging about 60 feet in height—five residential floors atop a commercial floor (Figure 10-7).

• Include new office buildings at major intersections along the primary commercial streets in residential districts. Office buildings are densely occupied over a period of nine or ten hours a day, five days a week, so they substantially bolster demand for businesses that benefit neighborhood residents. Office buildings enhance transit efficiency by creating bi-directional demand. Yonge Street in Toronto and Montague Street in Brooklyn are examples of non-CBD commercial streets enlivened by the presence of office buildings.

On Brooklyn's Montague Street, neighborhood residents stroll, meet neighbors, socialize in cafes, smell the aromas of many restaurants, and browse in bookstores, art galleries, and specialty food shops. Montague Street's visitors stroll not only *on* the street but *to* the street, for Montague has not one parking lot on its four-block length (and it isn't congested with traffic). Suburb-style commercial development offers not the pleasure of the stroll, but the tedium of the bituminous trek from car to store; shopping is nothing more than a chore in these parking-lot environments. Suburb-style commercial development will never charm middle-class homeseekers into urban neighborhoods. In the revitalized neighborhood, vibrant retail streets and high-density residential development reinforce one another.

Enlightened city policymakers will promote more than the mere revival of basic retailing on their gray-zone commercial streets; they will promote the revival of the urban experience that is offered by lively commercial streets. City policymakers have been instrumental in killing the urban experience; now they must face their obligation to restore it.

3. Transit

As noted in Chapter 5, America's cities hold a surplus of jobs, and those jobs are concentrated in the CBD. Therefore, any serious strategy for neighborhood revitalization must include housing for the downtown workforce, and good connections between housing and downtown. If and when federal and state governments get serious about revitalizing inner-city neighborhoods, they will provide for the neighborhoods what

10-7a. West Broadway—existing condition (2000).

Figure 10-7. West Broadway—existing and potential. Primary commercial avenues are typically broad enough to be defined by street-wall buildings 50 to 80 feet in height, at densities that will help sustain retailing and rail transit.

they provide for developing suburbs—generous funding for transportation infrastructure. In the case of inner-city neighborhoods, however, this infrastructure must take the form of centralized rail transit.

Combine the neighborhood density gradient suggested in Figure 10-1 with the centralized rail-transit configuration suggested in Chapter 6; then about 260,000 CRR households will be situated within a quarter mile of a rail-transit line with closely spaced stations. If those 260,000 households produce just 130,000 rail commutes each workday (a conservative assumption in the context of commercial recentralization), then the rail system will be accommodating 1.4 million passenger trips per route-mile annually, a better performance than any new-generation light-rail system in America.[21] (Portland's highly touted MAX garners half as many trips per route mile.) At 1.4 million annual passenger-trips per route mile, our hypothetical system outperforms some rapid-rail systems—San Francisco's BART, Miami's Metrorail, and Baltimore's Metro. And our ridership is even stronger when we factor in the many commuters who live

10-7b. West Broadway—potential condition.

farther than a quarter-mile from the line but nonetheless walk and ride. (Manhattanites walk one-third of a mile to a station, on average, and a half-mile is not uncommon for rail commuters.)[22] Add commuters who park and ride or kiss and ride, and commuters who transfer from feeder buses, and our hypothetical rail system is easily carrying as many passengers per route mile as the strongest of America's new-generation rapid-rail systems. Add non-work travelers, airport customers, and downtown residents (downtown land is excluded from the CRR), and our hypothetical system is outperforming all of America's new-generation systems—light rail and heavy.*

Households in the lowest-density zone—Zone 1 in Figure 10-1—would rely on buses for transit, but, even in this zone, significant increases in ridership would accompany the service improvements fostered by density enhancement. Extant densities as low as six or seven units per acre would rise to 16 or more where detached houses give way to townhouses and

---

*Such a high volume of passengers would choke a single downtown tunnel unless the several lines of the system remain separate or merge into two lines rather than a single line. Automation would help also, allowing shorter headways at higher speeds.

flats, and this increase can be expected to triple the rate of transit ridership according to a study of metropolitan areas in the Northeast. This
expectation is consistent with the conventional wisdom that, under conditions not uncommon in most cities, 15 units per net acre is the threshold density that sustains frequent bus service on closely spaced routes,
and the superior service motivates drivers to become riders.[23]

In the revitalized city, only a few pockets of green-zone land remain too
low in density to sustain good transit service, but ridership improves
even in these areas because they are proximate to the neighborhoods in
which a vastly improved transit system operates.

4. Public Realm

Baltimore's harbor districts undergo gentrification now that open space
and recreation have replaced the waterfront's derelict industrial rem-
nants. Meanwhile, thousands of inland residential acres decay, even
many that are covered by rowhouses similar to those sought by harbor-
district gentrifiers. Neighborhoods deprived of waterfronts or other substantial natural features are severely handicapped in the competition for
middle-class households. In his examination of gentrification in American
cities, Phillip Clay reported that significant natural features—rivers, lakes,
hilly terrain—are present in 78 percent of gentrifying neighborhoods.[24]

Manhattan's Murray Hill and SoHo prove that landlocked pure-city
neighborhoods can attract and retain affluent residents with little more
than urban vitality, which by itself exerts a magnetic force on urbanites.
But a typical gray zone's chances of attracting middle-class households in
large numbers would be greatly enhanced by a significant natural feature.

We find in Philadelphia that natural features can be created anew, and
they needn't be significant in size to be significant in impact.
Philadelphia's eight-acre Rittenhouse Square is the neighborhood parlor,
exquisitely designed and richly adorned with shade trees, flower beds,
bronze sculptures, a pool, a fountain, comfortable benches, and colorful
people. In Jane Jacobs' words, Rittenhouse is "the best known of [William]
Penn's four squares...a beloved, successful, much-used park, one of
Philadelphia's greatest assets today, the center of a fashionable neighborhood..."[25] A small park with a large effect, Rittenhouse Square exudes its
charm throughout the neighborhood (Figure 10-8).

The neighborhood surrounding Rittenhouse Square also provides guidance for the redesign of America's gray zones. First and foremost, the
neighborhood is high-density—the highest in Philadelphia, and property

Figure 10-8. Rittenhouse Square Park, Philadelphia. This exquisite eight-acre park is the neighborhood parlor.

values are among the highest in Philadelphia. The neighborhood's residential streets are tree-lined and quiet. Many are narrow, little more than alleys, and many are offset at intersections, discouraging through traffic. Plentiful commercial amenities, sustained by the high density of middle and upper income residents, are concentrated primarily on Walnut Street, adjacent to the square, and on Chestnut Street, a block north of the square, but small pockets of convenience retailers and restaurants are scattered throughout the neighborhood.

Since a parlor park is an appropriate place for high densities, (including highrise apartments on the north side, where they won't shadow the park) it should be situated within 1,000 feet of the primary commercial/transit street. It should be positioned and designed to maximize opportunities to walk through it en route to the primary commercial street. The park should be exploited for its ability to attract affluent home buyers.

The affluence that surrounds Rittenhouse Square ensures the maintenance and appeal of the park. The neighborhood focuses on this park rather than on the nearby Schuylkill waterfront (long separated from the neighborhood by railroad tracks and weedy terrain). This shows us that a well-designed and maintained man-made park can substitute for a natural feature as the heart of a thriving neighborhood.

A park like Rittenhouse Square would be an extravagance in a low-density neighborhood, but for a neighborhood on the path to revitalization, it represents a prudent investment with the power to attract affluence. Multimillion-dollar apartments overlook the square; a similarly appealing park will attract a revitalizing neighborhood's wealthiest newcomers. Elsewhere in Philadelphia, Society Hill's experience with renewal teaches us that a relatively few affluent newcomers can reverse the negative image of a derelict neighborhood.

The streets of the revitalized neighborhood deserve no less attention than the focal-point park. The primary commercial street must retain (or regain) its traditional pedestrian-friendly arrangement—street-walls of commercial-residential buildings with closely spaced entrances and generous display windows, such as the streets of Manhattan's SoHo. But SoHo owes much of its appeal to narrow streets, easily crossed and easy to see across; most commercial streets are much wider. Width of right-of-way and volume of traffic pose a significant challenge to the enhancement of the commercial street.

Chicago officials narrowed the vehicle pavement along downtown's State Street when they banished automobiles in 1979, but they couldn't reduce the width of the right-of-way or the distance between the buildings that spatially define the street.[26] Therefore, sidewalks were widened as vehicle pavement was narrowed. In the mid-1990s, less than two decades after State Street's sidewalks were widened, the city narrowed them in order to restore access to private vehicles, and also to restore the traditional scale of the sidewalks, which had become too wide, out of scale with pedestrian volumes—vacuous. The lesson of State Street is that sidewalks should be widened judiciously, only at crosswalks in most cases, where the alteration reduces pedestrians' physical contact with vehicle pavement. (Retailers benefit from on-street parking where pavements remain wide, between crosswalks.) Where two-way commercial streets carry buses, it is impractical to narrow the vehicle pavement to less that four lanes at any point, but the sidewalks of intersecting streets can be widened adjacent to the main street.

The widened portions of sidewalks must be enhanced with accouterments—well designed street lamps, newspaper kiosks, and transit stations—and they should be paved with brick or granite pavers. All of this is necessary to minimize the unpleasantness of the street-crossing experience. Sidewalk pavement, street furniture, trees, transit stations, civic art, all should impart an image of prestige and endurance. America's revitalized urban public realm is worthy of streets as lavishly adorned as Europe's grand boulevards. Affluent residents of the repopulated city provide the tax base that sustains a suburb public realm, which in turn attracts affluent residents, and benefits all residents.

Away from the neighborhood's primary street, the hierarchy of streets should be reinforced so that secondary streets are conspicuously distinguishable from tertiary streets, so that north-south streets are distinguishable form east-west streets. Building setbacks, landscaping, and paving configurations (sidewalk widths and positions relative to street curbs) should all serve to highlight the street's position in the hierarchy. Some streets should be interrupted by the imposition of a new park to curtail through traffic; this device is valid beyond the great focal-point park.

Back in the 1960s, architects and planners taught us much about the design of the urban public realm (e.g. Gordon Cullen, *Townscape*; Edmund Bacon, *Design of Cities*; Kevin Lynch, *The Image of the City*). But this knowledge is largely unapplied and, with the "New Urbanism," the tenor of literature on the subject of metropolitan development has turned from the improvement of cities to the improvement of suburbs. Now is the time to revisit the classic texts of the 1960s and to apply the nation's place-making wisdom to the urban rather than the suburban environment.

TACTICS

A whole-city rather than targeted-neighborhoods strategy of redevelopment was suggested above, but the strategy must begin with a few targeted gray-zone neighborhoods, where resources would be concentrated to achieve a comprehensive and convincing result. It is beyond the scope of this book to specify a detailed program of land redevelopment and marketing, but some commonsense tactics shed light on the challenges and possibilities:

Until rail transit is running and renewal is well under way, the revitalizing neighborhood has little to offer, therefore substantial incentives are needed to initiate the influx of new residents and retailers. The incentives include generous subsidies for mixed-use pilot projects developed at high-visibility locations (i.e., the primary commercial/transit street). The best housing values in the metropolis should be found in the pilot developments, thanks to generous development subsidies accompanied by other incentives such as property-tax abatements for early buyer-occupants. Strong incentives are needed to fill housing units quickly, thereby lending viability to retailing and transit. Development subsidies and tax abatements are standard operating procedure for urban revitalization attempts; serious revitalization initiatives would differ only in the density and scale of development.

A serious revitalization effort would derive its financial viability from upzoning and from the promise of infrastructure improvements, both of which produce the property appreciation that finances pilot developments (through tax proceeds and through the sale and lease of publicly owned land). Prior to rezoning for higher densities, city officials would gain ownership or control over as much strategically located land as possible in order to minimize development costs. (As they planned and built their Yonge Street subway line, Toronto officials acquired adjacent land so they could control development and capture the added value for public benefit. It is not uncommon for transit agencies in the United States to influence station-area development by means of land ownership and public-private development partnerships.)[27] Upzoning and infrastructure investment would entice key retailers—grocers and pharmacists—to the pilot developments, but subsidies would be necessary also, in the short term, until the neighborhood gains enough residents to sustain retailing.

Commercial subsidization would be formulated to benefit neighborhood business owners displaced by renewal. Condominium ownership of commercial space would shield independent business owners from the eventual onslaught of highly capitalized retail corporations. (Tom Shachtman studied business patterns in New York City's Chelsea district and found that small-business owners who also own their premises are resistant to displacement caused by chain retailers' ability to pay high rents.)[28] Undeveloped land would be available to retailers for their customers' parking until the neighborhood matures and the parking lots are needed for development, by which time a walk-in trade has been established. No incentive, however, would be designed to perpetually maintain—to entrench—businesses unable to compete in a high-vitality urban market.

MASTER PLAN

A neighborhood revitalization plan would entail at least one substantial pilot development, and as many as three or four, in strategic locations. To ensure diversity of scale and architecture, each pilot development would be parceled out to several developers. (Battery Park City's residential component consists, deliberately, of many small developments.) For reasons outlined in Chapter 2, most pilot developments would include at least one substantial residential/commercial building on a one-acre lot, more or less. (The lots underlying Manhattan's great apartment buildings—the San Remo, the Dakota, and the Ansonia—are about an acre in size.) Pilots would include several smaller buildings and individual townhouses also.

Pilot developments (and to a lesser degree all development) would be guided by a master plan that dictates not only density (within a range) but also building mass to ensure urban rather than suburban ground coverage, and positive spatial definition of streets and public spaces. The master plan defines minimum and maximum lot sizes to ensure diversity of scale, and it is formulated to ensure diversity of housing types. The master plan controls parking facilities, forbids blank pedestrian-hostile walls, and coordinates the locations of loading docks to maximize their utility and minimize their visual impact. Building materials are controlled to ensure private development worthy of a public realm rejuvenated at considerable public expense.

PROMOTION

It seems that very little time, measured in days or weeks rather than months, lapses between printed and televised news reports of various events—both petty and consequential—at the Mall of America. City officials must be equally adept and aggressive with a promotional campaign to back their investment in neighborhood revitalization. At least three important groundbreakings—rail transit, parlor park, and pilot project— are worthy of opulently staged high-image productions irresistible to the media. Nationally known public officials will be drawn to the earliest of the nation's serious revitalization efforts because these efforts signal a dramatic departure from the urban status quo.

Beyond that, the city's publicity machine should do the following: Publicize every major and minor event in the progress of the rail transit line, from the laying of the first rail to the emergence of the first station to the ribbon-cutting and official first ride. During design and construction, keep the completion date high in public consciousness. Provide special buses on the future route, buses emblazoned with the well-publicized name of the route (Green Line or Red Line or Broadway Line or whatever). Run the buses at frequent intervals and with priority at intersections; approximate the impending rail service as closely as possible. The special buses are highly visible downtown, where they offer promotional brochures and free express rides to the pilot developments, which are labeled with billboards announcing the future sites of supermarket, pharmacy, and cinema.

Don't forget those too busy to get on the bus. Set up a promotional extravaganza in the lobby of the most accessible and heavily trafficked building available downtown. Display large-scale models of the pilot projects and some of their components. Graphically prove that urbane streets and mature trees are not mutually exclusive. Display large-scale models of townhouse concepts, demonstrating that custom townhouses can still be constructed on individual lots just as they once were (and still are occasionally) in the most prestigious neighborhoods of Boston, New York, Philadelphia, Chicago, and San Francisco. With rendered floor plans and perspective drawings, demonstrate that a townhouse can be spatially exciting, that it can accommodate an attached alley-access garage with an office, studio, or small apartment above. Demonstrate that the walled townhouse garden (back yard) is an ideal place for toddlers to play and for adults to relax and cultivate flowers. (Gardens are often featured in the real estate advertisements for Manhattan's and Brooklyn's multimillion-dollar townhouses.)[29]

Focus the promotional campaign especially on suburban commuters to downtown jobs. Advertise lifestyle. Expose the pleasures of city life. Contrast the advantages of city life with the burdens of suburban life. Broadcast images of city-man strolling with his family on a waterfront promenade while suburb-man mows the lawn; city-man relaxing, reading the paper in a fast-moving train while suburb-man idles in traffic.

Publicize homeownership programs and incentives. Even though high-cost housing requires special promotional initiatives, advertise it alongside the advertisements for middle-income housing. Advertise the most opulent units, the seven-figure ones. Nothing will attract middle-class homebuyers more powerfully than the promise of rich neighbors. Build the first high-cost housing units where they will be most marketable and visible—in midrise and highrise buildings overlooking the parlor park. As repugnant as it may seem to equity planners, subsidize high-end units as necessary to move some of them quickly. Subsequent units will move at market prices, and housing of more modest cost will move quickly as middle-income households buy with confidence.

Generously subsidize the pilot developments' commercial assets because their quick completion is important to the appeal of the neighborhood. Quick completion of the parlor park boosts the image of the neighborhood, and it provides a staging area for media-worthy events such as charitable fundraisers. (Charitable events are a mainstay of the Mall of America's publicity machine.) Quick completion of Battery Park City's public spaces and visible infrastructure is credited for the marketability and financial success of the housing component.

Market forces will soon take over to complete the process of revitalization. Extravagant subsidies, however, are needed to initiate the process. Extravagant subsidies feed the middle-class growth of suburbs; extravagant subsidies produce the low-cost housing that entrenches poverty in cities. Revitalization entails the redirection of subsidies, in a direction that is socially and environmentally sane. Revitalization entails an economically rational redirection of subsidies, from productive exurban farmland to stagnating gray-zone land where extravagant value is pent up.

SOCIAL CONSIDERATIONS

Some low-income households will succumb to displacement from the revitalizing neighborhood as property values rise and derelict buildings fall. Revitalization is therefore a mechanism for the dispersal of poverty, but it needn't be a mechanism for the elimination of poverty. The nation's great and affluent urban neighborhoods accommodate measurable numbers of poverty-level households. Manhattan's Upper East Side recorded a poverty rate of 6 percent in the 1990 Census, with individual tracts ranging from 1 percent to 16 percent, and most tracts above 4 percent.[30] If an exemplary urban district can thrive with a 6 percent poverty rate, then another can probably thrive with an 8 percent rate—the 1990 rate for the Twin Cities metro area, and the rate appropriate for the central districts, whose poverty burden shouldn't noticeably exceed that of the metropolitan area.

At least two sources of low-income housing are available in the revitalized neighborhood. First, public housing authorities and nonprofit housing organizations control substantial inventories of land and housing in the typical gray zone. The nation's housing authorities are converting some of their holdings into mixed-income communities. Poverty-level households will be overrepresented in these communities, and market-rate units will be occupied by households at the moderate rather than middle or upper segments of the middle class. As for the nonprofits, many have been irresponsible to further entrench poverty in high-poverty neighborhoods, but in gentrifying neighborhoods the activities of the nonprofits can be legitimized. Some residents displaced by renewal would move to new apartments built by the nonprofits on upzoned land that they control, land heretofore occupied by low-density housing.

The second source of low-income housing lies within housing programs such as New York City's 80-20 program. If nonprofits' and public housing authorities' inventories of units are inadequate to accommodate displaced residents with positive records of tenancy, then developers should accommodate them in some of their new predominantly middle-class buildings. In New York City, developers in select neighborhoods are offered financial incentives to dedicate 20 percent of their units to low-income households. The low-income beneficiaries are carefully selected and their apartments are indistinguishable from market-rate units in the same building. In New York City, the program is targeted on affluent areas, such as Battery Park City, which can easily withstand the introduction of a few dozen low-income households. Pilot developments in a revitalizing gray zone might include one or two 80-20 (or 85-15) buildings to accommodate select households displaced in subsequent stages of renewal.

All housing types should be available to both owners and renters, but ownership should be valued by policymakers. Incumbent homeowner-occupants of modest income should be sheltered from tax increases associated with property value appreciation, allowing them to stay put if they wish, for a finite period, up to five years more or less. After that they make a choice: pay the costs or reap the rewards associated with precious land. Many such homeowners will quickly cash in on the value added by upzoning and renewal, and many will stay in the neighborhood, in new higher-density lower-maintenance housing. Special housing opportunities should be offered to induce modest-income homeowners to sell and relocate to higher-density housing in the neighborhood.

As noted in previous chapters, concentrations of low-income housing must be avoided. In the renewed neighborhood, privately held residential land (other than that controlled by nonprofits) is redeveloped primarily with market-rate housing, and low-income housing is developed with public subsidy. It is therefore feasible and reasonable to control the quantity and location of that housing. In order to socially recondition dysfunctional urban neighborhoods and their schools, disruptive and at-risk households should be offered relocation incentives.

Urban liberals confronted with this formula for revitalization might consider the cure worse than the disease. But policymakers serious about rectifying the social and environmental maladies of the metropolis—city and suburb—will be hard pressed to argue that lesser measures are sufficient. A 35-year history of lesser measures leaves us with urban neighborhoods unfit for the middle class. Urban policymakers feed the growth of suburbs with their lesser measures.

AN OFFER YOU CAN'T REFUSE

For about $250,000 you can buy a handsome new 1,900-square-foot apartment in BayHill condominiums, eight miles west of downtown Minneapolis in the developing suburb of Minnetonka. Your apartment overlooks a parking lot and a new townhouse development. Your commute to downtown is on Interstate 394, one of the Twin Cities' notoriously congested freeways. BayHill's developer advertises that "you can literally walk to restaurants and shops," but "shops" implies some measure of charm that is entirely absent from BayHill's retail array. The stores and restaurants—chain outlets in one-story buildings—are separated from your apartment by parking lots and loading docks, not a pleasant walk.

Urban neighborhood revitalization will succeed if participating developers can offer a similar apartment at a similar price in a safe and civil neighborhood with greater amenity, including:

• an array of shops and restaurants, and a cinema, in a pedestrian-friendly environment within walking distance

• a delightful nearby park conducive to socializing, people watching, relaxing, and family recreation.

• a convenient, quick, and comfortable transit commute to downtown.

A revitalized downtown would supplement this list of amenities with easily accessible theaters, museums, specialty retailers, and waterfront promenades, all in a lively urban environment little adulterated by parking lots and garages.

WINNERS AND LOSERS

The principal winners in the transition to a recentralized metropolis would include:

• People who find real cities—places such as New York, San Francisco, Paris, and Toronto—exhilarating,

• People who don't drive,

• Households that would prefer to minimize their investment in personal vehicles, e.g., two-adult households that would prefer to own just one vehicle,

• Suburbanites, particularly homeowners in developing suburbs, who prefer seclusion to commercial development and apartment buildings,
• Gray-zone property owners.

The principal losers would include:
• Urban politicians empowered by the poor,
• People who feel entitled to a low-density living environment in the heart of the metropolis,
• People sentimentally attached to obsolete urban housing,
• Class-obsessed liberals who resent exclusive large-lot suburbs,
• Landowners and speculators in and beyond developing suburbs (although detached-house development would continue).

The winners outweigh the losers in numbers if not in political strength. Each of the general components of recentralization already has significant political support: Metropolitan environmentalists agree that roadway development should be curtailed and that growth should be redirected toward the center. Political conservatives agree that cities should be more fiscally responsible and self-sufficient. Urban liberals insist that the urban poor should have access to suburban housing. Urbanites in every metropolis admire the nation's few remaining vibrant neighborhoods. Suburbanites wish to be left alone, spared the apartment buildings and commercial development that is increasingly foisted upon them. Suburbanites who enjoy the fruits of decentralization have much to gain from recentralization. Opposition to growth is strong and growing stronger in the nation's suburbs, and this opposition should be respected.

It is only in the specifics that recentralization differs from established agendas. Recentralization argues, for example, that suburban roadway development should give way to centralized rather than regional rail transit. Recentralization argues that the urban poor should be given housing opportunities in existing rather than new suburban housing. Recentralization argues that much of the city's housing, not just the most dilapidated and decrepit shacks, is obsolete. Thus recentralization is not a radical concept. The trendy New Urbanism is more radical because it attempts to create urbanity where it never existed. The restoration of urban vitality where it existed a few decades ago is the more rational and pragmatic concept.

HIGH-SPEED RAIL

The recentralization agenda will gain the support of at least one politically powerful interest group whose numbers are growing—air travelers. Crowded airports, jammed airplanes, and delayed flights have become a national nightmare so frightening that high-speed rail has at long last achieved political viability. Even those who might never ride high-speed trains will support them for their potential to relieve the nation's congested airports and airplanes.*

Potential high-speed rail corridors exist in most of the nation's regions, but the enormous investment will be productive enough to measurably relieve the growth in air travel only in corridors connecting metropolitan regions with massive and dense congregations of workers and residents near Amtrak stations. Amtrak launched its initial high-speed train—Acela—in the corridor centered by New York City, where millions of residents and workers have easier and faster access to Penn Station than to any airport.

Consider the options for a businessman traveling from an office in Midtown Manhattan to one in downtown Washington, D.C.: Acela Express travels from Penn Station to Union Station (235 miles away) in 2 hours and 30 minutes, compared to 1 hour and 15 minutes for the commercial flight from LaGuardia Airport to Washington National. But an air traveler must add nearly two hours on the ground: transportation between airport and CBD at both ends of the journey, plus airport check-in and boarding. This increases the duration of the journey to three hours—longer than it takes Acela to make its trip. The Amtrak passenger also must add ancillary travel and boarding time to his principal trip time, but for a CBD-to-CBD trip, these ancillary activities add less than an hour. All in all, the train traveler whose points of origin and destination are near Amtrak stations pays a premium of well under an hour. Under these conditions, Amtrak can set its prices at a profitable level and count on a meaningful market share. (In January 2001, Amtrak charged $286 for a

---

*Air travelers would be joined in their support of high-speed rail by all metropolitan residents who suffer increasing levels of airport noise. The number of nighttime takeoffs and landings at Minneapolis-Saint Paul International Airport increased from 10,908 in 1994 to 18,756 in 1999, an assault on the quality of life of all metropolitan households situated under flight paths. (Dan Wascoe Jr., "Night Flights, Noise Soaring," *Minneapolis Star Tribune*, 12 May 2000, p. 1.)

New York-Washington, D.C. midweek round trip, compared to Delta Airline's $405.)

Proposed high-speed trains on longer corridors such as Chicago-Saint Louis—300 miles—cannot compete with airlines if they are slowed down by numerous small-city and suburban stops, nor can they compete if few potential passengers live or work near an Amtrak station. High-speed trains in lengthy corridors connecting sparsely settled cities will offer infrequent service and they will fail to noticeably affect the growth in air travel. (Amtrak realistically expects to measurably improve its 30 percent market share of rail/air travel between New York City and Boston once Acela Express is running 10 round trips daily, as planned. Amtrak already enjoys a 70 percent share of the New York-Washington, D.C., market thanks to Metroliner, the semi-high-speed train that has been providing hourly service for several years.)[31]

The recentralized metropolis will ensure the restoration of downtown's vital point-of-entry status not only by providing a fast rail-transit connection from airport to CBD, but also by facilitating high-speed rail service—several trains daily—to a downtown station. Metropolitan recentralization represents the only hope for the development of a viable multimodal system of national, regional, and local transportation. The recentralization agenda is a holistic national transportation agenda with profound social and environmental benefits.

SMART GROWTH

Beyond the specific winners cited above—urbanites, non-drivers, recluse suburbanites, gray-zone landowners, and travelers—the whole of metropolitan society would reap the social and environmental benefits associated with recentralization. Land developers and people in the construction industry, and business people generally, would shift their economic activities from suburbs to cities. This shift would advantage some and disadvantage others, but it would not diminish the total amount of economic activity in the metropolis. Recentralization would increase economic activity according to those who argue that distressed cities burden their entire metropolitan areas economically.

Intolerable roadway congestion and intensifying criticism of sprawl impel more and more elected officials to propose "smart growth" policies in one form or another. When state and federal officials recognize that growth policy isn't smart unless it repopulates depleted central neighborhoods they will, by means of transportation policy, housing policy, tax policy, and any other policy at their command, compel cities to accommodate growth. They will, for example, stop the flow of state and federal money to programs that prop up obsolete low-density housing in central neighborhoods.

State and federal officials must recognize that city officials and neighborhood activists cannot be trusted to act in the best social and environmental interest of the city and metropolis. Just as state and federal officials have taken control of failing urban schools, they must find ways to seize control of the failing cities and neighborhoods that ceaselessly suck tax dollars out of state and federal coffers. David Rusk predicts that "state governments will step in to take over more and more functions of the local government and school system." The state of New Jersey has intervened in the governance of Camden, granting a state-appointed chief executive the power to veto city governmental actions.[32] Presidents, governors, mayors, and legislative bodies at all levels have done much to devitalize cities since World War II, but now the "smart-growth" agenda is in ascendance. America's leadership will begin to heal the social and environmental maladies of the metropolis when they realize smart growth begins with metropolitan recentralization.

INTRODUCTION NOTES:

1. Paul S. Grogan, Comeback Cities: *A Blueprint for Urban Neighborhood Revival* (Boulder, CO: Westview, 2000).

2. Brian J.L. Berry, ed. *Urbanization and Counterurbanization*, 1976, p. 24; Chris Kelley, "In Search of New Life for Smaller Cities," *Dallas Morning News*, 3 December 1995, p. 1A.

3. Rick Bragg, "It's the Traffic, Not the Heat, That Makes Miami Torpid," *New York Times*, 1 August 1999, website edition.

4. Gillece quoted by Jay Hancock, "Cost-Conscious Firms Looking to Urban Core," *Baltimore Sun*, 16 May 1999, p. D1. Ray Suarez's comment delivered in the Opening General Session of the American Planning Association's year 2000 National Planning Conference in New York City, 16 April 2000.

5. Brendan I. Koerner, "Cities That Work," *U.S. News & World Report*, 8 June 1998, p. 28.

6. John Holusha, "Dot-Coms Accounted for 25% of First-Quarter Leases," *New York Times*, 23 April 2000, Real Estate section, p. 4.

7. Sharon Sayles Belton, "Minneapolis: A City that Works," State of the City Address transcript dated 11 February 1999.

CHAPTER 1 NOTES

1. Jane Jacobs, *The Death and Life of Great American Cities* (New York: Random House, 1961), p. 249.

2. Minneapolis Planning Department, *Minneapolis Neighborhood Housing Comparison, 1984, 1989, 1994*, Working Copy, 19 September 1994; Minneapolis Planning Department, *State of the City 1998*, January 1999, p. 8.

3. M.W. Newman, "Minneapolis," *Saturday Review*, 21 August 1976, pp. 14-15.

4. *Money*, September issues, 1989-1994.

5. Paul Goldberger, "The Rise of the Private City," in *Breaking Away: The Future of Cities*, Julia Vitullo-Martin, ed. (New York: The Twentieth Century Fund Press, 1996), p. 136.

6. Dirk Johnson, "Nice City's Nasty Distinction: Murders Soar in Minneapolis," *New York Times*, 30 June 1996, p. 1.

7. Bob von Sternberg, "Twin Cities' Edge in City Rankings Has Disappeared," *Minneapolis Star Tribune*, 17 July 1996, p. A1; Bob von Sternberg , "Fearing the City's Future," *Minneapolis Star Tribune*, 20 August 1995, p. 1.

8. Bob von Sternberg, "18-Year-Old Gives Up in 2nd Newton Av. Shooting," *Minneapolis Star Tribune*, 14 June 1996, p. B1. Eight blocks away, later in the same month, a 16-year-old boy was killed and his younger brother wounded as they sat on another front porch (on the 700 block of Morgan Avenue), reported by Maria Elena Baca and Neal Shankman, "Teen Killed, Brother Hurt in Shooting; Arrests Made," *Minneapolis Star Tribune*, 26 June 1996, p. B7. In August of that summer a man was shot and killed as he played dice on a North Side front porch, reported on WCCO *10:00 p.m. News*, 24 August 1996.

9. Minneapolis Planning Department, *Willard-Hay Planning Information Base*, Summer 1992, pp. 14, 19.

10. Minneapolis Police Department, Crime Analysis Unit, homicide reports for 1995 and 1996

11. Tatsha Robertson, "Never Numb to Violence," *Minneapolis Star Tribune*, 10 June 1996, p. A1.

12. Jane Jacobs, *The Death and Life of Great American Cities* (New York: Random House, 1961), p. 209.

13. Jane Jacobs, *The Death and Life of Great American Cities* (New York: Random House, 1961), p. 150.

14. Jane Jacobs, *The Death and Life of Great American Cities* (New York: Random House, 1961), p. 338.

15. Parsons Brinckerhoff Quade & Douglas, Transportation Research Board of the National Research Council: *TCRP Report 16: Transit and Urban Form, Volume 1* (Washington, D.C.: National Academy Press, 1996), p. 15 of Part 1; Regional Plan Association, "Where Transit Works," *Regional Plan News*, August 1976, p. 6.

16. Jane Jacobs, *The Death and Life of Great American Cities* (New York: Random House, 1961), p. 212.

17. U.S. Census Bureau, Census 2000 PHC-T-5, Table 2; Minneapolis Planning Department, State of the City 2000, pp. 12, 42.

18. Economic Research Corporation, "Market Study of Neighborhood Commercial Areas and Nodes: City of Minneapolis," June 1996, p 17. A few of Minneapolis' "district" (as opposed to "neighborhood") commercial areas offer a full range of convenience merchandise.

19. Economic Research Corporation, "Market Study of Neighborhood Commercial Areas and Nodes: City of Minneapolis," June 1996, p. 17. One-thousand families sustained the typical neighborhood commercial area in the 1950s according to Carole Zellie, "Neighborhood Commercial Centers," Draft, 20 June 1993. A trade-area population of 18,000 sustains an enhanced commercial street with entertainment venues according to Norval White and Elliot Willensky, AIA Guide to New York City (New York: Macmillan, 1978), p. 302.

20. Carole Zellie, "Neighborhood Commercial Centers," Draft, 20 June 1993.

21. Marjorie Valbrun, "The Razing of an Unfulfilled Promise," *Philadelphia Inquirer,* 30 April 1995, p. B1.

22. Harry S. Jaffe and Tom Sherwood, *Dream City: Race, Power, and the Decline of Washington*, D.C. (New York: Simon & Schuster, 1994), p. 82.

23. Laura S. Washington, "In Englewood, Familiar Feelings of Misunderstanding and Mistrust," *Chicago Tribune*, 30 August 1998, Perspective section, p. 1.

24. R.L. Polk & Co., *Minneapolis City Directory 1955*; Author's inventory, 25 April, 2001.

25. R.L. Polk & Co., *Minneapolis City Directory 1964*; Author's inventory, 25 April 2001.

26. Willard Hay's 2000 population was 9,277 persons in approximately 3,150 housing units on 680 acres according to the City of Minneapolis, "1990 to 2000 Population Change by Neighborhood," April 2001; and *Minneapolis Neighborhood Housing Comparison 1984, 1989, 1994*, Working Copy, 19 September 1994. Willard-Hay net housing density is 3,150 housing units/310 acres=approximately 10 units per acre according to author's calculation.

CT-126's 2000 population was 12,895 persons in 9,044 housing units, on 44.1 acres, which translates to 205 units per acre (gross density), according to New York City Planning Department, Table PL-4B, April 2001; and U.S. Census Bureau, Census 2000, Table GCT-H5 for New York County, New York. CT-126 net residential density is 9,044 housing units/27.2 acres=332 units per acre according to author's calculation, based on *Block and Lot Maps: Manhattan Community District 8 Atlas,* New York City Planning Department, 1989, and partial land-use map 1"=600' from George Minicucci, New York City Planning Department, received 20 October 1995.

27. Minneapolis Planning Department, *The Minneapolis Plan: The City of Minneapolis' Comprehensive Plan*, adopted March 24, 2000, pp. 1.4.31-32.

28. "Alternative land uses" and "a great city" noted in Minneapolis Planning Department, *The Minneapolis Plan: A Workbook for Citizen Comment*, June 1997, pp. 54, 129. "Maintain areas" noted in Minneapolis Planning Department, *The Minneapolis Plan: The City of Minneapolis' Comprehensive Plan*, adopted March 24, 2000, p. 1.4.40.

29. Parsons Brinckerhoff Quade & Douglas, Transportation Research Board of the National Research Council: *TCRP Report 16: Transit and Urban Form, Volume 1* (Washington, D.C.: National Academy Press, 1996), p. 9 of Part 1. The probability of walking to work increases as density increases, and the probability is greater in a mixed-use environment than in a single-use environment according to Michael Burnick and Robert Cervero, *Transit Villages in the 21st Century* (New York, McGraw-Hill, 1997), Figure 4.7 on p. 89, see also pp. 121, 126-27.

30. Car ownership among welfare recipients reported by Leonard Inskip, "Welfare Reform Will Stall for Many Unless Transportation Improves," *Minneapolis Star Tribune*, 25 March 1997, p. A13. Lost households and gained automobiles noted in Minneapolis Planning Department, *State of the City 1996*, pp. 4, 10, 64.

31. Regional Plan Association, "Where Transit Works," *Regional Plan News*, August 1976, p. 7.

32. New York City Department of City Planning, *Socioeconomic Profiles*, March 1993, pp. 281, 284-85; 1990 Census of Population and Housing, Minneapolis STF 3A; Minneapolis Planning Department, *State of the City 1996*, p. 54.

33. Regional Plan Association, "Where Transit Works," *Regional Plan News*, August 1976, p. 7.

34. TCRT Route 20 pocket schedule effective November 24, 1957; Metro Transit pocket schedules effective 31 March 2001 for Routes 14, 19, and 20; Discussion with John Dillary, MCTO, 22 July 1997.

35. In Willard-Hay, Routes 14, 19, 20, and 55 run through, or on the bordering streets of, Willard-Hay; In CT-126, Route M15 provides service to Midtown and Downtown, route M30 provides service to Midtown. (Additional routes provide crosstown and uptown service.) Sources: Metro Transit pocket schedules effective 31 March 2001 for Routes 14, 19, 20; effective 1 October 2000 for Route 55; New York City Transit, Bus Timetables effective September 2000 for Route M15, effective January 2001 for Route M30. "Most ride the subway" according to New York City Planning Department, *Socioeconomic Profiles*, March 1993.

36. New York City Planning Department, DCP 1990 # 36, p. 25, and DCP 1990 #2, p. 28; *Statistical Abstract of the United States 1993*, p. 8, 723.

37. New York City Planning Department, *Socioeconomic Profiles*, March 1993, p. 136.

38. Urban Land Institute, *Land Use Digest 9*, September 1995, p. 3; San Francisco Planning Department, *Housing Information Series*, 1995, p. 28.

39. Quote from Barbara W. Moore and Gail Weesner, *Beacon Hill: A Living Portrait* (Boston: Centry Hill Press, 1992), pp. 5-6. Townhouse prices reported by Carey Goldberg, "Behind Curtains of Boston's Best Neighborhood, a New Elite," *New York Times*, 18 February 1999, p. A16.

40. San Francisco Planning Department, *Housing Information Series*, August 1995, p. 28; Minneapolis Planning Department, *State of the City 1996*, p. 23.

41. Morgenthau is quoted by David Ward, *Poverty, Ethnicity, and the American City, 1840-1925* (Cambridge: Cambridge University Press, 1989), p. 111.

42. David Ward, *Poverty, Ethnicity, and the American City, 1840-1925* (Cambridge: Cambridge University Press, 1989), Gould quoted on p. 67; Veiller quoted on p. 76; see also pp. 109-112, 136.

43. David Ward, *Poverty, Ethnicity, and the American City, 1840-1925* (Cambridge: Cambridge University Press, 1989), p. 75.

44. Richard Plunz, *A History of Housing in New York City* (New York: Columbia University Press, 1990), pp. 13-16.

45. Jacob A. Riis, *How the Other Half Lives* (New York: Dover Publications, 1971 edition), pp. 6, 85.

46. David Ward, Poverty, *Ethnicity, and the American City, 1840-1925* (Cambridge: Cambridge University Press, 1989), p. 75.

47. Richard Plunz, *A History of Housing in New York City* (New York: Columbia University Press, 1990), p. 16.

48. Jacob A. Riis, *How the Other Half Lives* (New York: Dover Publications, 1971 edition), p. 6.

49. David Ward, *Poverty, Ethnicity, and the American City, 1840-1925* (Cambridge: Cambridge University Press, 1989), p. 111.

50. David Ward, *Poverty, Ethnicity, and the American City, 1840-1925* (Cambridge: Cambridge University Press, 1989), pp. 35, 107, 138.

51. David Ward, *Poverty, Ethnicity, and the American City, 1840-1925* (Cambridge: Cambridge University Press, 1989), Riis quoted on p. 106, see also pp. 107-109.

52. Jane Jacobs, *The Death and Life of Great American Cities* (New York: Random House, 1961), p. 205.

53. The Upper East side is the most densely populated according to Editorial, "An Open Letter to the Mayor," *Our Town*, 14 October 1998; (The Upper West Side appears to have a slightly higher average net housing density; the land area of Riverside Park is included in the gross density.)

54. Kenneth Baar, "The National Movement to Halt the Spread of Multifamily Housing, 1890-1926," *Journal of the American Planning Association* 58, no. 1 (Winter 1992), p. 42.

55. Kenneth Baar, "The National Movement to Halt the Spread of Multifamily Housing, 1890-1926," *Journal of the American Planning Association* 58, no. 1 (Winter 1992), quoting Harvard Professor Ford on p. 43, and Hayes on p. 41.

56. Kenneth Baar, "The National Movement to Halt the Spread of Multifamily Housing, 1890-1926," *Journal of the American Planning Association* 58, no. 1 (Winter 1992), pp. 45-46.

57. George Galster and Jennifer Daniell, "Housing" in *Reality and Research: Social Science and U.S. Urban Policy Since 1960* (Washington, D.C.: Urban Institute Press, 1996), p. 87.

58. Simon Eisner, Arthur Gallion, and Stanley Eisner, *The Urban Pattern*, 6th Edition (New York: Van Nostrand Reinhold, 1993), p. 124.

59. Marjorie Valbrun "The Razing of an Unfulfilled Promise," *Philadelphia Inquirer*, 30 April 1995, p. B1.

60. Simon Eisner, Arthur Gallion, and Stanley Eisner, *The Urban Pattern*, 6th Edition (New York: Van Nostrand Reinhold, 1993), pp. 124, 340.

61. Joyce Cohen, "Kips Bay: Cohesive, With a Relaxed Ambience," *New York Times*, 18 April 1999, Real Estate section, website edition. Nora Ephron interviewed by Charlie Rose, originally aired 18 December 1998, *Charlie Rose* Transcript #2375, copyright 1999, Rose Communications.

62. Karen W. Bressler, "On the Upside," *Eastside Resident*, 3-10 September 1997, p. 55.

63. Ray Oldenburg, *The Great Good Place* (New York: Paragon House, 1989), pp. xvi, xv.

64. Anthony Lappe, "Two-Way Street," *New York Times*, 18 October 1998, Section 14, p. 1.

65. Min Zhou, *Chinatown: The Socioeconomic Potential of an Urban Enclave* (Philadelphia: Temple University Press, 1992), pp. 210-211.

66. Donald N. Rothblatt and Daniel J. Garr, *Suburbia: An International Assessment* (New York: St. Martin's, 1986), p. 173.

67. Simon Eisner, Arthur Gallion, and Stanley Eisner, *The Urban Pattern*, 6th Edition (New York: Van Nostrand Reinhold, 1993), p. 122.

68. Simon Eisner, Arthur Gallion, and Stanley Eisner, *The Urban Pattern*, 6th Edition (New York: Van Nostrand Reinhold, 1993), "freedom of movement" quote from p. 122. The authors apparently assume that urban transportation is automobile transportation when they impugn high densities (which they call "crowding") as a negative influence: "Crowding of people and buildings is a negation of every contemporary means of communication and transportation at our command." (p. 125)

Eisner, Eisner, and Gallion repeatedly decry "congestion," (e.g., pp. 125, 186, 340), but they fail to clarify whether they mean roadway congestion or sidewalk congestion or some other kind of congestion or all of the above. If roadway congestion bothers them, then it is strange they do not vigorously discourage automobile-dependent development practices.

69. Cuomo quoted in interview: "Housing," *Architecture*, August 1997, p. 44.

70. Oscar Newman, *Defensible Space: Crime Prevention Through Urban Design* (New York: Macmillan, 1972), p. 193.

71. Flynn McRoberts and Linnet Myers, "Out of the Hole, Into Another," *Chicago Tribune*, 23 August 1998, pp. 1, 16.

72. Melita Marie Garza, "Old Problems Plague New Low-Rises," *Chicago Tribune*, 20 September 1999, p. 1.

73. Harold R. Holzman, Tarl Roger Kudrick, and Kenneth P. Voytek, "Revisiting the Relationship Between Crime and Architectural Design: An Analysis of Data from HUD's 1994 Survey of Public Housing Residents," Cityscape 2, no. 1 (February 1996), p. 116.

74. Harold R. Holzman, Tarl Roger Kudrick, and Kenneth P. Voytek, "Revisiting the Relationship Between Crime and Architectural Design: An Analysis of Data from HUD's 1994 Survey of Public Housing Residents," *Cityscape* 2, no. 1 (February 1996), p. 116.

75. Harold R. Holzman, Tarl Roger Kudrick, and Kenneth P. Voytek, "Revisiting the Relationship Between Crime and Architectural Design: An Analysis of Data from HUD's 1994 Survey of Public Housing Residents," *Cityscape* 2, no. 1 (February 1996), quote "our findings suggest" from p. 122, see also pp. 116-118. HUD's findings do not indict traditional urban townhouse blocks, but rather public housing "townhouses," which are removed from the street, surrounded by the same sort of indefensible space that surrounds high-rise public housing.

76. Marjorie Valbrun, "The Razing of an Unfulfilled Promise," *Philadelphia Inquirer*, 30 April 1995, p. B1; Richard Moe and Carter Wilkie, *Changing Places: Rebuilding Community in the Age of Sprawl* (New York: Henry Holt, 1997), p. 117.

77. National Digest, "Cisneros Announces Plan to Revitalize Blighted Areas," *Minneapolis Star Tribune*, 12 July 1996, p. A4. In 1995 HUD provided a grant to the Manchester Citizens Corporation (a neighborhood organization in Pittsburgh) to replace blighted public housing with single-family homes, according to Richard Moe and Carter Wilkie, *Changing Places: Rebuilding Community in the Age of Sprawl* (New York: Henry Holt, 1997), p. 129.

78. Curtis Johnson comments at Minnesota Citizens League, Mind-Opener breakfast, St. Paul, 17 December 1996.

79. Minneapolis Zoning Code, reprinted 1993, p. 2170 (R2B zoning district).

80. Jane Jacobs, *The Death and Life of Great American Cities* (New York: Random House, 1961), p. 150.

CHAPTER 2 NOTES

1. Richard Lourie, "To Engage With New York: the World of Cafes," *New York Times*, 26 January 2001, p. B31.

2. Marvin Olasky, *The Tragedy of American Compassion* (Washington, D.C.: Regnery, 1992), p. 180, quoting Time magazine, 17 May 1968, p. 32.

3. Jane Jacobs, *The Death and Life of Great American Cities* (New York: Random House, 1961), pp. 32-33.

4. CBS, *48 Hours*, "Can Justin Be Saved?" 1 February 1996.

5. Anastasia Loukaitou-Sideris, "Hot Spots of Bus Stop Crime," *Journal of the American Planning Association* 65, no. 4 (Autumn 1999), p. 397.

6. Jane Jacobs, *The Death and Life of Great American Cities* (New York: Random House, 1961) quote from p. 33, North End density noted on p. 203, density and "sidewalk safety" noted on p. 209.

7. Jane Jacobs, *The Death and Life of Great American Cities* (New York: Random House, 1961), p. 203.

8. Jeff Minter, "Reinventing Roxbury's Dudley Square," *Urban Land*, January 1995, p. 34.

9. Jane Jacobs, *The Death and Life of Great American Cities* (New York: Random House, 1961), pp. 202-203.

10. Jane Jacobs, *The Death and Life of Great American Cities* (New York: Random House, 1961), p. 202.

11. Jane Jacobs, *The Death and Life of Great American Cities* (New York: Random House, 1961), p. 204.

12. Anastasia Loukaitou-Sideris, "Hot Spots of Bus Stop Crime," *Journal of the American Planning Association* 65, no. 4 (Autumn 1999), p. 404.

13. George L. Kelling and Catherine Coles, *Fixing Broken Windows: Restoring Order and Reducing Crime in Our Communities* (New York: Free Press, 1996), pp. 197-98.

14. George L. Kelling and Catherine Coles, *Fixing Broken Windows: Restoring Order and Reducing Crime in Our Communities* (New York: Free Press, 1996), p. 136.

15. Detached houses are considered to dominate the block if they account for a plurality of the structures on the block. The area defined as the "block" is the strip of properties on both sides of the street, between adjacent street intersections, containing the murder site.

16. Minneapolis Police Department Crime Analysis Unit, printout dated October 2, 1996; a murder attributed to a residential address occurred on the property of that address, or on a part of a street or alley closer to that address than to others. Distribution of housing units among the various types is indicated in Minneapolis Planning Department, *State of the City 1996*, p. 12.

Some sites that are counted as one-family detached houses may be duplex conversions that have only one entry door and address; most are, because of their size and appearance, conspicuously one-unit houses.

17. Crime data refer to FBI index crimes, from *Statistical Abstract of the United States* annual crime rate summaries for years 1990 through 1997, and from U.S. Department of Justice, FBI, *Crime in the United States* annual reports for years 1998 and 1999.

18. Harold R. Holzman, et.al., "Revisiting the Relationship between Crime and Architectural Design," *Cityscape* 2, no. 1 (February 1996): 122.

19. Mary Ellen Burns, "A HUD Strikeout," *New York Times*, 23 April 1996, p. A17.

20. Andrew Cuomo interview, *Architecture*, August 1997, p. 47; Michael Janofsky, "HUD and Its New Chief Face His High Ambitions," *New York Times*, 13 April 1997, p. 12, noting that demolitions outpace the availability of replacement housing in Chicago and Baltimore; "Very-low-income renters" noted by HUD, *Characteristics of HUD-Assisted Renters*, May 1997, Forward.

21. 1.7 million households noted by Howard Husock, "Let's End Housing Vouchers," *City Journal*, Autumn 2000, p. 84; Characteristics of Section-8 units noted in HUD, *Characteristics of HUD-Assisted Renters*, May 1997, pp. 20, 22.

22. Jane Jacobs, *The Death and Life of Great American Cities* (New York: Random House, 1961), p. 209.

23. Myron Orfield, *Metropolitics: A Regional Agenda for Community and Stability* (Washington, D.C.: Brookings Institution Press, and Cambridge: Lincoln Institute of Land Policy, 1997), Maps 2-2, 2-3, 3-7.

24. John S. Adams and Barbara VanDrasek, *Minneapolis-St.Paul: People, Place, and Public Life* (Minneapolis: University of Minnesota Press, 1993), p. 95.

25. John Clubbe, *Cincinnati Observed: Architecture and History* (Columbus: Ohio State University Press, 1992), p. 291.

26. Myron Orfield, Metropolitics: *A Regional Agenda for Community and Stability* (Washington, D.C.: Brookings Institution Press, and Cambridge: Lincoln Institute of Land Policy, 1997), Maps 2-2, 2-3.

27. David P. Varady and Jeffrey A. Raffel, *Selling Cities: Attracting Homebuyers through Schools and Housing Programs* (Albany: State University of New York Press, 1995), pp. 177, 194-198.

28. Veiller's extreme example of 329 dwelling units per net acre was equaled in 1990 in census tract 126; in 1890, Tenth ward population density was 522 persons per acre-the Lower East Side's maximum according to Jacob Riis, *How the Other Half Lives* (New York: Dover, 1971 edition of 1901 text), Appendix. Unless tenement occupancy rates averaged less than 4.25 persons per unit in 1890, Upper East Side housing densities of 1990 match or exceed those of the Lower East Side in 1890; and testimony about occupancy rates far exceeding 4.25 in tenement units is abundant. Veiller's block, for example, housed 4.6 persons per dwelling unit, on average. (see also David Ward, 1989; and Richard Plunz, 1990)

29. The Upper East Side has a gross housing density of approximately 123 units per acre, excluding Roosevelt Island; compared to a gross density of 128 units per acre, excluding the Penn Central rail yard and excluding Riverside Park, in Community District 7, the Upper West Side. Net densities of roughly 200 units per acre are calculated using a multiplier of 1.67, based on CT-126 calculations.

30. Nine buildings reported by Peter Hellman, "Co-Op Board Hell," *New York* magazine, 6 November 1995 p. 31; Heiress apartment reported by Associated Press, "Asking Price: $35 Million," *Minneapolis Star Tribune*, 21 February 1996, p. A16.

31. Larry R. Ford, *Cities and Buildings: Skyscrapers, Skid Rows, and Suburbs* (Baltimore: Johns Hopkins University Press, 1994), p. 214.

32. Larry R. Ford, *Cities and Buildings: Skyscrapers, Skid Rows, and Suburbs* (Baltimore: Johns Hopkins University Press, 1994), p. 214.

33. Christopher Mason, "West of Eden: How CPW Suddenly Became the Glammiest Address in Town," *New York* magazine, 2 September 1996, p. 24.

34. Andrew Alpern, *New York's Fabulous Luxury Apartments* (New York: Dover Publications, 1975), p. 1.

35. Peter Hellman, "Co-Op Board Hell," *New York* magazine, 6 November 1995, p. 28; Christopher Mason, "West of Eden: How CPW Suddenly Became the Glammiest Address in Town," *New York* magazine, 2 September 1996, p. 26; Madonna reported in *The New York Observer*, 25 August-1 September 1997, p. 25.

36. Peter Hellman, "Co-Op Board Hell," *New York* magazine, 6 November 1995, pp. 28-33.

37. Peter Hellman, "Co-Op Board Hell," *New York* magazine, 6 November 1995, p. 29, 31; Manhattan's East Side average 3-bedroom apartment sales prices reached $1.15 million in 1994 according to Urban Land Institute, *Land Use Digest 9,* September 1995, p. 3; Four Upper East Side townhouses sold in the first half of 1995 for more than $5 million each, including one on East 64th Street bought by fashion designer Gianni Versace for $7.5 million. Seven-figure prices are the rule for Upper East Side townhouses, and are unexceptional for apartments in the district, according to Tracie Rozhon, "Some Manhattan Town House Prices Top $5 Million," *New York Times,* 24 November 1995, p. B21.

38. Larry R. Ford, *Cities and Buildings: Skyscrapers, Skid Rows, and Suburbs* (Baltimore: Johns Hopkins University Press, 1994), p. 214.

39. New York City Planning Department, *Socioeconomic Profiles,* March 1993, p. 272.

40. (no byline) "Hometown New York," *New York* magazine, 23-30 December 1996, p. 117.

41. Gross housing density is about 25 to 30 units per acre according to New York City Planning Department, DCP 1990 #2.

42. New York City Planning Department, DCP 1990 #313.

43. 25 to 30 occupied housing units per acre (gross) according to New York City Planning Department, DCP 1990 #2; Minneapolis Planning Department, *State of the City 1996,* pp. 12, 54.

44. Oscar Newman, *Defensible Space: Crime Prevention through Urban Design* (New York: Macmillan, 1972), pp. 39, 46-47.

45. *Minneapolis Zoning Code* adopted 1999, p. 247.

46. Andrew Alpern, *New York's Fabulous Luxury Apartments* (New York: Dover Publications, 1975), p. 30; Michael Gabriel, *Apartment Sales Guide: Condos & Co-ops, Manhattan 2000* (New York: Gabriel Productions, Inc., 2000).

47. The fourth wall of the typical grand apartment building fronts a service alley, but the effect is mitigated by setbacks and landscaped courts that provide substantial daylight exposure and decent views to the backside rooms. (In many buildings, apartments have two exposures; main rooms are exposed to the street, and bedrooms, bathrooms, kitchens, and servants' rooms are exposed to the alley or court.)

48. Sales data for March 1999, from Steven Knoble, president, Cooperative Data Corp., telephone discussion 27 October 2000; Alwyn Court has 75 units on 0.3 acres; units range in size from about 950 square feet to about 1,600 square feet.

49. Boston Zoning Code Section 28-1, cited in Lawrence W. Kennedy, *Planning the City Upon a Hill: Boston Since 1630* (Amherst: University of Massachusetts Press, 1992), p. 227; Paul Goldberger, "The Rise of the Private City" in *Breaking Away,* Julia Vitullo-Martin, ed. (New York: Twentieth Century Fund Press, 1996) p. 135.

50. New York City Planning Department, Socioeconomic Profiles, March 1993, pp. 276, 282.

51. Michael Gabriel, *Gabriel's Apartment Sales Guide: Condos & Co-ops* (New York: Gabriel Productions, Inc., 2000), p. 287.

52. Jane Jacobs, *The Death and Life of Great American Cities* (New York: Random House, 1961), p. 200.

53. Tom Wolfe, *A Man in Full* (New York: Farrar, Straus and Giroux, 1998), p. 171.

54. 2001 inventory of Olive Garden and Chi-Chi's restaurants from *Quest Dex Yellow Pages,* Minneapolis, January 2001-2002; 1997 survey of independent restaurants from U.S. West Yellow Pages for Minneapolis and St. Paul and suburbs, 1997; only restaurants in the seven-county metro area were counted.

In the low-density city, high levels of automobile ownership substitute somewhat for proximity in promoting variety, but automobility only partially compensates for high densities. On most occasions restaurant patrons, including car owners, favor restaurants not too distant from their homes, a situation that advantages popular restaurants in low-density areas.

55. Jane Jacobs, *The Death and Life of Great American Cities* (New York: Random House, 1961), p. 200.

56. Kenneth T. Jackson, ed., *Encyclopedia of New York City* (New Haven: Yale University Press, 1995), p. 677.

57. David Denby, "Capital Culture," *New York* magazine, 23-30 December 1996, p. 72.

58. Paul Goldberger, "The Rise of the Private City" in *Breaking Away: The Future of Cities*, Julia Vitullo-Martin, ed. (New York: Twentieth Century Fund Press, 1996), p. 146.

59. Todd S. Purdum, "Where the Screen is King, the Stage is Queen," *New York Times*, 14 March 1999, Section 2, p. 1; Neil Strauss, "Knitting Factory Goes Hollywood," *New York Times*, 15 June 2000, p. B3.

60. Frank Rich, "A Detour in the Theater That No One Predicted," *New York Times*, 18 October 1998, Section 2, Arts and Leisure, p. 1 (quote on p. 7).

61. The creation of *Rent* is described in *Newsweek*, 13 May 1996, p. 56. Pulitzer Prize winners reported by Robin Pogrebin, "Nary a Drama on Broadway," *New York Times*, 28 December 1999, p. B1 ("The Living Arts" section)

62. Heidi Landecker, "Art Transplant," *Architecture*, March 1998, p. 105. A 1984 study found that Lincoln Center alone was generating more than $500 million in annual sales at the ticket office and in nearby hotels and restaurants. Indirect benefits such as real estate improvements and their effects brought the total to more than $1 billion in overall annual economic impact, according to Nathan Leventhal, "Lifeblood of the City: The Arts in New York" in B*reaking Away: The Future of Cities*, Julia Vitullo-Martin, ed. (New York: Twentieth Century Fund Press, 1996), pp. 190-1.

63. New York City Planning Department, *1997 Annual Report on Social Indicators*, p. 16.

64. *Statistical Abstract of the United States 1993*, pp. 42-44, 452; *Statistical Abstract of the United States 1996*, p. 455.

65. The Gallup Poll, "Public Releases from Gallup Poll Results," poll conducted 6 September 1997, noted by Peter Reinharz, "The Crime War's Next Battle," *City Journal*, Winter 1998, p. 49.

66. San Francisco Planning Department, "Multimedia in San Francisco," August 1997, pp. 23, 25, 27.

67. *CBS Evening News*, "Eye on America," 22 October 1998. "Many who've gained wealth in Silicon Valley chose to live in San Francisco," according to University of Minnesota geographer John Adams, quoted by David Peterson, "Some Metro Counties Among the Wealthiest," *Minneapolis Star Tribune*, 22 November, 2000 (web edition).

68. Carey Goldberg, "Behind the Curtains of Boston's Best Neighborhood, a New Elite," *New York Times*, 18 February 1999, p. A16.

69. Many low-density urban neighborhoods suffer bothersome levels of through traffic, according to Oscar Newman, *Creating Defensible Space* (Washington, D.C.: HUD's Office of Policy Development and Research, April 1996), p. 31.

70. Except in the case of highway overload, which in 1996 was diverting traffic onto Brooklyn Height's normally quiet streets and upsetting residents accustomed to tranquility, reported in *Brooklyn Heights Paper*, 28 June-11 July 1996, p. 1.

71. Greg Girard and Ian Lambot, *City of Darkness: Life in Kowloon Walled City* (Haslemere, Surrey, England: Watermark Publications [UK] Ltd., 1993), pp. 9-10.

72. Jan Morris, *Hong Kong* (New York: Random House, 1988), pp. 294-295.

73. Greg Girard and Ian Lambot, *City of Darkness: Life in Kowloon Walled City* (Haslemere, Surrey, England: Watermark Publications [UK] Ltd., 1993), p. 210.

74. Greg Girard and Ian Lambot, *City of Darkness: Life in Kowloon Walled City* (Haslemere, Surrey, England: Watermark Publications [UK] Ltd., 1993), p. 72.

75. Greg Girard and Ian Lambot, *City of Darkness: Life in Kowloon Walled City* (Haslemere, Surrey, England: Watermark Publications [UK] Ltd., 1993), p. 167.

76. Greg Girard and Ian Lambot, *City of Darkness: Life in Kowloon Walled City* (Haslemere, Surrey, England: Watermark Publications [UK] Ltd., 1993), dust jacket notes.

77. Walled City demolition noted by Greg Girard and Ian Lambot, *City of Darkness: Life in Kowloon Walled City* (Haslemere, Surrey, England: Watermark Publications [UK] Ltd., 1993), p. 211; Raymond Rosen demolition noted by Marjorie Valbrun, "The Razing of an Unfulfilled Promise, *Philadelphia Inquirer*, 30 April 1995, p. B1.

78. Greg Girard and Ian Lambot, *City of Darkness: Life in Kowloon Walled City* (Haslemere, Surrey, England: Watermark Publications [UK] Ltd., 1993), p. 208.

79. Greg Girard and Ian Lambot, *City of Darkness: Life in Kowloon Walled City* (Haslemere, Surrey, England: Watermark Publications [UK] Ltd., 1993), pp. 202-207.

CHAPTER 3 NOTES

1. Reid Ewing, "Is Los Angeles-Style Sprawl Desirable?" *Journal of the American Planning Association 63*, no. 1 (Winter 1997), p. 107.

2. 9,600 suburban jurisdictions plus 168 urban jurisdictions in 168 metropolitan areas noted by David Rusk, *Inside Game Outside Game: Winning Strategies for Saving Urban America* (Washington, D.C., Brookings Institution Press, 1999), p. 67.

3. Donald N. Rothblatt and Daniel J. Garr, *Suburbia: An International Assessment* (New York: St. Martin's Press, 1986), p. 16.

4. James E. Vance Jr., *The Continuing City: Urban Morphology in Western Civilization* (Baltimore: Johns Hopkins University Press, 1990), pp. 297, 352, 356-60, 371.

5. James E. Vance Jr., *The Continuing City: Urban Morphology in Western Civilization* (Baltimore: Johns Hopkins University Press, 1990), pp. 356-60, 410-11.

6. Kenneth T. Jackson, *Crabgrass Frontier: The Suburbanization of the United States* (New York: Oxford University Press, 1985), pp. 113, 183-84.

7. *Statistical Abstract of the United States 1999*, Table 678, p. 428.

8. *Statistical Abstract of the United States 1999*, Table 678, p. 428; Paul L. Knox, *Urbanization: An Introduction to Urban Geography* (Englewood Cliffs, New Jersey: Simon & Schuster, Prentice-Hall, 1994), p. 127; San Francisco Planning Department, July 1996," San Francisco Economy, p. 2; Minneapolis Planning Department, *State of the City 1996*, p. 39.

9. Paul L. Knox, *Urbanization: An Introduction to Urban Geography* (Englewood Cliffs, New Jersey: Simon & Schuster, Prentice-Hall, 1994), p. 127.

10. Alexander Garvin, *The American City: What Works, What Doesn't* (New York: McGraw-Hill, 1996), p. 126.

11. Alexander Garvin, *The American City: What Works, What Doesn't* (New York: McGraw-Hill, 1996), p. 126; Bessie C. Economou, "[Pittsburgh] Background and Context," in *Cities Reborn*, Rachelle L. Levitt, ed. (Washington, D.C.: Urban Land Institute, 1987), p. 111.

12. Bessie C. Economou, "[Pittsburgh] Background and Context," in *Cities Reborn*, Rachelle L. Levitt, ed. (Washington, D.C.: Urban Land Institute, 1987), p. 111.

13. Bessie C. Economou, "[Pittsburgh] Background and Context," in *Cities Reborn*, Rachelle L. Levitt, ed. (Washington, D.C.: Urban Land Institute, 1987), p. 110.

14. Jill Schachner Chanen, "New Sparkle for a Gritty Chicago Area," *New York Times*, 20 April 1997, Real Estate section, p. 32.

15. Jane Jacobs, *The Economy of Cities* (New York: Random House, 1969), p. 24-27; Perkins, Dexter, Jr. and Patricia Daly, "A Hunter's Village in Neolithic Turkey," *Scientific American*, November 1968, p. 97; Peter J. Ucko and G.W. Dimbleby eds., *The Domestication and Exploitation of Plants and Animals* (Chicago: Aldine Publishing Co., 1969), pp. 17-29, 73-100, 367. Pigs in New York City noted by Jacob Riis, *How the Other Half Lives* (New York: Dover Publications, 1971 edition), p. 6.

16. James E. Vance Jr., *The Continuing City: Urban Morphology in Western Civilization* (Baltimore: Johns Hopkins University Press, 1990), p. 354.

17. Joe Hallett, "Steel Comes to the Farmland," *Cleveland Plain Dealer Sunday Magazine*, 17 November 1996, pp. 10-11.

18. H.V. Savitch, *Post-Industrial Cities: Politics and Planning in New York, Paris, and London* (Princeton, New Jersey: Princeton University Press, 1988), p. 129.

19. Roberta Brandes Gratz, "Notown," *Preservation*, May/June 1999, pp. 38-45, 114-16; Detroit's industrialization efforts are described also by Detroit Central Business District Foundation, "Mayors of the City of Detroit," *Destination Detroit*, Summer 2000, p. 20.

20. R.J. King, "Ford Plans Auto Parts Plant, *Detroit News*, 20 October 1997, p. D1.

21. Minneapolis industrial development reported by Neal St. Anthony, "Green Tree May Leave St. Paul for Greener Pastures," *Minneapolis Star Tribune*, October 1, 1999, p. D2 and Kevin Diaz, "Upbeat Mayor Says City Is Doing Great," *Minneapolis Star Tribune,* 12 February 1999, p. B1. Industrial retention and expansion programs described by Neil S. Meyer, *Saving and Creating Good Jobs: A Study of Industrial Retention and Expansion Programs* (Washington, D.C.: U.S. Department of Housing and Urban Development, June 1999). Planned manufacturing districts in Chicago and Portland, Oregon, to retain jobs for local people without college degrees noted by Nathan Landau, letter to the editor, *New York Times*, 11 October 1998, Business section, p. 28. Industrial retention in Philadelphia noted by Buzz Bissinger, *A Prayer for the City* (New York: Random House, 1997), pp. 50, 335-64.

22. Ford plant payroll noted in *Minnesota Department of Administration/ MnSCU/UAW/Ford Technical Training Facility Predesign Manual* by Setter Leach & Lindstrom, November 1996, Appendix B; The Ford plant has 1,984 local employees, and "because of its age, it has an uphill battle to compete with the new Toyota truck plant that is being built in Evansville, Indiana," according to *Twin Cities Metro Report, 1999-2000 Millennium Edition* (St. Louis Park, MN: Cherbo Publishing Group), p. 15.

23. Ramsey County Assessor's office, 14 June 1999.

24. Tom Shachtman, *Around the Block: The Business of a Neighborhood* (New York: Harcourt Brace, 1997), pp. 189-90.

25. Ratcliff quoted by Jane Jacobs, *The Death and Life of Great American Cities* (New York: Random House, 1961), pp. 165-66.

26. Hudson's noted by Ron French, "It's History: Razing Paves Way for Renewal," *The Detroit News and Free Press*, October 25, 1998, p 1A; and in "Planning News" (no byline) Planning, December 1998, p. 27. Crowley's and Kern's noted by Roberta Brandes Gratz, "Notown," *Preservation*, May/June 1999, pp. 38-45, 114-16.

27. Donald N. Rothblatt and Daniel J. Garr, *Suburbia: An International Assessment* (New York: St. Martin's Press, 1986), pp. 25-27.

28. Alexander Garvin, *The American City: What Works, What Doesn't* (New York: McGraw Hill, 1996) pp. 128-129.

29. Linda Mack, "The Conservatory becomes Nicollet," *Architecture Minnesota*, January-February 1988, p. 43.

30. Neal St. Anthony, "Donaldsons Will Be Acquired for $163 Million," *Minneapolis Star Tribune*, 28 August 1987, p. 10A; Janet Moore, "As Projects Loom, Some Ask if City Should Add Retail," *Minneapolis Star Tribune,* 10 September 2000, p. D1.

31. Jeff Strickler and Kevin Duchschere, "Movies Downtown: Going Dark," *Minneapolis Star Tribune*, 14 April 1999, p. B1; Kevin Duchschere, "World Trade Center Watches Retail Vanish," *Minneapolis Star Tribune*, 26 September 1998, p. D1; Melissa Levy, "St. Paul Eyes Wabasha Street as Solution to Downtown Woes," *Minneapolis Star Tribune*, 10 September 2000, p. D1; Virginia Rybin, "Deal Keeps Dayton's in Downtown," *Saint Paul Pioneer Press*, 11 January 2001, p. 1. Absence of department stores in downtowns Kansas City, Detroit, Phoenix, Baltimore, and "more downtowns don't have a major department store than have one," reported by Jim McCartney, "Major Department Store Helps Set St. Paul Apart," *Saint Paul Pioneer Press*, 11 January 2001, p. 1.

32. Vacancy rates reported by Melissa Levy, "Minneapolis Building Boom Drives Downtown Retail Space Demand," *Minneapolis Star Tribune*, 11 January 2000, p. D8. St. Paul retail space removed from market noted by Colliers Towle Real Estate, 2001 *Towle Report*, p. 28.

33. Eight theaters with more than 24,000 seats noted in "National Register of Historic Places Inventory—Nomination Form" for Grand Circus Park Historic District, stamped received 14 January 1983; Closing of RenCen cinema noted by Shawn D. Lewis, "Movies Due to Roll Again in Detroit," *Detroit News*, 2 March 2001, p. D1.

34. 1955 city directories by Minneapolis Directory Company indicate 16 cinemas in downtown Minneapolis and 7 in downtown St. Paul, plus 27 neighborhood theaters in Minneapolis and 16 in St. Paul; Jeff Strickler and Kevin Duchschere, "Movies Downtown: Going Dark," *Minneapolis Star Tribune*, 14 April 1999, p. B1.

35. 1955 inventories from Minneapolis Directory Company, Minneapolis and St. Paul city directories; Year 2000 inventories from "The Movie Guide," *Minneapolis Star Tribune*, 9 January 2000, Entertainment section, indicating that nine cinemas with 19 screens exist in the two cities (after the closing of the six-screen Skyway at the end of March 1999). The total metro-area supply is "now" (3 February 1999) approximately 370 screens, according to Colliers Towle Real Estate, *Towle Report* 1999, p. 29. Author assumes fewer than 40 old screens remain in freestanding towns. The *Towle Report* notes that 144 new screens are planned or under construction in 1999. (This number perhaps includes several screens envisioned in downtown Minneapolis, Block E.) "Gone without a trace" quote from Editorial, "Final Reel in Detroit," *Detroit News*, 23 December 2000. "Only one movie theater" reported by Eric Schmitt, "Most Cities in U.S. Expanded Rapidly over Last Decade," *New York Times*, 7 May 2001, p. 1. Suburban inventory from "Movie Guide," *Detroit News*, 6 May 2001.

36. WCCO television, 5:30 p.m. news broadcast, 1 April 2001.

37. Rick Pearson, "Chicago Now 2nd City to Suburbs," *Chicago Tribune*, 14 February 1999, p.1.

38. Alan Black, *Urban Mass Transportation Planning* (New York: McGraw-Hill, 1995), p. 178.

39. William C. Wheaton, "Office Growth in the 1990s: Downtowns versus Edge Cities," *Urban Land*, April 1996, p. 67; Peter Gordon and Harry W. Richardson, "Where's the Sprawl," *Journal of the American Planning Association* 63, no. 2 (Spring 1997), p. 276.

40. Nearly one in five of Detroit's downtown office buildings is vacant according to a 1993 study by Detroit's Central Business District Association, reported by Michael Rubinkam, "Philadelphia Studying Rash of Building Cave-Ins," *Detroit Free Press*, 29 August 2000, p. 5A. Camilo Jose Vergera reported by James Bennet, "A Tribute To Ruin Irks Detroit," *New York Times*, 10 December 1995, p. 22.

41. Office square footage numbers exclude buildings of less than 20,000 square feet and they exclude government buildings. Detroit's numbers exclude New Center One, which is a couple of miles north of the CBD. Data from *January 2000 Metropolitan Detroit Office Market Summary*, by the Hayman Company, Troy, MI.

42. Downtown Minneapolis and metro-area year-2000 data from Greater Minneapolis Convention and Visitors Association, *Minneapolis Meeting Planner's Guide, 2000-2001;* Interstate 494 strip data from Minnesota Monthly Publications, *The Official Visitor's Guide to Minnesota's Twin Cities,* Spring/Summer 2000, pp. 42-46, and from Greater Minneapolis Convention and Visitors Association, *Minneapolis Meeting Planner's Guide, 2000-2001;* 1979-88 data from Minneapolis City Planning Department, "Hotels and Motels in the Twin Cities 1979-1988"; 1954 data from Minneapolis Convention and Visitor's Bureau, *Convention Facilities in Minneapolis, City of Lakes,* (undated, Minneapolis Public Library Special Collections assumes publication date is 1954).

43. Detroit's 1961 inventory from Socony Mobil Oil Company, Inc., *Mobil Travel Guide: Great Lakes Area* (New York: Simon and Schuster, 1961); Year 2000 information from Metropolitan Detroit Convention and Visitors Bureau website, and Ameritech, Detroit Area 1999-2000 *Yellow Pages,* August 1999. Hotels in New Center and other locations beyond practical walking distance of the CBD are excluded. There are 31,879 hotel rooms in Wayne, Oakland, and Macomb counties according to George Weeks and Karen Talaski, "Detroit Wants 2004 Convention," *Detroit News,* 17 August 2000, p. 6A.

44. Chris Kelley, "Learning From Detroit," *Dallas Morning News,* 6 December 1995, p. 1A.

45. Robert Puentes' comments at seminar "Job Growth Without Housing?" American Planning Association, National Planning Conference, New Orleans, 11 March 2001. (Puentes is a demographic analyst at the Brookings Institution.)

46. U.S. Bureau of the Census, *Census of Housing,* 1970 and 1990; U.S. Census Bureau website, "Census 2000 Housing Units."

47. Chris Kelley, "Learning From Detroit," *Dallas Morning News,* 6 December 1995, p. 1A.

48. Chris Kelley, "Learning From Detroit," *Dallas Morning News,* 6 December 1995, p. 1A; U.S. Census Bureau, Census 2000, PHC-T-5, Table 2.

49. Pennsylvania Horticultural Society, *Urban Vacant Land: Issues and Recommendations* (Philadelphia: Pennsylvania Horticultural Society, September 1995), pp. 53-54.

50. Population loss noted in *Statistical Abstract of the Unites States 1993,* p. 44; Housing unit loss noted in *University of Pennsylvania Law Review,* May 1995, p. 1345; "City officials said Philadelphia now has about 20,000 vacant lots and more than 30,000 vacant houses" according to Michael Rubinkam, "Philadelphia Studying Rash of Building Cave-Ins," *Detroit Free Press,* 29 August 2000, p. 5A. One current estimate puts Philadelphia's number of abandoned houses at more than 50,000, and a 1999 study commissioned by the Pennsylvania Horticultural Society identified 30,900 vacant residential lots in the city according to Mark Alan Hughes, "Dirt into Dollars," *Brookings Review,* Summer 2000, p. 38,.

51. Mark Alan Hughes, "Dirt into Dollars," *Brookings Review,* Summer 2000, pp. 37, 39.

52. *Statistical Abstract of the United States 1993,* p. 43; Peter Marcuse, "Abandonment, Gentrification, and Displacement: the Linkages in New York City," in Neil Smith and Peter Williams, eds., *Gentrification of the City* (Boston: Allen & Unwin, 1986), p. 158.

53. Baltimore rowhouses reported by Jim Haner, "Crumbling Houses, Unpaid Bills," *Baltimore Sun,* 16 May 1999, p. 1. In New Orleans "37,000 housing units are now vacant" according to Kristina Ford, executive director of New Orleans Planning Commission, "Tempering the Zeal for Preservation," *New York Times,* 4 September 1999, p. A13 (editorial page).

54. Pennsylvania Horticultural Society, *Urban Vacant Land* (Philadelphia: Pennsylvania Horticultural Society, September 1995), p. 15.

55. American News Service, "City Willing To Sell Vacant Lots for One Dollar," *Commuter News* (New Jersey/New York), 13 October 1998, p. 7.

56. Baltimore reported by Tracie Rozhon, "Undercrowded Baltimore Aims a Wrecking Ball at Derelict Row Houses," *New York Times,* 13 June 1999, National section, (www); Philadelphia noted in Nathan Gorenstein, "Fiscal Realities of Fight on Blight," *Philadelphia Inquirer,* 24 September 2000, p. B1.

57. Boston noted in Peter Medoff and Holly Sklar, *Streets of Hope: The Fall and Rise of an Urban Neighborhood* (Boston: South End Press, 1994), pp. 4, 81; Chicago noted in AP, "Federal Investigation Reveals a Mountain of Graft in Chicago," *The Boston Sunday Globe,* 14 January 1996, p. 19.

58. Donald N. Rothblatt and Daniel J. Garr, *Suburbia: An International Assessment* (New York: St. Martin's Press, 1986), p. 31.

59. Kenneth T. Jackson, *Crabgrass Frontier: The Suburbanization of the United States* (New York: Oxford University Press 1985), p. 203-09. The exclusion of half of Detroit and one third of Chicago noted by Michael H. Shcill and Susan M. Wachter, "The Spatial Bias of Federal Housing Law and Policy: Concentrated Poverty in Urban America," *University of Pennsylvania Law Review* 143, no. 5 (May 1995): 1311.

60. Kenneth T. Jackson, *Crabgrass Frontier: The Suburbanization of the United States* (New York: Oxford University Press, 1985), p. 209.

61. Kenneth T. Jackson, *Crabgrass Frontier: The Suburbanization of the United States* (New York: Oxford University Press, 1985), p. 293.

62. Mayor Belton's comments at Citizens League Mind-Opener Breakfast Series, St. Paul, 20 December 1996. Mayor Coleman noted by Anthony Lonetree, "St. Paul DFLers Endorse 3 for Council," *Minneapolis Star Tribune,* 13 April 1997, p. B2.

63. Steve Brandt, "Minneapolis Kondirator Agreement May Be Near," *Minneapolis Star Tribune,* 23 March 2000, p. B1; Steve Brandt, "$8.75 Million Settles Suit Over Shredder," *Minneapolis Star Tribune,* 25 March 2000, p. 1.

64. Tort reform reported by John Tierney, "In Tort City, Falling Down Can Pay Off," *New York Times,* 15 April 2000, p. B1.

65. Donald N. Rothblatt and Daniel J. Garr, *Suburbia: An International Assessment* (New York: St. Martin's Press, 1986), p. 11.

66. Myron Orfield, *Metropolis: A Regional Agenda for Community and Stability* (Washington, D.C.: Brookings Institution Press, and Cambridge: Lincoln Institute of Land Policy, 1997), p. 74.

67. Rick Pearson, "Chicago Now 2nd City to Suburbs" *Chicago Tribune,* 14 February 1999, p. 1.

68. Rick Pearson, "Chicago Now 2nd City to Suburbs," *Chicago Tribune,* 14 February 1999, p. 1.

69. Rick Pearson, "Chicago Now 2nd City to Suburbs," *Chicago Tribune,* February 14, 1999, p. 1, James "Pate" Philip's quote on p. 9 section 1 continuation (Philip is DuPage County Republican Chairman and state Senate GOP leader.)

70. Ten most poverty-ridden tracts reported by John Tichy and William J. Craig, *Income and Poverty: What the 1990 Census Says About Minnesota,* (Minneapolis: Center for Urban and Regional Affairs, 1995), p. 71. Combined poverty rates calculated from data in Metropolitan Council, *Community Profiles: Housing, Population and Households,* July 1993.

71. 1970 vs. 1993 & 1995 poverty rates noted in HUD, *The State of the Cities 1997,* June 1997, p. 33. Cities contain half of metro low-income families noted in HUD, *State of the Cities 1998,* June 1998, p. 9. Minneapolis data from Minneapolis Planning Department, *The State of the City 1993,* pp. 25, 28-33.

72. Tripling of extreme poverty noted by Michael H. Schill and Susan M. Wachter, "The Spatial Bias of Federal Housing Law and Policy: Concentrated Poverty in Urban America," *University of Pennsylvania Law Review* 143, no. 5 (May 1995): p. 1287. Minneapolis data from John S. Adams, Barbara J. VanDrasek, and Laura J. Lambert, *The Path of Urban Decline* (Minneapolis: Center for Urban and Regional Affairs, 1995), p. 40.

73. 1960-1990 median family income noted by William Lucy and David Phillips, "Why Some Suburbs Thrive," *Planning*, June 1995, p. 20. Median household income higher in suburbs noted in HUD, *State of the Cities 1998*, June 1998, p. 9.

74. HUD, *State of the Cities 2000*, June 2000, p. 30.

75. HUD, *State of the Cities 1997*, June 1997, p. 39.

76. Two-parent families 1970-1990 noted in HUD, *State of the Cities 1997*, June 1997, p. 39. Exodus continues noted in HUD, *State of the Cities 1998*, June 1998, p. v.

77. Metropolitan Council, *Community Profiles*, July 1993.

78. (byline: *Los Angeles Times*) "Kids Do Better in School When Dad Is Involved, Study Shows," *Minneapolis Star Tribune*, 3 October 1997, p. A19; Oscar Newman, *Creating Defensible Space* (Washington, D.C.: HUD, 1996), p. 28.

79. Poverty rates noted in U.S. Census Bureau, *Poverty in the United States: 1999*, September 2000, p. vii and Table B-3. Child poverty is five times higher in single-parent families according to Isabel V. Sawhill, "Welfare Reform and Reducing Teen Pregnancy," *The Public Interest*, no. 138, Winter 2000, p. 42. Family composition is a more reliable predictor according to Kay S. Hymowitz, "The Children's Defense Fund: Not Part of the Solution," *City Journal*, Summer 2000, p. 35. "Half of children who live in female-headed households remain in poverty," according to editorial, "Rising Tide," *Minneapolis Star Tribune*, 29 September 2000, p. A18.

80. Shine quoted by Chris Kelley, "Learning From Detroit," *The Dallas Morning News*, 6 December 1995, p. 1A.

81. Daniel Patrick Moynihan (1965) quoted by William J. Bennett, *The Index of Leading Cultural Indicators* (New York: Touchstone, 1994), p. 53.

82. Oscar Newman, *Defensible Space: Crime Prevention Through Urban Design* (New York: Macmillan, 1972), p. 193.

83. William J. Bennett, *The Devaluing of America: The Fight for Our Culture and Our Children* (New York: Summit, 1992), pp. 136-37.

84. Lykken is quoted by Daniel Wiener, "'U' Professor Tackles Antisocial Personalites," *Minneapolis Star Tribune*, 21 January 1996, p. 15F. Lykken examines "father absence" as a factor in antisocial behavior in *The Antisocial Personalities* (Hillsdale NJ: Lawrence Erlbaum, 1995), pp. 197-212.

85. Blankenhorn interview on CBS, *48 Hours*, 22 February 1996.

86. Kay S. Hymowitz, "The Teen Mommy Track," *City Journal*, Autumn 1994, p. 29.

Sociologist Elijah Anderson explains that sexually aggressive boys and young men in the inner city are more leery of households with fathers than of households without. Anderson notes that a two-parent family is a "durable team," but a fatherless household is perceived as an "unprotected nest," Elijah Anderson, *Code of the Street: Decency, Violence, and the Moral Life of the Inner City* (New York: W.W. Norton, 1999), pp. 160-62.

In a 1999 essay called "Deconstructing the Essential Father," psychologists Louise B. Silverstein and Carl. F. Auerbach set out to dispel the "neoconservative" notion that fathers are important to positive child development, asserting that "neither a father nor a mother is essential." But, in the end, they contradict themselves, admitting, "it is essential to strengthen the father-child bond . . ." (Louise B. Silverstein and Carl F. Auerbach, "Deconstructing the Essential Father," *American Psychologist*, June 1999, pp. 397, 404.)

87. William J. Bennett, *The Index of Leading Cultural Indicators* (New York: Touchstone, 1994), p. 50.

88. The Urban Institute defines an underclass area as one with a high proportion—one standard deviation above the national mean—of the following social and economic conditions: families headed by a female, unemployed or underemployed males, teenage high-school dropouts, and households receiving public assistance; the Urban Institute's definition refers to a census tract or larger area, according to John S. Adams, Barbara J. VanDrasek, and Laura J. Lambert, *The Path of Urban Decline* (Minneapolis: Center for Urban and Regional Affairs, 1995), p. 20.

89. Harold R. Holzman, Tarl Roger Kudrick, and Kenneth P. Voytek, "Revisiting the Relationship Between Crime and Architectural Design," *Cityscape 2,* no. 1 (February 1996), p. 114.

90. Douglas Massey and Nancy Denton quoted by Anthony Downs, *New Visions for Metropolitan America* (Washington, D.C.: Brookings Institutions Press, and Cambridge: Lincoln Institute of Land Policy, 1994), p. 26. Researchers at the Urban Institute are quoted by Alan J. Abramson, Mitchell S. Tobin, and Matthew R. VanderGoot, "The Changing Geography of Metropolitan Opportunity," *Housing Policy Debate 6,* no. 1 (1995), p. 67.

91. Wilson cited by Leon Dash, *Rosa Lee: A Mother and Her Family in Urban America* (New York: Harper Collins, Basic Books 1996), p. 96.

92. Archie Anderson quoted on "Little Criminals," *Frontline,* WGBH, 1997, broadcast 13 May 1997 on KTCA Twin Cities.

93. Leon Dash, *Rosa Lee: A Mother and Her Family in Urban America* (New York: Harper Collins, Basic Books 1996), pp. 124-26, 255.

94. William J. Bennett, *The Index of Leading Cultural Indicators* (New York: Touchstone, 1994), p. 8.

95. Anthony Downs, *New Visions for Metropolitan America* (Washington, D.C.: Brookings Institution Press, and Cambridge: Lincoln Institute of Land Policy, 1994), pp. 71-73, Figures 5-1, 5-2, 5-3.

96. U.S. Department of Justice, FBI, *Crime in the United States 1999,* 15 October 2000, Table 16.

97. John J. DiIulio Jr., "The Question of Black Crime," *Public Interest,* Fall 1994, p. 3.

98. Leon Dash, *Rosa Lee: A Mother and Her Family in Urban America* (New York: Harper Collins, Basic Books, 1996), pp. 125, 153-57.

99. Leon Dash, *Rosa Lee: A Mother and Her Family in Urban America* (New York: Harper Collins, Basic Books, 1996), pp. 153, 159-60, 167.

100. HUD, *State of the Cities 1999,* p. x; See also *State of the Cities 1998,* p. 9, noting that when families are asked why they flee cities, they cite crime and poor schools.

101. "Report Card on the Schools," *Philadelphia Inquirer,* 24 September 2000; Allie Shah, "State Lists Struggling Schools," *Minneapolis Star Tribune,* 21 December 2000, p. 1; Allie Shah, "Schools Take Aim at the Success Gap," *Minneapolis Star Tribune,* 12 February, 2001, p. 1.

102. Mark Hornbeck and Brian Harmon, "Reform Can Work in Big City Schools," *Detroit News and Free Press,* 21 March 1999, p. 1, see also accompanying articles; Council of the Great City Schools, *Urban Educator* 8, no. 3, (April 1999); Pam Belluck, "Cleveland Voucher Program Is Blocked at Start of School," *New York Times,* 25 August 1999, p. A12; Francis X. Clines, "Philadelphia's Troubled Schools Reopen as a Showdown With Teachers Nears," *New York Times,* 10 September 2000, p. 18; National Digest, "Ex-Governor Named L.A. Schools Chief," *Minneapolis Star Tribune,* 7 June 2000, p. A4.

103. Elijah Anderson, *Code of the Street: Decency, Violence, and the Moral Life of the Inner City* (New York: W.W. Norton, 1999), pp. 316-17.

104. Syl Jones, "A System that Shames Black Kids for Doing Well," *Minneapolis Star Tribune,* 25 October 1996.

105. Elijah Anderson, *Code of the Street: Decency, Violence, and the Moral Life of the Inner City* (New York: W.W. Norton, 1999), p. 317.

106. Mr. Johnson quoted by Betty DeRamus, "Detroit Cop's New Mission: Saving Boys from Bullets," *Detroit News*, 3 August 2000, p. 1C.

107. Genco noted in Juan Gonzales, "Gang Parleys Cool Off School," *New York Daily News*, 4 June 1999, p. 6; Alex Kotlowitz, *There Are No Children Here: The Story of Two Boys Growing Up in the Other America* (New York: Anchor Books, division of Random House, 1992), pp. 221-22.

108. Cofield quoted by Brian Harmon, "Detroit School Security Short," *The Detroit News and Free Press*, 26 September 1999, pp. C1, C6.

109. Baltimore's $5 million plus police force budget noted in Erik Larson, "Where Does the Money Go?" *Time*, 27 October 1997, p. 88; List of districts with "sizable police forces" noted in Brian Harmon, "Detroit School Security Short," *The Detroit News and Free Press*, 26 September 1999, pp. C1, C6; 3,200 officers in New York noted in (no byline) "NYC Police Department to Manage School District Security Force," *Urban Educator*, Vol. 7, No. 6, October 1998a, (published by Council of the Great City Schools, Washington, D.C.)

110. Associated Press, "Mass Tragedy Spares Schools in Cities," *Minneapolis Star Tribune*, 23 May 1999, p A16.

111. Rapes in St. Paul reported by Paul Gustafson, "St. Paul Teen Pleads Guilty to Raping Girl in High School," *Minneapolis Star Tribune*, 22 March 2000, and Heron Marquez Estrada and Duchesne Paul Drew, "3 Students Charged with Rape at St. Paul School," *Minneapolis Star Tribune*, 11 October 2000, p. B1, and Paul Gustafson, "18-Year-Old Pleads Guilty in Rape Case at St. Paul Central," *Minneapolis Star Tribune*, 7 February 2001.

112. Two incidents involving packs of boys reported by Edward Wyatt, "Report Faults School's Inaction in Attacks," *New York Times*, 22 September 2000, p. B6. Seven-year-old Brooklyn victim reported by Elissa Gootman, "2 Held in Abuse of Boy, 7, on Bus," *New York Times*, 7 October 2000, p. B3. Twelve-year-old Staten Island victims reported by Elissa Gootman, "Staten Island: Abuse Alleged on School Bus," *New York Times*, 13 October 2000, p. B6. Incidents in spring 2001 reported by Edward Wyatt, "School failed to Tell Police of Sex Attack," *New York Times*, 26 May 2001, p. B1, see also Edward Wyatt's articles of May 4, May 23, and June 3.

113. Assaults on teachers in Minneapolis reported on *Channel 5 Eyewitness News*, 7 June 2000. Philadelphia schools noted by Kay S. Hymowitz, "Philadelphia's Blackboard Jungle," *City Journal*, Winter 2001, p. 12. In the New York City metropolis, "the teacher salary gap between the city and the closest suburban counties…was more than 40 percent" in 1997-98, according to Sol Stern, "The Vanishing Teacher and Other UFT Fictions," *City Journal*, Spring 2000, p. 26.

114. (byline: *Los Angeles Times*), "Teacher Critically Injured by Stray Shot," *Minneapolis Star Tribune*, 23 February 1996, p. A18; Kevin Duchschere, "No One Injured in Gunplay Near J.J. Hill School," *Minneapolis Star Tribune*, 23 February 1996, p. B7.

115. Bill Dedman, "Teen-Age Girl in Chicago Embarks on New Experience: School," *New York Times*, 17 October, 1997, p. A17. Detroit rapes reported in National News Briefs, "Detroit Calls for Help After Rapes of 8 Girls," *New York Times*, 23 November 1999, p. A21. Queens boy reported in (no byline) "Queens Boy Injured by a Stray Bullet," *New York Times*, 8 October 2000, p. 39. South-central Los Angeles noted by William J. Bennett, *The Devaluing of America: The Fight for Our Culture and Our Children* (New York: Summit, 1992), pp. 131-32.

116. Editorial, "Suburban sprawl," *Minneapolis Star Tribune*, 20 November 1998, p. A30.

117. William J. Bennett, *The Index of Leading Cultural Indicators* (New York: Touchstone, 1994), p. 123; *Statistical Abstract of the United States 1993*, p. 471.

118. U.S. Department of Transportation, *Journey-To-Work Trends*, 1993, p. P-5.

119. David C. Hodge, "My Fair Share: Equity Issues in Urban Transportation" in *Geography of Urban Transportation* 2nd edition, Susan Hanson, ed. (New York: Guilford Press, 1995), pp. 371-72.

120. Jean Hopfensperger, "Expanded Mass Transit System Called Critical to Welfare Changes," *Minneapolis Star Tribune*, 6 February 1997, p. B3.

121. Jean Hopfensperger, "Welfare Workers Surveyed," *Minneapolis Star Tribune*, 29 March 1999, p. B1.

122. Alice Newell got a new job in the city but to get to that job she has to wait at a bus stop across the street from gun-toting drug dealers, according to Robyn Meredith, "Jobs Out of Reach for Detroiters Without Wheels," *New York Times*, 26 May 1998, p. A12.

123. Transit information from Metro Transit pocket schedules, Routes 19 and 14 effective 16 September 2000, and phone calls to Metro Transit information and Maple Grove Transit System, 18 September 2000. (Some of the Near North residents for whom two transfers would be necessary could eliminate one of those transfers by walking a half mile or farther to a bus stop on West Broadway).

124. Jeff Strickler and Kevin Duchschere, "Movies Downtown: Going Dark," *Minneapolis Star Tribune*, 14 April 1999, p. B1.

125. The national average cost of owning/operating an automobile was $6,100 annually in 1999 according to Roy Kienitz, executive director, Surface Transportation Policy Project, Washington, D.C., in a panel discussion called "Fact or Fiction: Transportation Policy" at "Growing Smart in Minnesota" conference, Minneapolis, 11 June 1999, sponsored by 1000 Friends of Minnesota.

126. Unlimited work commutes and other MTA travel for one: $63 per 30 days of unlimited travel in the five boroughs = $766.50/year (MTA "The Map," July 1998); Car rental: New York Rent-A-Car weekly rate from any of a dozen Manhattan locations, for a mid-size car, unlimited mileage, no discounts = $319 for June 1999, per 2 June 1999, phone inquiry.

127. Because of differences in the quality of transit, the national average cost of transportation, per household, was 43 percent higher in Dallas than in New York City in 1998, and 45 percent higher in Houston and in Minneapolis than in New York, according to HUD, *State of the Cities 2000*, June 2000, p. 67.

128. Text of J.C. Watts speech printed in *New York Times*, 5 February 1997, p. A15.

129. County official quoted by Jean Hopfensperger, "Expanded Mass Transit System Called Critical to Welfare Changes," *Minneapolis Star Tribune*, 6 February 1997, p. B3. Family Options program reported by H.J. Cummins, "State Ranks Third in Nation in Child Welfare Measures," *Minneapolis Star Tribune*, 18 May 1999, p. B1.

130. Leonard Inskip, "Loan Program Helps Poor Families Maintain A Car, A Job-and Dignity," *Minneapolis Star Tribune*, 22 August 1995, p. 11A.

131. Amy Waldman, "Citing Oil Price, Schumer Urges Using Reserve," *New York Times*, 4 October 1999, p. B6; Bruce Lambert, "Gas May Reach $2.25 a Gallon, Schumer Warns," *New York Times*, 30 May 2000, p. B6; Richard W. Stevenson and Neela Banerjee, "Clinton Approves Releasing Some Oil from U.S. Reserve," *New York Times*, 23 September 2000, p. 1; Michael Cooper, "Democrats Lash Back at Cheney on Oil," *New York Times*, 23 September 2000, p. A11, noting that Bush favors Alaskan production.

132. Philip Langdon, *A Better Place to Live: Reshaping the American Suburb* (Amherst: University of Massachusetts Press, 1994), p. 78.

133. 24 percent of respondents preferred suburbs at a time when approximately half of Americans lived in suburbs. Pollsters asked "If you could live anywhere in the United States that you wanted to, would you prefer a city, suburban area, small town or farm?" Preferences were as follows: 19% city; 24% suburban area; 34% small town; 22% farm; 1% no opinion, according to Andrew Kohut and Linda DeStefano, "Cities Enjoy New Popularity; New York Tops the List as Best and Worst," *The Gallup Report* no. 289, October 1989, p. 24. If a significant number of the 24 percent who preferred suburbs were city-dwellers or rural folk, then significantly less than half of suburban respondents were satisfied with their living environment. Forty-eight percent of Americans would like to live in a small town according to Sidney N. Brower, *Good Neighborhoods: A Study of In-Town and Suburban Residential Environments* (1996), reviewed by Charles Bohl in *Urban Land*, February 1999, p. 108.

134. Alan Ehrenhalt, *The Lost City: Discovering the Forgotten Virtues of Community in the Chicago of the 1950s* (New York: Harper Collins, Basic Books, 1995), pp. 98-99.

135. Ronald P. Formisano, *Boston Against Busing* (Chapel Hill: University of North Carolina Press, 1991), p. 17.

136. The guidebook is for teachers of grades 7-12, New York State Education Department, *Energy Conservation Education for New York State* (undated), pp. 14-1, 14-6.

137. *CBS Evening News,* 27 July 1999; J. Raloff, "Cars' Ammonia May Sabotage Tailpipe Gains," *Science News,* 26 August 2000.

138. HUD, *State of the Cities 2000,* June 2000, p. 65; EPA, "National Air Quality and Emissions Trends Report," 1998, Table A-15; American Lung Association, "August Medical Release: Long-term Ozone Linked to Reduced Lung Function Growth in Children," 19 August 1999.

139. The air in metro areas nationwide...reported by Tom Meersman, "EPA Study Catalogs Polluted Urban Air," *Minneapolis Star Tribune,* 11 December 1998, p. 1. MPCA concluded that air pollution causes 4 to 11 cancers per 100,000 people reported by Tom Meersman, "Elevated Levels of Toxins in the Air Reported," *Minneapolis Star Tribune,* 16 November 1999, p. B1; Vehicles are responsible for half of pollutants noted by MPCA official Leo Raudys on KTCA television, *Newsnight Minnesota,* 16 November 1999.

140. 766 accidents involving seagoing vessels spilled 5.8 million gallons of oil in the first half of 1989, not including the 11 million gallons spilled by the Exxon *Valdez* in March 1989; illegal but intentional dumping of the byproducts of petroleum handling and processing pose "a greater threat to the health of oceans and marine life than headline-grabbing oil spills," according to Steve Nadis and James J. Mac Kenzie, *Car Trouble* (Boston: Beacon Press, 1993), pp. 16-17 (Greenpeace ad noted on p. 19). Oil slick in Gulf of Mexico noted in (no byline) "Oil Pipeline Breaks, Fouling Gulf of Mexico," *New York Times,* 23 January 2000 (website edition).

141. EPA fine against pipeline operator Koch Industries reported by Matthew L. Wald, "Conglomerate, Accused of Allowing Spills to Cut Costs, Is Fined $30 Million." *New York Times,* 14 January 2000 (website edition). Fatal pipeline leak in Bellingham reported in (no byline) "Operator of Pipeline Faces a Record Fine," *New York Times,* 3 June 2000 (website edition).

142. Gasoline spills from Minnesota refinery noted by Tom Meersman, "Koch Forges Plan to Cut Emissions at Refinery," *Minneapolis Star Tribune,* 15 April 1999, p. A1. Air pollution from refineries noted by Tom Meersman, "Koch Agrees to $4.5 Million in New Fines," *Minneapolis Star Tribune,* 26 July 2000, p. 1). Gasoline tank truck accidents noted in Randy Kennedy, "Tanker Fire On L.I. Linked to Old Defect," *New York Times,* 14 October 2000, p. B1.

143. Tom Meersman, "Most Heed New Rules on Gasoline Storage," *Minneapolis Star Tribune*, 22 December 1998, p. B1.

144. Tri-state A.M. report (no byline), "Smoke From Tire Fire Spreads Across Counties," *Cincinnati Enquirer*, 22 August 1999, p. B2.

145. 270 million tires noted on ABC News, *World News Tonight*, 30 August 2000. Tires in New York noted in Metro Briefing (AP) "Albany: 25 Million Rotting Tires," *New York Times*, 10 October 2000, p. B9; Public health officials in Minnesota reported by Jill Burcum, "Deadly Mosquito Virus is Headed This Way," *Minneapolis Star Tribune*, 25 April 2001, p. B1.

146. Vehicles retired noted in *Statistical Abstract of the United States 1993*, p. 617. Philadelphia noted in National Digest (no byline), "Philadelphia Clears Abandoned Cars," *Minneapolis Star Tribune*, 31 May 2000, p. A4.

147. Developed land area in the Twin Cities metropolis grew from 350 to 740 square miles according to (no byline) "Snapshot of Minnesota's Environment—Earth Day," *Minneapolis Star Tribune*, 16 April, 1995, p. 10A. Three million acres of rural land are lost to development annually according to Dan Glickman, quoted on *ABC World News Tonight*, 25 April 2000.

148. Minneapolis Zoning Code 1991, p. 2245; Apple Valley requirement is one 9' by 20' parking space for every 150 square feet of office space up to 6,000 square feet, plus one space for every 200 square feet over and above 6,000 square feet, according to Apple Valley assistant planner, telephone inquiry 8 January 1996.

149. Donald N. Rothblatt and Daniel J. Garr, *Suburbia: An International Assessment* (New York: St. Martin's Press, 1986), p. 124. Fairfax County noted on CBS Evening News, 13 June 1999. Shortage of recreational land in metro Detroit noted by Edward L. Cardenas, Kevin Lynch, and Joel Kurth, "Metro Suburbs Run Out of Places for Kids to Play," *Detroit News*, 13 April 2000, p. 1.

150. The Minneapolis Chain of Lakes and St. Paul's Como Park each "has drawn more than 2 million annual visitors in recent years," and the new $17 million Lake Minnetonka Regional Park had only 86,000 visitors in 1998; state senator Gen Olson, R-Minnetrista said of Lake Minnetonka Regional Park: "I almost never see anyone going in." St. Croix Bluffs park in Washington County also cited as a little used suburban park, reported by David Peterson, "Foes: Park Is No 'Crown Jewel'" *Minneapolis Star Tribune*, 7 June 1999, p. B1.

151. Andrew C. Revkin, "Studying Human Impact on Nature Where Swamp and Suburbia Meet," *New York Times*, 7 September 1997, p. 20.

152. Chester L. Arnold and C. James Gibbons, "Impervious Surface Coverage: the Emergence of a Key Environmental Indicator," *Journal of the American Planning Association* 62, no. 2 (Spring 1996), p. 243-258. Species extinction due to suburbanization noted in (byline: Associated Press) "Extinction Risk to Species Around the World Grows," *Minneapolis Star Tribune*, 29 September 2000, p. A20.

153. Hydrologic disruption noted in Chester L. Arnold and C. James Gibbons, "Impervious Surface Coverage: The Emergence of a Key Environmental Indicator," *Journal of the American Planning Association* 62, no. 2 (Spring 1996), p. 243-258. Flooding reported in Sierra Club, "Sprawl Hurts Us All" (undated); See also Tom Meersman, "Streams' Water Quality Questioned," *Minneapolis Star Tribune*, 5 April 2000, p. B1.

154. Rain cycles noted on ABC News, *World News Tonight*, broadcast 3 July 1998. Heat island effect noted in Kenneth Chang, "Scientists Watch Cities Make Their Own Weather," *New York Times*, 15 August 2000, p. D1. Deaths attributed in part to heat island effect noted on CBS Evening News, 17 September 2000.

155. Costs of sprawl are discussed in Robert Burchell, et. al., Transportation Research Board of the National Research Council, *TCRP Report 39: The Costs of Sprawl Revisited* (Washington, D.C.: National Academy Press, 1998). $10 billion annual cost of air pollution noted in Michael Bernick and Robert Cervero, *Transit Villages in the 21st Century* (New York: McGraw Hill, 1997), p. 44. Cost of congestion in New Jersey noted in HUD, *State of the Cities 2000*, endnote 29.

156. Fox Butterfield, "2 Economists Give Far Higher Cost of Gun Violence," *New York Times*, 15 September 2000, p. A20.

157. "High Density Planned" development is lower in cost than low and medium densities—planned or unplanned, according to a 1974 analysis by the Real Estate Research Corporation, but that analysis has been criticized for underestimating demand for services in high-density development and for commingling the effects of high density and small dwelling units, according to Robert Burchell, et. al., Transportation Research Board of the National Research Council, *TCRP Report 39: The Costs of Sprawl Revisited* (Washington, D.C.: National Academy Press, 1998).

158. Associated Press, "Rising Energy Imports Increase Trade Deficit to Record $33.3 Billion," *Minneapolis Star Tribune*, 21 March 2001, p. D4.

159. Francis X. Clines and Steven Lee Myers, "Attack on Iraq: The Overview," *New York Times*, 17 December 1998 (website edition).

160. President George H.W. Bush said, "Needless to say, we view this situation with the utmost gravity…We remain committed to take whatever steps are necessary to defend our long-standing vital interests in the Gulf" quoted on "War In The Gulf," *CNN News* videotape.

161. Hussein would have gained control of 40 percent of the world's oil if he had continued beyond Kuwait to capture Saudi Arabia's ports according to Brent Scowcroft interview, "The Gulf War Part I," *Frontline* broadcast 9 January 1996. Atkinson quote from Rick Atkinson, *Crusade: The Untold Story of the Persian Gulf War* (Boston: Houghton Mifflin, 1993), p. 499.

162. Senator Bob Smith, New Hampshire Republican, criticized the Clinton administration's military spending in the Balkans and explained Congressional reluctance to intervene in Kosovo in 1999: "What is the national security interest of the U.S.? I don't think there is any," *Nightline*, ABC News, 27 March 1999. After a March 1999 White House briefing on the situation in the Balkans, Senate Majority Leader Trent Lott said he wasn't sure the security of the United States is at Stake in Kosovo, *CBS Evening News*, 18 March 1999. In May 2000, the Clinton administration agreed with Republicans that no "vital national interest" compels the United States to commit combat troops or peacekeepers to Sierra Leone, where the United Nations struggled to quell a national bloodbath in which tens of thousands of innocents had been killed or maimed, and machetes were used routinely to hack limbs off children, according to Associated Press, "Sierra Leone Rebels, U.N. Together Tour Areas of Fighting," *Minneapolis Star Tribune*, 8 May 2000, p. A4.

163. Chris Christoff, "Bush: More Crude Oil Needed," *Detroit Free Press*, 28 June 2000, p. B1.

164. Bettina H. Aten and Geoffrey J.D. Hewings, "Transportation and Energy," in *Geography of Urban Transportation Second Edition*, Susan Hanson, ed. (New York: Guilford, 1995) Fig. 14.4, p. 346 and Fig. 14.2, p. 345. "Imports have risen to record levels—above 50 percent of consumption," and "dependence of foreign sources will grow," according to Matthew L. Wald, "Oil Imports Are Up, Fretting About It Is Down," *New York Times*, 26 January 1997, p. E3.

165. The World Resources Institute calculated in the mid-1990s that if Americans cut their petroleum consumption by one-eighth, our dependence on Arabian Gulf imports would end, according to Steve Nadis and James MacKenzie 1993, *Car Trouble*, 1993, p. xvi.

166. Nigeria noted in Norimitsu Onishi, "In the Oil-Rich Nigeria Delta, Deep Poverty and Grim Fires," *New York Times,* 11 August 2000 (national edition), p. A1. Angola noted in Rachel L. Swarns, "In Big Offshore Oil Discoveries, Frail Visions of a Redeemed Angola," *New York Times,* 24 September 2000, p. 14, noting also that oil accounts for 90 percent of Angola's export income.

167. *CBS Evening News,* 1 February 1999.

168. Some stipulated that other countries would also have to contribute to a global warming solution, according to (byline *Los Angeles Times*) "Most Back Higher Gas Prices to Fight Global Warming," *Minneapolis Star Tribune,* 21 November 1997, p. A4. Exploitive practices in clothing factories noted on *NBC Dateline,* 20 October 1996.

CHAPTER 4 NOTES

1. Joel Garreau, *Edge City: Life on the New Frontier,* (New York: Doubleday, Anchor Books, 1991), p. 8.

2. Joel Garreau, *Edge City: Life on the New Frontier,* (New York: Doubleday, Anchor Books, 1991), pp. 5, 8.

3. Valerie A. Haines, "Energy and Urban Form: A Human Ecological Critique," *Urban Affairs Quarterly* 21, no. 3 (March 1986), pp. 337, 345-346.

4. Joel Garreau, *Edge City: Life on the New Frontier,* (New York: Doubleday, Anchor Books, 1991), pp. 426-438

5. Urban Land Institute, "Myths and Facts about Transportation and Growth," 1989, Myth/Fact no. 4.

6. Metropolitan Council, *Metro 2015 Vision & Goals,* November 1992, pp. 22-23. In April 2000 the Metropolitan Council approved a package of transportation and transit spending that aims to make transit more attractive to suburbanites. The package includes transit hubs near business sites in developing suburbs, according to David Peterson, "Met Council Aims Money at Transit," *Minneapolis Star Tribune,* 13 April 2000, p. 1. Seattle's transit authority formally adopted a multiple-centers development policy in the mid-1990s, according to Chris Bushell, ed., *Jane's Urban Transport Systems 1998-99* (Alexandria, Virginia: Jane's Information Group, 1998), p. 315. The San Francisco Bay Area Rapid Transit rail system (BART) is a manifestation of a 1956 plan that envisioned a "multicentered" metropolitan form, according to Michael Bernick and Robert Cervero, *Transit Villages in the 21st Century* (New York: McGraw-Hill, 1997), p. 174.

7. "Oil is becoming more rather than less plentiful," according to Sarah A. Emerson, "Resource Plenty: Why Fears of an Oil Crisis are Misinformed," *Harvard International Review* 19, no. 3 (Summer 1997): 13.

8. Joel Garreau, *Edge City: Life on the New Frontier,* (New York: Doubleday, Anchor Books, 1991), p. 127.

9. U.S. Department of Transportation, *Journey-To-Work Trends in the United States and its Major Metropolitan Areas 1960-1990,* 1993, p. 2-8; Robert Cervero, "Jobs-Housing Balance Revisited," *Journal of the American Planning Association* 62, no. 4 (Autumn 1996), p. 494.

10. Gregor W. Piney, "Census Says Commutes Are Lonelier, a Little Longer," *Minneapolis Star Tribune,* 17 June 1994, p 1B.

11. Trip length data reported by Patricia S. Hu and Jennifer R. Young, "Summary of Travel Trends: National Personal Transportation Survey," Draft, Oak Ridge National Laboratory for the U.S. Department of Energy, 8 January 1999, p. 12. "Locational changes" quote is from Energy Information Administration, *Consumption Patterns for Household Vehicles* 1991, p. 25, citing 1983 and 1990 National Personal Transportation Surveys.

12. Patricia S. Hu and Jennifer R. Young, "Summary of Travel Trends: 1995 National Personal Transportation Survey," Draft, Oak Ridge National Laboratory for the U.S Department of Energy, 8 January 1999, pp. 12-13.

13. The U.S. population increased 32 percent from 1969 to 1995, while the number of person trips increased 161 percent. "A typical household traveled . . . more . . . trips" in 1995 than in previous survey years, according to Patricia S. Hu and Jennifer R. Young, "Summary of Travel Trends: 1995 Nationwide Personal Transportation Survey," Draft, Oak Ridge National Laboratory for the U.S. Department of Energy, 8 January 1999, pp. 7, 12.

14. Metropolitan Council, *1990 Travel Behavior Inventory Summary Report*, June 1994, pp. vi, 3, 58, noting 10 million miles added between 1970 and 1990.

15. Patricia S. Hu and Jennifer R. Young, "Summary of Travel Trends: 1995 Nationwide Personal Transportation Survey," Draft, Oak Ridge National Laboratory for the U.S. Department of Energy, 8 January 1999, p. 9; "Sprawl as a Primary Cause of Congestion," Surface Transportation Policy Project (undated); "Transit Use Still Growing, But So Are Traffic Delays," *Planning*, June 2001, p. 29. In Los Angeles, "the population between 1980 and 1997 increased 37 percent to more than 14 million. The number of miles being traveled on roadways increased 75 percent," according to Barbara Whitaker, "Los Angeles Loses Dubious Distinction: Worst Summer Smog Day," *New York Times*, 5 September 1999, p. 25.

16. Jay Hancock, "Cost-Conscious Firms Looking to Urban Core," *Baltimore Sun*, 16 May 1999, p. D1.

17. Metropolitan Council, *1990 Travel Behavior Inventory Summary Report*, June 1994, p. 4.

18. Robert Cervero, "Jobs-Housing Balance Revisited," *Journal of the American Planning Association* 62, no. 4 (Autumn 1996), p. 496.

19. Robert Cervero, "Jobs-Housing Balance Revisited," *Journal of the American Planning Association* 62, no. 4 (Autumn 1996), p. 496-497.

20. Joel Garreau, *Edge City: Life on the New Frontier*, (New York: Doubleday, Anchor Books, 1991), pp. 6-7, 436.

21. San Jose's 1960 population was 204,000 according to *Statistical Abstract of the United States 1976*.

22. Robert Cervero, "Jobs-Housing Balance Revisited," *Journal of the American Planning Association* 62, no. 4 (Autumn 1996), p. 494; U.S. Department of Transportation, *Journey-To-Work Trends in the United States and its Major Metropolitan Areas 1960-1990* (published 1993), p. P-12.

23. Robert Cervero, "Jobs-Housing Balance Revisited," *Journal of the American Planning Association* 62, no. 4 (Autumn 1996), p. 497.

24. Robert Cervero, "Jobs-Housing Balance Revisited," *Journal of the American Planning Association* 62, no. 4 (Autumn 1996), p. 503. Garreau's "edge cities" are not necessarily co-extensive with the cities that Cervero analyzed. Garreau defines an "edge city" generally as a recently developed (after 1960) business concentration of five million or more square feet of office space and a half million or more square feet of retail space (Garreau 1991, pp. 6-7). Garreau's "edge cities," therefore, might include a small portion of a municipality, or they might include multimunicipality regions, such as the "Redwood City-southern San Mateo County area." Cervero analyzed cities traditionally defined—geographic units outlined by municipal boundaries (Cervero, 1996, pp. 494-495). Presumably, most of Garreau's "edge cities" lie within the municipal boundaries of the cities studied by Cervero, so that, with the exception of San Jose, Garreau's "edge cities" are dominant factors affecting the commuting trends analyzed by Cervero. Cervero studied cities in eight of the nine counties surrounding San Francisco and San Pablo bays. Garreau limited his inventory to locales south of the San Pablo/Suisun Bay estuary that leads to the Sacramento River, roughly the southerly two-thirds of the area that Cervero analyzed (Cervero 1996, p. 496; Garreau 1991, p. 305).

25. Robert Cervero, "Jobs-Housing Balance Revisited," *Journal of the American Planning Association* 62, no. 4 (Autumn 1996), p. 495.

26. Robert Cervero, "Jobs-Housing Balance Revisited," *Journal of the American Planning Association* 62, no. 4 (Autumn 1996), p. 503.

27. Robert Cervero, "Jobs-Housing Balance Revisited," *Journal of the American Planning Association* 62, no. 4 (Autumn 1996), p. 503, 505.

28. Robert Cervero, "Jobs-Housing Balance Revisited," *Journal of the American Planning Association* 62, no. 4 (Autumn 1996), p. 498.

29. Robert Cervero, "Jobs-Housing Balance Revisited," *Journal of the American Planning Association* 62, no. 4 (Autumn 1996), p. 503.

30. Joel Garreau, *Edge City: Life on the New Frontier* (New York: Doubleday, Anchor Books, 1991), p. 7.

31. Robert Cervero, "Jobs-Housing Balance Revisited," *Journal of the American Planning Association* 62, no. 4 (Autumn 1996), p. 502-03.

32. State University of New York—Buffalo, Department of Environmental Design and Planning, *An Analysis of Rapid Transit Investments: The Buffalo Experience*, Final Report, July 1981, p. 76 (sponsored by the U.S. Department of Transportation, Urban Mass Transportation Program).

33. Work and work-related trips, combined, make up the plurality of all household trips, and they grew in length by the largest percentages from 1983 to 1990, according to the Energy Information Administration, *Consumption Patterns of Household Vehicles-1991*, pp. 25-26, citing 1983 and 1990 data. "In 1995, commuting had the largest share of vehicle travel for all purposes," according to Patricia S. Hu and Jennifer R. Young, "Summary of Travel Trends: 1995 National Personal Transportation Survey," Draft, Oak Ridge National Laboratory for the U.S Department of Energy, 8 January 1999, p. 13.

34. Robert Cervero, "Jobs-Housing Balance Revisited," *Journal of the American Planning Association* 62, no. 4 (Autumn 1996), p. 498.

35. "The fact that 70 percent of commuting households have two or more workers suggests that living near work is no longer a simple option," according to Alan E. Pisarski, *Commuting In America II: The Second National Report on Commuting Patterns and Trends* (Lansdowne, Virginia: Eno Transportation Foundation, 1996), p. xiii.

36. Robert W. Burchell, et.al., Transportation Research Board of the National Research Council, *TCRP Report 39: The Costs of Sprawl—Revisited* (Washington, D.C.: National Academy Press, 1998), p. 25.

37. *Statistical Abstract of the United States 1999*, p. 421.

38. U.S. Department of Transportation, *1995 Status of the Nation's Surface Transportation System: Conditions and Performance*, p. 36.

39. U.S. Department of Transportation, *1995 Status of the Nation's Surface Transportation System: Condition & Performance*, p. 36; "Thirty percent of workers are in contingent jobs—part-time, temporary, on-call or contract work," according to Molly Ivins, "Labor Day Celebration Should Focus on Those Who Actually Work," *Minneapolis Star Tribune*, 5 September 1999, p. A27.

40. Median years of job tenure for men aged 25 and older decreased by six months, from 6.4 to 5.9 years, between 1983 and 1991. Women's median job tenure was only 4.8 years in 1991, according to "Work Force Stability in the U.S." extracted from "Report on the American Workforce," U.S. Department of Labor, 1995.

41. Robert Cervero, "Jobs-Housing Balance Revisited," *Journal of the American Planning Association* 62, no. 4 (Autumn 1996), p. 496.

42. Only a small percentage of Pleasanton's new jobs were held by Pleasanton residents, according to Robert Cervero, "Jobs-Housing Balance Revisited," *Journal of the American Planning Association* 62, no. 4 (Autumn 1996), pp. 503, 505.

43. Robert Cervero, "Jobs-Housing Balance Revisited," *Journal of the American Planning Association* 62, no. 4 (Autumn 1996), pp. 492-3, 505.

44. Robert Cervero, "Jobs-Housing Balance Revisited," *Journal of the American Planning Association* 62, no. 4 (Autumn 1996), p. 493.

45. Jim Solem interview, *Newsnight Minnesota*, KTCA-TV, 23 October 1996.

46. Robert Cervero, "Jobs-Housing Balance Revisited," *Journal of the American Planning Association* 62, no. 4 (Autumn 1996), pp. 497-98.

47. Robert Cervero, "Jobs-Housing Balance Revisited," *Journal of the American Planning Association* 62, no. 4 (Autumn 1996), p. 492.

48. Robert Cervero, "Jobs-Housing Balance Revisited," *Journal of the American Planning Association* 62, no. 4 (Autumn 1996), p. 505.

49. Joel Garreau, *Edge City: Life on the New Frontier* (New York: Doubleday, Anchor Books, 1991), pp. 108, 221-22, 227-28.

50. U.S. Department of Commerce and HUD, *American Housing Survey for the United States in 1995* (published 1997), Table 9-11, p. 448. Only nine percent of survey respondents cited "reasonable commute time" as an important quality-of-life factor, among 10 factors listed, and the presence of recreational opportunities, and of colleges and universities, were among the nine factors that scored higher, according to James A. Segedy, "How Important Is 'Quality of Life' in Location Decisions and Local Economic Development," *Dilemmas Of Urban Economic Development*, Urban Affairs Annual Reviews, No. 47, 1997, p. 65, Figure 3-3.

51. Alan Black, *Urban Mass Transportation Planning* (New York: McGraw-Hill, 1995), p. 296.

52. Robert Cervero, "Jobs-Housing Balance Revisited," *Journal of the American Planning Association* 62, no. 4 (Autumn 1996), p. 493.

53. U.S. Department of Transportation, *Journey-To-Work Trends in the United States and its Major Metropolitan Areas 1960-1990*, pp. ES-2, 2-3

54. *Statistical Abstract of the United States 1993*, p. 916.

55. Rosemount's population in 1960 = 2,012; 1970 = 4,034; 1980 = 5,083; 1990 = 8,622; 2000 = 14,619 according to Minnesota State Demographics Office, Census 2000, "Excerpts from Population and Race for Cities."

56. Robert Cervero, "Jobs-Housing Balance Revisited," *Journal of the American Planning Association* 62, no. 4 (Autumn 1996), p. 498. Seventy-five percent of San Francisco's employed residents worked the city in 1995, according to San Francisco Planning Department, *San Francisco Economy*, July 1996, p. 5.

57. Robert Cervero, "Jobs-Housing Balance Revisited," *Journal of the American Planning Association* 62, no. 4 (Autumn 1996), p. 498.

58. Robert Cervero, "Jobs-Housing Balance Revisited," *Journal of the American Planning Association* 62, no. 4 (Autumn 1996), p. 497.

59. Robert Cervero, "Jobs-Housing Balance Revisited," *Journal of the American Planning Association* 62, no. 4 (Autumn 1996), p. 495. (The Bay Area had 2,890,000 jobs in 1995 according to San Francisco Planning Department, *San Francisco Economy*, July 1996, p. 3.)

60. Patricia S. Hu and Jennifer R. Young, "Summary of Travel Trends: 1995 National Personal Transportation Survey," Draft, Oak Ridge National Laboratory for the U.S Department of Energy, 8 January 1999, p. 44.

61. Longtime Northfield resident Richard Peterson described Northfield commuters to Burnsville in a conversation on 22 April 1997. Keith Rosdahl, project manager for Parsons Electric, commutes about 40 minutes from Elk River, a town 30 miles northwest of downtown Minneapolis, to his office in Fridley, nine miles north of downtown Minneapolis, and north of Interstate 694. Rosdahl says that because traffic congestion increases substantially inside the beltway, the trip into downtown would take at least twenty minutes longer (conversation 17 June 1999).

62. Lawley Publications, *The Urban Transportation Monitor,* 3 February 1995, pp. 2, 16.

63. Metropolitan Council, *1990 Travel Behavior Inventory Summary Report,* June 1994, p. 32.

64. U.S. Department of Transportation, *Journey-To-Work Trends in the United States and its Major Metropolitan Areas 1960-1990* (published 1993), pp. 2-6.

65. Metropolitan Council, *Travel Behavior Inventory Summary Report,* June 1994, p. 33.

66. Data from Patricia S. Hu and Jennifer R. Young, "Summary of Travel Trends: 1995 National Personal Transportation Survey," Draft, Oak Ridge National Laboratory for the U.S Department of Energy, 8 January 1999, increased household VMT noted on p. 7, increased daily VMT per driver noted on p. 9, decreased vehicle occupancy noted on p. 27.

67. American Public Transit Association, *1999 Transit Fact Book,* p. 20.

68. Steve Nadis and James J. MacKenzie for the World Resources Institute, *Car Trouble,* 1993, p. 34.

69. Charles River Associates, Transportation Research Board of the National Research Council, *TCRP Report 27: Building Transit Ridership, An Exploration of Transit's Market Share and the Public Policies That Influence It* (Washington, D.C.: National Academy Press, 1997). p. 18.

70. American Public Transit Association, *1993 Transit Fact Book, p. 64; Statistical Abstract of the United States 1993,* pp. 8, 393.

71. U.S. Department of Transportation, *Journey-To-Work Trends in the United States and its Major Metropolitan Areas 1960-1990* (November 1993), p. 2-2. "Since the U.S. Congress passed the Urban Mass Transportation Act in 1964, mass transit as a percentage of total passenger miles traveled has decreased from 5.2 percent in 1965 to 2.3 percent in 1994. Mass transit produces only 1 percent of the total surface transportation passenger miles," according to Floyd Lapp, "Auto vs. Transit," *Journal of the American Planning Association* 65, no. 4 (Autumn 1999), p. 444.

72. Steve Nadis and James J. MacKenzie for the World Resources Institute, *Car Trouble* (1993), p. 35; Charles River Associates, Transportation Research Board of the National Research Council, *TCRP Report 27: Building Transit Ridership, An Exploration of Transit's Market Share and the Public Policies That Influence It* (Washington, D.C.: National Academy Press, 1997), p. 19, Table 13; Urban Land Institute, "Myths and Facts about Transportation and Growth," 1989, Myth/Fact no. 5.

73. Charles River Associates, Transportation Research Board of the National Research Council, *TCRP Report 27: Building Transit Ridership, An Exploration of Transit's Market Share and the Public Policies That Influence It* (Washington, D.C.: National Academy Press, 1997), p. 19, Table 13; Urban Land Institute, "Myths and Facts about Transportation and Growth," 1989, Myth/Fact no. 5

74. Parsons Brinckerhoff Quade & Douglas, Inc., Transportation Research Board of the National Research Council, *TCRP Report 16: Transit and Urban Form,* Volume 1 (Washington, D.C.: National Academy Press, 1996), p. 5.

75. Regional Plan Association, "Where Transit Works," *Regional Plan News,* August 1976, p. 2.

76. Parsons Brinckerhoff Quade & Douglas, Inc., Transportation Research Board of the National Research Council, *TCRP Report 16: Transit and Urban Form,* Volume 1 (Washington, D.C.: National Academy Press, 1996), p. 5.

77. Michael Bernick and Robert Cervero, *Transit Villages in the 21st Century* (New York: McGraw-Hill, 1997), p. 123.

78. Portland Metro, *2040 Framework Plan,* Fall 1996/Winter 1997, p. 2; Alan Black, *Urban Mass Transportation Planning* (New York: McGraw-Hill, 1995), p. 358.

79. Downtown Los Angeles is home to heavy transit traffic because of the many bus transfers there, according to Anastasia Loukaitou-Sideris, "Hot Spots of Bus Stop Crime," *Journal of the American Planning Association*, 65, no.4 (Autumn 1999), p. 401. Personal Rapid Transit (PRT) would, in concept, provide direct service from all points to all others, but research and development funded by the federal government as long ago as 1963 has thus far produced no results of any substance. Transit planner Alan Black considers prospects for a true PRT system to be unpromising at best; Alan Black, *Urban Mass Transportation Planning* (New York: McGraw-Hill, 1995), pp. 154-158.

80. Vehicle ownership rates among all metro areas ranged from 89 to 95 percent in 1995, according to Patricia S. Hu and Jennifer R. Young, "Summary of Travel Trends: 1995 Nationwide Personal Transportation Survey," Draft, Oak Ridge National Laboratory for the U.S. Department of Energy, 8 January 1999, p. 32.

81. Alan Black, *Urban Mass Transportation Planning* (New York: McGraw-Hill, 1995), pp. 187, 294; Charles River Associates, Transportation Research Board of the National Research Council, *TCRP Report 27: Building Transit Ridership, An Exploration of Transit's Market Share and the Public Policies That Influence It* (Washington, D.C.: National Academy Press, 1997), pp. 6, 36.

82. Many transit systems feed suburban rail stations or transit centers with feeder buses so that some passengers must transfer prior to reaching the CBD, but in those situations, a second transfer is required to reach most non-CBD destinations.

83. Appletree Square and Carlson Center.

84. Metropolitan Council, *Regional Blueprint*, adopted 1996, p. 51.

85. Commentary by Natalio Diaz, *Minneapolis Star Tribune*, 21 July1993.

86. City of Minneapolis, *Transit Planning and Funding Strategy Interim Report*, 31 October 1996, pp. 21-22.

87. Chris Bushell, ed., *Jane's Urban Transport Systems 15th Edition*, 1996-97 (Alexandria, Virginia: Jane's Information Group, 1996), p. 333.

88. Mark Brunswick, "Bus Links Ex-Welfare Recipients to Jobs," *Minneapolis Star Tribune*, 27 January 2000, p. B1.

89. Alan Black, *Urban Mass Transportation Planning* (New York: McGraw-Hill, 1995), pp. 88-89.

90. Anthony Downs, *New Visions for Metropolitan America* (Washington, D.C.: The Brookings Institution, and Cambridge, Massachusetts: Lincoln Institute of Land Policy, 1994), p. 160.

91. City of Minneapolis, *Transit Planning and Funding Strategy Interim Report*, 31 October 1996, p. 6. Transit service decentralization is described also by Minneapolis Planning Department, *State of the City 1995*, p. 90.

92. Charles River Associates, Transportation Research Board of the National Research Council, *TCRP Report 27: Building Transit Ridership, An Exploration of Transit's Market Share and the Public Policies That Influence It* (Washington, D.C.: National Academy Press, 1997), p. 19, Table 13, and Urban Land Institute, "Myths and Facts about Transportation and Growth" (1989), Fact #6.

93. Chris Bushell, ed., *Jane's Urban Transport Systems 17th Edition*, 1998-99 (Alexandria, VA: Jane's Information Group, 1998) p. 265.

94. Regional Plan Association, "Where Transit Works," *Regional Plan News*, August 1976, p. 7.

95. The manager of Metro Commuter Services says that lower bus ridership in St. Paul reflects greater service cuts in St. Paul than in Minneapolis when the transit budget was reduced two years ago, according to Laurie Blake, "Report Offers Remedies for St. Paul Parking Woes," *Minneapolis Star Tribune*, 16 December 1997, p. B2.

96. *Statistical Abstract of the United States 1993*, p. 735.

97. H.V. Savitch, *Post-Industrial Cities: Politics and Planning in New York, Paris, and London* (Princeton: Princeton University Press, 1988), pp. 125, 149.

98. H.V. Savitch, *Post-Industrial Cities: Politics and Planning in New York, Paris, and London* (Princeton: Princeton University Press 1988), p. 149; more than 100 million square feet surmised from Savitch's statement that the workforce far exceeded one million in 1982 (p. 313).

99. Joel Garreau, *Edge City: Life on the New Frontier* (New York: Doubleday, Anchor Books, 1991), p. 116.

100. Average city has 25 percent of its land vacant according to U.S. House of Representatives, 96th Congress 2nd Session, Committee on Banking, Finance, and Urban Affairs, Subcommittee on the City, *Compact Cities*, 1980, p. 10. Portland noted by Marcia D. Lowe for Worldwatch Institute, Worldwatch Paper 105, *Shaping Cities: the Environmental and Human Dimensions*, October 1991, p. 26.

101. At the beginning of 2001, Twin Cities metro area office inventory is 61.8 million square feet (rentable area), excluding government and medical office space; retail inventory is 46 million square feet in multi-tenant buildings more than 30,000 square feet (over 20,000 square feet in downtowns), plus an estimated six million in single tenant buildings like Wal-Mart, according to Colliers Towle Real Estate, *2001 Towle Report*. It is assumed here that medical office space and small freestanding stores add roughly 11.2 million square feet for a total of 125 million. If small freestanding stores bring the total above 125 million, that does not invalidate the author's conclusions, because Minneapolis has about 25 linear miles of secondary commercial streets (such as Lowry and Chicago) which are disregarded in this analysis; these streets have the capacity to absorb several million square feet of small stores.

102. Minneapolis Planning Department, *State of the City 2000* (January 2001), p. 42.

103. *The American Experience*, "New York Underground" broadcast on KTCA TV 17 February 1997.

104. Alan Black, *Urban Mass Transportation Planning* (New York: McGraw-Hill, 1995), p. 248.

CHAPTER 5 NOTES

1. Regional Plan Association, "Where Transit Works," *Regional Plan News*, August 1976, p. 7.

2. Stacy C. Davis, Oak Ridge National Laboratory, *Transportation Energy Data Book: Edition 17*, September 1997, Table 4.3.

3. Metropolitan Council, *1990 Travel Behavior Inventory Summary Report*, June 1994, pp. 30, 33, 44, 45.

4. Myron Orfield, *Metropolitics: A Regional Agenda for Community and Stability* (Washington, D.C.: Brookings Institution Press, and Cambridge, Massachusetts: Lincoln Institute of Land Policy, 1997), p. 84.

5. Metropolitan Council, *1990 Travel Behavior Inventory Summary Report*, June 1994, p. 29.

6. Suburbanites' rates of transit travel noted in Anthony Downs, *New Visions for Metropolitan America* (Washington, D.C.: Brookings Institution Press, and Cambridge, Massachusetts: Lincoln Institute of Land Policy, 1994), pp. 156, 160.

7. 1990 Census SSTF20.

8. Metropolitan Council, *1990 Travel Behavior Inventory Summary Report*, June 1994, pp. 16, 44; Metropolitan Council, Community Profiles: Housing, Population and Households, July 1993. The central cities' share of seven-county metro area population has shrunk to 25 percent in 2000, according to the U.S. Census Bureau.

9. San Francisco had 526,000 jobs and 382,000 employed residents for a jobs-to-employed residents ratio of 1.38 to 1 according to the San Francisco Planning Department, *San Francisco Economy*, July 1996, p. 5. Minneapolis had 290,400 jobs and 199,500 employed residents in 1995, for a ratio of 1.46 to 1 according to the Minneapolis Planning Department, *State of the City 1996*, pp. 32-33.

10. San Francisco Planning Department, *San Francisco Economy*, July 1996, p. 5.

11. Toronto Planning and Development Department, "Bay Street Corridor Residential Intensification Zone" May 1988, p. 1.

12. MCTO pocket schedules, effective March 22, 1997, for routes 6, 12, and 28. Route 17 buses, which travel a portion of Hennepin Avenue and turn off at 24th Street, are not included in the 171 buses/day count.

13. Regional Plan Association, "Where Transit Works," *Regional Plan News*, August 1976, p. 7.

14. Alan Black, *Urban Mass Transportation Planning* (New York: McGraw-Hill, 1995), p. 212.

15. Parsons Brinckerhoff Quade & Douglas, Inc., Transportation Research Board of the National Research Council, *TCRP Report 16: Transit and Urban Form*, Volume 1, 1996, p. 15 of Part 1.

16. Minneapolis routes 4 and 18 to the north of downtown; San Francisco routes K, M, and L to the southwest quadrant of the city.

17. 1990 Census, SSTF20 for San Francisco, STF3A for Minneapolis.

18. Healthy City Office, City of Toronto, "Evaluating the Role of the Automobile," September 1991, p. 102.

19. Regional Plan Association, "Where Transit Works," *Regional Plan News*, August 1976, p. 6.

20. Paul Knox, *Urbanization: An Introduction to Urban Geography* (Englewood Cliffs, New Jersey: Simon and Schuster, Prentice-Hall, 1994), p. 128.

21. Anthony Downs, *New Visions for Metropolitan America* (Washington, D.C.: Brookings Institution Press, and Cambridge, Massachusetts: Lincoln Institute of Land Policy, 1994), p. 143; *Statistical Abstract of the United States 1993*, p. 42.

22. Larry R. Ford, *Cities and Buildings: Skyscrapers, Skid Rows, and Suburbs* (Baltimore: Johns Hopkins Press, 1994), pp. 217-218.

23. Metropolitan Council, "Regional Population, Household and Residential Construction Trends," April 1998, and "Residential Building Permits Issued in the Twin Cities Metropolitan Area," 1995 through 1999.

24. Minneapolis had 77,650 "Single Family Detached Houses" in October 1998, 980 more than the 76,670 in November 1993, according to Minneapolis Planning Department, *State of the City 1993*, p. 40, and *State of the City 1998*, pp. 8-9; Minneapolis and St. Paul issued permits for 6,410 detached houses from the beginning of 1970 through the end of 1999 according to Metropolitan Council, "Regional Population, Household and Residential Construction Trends," April 1998, and "Residential Building Permits Issued in the Twin Cities Metropolitan Area," 1995 through 1999.

25. Allen Short, "Minneapolis Panel Backs Disputed Housing Project," *Minneapolis Star Tribune*, 14 December 1993, p. B7.

26. McDonald also touted the semi-suburban density of 11 to 14 residential units per acre as an ideal for Minneapolis, "Growing Smart in Minnesota" conference, Minneapolis, 11 June 1999.

27. City of Minneapolis, *Consolidated Plan for Housing and Community Development*, Fiscal Year 99, pp. 38, 41.

28. Richard Moe and Carter Wilkie, *Changing Places: Rebuilding Community in the Age of Sprawl* (New York: Henry Holt and Company, 1997), p. 127.

29. Greater Minneapolis Metropolitan Housing Corporation (GMMHC) undated promotional brochure.

30. Steve Brandt, "At Home Along Hiawatha," *Minneapolis Star Tribune*, 14 August 1995, p. B1.

31. Diane Corcelli and Victor Dubina, "Cleveland's Rejuvenated Neighborhoods," *Urban Land*, April 1996, p. 51.

32. Detroit programs noted by Roberta Brandes Gratz, "Notown," *Preservation*, May/June 1999, p. 114. Oakland information from observations on 12 December 1999, and telephone discussion with Nancy Nadel, 3rd District Council Representative, on 15 December 1999, and undated flier by East Bay Asian Local Development Corporation, entitled "Bayport Village: Attractive and Affordable Single-Family Homes," received January 10, 2000, noting that there are "71 single-family homes" in Bayport Village. Watts, Los Angeles, noted by William H. Hudnut III, *Cities on the Rebound: A Vision for Urban America* (Washington, D.C.: Urban Land Institute, 1998), p. 80. Additional examples of government-subsidized detached-house developments in American cities are described by Diane R. Suchman, Developing *Infill Housing in Inner-City Neighborhoods: Opportunities and Strategies* (Washington, D.C.: Urban Land Institute, 1997).

33. Cleveland's Mount Pleasant Now Development Corporation noted by William H. Hudnut III, *Cities on the Rebound: A Vision for Urban America* (Washington, D.C.: Urban Land Institute, 1998), p. 81. Chicago HomeStart program reported by Jeanette Almada, "Building High Hopes 'New Homes For Chicago' Jump-Starts Neighborhood Residential Development," *Chicago Tribune*, November 21, 1999, Real Estate section, p. 1.

34. GMMHC's 100 units per year noted in editorial, "City Housing," *Minneapolis Star Tribune*, 23 February 1995, p. 16A. In "the inner city" noted in GMMHC Mission Statement dated 31 December 1996.

35. Rick Pearson, "Chicago Now 2nd City to Suburbs," *Chicago Tribune*, 14 February 1999, p. 1. Chicago's population increased by 112,290 residents (4 percent) between 1990 and 2000, according to the U.S. Census Bureau.

36. The Metropolitan Council adopted "a policy emphasis on increasing the housing density in the newly urbanizing areas . . ."according to Metropolitan Council, *Regional Blueprint*, 24 January 1997, p. 3. A 25-year growth of 18,429 households in Minneapolis and St. Paul, which is 5.8 percent of the 319,973 households forecast for the whole metro area, indicated in Metropolitan Council's "Preliminary Forecasts of Population, Households and Employment-Regional Growth Strategy," March 1997.

37. New York City Planning Department, *Demographic Profiles*, August 1992, p. 10; New York City Planning Department, DCP 1990 #6; San Francisco Planning Department August 1995, *Housing Information Series*, p. 12.

38. U.S. Census Bureau, Census 2000; 46.7 square miles land area noted in *Statistical Abstract of the United States 1999*, Table 48.

39. The city intends to maintain a small portion of Hunter's Point Navy ship repair yard in industrial use, according to San Francisco Planning Department, "Hunters Point Shipyard," February 1996, pp. II.X.3, 5, 7, 17. San Francisco's waning industrial sector noted by San Francisco Planning Department, "San Francisco Economy," July 1996, p. 3.

40. City and County of San Francisco 1990 Census, 1980 to 1990 Comparison of Ethnic Breakdown and Housing Units—by Census Tract.

41. San Francisco Planning Department, *San Francisco's Neighborhoods: Evolving Economic Activities*, June 1998, pp. 76-77.

42. Alan Black, *Urban Mass Transportation Planning* (New York: McGraw-Hill, 1995), p. 180.

43. Annie Nakao, "S.F.: Diverse City," *San Francisco Examiner,* 22 November 1998, p. 1.

44. San Francisco Planning Department, *Citywide Travel Behavior Survey 1993,* p. 3; Urban Land Institute, *Myths and Facts about Transportation and Growth,* 1989, Fact 6.

45. San Francisco Planning Department, *1997 Housing Inventory,* June 1998, p. 26

46. Annie Nakao, "S.F.: Diverse City," *San Francisco Examiner,* 22 November 1998, p. 1.

47. U.S. Census Bureau, Census 2000; Land areas from *Statistical Abstract of the United States 1999,* Table 48.

48. U.S. Department of Justice, *Crime in the United States 1999,* October 2000, Table 8.

49. San Francisco Planning Department, *Neighborhood Commercial—Master Plan Amendments,* undated, p. 25.

50. Minneapolis and St. Paul's year 2000 combined density is about 2,778 housing units per square mile; 256,000 new households plus vacancies = approximately 260,000 units, plus 300,000 in 2000 = 560,000/108 square miles = 5,185 units/square mile.

51. Parsons Brinckerhoff Quade & Douglas, Inc., Transportation Research Board of the National Research Council, *TCRP Report 16: Transit and Urban Form,* Volume 1 (Washington, D.C.: National Academy Press, 1996), p. 15 of Part 1.

52. Minneapolis Community Development Agency official says it costs an average of $8,000 to demolish a house, according to David Chanen, "Activist Could Be Setting Hawthorne Neighborhood Houses on Fire, Police Say," *Minneapolis Star Tribune,* 5 February 1998, p. B3. The cost per unit for duplexes is assumed to be slightly more than half of the cost per single house, and the cost per unit for small frame apartment buildings is assumed to be slightly less than half the cost per single house.

53. The average cost of a residential lot is $73,000 in central Scott County, $84,500 in northern Washington County and $104,000 in northwestern Hennepin County, according to David Peterson, "Builders Say Rules Lift Cost of Land," *Minneapolis Star Tribune,* 23 February 2000, p. 1.

54. Minneapolis Planning Department, *State of the City 1999,* p. 8.

55. Barbara W. Moore and Gail Weesner, *Beacon Hill: A Living Portrait* (Boston: Century Hill Press, 1992), pp. 16, 18-19.

56. Christopher Gray, "Park Avenue Without Doorman," *New York Times,* 8 May 1994, p. 8.

57. Parsons Brinckerhoff Quade & Douglas, Inc., Transportation Research Board of the National Research Council, *TCRP Report 16: Transit and Urban Form* Volume 2 (Washington, D.C.: National Academy Press, 1996), p. 99 of Part 4.

58. Peter Leyden. "'60s Walk-Ups are in Limbo in '90s Market," *Minneapolis Star Tribune,* 24 January 1994, p. B1.

59. 1990 Census data indicates a poverty rate of 18.5 percent in Minneapolis and 16.7 percent in St. Paul; the average for both cities was 17.7 percent, according to Metropolitan Council, Community Profiles, 1993.

60. Developed suburbs would grow by 8 percent; target density for developing suburbs is three units per acre (including local streets and parks) according to the *Metropolitan Council's Regional Blueprint,* adopted 19 December 1996, p. 69.

61. Michael Southworth, "Walkable Suburbs? An Evaluation of Neotraditional Suburbs at the Urban Edge," *Journal of the American Planning Association 63,* no. 1 (Winter 1997), p. 44.

62. Michael Southworth, "Walkable Suburbs? An Evaluation of Neotraditional Suburbs at the Urban Edge," *Journal of the American Planning Association 63,* no. 1 (Winter 1997), p. 43.

63. Andres Duany and Elizabeth Plater-Zyberk—Kentlands' planners—and Jeff Speck wrote a book called *Suburban Nation* (2000), which is in effect two books. The first book spells out the evils of automobile dependence. The second book explains how to create a neotraditional suburb. By combining the two books under a single title, the authors imply that neotraditional suburbs rectify the evils of automobile dependence. The authors provide no data to demonstrate that Kentlands or any other neotraditional suburb reduces automobile dependence to any meaningful degree. The closest they come is to proclaim that commercial and institutional land uses in a neotraditional suburb require only 60 percent of the number of parking spaces that are required in a typical post-war suburb (p. 208), and this assertion appears to be speculation because it is unsupported by evidence or data. Even if the assertion is true, 60 percent of a huge number of parking spaces is still a lot of parking spaces. The authors cite the construction of 81 new houses in Cleveland as a good thing, for which they are proud to take some credit (p. 185).

64. Dan Wascoe Jr., "Affordable Housing Goals Require More Money, Group Says" *Minneapolis Star Tribune*, 8 January 1996, p. B1.

65. Minnesota Citizens League, Mind Opener series, St. Paul, 28 March 1995.

66. North Metro Mayors Association, *Housing Challenge 2020*, p. 1.

67. Article 3, Section 2 of the Metropolitan Livable Communities Act authorizes state income tax credits for buyers of houses in distressed neighborhoods.

68. George Galster and Jennifer Daniell, "Housing," in *Reality and Research: Social Science and U.S. Urban Policy Since 1960*, George Galster, ed. (Washington, D.C.: The Urban Institute Press, 1996) pp. 90-91.

69. "Suburban Report," *Chicago Tribune*, 19 April 1998, p. 9L (Real Estate section).

70. Mike Kaszuba, "In Shorewood, There's No Doubt Who's Boss," *Minneapolis Star Tribune*, 6 June 1998, p. B1.

71. Minnesota Chapter, American Planning Association, "Showdown in the Suburbs," *Planning Minnesota*, September 1998, p. 7.

72. Linda Mack, "Sprawl A Hot Topic As Suburbs Boom," *Minneapolis Star Tribune*, 8 August 1999, p. A17.

73. Fifty-four percent of respondents oppose townhouses; 78 percent oppose apartment buildings in their neighborhoods, 10 percent are "not sure," and only 12 percent "support" them, according to the National Association of Home Builders, *Smart Growth*, 1999, p. 16. Effective opposition to multi-unit development by detached-house residents noted by Robert Cervero, "Jobs-Housing Balance Revisited," *Journal of the American Planning Association* 62, no. 4 (Autumn 1996), p. 507. See also Mike Kaszuba, "Affordable Housing Conflict Resurfaces," *Minneapolis Star Tribune*, 16 March 1997, pp. B1, B7.

74. Dennis Cassano, "It's Not Just Country Anymore," *Minneapolis Star Tribune*, 4 March 1996, p. A1.

75. Dennis Cassano, "St. Croix County Survey Aids Planning," *Minneapolis Star Tribune*, 15 July 1996, p. B4.

76. James Howard Kunstler, *Home From Nowhere* (New York: Simon & Schuster, 1996), Calthorpe theory on pp. 16-17; "subnormal" developers and home buyers noted on p. 97.

77. James Howard Kunstler, *The Geography of Nowhere* (New York: Simon & Schuster, 1993), p. 14.

78. Philip Langdon, *A Better Place to Live: Reshaping the American Suburb* (Amherst: University of Massachusetts Press, 1994), p. 49.

79. Alan Ehrenhalt, *Lost City: Discovering the Forgotten Virtues of Community in the Chicago of the 1950s* (New York: Basic Books, 1995), p. 212.

80. Alan Ehrenhalt, *Lost City: Discovering the Forgotten Virtues of Community in the Chicago of the 1950s* (New York: Basic Books, 1995) p. 234.

81. Iver Peterson, "After Decades of Disregard, the Suburbs Win Converts," *New York Times*, December 5, 1999, New York Region section (www).

82. Curt Brown, "Displaced by Storm, Woodbury Neighbors Still Have Community," *Minneapolis Star Tribune*, 7 June, 1998, p. A22.

83. David P. Varady and Jeffrey A. Raffel, *Selling Cities: Attracting Homebuyers Through Schools and Housing Programs* (Albany: State University of New York Press, 1995), pp. 6, 62.

84. Metropolitan Council transit spending noted in David Peterson, "Met Council Aims Money at Transit," *Minneapolis Star Tribune*, April 13, 2000, p. 1.

85. Diane R. Suchman, *Developing Infill Housing in Inner-City Neighborhoods: Opportunities and Strategies* (Washington, D.C.: Urban Land Institute, 1997), p. 2; Michael Bernick and Robert Cervero, *Transit Villages in the 21st Century* (New York: McGraw-Hill, 1997), pp. 139, 147.

86. Peter O. Muller, "Transportation and Urban Form: Stages in the Spatial Evolution of the American Metropolis," in *The Geography of Urban Transportation*, 2nd Edition, Susan Hanson, ed. (New York: Guilford, 1995) p. 38.

87. Editorial, "Affordable Housing: Our Conclusion," *Southwest Journal*, 29 November-2 December 1999, p. 6.

88. San Francisco Planning Department, *San Francisco's Neighborhoods: Evolving Economic Activities*, June 1998; San Francisco Planning Department, "1997 Housing Inventory," June 1998; Christina Guinot, *Relocating to the San Francisco Bay Area and Silicon Valley* (Rocklin, California: Prima Publishing, 1999)

89. On March 22, 2000, the Metropolitan Council agreed to expand the land supply, acting under pressure by housing developers who warned that a land shortage is driving housing prices up, reported by David Peterson, "Outer Suburbs Will Get More Room to Grow," *Minneapolis Star Tribune*, 23 March 2000, p. B1.

CHAPTER 6 NOTES

1. David C. Hodge, "My Fair Share: Equity Issues in Urban Transportation," in *The Geography of Urban Transportation*, 2nd Edition, Susan Hanson, ed. (New York: The Guilford Press, 1995), p. 374.

2. Jessica Gross, "Over Land and Water," *Minnesota Real Estate Journal*, 16 October 1995, p. 1 (assistant city administrator Barry Stock is quoted on p. 8).

3. Editorial, "Opportunity Spans the River," *Minnesota Real Estate Journal*, 16 October 1995, p. 3

4. Jessica Gross, "Over Land and Water," *Minnesota Real Estate Journal*, 16 October 1995, p. 1, (quote on p. 8).

5. Coralie Carlson, "Census Figures Indicate Continued Population Drop in Minneapolis, St. Paul," *Minneapolis Star Tribune*, 30 June 1999, p. B3; Rand McNally's *Minneapolis St. Paul City Map*, 1997, shows local streets in the eastern third of the municipality, near Interstate 35W, and mostly undeveloped land in the western two-thirds. At mid-1999, new streets have materialized in the western portion, which is near the new Bloomington Ferry Bridge.

6. Kathleen Ingley, "A Taking of Public Land?" *The Arizona Republic*, 18 January 1999, p. 1.

7. Kenneth T. Jackson, ed., *The Encyclopedia of New York City* (New Haven: Yale University Press, 1995), pp. 156-157.

8. Oakland Daily Evening Tribune, 12 December 1876, quoted in Kenneth T. Jackson, *Crabgrass Frontier: The Suburbanization of the United States* (New York: Oxford University Press, 1985), p. 40.

9. Kenneth Jackson, *Crabgrass Frontier: The Suburbanization of the United States* (New York: Oxford University Press, 1985), p. 120; Shaker Heights described by Jane Wood, "Shaker Heights, Then and Now," *Urban Land*, April 1996, pp. 26-28.

10. Editorial, "Opportunity Spans the River," *Minnesota Real Estate Journal*, 16 October 1995, p. 3.

11. Stuart F. Chapin and Edward J. Kaiser, *Urban Land Use Planning*, 3rd Edition (Chicago: University of Illinois Press, 1979), p. 59.

12. Peter O. Muller, "Transportation and Urban Form" in *The Geography of Urban Transportation*, 2nd Edition, Susan Hanson, ed. (New York: Guilford, 1995). p. 43.

13. Janet Moore, "Richfield May Drive Changes on I-494 Strip," *Minneapolis Star Tribune*, 10 June 1998, p. 1.

14. David Gurin's comments at Minnesota Citizens League forum, St. Paul, May 1, 1996.

15. U.S Department of Transportation, Federal Highway Administration, *Highway Statistics 1995*, Table HM-47, p. V-36.

16. Jessica Gross, "Over Land and Water," *Minnesota Real Estate Journal*, 16 October 1995, pp. 1,8, paraphrasing MNDOT spokesman Kent Barnard.

17. Jessica Gross, "Over Land and Water," *Minnesota Real Estate Journal*, 16 October 1995, p. 1.

18. Freeway mileage noted in U.S. Department of Transportation, Federal Highway Administration, *Highway Statistics 1996*, Table HM-50. Rail transit mileage noted in Robert Bernick and Robert Cervero, *Transit Villages in the 21st Century* (New York: McGraw-Hill, 1997), Tables 3.1, 3.2, and 3.3; and Tony Pattison, ed., *Jane's Urban Transport Systems*, 18th Edition (Alexandria, Virginia: Jane's Information Group, 1999). Atlanta freeway mileage from author's calculation based on information in Ronald L. Mitchelson and James O. Wheeler, "Analysis of Aggregate Flows: The Atlanta Case," in *Geography of Urban Transportation*, 2nd Edition, Susan Hanson, ed. (New York: The Guilford Press, 1995) p. 129-30, 144.

19. Vancouver ratio = 106:35 counting only that portion of commuter rail that is within the same reach as Skytrain; "The region only has about 106 miles of freeway," according to Parsons Brinckerhoff Quade and Douglas, Inc., Transportation Research Board of the National Research Council, *TCRP Report 16: Transit and Urban Form*, Volume 2, p. 100 of Part IV; Chris Bushell, ed. *Jane's Urban Transport Systems* 17th Edition (Coulsdon, Surrey, UK: Jane's Information Group Limited, 1998) pp. 355-57, 364-66; MapArt Greater Toronto 1988, and MapArt Ontario 2000 maps; Toronto rail transit mileage includes 35 miles metro, 69 miles GO train, and 2 miles light rail = 106 miles rail transit versus 82 miles expressway.

20. Transit accounts for negligible use of metropolitan roadways according to David C. Hodge, "My Fair Share: Equity Issues in Urban Transportation," in *The Geography of Urban Transportation*, 2nd Edition, Susan Hanson, ed. (New York: Guilford, 1995), p. 366. Interstate 35W noted in MN/DOT project description dated 18 November 1996. At least 257,000 vehicles (with an average of 1.3 occupants) use the freeway each day, according to MN/DOT 1994 Traffic Volumes maps.

21. ABC News, *This Week*, 8 November 1998.

22. Federal Highway Administration, *Highway Statistics 1995*, November 1996, p. V-84.

23. WGBH Boston, *The American Experience*, "New York Underground" (1997).

24. "Trains are sexy" quote in Alan Black, *Urban Mass Transportation Planning* (New York: McGraw-Hill, 1995), p. 117. "Life failure" noted in Joel Garreau, *Edge City: Life on the New Frontier* (New York: Doubleday, Anchor Boods, 1991), p. 130.

25. Regional Plan Association, *The Renaissance of Rail Transit in America*, June 1991, p. 75.

26. Regional Plan Association, *The Renaissance of Rail Transit in America*, June 1991, p. 84; The steepest decline in passenger trips per vehicle mile of transit route was for bus transit (1984 to 1993), according to Michael Bernick and Robert Cervero, *Transit Villages in the 21st Century* (New York: McGraw-Hill, 1997), p. 58.

27. Fred Hansen quote and "MAX has almost as many riders on Saturdays" in Gordon Oliver, "Portland Revs Up for Action," *Planning*, August 1994. "6,500 new transit riders" noted in Regional Plan Association, *The Renaissance of Rail Transit in America*, 1991, p. 52.

28. Parsons Brinckerhoff Quade & Douglas, Inc., Transportation Research Board of the National Research Council, *TCRP Report 16: Transit and Urban Form*, Volume 2 (Washington, D.C: National Academy Press, 1996), p. 87 of Part 4.

29. Commuter rail traveled at 33.8 mph. According to the American Public Transit Association, *Transit Fact Book* (Washington, D.C.: American Public Transit Association, 1999), p. 16. The APTA's numbers presumably include light rail that does not have exclusive R.O.W., and buses that do.

30. National averages from American Public Transit Association, *1999 Transit Fact Book*, January 1999, pp. 63, 71, 73. San Diego noted in Chris Bushell, Tony Pattison, eds., *Jane's Urban Transport Systems*, 17th and 19th editions (Alexandria, Virginia: Jane's Information Group, 1998, 1999, and 2000).

31. Parsons Brinckerhoff Quade & Douglas, Inc., Transportation Research Board of the National Research Council, *TCRP Report 16: Transit and Urban Form*, Volume 2 (Washington, D.C: National Academy Press, 1996), p. 109 of Part 4.

32. Chris Bushell, ed., *Jane's Urban Transport Systems*, 17th Edition (Alexandria, Virginia: Jane's Information Group, 1998), p. 265.

33. Capacity comparisons noted in Alan Black, *Urban Mass Transportation Planning* (New York: McGraw-Hill, 1995), p. 121. Washington, D.C. Metro noted in Regional Plan Association, *The Renaissance of Rail Transit in America*, June 1991, p. 77. New York City subway noted in Michael Bernick and Robert Cervero, *Transit Villages in the 21st Century* (New York: McGraw-Hill, 1997), p. 58.

34. Regional Plan Association, *The Renaissance of Rail Transit in America*, June 1991, p. 5.

35. State University of New York, "An Analysis of Rapid Transit Investments: The Buffalo Experience," Final Report, July 1981, p. 85.

36. James E. Vance Jr., *The Continuing City: Urban Morphology in Western Civilization* (Baltimore: Johns Hopkins University Press, 1990), p. 401.

37. Parsons Brinckerhoff Quade & Douglas, Inc., Transportation Research Board of the National Research Council, *TCRP Report 16: Transit and Urban Form*, Volume 2 (Washington, D.C: National Academy Press, 1996), pp. 72, 90 of Part 4. Portland's second line had reportedly generated $1 billion in real estate development by the time it opened in September, 1998, according to editorial, "Our Perspective: Hiawatha Line," Minneapolis Star Tribune, 27 September 1998, p. A22.

38. Gordon J. Fielding, "Transit in American Cities" in *Geography of Urban Transportation*, 2nd Edition, Susan Hanson, ed. (New York: Guilford Press, 1995), p. 295.

39. Parsons Brinckerhoff Quade & Douglas, Inc., Transportation Research Board of the National Research Council, *TCRP Report 16: Transit and Urban Form*, Volume 1 (Washington, D.C: National Academy Press, 1996), p. 28 of Part 1.

40. Parsons Brinckerhoff Quade & Douglas, Inc., Transportation Research Board of the National Research Council, *TCRP Report 16: Transit and Urban Form*, Volume 1 (Washington, D.C: National Academy Press, 1996), p. 31 of Part 1.

41. Alan Black, *Urban Mass Transportation Planning* (New York: McGraw-Hill, 1995), pp. 238, 393, Toronto official's quote on p. 242.

42. San Francisco Planning Department, *Transportation Element of the Master Plan of the City and County of San Francisco*, Adopted July 1995, p. I.4.26. "There's insufficient parking for nearly 145,000 downtown [Minneapolis] commuters, 60 percent of whom drive into town alone," according to Neal St. Anthony, "Grabarski Has Plenty of Ideas for Improving Downtown," *Minneapolis Star Tribune*, 4 December 1998, p. D1.

43. Six-minute headways according to schedule posted at Market Street terminus of California Street line, 23 January 1997.

44. Parsons Brinckerhoff Quade & Douglas, Inc., Transportation Research Board of the National Research Council, *TCRP Report 16: Transit and Urban Form*, Volume 1 (Washington, D.C: National Academy Press, 1996), p. 27 of Part 1; New York City Department of City Planning, *1997 Annual Report on Social Indicators*, p. 17.

45. Parsons Brinckerhoff Quade & Douglas, Inc., Transportation Research Board of the National Research Council, *TCRP Report 16: Transit and Urban Form* (Washington, D.C: National Academy Press, 1996), Volume 1, p. 31 of Part 1, and Volume 2, p. 37 of Part 4.

46. Daniel Immergluck, "Urban Advantages: Sustaining Retail Activity in a Modest Income Neighborhood," *Woodstock Institute,* February 1995, pp. ii, 18.

47. Parsons Brinckerhoff Quade & Douglas, Inc., Transportation Research Board of the National Research Council, *TCRP Report 16: Transit and Urban Form*, Volume 1 (Washington, D.C: National Academy Press, 1996) p. 27 of Part 1; Michael Bernick and Robert Cervero, *Transit Villages in the 21st Century* (New York: McGraw-Hill, 1997), pp. 157-60.

48. Robert R. Kiley, "New York Underground: Rescuing the MTA" in *Breaking Away: The Future of Cities,* Julia Vitullo-Martin, ed. (New York: Twentieth Century Fund Press, 1995) p. 168.

49. David C. Hodge, "My Fair Share: Equity Issues in Urban Transportation" in *Geography of Urban Transportation*, 2nd Edition, Susan Hanson, ed. (New York: The Guilford Press, 1995) pp. 367-369.

50. Seventy-three percent of BART's passengers arrive at stations in cars according to Alan Black, *Urban Mass Transportation Planning* (New York: McGraw-Hill, 1995), p. 240.

51. Alan Black, *Urban Mass Transportation Planning* (New York: McGraw-Hill, 1995), p. 59.

52. Peter O. Muller, "Transportation and Urban Form" in *The Geography of Urban Transportation*, 2nd Edition, Susan Hanson, ed. (New York: Guilford, 1995), pp. 36-37.

53. Terence O'Donnell, Tri-Met, "The Right Track: The Story of MAX," January 1988; Alan Black, *Urban Mass Transportation Planning* (New York: McGraw-Hill, 1995), p. 103.

54. Alan Black, *Urban Mass Transportation Planning* (New York: McGraw-Hill, 1995), p. 71.

55. "Congestion-relieving tool" quote by Metropolitan Council Chairman Ted Mondale, "Buses Help a Lot in Reducing Congestion," *Minneapolis Star Tribune,* 11 May 2001, p. A26. Two and a half percent according to Metropolitan Council, *1990 Travel Behavior Inventory Summary Report*, p. v. Governor Jesse Ventura's opinion revealed in his speech to the *Growing Smart in Minnesota* conference, Minneapolis, 11 June 1999. Senate Majority Leader Dick Day (Republican from Owatonna) quote "put 'em where cars travel...." from a debate about transportation issues on NewsNight Minnesota, Citizens Forum, KTCA TV, Twin Cities, 22 March 2000.

56. Chris Bushell, ed., *Jane's Urban Transport Systems*, 17th Edition (Alexandria, Virginia: Jane's Information Group, 1998), p. 265.

57. Tract 036002 @ 112.584 housing units per acre (New York City Planning Department, DCP 1990 #2, p. 15)

58. St. Louis' MetroLink expansion noted in Bi-State Development Agency's *Fiscal 2000 Annual Report,* and proposed route diagrams. San Diego extensions described by Metropolitan Transit Development Board, "Mission Valley East Light Rail Transit Project," January 2001, "Proposed Mid-Coast Segment," January 2001, and "Proposed South Bay LRT Extensions," November 2000. Additional system extensions reported on transit agency websites in May 2001.

59. Chris Bushell, ed., *Jane's Urban Transport Systems,* 17th Edition (Alexandria, Virginia: Jane's Information Group, 1998), p. 245.

60. Portland, Oregon, *Tri-Met,* "Meet MAX," June 1994, p. 12.

61. San Francisco Muni, Fall 1996 Timetables.

62. Muni, *San Francisco Street and Transit Map,* 1996; BART December 1996 Schedule.

63. Peter Gordon and Harry W. Richardson, "Are Compact Cities a Desirable Planning Goal?" *Journal of the American Planning Association* 63, no. 1 (Winter 1997), p. 98.

64. Gordon J. Fielding, "Transit in American Cities" in *Geography of Urban Transportation,* 2nd Edition, Susan Hanson, ed. (New York: Guilford, 1995), pp. 293-96; Genevieve Giuliano, "Land Use Impacts of Transportation Investments: Highway and Transit" in *Geography of Urban Transportation,* 2nd Edition, Susan Hanson, ed. (New York: Guilford, 1995), pp. 332-35.

65. Gordon Oliver, "Portland Revs Up for Action," *Planning,* August 1994.

66. Richard Moe and Carter Wilkie, *Changing Places: Rebuilding Community in the Age of Sprawl* (New York: Henry Holt, 1997), p. 232.

67. David Goldberg, "Heads Up, Atlanta," *Planning,* July 1998, p. 20 (see p. 21). Residents of the Atlanta metropolis drive an average of 35 miles a day, more than anywhere else in the nation, according to David Firestone, "Suburban Comforts Thwart Atlanta's Plans to Limit Sprawl," *New York Times,* 21 November 1999, p. 1.

68. Commuter rail is an exception

69. Regional Plan Association, "Where Transit Works," *Regional Plan News,* August 1976, p. 7.

70. Parsons Brinckerhoff Quade & Douglas, Inc., Transportation Research Board of the National Research Council, *TCRP Report 16: Transit and Urban Form,* Volume 1 (Washington, D.C: National Academy Press, 1996), pp. E-4, 17, 25, 30 of Part 2.

71. Tony Pattison, ed., *Jane's Urban Transport Systems,* 19th Edition (Alexandria, Virginia: Jane's Information Group, 2000).

72. San Francisco Planning Department of the City and County, Transportation Element of the Master Plan, adopted July, 1995, p. I.4.46.

73. Parsons Brinckerhoff Quade & Douglas, Inc., Transportation Research Board of the National Research Council, *TCRP Report 16: Transit and Urban Form,* Volume 1 (Washington, D.C: National Academy Press, 1996), p. E-4 of Part 2.

74. James E. Vance, *The Continuing City: Urban Morphology in Western Civilization* (Baltimore: Johns Hopkins University Press, 1990), p. 401.

75. Rachelle L. Levitt, ed., *Cities Reborn* (Washington, D.C.: Urban Land Institute, 1987), p. 193.

76. Parsons Brinckerhoff Quade & Douglas, Inc., Transportation Research Board of the National Research Council, *TCRP Report 16: Transit and Urban Form,* Volume 1 (Washington, D.C: National Academy Press, 1996), p. 30 of Part 1. Contra Costa County growth noted by Spencer Michaels, "Sprawling America," on PBS, *NewsHour,* May 26, 1999.

77. Gordon J. Fielding, "Transit in American Cities" in *Geography of Urban Transportation,* 2nd Edition, Susan Hanson, ed. (New York: Guilford, 1995), p. 303; Genevieve Giuliano, "Land Use Impacts of Transportation Investments: Highway and Transit" in *Geography of Urban Transportation,* 2nd Edition, Susan Hanson, ed. (New York: Guilford, 1995), pp. 333.

78. Parsons Brinckerhoff Quade & Douglas, Inc., Transportation Research Board of the National Research Council, *TCRP Report 16: Transit and Urban Form,* Volume 2 (Washington, D.C: National Academy Press, 1996), pp. 50, 59, 61, 63 of Part 4.

79. Urban Land Institute, "Connection: Linking Transportation and Land Use," Summer 1995, p. 4.

80. Tri-Met, "Beyond the Field of Dreams," March 1995, p. 14; See also Parsons Brinckerhoff Quade & Douglas, Inc., Transportation Research Board of the National Research Council, *TCRP Report 16: Transit and Urban Form*, Volume 2 (Washington, D.C: National Academy Press,) 1996, p. 90 of Part 4.

81. Michael Bernick and Robert Cervero, *Transit Villages in the 21st Century* (New York: McGraw-Hill, 1997), p. 154-55.

82. Kunz, Andy, "New Urbanism and Transportation Choices," *The Town Paper*, Lakelands Edition, (Gaithersburg, MD) October/November 2000, p. 10.

83. Michael Bernick and Robert Cervero, *Transit Villages in the 21st Century* (New York: McGraw-Hill, 1997), p. 74.

84. Ronald L. Mitchelson and James O. Wheeler, "Analysis of Aggregate Flows: The Atlanta Case" in *The Geography of Urban Transportation*, 2nd Edition, Susan Hanson, ed. (New York: The Guilford Press, 1995), p. 159.

85. Parsons Brinckerhoff Quade & Douglas, Inc., Transportation Research Board of the National Research Council, *TCRP Report 16: Transit and Urban Form*, Volume 2 (Washington, D.C: National Academy Press, 1996), p. 91 of Part 4; Douglas R. Porter, "Transit-Focused Development: A Progress Report," *Journal of the American Planning Association*, Autumn 1998, pp. 474-88.

86. Parsons Brinckerhoff Quade & Douglas, Inc., Transportation Research Board of the National Research Council, *TCRP Report 16: Transit and Urban Form*, Volume 2 (Washington, D.C: National Academy Press, 1996), pp. 37, 45 of Part 4; Douglas R. Porter, "Transit-Focused Development: A Progress Report," *Journal of the American Planning Association*, Autumn 1998, pp. 475-88.

87. Michael Bernick and Robert Cervero, *Transit Villages in the 21st Century* (New York: McGraw-Hill, 1997), p. 115.

88. Cervero quote from Michael Bernick and Robert Cervero, *Transit Villages in the 21st Century* (New York: McGraw-Hill, 1997), p. 98. "Less than 5 percent" noted in Anthony Downs, *New Visions for Metropolitan America* (Washington, D.C.: The Brookings Institution, 1994), p. 160, footnote 23.

89. Michael Bernick and Robert Cervero, *Transit Villages in the 21st Century* (New York: McGraw-Hill, 1997), p. 111.

90. Joel Garreau, *Edge City: Life on the New Frontier* (New York: Doubleday, Anchor Books, 1991), pp. 131-32.

91. Cervero quote from Michael Bernick and Robert Cervero, *Transit Villages in the 21st Century* (New York: McGraw-Hill, 1997), p. 111. Metro-area transit-use data from Alan Pisarski, *Commuting in America II* (Lansdowne, Virginia: Eno Transportation Foundation, 1996), p. 64.

92. Chris Bushell, ed., *Jane's Urban Transport Systems*, 17th Edition (Alexandria, Virginia: Jane's Information Group, 1998), p. 17.

93. More than 80 percent of suburban BART users arrive at their stations in cars according to Michael Burnick and Robert Cervero, *Transit Villages in the 21st Century* (McGraw-Hill, 1997), p. 7. Parking at BART stations noted in *The Urban Transportation Monitor*, 3 February 1995, p. 5.

94. Twin Cities light rail noted by Robert Whereatt, "Legislator Sues Ventura Over Light Rail Project," *Minneapolis Star Tribune*, 30 December 1999, p. B3. BART noted in Alan Black, *Urban Mass Transportation Planning* (New York: McGraw-Hill, 1995), pp. 263-65.

95. DFL gubernatorial candidate Mark Dayton in a political advertisement aired on WFTC TV, 14 September 1998.

96. The Buffalo region's stagnant economy could not sustain commercial growth in the CBD, fed by a federally funded rail line, and in the suburbs, fed by federally funded highways, simultaneously. "Encouraged by conflicting programs supported by HUD, EDA, and DOT, suburban areas compete with urban areas for the same resources," according to State University of New York, "An Analysis of Rapid Transit Investments: The Buffalo Experience," Final Report, July 1981, pp. 25, 85

97. William F. Eager, "Transportation and Growth: Separating Myth from Fact," *Urban Land*, February 1996, p. 7.

98. Metropolitan Council, *Metropolitan Development and Investment Framework*, 1988, p.34.

99. Robert Caro, *The Power Broker: Robert Moses and the Fall of New York* (New York: Random House, Vintage Books, 1974), p. 519.

100. Metropolitan Council, *Transit Redesign 1996*, p. IX1.

101. (no byline) "Hwy. 169 Bypass to Open at Shakopee," *Minneapolis Star Tribune*, 20 November 1996, p. B3.

102. David Peterson, "$1.3-Billion Package OK'd," *Minneapolis Star Tribune*, 30 September 1999, p. 1.

103. Chapter 479 of House File No. 2891, Article 1, Section 2, Subd. 3 (page 3, lines 12-30). The appropriation is a "one-time infusion" of money from the state's $1.8 billion surplus, according to Robert Whereatt and Laurie Blake, "House OKs $425 Million Transportation Bill," *Minneapolis Star Tribune*, 22 March 2000, pp. B1, B5.

104. Congestion is interfering with access to nearby businesses; scheduled enhancements include the construction of a new interchange at the intersection of Interstate 70 and Highway 94, 15 miles northwest of the city; the city and the county each will lend $1 million, reported by Bill Bell Jr., "Financing Plan Lets I-70, Highway 94 Work Begin Soon Instead of Year 2000," *St. Louis Post-Dispatch*, 5 September 1998, Local News section, p. 11.

105. Safety concerns noted in MN/DOT, "I-35W/Highway 62 Improvements and HOV Lane Project: Technical Memorandum," November 1996. $100 million cost reported by Laurie Blake, "Hearing on Crosstown Yields Little," *Minneapolis Star Tribune*, 19 January 2001, p. 1.

106. Urban interstates' fatality rate is one-sixth that of rural roads, according to Frank Markowitz and Michelle DeRobertis, "The Road to Safety," *Planning*, December 1998, p. 4. A motorist's chance of being killed in a traffic accident on a two-lane highway is four times his chance on an interstate freeway, according to NBC *Dateline*, February 21, 1997.

107. A 1996 study by the Transportation Research Board concluded, based on 10 North American light rail systems, that the rail systems are safer than highways, reported by Ken Leiser and Phil Sutin, "Expect Accidents, But No Blood Alley," *St. Louis Post-Dispatch*, 16 May 1999, p. A8. Accidents concern highway officials because of delays according to (no byline) "Houston METRO and Partners Celebrate MAP's 10 Years," *Public Roads*, Volume 63, No. 3 (November/December 1999), published by the Federal Highway Administration, U.S. Department of Transportation, p. 56.

108. State representative Carol Molnau (Republican, Chaska) comments in a debate about transportation issues on *NewsNight Minnesota*, Citizens Forum, KTCA TV, 22 March 2000.

109. David Goldman and Pam Perry, *The Insiders' Guide to Metro Atlanta*, 2nd Edition (Macon, Georgia: Macon Telegraph Publishing Co., and Manteo, North Carolina: The Insiders' Guides Inc., 1996), pp. 19-20.

110. Laurie Blake, "A Change in Direction on Lanes for Car Pools," *Minneapolis Star Tribune*, 5 November 1998, p. B2. In Minnesota, Governor Jesse Ventura called for removal of HOV lanes during his gubernatorial campaign. Republican state representative Doug Reuter (Owatonna) called HOV lanes "a failed experiment in behavior modification," according to Robert Whereatt, "2 Legislators Question Sanity of Sane Lanes, Ramp Meters," *Minneapolis Star Tribune*, 16 December 1998, p. B1. A plurality of Minnesota state legislators surveyed by the *Minneapolis Star Tribune* at the end of 1998 supported the conversion of HOV lanes to open access lanes, according to Robert Whereatt, "Subjects that Strike a Nerve," *Minneapolis Star Tribune*, 3 January 1999, p. A13.

111. Parsons Brinckerhoff Quade & Douglas, Inc., Transportation Research Board of the National Research Council, *TCRP Report 16: Transit and Urban Form*, Volume 2 (Washington, D.C: National Academy Press, 1996), p. 33 of Part 4.

112. Texas Transportation Institute, "2001 Urban Mobility Study," May 2001, Tables A-6, A-7,-A-9. (no byline), "EPA Funds Air Quality Study of Houston's No. 1 Smog," *Planning*, March 2000, p. 27. Houston's status as the nation's largest city without rail transit will change in 2004 with the completion of a light rail line recently approved by voters.

113. Representative Ken Wolf (Republican, Burnsville) letter to the editor, *Minneapolis Star Tribune*, 3 April 1996, p. 8A.

114. Mike Blahnik, "Intelligent Transportation Systems Given Radio Spectrum Spot by FCC," *Minneapolis Star Tribune*, 22 October 1999, p. A9.

115. *CBS Evening News*, 7 August 1997 and 4 October 1998.

116. San Francisco City and County Planning Department, *Citywide Travel Behavior Survey 1993*, Summary Findings Phase I, pp. 2-4.

117. San Francisco Planning Department of the City and County, *Transportation Element of the Master Plan of the City and County of San Francisco*, Adopted July 1995, p. I.4.3

118. San Francisco Planning Department of the City and County, *Transportation Element of the Master Plan*, July 1995, pp. I.4.5-I.4.6

119. Charles River Associates, Transportation Research Board of the National Research Council, *TCRP Report 27: Building Transit Ridership: An Exploration of Transit's Market Share and the Public Policies That Determine It* (Washington, D.C.: National Academy Press, 1997), p. 7.

120. Worldwatch Institute, *Worldwatch Paper 105*, October 1991, p. 16.

121. Learry Beastley, " 'Living First' in Downtown Vancouver," *Zoning News*, April 2000.

122. William C. Wheaton, "Office Growth in the 1990s: Downtown Versus Edge Cities," *Urban Land*, April 1996, p. 67.

123. Perimeter Mall situation noted at Growing Smart in Minnesota conference, Minneapolis, 11 June 1999. "Hewlett Packard Co. scrapped an expansion plan because of the mobility crisis of gridlocked traffic" according to Linda Mack, "Sprawl A Hot Topic As Suburbs Boom," *Minneapolis Star Tribune*, 8 August 1999, p. A17. At Research Triangle Park, new roads, and even a new rail system, are proposed to serve the SBC, according to David J. Morrow, "Corporate Park's Bucolic Appeal is Lost in Traffic," *New York Times*, 16 May 1999, p. 22.

124. Charles Walston, "Ready to Govern," *Atlanta Journal-Constitution*, 10 January 1999, p. A1.

125. Subcommittee on the City, a subcommittee of the U.S. House of Representatives' Committee on Banking, Finance, and Urban Affairs, *Compact Cities: Energy Saving Strategies for the Eighties*, 1980, pp. VIII, 79.

126. Dennis J. McGrath, "Bloomington Asks State to Forgive $50 Million Loan for Mall of America," *Minneapolis Star Tribune*, 11 April 1995, p.1A.

127. David Firestone, "Suburban Comforts Thwart Atlanta's Plans to Limit Sprawl," *New York Times*, 21 November 1999, p. 1.

128. Joel Garreau, *Edge City: Life on the New Frontier* (New York: Doubleday, Anchor Books, 1991), p. 108, see also pp. 221-222, 227-228.

129. Decline from 19 to 12 percent noted in Peter Gordon and Harry W. Richardson, "Are Compact Cities a Desirable Planning Goal?" *Journal of the American Planning Association* 63, no. 1 (Winter, 1997), p. 100. "The trend" quote from Peter Gordon and Harry W. Richardson, "Beyond Polycentricity: The Dispersed Metropolis, Los Angeles, 1970-1990," *Journal of the American Planning Association* 62, no. 3 (Summer 1996), p. 292.

130. Peter Gordon and Harry W. Richardson, "Beyond Polycentricity: The Dispersed Metropolis, Los Angeles, 1970-1990," *Journal of the American Planning Association* 62, no. 3 (Summer 1996), pp. 289-90, quote "just as ..." on p. 290.

131. Joel Garreau, *Edge City: Life on the New Frontier* (New York: Doubleday, Anchor Books, 1991), p. 8.

132. Joel Garreau, *Edge City: Life on the New Frontier* (New York: Doubleday, Anchor Books, 1991), p. xxiii.

133. Joel Garreau, *Edge City: Life on the New Frontier* (New York: Doubleday, Anchor Books, 1991), p. 235.

134. Joel Garreau, *Edge City: Life on the New Frontier* (New York: Doubleday, Anchor Books, 1991), Detroit noted on p. 116; "But so what" from p. 132.

135. H.V. Savitch, *Post-Industrial Cities: Politics and Planning in New York, Paris, and London* (Princeton, New Jersey: Princeton University Press, 1988), p. 150; Chris Bushell, ed., *Jane's Urban Transport Systems*, 17th Edition (Alexandria, Virginia: Jane's Information Group Inc., 1998), p. 264.

136. Chris Bushell, ed., *Jane's Urban Transport Systems*, 15th Edition (Alexandria, Virginia: Jane's Information Group Inc., 1996), pp. 278-79; H.V. Savitch, *Post-Industrial Cities: Politics and Planning in New York, Paris, and London* (Princeton, New Jersey: Princeton University Press, 1988), p. 130.

137. H.V. Savitch compares the decentralization of Paris to that of American cities: "New towns and suburban growth poles were a method of channeling population and development into designated locales. The French approach should not be mistaken for American suburban development, which rises helter-skelter around a central city. Far from that, Delouvrier promoted the concentration of resources and people within confined spaces. Apart from these spaces, land was left relatively open for either farming or recreation. Planning was the decisive and directive edge for inaugurating a new region." (H. V. Savitch, *Post-Industrial Cities: Politics and Planning in New York, Paris, and London* [Princeton, New Jersey: Princeton University Press, 1988], pp. 102-03; see also pp. 100-108, 130, 136, 147-49, 159-60.)

CHAPTER 7 NOTES

1. Tommy G. Thompson, "Welfare Reform's Next Step," *Brookings Review*, Summer 2001, p. 3.

2. Percentage of single-parent families tripled according to William J. Bennett, *The Index of Leading Cultural Indicators: Facts and Figures on the State of American Society* (New York: Touchstone, 1994), p. 50. "Bedrock of a stable community" quote reported by Brendan I. Koerner, "Cities That Work," *U.S. News and World Report*, 8 June 1999, p. 28, citing a HUD *State of the Cities* report.

3. U.S. Census Bureau, "Profiles of General Demographic Characteristics," May 2001. Incomes noted by William J. Bennett, *The Index of Leading Cultural Indicators: Facts and Figures on the State of American Society* (New York: Touchstone, 1994), p. 53.

4. George Kranzler, *Hasidic Williamsburg: A Contemporary American Hasidic Community* (Northvale, New Jersey: Jason Aronson,Inc., 1995), p. 153, delinquency rate noted on p. 75.

5. Kevin Diaz, "No End in Sight for Housing Crunch," *Minneapolis Star Tribune*, 26 August 1997, p. 1.

6. David Rusk, *Inside Game Outside Game: Winning Strategies for Saving Urban America* (Washington, D.C.: Brookings Institution Press, 1999), pp. 139-40.

7. Chris Graves, "Year-old Boy Dies in Six-story Fall in Minneapolis," *Minneapolis Star Tribune,* 6 September 1998, p. A12.

8. Buzz Bissinger, *A Prayer for the City* (New York: Random House, 1997), p. 291.

9. Greater Minneapolis Metropolitan Housing Corporation, "Lyn Park-The Suburb in the City," undated. New high-density projects for low-income people and families are found in or at the edge of downtown in some cities, but these are exceptional; see Tom Jones, William Pettus, and Michael Pyatok, *Good Neighbors: Affordable Family Housing* (New York: McGraw-Hill, 1997).

10. Richard Plunz, *A History of Housing in New York City* (New York: Columbia University Press, 1990), pp. 216, 219. (Urban Renewal occasionally suburbanized neighborhoods on behalf of the non-poor as well.)

11. Techwood/Howell's net density prior to redevelopment was less than 16 units per acre according to Larry Keating, "Redeveloping Public Housing," *Journal of the American Planning Association* 66, no. 4 (Autumn 2000), p. 384. Density reductions in Baltimore, Columbus, Atlanta, Oakland, Milwaukee, and El Paso noted by Arthur J. Naparstek, et. al., Hope VI: *Community Building Makes a Difference* (Washington, D.C.: HUD, February 2000), pp. 10-53. Density reduction in Chicago noted by Susan Popkin, et. al., *The Hidden War: Crime and the Tragedy of Public Housing in Chicago* (New Brunswick, New Jersey: Rutgers University Press, 2000), pp. 83, 183.

12. Philadelphia example noted by John R. Gibbons, "Inner-City Innovation in Philadelphia," *Urban Land*, October 1998, p. 18. For additional examples of density reduction and restoration of derelict low-density buildings by nonprofit housing developers in concert with city agencies, see Steve Brandt, "Rehabbing Phillips Housing Illustrates Some Quandaries of Redeveloping City's Core," *Minneapolis Star Tribune*, 27 June 2000, p. B1.

13. *RS Means Square Foot Costs*, 18th Edition-1997 (Kingston, Massachusetts: R.S. Means Co, 1996) pp. 78, 80, 82.

14. John R. Gibbons, "Inner-City Innovation in Philadelphia," *Urban Land*, October 1998, p. 18.

15. Diane R. Suchman (with Margaret B. Sowell), *Developing Infill Housing in Inner-City Neighborhoods: Opportunities and Strategies* (Washington, D.C.: Urban Land Institute, 1997), p. 48; Manufactured Housing Institute, "MHI Developer Resources: Urban Design Project," (www mrghome.org, 26 February 2000).

16. Phillip L. Clay, *Neighborhood Renewal* (Lexington, Massachusetts: D.C. Heath, 1979), p. 18.

17. Tracie Rozhon, "The Reconstruction of a 5-Story Mansion Manque," *New York Times*, 20 October 1996, Real Estate section, p. 7; Larry Beasely, "'Living First' in Downtown Vancouver," *Zoning News*, April 2000, p. 1.

18. Regional Plan Association, "Where Transit Works," *Regional Plan News*, August 1976, p. 6.

19. Anastasia Loukaitou-Sideris, "Hot Spots of Bus Stop Crime," *Journal of the American Planning Association* 65, no. 4 (Autumn 1999), pp. 395, 399. The author notes that most of the respondents to her survey are captive riders, half of whom feel unsafe at bus stops, and 31.1 percent of whom claimed to have been the victim of a crime in the five years preceding the survey (p. 400).

20. New York City ridership noted by George L. Kelling and Catherine M. Coles, *Fixing Broken Windows: Restoring Order & Reducing Crime in Our Communities* (New York: The Free Press, 1996), pp. 119-120. Service reductions in San Diego noted by Chris Bushell, *Jane's Urban Transport Systems,* 15th Edition (Alexandria, Virginia: Jane's Information Group, 1996), p. 317.

21. Michael Cooper, "Train Suspect Mentally Ill, Officials Say," *New York Times,* 30 April 1999, p. A27; C.J. Chivers, "Man Charged in Subway Robberies of Women," *New York Times,* 14 April 2000, Metropolitan Desk (www.nytimes.com).

22. Woman shot in head reported by Steve Berg, "Rude, Coarse and Selfish: Got a Problem With That?" *Minneapolis Star Tribune,* 9 March 1997, p. 1. Man killed reported by David Shaffer, "Suspect Charged in Death of Man Pushed Off Bus," *Minneapolis Star Tribune,* 21 September 2000, p. B5.

23. "Transit riders have always had to put up with the annoying habits, bad behavior and inconsiderateness of fellow commuters: Folks who . . . strew garbage, smoke, eat or blast their radios," writes Michael Cabanatuan, "Mass Transit Latest Stop For Cell-Phone Discord," *San Francisco Chronicle,* 13 December 1999, p. 1.

24. Tamar Jacoby, *Someone Else's House: America's Unfinished Struggle for Integration* (New York: Basic Books, 1998), p. 502.

25. Michael Bernick and Robert Cervero, *Transit Villages in the 21st Century* (New York: McGraw-Hill, 1997), p. 174.

26. Michael Bernick and Robert Cervero, *Transit Villages in the 21st Century* (New York: McGraw-Hill, 1997), p. 193.

27. Michael Bernick and Robert Cervero, *Transit Villages in the 21st Century* (New York: McGraw-Hill, 1997), pp. 52, 66.

28. Kathy Scruggs, "Marta Shooting Claims Life of 2nd Businessman," *Atlanta Journal and Constitution,* 5 July 1991, p. A1.

29. Charles Haddad, "Empty Buildings A Silent Witness to Shift North," *Atlanta Journal and Constitution,* 5 June 1991, p. C1.

30. Ross Miller, *Here's the Deal: The Buying and Selling of a Great American City* (New York: Alfred A. Knopf, 1996), Daley quote from p. 193, see also pp. 131, 175-76.

31. Ross Miller, *Here's the Deal: The Buying and Selling of a Great American City* (New York: Alfred A. Knopf, 1996), p. 10.

32. Ross Miller, *Here's the Deal: The Buying and Selling of a Great American City* (New York: Alfred A. Knopf, 1996), p. 193.

33. Ross Miller, *Here's the Deal: The Buying and Selling of a Great American City* (New York: Alfred A. Knopf, 1996), pp. 176-77.

34. David Dunkelman, *Your Guide to Toronto Neighborhoods* (Toronto: Maple Tree, 1999), pp. 3-129, 227, 243.

35. Regional Plan Association, "Where Transit Works," *Regional Plan News,* August 1976, p. 7.

36. Oscar Newman, *Creating Defensible Space* (Rutgers University: Center for Urban Policy research, 1996).

37. Marlys McPherson and Glenn Silloway, "The Role of the Small Commercial Center in the Urban Neighborhood," *Urban Neighborhoods: Research and Policy,* Ralph B. Taylor, ed. (New York: Praeger, 1986), p. 171.

38. Marlys McPherson and Glenn Silloway, "The Role of the Small Commercial Center in the Urban Neighborhood," *Urban Neighborhoods: Research and Policy,* Ralph B. Taylor, ed. (New York: Praeger, 1986), p. 172.

39. Robert Caro, *The Power Broker: Robert Moses and the Fall of New York* (New York: Vintage, 1975), p. 489; Elijah Anderson, *Code of the Street: Decency, Violence, and the Moral Life of the Inner City* (New York: W.W. Norton, 1999), p. 22; William H. Whyte, *The Social Life of Small Urban Spaces* (Washington, D.C.: The Conservation Foundation, 1980), p. 62; Martin Fuller, "The Magic Fountain," *Progressive Architecture*, November 1978, p. 81.

40. James Sterngold, "Los Angeles Plans to Offer Public Toilets," *New York Times*, 26 July 2001, p. A14.

41. Min Zhou, *Chinatown: The Socioeconomic Potential of an Urban Enclave* (Philadelphia: Temple University Press, 1992), p. 203.

42. John Wier, "Low Rent Allure," *New York* magazine, 23-30 December 1996, p. 60.

43. James E. Rosenbaum, "Changing the Geography of Opportunity by Expanding Residential Choice: Lessons from the Gautreaux Program," *Housing Policy Debate*, 6, no. 1 (1995) p. 234.

44. *Federal Register*, 23 January 1989, p. 3240.

45. National Law Center on Homelessness & Poverty, "No Room for the Inn," December 1995, p. 129; Kenneth T. Jackson, *Crabgrass Frontier: The Suburbanization of the United States* (New York: Oxford University Press, 1985), p. 301.

46. Michael J. Weiss, *The Clustering of America* (New York: Harper and Row, 1988), p. xiv.

47. Alan Dubrow and Priscilla Celano, chairman and district manager of Brooklyn's Community Board No. 12, quoted in New York City Planning Department, NYC DCP # 96-18, *Community District Needs: Brooklyn*, August 1996, p. 250.

48. It's not that most Americans consciously seek the neighborhood that best represents their economic station in life, but rather that most Americans are naturally drawn to neighborhoods that offer the general location, amenities, character, and housing type they prefer, and then they buy into the best such neighborhood they can afford. (Americans would rather occupy an average house in a good neighborhood than a good house in an average neighborhood, according to a 1994 survey by Fannie Mae.) Housing demand is sufficiently strong in high-appeal neighborhoods that substandard housing is purchased by households that can afford to upgrade or replace it. In low-appeal neighborhoods, the best housing stagnates or depreciates in value. The result is economic stratification among neighborhoods, which the private housing markets do not discourage.

49. Heathrow incident reported by Alecia Swasy, "Exclusive Town Panics As Plunging Home Prices Smash Social Barriers." *Wall Street Journal*, 22 November 1993, p. B1. Huntington Beach incident reported on CBS News *48 Hours*, 15 July 1999. Haverhill situation noted by Jeanne Schinto, *Huddle Fever: Living in the Immigrant City* (New York: Alfred A. Knopf, 1995), p. 12.

50. Edward G. Goetz, Hin Kin Lam, and Anne Heitlinger, *There Goes the Neighborhood?* (Minneapolis: Center for Urban and Regional Affairs, and Neighborhood Planning for Community Revitalization, 1996), p. 11. "Rural habits" such as storing junk on property are often blamed for discord in urban neighborhoods, according to James E. Vance Jr., *The Continuing City: Urban Morphology in Western Civilization* (Baltimore: Johns Hopkins University, 1990), p. 309.

51. John P. Marquand, *The Late George Apley* (The Modern Library, Random House, New York, 1936), pp. 17, 26.

52. Kenneth T. Jackson, *Crabgrass Frontier: The Suburbanization of the United States* (New York: Oxford University Press, 1985), p. 198.

53. Chuck Shepherd, "News of the Weird," *Minneapolis Star Tribune*, 19 September 1996, p. E17.

54. Author's observation, 11 June 2000 and 21 May 2001.

55. Stephanie W. Greenberg and William M. Rohe, "Informal Social Control and Crime Prevention in Modern Urban Neighborhoods" in *Urban Neighborhoods: Research and Policy,* Ralph B. Taylor ed. (New York: Praeger, 1986), p. 85. Sociologist Herbert Gans had reached a similar conclusion in 1961, "A mixing of all age and class groups is likely to produce at best a polite but cool social climate, lacking the consensus and intensity of relations that is necessary for mutual enrichment. Instances of conflict are as probable as those of cooperation." (Gans is quoted by Howard Husock, "A Critique of Mixed Income Housing: The Problems with Gautreaux," *The Responsive Community,* Spring 1995, p. 37.)

56. Mary Schmich, "Everyone Equal in Cabrini-Green Supermarket," *Chicago Tribune,* 4 June 2000, Section 4, p. 1.

57. Thomas McMahon, Larian Angelo, and John Mollenkopf, "The Disappearing Urban Middle Class," excerpt from "Hollow in the Middle: The Rise and Fall of New York City's Middle Class" prepared for the New York City Council in December 1997, excerpt printed in the *Union Institute's Social Policy,* Vol. 28, no. 4, (Summer 1998), p. 33.

58. David Hackett, executive director of President Kennedy's Committee on Juvenile Delinquency and Youth Crime, quoted by Daniel P. Moynihan, *Maximum Feasible Misunderstanding: Community Action in the War on Poverty* (New York: The Free Press, 1970), p. 71.

59. David Rusk, *Inside Game Outside Game: Winning Strategies for Saving Urban America* (Washington, D.C.: Brookings Institution Press, 1999), p. 81.

60. Elijah Anderson, *Code of the Street: Decency, Violence, and the Moral Life of the Inner City* (New York: W.W. Norton, 1999), pp. 18, 26; Phillip L. Clay, Neighborhood Renewal (Lexington, Massachusetts: D.C. Heath, 1979), p. 38.

61. George L. Kelling and Catherine M. Coles, *Fixing Broken Windows: Restoring Order and Reducing Crime in Our Communities* (New York: The Free Press, 1996), pp. 99-100.

62. George L. Kelling and Catherine M. Coles, *Fixing Broken Windows: Restoring Order and Reducing Crime in Our Communities* (New York: The Free Press, 1996), pp. 99-100.

63. Howell S. Baum, "Ethical Behavior Is Extraordinary Behavior: It's the Same as All Other Behavior," *Journal of the American Planning Association* 64, no. 4 (Autumn 1998), p. 417.

64. Diane R. Suchman and Margaret B. Sowell, *Developing Infill Housing in Inner-City Neighborhoods: Opportunities and Strategies* (Washington, D.C.: Urban Land Institute, 1997), p. 63.

65. Oscar Newman, *Defensible Space: Crime Prevention Through Urban Design* (New York: Macmillan, 1972), p. 189.

66. Zane L. Miller and Bruce Tucker, *Changing Plans for America's Inner Cities: Cincinnati's Over-the-Rhine and Twentieth-Century Urbanism* (Columbus: Ohio State University Press, 1998), p. 141.

67. Buzz Bissinger, *A Prayer for the City* (NewYork: Random House, 1997), p. 166.

68. Buzz Bissinger, *A Prayer for the City* (NewYork: Random House, 1997), pp. 169-72. In Code of the Street, Elijah Anderson quotes a young woman in another Philadelphia neighborhood troubled by a Section-8 building, "The mothers have no control over their kids whatsoever." (p. 58)

69. Michael Patrick MacDonald, *All Souls: A Family Story from Southie* (Boston: Beacon Press, 1999).

70. Oscar Newman, *Defensible Space: Crime Prevention Through Urban Design* (New York: Macmillan, 1972), pp. 38, 198. Newman noted that ". . . low-income families with children-particularly those on welfare . . ." are especially troublesome. (p. 193).

71. Cisneros quoted in *Urban Land,* January 1994, p. 22. Dreier's comments in *Journal of the American Planning Association* 63, no. 1 (Winter 1997), p. 20. Latimer's prescription described in "Promises Deferred," Livable Communities Housing Task Force, undated, pp. 5, 13, 15. Freeman reported by Dane Smith, "Freeman Offers an Agenda on Issues Facing the Metro Area," *Minneapolis Star Tribune,* 26 March 1998. Rusk and Orfield noted in David Rusk, *Inside Game, Outside Game: Winning Strategies for Saving Urban America* (Washington, D.C.: Brookings Institution Press, 1999).

72. Myron Orfield, *Metropolitics: A Regional Agenda for Community and Stability* (Washington, D.C.: Brookings Institution Press, and Cambridge: Lincoln Institute of Land Policy, 1997), p. 130.

73. MLCA affordability guidelines noted in Edward G. Goetz and Lori Mardock, *Losing Ground: The Twin Cities Livable Communities Act and Affordable Housing,* (Minneapolis: Center for Urban and Regional Affairs, 1998), p. 9. Minneapolis' median home sales price was $79,900 in the first quarter of 1996 and $82,148 in the first quarter of 1997, and only Calhoun-Isles and Southwest had median home sale prices above $120,000 in first quarter 1996 or 1997; insufficient house sales data for three of eleven districts: Central (downtown), University, and Phillips, according to Minneapolis Planning Department, *State of the City 1997,* p. 14. It is assumed that house values in severely distressed Phillips are among the lowest in the city.

  For the Metropolitan Council's explanation of affordability criteria, see Metropolitan Council, "Metropolitan Livable Communities Act Negotiated Affordable and Life-Cycle Housing Goals-1996," Introduction.

74. MLCA rental affordability guideline for efficiency apartments was $475 in 1996, ranging up to $735 for three-bedroom apartments, according to Guy Peterson, Metropolitan Council, telephone discussion 24 October 2000; Minneapolis neighborhood income data and city-wide rental rates from Minneapolis Planning Department, *State of the City 1997,* pp. 4, 15, noting that the median rent for all apartments in Minneapolis was $445 in the first half of 1996 and $475 in the first half of 1997.

75. Besides West Ridge's six public housing replacement units and its 14 units for households earning 50 percent of median income, 37 rental apartments are set aside for moderate-income households, those earning 60 percent of the metro-area median, which in 1989 was $36,678. Sixty percent of $36,678 = $22,007, well above the poverty threshold and above the median income of many Minneapolis neighborhoods, according to Minneapolis Planning Department, *State of the City 1996,* p. 9. The MLCA "will fail to address the current shortage of affordable housing in suburban areas of the metropolitan area," according to Edward G. Goetz and Lori Mardock, *Losing Ground: The Twin Cities Livable Communities Act and Affordable Housing,* (Minneapolis: Center for Urban and Regional Affairs, 1998), p. 31.

76. The median home value in Minneapolis was $69,000 in 1996, according to the *Minneapolis Star Tribune,* 13 September 1996, p. B1. The median value of houses in Near North was $46,000 in the first quarter of 1996, according to the Minneapolis Planning Department, *State of the City 1996,* p. 23.

77. Livable Communities Task Force, "Promises Deferred" (undated) p. 5; John W. Wright, *The American Almanac of Jobs and Salaries,* (New York: Avon Books, 1996), pp. 575-76. Some housing-mobility initiatives exacerbate concentrated inner-city poverty by subsidizing the development of new suburban housing for households with incomes well above the poverty threshold, according to Michael H. Schill and Susan M. Wachter, "The Spatial Bias of Federal Housing Law and Policy: Concentrated Poverty in Urban America," *University of Pennsylvania Law Review* 143, no. 5 (May 1995), p. 1334, note 193.

78. Gans is cited in Phillip L. Clay, *Neighborhood Renewal* (Lexington, Massachusetts: D.C. Heath, 1979), p. 4.

79. James E. Rosenbaum, "Changing the Geography of Opportunity by Expanding Residential Choice: Lessons from the Gautreaux Program," *Housing Policy Debate*, vol. 6, issue 1, (1995), p. 232.

80. James E. Rosenbaum, "Changing the Geography of Metropolitan Opportunity by Expanding Residential Choice: Lessons from the Gautreaux Program," *Housing Policy Debate* vol. 6, no. 1, (1995), pp. 233, 237, 243-44; aside from the five MTO cities, Gautreaux-like programs were implemented in Dallas, Cincinnati, and Hartford (p. 232).

81. James E. Rosenbaum, "Changing the Geography of Metropolitan Opportunity by Expanding Residential Choice: Lessons from the Gautreaux Program," *Housing Policy Debate* vol. 6, no. 1, (1995), p. 255.

82. Susan Popkin, et.al., *The Hidden War: Crime and the Tragedy of Public Housing in Chicago* (New Brunswick, New Jersey: Rutgers University Press, 2000) p. 185.

83. Edward G. Goetz, Hin Kin Lam, and Anne Heitlinger, *There Goes the Neighborhood?* (Minneapolis: Center for Urban and Regional Affairs, and Neighborhood Planning for Community Revitalization, 1996), p. 4.

84. Randy Furst, "Sharing the Wealth or Cutting Ties," *Minneapolis Star Tribune*, 12 July 1996, p. B3.

85. Peter Dreier, "The New Politics of Housing: How to Rebuild the Constituency for a Progressive Federal Housing Policy," *Journal of the American Planning Association* 63, no. 1, (Winter 1997) pp. 17-19; Alan J. Abramson, Mitchell S. Tobin, and Matthew R. VanderGoot "The Changing Geography of Metropolitan Opportunity: The Segregation of the Poor in U.S. Metropolitan Areas, 1970 to 1990," *Housing Policy Debate* vol. 6, no. 1, (1995): 49-50.

86. James E. Rosenbaum, "Changing the Geography of Metropolitan Opportunity by Expanding Residential Choice: Lessons from the Gautreaux Program," *Housing Policy Debate* vol. 6, no. 1 (1995), p. 256.

87. Dan Wascoe Jr., "Affordable Housing Goals Require More Money, Group Says," *Minneapolis Star Tribune*, 8 January 1997, p. B1; Minneapolis Planning Department, *State of the City 1996*, p. 6.

88. Latimer reported by Dan Wascoe Jr., "Affordable Housing Goals Require More Money, Group Says," *Minneapolis Star Tribune*, 8 January 1997, p. B1. Montgomery County noted by David Rusk, *Inside Game Outside Game: Winning Strategies for Saving Urban America* (Washington, D.C.: Brookings Institution, 1999), pp. 189-90.

89. Community Resources Partnership, Inc., Community Partners, September 1996, p. iii.

90. Myron Orfield, *Metropolitics: A Regional Agenda for Community and Stability* (Washington, D.C.: Brookings Institution Press, and Cambridge: Lincoln Institute of Land Policy, 1997), p. 76.

91. Lizette Alvarez, "House Passes Bill to Replace System of Public Housing," *New York Times*, 15 May 1997, p. 1.

92. Cuomo quote in Interview, *Architecture*, August 1997, p. 47.

93. Julia Vitullo-Martin, "Housing and Neighborhoods" *Breaking Away*, 1995, p. 117.

94. Jennifer Preston, "Bulldozers in Camden Make Room for Affordable Homes," *New York Times*, 30 August 1996, p. B5. Bankruptcy noted in National Digest, "Camden, N.J. Faces Bankruptcy," *Minneapolis Star Tribune*, 21 July 1999, p. A4.

95. Timothy Egan, "Urban Mayors Share the Burden of Coping With Prosperity," *New York Times*, 13 June 2000 (www.nytimes.com).

96. Anthony Downs, *New Visions for Metropolitan America* (Washington, D.C.: Brookings Institution Press, and Cambridge: Lincoln Institute of Land Policy, 1994), p. 20.

97. Peter D. Salins, "Cities, Suburbs, and the Urban Crisis," *The Public Interest*, Fall 1993, p. 99.

98. Peter Dreier, "The New Politics of Housing: How to Rebuild the Constituency for a Progressive Federal Housing Policy," *Journal of the American Planning Association* 63, no. 1 (Winter 1997), pp. 13-14, 17.

99. Peter Dreier, "The New Politics of Housing: How to Rebuild the Constituency for a Progressive Federal Housing Policy," *Journal of the American Planning Association* 63, no. 1 (Winter 1997), p. 15.

100. Peter Dreier, "The New Politics of Housing: How to Rebuild the Constituency for a Progressive Federal Housing Policy," *Journal of the American Planning Association* 63, no. 1 (Winter 1997), p. 15.

101. Peter Dreier, "The New Politics of Housing: How to Rebuild the Constituency for a Progressive Federal Housing Policy," *Journal of the American Planning Association* 63, no. 1 (Winter 1997), pp. 13-14.

102. Housing replacement statute was enacted in 1989, authored by Minneapolis representative Karen Clark, according to Kevin Diaz, "Low-Income Housing Proposal Divides Minneapolis Council," *Minneapolis Star Tribune*, 12 March 1994, p. B1-B2. Housing replacement statute was repealed in 1995 according to Martiga Lohn and Linda Picone, "Task Force Recommends More Money for Affordable Housing, Including NRP Funds," *Southwest Journal*, 14-27 July 1999, p. 2. Central-city legislators opposed the repeal of the housing replacement statute in 1995 according to Minnesota state representative Todd Van Dellum (from a suburban district) in a speech to Citizens League, "Housing Policy" Forum, 4 April 1995. Minneapolis representative Karen Clark opposed repeal of the replacement statute, and Minneapolis City Council voted against recommending repeal of the according to Kevin Diaz, "Low-Income Housing Proposal Divides Minneapolis Council," *Minneapolis Star Tribune*, 12 March 1994, pp. B1-B2, noting also that the city council voted against asking the legislature to distribute replacement housing regionally at state expense. Minneapolis City Council adopted a "no net loss" policy according to Scott Russell and Sarah Tellijohn, "Affordable Housing: One Year Later," *Southwest Journal*, 9-22 October 2000, p. 1.

103. St. Paul officials noted in (no byline) "Low-Income Apartment Building to be Turned Over to Nonprofit," *Minneapolis Star Tribune*, 20 March 1998, p. B3. Mayor Sayles Belton's remark is from her 1999 State of the City address: "Minneapolis: A City That Works," 11 February 1999, p. 13.

104. Kevin Diaz, "Flophouse Residents Have an Ally Against Developers: The City," *Minneapolis Star Tribune*, 24 July 1999, p. 1.

105. State representative Todd Van Dellum in a speech to the Citizens League: "Housing Policy," 4 April 1995.

106. Kevin Duchschere, "Coleman Veto of Low-Income Housing Plan is Overridden," *Minneapolis Star Tribune*, 22 April 1999, p. B3.

107. Mayor Sayles Belton's quotes are from her 1999 State of the City Address, "Minneapolis: A City That Works," 11 February 1999, p. 13. "Sayles Belton vowed to double city spending on affordable housing, according to Kevin Diaz, "Sayles Belton Asks For a 7.1% Increase in Tax Collections," *Minneapolis Star Tribune*, 13 August 1999, p. B1. Council's approval of budget increase and tax hike noted in "Council, Mayor Approve Budget," *FYI Information* (A biweekly publication by the city of Minneapolis), 27 December 1999, p. 1. The city of Minneapolis spends (in 1999) an estimated $7 million annually on housing for people with the lowest incomes, and Mayor Sayles Belton recommended increasing city expenditures for affordable housing to $15 million annually, according to Kevin Diaz, "MCDA Calls Affordable Housing Report 'Problematic,'" *Minneapolis Star Tribune*, 17 August 1999, p. B3.

108. MCDA executive director Steve Cramer's quote is from Scott Russell and Sarah Tellijohn, "Affordable Housing: One Year Later," *Southwest Journal*, 9-22 October 2000, p. 1. Niland's position reported by Kevin Diaz, "Minneapolis Officials Back Low-Income Housing Plan," *Minneapolis Star Tribune*, 16 June 1998, p. B1.

109. In the year 2000, the 10 metro-area districts with the lowest median residential sales prices were all in Minneapolis and St. Paul (the metro is divided into 24 city districts and 77 suburban districts), and the core cities had only one district in highest-priced 10, according to the Minneapolis Area Association of Realtors, reported by Steve Brandt and Mary Lynn Smith, "For Cities, Big Home-Price Gains," *Minneapolis Star Tribune*, 4 March 2001, p. B1. Apartment rents noted in Collier Towle Real Estate, *2001 Towle Report, p. 35;* and in *Apartment Search Profiles* quarterly reports, 1996 through 2000, by Apartment Search, Edina, Minnesota; and Minneapolis Planning Department, *State of the City 2000,* p 21. David Browner of Apartment Search said that Minneapolis' average rent is likely lower than stated in his company's reports because public housing and small buildings of a dozen or fewer units are excluded from the data. These buildings are common in gray zones and they provide the lowest rents in the city. (Telephone discussion with David Browner, 25 October 2000).

110. Minneapolis Affordable Housing Task Force Report, 15 July 1999, city's resolution noted on p. 58, family priority noted on p. 16. Population loss noted in Minneapolis Planning Department, *State of the City 1998*, p. 2; p.131 lists "Develop and Implement an Affordable Housing Strategy" as one of the mayor's "1999 Priorities." There is no mention of a middle-class housing priority or strategy.

The city's surplus of low-income and very-low-income units outweighs its shortage of extremely-low-income units by 17,000, according to City of Minneapolis, Consolidated Plan for Housing and Community Development, Fiscal Year 1995, p. 321.

111. Minneapolis Affordable Housing Task Force Report, 15 July 1999, p. 59. HUD makes up to 20 percent of its HOPE VI funds available for social services, according Diane R. Suchman and Margaret B. Sowell, *Developing Infill Housing in Inner-City Neighborhoods: Opportunities and Strategies* (Washington, D.C.: Urban Land Institute, 1997), pp. 64-65.

112. Peter Dreier, "The New Politics of Housing: How to Rebuild the Constituency for a Progressive Federal Housing Policy," *Journal of the American Planning Association* 63, no. 1 (Winter 1997), p. 19.

113. Mike Kaszuba, "Fear of Decay Goes Beyond City Limits," *Minneapolis Star Tribune*, 20 October 1996, p. 1B, noting that Brooklyn Center officials planned to develop houses that would sell for prices starting at $120,000. The 1995 median in Lind-Bohanon-the adjacent Minneapolis neighborhood-was $52,500 according to data from Minneapolis Assessor, received 20 July 1996.

114. Mike Kaszuaba, "Brooklyn Park's Deal to Raze Apartments Raises Eyebrows," *Minneapolis Star Tribune,* 27 May 1998, p. 1. Hennepin County District Judge Thomas Carey ordered a temporary injunction against the demolition on June 30, citing the city's failure to meet standards for establishing the buildings as "distressed rental housing projects," a designation needed to use tax-increment financing, according to Mark Brunswick, "Brooklyn Park Deal to Raze Complex Is Blocked," *Minneapolis Star Tribune,* 2 July 1998, p. B1.

115. Mayor Sayles Belton's comments to Citizens League "Mind Opener Breakfast Series," St. Paul, 20 December 1996.

116. Mark Alan Hughes, "A Mobility Strategy for Improving Opportunity," *Housing Policy Debate* vol. 6, no. 1 (1995): 286.

117. Kevin Diaz, "Minneapolis Defers Vote on Housing Principles," *Minneapolis Star Tribune*, 9 June 1995, p. 2B.

118. Steve Brandt, "Lucy Mae Hollman's Moving Again," *Minneapolis Star Tribune*, 4 May 1999, p. 1.

119. Chicago homeowner quote reported by Flynn McRoberts and Abdon M. Pallasch, "Neighbors Wary of New Arrivals," *Chicago Tribune*, 28 December 1998, p. 1; Philadelphia complaint noted by Howard Husock, "Let's End Housing Vouchers," *City Journal*, Autumn 2000, p. 84.

120. Wolfgang Saxon, "Zachary Fisher, 88, Dies: Helped Alter New York Skyline," *New York Times*, 5 June 1999, p. C16.

121. John S. Adams, "Housing Submarkets in an American Metropolis," in *Our Changing Cities*, John Fraser Hunt, ed. (Baltimore: Johns Hopkins University Press, 1991), p. 124.

122. Edward Lewine, "The Great Divide," *New York Times*, 19 October 1997, Section 14, p. 1 (quote on p. 20).

123. Minneapolis Affordable Housing Task Force Report, 15 July 1999, p. 28.

CHAPTER 8 NOTES

1. Unnamed planner quoted by Steven Greenhouse, "Why Paris Works," *New York Times Magazine*, 19 July 1992, p. 16.

2. Kenneth Jackson, *Crabgrass Frontier: The Suburbanization of the United States* (New York: Oxford University Press, 1985), pp. 9, 102.

3. Alex Marshall, "Eurosprawl," *Metropolis*, January/February 1995, p. 79.

4. H.V. Savitch, *Post-Industrial Cities: Politics and Planning in New York, Paris, and London* (Princeton: Princeton University Press, 1988), quote from p. 120, see also pp. 115, 119.

5. H.V. Savitch, *Post-Industrial Cities: Politics and Planning in New York, Paris, and London* (Princeton: Princeton University Press, 1988), pp. 103-05, 120.

6. Steven Greenhouse, "Why Paris Works," *New York Times Magazine*, 19 July 1992.

7. Steven Greenhouse, "Why Paris Works," *New York Times Magazine*, 19 July 1992, pp. 16, 49; Statistical Abstract of the United States 1993, p. 194.

8. Public housing demolition noted by Marie Christine Loriers, "An Occasion for Architecture," *Progressive Architecture*, July 1987, p. 87. Suburban social problems noted by Steven Greenhouse, "Why Paris Works," *New York Times Magazine*, 19 July 1992, p. 29.

9. Thomas Kessner, *Fiorello H. LaGuardia and the Making of Modern New York* (New York: McGraw-Hill, 1989), pp. 334-35.

10. Property tax exemptions proposed by Wagenius was enacted into law (273.80 Distressed Homestead Reinvestment Exemption) with a five-year exemption period, which applies only to "detached single-family dwellings" in Minnesota's cities "of the first class," according to Minnesota House of Representatives, *Session Weekly*, 27 February 1998, p. 15. MCDA program reported by Neal Gendler, "Deferred Rehab Loan Program Offered in Minneapolis," *Minneapolis Star Tribune*, 20 November 1998, p. B7. Federally funded Single Family HOME Program noted in City of Minneapolis, *Consolidated Plan for Housing and Community Development*, Fiscal Year 1999, p. 41.

11. Jeanette Almada, "Building High Hopes: 'New Homes for Chicago' Jump-Starts Neighborhood Residential Development," *Chicago Tribune*, 21 November 1999, Real Estate section, p. 1.

12. David P. Varady and Jeffrey A. Raffel, *Selling Cities: Attracting Homebuyers through Schools and Housing Programs* (Albany: State University of New York Press, 1995), pp. 140-43, 155.

13. David P. Varady and Jeffrey A. Raffel, *Selling Cities: Attracting Homebuyers through Schools and Housing Programs* (Albany: State University of New York Press, 1995), pp. 12, 22, 29, 47-49.

14. David P. Varady and Jeffrey A. Raffel, *Selling Cities: Attracting Homebuyers through Schools and Housing Programs* (Albany: State University of New York Press, 1995), pp. 54-55 Table 3.1.

15. Alexander Garvin, *The American City: What Works, What Doesn't* (New York: McGraw Hill, 1996), pp. 302-07; Rachelle Garbarine, "Financing is Ready for 3 Mixed-Income Buildings," *New York Times,* 5 September 1997, p. B6; Peter Malbin, "Battery Park City: An Urban Suburb, with Yacht Basin," in *If You're Thinking of Living In . . . : All About 115 Great Neighborhoods In & Around New York,* Michael J. Leahy, ed. (New York: Random House, 1999) pp. 3-6, noting median household income of $110,000.

16. Numbers derived from data in Metropolitan Council, *Community Profiles,* July 1993; and Metropolitan Council, "Preliminary Forecasts of Population, Households and Employment, Regional Growth Strategy," March 1997.

17. Neighborhood Preservation Loan Program described by Greg Baron, Minnesota Housing Finance Agency (MHFA), telephone discussion 3 February 1995; Year 2000 data from Kathy Aanerud, MHFA, fax received 21 May 2001.

18. North Metro Mayors Association, *Housing Challenge 2020,* November 1996, p. 10; City of Minneapolis, *Consolidated Plan for Housing and Community Development,* Fiscal Year 1199, p. 41.

19. Laurie Blake, "Soundproofing Muffles Some Airport Noise Protest," *Minneapolis Star Tribune,* 9 May 1995, p. 1B; (no byline) "Residents Near Airport Applaud Soundproofing," *Minneapolis Star Tribune,* 3 November 1998, p. B2; Scott Russell, "Coming Soon to Your Neighborhood?" *Southwest Journal,* 26 February-11 March 2001, p. 1.

20. Mike Kaszuba, "Is American Dream Moving Farther Out?" *Minneapolis Star Tribune,* 5 August 1992, p. 1.

21. Kale Williams, "Housing Mobility As an Anti-Poverty Strategy," *The Responsive Community,* Summer 1995, pp 89-90.

22. Edward G. Goetz, Hin Kin Lam, and Anne Heitlinger, *There Goes the Neighborhood?* (Minneapolis: Center for Urban and Regional Affairs, and Neighborhood Planning for Community Revitalization, 1996), pp. 10, 24-26.

23. Qing Chen, "Spatial and Social Dimensions of Commuting," *Journal of the American Planning Association* 66, no. 1 (Winter 2000), pp. 74, 80.

24. Katy Reckdahl, "Little Monrovia," *City Pages,* 5 January 2000, p. 4.

25. (no byline) "Shifting Immigrant Settlement: The Suburbs Beckon," *Urban Research Monitor* 4, no. 6 (January/February 2000), p. 1, review of "Neighborhood Opportunity Structures of Immigrant Populations, 1980 and 1990" by George Galster, Kurt Metzger, and Ruth Waite, *Housing Policy Debate,* Volume 10, Issue 2, 1999; and "Immigrant Groups in the Suburbs" by Richard Alba, John Logan, Brian Stults, Golbert Marzan, and Wenquan Zhang, *American Sociological Review,* Volume 64, Issue 3, 1999.

26. "Immigrants bring their kids to suburbs for the educational opportunities just like everybody else," according to Lawrence Osborne, "Migration of the Melting Pot," *New York Times Magazine,* 9 April 2000, p. 97.

27. Urban versus rural poverty exit rates noted by Terry K. Adams, Greg J. Duncan, and William L. Rodgers, "The Persistence of Urban Poverty" in *Quiet Riots,* Fred R. Harris and Roger W. Wilkins, eds. (New York: Pantheon Books, 1988), p. 94. Welfare caseload reductions noted in HUD, *The State of the Cities 1998,* June 1998, p. 11; and by Bruce Katz and Katherine Allen, "Cities Matter: Shifting the Focus of Welfare Reform," *Brookings Review,* Summer 2001, p. 31.

28. Kay S. Hymowitz, "The Teen Mommy Track," *City Journal,* Autumn 1994, p. 25.

29. Marvin Olasky, *The Tragedy of American Compassion* (Washington, D.C.: Regnery, 1992), pp. 35-41.

30. Richard Meryhew, "Bronx Man Makes Good with Minnesotans' Help," *Minneapolis Star Tribune,* 3 June 1996, p. 1B.

31. Diane R. Suchman (with Margaret B. Sowell), *Developing Infill Housing in Inner-City Neighborhoods: Opportunities and Strategies* (Washington, D.C.: Urban Land Institute, 1997), pp. 3, 42.

32. Andres Duany, Elizabeth Plater-Zyberk, and Jeff Speck, *Suburban Nation: The Rise of Sprawl and the Decline of the American Dream* (New York: North Point Press, 2000), p. 172.

33. Anemona Hartocollis, "Parents Want High Schoolers Closer to Home," *New York Times*, 11 October 2000, p. 1.

34. J.M. Almonor and J.G. Shulman, "School District Boundaries Carve Ethnic Enclaves," *Minneapolis Star Tribune*, 17 November 1997, p. A13.

35. Anemona Hartocollis, "Teacher Hiring Plan Is More Than a Matter of Decree," *New York Times*, 2 September 2000, p. B1; Abby Goodnough, "Schools Chief Says State Rule Hinders Hiring," *New York Times*, 16 October 2000, p. B1.

36. David P. Varady and Jeffrey A. Raffel, *Selling Cities: Attracting Homebuyers through Schools and Housing Programs* (Albany: State University of New York Press, 1995), p. 205.

37. Sara Mosle, "The Stealth Chancellor," *New York Times Magazine*, 31 August 1997, p. 32.

38. Sara Mosle, "The Stealth Chancellor," *New York Times Magazine*, 31 August 1997, p. 56.

39. Erik Larson, "Where Does the Money Go?" *Time*, 27 October 1997, p. 92.

40. Heather Mac Donald, "How Gotham's Elite High Schools Escaped the Leveler's Ax," *City Journal*, Spring 1999, p.74. Mac Donald quotes the *Washington Post's* Jonathan Yardley: "[urban educators] assume that the only way to make schools genuinely democratic is to make them genuinely inferior." Superintendent Carol Johnson quoted by Allie Shah, "Schools Take Aim at the Success Gap," *Minneapolis Star Tribune*, 12 February 2001, p. B1. See also Allie Shah, "Help for Minority Students Will Benefit All, Schools Say" *Minneapolis Star Tribune*, 13 February 2001, p. B1.

41. Anemona Hartocollis, "The New, Flexible Math Meets Parental Rebellion," *New York Times*, 27 April 2000, p. 1.

42. David P. Varady and Jeffrey A. Raffel, *Selling Cities: Attracting Homebuyers through Schools and Housing Programs* (Albany: State University of New York Press, 1995), pp. 205-206.

43. Erik Larson, "Where Does the Money Go?" *Time*, 27 October 1997, pp. 88-93.

44. Thomas Sowell, "Superficial Help, At Cost of a Profound Loss," *Minneapolis Star Tribune*, 1 May 2000, p. A13.

45. David P. Varady and Jeffrey A. Raffel, *Selling Cities: Attracting Homebuyers through Schools and Housing Programs* (Albany: State University of New York Press, 1995), p. 230.

46. Letter to the Editor, *Detroit Free Press*, 20 October 1997, p. 12A

47. Linda Sauer, "Choosing Suburbs Doesn't Make Them Racists," *Minneapolis Star Tribune*, 23 October 1998, p. A26. Sauer, a resident of the developing suburb Maple Grove, and a senior scientist at the University of Minnesota, wrote: "For years I have been reading in your paper about 'horrible' people who live in the suburbs. . . . We're not racist. We're caring parents."

The *Star Tribune* article referenced in Sauer's letter appeared on 19 October 1998, p. B1: "Plan for Edina School With Minneapolis Pupils Is Resisted," by Mark Brunswick, who cited Edina's "lack of diversity," and wrote: "Some residents of the Morningside area of Edina would rather see Minneapolis water in their neighborhood than Minneapolis schoolkids."

48. (no byline) "Basic Skills Test Results" *Minneapolis Star Tribune*, 29 April 1999, pp. A16-A18. The oft-heard rationale that urban schools' test results are suppressed by the unique mission of educating immigrants is suspect: zero percent of the students at Minneapolis' Broadway school are "limited English proficient, yet the school produced the state's worst test results according to district data. Samuel G. Freedman, who has researched and written about public education, cites Queens' Newton High School, which educates children from 125 countries speaking 43 languages, as an example of excellence. Newton sends about 85 percent of its graduates to college. ("Broken but Not Unfixable," *New York Times*, 30 April 1999, p. A31).

49. Norimitsu Onishi, "Four Teen-agers Charged in Rape of Girl in a Classroom in Queens," *New York Times*, 21 May 1997, p. 1.

50. William J. Bennett, *The Devaluing of America: The Fight for Our Culture and Our Children* (New York: Summit, 1992), p. 90.

51. David P. Varady and Jeffrey A. Raffel, *Selling Cities: Attracting Homebuyers through Schools and Housing Programs* (Albany: State University of New York Press, 1995), pp. 215, 218, 242.

52. Former Secretary of Education William Bennett suggests that even in a bad neighborhood, a good school can attract middle-class students. Bennett cites Dayton Ohio's Edison Elementary School, which is, according to Bennett, "in the worst section of Dayton," but, thanks to the academic achievement elicited by an outstanding principal, it is "sought out by parents all over Dayton." (William J. Bennett, *The Devaluing of America: The Fight for Our Culture and Our Children* [New York: Summit, 1992], pp. 83-84)

53. David P. Varady and Jeffrey A. Raffel, *Selling Cities: Attracting Homebuyers through Schools and Housing Programs* (Albany: State University of New York Press, 1995), pp. 230, 253-54. In the aftermath of the expulsion of seven black students for fighting at a high school football game in Decatur, Illinois, the Rev. Jesse Jackson criticized schools' "zero tolerance" policies and asked the Clinton administration to investigate their effect on minority students. Jackson and other civil-rights leaders asked the Department of Education to gather information, according to race, on expulsions and suspensions. (Dirk Johnson, "Jackson Arrested in Protest Over Expulsions of Students," *New York Times*, 17 November 1999, p. A16)

54. Brian C. Anderson and Matt Robinson, *City Journal*, Autumn 1998, p. 55, quote on p. 62.

55. Brian C. Anderson and Matt Robinson, "Willie Brown Shows How Not to Run a City," *City Journal*, Autumn 1998, p. 55.

56. Heather Mac Donald, "How Gotham's Elite High Schools Escaped the Leveler's Ax," *City Journal*, Spring 1999, p. 68; Craig Horowitz, "The Upper West Side of Suburbia," *New York* magazine, 18 November 1996, p. 49; David P. Varady and Jeffrey A. Raffel, *Selling Cities: Attracting Homebuyers through Schools and Housing Programs* (Albany: State University of New York Press, 1995), p 243; Allie Shah, "St. Paul School Faces Hard Question: Who's Gifted?" *Minneapolis Star Tribune*, 20 March 2000, p. 1, noting that school administrators in St. Paul wanted to increase the number of minority and poor students in the elite Capitol Hill Magnet School so they abandoned the traditional practice of testing intellectual ability and employed a test "designed to add more minority and poor children to the ranks of the gifted." Under the old admissions regime, test scores were consistently above average, but the new batch of students tested "all over the map, ranging from the highest levels to a score so low that remedial education could be warranted." Teachers complain that they must now work to keep students focused on learning and that lessons now take more time. Some officials worry that high-achieving students will become bored while waiting for other students to catch up.

57. David P. Varady and Jeffrey A. Raffel, *Selling Cities: Attracting Homebuyers through Schools and Housing Programs* (Albany: State University of New York Press, 1995), pp. 241-42.

CHAPTER 9 NOTES

1. Daniel Patrick Moynihan, "Putting Pizzazz Back in Public Works," *New York Times*, 6 March 1998, p. A23.

2. Jane Jacobs, *The Death and Life of Great American Cities* (New York: Random House, 1961), p. 150.

3. Peter Medoff and Holly Sklar, *Streets of Hope: The Fall and Rise of an Urban Neighborhood* (Boston: South End Press, 1994), p. 266.

4. (no byline) "Group Celebrates 20 Years of Giving Residents Hope," *Minneapolis Star Tribune*, 6 October 1997, p. B6.

5. John Kain and William Apgar, *Housing and Neighborhood Dynamics: A Simulation Study* (Cambridge: Harvard University Press, 1985) pp. 128-29. See also John Sullivan, "Fiasco in Urban Renewal: A Case Study in Brooklyn," *New York Times*, 3 January 2000, p. B4.

6. In 2001, *Minneapolis Star Tribune* reporter Steve Brandt concluded that Minneapolis' modest population growth in the 1990s is attributable to national and regional forces rather than programs such as NRP (Steve Brandt, "With Strong Growth in Core Cities, How Much Effort to Public Efforts?" *Minneapolis Star Tribune*, 30 March 2001, p. A8). 1998 analysis of NRP reported by Steve Brandt, "Spending Millions With Unclear Results," *Minneapolis Star Tribune*, 30 January 1998, p. 1.

7. David Rusk, *Inside Game, Outside Game: Winning Strategies for Saving Urban America* (Washington, D.C.: Brookings Institution Press, 1999), pp. 41, 58, 60.

8. Avis C. Vidal, "CDCs as Agents of Neighborhood Change: The State of the Art," in *Revitalizing Urban Neighborhoods*, W. Dennis Keating, Norman Krumholz, and Philip Star, eds. (Lawrence: University Press of Kansas, 1996), p. 156.

9. Minneapolis Planning Department, *State of the City 1996*, January 1997, p. 166.

10. Minneapolis Planning Department, staff comment at "Learning From" meeting, 23 October 1997.

11. Rip Rapson and Gretchen Nichols, *Defining Community: A Neighborhood Perspective* (Minneapolis: Design Center for American Urban Landscape, University of Minnesota, 1996), quote from p. 13, downzoning noted on p. 9.

12. Mary Ellen Egan and Kim Nauer, "Mapping the Future," *City Limits*, October 1995, p. 17, quoting Darlene Walser, Jordan Area Community Council.

13. Minneapolis Planning Department, *The Minneapolis Plan: The City of Minneapolis Comprehensive Plan*, adopted March 24, 2000, pp. 1.4.29, 1.4.40.

14. Minneapolis Planning Department, *The Minneapolis Plan: Workbook for Citizen Comment*, June 1997, p. 47.

15. Cramer's commitment to rehabilitation noted by Ken Eisinger, "Board-ups Eyed for Affordable Housing," *Minneapolis Star Tribune*, 14 August 1999, pp. B1-B2. HUD's role noted in *Minneapolis Star Tribune*, 4 August 1995, p. B7.

16. Cleveland noted in Diane Corcelli, "Cleveland's Rejuvenated Neighborhoods," *Urban Land*, April 1996, p. 44. Cincinnati noted in David P. Varady and Jeffrey A. Raffel, *Selling Cities: Attracting Homebuyers through Schools and Housing Programs* (Albany: State University of New York Press, 1995), pp. 133-34.

17. Minneapolis Planning Department, *Minneapolis Neighborhood Housing Comparison*, Working Copy, September 19, 1994: NRP, Planning Information Base, for all Near North neighborhoods except Sumner-Glenwood (public housing), 1992 and 1994.

18. David P. Varady and Jeffrey A. Raffel, *Selling Cities: Attracting Homebuyers through Schools and Housing Programs* (Albany: State University of New York Press, 1995), p. 182, 193. A for-profit developer built 21 townhouses in 1997 and 15 detached houses in 1999 in the East End, all priced at about $300,000 and above; the city has provided tax abatements and an infrastructure grant to the 1999 development, according to John Eckberg, "Upscale Housing in a Downscale Cincinnati Area," *New York Times*, 25 April 1999.

19. Peter Medoff and Holly Sklar, *Streets of Hope: The Fall and Rise of an Urban Neighborhood* (Boston: South End Press, 1994), pp. 100, 108, 151.

20. Peter Medoff and Holly Sklar, *Streets of Hope: The Fall and Rise of an Urban Neighborhood* (Boston: South End Press, 1994), p. 110.

21. Nina Walfoort, "New Land-use Plan Still Needs Scrutiny, Aldermen Contend," *Louisville Courier-Journal*, 18 September 1996, p. B1.

22. "The last 24 hours have been kind . . ." noted in *Chicago Tribune* "A Little Slice of Innocence," 1 June 1997. Fifteen-year-old girl killed noted in Tom McCann, "Girl Dies After Cabrini Shooting; Suspect Is 13," *Chicago Tribune*, 28 April 2000, Metro Chicago section p. 3. Additional sources for Cabrini-Green crime reports include Alex Kotlowitz, *There Are No Children Here* (New York: Anchor Books, 1992) p. 25; and reports in the *Chicago Tribune* on the following dates: 5 and 6 March 1997; 12 and 17 April 1997; 1 June 1997; 1, 10, 12, 13, 30 October 1997; 7 and 20 November 1997; 18 and 20 December 1997; 26 March 1998; 1 and 2 June 1998; 28 and 29 November 1999; 28 April 2000; 28 May 2000, all from internet archives, search words "Cabrini Green." Pregnancies of 10-year-old girls noted in Lola Smallwood, "Teen Mom Drop is Birth of Hope," *Chicago Tribune*, 17 March 1998, Metro Chicago section p. 1. Seven percent unemployment noted in Mary Schmich, "As Cabrini Fades, Will the Poor Become Ghosts?" *Chicago Tribune*, 31 July 1998, p. 1. Girl X information from Associated Press, "Suspect Arraigned in Assault on Girl X," *Minneapolis Star Tribune*, 5 April 1997, p. A17.

23. The Cabrini-Green Local Advisory Council filed a lawsuit in 1996 seeking to block demolition of Cabrini buildings unless all public-housing units were replaced on site, reported by Noreen S. Ahmed-Ullah, "Residents Are Warned to Monitor Cabrini-Green Development Plans," *Chicago Tribune*, 8 June 2000, Metro Chicago section p. 5. See also Flynn McRoberts, J. Linn Allen, and Cindy Richards, "When Two Worlds Collide at Cabrini," *Chicago Tribune*, 30 July 1998, p. 1 of Metro Chicago section; Karen Craven and Diane Struzi, "5 Evicted from 3-Flat Near Cabrini-Green," *Chicago Tribune*, 20 April 1999, News section p. 1; Robert Sharoff, "Chicago Tries to Upgrade a Neighborhood," *New York Times*, 10 September 2000, p. 47; and Robert A. Axelrod, "Breaking Ground in Chicago's Downtown," *Urban Land*, October 1998, p. 77.

24. Protest against demolition noted in editorial, "Affordable Housing," *Minneapolis Star Tribune*, 13 June 1999, p. A28. Clarence Hightower's advisory group proposed a density of only six to 10 units per acre, according to Steve Brandt, "Moderate Housing is Axed from Plan," *Minneapolis Star Tribune*, 13 December 1997, p. B1. Activists demanded that at least half of new units be subsidized, according to Kevin Diaz, "Sayles Belton Pledges to Speed Housing Plan," *Minneapolis Star Tribune*, June 19, 1999, p. 1.

25. Roberta Brandes Gratz, *The Living City* (New York, Simon & Schuster, Touchstone, 1989), p. 79.

26. Abramovitz quoted in Peter Medoff and Holly Sklar, *Streets of Hope: The Fall and Rise of an Urban Neighborhood* (Boston: South End Press, 1994), p. 206.

27. Peter Medoff and Holly Sklar, *Streets of Hope: The Fall and Rise of an Urban Neighborhood* (Boston: South End Press, 1994), p. 193.

28. Peter Medoff and Holly Sklar, *Streets of Hope: The Fall and Rise of an Urban Neighborhood* (Boston: South End Press, 1994), p. 193.

29. "It takes a village . . ." from Peter Medoff and Holly Sklar, *Streets of Hope: The Fall and Rise of an Urban Neighborhood* (Boston: South End Press, 1994), p. 174; see also p. 197.

Psychologists Louis B Silverstein and Carl F. Auerbach claim that the superiority of the traditional family is a myth promoted by "neoconservatives" as a "reaction to [the] loss of male power and privilege." "We see the argument that fathers are essential as an attempt to reinstate male dominance . . ." Predictably, the psychologists invoke "institutionalized racism" as a root cause of the social distress that is associated with father absence in urban America. (Louis B Silverstein and Carl F. Auerbach, "Deconstructing the Essential Father," *American Psychologist*, June 1999, pp. 397-407.)

30. Peter Duffy, "Paradise Lost?" *Eastside Resident,* August 27-September 2, 1997, p. 6.

31. Neil Smith, "New City, New Frontier," in *Variations on a Theme Park*, Michael Sorkin, ed. (New York: Hill and Wang, 1992), p. 91.

32. Brian J.L. Berry, "Islands of Renewal in Seas of Decay," in *The New Urban Reality*, Paul E. Peterson, ed. (Washington ,D.C.: The Brookings Institution, 1985), p. 92.

33. John Kain and William Apgar, *Housing and Neighborhood Dynamics: A Simulation Study* (Cambridge: Harvard University Press, 1985), p. 112; Myron Orfield, *Metropolitics* (Washington, D.C.: Brookings Institution Press, and Cambridge: Lincoln Institute of Land Policy, 1997), p. 76.

34. John Kain and William Apgar, *Housing and Neighborhood Dynamics: A Simulation Study* (Cambridge: Harvard University Press, 1985), p. 111.

35. Zane L. Miller and Bruce Tucker, *Changing Plans for America's Inner Cities: Cincinnati's Over-the-Rhine and Twentieth-Century Urbanism* (Columbus: Ohio State University Press, 1998), pp. 114, 161.

36. Neil Smith, "New City, New Frontier," in *Variations on a Theme Park, Michael Sorkin,* ed. (New York: Hill and Wang, 1992), pp. 85-86.

37. Eric Wieffering, "The Twisted Economics of Minneapolis Neighborhood Nonprofits and Low-income Housing," *Corporate Report Minnesota*, March 1994, p. 61; "disdain" noted by Terry Fiedler in "Editor's Note," p. 4.

38. Peter Medoff and Holly Sklar, *Streets of Hope: The Fall and Rise of an Urban Neighborhood* (Boston: South End Press, 1994), p. 186.

39. Peter Medoff and Holly Sklar, *Streets of Hope: The Fall and Rise of an Urban Neighborhood* (Boston: South End Press, 1994), pp. 52-53, 109, 113.

40. Peter Medoff and Holly Sklar, *Streets of Hope: The Fall and Rise of an Urban Neighborhood* (Boston: South End Press, 1994), pp. 5, 131, 147, 155, 157, 159. 264-65. Association of Neighborhood Housing Developers noted by Heather Mac Donald, "The Billions of Dollars That Made Things Worse," *City Journal*, Autumn 1996, p. 42.

41. Zane L. Miller and Bruce Tucker, *Changing Plans for America's Inner Cities: Cincinnati's Over-the-Rhine and Twentieth-Century Urbanism* (Columbus: Ohio State University Press, 1998), p. 102, 118.

42. Cherryhomes noted by Eric Wieffering, "Housing That Sucks," *Twin Cities Reader,* 23-29 March 1994, p. 12. Cramer noted by Kevin Diaz, "City Won't Spend $300,000 to Reopen 70 Housing Units," *Minneapolis Star Tribune*, 28 July 1999, p. 1. Former St. Paul Mayor Jim Scheibel is now the executive director of the nonprofit developer Project for Pride in Living, according to Steve Brandt, "Rehabbing Phillips Housing Illustrates Some Quandaries of Redeveloping City's Core," *Minneapolis Star Tribune*, 27 June 2000, p. B1.

43. Eric Wieffering, "The Twisted Economics of Minneapolis Neighborhood Nonprofits and Low-income Housing," *Corporate Report Minnesota*, March 1994, p. 61 (see pp. 66-67).

44. Eric Wieffering, "Housing That Sucks," *Twin Cities Reader,* 23-29 March 1994, p. 12, quote on p. 13.

45. Terry Pristin, "In Bedford-Stuyvesant, The Boom Remains a Bust," *New York Times,* 29 May 2000, p. B1; David Rusk, *Inside Game, Outside Game: Winning Strategies for Saving Urban America* (Washington, D.C.: Brookings Institution Press, 1999), p. 25.

46. Eric Wieffering, "The Twisted Economics of Minneapolis Neighborhood Nonprofits and Low-income Housing," *Corporate Report Minnesota*, March 1994, p. 61, quote on p. 67.

47. Minnesota Council of Nonprofits, *Minnesota Nonprofit Directory*, 1996-1998, p. 46.

48. Zane L. Miller and Bruce Tucker, *Changing Plans for America's Inner Cities: Cincinnati's Over-the-Rhine and Twentieth-Century Urbanism* (Columbus: Ohio State University Press, 1998), p. 116, 133.

49. Peter Medoff and Holly Sklar, *Streets of Hope: The Fall and Rise of an Urban Neighborhood* (Boston: South End Press, 1994), p. 159.

50. Alice S. Baum and Donald W. Burns 1993, *A Nation in Denial: The Truth About Homelessness* (Boulder: Westview Press, 1993), pp. 2-3.

51. C. Dugger, "A Roof for All, Made of Rulings and Red Tape," *New York Times*, 4 July 1993, p. 1 (see p. 28).

52. U.S. Department of Commerce and HUD, *American Housing Survey for the United States in 1995*, July 1997, Tables 1B-7 and 1C-7; Minneapolis Planning Department, *State of the City 1998*, January 1999, p. 16.

53. "People's Summit on Affordable Housing," KTCA, 3 December 1997.

54. The Minneapolis Affordable Housing Task Force, convened in 1998 and composed largely of housing advocates and nonprofit housing developers, proposed an affordable-housing budget based on a cost of $128,000 per unit, the 1998 Twin Cities metro median for single-family houses: *Minneapolis Affordable Housing Task Force Report*, 15 July 1999, p. 16. 1998 median value reported by Jim Buchta, "Home Prices Just Keep Going Up," *Minneapolis Star Tribune*, 11 February 1999, p. 1. Inflated construction costs for Minneapolis' Project for Pride in Living units reported by Steve Brandt, "Rehabbing Phillips Housing Illustrates Some Quandaries of Redeveloping City's Core," *Minneapolis Star Tribune*, 27 June 2000, p. B1.

55. *Minneapolis Affordable Housing Task Force Report*, 15 July 1999, p. 1.

56. U.S. Conference of Mayors' Status Report on Hunger and Homelessness in American Cities, 1998, cited in "There's No Place Like Home" report by Housing America and Doc4Kids.

57. Donna Etienne interview, 6 August 1999; Ms. Etienne also noted that fast-food restaurants take too much of her clients' food budget.

58. Elijah Anderson, *Code of the Street: Decency, Violence, and the Moral Life of the Inner City* (New York: W.W. Norton, 1999) pp. 45, 163-65.

59. Rachel Bratt, professor of urban policy at Tufts University, says, ". . . we do not have the luxury of bemoaning larger economic trends that may be beyond the reach of local nonprofits. The only reasonable response is to . . . do whatever is possible to try to meet the need and alleviate human suffering." (Rachel G Bratt, "Community Based Housing Organizations." in *Revitalizing Urban Neighborhoods*, W. Dennis Keating, Norman Krumholz, and Philip Star, eds. [Lawrence: University Press of Kansas, 1996], p. 181.)

60. Edward G. Goetz, Hin Kin Lam, and Anne Heitlinger, *There Goes the Neighborhood?* (Minneapolis: Center for Urban and Regional Affairs and Neighborhood Planning for Community Revitalization, 1996), pp. 71-72.

61. Edward G. Goetz, Hin Kin Lam, and Anne Heitlinger, *There Goes the Neighborhood?* (Minneapolis: Center for Urban and Regional Affairs and Neighborhood Planning for Community Revitalization, 1996), p. 42; 1999 value and tax from telephone inquiry to Hennepin County property tax office, 19 July 1999.

62. Kevin Duchschere, "St. Paul Council OKs Affordable-housing Project," *Minneapolis Star Tribune*, 16 December 1998, p. B2; Pat Burson, "From Blight to Bright Future," Saint Paul Pioneer Press, 21 February 2000, p. 1; Median price of Twin Cities detached houses was $128,000 in 1998, according to Jim Buchta, "Home Prices Just Keep Going Up," *Minneapolis Star Tribune*, 11 February 1999, p. 1.

63. Peter Medoff and Holly Sklar, *Streets of Hope: The Fall and Rise of an Urban Neighborhood* (Boston: South End Press, 1994), pp. 50-51, 160.

64. Lawrence W. Kennedy, *Planning the City Upon a Hill* (Amherst: University of Massachusetts Press, 1992), pp. 201, 231.

65. David P. Varady and Jeffrey A. Raffel, *Selling Cities: Attracting Homebuyers through Schools and Housing Programs* (Albany: State University of New York Press, 1995), p. 198.

66. David P. Varady and Jeffrey A. Raffel, *Selling Cities: Attracting Homebuyers through Schools and Housing Programs* (Albany: State University of New York Press, 1995), pp. 179, 182-83.

67. "Permanent low-income . . . ghetto" statement by Karla Irvine, executive director of Housing Opportunities Made Equal, quoted in Zane L. Miller and Bruce Tucker, *Changing Plans for America's Inner Cities: Cincinnati's Over-the-Rhine and Twentieth-Century Urbanism* (Columbus: Ohio State University Press, 1998), p. 161; Councilman Tarbell quoted by Rosemary Goudreau, "Councilman Gives Account of Fatal Chase," *Cincinnati Enquirer*, 14 April 2001, Local News, p. 1.

68. Zane L. Miller and Bruce Tucker, *Changing Plans for America's Inner Cities: Cincinnati's Over-the-Rhine and Twentieth-Century Urbanism* (Columbus: Ohio State University Press, 1998), p. 61.

69. Zane L. Miller and Bruce Tucker, *Changing Plans for America's Inner Cities: Cincinnati's Over-the-Rhine and Twentieth-Century Urbanism* (Columbus: Ohio State University Press, 1998), pp. 56-57, 69.

70. Zane L. Miller and Bruce Tucker, *Changing Plans for America's Inner Cities: Cincinnati's Over-the-Rhine and Twentieth-Century Urbanism* (Columbus: Ohio State University Press, 1998), p. 161.

71. Zane L. Miller and Bruce Tucker, *Changing Plans for America's Inner Cities: Cincinnati's Over-the-Rhine and Twentieth-Century Urbanism* (Columbus: Ohio State University Press, 1998), p. xix.

72. Norman Krumholz, "The Provision of Affordable Housing in Cleveland," in *Affordable Housing and Urban Redevelopment in the United States, Urban Affairs Annual Reviews* #46, 1997, pp. 52-72, quote on p. 65.

73. David P. Varady and Jeffrey A. Raffel, *Selling Cities: Attracting Homebuyers through Schools and Housing Programs* (Albany: State University of New York Press, 1995), p. 128.

74. Sidney Brower, "Planners in the Neighborhood: A Cautionary Tale," in *Urban Neighborhoods: Research and Policy*, Ralph B. Taylor, ed. (New York: Praeger, 1986), pp. 181-214 (quote on p. 205).

75. William M. Rohe and Lauren B. Gates, "Neighborhood Planning in America: Accomplishments and Limitations," in *Urban Neighborhoods: Research and Policy*, edited by Ralph B. Taylor, (New York: Praeger, 1986), p. 30.

76. Susan S. Fainstein and Clifford Hirst, "Neighborhood Organizations and Community Planning: The Minneapolis Neighborhood Revitalization Program," in *Revitalizing Urban Neighborhoods*, W. Dennis Keating, Norman Krumholz, and Philip Star, eds. (Lawrence: University of Kansas Press, 1996), p.106.

77. Susan S. Fainstein and Clifford Hirst, "Neighborhood Organizations and Community Planning: The Minneapolis Neighborhood Revitalization Program," in *Revitalizing Urban Neighborhoods*, W. Dennis Keating, Norman Krumholz, and Philip Star, eds. (Lawrence: University of Kansas Press, 1996) p. 105.

78. Howell S. Baum, "Ethical Behavior is Extraordinary Behavior," *Journal of the American Planning Association* 64, no. 4 (Autumn 1998), pp. 414-15.

79. Myron Orfield, *Metropolitics* (Washington, D.C.: Brookings Institution Press, and Cambridge: Lincoln Institute of Land Policy, 1997), p. 76. Daniel Patrick Moynihan reported the election farce associated with the federal government's Community Action Program, "The device of holding elections among the poor to choose representation for the [neighborhood] governing boards made the program look absurd. The turnouts in effect declared that the poor weren't interested." (Daniel P. Moynihan, *Maximum Feasible Misunderstanding: Community Action in the War on Poverty* [New York: The Free Press, 1970,] p. 137.

80. Peter Medoff and Holly Sklar, *Streets of Hope: The Fall and Rise of an Urban Neighborhood* (Boston: South End Press, 1994), pp. 74-75.

81. Urban Land Institute, ULI Advisory Services, "Roxbury Massachusetts," 12-17 June 1994, p. 44.

82. Peter Medoff and Holly Sklar, *Streets of Hope: The Fall and Rise of an Urban Neighborhood* (Boston: South End Press, 1994), "true inclusive participation noted on p. 257; "this meeting will be geared . . ." noted on p. 49. See also Rohe and Gates, "Neighborhood Planning in America: Accomplishments and Limitations," in *Urban Neighborhoods: Research and Policy*, Ralph B. Taylor, ed. (New York: Praeger, 1986), p. 27, noting poor meeting attendance.

83. Curt Brown, "Advocate Fights to Keep Roofs Over Others' Heads," *Minneapolis Star Tribune*, 20 June 1999, p. B1.

84. Michael Patrick MacDonald, *All Souls: A Family Story in Southie* (Boston: Beacon Press, 1999), p. 3.

85. Howell S. Baum, "Ethical Behavior is Extraordinary Behavior," *Journal of the American Planning Association* 64, no. 4 (Autumn 1998), pp. 414-15, 418.

86. Zane L. Miller and Bruce Tucker, *Changing Plans for America's Inner Cities: Cincinnati's Over-the-Rhine and Twentieth-Century Urbanism* (Columbus: Ohio State University Press, 1998), pp. 112, 153-54.

87. Zane L. Miller and Bruce Tucker, *Changing Plans for America's Inner Cities: Cincinnati's Over-the-Rhine and Twentieth-Century Urbanism* (Columbus: Ohio State University Press, 1998), p. 112.

88. Zane L. Miller and Bruce Tucker, *Changing Plans for America's Inner Cities: Cincinnati's Over-the-Rhine and Twentieth-Century Urbanism* (Columbus: Ohio State University Press, 1998), p. 159, Gray gained control noted on p. 118.

89. Zane L. Miller and Bruce Tucker, *Changing Plans for America's Inner Cities: Cincinnati's Over-the-Rhine and Twentieth-Century Urbanism* (Columbus: Ohio State University Press, 1998), p. 151, middle-income people would object noted on p. 117.

90. Zane L. Miller and Bruce Tucker, *Changing Plans for America's Inner Cities: Cincinnati's Over-the-Rhine and Twentieth-Century Urbanism* (Columbus: Ohio State University Press, 1998), "sided almost from the outset" on p. 125; deference to neighborhood autonomy noted on p. 118, see also p. 127.

91. Myron Orfield, *Metropolitics* (Washington, D.C.: Brookings Institution Press, and Cambridge: The Lincoln Institute of Land Policy, 1997), quote on p. 57; preferences for racially integrated neighborhoods noted on p. 83, which includes the following observation: "African Americans ... express a strong distaste for neighborhoods that are entirely African-American."

92. Zane L. Miller and Bruce Tucker, *Changing Plans for America's Inner Cities: Cincinnati's Over-the-Rhine and Twentieth-Century Urbanism* (Columbus: Ohio State University Press, 1998), p. 139.

93. Zane L. Miller and Bruce Tucker, *Changing Plans for America's Inner Cities: Cincinnati's Over-the-Rhine and Twentieth-Century Urbanism* (Columbus: Ohio State University Press, 1998), p. 166.

94. Paul L. Knox, *Urbanization: An Introduction to Urban Geography* (Englewood Cliffs, New Jersey: Simon and Schuster, Prentice-Hall, 1994), p. 351.

95. Knox quote in Paul L. Knox, *Urbanization: An Introduction to Urban Geography* (Englewood Cliffs, New Jersey: Simon and Schuster, Prentice-Hall), 1994, p. 351; Mailer quote in Kenneth T. Jackson, ed. *Encyclopedia of New York City* (New Haven: Yale University Press, 1995), p. 805.

96. Allan Jacobs and Donald Appleyard, "Toward an Urban Design Manifesto" in *The City Reader*, Richard T. LeGates and Frederic Stout, eds. (New York: Routledge, 1996), p. 170; Zane L. Miller and Bruce Tucker, *Changing Plans for America's Inner Cities: Cincinnati's Over-the-Rhine and Twentieth-Century Urbanism* (Columbus: Ohio State University Press, 1998), p. 152.

97. Daniel P. Moynihan, *Maximum Feasible Misunderstanding: Community Action in the War on Poverty* (New York: The Free Press, 1970), pp. 73, 76.

98. Community Action Programs described by Daniel P. Moynihan, *Maximum Feasible Misunderstanding* (New York: The Free Press, 1970), pp. 73, 76; Bedford-Stuyvesant Restoration Corporation noted in David Rusk, *Inside Game, Outside Game: Winning Strategies for Saving Urban America* (Washington, D.C.: The Brookings Institution Press, 1999), p. 25. National Affordable Housing Act noted by Rachell G. Bratt, "Community-Based Housing Organizations," in *Revitalizing Urban Neighborhoods*, W. Dennis Keating, Norman Krumholz, and Philip Star, eds. (Lawrence: University Press of Kansas, 1996), p. 181. HUD's 203(k) program noted by John Sullivan, "Fiasco in Urban Renewal: A Case Study in Brooklyn," *New York Times*, 3 January 2000, p. B4.

99. Heather Mac Donald, "The Billions of Dollars That Made Things Worse," *City Journal*, Autumn 1996, "welfare state" quote from p. 29, Schrank quote from p. 33, Pifer quote from p. 26.

100. Daniel P. Moynihan, *Maximum Feasible Misunderstanding: Community Action in the War on Poverty* (New York: The Free Press, 1970), "invented a new level," p. 42; "public disorder," p. 180; program director in Newark noted on p. 156; "no ends are accomplished," p. 133; "power of rioting," pp. xxvi-xxvii; Metropolitan Applies Research Center study noted on p. xxxvi; Chicago gangs noted by Heather Mac Donald, "The Billions of Dollars That Made Things Worse," *City Journal*, Autumn 1996, p. 31. Paul Grogan, once a national leader in the CDC movement, has admitted that the community action era was one marked by a "riot ideology" of "racial demagoguery, demands for patronage, hints of unrest if demands aren't met, a preference for confrontation over visible results." (Paul Grogan and Tony Proscio, *Comeback Cities: A Blueprint for Neighborhood Revival* [Boulder, Colorado: Westview Press, 2000], pp. 66-67.)

101. Daniel P. Moynihan, *Maximum Feasible Misunderstanding: Community Action in the War on Poverty* (New York: The Free Press, 1970), quote from p. 112; conflict between blacks and Puerto Ricans noted on p. 114.

102. Tamar Jacoby, *Someone Else's House: America's Unfinished Struggle for Integration* (New York: Basic Books, 1998), "separatist hatred" and "poisonous levels" quotes from p. 186; activists not supported by parents noted on p. 180; Ford Foundation support noted on pp. 189, 196.

103. Tamar Jacoby, *Someone Else's House: America's Unfinished Struggle for Integration* (New York: Basic Books, 1998), "bigotry from black extremists" quote from p. 210; "spiral of hatred" quote from p. 214; student attacks incited by militant teacher noted on p. 188; teachers fired because of race noted on pp. 189, 191, 195.

104. Tamar Jacoby, *Someone Else's House: America's Unfinished Struggle for Integration* (New York: Basic Books, 1998), pp. 180, 197, 216-20.

105. Bundy's "disruption" quote from Tamar Jacoby, *Someone Else's House: America's Unfinished Struggle for Integration* (New York: Basic Books, 1998), p. 215. Bundy's "The foundation is a creature" quote from Heather Mac Donald, "The Billions of Dollars That Made Things Worse," *City Journal*, Autumn 1996, p. 33.

106. Heather Mac Donald, "The Billions of Dollars That Made Things Worse," *City Journal*, Autumn 1996, p. 33.

107. Heather Mac Donald, "The Billions of Dollars That Made Things Worse," *City Journal*, Autumn 1996, "the impulse" on p. 42; "once an agent" on p. 26.

108. Peter Dreier, "The New Politics of Housing," *Journal of the American Planning Association* 63, no.1 (Winter 1997), p. 10.

109. Peter Medoff and Holly Sklar, *Streets of Hope: The Fall and Rise of an Urban Neighborhood* (Boston: South End Press, 1994), pp. 5, 131, 157, 164.

110. Peter Medoff and Holly Sklar, *Streets of Hope: The Fall and Rise of an Urban Neighborhood* (Boston: South End Press, 1994), "adequate funding" quote on p. 273; see also pp. 44, 61-61

111. Peter Medoff and Holly Sklar, *Streets of Hope: The Fall and Rise of an Urban Neighborhood* (Boston: South End Press, 1994), p. 146.

112. Heather Mac Donald, "The Billions of Dollars That Made Things Worse," *City Journal*, Autumn 1996, p. 38.

113. Michael Tomasky, "The Next Big Things," *New York* magazine, 17 May 1999, pp. 42-43.

114. George E. Peterson, "Intergovernmental Financial Relations" in *Reality and Research: Social Science and U.S. Urban Policy Since 1960*, George Galster, ed. (Washington, D.C.: Urban Institute Press, 1996) p. 209

115. Siegel quoted by Jeffrey Goldberg, "The Decline and Fall of the Upper West Side," *New York* magazine, 25 April 1994, p. 39.

116. Zane L. Miller and Bruce Tucker, *Changing Plans for America's Inner Cities: Cincinnati's Over-the-Rhine and Twentieth-Century Urbanism* (Columbus: Ohio State University Press, 1998), pp. 125, 131.

117. Daniel P. Moynihan, *Maximum Feasible Misunderstanding: Community Action in the War on Poverty* (New York: The Free Press, 1970), p. 130.

118. Myron Orfield, *Metropolitics* (Washington, D.C.: Brookings Institution Press, and Cambridge: Lincoln Institute of Land Policy, 1997), p. 179.

119. P.L. Baden, "Fraser Says He'll Lead Cities to New Governance Style," *Minneapolis Star Tribune*, 2 December 1992, p. B1.

120. Mayor Donald Fraser's letter to Metropolitan Council Chair Mary Anderson, 14 July 1992.

121. Attorney General Skip Humphrey's speech at American Institute of Architects, Minnesota chapter, convention symposium "Reducing Crime Through Design," 13 November 1997.

122. Fraser quoted by Kevin Diaz, "Sayles Belton Wants City to Realign Social Services," *Minneapolis Star Tribune*, 3 December 1997, p. B1, noting that Fraser was reflecting on his 14-year legacy of creating programs for women and children.

123. Jane Jacobs, *The Death and Life of Great American Cities* (New York: Random House, 1961), p. 95.

124. Matthew Purdy, "Left to Die, the South Bronx Rises From Decades of Decay," *New York Times*, 13 November 1994, p. 1.

125. Myron Orfield, *Metropolitics* (Washington, D.C.: Brookings Institution Press, and Cambridge: Lincoln Institute of Land Policy, 1997), p. 4.

126. WCCO 10:00 p.m. News, 6 August 1996.

127. Minneapolis Community Development Agency, "New Developments," 10 February 2000. Back Bay values noted in Barbara W. Moore and Gail Weesner, *Back Bay* (Boston: Century Hill Press, 1995), p. 18.

128. Rector cited by John J. DiIulio, Jr., "Comment on Douglas S. Massey . . ." in *University of Pennsylvania Law Review* 143, no. 5 (May 1995), p. 1278.

129. John S. Adams, Barbara J. VanDrasek, and Elvin K. Wyly, *Minnesota Housing: Shaping Community in the 1990s* (Minneapolis: Center for Urban and Regional Affairs, 1996), p. 106.

130. In West Palm Beach, Florida, the historic black Northwest neighborhood is deteriorating, but nearby City Place revitalization makes Northwest's houses more appealing and marketable. Many Northwest homeowners would prefer to sell now that they might do so profitably, but defenders resist gentrification, according to Kristina Ford (executive director of the New Orleans Planning Commission), "Tempering the Zeal for Historic Preservation," *New York Times*, 4 September 1999, p. A13.

131. Peter Medoff and Holly Sklar, *Streets of Hope: The Fall and Rise of an Urban Neighborhood* (Boston: South End Press, 1994), pp. 53, 161. "Give us a hand" quote in New Day Films, Holding Ground Productions, 1996, "Holding Ground" videotape.

132. Mary Lynn Smith, "Frogtown Hopes Factory is a Nice Fit," *Minneapolis Star Tribune*, 15 February 1999, p. B1.

133. Mary Lynn Smith, "Frogtown Hopes Factory is a Nice Fit," *Minneapolis Star Tribune*, 15 February 15 1999, p. B1.

134. Metropolitan Council, *1990 Travel Behavior Inventory Summary Report*, June 1994, pp.46, 48.

135. Lourdes Medrano Leslie, "St. Paul Asks Frogtown Group to Return Money," *Minneapolis Star Tribune*, 18 September 2000, p. B1.

136. Michael E. Porter, "The Competitive Advantage of the Inner City," *Harvard Business Review,* May-June 1995, p. 65.

137. Mary Schmich, "Everyone Equal in Cabrini-Green Supermarket," *Chicago Tribune*, 4 June 2000, Section 4 p. 1

138. Michael E. Porter, "The Competitive Advantage of the Inner City," *Harvard Business Review*, May-June 1995, pp. 65, 70.

139. Michael E. Porter, "The Competitive Advantage of the Inner City," *Harvard Business Review*, May-June 1995, pp. 69-70. The failures of a Minneapolis nonprofit were reported in the *Minneapolis Star Tribune*, "An important Urban Ventures mission is to help restart the neighborhood's economic engine, so that families can support themselves and own homes. That's a tough job. A promised Bridgeman's didn't open. A promising business relocation failed because of inadequate operational skills. One firm moved to a suburb…" (Leonard Inskip, "Urban Ventures Finds Roles in Faith, Sports in Tackling Problems," *Minneapolis Star Tribune*, 22 June 1999, p. A13.)

140. Michael E. Porter, "The Competitive Advantage of the Inner City," *Harvard Business Review,* May-June 1995, p. 71.

141. Andres Duany, Elizabeth Plater-Zyberk, and Jeff Speck, *Suburban Nation: The Rise of Sprawl and the Decline of the American Dream* (New York: North Point Press, 2000), pp. 174-75.

142. James Howard Kunstler, *Home From Nowhere: Remaking Our Everyday World for the 21st Century* (New York: Simon and Schuster, Touchstone, 1996), pp. 171-72. Housing construction (mostly townhouses) is now occurring where envisioned by the Atlantic Center plan.

143. Diane R. Suchman (with Margaret B. Sowell) *Developing Infill Housing in Inner-City Neighborhoods: Opportunities and Strategies* (Washington, D.C.: Urban Land Institute, 1997), p. 43.

144. Twin Cities suburban land prices doubled between 1996 and 2000 according to David Peterson, "Builders Say Rules Lift Cost of Land," *Minneapolis Star Tribune*, 23 February 2000, p. A1.

CHAPTER 10 NOTES

1. Oath of the Athenian City State, quoted by Marcia D. Lowe, *Shaping Cities: The Environmental and Human Dimensions* (Washington, D.C.: Worldwatch Institute, October 1991), p. 57.

2. Katherine Kersten, "Teen Challenge Operates on Faith but Then Pays For It," *Minneapolis Star Tribune*, 17 November 1999, p. A19.

3. David Rusk, *Inside Game Outside Game: Winning Strategies for Saving Urban America* (Washington, D.C.: Brookings Institution Press, 1999), pp. 53, 147-51, 168-69, 185.

4. Parsons Brinckerhoff Quade & Douglas, Inc., Transportation Research Board of the National Research Council, *TCRP Report 16: Transit and Urban Form*, Volume 2 (Washington, D.C.: National Academy Press, 1996), p. 105 of Part 4.

5. The suburban average value per owner-occupied unit was 127 percent of the Minneapolis average in 2000. If this percentage is applied to the aggregate value of *all* Minneapolis units and combined with a 220 percent increase in the number of units, the result is an aggregate value of $33.5 billion. Minneapolis housing counts and aggregate value reported by Minneapolis Planning Department, *State of the City 2000*, (January 2001), pp. 12, 16.

6. Added tax revenue includes city, county, and school district levies. Rate information from Joel Jacobson, Minneapolis Assessor's Office. 18 May 2001.

7. Jane Jacobs, *The Death and Life of Great American Cities* (New York: Random House, 1961), p. 98.

8. Roman A. Cybriwsky, et. al., "The Political and Social Construction of Revitalized Neighborhoods" in *Gentrification of the City*, Neil Smith and Peter Williams, eds. (Boston: Allen & Unwin, 1986), p. 102.

9. Roman A. Cybriwsky, et. al., "The Political and Social Construction of Revitalized Neighborhoods" in *Gentrification of the City*, Neil Smith and Peter Williams, eds. (Boston: Allen & Unwin, 1986), p. 94; Jonathan Barnett, *The Fractured Metropolis: Improving the New City, Restoring the Old City, Reshaping the Region* (New York: Harper Collins, Icon, 1995), 1995, p. 134.

10. Minneapolis Planning Department, *Willard-Hay Neighborhood Planning Information Base*, Summer 1992, p. 2.

11. "An Interview With Paul Bauknight, Jr." *Construction Market Data*, 29 April 1996,. pp. 14-15.

12. Patricia Leigh Brown, "Higher and Drier, Illinois Town is Reborn," *New York Times*, 6 May 1996, p. 1.

13. Jonathan Barnett, *The Fractured Metropolis: Improving the New City, Restoring the Old City, Reshaping the Region* (New York: Harper Collins, Icon, 1995).

14. Michael E. Porter, "The Competitive Advantage of the Inner City," *Harvard Business Review*, May-June 1995, pp. 55-56.

15. Michael E. Porter, "The Competitive Advantage of the Inner City," *Harvard Business Review*, May-June 1995, p. 57.

16. Seward's one-mile stretch of East Franklin Avenue has 27 consumer businesses, aside from gas stations and car repair shops, for an average of 1.1 businesses per block face. The one-mile stretch is 12 blocks, or 24 block fronts, in length. One-story buildings and parking lots are plentiful (windshield survey, 8 February 2000). Montague Street in Brooklyn Heights has 80 consumer establishments, no gas stations or auto repair shops, on a four-block stretch-8 block fronts (August 1996 shoe leather survey).

17. Tracie Rozhon, "Murray Hill Story: What's Worth Keeping," *New York Times*, 12 October 2000, p. F12.

18. Paul Goldberger's "forward" in *The New American Townhouse* by Alexander Gorlin (New York: Riozzoli, 1999), p. 8.

19. Author's observations, 23 March 2000.

20. Tom Shachtman, *Around the Block: The Business of a Neighborhood* (New York: Harcourt Brace, 1997).

21. "Thirty-seven percent" and "nearly 55 percent" of surveyed residents of two apartment buildings within a quarter-mile of BART's Pleasant Hill station commuted routinely on BART, according to Michael Bernick and Robert Cervero, *Transit Villages in the 21st Century* (New York: McGraw-Hill, 1997), p. 194.

22. Some who live one-quarter mile from a rail line would live somewhat farther from the nearest station. Walking distance is discussed by Michael Bernick and Robert Cervero, *Transit Villages in the 21st Century* (New York: McGraw-Hill, 1997), pp. 126-27.

23. Michael Bernick and Robert Cervero, *Transit Villages in the 21st Century* (New York: McGraw-Hill, 1997), p. 75; Regional Plan Association, "Where Transit Works," *Regional Plan News*, August 1976, p. 4.

24. Phillip L. Clay, *Neighborhood Renewal* (Lexington Massachusetts: D.C. Heath and Company, 1979), p. 47.

25. Jane Jacobs, *The Death and Life of Great American Cities* (New York: Random House, 1961), p. 92.

26. Robert Sharoff, "Putting 'That Great' Back in State Street," *New York Times*, 14 May 2000, Real Estate section p. 43.

27. Bernick, Michael and Robert Cervero, *Transit Villages in the 21st Century* (New York: McGraw-Hill, 1997), pp. 138. 221-22; Diane R. Suchman, *Developing Infill Housing in Inner-City Neighborhoods* (Washington, D.C.: Urban Land Institute, 1997), p. 46.

28. Tom Shachtman, *Around the Block: The Business of a Neighborhood* (New York: Harcourt Brace, 1997).

29. Such is the appeal of Manhattan's townhouses that they reached an average sales price of $2.5 million in 1999, according to Allyn Thompson, "Through the Roof," *East Side Resident*, 19-25 April 2000, p. 18.

30. New York City Planning Department, "Economic Development Indicators" (DCP 1990 # 313), pp. 25-26.

31. National Railroad Passenger Corporation, "Amtrak Makes History With Launch of Acela Express," press release dated 16 November 2000.

32. David Rusk, *Inside Game, Outside Game* (Washington, D.C.: Brookings Institution Press, 1999), p. 99. New Jersey's intervention in Camden reported by Iver Peterson, "State Will Appoint Manger to Run Camden's Government," *New York Times*, 25 May 2001, p. B1.

Index